Trading
Beyond the Mountains

Richard Somerset Mackie

Trading
Beyond the Mountains

THE BRITISH FUR TRADE ON THE PACIFIC
1793–1843

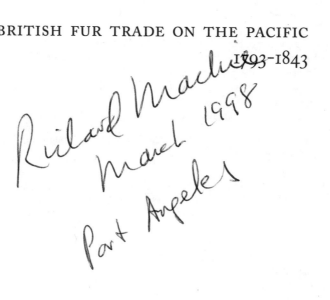

UBCPress / Vancouver

Printed in Canada on acid-free paper ∞
ISBN 0-7748-0559-5

Canadian Cataloguing in Publication Data

Mackie, Richard 1957-
  Trading beyond the mountains

  Includes bibliographical references and index.
  ISBN 0-7748-0559-5

  1. Simpson, George, Sir, 1792?-1860. 2. Hudson's Bay Company – History. 3. Fur trade – British Columbia – Pacific Coast – History. 4. Fur trade – United States – Pacific Coast – History. 5. Northwest Coast of North America. I. Title.
FC3207.M32 1996   971.1'1'02   C96-910486-3
FI060.8.M32 1996

Financially assisted by the Province of British Columbia through the British Columbia Heritage Trust.

UBC Press gratefully acknowledges the ongoing support to its publishing program from the Canada Council, the Province of British Columbia Cultural Services Branch, and the Department of Communications of the Government of Canada.

UBC Press
University of British Columbia
6344 Memorial Road
Vancouver, BC v6T 1Z2
(604) 822-3259
Fax: 1-800-668-0821
E-mail: orders@ubcpress.ubc.ca
http://www.ubcpress.ubc.ca

To Cathy, Juliet, and Raphael

Contents

Figures, Maps, and Tables

Acknowledgments

$\mathbf{M}$y original and perhaps greatest debt is to my brother Alexander. In October 1981, Al, an archaeologist, asked if I could provide him with biographical details about a west coast fur trader named George Blenkinsop. Al had found Blenkinsop's unpublished 1874 report and census on the Indians of Barkley Sound, on Vancouver Island's west coast, but he knew little about the author, and he asked if I could do some research for him at the British Columbia Archives. I had recently returned from Scotland, where I had acquired an undergraduate degree in medieval history. After a few days at the archives I was hooked. I found that Blenkinsop, even when he worked for the Hudson's Bay Company, was much more than a fur trader: he worked as a lumberman, farmer, and coal miner, and provided commodities for export to Pacific markets. His occupational diversity seemed to contradict almost everything written at that time about the west coast fur trade. A year later, I began graduate work in history at the University of Victoria intending to write Blenkinsop's biography. After a few months of fruitful research on Blenkinsop and his contemporaries, I decided to broaden my study to include the economic history of Vancouver Island during the Hudson's Bay Company's era. I suspected that Blenkinsop, an emigrant Cornishman with wide commercial interests, was typical of his generation.

I completed my master's degree in 1984, and a year later enrolled in the Ph.D. program at the University of British Columbia, determined to locate the origins of the economic patterns I had detected at the western edge of Canada at the very end of the fur trade era. This book is the result of that search. With Cole Harris's encouragement, I travelled back in time to the fur trades of the Columbia River, New Caledonia, Red River, Hudson Bay, and the St. Lawrence River, and somewhere along the way I grasped Harold Innis's analysis of the workings of the northern fur trade. At the end of the journey I felt almost like a Canadian – something that does not always come naturally to a Vancouver Islander.

It is a pleasure to acknowledge support from the institutions and granting agencies that have assisted me since the start of this project. I entered the doctoral program at the University of British Columbia with an Ireland Scholarship offered by the government of British Columbia. Subsequently I received the Norman MacKenzie Fellowship, the Tina and Morris Wagner Foundation Fellowship, a travel grant from the Ewart Foundation of the University of Manitoba, the Native Daughters of British Columbia Scholarship, and a doctoral fellowship from the Social Sciences and Humanities Research Council of Canada. I am grateful to these funding agencies and to those who recommended me. A grant from the British Columbia Heritage Trust helped pay the cost of publication.

I am indebted to some members of the history and geography departments at the University of British Columbia. Peter Ward steered me away from some of the bogs and swamps of the doctoral landscape, and shepherded the project through to the end. Keith Ralston, Roderick Barman, Jeremy Mouat, Tina Loo, and Jim Winter of the history department supported my work. I found a congenial home in the geography department, where some of the best university traditions persist and flourish. Cole Harris and Graeme Wynn joined my doctoral committee and welcomed me to the rich intellectual and social life of the department. Among their students I am grateful to Wayne (and Connie) Wilson, Dan Clayton, Ken Favrholdt, David Demeritt, and Averill Groeneveld-Meijer. I could also always count on tapping Bob Galois's awesome knowledge of the British Columbian past.

I cannot begin to thank Cole Harris for all his encouragement. It was a privilege to be associated with him, his learning and high standards, and the rich tradition of historical geography at UBC. I also thank him and Muriel Harris for inviting me to stay at the old ranch house in New Denver, where I wrote the first draft of what became this book between September and December 1991. Nancy and John Anderson were generous with their hospitality at New Denver. Cole also introduced me to Eric Leinberger of UBC's geography department, who drew the maps in this book. They were funded by the Social Sciences and Humanities Research Council through a grant to the Historical Geography of British Columbia Project.

UBC, however, was merely an anchor to my ship, which drifted all over British Columbia during the completion of this project: I lived in Victoria, Vancouver, Sidney, Pender Island, Bamfield, Salt Spring Island, Errington, and Courtenay. My parents, George and Gillian, gave frequent support and assistance along the way, and Paddy Mackie, my cousin, was always positive and helpful during my visits to Vernon and Sugar Lake. I am particularly grateful to David, Jon, and Winifred Spalding, who made my stay on Pender Island rewarding and recuperative.

This book is based on research undertaken at a number of institutions. I thank the archives of the Hudson's Bay Company for permission to quote from their records. Anne Morton, Shirlee Anne Smith, Debra Moore, Michael Moosberger, Judith Beattie, and Tammy Hannibal were generous with their knowledge and time during my three visits to Winnipeg. I learned recently that my English grandparents were shareholders in the Hudson's Bay Company, and I must belatedly thank Mary Mackie, my grandmother, for sending *The Beaver* magazine to Canada when I was young. The British Columbia Archives have been a home away from home since I first opened their solid ornamental doors in 1981. Brian Young, David Mattison, Kathy Bridge, Cathy Henderson, Brent McBride, Fran Gundry, and the rest of the staff have been consistently helpful and companionable. I must also thank the staffs of the many institutions that provided copies of the original sketches and watercolours that illustrate this book, namely the British Columbia Archives, Hudson's Bay Company Archives, National Archives of Canada, the Special Collections Division of the University of British Columbia, Royal Ontario Museum, the American Antiquarian Society, Boston Museum of Fine Arts, Bancroft Library at Berkeley, the Bishop Museum in Honolulu, and the Stark Museum of Art in Orange, Texas. I am also grateful to the staffs of the Parksville and Courtenay branches of the Vancouver Island Regional Library for their cheerful assistance.

In 1992 I devised and taught a course in the history of the Canadian fur trade at the University of Victoria, and in 1994 I taught introductory Canadian history at North Island College in Campbell River. I thank all my students for promoting clarity and focus.

Cathy Richardson has been a source of inspiration and happiness for the past few years, and our daughter, Juliet, has been a delight.

Jean Wilson of UBC Press acted as capable midwife to this project, and I have come to depend on her timely and sensible advice and support. It has been a pleasure to work with her and also with Holly Keller-Brohman. For their encouragement along the way I also thank Peter Murray, Dan Marshall, Allan and Betty Brooks, Jean Barman, Wendy Wickwire, Margaret Ormsby, Maria Tippett, Grant Keddie, Irene Moorhouse (Bekes), Lloyd Keith, Mavis Erickson, Harry Duckworth, John Selwood, April McIlhagga, Kitty Bernick, Cheryl Coull, John Lutz, Allan Pritchard, John Adams, Tom Norris, Lorne Hammond, Susan Johnston, Gordon Lafortune, Patrick Dunae, Allan Smith, Rod Fotheringham, Quentin Mackie, Marty Magne, Steve and Laurie Acheson, Liz Vibert, Cairn Crockford, Bruce Watson, Alex Christie, Kitty Lloyd, and Jane Watson. Jamie Morton shared his extensive unpublished writing on the Columbia Department fur trade. I owe my sincere thanks to Bill Swagerty of the University of Idaho.

Introduction

From the advantages the country possesses it bids fair
to have an extensive commerce, on advantageous terms, with
many parts of the Pacific. It is well calculated to produce the
following staple commodities – furs, salted beef and pork, fish,
grain, flour, wool, hides, tallow, timber and coals; and in return
for these – sugars, coffee, and other tropical productions,
may be obtained at the Sandwich Islands.

– JOHN DUNN, 1844[1]

This is a study in commercial policy, environmental adaptation, and capitalist success. It concerns the fifty years between 1793 and 1843, when fur traders from Montreal and Hudson Bay explored and dominated the non-Native economy of much of the Pacific coast and cordilleran interior of western North America – the region fur traders came to know as the Columbia Department. This was the westernmost administrative division of the British land-based fur trade (Map 1). On the Pacific, British fur traders found an unexploited region of natural abundance ripe for the application of their acquisitive commercial culture. This book concerns the origin, impetus, and extent of economic development in the Columbia Department in these years, the markets to which exports were destined, the first stages of economic diversification within a fur trade region, the formation of a distinctive regional economy, and, finally, the central role played by Native traders and workers in these changes.

This book also traces the history of an idea from its origins to its fruition. This was the idea of a British, transcontinental commerce connecting the Canadian colonies or Hudson Bay with the Pacific, an idea much older than the political idea of a continental confederation within British North America. The Montreal-based North West Company (NWC) and the London-based Hudson's Bay Company (HBC) applied this idea to the Pacific coast in the late eighteenth and early nineteenth centuries. The Northwesters did much of the initial exploration of the region, located workable transport routes, and glimpsed its larger

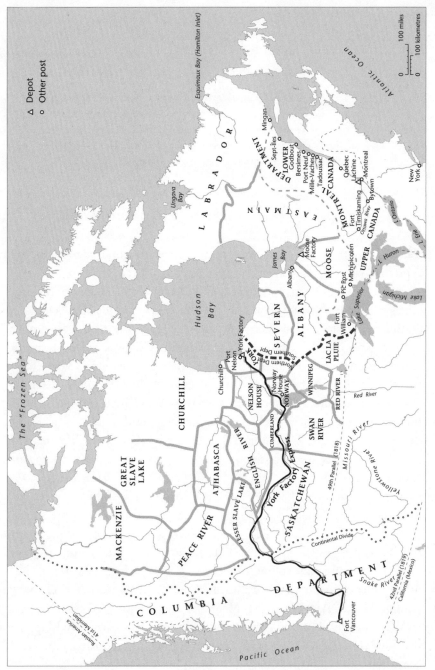

MAP 1 Hudson's Bay Company districts, 1830 (after Arrowsmith)

potential. Led by Alexander Mackenzie and the London geographer and theorist Alexander Dalrymple, they devised a scheme for the export of natural resources from the west coast to Pacific markets. While the NWC experimented with a trans-Pacific commerce, it was left to the HBC to capitalize on it.

The Northwesters exported only fur from the region, a commodity they shipped to Canton to avoid the long overland route back to Montreal and to profit from the wealthy Chinese fur market. Before their merger with the HBC in 1821, they were unable to export any other commodity. By contrast, the HBC subsequently shipped Columbia Department furs to London, and other commodities to Pacific markets, principally salmon and lumber. Through its trade in fur, the British company tied this region and its produce to London, the global centre of commerce and finance; through its exports of salmon and lumber, it connected the region to emerging Pacific markets.

This book, then, concerns the whole range of commercial activities undertaken by the British fur traders on the north Pacific Ocean before Fort Victoria was built in 1843, an event that signalled the end of the British fur trade on the Columbia River. For almost half a century the Columbia River provided the hope, the focus, and the headquarters of the British fur trade on the Pacific.

This study begins in 1793, the year Alexander Mackenzie reached the Pacific Ocean at Bella Coola. It includes the quiet years of exploration between 1793 and 1811, when Mackenzie, Simon Fraser, and David Thompson came to grips with the physical geography of the cordilleran interior north of and including the Columbia River, and devised an ambitious scheme for the commercial development of the region. This book also includes a brief discussion of the maritime sea otter trade of the North West Coast, a trade that was dominated until the 1830s by American traders out of Boston.

Before 1821, the Northwesters exported a single commodity (animal fur) from the watersheds of two great rivers (the upper Fraser and lower Columbia), and shipped most of their furs to one great fur market (Canton). The Northwesters lost money on this venture owing to high transport, commission costs, and competition with the HBC elsewhere on the continent. Due to such losses, the two companies merged in 1821, with the HBC effectively taking over the Montreal-based firm.

The Pacific fur trade appeared so unpromising that, after the merger, the HBC considered abandoning the lower Columbia region. Instead, between 1821 and 1843, the company, strengthened by the addition of canny former Northwesters, consolidated its operations in the entire Columbia Department through the application of several venerable commercial strategies of the Canadian fur trade. It extended its fur trade to all the major rivers of the region, from the Yukon watershed in the north to the Sacramento and Colorado river systems in the south (Map 2). It also forced American traders to vacate the North West Coast, the lower Columbia, and much of the southern interior. To support this massive trade extension, the HBC developed substantial provision trades in agricultural produce and salmon on the lower Columbia and Fraser rivers. The company took advantage of the possibility of seaborne transport to develop markets at Oahu (Hawaii), Yerba Buena (San Francisco), and Sitka (in present-day Alaska). To these places the company exported salmon, lumber, flour, and other country produce on its Pacific fleet of ships. As fur trader John Dunn wrote in 1844, the HBC had effectively set to work a 'vast and complex machinery of internal and coasting commerce.'[2]

Natural conditions favoured these commercial developments on the Pacific coast. East of the Rockies, on Hudson Bay and in Rupert's Land – constrained by a hostile climate, great distances, and transport limitations – the company could export only fur, while on the west coast the 'fur' traders successfully turned to general commerce and resource development.

This commercial transformation was conceived by Alexander Mackenzie and other Northwesters before 1821, but it was applied most effectively by Governor George Simpson of the HBC, who demanded that farming and Native provision trades carry the burden of all other economic activity west of the Rocky Mountains. Commercial policy was put into practice by an able Columbia River management, led by John McLoughlin who, with Simpson, initiated export trades in salmon and lumber, tested new markets for Columbia produce, and decided on Oahu as the most promising market. McLoughlin's assistant, James Douglas, also played a significant role in managing the daily operations of the fur, salmon, lumber, and agricultural trades from the Fort Vancouver headquarters. This new regional economy on the Pacific depended on a

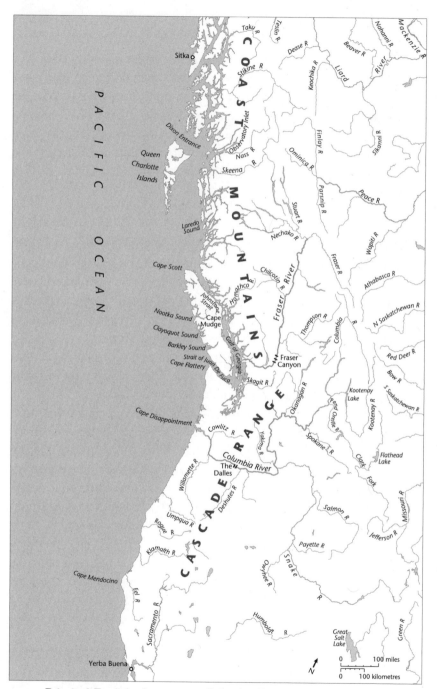

MAP 2 Principal English place-names, Columbia Department

permanent non-Native workforce of about 600, as well as many Native workers and traders.

Statements made by Simpson and others suggest that they were well aware of the larger commercial potential of the region at a time when the fur trade of the entire continent showed signs of decline. In 1822, the London-based Governor and Committee (G&C) of the HBC referred to 'the possibility of bringing other articles as well as Peltries to a profitable market' on the Pacific. Two years later, Simpson referred to the need to look beyond 'the mere trafficking with Indians,' and in 1840 Douglas speculated on the need to extend the company's views 'beyond the mere traffic in peltries' on the west coast. Such wishes were based on the region's abundant resources and on the company's tradition of resource exploitation for provision supply. The company's traders, wrote a British resident of the Mexican province of California in 1839, were 'always the first to take advantage of new and remote markets.' Contemporaries were full of praise for the commercial potential of the region. 'For general adaptation for commerce,' Dunn wrote in 1844, the Columbia Department could 'scarcely be surpassed by any country in the world.'[3]

The fur traders, of course, did not leave their considerable experience behind them when they reached the Pacific. They applied a set of tested commercial strategies, developed gradually in the Montreal and Hudson Bay fur trades, that were aimed at increasing profit and countering commercial competition: promoting able and entrepreneurial personnel, finding new forms of country produce either through the Indian trade or through agricultural development, extending the fur trade to new regions, selectively overhunting frontier regions to evict competitors, and locating fresh markets for new exports. Several of these strategies had been implemented, boldly but unprofitably, on the lower Columbia River before 1821 by the NWC.[4] After 1821, the HBC applied its capital and accumulated expertise to the diverse resources and commercial potential of the whole Pacific coast with impressive results. The company embarked on an ambitious and highly competitive trade extension on the coast and in the interior, followed up, on the coast alone, by a vigorous policy of resource development aimed at supplying provisions, cutting costs, and capitalizing on new markets.

The company's established commercial policies were united on the Pacific coast with a larger trading scheme, devised in the late eighteenth century by Alexander Dalrymple and Alexander Mackenzie, and inspired by British maritime explorers and fur traders from James Cook to John Meares. This ambitious geopolitical strategy originally entailed the creation of an all-British Pacific commerce uniting the capital, commodities, expertise, and discoveries of the East India, North West, and Hudson's Bay companies. Fur and fish from the Pacific coast were to be marketed in China through a united British mercantile effort. Before 1821, the NWC attempted a variation on this scheme, marketing Columbia region fur in Canton through American merchants, but such exports were unprofitable owing to the poor quality of Columbia pelts, high port fees at Canton, and high commission fees charged by the American intermediary. The HBC's attempt was more successful. With the disappearance of sea otter, the company abandoned the China scheme and established an agency in Honolulu in 1833 where country produce from the Columbia Department, together with British manufactured goods, were sold wholesale and retail. The opening of the Hawaiian agency represented the fruition of Alexander Mackenzie's scheme of a British commerce linking the Columbia River and adjacent Pacific markets.

This book considers the two periods, 1811-13 and 1834-6, when land-based American fur traders mounted serious commercial opposition against the British fur traders west of the Rocky Mountains. Neither attempt was successful: in 1813, the NWC bought out John Jacob Astor's Pacific Fur Company, which for two short years had traded fur on the Columbia and Fraser; in 1837, the HBC took over Nathaniel Wyeth's Columbia River Fishing and Trading Company, which since 1834 had built posts and traded furs on the Columbia and Snake rivers. American fur traders were no match for their well-capitalized, experienced, and competitive British counterparts in the region beyond the Rocky Mountains.

The political status of the Columbia Department remained undecided between the Anglo-American Convention of 1818 and the Oregon Treaty of 1846. In these years, British and American merchants had the same rights and privileges in the vast region between the forty-second parallel and the Russian possessions to the north. In the negotiations preceding the Oregon Treaty, the HBC hoped that its one-sided commercial success over rival American fur traders would translate into a powerful territorial and political claim on behalf of Great Britain. Such would not be the case, even though the company's commercial achievement on the Pacific had provoked the admiration, and sometimes the envy, of visiting American traders, missionaries, and government officials since the 1820s.[5] But in 1846, the forty-ninth parallel was extended to the Pacific, cutting off the HBC's important forts, farms, fisheries, and export trades on the lower Columbia River and Puget Sound. That year, the British government abandoned a region that its own merchants had publicized to the commercial world.

The emergence of a general maritime commerce on the Pacific after 1821 resulted from a number of causes. The NWC's early efforts were important, as was the HBC's mastery of the strategies, skills, and provisions required to operate in solitude. In their markets and transport routes, the maritime fur traders lent a useful precedent. Extensive Native trade networks and ready maritime access were conducive to commercial endeavour. The HBC's own transport system permitted idle vessels to visit Pacific markets in winter months. Their legal monopoly of what contemporaries called the 'Indian trade' also contributed. This monopoly applied to the company's British rivals only, but on the Pacific coast the Indian trade itself was much more varied and full of commercial potential than in the landlocked regions east of the Rockies. The threat of American competition was always real, and the appearance of an Astor or a Wyeth was always possible. But the likelihood of American success in the fur, salmon, and lumber trades diminished as the company broadened its commercial base and monopolized the Indian trade of the Columbia Department.

Between 1793 and 1843, a regional economy emerged on the west coast. This new economy was linked by finance to Montreal and later to London; tied by precedent and personnel to the St. Lawrence River valley and Rupert's Land; separated from those regions by labour, transport, and market conditions; and based increasingly on exports to Pacific markets. The Pacific coast offered a commercial opportunity not available in Rupert's Land until the railway era. The HBC's business on the Pacific was as much concerned with resource development as with finding new sources of fur, though the fur trade remained the major source of profit from the Columbia Department as a whole.[6]

In 1843, the company's coastal operations on the lower Fraser and Columbia rivers and in California were characterized by a general export commerce, while its interior operations from California to the Yukon River continued to specialize in the fur trade. This fundamental commercial division between the coast and the interior characterized the Columbia Department fur trade. In several coastal areas, the company had colonized Native economies and redirected their abundant produce to foreign markets.

To locate the economic base of the North West and HBC's operations, I examined published historical works as well as the primary correspondence of the British, Canadian, and American companies involved. These letters, especially the 'Country Correspondence,' provide the basic history of new commercial policies and the new export trades that resulted. Important among them are the scattered but substantial dispatches of the HBC's Oahu agency. Most of these letters are of a routine nature and remain unpublished, but a few key series have been printed: volumes three, four, six, and seven of the Hudson's Bay Record Society series, edited by Harvey Fleming and E.E. Rich, and introduced by Harold Innis and W. Kaye Lamb.[7] I have made scant use of the many fort journals that survive at the Hudson's Bay Company and British Columbia archives. Each of these will eventually be examined and analyzed in greater detail than is now possible in a general history of this kind. I have consulted, for this pre-colonial period, the books, letters, and journals of missionaries, botanists, and naval and army officers from several countries. Of critical importance is Governor George Simpson's published and unpublished correspondence relating to his three visits to the Columbia Department.[8]

The finest collection of nineteenth-century business correspondence in existence, at the HBC archives, provides the narrative thread of the book. No comparable source exists for the Native side of the Columbia Department fur trade. My background in archaeology lends the book, I hope, a certain materialist emphasis. It is, however, primarily a study in the history of commerce and historical geography; it is intended to provide a narrative baseline for further research in a number of regions and disciplines.

This study fills a void. In the last two decades, two historical geographers, James R. Gibson and Arthur J. Ray, have worked to the north, south, east, and west of the Columbia Department. Ray's work is set in

Rupert's Land and elsewhere east of the Rockies,[9] while Gibson has written about the Russian and American maritime fur trades to the north and on the Pacific, and with the HBC's farms in the southern part of the department.[10] Three historians, John S. Galbraith, Barry M. Gough, and Robin A. Fisher, have written respectively about the Hudson's Bay Company's frontier policies, British commercial, naval, and political policy on the Pacific, and Native-European relations in this era.[11] These valuable works have left largely untouched the commercial geography and history of the NWC and the HBC in the Columbia Department.

American historians, by and large, have been preoccupied with their own stories: Lewis and Clark's expeditions, the abortive schemes of Astor and Wyeth, the 'mountain men' of the Rockies and the western fur trade companies, the Oregon Trail and the tribulations of the overland immigrants, these immigrants' relations with John McLoughlin, the 'Father of Oregon,' and the diplomatic history of the Oregon Crisis. American fur trade scholars have produced an impressive body of scholarship relating to the policies and motives of the American fur trade companies of the upper Missouri and Rocky Mountains.[12]

In all these works, the British fur trade on the Pacific has been treated as a sort of dark age: an era scarcely relevant to British, Canadian, or American history, or connected in any meaningful way to subsequent BC history. The 1846 Treaty and subsequent loss of the southern part of the Columbia Department explains the Canadian disinterest in the region. It was also an era easily forgotten by a nationalist American historiography. The Oregon Trail migrations of the early 1840s provided an evocative founding myth of a promised land won through endurance and struggle: the surmounting of physical hardship by American overlanders and settlers, the breaking of Native resistance by American military force, and the defeating of a stubborn, well-rooted British commerce by American diplomatic expertise.

Trading
Beyond the Mountains

CHAPTER I

The North West Passage
by Land

*It was amid these inlets that Vancouver, in about 1793, strove for
several years to solve a great geographical problem; and the result of
his explorations effectually set at rest the fanciful speculations of the
carpet-geographers of Europe, founded on the mythical relations of
De Fuca and De Fonte.*

— ALEXANDER CAULFIELD ANDERSON, 1882[1]

The British land-based fur trade west of the Rocky Mountains
originated with the cordilleran explorations and policies of the North
West Company between 1793 and 1821. Officials of this company, inspired by Alexander Mackenzie and encouraged by the London-based
geographer Alexander Dalrymple, devised a model for the territorial control and commercial exploitation of the Pacific region of the fur trade.
The Northwesters put their model in place through the explorations
of Mackenzie, Fraser, and Thompson between 1793 and 1811, through
their timely purchase of John Jacob Astor's Pacific Fur Company in
1813, and through their 'Columbia Adventure' of the years between 1813
and 1821.

The Montreal-based fur traders displayed a resolute consistency of
commercial purpose. They based their model on their own knowledge,
gained through exploration and trade, and on the knowledge of the
region revealed by the coastal explorations and surveys of naval explorers James Cook and George Vancouver, and of the British sea otter
traders who followed. British fur traders, politicians, and theorists had
long sought a North West Passage by land or sea: a viable route to the
Pacific and a trade link with the Orient. Such a passage was finally
located by the NWC in the early years of the nineteenth century.[2]

By the late eighteenth century, the search for a North West Passage had occupied European minds for more than 200 years. Merchants and explorers, mainly from Spain and Britain, had made sporadic attempts to find such a passage, known by its mythical name as the Strait of Anian. The shadowy, almost apocryphal voyages of the English adventurer Francis Drake, Greek pilot Juan de Fuca, and Spanish admiral Bartholemew de Fonte, among others, encouraged what Barry Gough terms the 'geographical theorists, commercial promoters, and artful strategists' who kept the idea of a North West Passage alive between the sixteenth and eighteenth centuries.[3]

The HBC made some of the first documented attempts to find the North West Passage. In 1719 Governor John Knight was sent by the company to find 'the Straights of Anian, and to make what Discoveries you possibly can, and to obtain all sorts of Trade and Commerce.' Knight and his ships subsequently disappeared north of Hudson Bay without a trace, and the loss did much to keep the company 'asleep by the frozen sea' for the next half century. A navigable passage through or around North America, however, remained of great commercial and political importance, and in 1745 parliament offered a reward of £20,000 to any British navigator who could find such a passage.[4]

In the 1770s, many still hoped that a North West Passage would unite the fur trade of the continent with the markets of the Pacific. This passage was speculated to take one of two forms: a northern, oceanic, navigable North West Passage, and a southern, overland, great river to the Pacific. This late search for the North West Passage was primarily British, conducted by the Royal Navy and the HBC,[5] while the search for an overland route originated in New France but was also advocated in Britain and in the American colonies by such military and political strategists as Robert Rogers and Jonathan Carver. Between 1765 and 1772, Major Rogers, commander of the post at Michilimackinac, urged the British government to locate a North West Passage by land. Rogers planned to explore from the Great Lakes to the head of the Mississippi, and down the mythical 'Ouragon' River to the Pacific. In 1765 he proposed to establish a communication with Japan, 'and perhaps with nearer and hitherto unknown Rich Countries in the East, where both British and American Commodities might fetch large prices, and a New and Valuable Commerce be Opened, and Secured to His Majesty's Subjects.'

Neither Rogers nor Jonathan Carver, who put forward a similar proposal in the early 1770s, received approval for their projects, and the revolutionary decades saw a temporary suspension of interest in American expansion to the Pacific.[6]

For a quarter century after 1776, the search for a North West Passage was conducted primarily by British and Canadian fur traders. The project was initiated from both London and Montreal. The government-sponsored explorations of James Cook (1776-9) and George Vancouver (1791-5) were part of this new push for a route to the Orient (Map 3). In July 1776, Captain Cook was instructed to find a North West Passage from the Pacific Ocean to Hudson Bay. He found instead an abundant sea otter population and Native peoples willing to hunt and trade them. Cook's men sold the sea otter pelts in Canton for fabulous prices, and his voyage alerted the commercial world to the riches of the Pacific coast fur trade.[7]

The 1780s were a decade of frenetic activity on the Pacific coast. After the publication of Cook's journal in 1781, ships of several nationalities visited the coast for the sea otter trade. In 1784, Captain James King, who commanded the Cook expedition after Cook's death in Hawaii in 1779, published a plan for a fur-trading commerce between China and the North West Coast involving the East India Company. King's call was heeded by British merchants who, to avoid the monopolies of the East India and South Sea companies, sailed to the North West Coast under Austrian and Portuguese flags of convenience. They left from ports such as London, Bombay, Calcutta, Canton, and Macao. Between 1785 and 1790, no less than thirty-three voyages were made to the North West Coast, twenty-six by British ships and seven by American.[8]

These visitors had read Cook and King and had embraced their blueprint for commerce. One was John Meares, who, following King, in 1790 proposed to establish a 'commercial communication,' 'forming a chain of trade between the Hudson's Bay, Canada, and the North West Coast of America,' in which beaver pelts would be shipped directly from there to Canton instead of overland from London to Russia.[9]

Such proposals, combined with the altercation between Meares and the Spanish at Nootka in 1789, prompted the British government to action. Vancouver's voyage revealed finally that a passage did not exist, at least on the North West Coast. What Captain Vancouver charted was

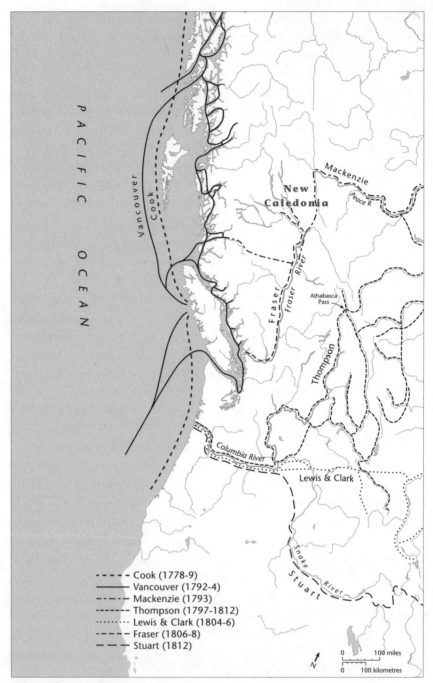

MAP 3 Major explorations, 1778-1812

not a North West Passage through the heart of the continent, but its near-namesake, the North West Coast, the Pacific littoral of the western cordillera. The sea otter trade and the coast's proximity to Oriental markets increased the desire to unite British commercial interests in North America and in the Pacific via an overland route.[10]

The search for a passage, and later for a practicable overland route, was concurrently undertaken by British fur traders, some of whom had settled in Montreal after the fall of New France, and others who settled there as loyalists during and after the American Revolution. The search for a passage took on a new urgency with the loss of the American colonies, when the British government emphasized its trade with India, China, and the Far East to compensate for the loss of settlement and governance in North America. 'The new search for an empire of trade, rather than of governance,' historian Edwin Rich wrote, 'like the earlier version of the same theme, toyed with visions of Far Cathay, and of a route thither.' Peter Pond, Alexander Henry, Alexander Mackenzie, and David Thompson were part of this new search for a route to the Orient.[11]

In 1781 Alexander Henry, influenced by Pond's important explorations, urged the British government to give the Montreal traders permission to conduct their search through Hudson Bay. He proposed a route from Montreal to the Cumberland House area of the HBC, and thence to the Pacific where 'an Establishment may be made in Some Convenient Bay, or harbour, where Shipping, may come to. In the mean Time a Small Vessell may be Built, for Coasting, and Exploring the Coast.' Furs would be sent back to Montreal. He thought the whole scheme could be put into effect for £13,320, and he concluded that

> there are many National advantages which may result from Discovery and Surveying these Remote, unknown Parts of America, and having a Communication, from other Rich Country's in the East and Easily, Conveyed across to Hudsons bay, where British Manufactorers, might be sent, To Thousands on the Continent, & fetch large Profits & a Valuable New Commerce be opened and Secured to his Majesty's subjects – as there is at present no appearance of a North west passage, for Ships.[12]

The principal late-eighteenth-century advocate of a North West Passage, by land and sea, was a geographer named Alexander Dalrymple

(1737-1808). A younger son of a Scottish baronet, Dalrymple joined the East India Company at the age of fifteen and became that company's hydrographer in 1779. In this capacity, he learned that North American fur was finding its way from London to Russia, and thence overland to China, to the benefit of Russian middlemen. Such fur, he reasoned, should instead be sent directly from the North West Coast to China through the combined efforts of the British fur companies and the East India Company, which possessed the British trade monopoly in the Orient. Dalrymple combined a knowledge of the East Indian trade, the British overland fur trade, and the most recent British maritime discoveries and expeditions to publish, in 1789, his *Plans for Promoting the Fur-Trade and Securing It to This Country by Uniting the Operations of the East India and the Hudson's Bay Companies*. China, he wrote, was the great mart for furs owing to its cold climate, but the country was 'too well inhabited to afford an asylum to animals, which abound only in wastes and wilds.' He reasoned that only the combined trade routes and monopolies of the Hudson's Bay and East India companies could exclude Russian middlemen from this trade and secure it for Britain.[13]

Dalrymple devised a scheme in which one ship would sail annually from London to Canton laden with British goods, and a second, copper-hulled vessel would sail annually from Canton 'for the NW Coast of America, to receive the Furs collected there by the Hudson Bay Company's Agents.' There, the vessel should 'remain in Harbour 'till after the Equinoctial Gales, and then return to China, where she will arrive in December and be ready to come home to England, in January or February.' The missing link was the region between Hudson Bay and the coast; but with the latest information obtained from British fur traders, he published a map in 1789 anticipating that the Saskatchewan River would become the link between Rupert's Land and the North West Coast. This was Dalrymple's overland North West Passage. His project for uniting the trade of the companies was scuttled, however, by the refusal of the East India Company to consider it.[14]

In 1790 Dalrymple continued his efforts, citing and synthesizing the recent discoveries of Cook, Meares, Portlock, and the Hudson's Bay and Canadian traders. 'The opinion therefore of a N.W. Passage,' he wrote early in 1790, 'is strongly confirmed by the concurrence of the antient Reports, the Indian Maps, and the opinion of those who have recently visited the N.W. Coast. The only allegations to the contrary that Capt. Middleton represents *Repulse Bay* to be shut up, and that Capt. Cook & Capt. Clerk [Clerke] could not find a Passage by *Strait* of *Anian* now called *Behring's Strait*.' He believed that explorations by land would be worthwhile and that the HBC had expressed their willingness to cooperate.[15] Dalrymple was also behind the British government's 1790 plan to send a detachment of the British military garrison at Quebec westward to explore the country between Canada and the coastline located by Cook.[16]

Dalrymple continued to wield great influence in London, and in 1795 he was appointed the Admiralty's first chief hydrographer. 'For Vancouver's voyage, as for Cook's, Alexander Dalrymple was in the centre of the web,' Rich wrote, 'industriously and persistently spinning plans for a route which would bring the furs of the prairies and of the Northwest out to the Pacific Coast and so to the China market.' Dalrymple's scheme influenced the Admiralty's decision to send Vancouver to the North West Coast; Vancouver carried specific instructions to find any water communication between the North West Coast, Canada, or Hudson Bay.[17]

Dalrymple's strategy, as it happened, was adopted by the Montreal fur traders. Between 1792 and 1798, the NWC embarked on an 'Adventure to China' in which fur was sent directly to Canton from London with the permission of the East India Company, or indirectly via American firms to Canton, in return for tea and other goods; these shipments, however, either lost money or made little.[18] In exploration as in other activities, the NWC surpassed the HBC in the late eighteenth century, sending Pond to the western prairies and Mackenzie to the Arctic and Pacific oceans. Mackenzie found the first overland route to the Pacific in 1793. Dalrymple, who probably knew Mackenzie, had by this time switched his attention to the Canadian fur trade company. There were real similarities in their projects, though Pond had also influenced Mackenzie greatly. Later, Dalrymple counselled David Thompson on an overland route.[19]

After 1801 the principal lobbyist for an overland route to the Orient was Mackenzie, now in London. In December of that year, he published an account of his explorations, assessing the implications of his and Vancouver's discoveries. Mackenzie announced that he had found a land passage to the Pacific Ocean, and more importantly, he set out a plan for the commercial development of the north Pacific coast – a plan little different from the one proposed by George Simpson twenty years later. Like Dalrymple, Mackenzie envisaged a union of commercial interests in which the HBC would be one of the partners. Hudson Bay, not Montreal (which was too distant), would be one end of the line of communication, and the Columbia River would be the other. In this way, he hoped to open a trade between the Pacific coast and the Chinese market.[20] He urged the government to pressure the HBC to this end:

> By opening the intercourse between the Atlantic and Pacific oceans, and forming regular establishments through the interior, and at both extremes, as well as along the coasts and islands, the entire command of the fur trade of North America, might be obtained, from latitude 48 North to the pole, except that portion of it which the Russians have in the Pacific. To this may be added the fishing in both seas, and the markets of the four quarters of the globe.
>
> Such would be the field for commercial enterprise, and incalculable would be the produce of it, when supported by the operations of that credit and capital which Great Britain so pre-eminently possesses. Then would this country begin to be remunerated for the expenses it has sustained in discovering and surveying the coast of the Pacific Ocean, which is at present left to American adventurers, who without regularity or capital, or the desire of conciliating future confidence, look altogether to the interest of the moment [and who] ... would instantly disappear before a well-regulated trade.[21]

Mackenzie, like many of his predecessors, hoped that the East India Company would relax its monopoly of Britain's trade in India and China, thereby allowing the new company to operate on the Pacific.

Weeks after the publication of his book, Mackenzie transmitted to the British government a proposal entitled *Preliminaries to the Establishment of a Permanent British Fishery and Trade in Furs &c on the Continent and West Coast of North America*. He sought a licence to form a company called 'The Fishery and Fur Company' to combine the Pacific fishery and sea otter trade with the fur trade of the interior. For this 'great national object,' Mackenzie wrote, he hoped to merge the Montreal-based North West and XY companies, and to negotiate with the Hudson's Bay, East India, and South Sea companies for licences to operate or trade in their charter territories. He planned to open a 'Sea Otter House' at 55° north latitude, a commercial, civil, and military base at Nootka, and a subordinate post at the mouth of the Columbia River, the lower reaches of which had been surveyed by Captain Vancouver.[22] Meanwhile, the British government and the HBC continued their arctic search for a North West Passage, in part to counter Russian activities; it was becoming increasingly clear, however, that only a more southerly overland fur trade route to the Pacific would be commercially viable.[23]

Although the British government did nothing about Mackenzie's precocious plan for commercial extension and colonization of the west coast of North America – even though pressed by Dalrymple[24] – Mackenzie's explorations and his book caused a stir in Canada, Britain, and the United States. He demonstrated that overland communication between the Atlantic and Pacific might be opened. He conceptualized a plausible commercial structure for the Pacific coast that, by 1809, included the formation of a commercial colony on the lower Columbia River.[25] The Northwesters pursued Mackenzie's plan by building posts in New Caledonia and exploring the Fraser and Columbia rivers. Thus, by the turn of the nineteenth century, Mackenzie, backed by Dalrymple and the British maritime explorers, had conceived a plan to export pelts from British North America westward across the Pacific to China. This commercial blueprint would remain at the heart of British plans for the region in the early nineteenth century.

The NWC followed Mackenzie's advice. Within a few years, the company's operations beyond the Rockies fell into two regions of considerable activity separated by an immense distance.

New Caledonia, the older district, centred around the upper Fraser River and its tributaries. It possessed a northern climate and a correspondingly rich fur trade. New Caledonia was located by Mackenzie during his 1793 exploration, and was named and explored in 1805 by Simon Fraser, who built posts at McLeod Lake (Fort McLeod 1805), Stuart Lake (Fort St. James, 1806), Fraser Lake on the Nechako River (Fort Fraser, 1806), and at the confluence of the Fraser and Nechako rivers (Fort George, 1807). These posts were meant to capture a rich new region of the fur trade and prevent Native traders from bartering the region's pelts down the Skeena and Nass rivers to the Pacific, where they were eagerly bought by American maritime traders and Russian traders to the north. The Northwesters faced the permanent difficulty of high costs of transport and provisions in a region so far distant from Montreal; New Caledonia received dressed moose or caribou skins (used for moccasins in hunting) from east of the Rockies via Leather (Yellowhead) Pass.[26]

The Columbia, the newer district, lay some 500 miles to the south. Commercially and spatially, the region contrasted markedly with landlocked and eastward-looking New Caledonia. While New Caledonia had been explored from the northern Rockies by Alexander Mackenzie and Simon Fraser, the Columbia had been approached from the central Rockies after 1807 by David Thompson; in 1811 he located Athabasca Pass. The Columbia's orientation was ultimately westward, toward the Pacific Ocean.[27]

After the publication of Mackenzie's book, it became important for British – and American – fur traders to locate an effective overland route to the mouth of the Columbia River. The expansionist Americans responded to the Dalrymple-Mackenzie plan by showing a political and commercial interest in the region. An American edition of Mackenzie's *Voyages from Montreal* appeared in 1802, and another two editions in 1803; a copy was bought by US President Jefferson, who read it late in 1802 and organized the Lewis and Clark expedition the following year to locate a more southerly, American, overland route to the Pacific. 'The object of your mission,' Jefferson instructed Meriwether Lewis in 1803, 'is to explore the Missouri river, & such principal stream of it, as, by it's course & communication with the waters of the Pacific Ocean, may offer the most direct and practicable water communication across the continent, for the purposes of commerce.' Lewis and Clark found Lewis Pass, an avenue (albeit a poor one) between the Missouri and Columbia river systems.[28]

The American success urged the NWC onwards. Mackenzie's 1793 route to the Pacific at Bella Coola, while tempting, was not a practical fur trade route – 'Canoes could never transport pelts over those formidable rapids, nor voyageurs carry packs through those tortuous defiles,' wrote Marjorie Campbell – and Fraser's river, with its precipitous canyon, did not provide such a route either.[29] In the first decade of the nineteenth century, NWC policy west of the Rockies served several interconnected ends: the extension of continental fur trade routes to the Pacific coast, the creation of a Pacific outlet for interior furs that otherwise had to be sent overland to Montreal at vast expense, the hope of access to Oriental markets, and the hope of determining the course of the Columbia River and its northern tributaries. The valuable sea otter trade of the North West Coast was an added attraction to the overland fur traders; indeed, it figured in Mackenzie's mature plan for the commercial development of the region. In 1809, he stated to the British Board of Trade that the Northwesters proposed to extend their trade to the Columbia River, where 'a Commercial Colony might be planted, from whence trade could be carried on and extended, not only with the interior, but along the Coast and its adjacent Islands.'[30] In 1811 the NWC published a book entitled *On the Origins and Progress of the North-West Company of Canada*, based on information provided by Duncan McGillivray. 'Not stopping here [at the Rockies], the Company have passed the Rocky Mountains, and have already established three or four posts on the streams which empty themselves into the Pacific Ocean. Their further design has been ... to explore the whole country to the west of the Rocky Mountains, and to form, upon the great river Columbia, which falls into the Pacific Ocean, in latitude 46° north, a grand establishment for the trade of the adjacent country.' They also wrote that the Columbia 'is the only river, in the whole extent of country, capable of navigation' on its lower reaches.[31]

After several years of remarkable explorations of the upper Columbia and its tributaries, David Thompson reached the mouth of the Columbia on 15 July 1811, having met his object of exploring the river 'to open out a passage for the interior trade with the Pacific Ocean.'[32] However, Thompson, who carefully mapped the southern interior and opened several posts, was not alone. Although his predecessors, Mackenzie and Fraser, had reached the Pacific in 1793 and 1808 without competition from other fur traders, the situation had changed by 1811. Mackenzie's book, together with the impetus given by the American purchase of Louisiana and the reports of the Lewis and Clark expedition, spurred direct American commercial activity: the formation in 1809 of Astor's Pacific Fur Company, whose vessel *Tonquin* reached the mouth of the Columbia on 22 March 1811.[33]

Astor's Pacific Fur Company was, in its main outlines, an American facsimile of the scheme of Mackenzie and the NWC, both conceptually and to the extent that it relied almost entirely on a mercenary workforce of the Canadian fur trade. Historian James Ronda notes that the North West Company 'provided the form and substance for Astor,' who had bought furs from the Northwesters in Montreal as early as 1787, was on close business terms with the Canadians and recruited some of those, Washington Irving wrote, who 'either through lack of interest and influence, or a want of vacancies, had not been promoted.' Hired in 1810, Alexander McKay (who had travelled with Mackenzie to the Pacific in 1793), Duncan McDougall, Donald Mackenzie, David Stuart, and Robert Stuart were 'British subjects experienced in the Canadian fur trade.'[34] These managers hired a group of able clerks at Montreal, some of whom – Ross Cox, Alexander Ross, and Gabriel Franchère – later wrote their Columbia River memoirs.[35] Ramsay Crooks, who succeeded Astor in charge of the American Fur Company, was also a Scot familiar with the Canadian fur trade. Reliance on the Canadian fur trade extended further than the managerial level: both the Lewis and Clark expedition and the Pacific Fur Company relied on an experienced French Canadian workforce.[36] Indeed, a recurrent motif of the Ross and Cox narratives was the Britishness of the Pacific Fur Company partners. For example, the complement that arrived on the *Tonquin* in 1811 to build Astoria consisted of 31 people: 17 British subjects, 11 Sandwich Islanders, and 3 Americans. 'These gentlemen were all British subjects,' Cox recalled, 'and, although engaged with Americans in a commercial speculation, and sailing under the flag of the United States, were sincerely attached to their king and the country of their birth.' Of the 86 Astorians sent overland to the Columbia in 1811 and 1812, 55 were 'Canadian voyageurs'; most of the others were Montreal Scots or traders from the Missouri.[37]

Astor may have benefitted from the NWC's commercial blueprint, personnel and management strategies, and cordilleran explorations, but he also took encouragement from the precedent of the Lewis and Clark expedition and the successes of the American maritime fur traders on the North West Coast. Like Mackenzie and the Northwesters, Astor regarded the lower Columbia as the preferable base of operations. The main difference was that Astor hoped to trap the fur resources of the southerly portions of the cordillera located by Lewis and Clark, while the British scheme had a more northerly focus. As Alexander Ross recalled, Astor hoped to build a chain of posts along the Missouri and Columbia rivers. He planned to sell furs from the drainages of these rivers to Oriental markets, to which he had the advantage of unhindered access, and, like Mackenzie, he planned to engage in the maritime fur trade.[38] 'One part of his plan,' Dunn stated, 'was that a vessel laden with goods for the Indian trade, should every year sail from New York to the Columbia; and, having discharged her cargo at the establishment there, take on board the produce of her year's trade; and thence proceed to Canton, bringing back the rich productions of China.'[39]

The Astorians were harassed by difficulties from the start. The Pacific Fur Company was, Alexander Ross recalled, 'an association which promised so much, and accomplished so little.' The party that arrived by the *Tonquin* was too small to venture up the Columbia, and they welcomed Thompson's arrival at Astoria in July 1812. 'Mr. Thompson, north-west-like, came dashing down the Columbia in a light canoe, manned with eight Iroquois and an interpreter, chiefly men from the vicinity of Montreal,' Ross recalled. A week later Thompson escorted the Astorians up the river: the Astorian party was 'too small to attempt anything of the kind by itself.' Astorian narratives show a consistent admiration for the larger and better-equipped Northwest crews.[40]

In its most important commercial aspects, the Pacific Fur Company was an unqualified disaster. The Astorians built a vessel, *Dolly*, for the coasting trade, but the vessel was too small and unseaworthy for ocean travel. 'There was a fatality attending the ships bound for Columbia,' Ross observed. The *Tonquin* was attacked and destroyed at Clayoquot Sound in 1811 with the loss of the entire crew; the Northwesters unanimously put the blame on Captain Jonathan Thorn, the strict and arrogant American captain of the vessel. In 1813 the supply vessel *Beaver* was severely damaged in a storm, and the *Lark* was wrecked in the same year off the island of Maui. These calamities all but ended the Astorians' hope of receiving goods and getting their furs to market. By the fall of 1813, the Pacific Fur Company had lost the enormous total of 61 men in its Columbia venture.[41]

The Astorians were critical of Astor's distant management. They accused him of appointing an unsuitable captain to the *Tonquin*, and they charged him with supplying trade goods of the worst quality. 'Instead of guns,' wrote Ross, 'we got old metal pots and gridirons; instead of beads and trinkets, we got white linen; and instead of blankets, molasses. In short, all the useless trash and unsaleable articles which had been accumulating in his shops and stores for half a century past, were swept together to fill his Columbia ships.' Astor, Ross argued, preferred to supply the Russians rather than his own people:

> It was a part of Mr. Astor's general plan to supply the Russian factories along the coast with goods; and it would appear, from the conduct of his captains, that to this he devoted his chief attention; reserving for them the choicest part of his cargoes, and for Columbia the mere refuse. This alone gave umbrage to the partners at Astoria; it soured their dispositions to see many articles which they stood in need of passing by their door.[42]

The Scottish partners on the Columbia River decided that Astor's policies were opposed to their best interests. The senior American partner in the company, Wilson Price Hunt, decided that 'the underhand policy of Astor and the conduct of his captains had ruined the undertaking.'[43] At Astoria in June 1813, the partners exercised their option of abandoning the enterprise within five years if it turned out impracticable or unprofitable. They decided to dissolve the concern and abandon the enterprise on 1 June 1814. In October 1813 Duncan McDougall sold the Pacific Fur Company's goods and furs to John George McTavish of the North West Company for $80,000. The agreement gave the Astorians the choice of remaining in the employ of the NWC or returning to Canada or the United States. Most of the Scottish Astorians joined the NWC, but, as Cox wrote, 'The Americans of course preferred returning to their own country, as did Mr. Gabriel Franchere and a few other Canadian clerks.'[44]

The Astorians were quite aware of the growing strength of the North West Company in the Columbia District. Duncan McDougall and Donald Mackenzie knew, late in 1812, that the NWC was 'now strong in numbers and well supplied with goods,' and in 1813 parties of Northwesters congregated at the mouth of the Columbia to meet the supply vessel. In the fall of 1813, at Fort Okanagan, Alexander Ross described seeing 'a strong party of North-westers, seventy-five in number, in a squadron of canoes, on their way to the mouth of the Columbia, in high glee, to meet their ship, the *Isaac Todd*, which was expected daily.' The Northwesters enjoyed efficient and established transport and supply connections with Montreal via New Caledonia, while the Astorians' connections with St. Louis were in their infancy; the first party of overland

Astorians did not reach the lower Columbia until February 1812. The Astorians were also influenced by outside events: in December 1812 they learned from the Northwesters of the outbreak of war between Great Britain and the United States. Officers of the Royal Navy, arriving in the Columbia shortly after the sale of the Pacific Fur Company, renamed Astoria Fort George.[45]

The Astorians did, however, make important innovations and discoveries in their short existence. On the lower Columbia they introduced *bateaux*: split or sawn cedar boats. Owing to the shortage of labour, they adopted the maritime fur traders' habit of hiring Kanakas (Native Hawaiians) at the Sandwich Islands. They extended the fur trade and conducted important explorations: in 1812 they sent Donald Mackenzie and Duncan McDougall to the source of the Willamette River. They found the valley to be very fertile and rich in beaver, and they learned of the 'Imp-qua' River but did not explore it. Robert Stuart's 1812 discovery of South Pass through the southern Rockies was their most lasting achievement. Much later, this pass would allow communication between the Missouri and Columbia watersheds. It was a southerly and in many ways superior answer to Thompson's Athabasca Pass, located a year earlier. 'A journey across the continent of North America might be performed with a waggon,' Stuart claimed. For the Oregon Trail immigrants and later American overlanders, South Pass became the doorway to Oregon.[46]

Despite this discovery, the NWC had been on the ascendant and the Astorians in retreat on the Columbia before 1813. The Northwesters had established a secure provision base nearby in New Caledonia, a rapid and safe brigade trail linking that district with the lower Columbia, and an effective transport system connecting the whole department with the districts east of the Rockies. They had built posts to rival the Astorians', they competed in every branch of business, their supply vessels reached the mouth of the Columbia safely and with goods of the best quality, and in 1813, they welcomed the renegade Northwesters of Astor's company back into their fold.

The NWC, secure on the Columbia with the purchase of the Pacific Fur Company but hindered by the long transport to Montreal, lost no time in putting Alexander Mackenzie's plan into effect. Since

Thompson's arrival they had expended their money, energy, and talent on gaining control of the region and establishing a trade connection with Canton. 'We have established a colony of British subjects on the Columbia River,' the company's suppliers announced in July 1815, 'for the purpose of carrying on the trade with China.' Four years earlier, the NWC had acquired a trade licence from the East India Company to sell their Columbia furs directly to China. The *Isaac Todd* arrived at the Columbia River from London in April 1814, George Simpson recalled, 'the first Ship that took any Produce of the North West Companys trade collected on the West side of the Rocky Mountains and carried it to China from whence she brought a Cargoe of Tea to England for account of the East India Compy.'[47] The *Isaac Todd* was followed by the supply vessels *Columbia* and *Colonel Allen* between 1814 and 1816. The licence from the East India Company to ship furs to Canton, however, had disallowed the NWC from sending a return shipment of its own goods to London from Canton, and the China Venture – not its Columbia River policies as such – produced great losses for the NWC. As Ross recalled, 'A voyage or two across the Pacific, however, convinced the north-westers that the project would not succeed. The port duties at Canton, connected with other unavoidable expenses, absorbed all the profits; and this branch of the trade was relinquished as unprofitable.'[48]

By the end of the decade, the NWC operated six posts on the lower Columbia River and its tributaries, posts that owed their existence largely to David Thompson's explorations (Map 4). They were Spokane House on the Spokane River (1810), Flathead House and Fort Kootenay (satellite posts of Spokane House), Fort George (1811), Fort Okanagan on the Okanagan River (1811), and Fort Nez Perces (also known as Fort Walla Walla) at the fork of the Walla Walla and Columbia rivers (1818). Of these, only forts George and Okanagan had been constructed by the Pacific Fur Company. The Northwesters kept some of the Astorians' innovations in transport and labour. In the interior they continued what Ross called the 'American system' of transporting goods by pack horse. It is true that the NWC sent, in 1813, a shipment of birchbark from Montreal to London and then around the Horn to the Columbia on the *Isaac Todd*, but this was a precautionary trial shipment, and thereafter the NWC constructed *bateaux* on the Columbia. The NWC breathed new life into Astor's moribund operations and integrated them

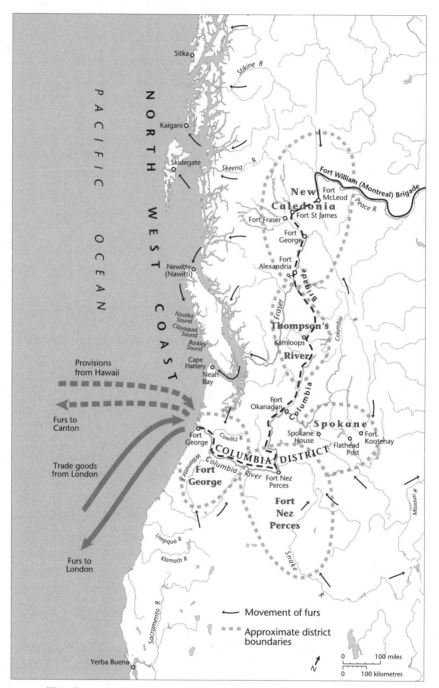

MAP 4 The Columbia Department of the North West Company, 1821

into the company's continental transport and labour networks and markets. Costs of labour were reduced and kept efficient. The Northwesters continued the Astorians' policy of hiring Kanakas at the Sandwich Islands. In 1817 the NWC hired Hawaiians, owing to a labour shortage caused directly by competition between the NWC and HBC east of the Rockies.[49]

The Northwesters also, in 1815, decided that the company's dispatches between Fort George and the interior should be 'entrusted to the natives,' as an economy measure. 'This custom was afterwards continued,' Ross recalled, 'a Columbia Indian was always ready to start in the capacity of courier, for the boon of a few strings of beads, or a few shots of ammunition.' Ross calculated that this saved the expense of sending a brigade of forty or fifty men. This policy of regarding Native people as a cheap source of labour became one of the most striking aspects of the NWC's and later the HBC's regimes west of the Rockies.[50]

The NWC continued to hire experienced voyageurs in Lower Canada and send them to the Columbia. Some left the company and trapped as independent freemen. In 1815 the company introduced large numbers of Iroquois Indians from Montreal so that they could teach others to trap and hunt fur: Astorians and Northwesters alike had been baffled and disturbed by the inability or unwillingness of Indians on the lower Columbia to hunt animals for them. 'The object in introducing them into the service of the traders was to make them act in the double capacity of canoe-men and trappers,' Ross recalled. Skilled Iroquois hunters and trappers soon became a standard feature of the the British fur traders' frontier policies in the Columbia Department.[51]

Iroquois hunters helped the NWC extend the fur trade to much of the Columbia basin before 1821. At its Fort William council meeting of 1815, the NWC resolved to send trapping parties up the Snake River, as Ross recorded:

> And the Columbia itself, in lieu of being confined to the northern branch and sea coast as had been the case since the [Pacific Fur Company] had the trade, would be extended on the south and east, towards California and the mountains, embracing a new and unexplored tract of country. To obviate the necessity of establishing trading posts, or permanent dwellings, among so many warlike and refractory tribes, formidable trapping parties were under chosen leaders, to range the country for furs; and the resources thus to be collected

were annually to be conveyed to the mouth of the Columbia, there to be shipped for the Canton market.[52]

In 1817 Donald Mackenzie embarked on the first Snake River expedition. Trapping and trading parties would be sent out from the lower Columbia to the upper Snake for the next thirty years, to the serious injury of American traders hoping to tap the Columbia fur trade via the upper Missouri and South Pass. In 1818 the NWC built Fort Nez Perces, being more central, Ross wrote, 'for the general business of the interior than that of David Thompson's Spokane House,' built in 1810.[53] Thus, the NWC's use of the Snake River differed fundamentally from the Pacific Fur Company's. Robert Stuart and the Astorians had regarded the Snake River mainly as a route to and from the United States, but the NWC and later the HBC would regard it solely as a frontier to be turned into a fur desert to discourage American overland interest in the Columbia.

Nearer to Fort George were a couple of tributaries with rich if limited fur resources. The Astorians had known of the excellent soil and fur trade of the Willamette Valley, and in 1816 the NWC sent a party of ten men, including Iroquois hunters, to hunt and trap in the valley. In 1818 these hunters got as far as the Umpqua River, and in the same year to the Cowlitz River on the Columbia's north bank, but on each occasion the Iroquois battled with the Native inhabitants to the detriment of the NWC's trade.[54]

These policies were aimed at getting furs from the Snake and lower Columbia to Fort George. Two further policies were formulated at the important 1815 Fort William council meeting. First, the whole of the NWC's business beyond the Rockies was divided into two separate districts, the Columbia and New Caledonia, with James Keith in charge of the Columbia and Donald Mackenzie of the interior. Second, New Caledonia would thereafter receive its annual supplies from the lower Columbia rather than overland from Montreal. These measures were put into effect in 1816, and they were 'hailed,' Ross wrote, 'as opening a new and extensive field for energy and enterprise.'[55]

There was still the problem of getting Columbian and New Caledonian furs to China. After the failure of their 'China Venture,' the Northwesters contracted, in 1814, with Perkins and Company of Boston to carry furs from the Columbia to Canton and to bring return cargoes to the Russian and Spanish settlements on the coast on the NWC's behalf. Such direct shipments allowed New Caledonia to be outfitted from Fort George. American intermediaries were hired, William McGillivray wrote in 1816, because 'the Partners of the North West Company do not understand the management of ships or captains; collecting and trading skins is their real business.'[56]

This second attempt to market Columbia furs in Canton, while effectively avoiding the East India Company monopoly, failed owing to a combination of high commission fees charged by Perkins and Company (about a quarter of the proceeds of the Canton venture), high expenses between the Columbia, Canada, Boston, and Canton, low beaver prices in Canton, and the poor quality of Columbia beaver.[57] HBC trader John Lee Lewes wrote in 1822 that beaver and land otter were numerous on the lower Columbia, but were also 'far inferior' to those procured on the east side of the Rocky Mountains. Pacific slope beaver were also inferior to those of Rupert's Land because, at first, they were less well cured.[58]

Although conceptually mature, the Northwesters' Chinese scheme was a financial disaster (Table 1). Despite its contract with Perkins, and a five-fold increase in returns from the Columbia District between 1813 and 1821, the NWC's shipments to Canton failed. So severe were its losses that the NWC considered abandoning the Columbia River trade altogether. The fabulous Canton prices of the maritime fur trade had applied to sea otter pelts, but this trade was in serious decline; as well, the NWC was reluctant to trade directly on the North West Coast after the destruction of Astor's *Tonquin*, which left the coastal fur trade in the hands of Boston merchants. The company was never completely able to bypass the East India Company monopoly. The Northwesters' China venture was a financial calamity, losing the company about £40,000[59] and contributing materially to the NWC's financial difficulties of 1821 and its merger with the HBC.

Despite the failure of the Canton venture, the work of the NWC after 1793 was innovative and bold. The company had vigorously pursued the late-eighteenth-century British model of trans-Pacific trade and absorbed Astor's nebulous Pacific operations. Mackenzie, Fraser, and Thompson had charted the courses of the Fraser and Columbia rivers, and their successors had extended the fur trade into their watersheds. The Lewis and Clark expedition of 1805-6 had been transitory, leaving

TABLE 1 North West Company profit and loss, China venture (£)

Year	Profit/Loss
1813	−26,041
1814	−19,277
1815	+9,000
1816	−6,247
1817	−6,905
1818	+286
1819	−6,822
1820	n/a
1821	+11,622

Source: H. Lloyd Keith, 'The North West Company's "Adventure to the Columbia": A Reassessment of Financial Failure,' unpublished ms., 1989

almost no physical presence, and the Pacific Fur Company was short-lived, its principal legacy being its experienced Scottish and Canadian workforce consisting of men with no or few American allegiances. The NWC had strengthened its presence west of the Rockies by buying Astor's operations, absorbing his workforce, and putting an end, for the time being, to American trading in the region. They had developed a transport system independent of that developed east of the Rockies, consisting of horse brigades and the Snake River parties, innovations the HBC would incorporate. They and the Astorians had introduced agriculture to the region, albeit on a limited scale, to lessen dependence on imported food and Native provisions; at Fort George on the lower Columbia, company personnel relied on imported food supplemented by their own potatoes and by salmon obtained in the Native trade.[60] Although they undertook fishing and farming at the interior posts, New Caledonia was, and would remain, notorious for privations caused by a lack of food. The Northwesters had not considered the export of provisions or agricultural foodstuffs from the Pacific: natural abundance did not automatically or immediately translate into a diverse commercial economy. Aside from its ambitious Canton venture, the NWC had not transcended the riverine mentality that had served it so well in its competitive westward expansion from the St. Lawrence River.

The NWC's business west of the Rockies was hindered from the beginning by the distance from Montreal and by the high cost of transport, problems that were not so severe for the HBC, which could send its vessels to bayside posts a thousand miles west and inland of Montreal. Potential profits were absorbed in transport expenses. In 1808 Duncan McGillivray wrote that 'The trade as it is carried on at present beyond the mountains, instead of getting any profit, is a very considerable loss to the Company, as the furs did not pay the transport to Montreal where they were shipped.' Even in Rupert's Land, the NWC was at a disadvantage: in 1821 William McGillivray reflected that the Montreal company had been unable to compete 'against a Chartered Company, who brought their goods to the Indian Country at less than one half the Expense that ours cost us.'[61] The expensive transport to Montreal only increased the need for a Pacific outlet. Until 1820, New Caledonia had received supplies and provisions from east of the Rockies, but the supply and fur brigades to and from Montreal were replaced with the Okanagan brigade route; the first fur brigade left Fort St. James for lower Fort George in June 1820. Thereafter, the New Caledonian operations of the NWC were merged with their lower Columbian operations, and what had been two trade systems became one.[62]

A rapid and efficient brigade route connected the Columbia and New Caledonia districts (Map 4). Devised by the Northwesters, the route followed the upper Fraser, Thompson River, Monte Creek ('Grand Prairie'), Okanagan Lake, Okanagan River, and the Columbia River.[63] Midway were two NWC establishments: Fort Alexandria on the Fraser (1821), and Kamloops or Thompson's River Post (1812).[64] The NWC had recognized four districts in the southern interior and Columbia watershed: Thompson's River District (Kamloops and Fort Okanagan), Spokane District (including Spokane House, Flathead House, and Fort Kootenay), Fort Nez Perces (Walla Walla) District, and Fort George District.[65] Some of this activity is visible in Alexander Ross's extraordinary 1821 map of the Columbia River basin, now housed at the British Museum (Map 5). He based it on the NWC's explorations and trade of the Columbia, Snake, and lower tributaries. It shows a vast interior region dominated by the Columbia River and its southern tributary, 'the Great Snake Branch.' For effect, Ross exaggerated the width of both rivers. The map shows the degree to which Ross and the Northwesters understood the region – its great rivers and tributaries as well as the main ethnographic divisions within the Columbia drainage. The limits of the map are the Pacific Ocean, the Rocky Mountains, the Spanish frontier to the south, and the southern edges of the North West Coast.[66]

The NWC's operations, headquartered on the Pacific at lower Fort George, were extensive. Fort George, Gough writes, was the 'linchpin of the transcontinental/trans-Pacific fur trade.'[67] A description of the post by Northwester Peter Corney has survived, describing the fort in

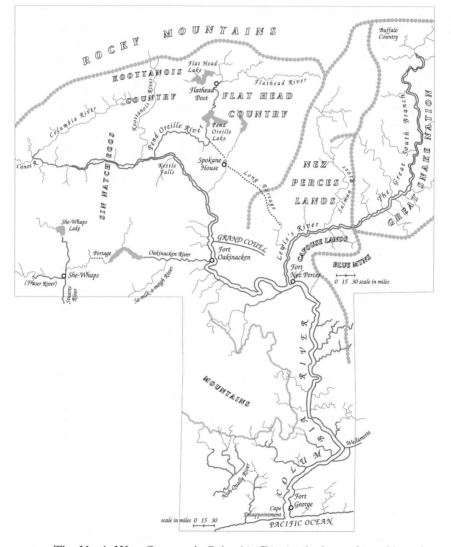

MAP 5 The North West Company's Columbia District (redrawn from Alexander Ross map, 1821)

late 1817: 'The whole of the settlers do not exceed 150 men, most of whom keep Indian women, who live inside of the fort with them. Nearly all the settlers are [French] Canadians. The clerks and partners are Scotch.' The fort was a square of about 200 yards, surrounded by pickets about fifteen feet high and protected by two bastions. On the Columbia River in front of the fort was a wharf with a crane for landing and shipping goods from the interior and from the Pacific:

> The Company's canoes arrive here from the interior, in the spring and fall; they bring the furs that are collected at the different posts on the west side of the stoney mountains, and take back stores for the posts. The canoes are manned by Euroque [Iroquois] Indians and Canadians, under the direction of a partner and several young clerks ... The Company have a train of posts from the Columbia River to the rocky or stoney mountains, and from thence to Montreal; all the furs that are collected at the west side of these mountains are brought to the Columbia, and sent from thence to China; and all that are collected on the east side are sent to Montreal, and from thence to England.[68]

Place-names on the Columbia River – for example, la Port de l'enfer (hell's gate), la Course de Satan (Satan's course), la Passage du Diable (the devil's passage), les Cornes du Démon (demon's horns) and les dalles des morts (the rapids of the dead) – reflected the river's treacherous rapids and canyons, and betrayed the origins of the voyageurs who navigated them. Numerous other locations, from the Grand Coulee to the Cascades, were named by lower Canadian voyageurs. By 1821 the southern tributaries of the Snake had been named the Piednoir, Portneuf, Bruneau, Owyhee, Malheur, Bruler, La Poudre, and Grand Ronde.[69] Voyageurs carried the goods around the portages and over the Rockies, and pack horses were used where possible. 'The goods were made into packages weighing eighty-four pounds,' Joseph William (Joe) McKay recalled; 'each package was called a piece; two pieces made a load for one horse, with which he was expected to travel about twenty miles a day; on portages where there were no horses each man in the brigade was expected to carry from eight to ten pieces one mile a day in quarter mile stages, two pieces at a time. Some of the voyageurs exhibited great strength. Poulet Paul of the Saskatchewan Brigade carried six pieces (504 pounds) one mile without resting. The returns of furs were baled

FIGURE 1 *Hauling Up a Rapid, Les Dalles des Morts*, Columbia River, 1845, a water-colour painted by twenty-five-year-old British army officer Henry Warre. Warre came overland to the Columbia in 1844 and compiled the best extant pictorial record of the western operations of the HBC. [BC Archives, PDP 57]

into neat packages, each weighing eighty-four pounds.'[70]

The NWC's position west of the Rockies was, then, based around two great river systems (the upper Fraser and the lower Columbia) connected by brigade, two markets (London and Canton), and one export (fur). Only Fort George was near the coast. The entire annual trade, storage, and transport of about twenty thousand parchment beaver and land otter was achieved by 230 employees based at ten posts.[71] The brigade routes were light rapid transit systems between distant points; they were not designed for bulk carriage. There were large uncharted areas in the NWC's field of operations, the most significant of which were the intricate coastal regions north of the Columbia River, including Puget Sound, the Gulf of Georgia, the lower Fraser, the whole of Vancouver Island, the North West Coast, and every river north of the Fraser, including the Skeena and Nass. Despite Fraser's journey of 1808, the NWC had, in 1821, only a vague idea of where the Fraser met the sea.

The Americans, absent on the lower Columbia in 1821, dominated the

sea otter trade of the North West Coast – that is, the coastline north
of Cape Flattery, including the west coast of Vancouver Island and the
Queen Charlotte Islands (Map 4). This trade was dominated by shrewd
Boston merchants, who traded sea otter pelts and an increasing number
of beaver from the peoples of the coast to the Cantonese market, and
supplied the Russian American Company on the north coast with foodstuffs and trade goods. Neither the NWC nor the HBC had control
over this sea otter trade, which, in any event, was in decline in 1821.[72]
The maritime fur traders had done their transactions on the outer coast,
leaving the labyrinthine inner coastline much as Vancouver had found
it in the 1790s. The NWC had no posts north of the Columbia in 1821
and had shown no interest in the coastal trade after the destruction of
the *Tonquin* at Clayoquot in 1811.

More serious than the declining sea otter trade was the diversification undertaken by the American maritime traders. They obtained 3,000
to 5,000 beaver skins annually from Native traders on the coast.[73] These
were continental pelts, most of which would otherwise have been traded
eastward to New Caledonia. The American maritime fur trade was
doomed, however, by the coordinated and well-capitalized commercial
strategies of the HBC. In the 1830s, the company would supplant the
American maritime fur trade along with one of its great specialists, Captain William Henry McNeill.

To the north, the Russian American Company operated a chain of
posts from their depot at Sitka. In 1821 they occupied five administrative districts: Unalaska, Kodiak, the Northern Islands, New Archangel
(Sitka), and Fort Ross in California. Like the Americans, the Russians
traded fur on the coast that originated in interior districts little known
to the NWC, like the Yukon, Taku, Stikine, Nass, and Skeena rivers.
But as Gibson points out, Russian participation in the maritime fur trade
did not extend south of Dixon Entrance, 'and it remained marginal fig-
uratively as well as literally.' The Mexicans obtained sea otter on the
California coast, but they did not trade actively on the North West Coast,
and Spanish claims to sovereignty had been circumscribed by the Nootka
Convention of 1794.[74]

In 1821 the political situation was as vulnerable as the commercial one.
Under the 1818 Anglo-American Convention, Great Britain and the
United States had agreed to share the Oregon Territory: both had the

right to the trade and 'joint occupancy' of the region west of the Rockies (between 42° and 54°40′ north latitude) for ten years, leaving 'sovereignty' (non-Native title, that is) undefined between California and Russian America. This meant that further American competition could be expected from Robert Stuart's South Pass. American political claims to the region were strengthened in 1819 with the Adams-Onis Treaty between the United States and Spain, in which the Americans inherited the tenuous Spanish claim of sovereignty between 42° and 54°40′ north latitude.[75]

The British fur traders' plans for the region had temporarily triumphed. American plans, similar in many respects, would remain dormant and thwarted for a generation after Astor's failure. Representatives of both nations continued to speak of the enormous geopolitical value of the lower Columbia. In September 1821, for example, an American congressional committee recommended the formal colonization of the Columbia. 'In a commercial point of view,' wrote John Floyd, the Columbia was 'a position of the utmost importance; the fisheries on that coast, its open ocean, and its position in regard to China, which offers the best market for the vast quantities of furs taken in those regions.' The Americans, in short, had assumed the late-eighteenth-century British perception of the region, and through Lewis and Clark and Astor they possessed a valid political claim to the lower Columbia.[76]

The commercial situation inherited by the HBC on the Pacific coast in 1821 was, then, both promising and fraught with problems. The NWC controlled the fur trade of the Columbia River but had lost money there. The Northwesters had strengthened Fort George and made it a depot for their Columbia business. Yet even with access to Pacific markets and with the abundant coastal resources at their disposal, the Northwesters had struggled. They adopted the provisioning pattern developed by American merchants involved in the maritime fur trade. After 1814 they sent their vessels to Monterey for provisions. They also went to Sitka for supplies, and as late as 1817-18 they were dependent on distant American suppliers for the most basic goods: they went to Honolulu to buy, slaughter, and pickle 100 barrels of pork. They had barely made a start toward agricultural self-sufficiency.[77] The Northwesters had avoided the maritime fur trade altogether, leaving it in the hands of Boston merchants. In fact, their oceanic operations depended largely on Boston merchants involved in the Canton and North West Coast trades, such as Perkins and Company and Bryant & Sturgis, who provided vessels and agents.

Native labour was restricted primarily to the fur trade, and to a lesser degree to the provision trade. Native people worked indirectly for the traders: they hunted and trapped animals on their own land and prepared pelts at their own settlements. Native women lived with traders at their posts; there was probably one for every NWC employee. They also provided provisions such as salmon. In April 1821, James Keith of Fort George wrote to his supplier, Perkins and Company, about the difficulties of obtaining a provision supply in this extremely remote region. Keith was dependent on the Chinook people of the lower Columbia for salmon, sturgeon, and wildfowl. 'The Winter has been unusually severe both as to the degree of cold & quality & duration of the snow,' he wrote:

> The fishery of the smelt being lately over the Natives begin to bring us a chance Sturgeon & wild fowl, which when more abundant will be gratifying to people from a long sea Voyage. Our horticultural labours in the experiment of the apple seed I am sorry to say did not succeed, though I believe as much owing to the want of the usual Conveniences, & using the requisite precautions as any defect of Climate, which by the bye is by no means one of the most invigorating or salubrious. Our Potatoes of which we raised upwards of 1000 Bushels last year, & which with our salted Salmon were [our] most valuable produce ...[78]

Keith, struggling to get a share of the produce of the Native economy, was unaware that the NWC no longer existed.

On 26 March 1821, the Hudson's Bay and North West companies had merged, retaining the name HBC and ending a period of competition that had not, however, extended across the Rockies. The HBC did not possess a single post west of the Rocky Mountains.[79] Control of the Columbia River fur trade passed from the Montreal-based branch of the British fur trade to the powerful London-based branch, which would reap the benefit of the Northwesters' audacious beginnings.

The new company was British, well-capitalized, with strong ties to the City of London, and a financial survivor of the competitive era. It held what A.C. Anderson called a 'vast command of capital.'[80] The company was run from London by a governor and a board of directors known as the Governor and Committee (G&C). In North America, it was supervised by departmental governors and the Northern Council of Rupert's Land. Two enormous departments were created out of the vast amalgamated territory of the rival companies: the Northern and Southern departments, each of which dwarfed the tiny Canadian colonies to the south and east of them (see Map 1). Each department was large enough, Alexander Ross recalled, 'for the territory of a crowned head.'[81] Each possessed an administrative centre known as a depot, where furs were gathered to await shipment to London, and where British trade goods were unloaded for distribution to the interior.[82] William Williams – one-time commander of an East India Company ship – was put in charge of the Southern Department, and George Simpson of the Northern. Previously in charge of the HBC's Athabasca District, Simpson had until a few years before been a sugar-broker's clerk in a London firm of West India merchants; he was thirty-four years old in 1821.[83] Almost from the start, the G&C placed a high degree of confidence in him. 'Sir George Simpson's rule is more absolute than that of any governor under the British crown,' his critic John McLean wrote in 1845; 'his influence with the committee enables him to carry into effect any measure he may recommend.' Another fur trader, John Tod, recalled that Simpson's long tenure as governor made him practically autocratic. Simpson also dominated the Northern Council of Rupert's Land, the orders of which were 'considered the statutes of the land.'[84] In December 1821 the HBC received political sanction to operate west of the Rockies when the government awarded it the exclusive British licence to trade with the Native peoples.[85] This legal monopoly did not apply, of course, to American merchants operating in the region.

The HBC had a very important advantage over its rivals: from a legal point of view, there was nothing stopping the company from exporting anything it liked. The British government's Royal Charter of 1670 had given the company the right to develop the resources of Hudson Bay and the rivers that drained into it. The government had granted the company the trade in furs and 'other considerable commodities':

The Fishing of all sortes of ffish Whales Sturgions and all other Royal ffishes in the Seas Bayes Islettes and Rivers within the premisses and the ffish therein taken together with the Royalty of the Sea upon the Coastes and the lymittes aforesaid And all Mynes Royall as well discovered as not discovered of Gold Silver Gemms and pretious Stones to bee found or discovered.

The Crown also gave the company the 'entire Trade and Trafficke' with the Native peoples of Rupert's Land, while all other British subjects were forbidden to 'visit, haunt, frequent, trade, traffic or adventure' within the drainage of Hudson Bay.[86] These and other privileges, common to English colonial companies formed in the seventeenth century, were confirmed and extended by parliament for the next two centuries. The company had examined a wide variety of 'Comodityes besides Furres' for their export potential in Rupert's Land soon after 1670, including walrus teeth, minerals, whale oil, turpentine, potash, and maple sugar,[87] but by the early eighteenth century furs had emerged as the sole substantial export. In the absence of bulky exports, company labourers at York Factory annually collected and stored beach stones as ballast for the homeward ship.[88]

The HBC, then, was a trading company with a comprehensive interest in natural resources, though only after its merger with the NWC and its expansion to the Pacific coast would it finally take ample advantage of the spirit of its charter. The NWC, on the other hand, was a fur-trading company pure and simple.[89] It did not have a clear charter right to engage in other export trades, and the length of its canoe route west of Montreal excluded all but light, valuable commodities. The NWC's interest in resource development extended, therefore, only to those resources necessary for local provisioning trades.

There was little immediate change in personnel or policy when news of the merger reached Fort George. The NWC had recruited a remarkable pool of talent and had promoted traders in proportion to their ability to develop new sources of both fur and provisions. Their commercial prowess was inherited by the HBC in the Columbia Department, the management of which between 1821 and 1858 was in the hands of old Northwesters: John Cameron, John Haldane, John McLoughlin, Peter Ogden, and James Douglas. A list of other old Northwesters in the Columbia Department between 1821 and 1843 reads like a roll call: Alexander Ross, James McMillan, John McLeod, Alexander McLeod, Richard Grant, John Stuart, Michel Laframboise, William Kittson,

Donald Manson, Samuel Black, Thomas McKay, François Payette, Finan McDonald, James Birnie. Some had worked for the Pacific Fur Company (Alexander Ross and Michel Laframboise); Black had even worked for the XY Company – the NWC's old competitor in Montreal. As Joe McKay recalled:

> The organization of the North-West Company was better suited to the circumstances and conditions of what might be called the Indian country than that of the Hudson's Bay Company, and the Directors of the United Company promptly adapted thereto what was best in each management, and proceeded to extend their business on a sounder and broader basis under the title of the older and more privileged one, namely, that of the Hudson's Bay Company.[90]

Nicholas Garry, an inspecting director of the HBC, observed in 1821 that, in comparison with the Northwesters, 'the old Hudson's Bay servants are too fond of old regulations to encourage a new branch of trade and innovations.'[91]

The merger also gave the HBC a vastly experienced pool of French Canadian, Scottish, Native, and Metis traders, labourers, and trappers, a workforce that gave the company great internal strength and advantages beyond the reach of American rivals. One of the HBC's early Snake River parties, according to Alexander Ross, consisted of forty-one men from east, and twelve from west of the Rockies: 'two Americans, seventeen Canadians, five half-breeds from the east side of the mountains, twelve Iroquois, two Abinakee Indians from Lower Canada, two natives from Lake Nipisingue, one Sauteaux from Lake Huron, two Crees from Athabasca, one Chinook, two Spokanes, two Kouttanais, three Flatheads, two Callispellums, one Palloochey, and one Snake Slave!' Ross was alarmed by the medley of dress, accents, and notions of the 1823 Snake Party.[92] In the 1830s, the American fur trader Nathaniel Wyeth summarized the advantages lent by this skilled workforce:

> In fact the traders of the Hudson's Bay Company have advantages over all competitors in the trade beyond the Rocky Mountains. That huge monopoly centers within itself not merely its own hereditary and long-established power and influence; but those of its ancient rival, now an integral part, the famous North-west Company. It has thus its races of traders, trappers, hunters and voyageurs, born and brought up in its service, and inheriting from preceding

generations its knowledge and aptitude in everything connected with Indian

life, and Indian traffic ... Their capital also, and manner in which their supplies are distributed at various posts, or forwarded by regular caravans, keep
their traders well supplied, and enable them to furnish their goods to the
Indians at a cheap rate.[93]

However, some of the new company's managers were first-generation
fur traders, often from mercantile backgrounds. Simpson had been a
London merchant; Douglas's father was a West Indies merchant.
McLoughlin came from a seigneurial background on the St. Lawrence
River, John Work grew up on a farm in Ireland, Peter Ogden was the
son of a Lower Canadian justice, and James Yale of Fort Langley was
also a Lower Canadian of bourgeois background. 'Indeed,' wrote Karl
Andreas Geyer, a German botanist who visited the Columbia in 1843-4,
'the officers of the Hudson's Bay Company are a group of rather substantial, educated men.'[94] Unlike some of their contemporaries who first
arrived on the Columbia by ship from Britain, they had prior continental
experience and were keenly aware of environmental and economic contrasts between Rupert's Land and the west coast.

Whatever their former experience, all applied themselves to the latent
commercial potential of the region. They became experts in matters of
geography, exploration, and Pacific trade; they developed a rigorously
competitive, mercantile, spatial mentality. An inventory of Fort Vancouver's library revealed such volumes as '*1 McKenzie's Voyage, 1 Universal
Geography, 1 Pope's Commercial Guide.*'[95]

In 1821 the HBC inherited the NWC's position west of the Rockies,
along with its skills and personnel, its problems of transport and supply, an essentially unexploited commercial position on the Pacific coast,
and the discoveries of the British maritime and overland explorers.
Americans hoping to trade in this region would face a company with a
specialized but extensive commercial experience in the fur trades of New
France, Hudson Bay, and Rupert's Land, a company supported by the
financial resources of the City of London, and one eager to absorb the
entire trade beyond the mountains.

CHAPTER 2

Managing
a New Region

Altho' the Country has been occupied upwards of Fourteen Years,
and immense sums of money expended therein I feel that as yet
we have done little more than Commenced operations on this
side the Continent.

— GEORGE SIMPSON, FORT GEORGE
(LOWER COLUMBIA RIVER), 1825[1]

At the time of the 1821 merger, the Columbia Department was in the hands of two Northwesters, John Dugald Cameron and John Haldane, chief factors in the amalgamated company. George Simpson and the Hudson's Bay Company's Governor and Committee were concerned about the state of the department. New Caledonia, the northern district, was safe. Historically and commercially, the district was an extension of the Rupert's Land fur trade: its fur-bearing animals were abundant and it was considered the nursery of the transmontane fur trade. New Caledonia was also distant from American competition on the lower Columbia and North West Coast, and it could be outfitted from York Factory without ruinous expense.[2]

The southern, or Columbia District, was another matter. The G&C considered abandoning it. Fur obtained there was generally inferior in quality to that from the north, the cost of provisioning by sea was immense, and the region was open to competitors. The North West Company, despairing of supplying the region overland from Montreal, had sent provisions and outfits by sea from London and Boston and had marketed the region's furs directly in Canton – and had lost £40,000 on its China adventure. In 1821 the HBC quickly cancelled the NWC's unprofitable contract with Perkins and Company. The Astorians had sent a vessel to trade on the North West Coast, but the *Tonquin* had been destroyed with great loss of life and property; the Northwesters had avoided the coast altogether. As a result, the valuable fur trade of the coast, located by Cook and explored and charted by Vancouver, remained firmly in the hands of American and Russian fur traders in 1821, and British merchants were absent.[3] Any attempt by the Hudson's Bay Company to enter the Pacific fur trade promised to be both dangerous and costly. Finally, owing to the 1818 Anglo-American Convention, the company's entire business west of the Rockies, in New Caledonia and on the lower Columbia, was subject to legitimate competition from American fur traders. East of the Rockies, where the forty-ninth parallel defined a line between British and American jurisdictions, such territorial competition was theoretically absent. The Columbia Department, therefore, was an open frontier where the company's monopoly of the Indian trade served only to exclude other British merchants.

In 1822, the company's G&C were so worried about the region's future that they ordered a partial strategic retreat. They decided that both the New Caledonia and Columbia districts should be supplied from York Factory, thus temporarily undoing one of the NWC's major policy initiatives west of the Rockies: the outfitting of New Caledonia from the Pacific depot at Fort George.[4] In February 1822, they asked Simpson to consider withdrawing from the lower Columbia to New Caledonia:

> But if by any improved arrangement the loss can be reduced to a small sum, it is worth a serious consideration, whether it may not be a good policy to hold possession of that Country, with the view of protecting the more valuable districts to the North of it; and we wish you to direct the attention of the council to this subject and collect all the information which you can obtain from individuals acquainted with the Country
>
> Should the result of all your enquiries be unfavourable to the plan of continuing the trade of Columbia it will be proper to consider, whether it will be better to continue the trading establishments there ... The Russians are endeavouring to set up claims to the North West Coast of America as low as Latitude 51, and we think it desirable to extend our trading operations as far to the West and North from Frazer's River in Caledonia, as may be practicable, if there appears any reasonable prospect of doing so profitably.[5]

By the fall of 1822, the G&C, acting on Simpson's advice, no longer considered withdrawing from the Columbia. In July, Simpson had told them that the Columbia trade had improved over the previous year. He praised John Haldane for his 'oeconomical and systematic arrangements,' he wrote that Haldane and 'every Gentleman conversant with the affairs of that Country are of opinion that it would not be politic to withdraw from that Country if it does not realize profits no loss is likely to be incurred thereby and it serves to check opposition from the Americans,' and he proposed that the Columbia be supplied directly from London. He also told John Cameron that it might be necessary to extend the trade to the North West Coast to keep the Russians 'at a distance.'[6] In September, the G&C, reflecting Simpson's opinions, outlined to Haldane and Cameron their proposals for the extension of trade, economic diversification, and the opening of a direct trade between the Pacific coast and Canton:

> We have to desire that you will transmit a full and detailed Statement of the Trade of the Columbia Department, your opinion as to the possibility of extending it, it being absolutely necessary that we should possess every information relative to the productions of the Country, in order to ascertain the possibility of bringing other articles as well as Peltries to a profitable market.
>
> You will likewise state whether you consider that a Vessell can be beneficially employed on the Coast, in collecting Furs, and procuring provisions from California or elsewhere for the Service of the Department, the size and description of Vessell best adapted to such purpose and in the event of it being considered in future advisable to forward the trade of the Columbia Department direct to Canton, you will also state whether any Officer in the department, [is] competent to take charge of the Goods and proceed with the ship as Super Cargo to Canton.[7]

The G&C briefly contemplated hiring the NWC's old Boston agents, Perkins and Company, to supply the Columbia with provisions and to market furs and other commodities in Canton.[8] Their decision to revert to a China venture resulted from the surprising £12,000 profit arising from the Northwesters' final shipment of Columbia furs to Canton, a profit that benefited the newly merged company.[9] If such a China trade were to be rejuvenated, it could only take place from Fort George on the lower Columbia. Such a plan in fact appeared in 1821 with the publication in London of *Voyages in the Northern Pacific* by Peter Corney, who had spent the years 1814-18 at Fort George with the Northwesters. His book was firmly in the tradition of Mackenzie, Dalrymple, and the British maritime fur traders. Corney thought the Northwesters and other

British merchants had not sufficiently challenged American commercial dominance of the Pacific trade between China and the Sandwich Islands (the Hawaiian Islands), and the North West Coast.[10]

In 1823, the G&C decided to transport the Columbia's complete outfits to Fort George every two years on a vessel from London. This arrangement would avoid all direct and indirect contact with Canton and Boston and allow the HBC to maintain entire control of the transport system and fur imports.[11] The company would now outfit the Columbia Department as it had outfitted posts on the bay for 150 years: the company's own vessels would deliver trade goods and other supplies to Fort George in exchange for furs destined for the London market. There was no place for American middlemen in this scheme. The circuit was longer than the Hudson Bay route, taking up to six months in each direction, and it differed also in that the Columbia ship would stop en route – at Honolulu, the new Pacific market. Thus, the company's Pacific policies of the 1820s broke with those of the NWC, but they benefited from the Northwesters' experience.

In the background were other, equally important, political reasons for retaining the lower Columbia. The region's principal explorers had been British fur traders employed by the NWC, whose personnel and ideals had passed over to the new company. The Northwesters had gained commercial control of the Columbia. In the 1820s, the Columbia River provided the only effective continental opening onto the Pacific coast of North America, the northern parts of which had been charted assiduously thirty years before by George Vancouver. British fur traders sought to solidify their right to a territory they had done much to explore and occupy. The nationalism and jingoism of Corney, Simpson, and others reflected the reality of their achievement.

Moreover, although the region was firmly in the hands of the British fur trade, it was also, politically, equally open to Americans, who might arrive at any time by land or sea to enjoy their trading rights. An extended British fur trade in the interior would ensure that American fur traders, working from the upper Missouri and Platte Rivers, would not move easily into the Columbia River watershed. Joint political status would be meaningless if the company could exert complete commercial control; a competitive British fur trade could keep Americans out of the region as effectively as political sovereignty, at least in the short term.

The threat from American fur traders would be greatly increased if they perceived the HBC dithering about the Columbia District. Although American traders had equal access to the region, they had abandoned it in 1813 with the sale of Astoria, and they had not returned. As Corney wrote in 1821, the American fur traders, and the whole trajectory of American westward expansion, were stuck beyond the Missouri on the eastern edge of an 'immense space of desert territory.' 'For several years past, it has been a favorite object of the American Government to open an easy communication from American western settlements to the Pacific Ocean.' Corney believed the Americans planned to revive Astor's strategy of opening a chain of posts to the Pacific; Lewis and Clark, after all, had crossed the continent by a route that connected the Missouri and Columbia river systems, and Robert Stuart had found a second and superior southerly route, South Pass.[12]

However, in 1821, the British fur traders controlled the best natural access to the Pacific coast via the Fraser and Columbia rivers, linked effectively by the Okanagan Brigade route. Both rivers arose in the northern Rockies and flowed, more or less, in a southwesterly direction through profitable fur territory to the ocean. This access was worth maintaining. The Columbia River was the natural line of communication within the department. By contrast, the route from St. Louis, disused since 1812, involved a lengthy journey through the little-known and notorious Snake Country. If the company had abandoned the lower Columbia in the 1820s, the fur trade of the North West Coast, the Columbia, and the whole of the interior, including that of New Caledonia, would have been vulnerable to American traders entering overland from the Missouri or from the lower Columbia itself.

After 1822, there was no more talk of abandoning the Columbia region. The company decided it was worth expanding for its commercial and political potential: to protect New Caledonia's fur trade, to maintain a British mercantile presence on the northern Pacific coast, to keep the Russians well to the north, to confront American traders in the southern interior and on the North West Coast, and to find new exports to Pacific markets.

These plans, like those advanced earlier by Mackenzie and the Northwesters, would have remained at a theoretical stage without a confidence born of a practical, material knowledge of the ways of the fur trade. In the early nineteenth century, only the North West and Hudson's Bay companies could be so confident. In 1821, the HBC inherited the expansionistic, territorial ambitions of the Canadian and British fur traders, as well as the daily skills of the fur trade. The British fur traders brought with them a distinctive set of commercial strategies worked out to the east of the Rockies over some 200 years, strategies identified in 1930 by Harold Innis in his book *The Fur Trade in Canada*. These strategies can be summarized as follows:

(1) exploring new regions in search of furs ('extending the trade')
(2) applying policies of overhunting or fur conservation, depending on the presence or absence of competition
(3) striving for monopoly control to cut costs
(4) devising both fixed (official) and variable (unofficial) standards of trade
(5) devising an effective 'Indian policy'
(6) searching for internal supplies of food ('provisions' or 'country produce')
(7) borrowing aspects of the material culture of Native people
(8) using inexpensive local labour, often Native or Metis
(9) encouraging traders' self-reliance and initiative
(10) devising forms of transportation suitable to cold climates, to the goods being transported, to immense distances, and to river travel
(11) producing local implements ('country-made trade goods')
(12) searching for export commodities other than fur.[13]

These strategies enabled British fur traders to develop the resources of new regions in conjunction with the Native inhabitants. They were the methods by which provisions were obtained, costs were reduced, export trades were developed, and, ultimately and inadvertently, regional economies were created. They countered the high overhead cost of transportation, personnel, and provision, and had been applied – sometimes sporadically, sometimes consistently – for almost two centuries before the fur trade reached the west coast.

High overhead costs were persistent, a result of the fur trade's isolation and expansionist nature. The traders' principal solutions to the problems were recurrent and replicative, shifting in location and details as the companies extended operations to new parts of the continent. Provisioning strategies, for example, were applied to very different environments: pemmican became the staple food of the Rupert's Land fur trade, salmon of the Columbia Department. That the fur trade operated successfully in such different regions as Hudson Bay and the Pacific coast suggests a flexible and adaptable commercial expertise.

After 1821, the sheer vastness and isolation of the HBC's domain made the uniform adoption of these commercial strategies of crucial importance – and Governor Simpson's unchallenged authority made them possible. Faced with a top-heavy and superfluous workforce in 1821, Simpson transformed the old cost-cutting strategies into coherent new policies for the continental fur trade.[14] These strategies allowed the fur trade to be prosecuted in remote places, including on the company's frontiers where they encountered American fur traders who generally lacked some or most of the British fur trade strategies.

Fur traders, who for want of a better term referred to the company's entire territory as 'the Country,' were well aware of the vast scale of their business. The NWC had extended its trade from the St. Lawrence to the Arctic ('Frozen') and Pacific oceans, and after 1821 the HBC controlled the greater part of British North America (Map 1). In 1843, for example, Simpson referred to the company's districts as extending 'from the Atlantic to the Pacific – from the shores of Labrador to the Polar Sea.'[15] No politician in the Canadian colonies or the United States could yet make such a territorial claim. Indeed, the transcontinental fact at the basis of Canadian nationhood ultimately owes more to the policies and economies of the Canadian and British fur trade companies than to the political and territorial ambitions of the original Canadian colonies.

In 1821, the HBC had great confidence in its commercial control and managerial expertise in the regions known as the 'Indian Country,' the company's territorial heartland held by charter or licence for the purpose of trade. The company had also inherited a large, diverse, and experienced pool of labour from the old North West, Hudson's Bay, Pacific Fur, and XY companies. This new company was well capitalized and could afford to charter ships in London and send them around the world to develop the fur trade of a new region and to ensure the absence of competitors – and could withstand a few years' losses to do so.

On the Pacific coast, the HBC applied its commercial strategies to local resources, labour supplies, and available markets with impressive results. The British fur traders reached the Pacific via a region of violent climatic extremes – brief and hot summers, frigid and sterile winters – and failed export trades. Without a railway or reliable winter road, the company had not been able to develop the resources of Rupert's Land beyond the trade in furs and a few other light, valuable animal products, like isinglass and castorum. A penurious environment and isolated location placed severe checks on commercial development; the fur trade had hardly diversified and the company's ambitions were sharply circumscribed.

On the west coast, conditions were favourable for the implementation of the Dalrymple-Mackenzie plan for a Pacific commerce. The accumulated competitive skills of an eighteenth-century interior fur trade were married with those of a nineteenth-century commercial maritime economy. Resources were abundant, the climate was conducive to agricultural undertakings, year-round ocean-borne transport was feasible, distant markets were accessible, and a large Native population was available for trade and work. The HBC would encounter little difficulty in locating a suitable market, which transpired to be Honolulu, not Canton. By the 1840s, the lower Columbia possessed a wide commercial base similar to what the Red River region, for example, would acquire only after the completion of the Canadian Pacific Railway forty years later.

Neither the Strait of Anian, nor the North West Passage, nor direct access to the Canton market would be located by the HBC after 1821. The reality was more modest and realistic, and more in keeping with the trajectory of actual fur trade experience. What was inherited was fur-rich New Caledonia, the temperate lower Columbia, and a maritime corridor, roughly but systematically charted by Captain Vancouver, densely populated by Native peoples whose lives intertwined with an abundant resource base bearing an enormous commercial potential. The wealth predicted by Dalrymple and others existed on the coast, but it was a more prosaic, less romantic wealth, consisting not of the spices and sugars of the Orient, but of shiploads of salmon and lumber. The coast was not the Orient, yet its products were destined for Pacific markets. The fur traders' overland North West Passage led not to the known wealth of the Orient, but to the unknown wealth of the North West Coast. In 1821, the region was suddenly controlled by a company whose name belied the real extent of its activities and of its territorial ambitions, a company anxious to establish Pacific and Oriental trade routes and to apply the tested commercial strategies of the continental fur trade to the natural abundance of the west coast.

CHAPTER 3

George Simpson and
a New Pacific Commerce

The enterprising spirit of the British merchant
shews itself conspicuous in all parts of the world
except on the North West Coast of America.

– GEORGE SIMPSON, 1825[1]

George Simpson visited the Columbia Department twice in the
1820s, imposing a strict set of economy measures and a workable vision
of economic development for the Pacific coast.[2] Elsewhere on the continent, the merger of the companies had resulted in an organization
top-heavy with employees, as well as duplicate posts and rival transport
systems dating from the period of competition with the North West
Company. After 1821, Simpson regularly toured the Northern Department, formulating and imposing 'rigid measures of economy' based on
the commercial strategies of the fur trade, including trade extension, fur
conservation, and personnel and wage reduction.[3] He harmonized the
accounting systems of the Hudson's Bay and North West companies and
everywhere promoted men of 'regularity & system.' No inhabitant of the
Indian Country had, he wrote, a right to extravagance. Simpson developed an intimate knowledge of the amalgamated company's vast territories. 'By these visits of inspection,' Harold Innis wrote, 'he was able to
gain a remarkable knowledge of the demands of the trade and to bring
the trade under the control of the organization.'[4]

Simpson's Columbia policy of the 1820s had two phases, correspond-
ing to his two visits of 1824-5 and 1828-9. In the first phase, he ordered
the extension of the fur trade; he arranged the trade's extension to the
North West Coast and to the southern interior to meet American com-

petitors. He also considered, briefly, the export of fur and other commodities directly to China. In the second phase, he called for economic
diversification and market expansion to make the most of the new territories. In 1828-9, Simpson initiated export trades in salmon and lumber to Pacific markets in Honolulu and California, trades that could be
carried on conveniently in the dead winter months when the company's
vessels were idle.

The massive trade extension of the 1820s entailed expenses unmatched
elsewhere on the continent. The company's venture into the maritime
fur trade meant the purchase of vessels, the hiring of qualified mariners,
and the imposition of a higher-priced standard of trade than was needed
in the noncompetitive interior and eastern districts. Despite these costs,
by 1829 the company was ready to challenge American coasters for commercial control of the North West Coast, new markets had been located,
and Simpson was poised to fulfil Mackenzie's ambition of marketing
local produce in Pacific markets. A new regional economy of the fur
trade was in the process of forming.

By the time of his first visit to the Columbia, Simpson had a pretty good
idea of what to expect. In September 1821, he had sent Archibald
McDonald to the Columbia, in the capacity of accountant, and asked
him to prepare a full and accurate report. McDonald met old Northwesters who had come to the lower Columbia originally with Astor's
company. 'We are called Americans,' Alexander Ross took pains to assure
him, 'but there were very few Americans among us – we were all Scotch-
men like yourselves.' In the spring of 1822, McDonald reported that an
expensive dependence on European provisions was the major cause of
the lack of profits, a situation inherited from the NWC. Reports on the
fur and provision trades on the lower Columbia improved steadily thereafter. In 1823, Simpson wrote that the Native people in the Columbia
were 'getting rapidly in the way of collecting Skins,' and a year later that
the provision trades were improving and that the Columbia business had
been brought nearly into a 'regular and organized train.' 'Mr Cameron
has brought very satisfactory reports from the Columbia by which it
appears that the Trade is encreasing, the expenses diminishing and the
natives becoming well disposed towards the Whites.'[5]

In August 1824, Simpson proposed to visit the Columbia, he said, 'to take a more accurate view of the Company's affairs and prospects in that country.' He complained that the Northern Council of Rupert's Land would gladly drop the Columbia: 'Our Council know so little about that Country having confined their attention to the mere trafficking with Indians and not taking an enlarged view of its affairs either in regard to political or Commercial prospects indeed there is a general feeling against it and I believe they would gladly throw up all interest in the trade on the West side of the Mountain (New Caledonia excepted) if left to themselves.'[6]

Simpson's first inspection of the Columbia Department was an epochal affair. It took him only eighty-four days to get from York Factory to the mouth of the Columbia.[7] For part of the journey he travelled with Dr. John McLoughlin, newly appointed to the charge of the department. Along the way, Simpson scrutinized the company's operations, never losing sight of the profit motive. He investigated a quicker and more economical route to the Pacific via the Saskatchewan River and David Thompson's Athabasca Pass, a route followed thereafter by the Fort Vancouver-York Factory Express. 'It appears extraordinary,' Simpson mused, 'how any human being should have stumbled on a pass through such a formidable barrier as we are now scaling and which nature seems to have placed here for the purpose of interdicting all communication between the East and West sides of the continent.' At the Committee's Punchbowl in the Rockies, Simpson shot a mountain goat and sheep and kept the skins in case they became 'an object of Trade worthy of our attention'; as an experiment he ate the mountain goat, the flesh of which he described as tough.[8] He asked John McLeod, in charge of Kamloops, to consider opening a trade in swan skins and quills, and instructed him to depend less on imported provisions and more on local fish, game, and horseflesh.[9]

As he worked his way to the coast, Simpson grew increasingly wrathful at the dormant agricultural and commercial opportunities around him. 'If my information is correct,' he wrote in October 1824, 'the Columbia Deptmt from the Day of its origin to the present hour has been neglected, shamefully mismanaged and a scene of the most wasteful extravagance and the most unfortunate dissention.'[10] Regarding the Spokane District, he wrote:

> The good people of Spokane District and I believe of the interior of the Columbia generally have for a length of time shewn an extraordinary predilec-

tion for European provisions without sufficiently considering the enormous price ... I do not know any part of the Country on the East side of the Mountain that affords such resources in the way of living as Spokane District; there is an abundance of Salmon besides a variety of other Fish to be had quite at home, plenty of Potatoes if trouble is taken to raise them, Game if required in short everything in the way of necessaries that an inhabitant of the Indian Country has a right to look for; why therefore squander large sums of money in this manner?[11]

On his way down the Columbia River, Simpson gave some thought to the fur trade of the Snake River, which, according to McLoughlin, the NWC had 'given up as a hopeless affair.' 'If properly managed,' Simpson told the G&C, 'no question exists that it would yield handsome profits as we have convincing proof that the country is a rich preserve of Beaver and which for political reasons we should endeavour to destroy as fast as possible.'[12] This would give American fur traders on the Missouri no incentive to enter the watershed of the Columbia River.

Simpson spent a long winter (1824-5) at Fort George, located on the south bank of the Columbia some seven or eight miles from the open Pacific. He spent part of the time going over the accounts with Archibald McDonald,[13] which gave him ample opportunity to give orders and vent his spleen – inseparable activities for Simpson. He raged against the extravagant habits formed on the lower Columbia during the Pacific Fur and NWC regimes. 'Every thing appears to me in the Columbia on too extended a scale *except the trade*.' He thought the district could be reduced from 136 to 76 men, and the number of pieces customarily sent upriver from Fort George could be reduced from 645 to 200; many were superfluous and unnecessary. Simpson also thought the excess goods at Fort George, inherited from the NWC, could be disposed of in California or the Sandwich Islands. The NWC had never collected its debts in California, totalling $4,500 – debts inherited by the new company.[14]

He found Fort George wanting both as a fur trade post and as a depot: 'The Establishment of Fort George is a large pile of buildings covering about an acre of ground well stockaded, and protected by flanking Bastions with two 18 Pounders, mounted in front, and having altogether an air or appearance of Grandeur, and Consequence which does not become or is not at all suitable to an Indian Trading Post.' Moreover, Fort George was cramped near the river mouth, a relic of the Pacific Fur Company era when visiting traders from the Pacific ocean afforded the only hope of obtaining supplies from the outside world.

Simpson also considered the post unsuited as a depot because of its poor potential as a farm, and he ordered the construction of a new post some ninety-six miles up the Columbia from Fort George at the spot where Lieutenant William Broughton of the Vancouver expedition had discontinued his survey of the river. The fur traders already knew the place as Jolie Prairie; it was, Simpson said, 'an admirable situation for a Farm where we expect to raise all the Corn [wheat] required for the Coasting trade.' He thought that a very large farm could be made there, and that thirty-five of the seventy men at Fort George could be spared for the new post. Clerk Alexander Mackenzie stated in April 1825 that the new fort possessed 'a more commodious situation' than the old, while Dunn recalled that Simpson chose the new location because it was more convenient for trade with a 'larger and richer tract of land for cultivation' and 'a more convenient landing place for cargoes from the ships.' Botanist David Douglas, who arrived by ship at the new post in the spring of 1825, wrote that 'The scenery from this place is sublime – high, well-wooded hills, mountains covered with perpetual snow, extensive meadows and plains of deep fertile alluvial deposit covered with a rich sward of grass and a profusion of flowering plants.' The move to Fort Vancouver took place in April 1825,[15] and Fort George was temporarily abandoned in June.

Knowledgeable Northern Council members, many of them old Northwesters, had told Simpson that the 'hostile character of the Natives' would prevent any extension of the company's activities to the North West Coast. This coast, after all, was the theatre of the still-active maritime fur trade, and the memory was fresh of the destruction of the Pacific Fur Company's ship *Tonquin* and her crew at Clayoquot. The entire coast north of Puget Sound was, Alexander Ross asserted, 'gloomy and forbidding.' The old guard warned Simpson that the Russians, to the north, kept their Native customers only by 'force of arms.'[16] In June 1825, John McLoughlin advised David Douglas not to accompany a company vessel to Nootka, but to botanize on the Columbia River instead, owing to the 'turbulent disposition of the natives' on the North West Coast, which made it necessary for fur traders to meet them 'armed and in a large party.'[17]

Simpson's stubborn attitude to the North West Coast was shaped by a knowledge of British explorations there and a respect for their achievement. Vancouver's surveys and Mackenzie's and Fraser's voyages to the Pacific had never been revisited, integrated, or tied together in any way. In its ten years on the lower Columbia, the NWC had never revisited Bella Coola or the lower Fraser; indeed, Europeans had abandoned the inside coast in the twenty or thirty years since Vancouver, Mackenzie, and Fraser. Vessels from Boston engrossed the fur trade of the whole coast, and an 1818 affray between the NWC's Iroquois hunters and the Cowlitz Indians had closed the overland access to Puget Sound. Simpson did not share the view that Native hostility made the coast forbidden territory. 'The Country north of this place as far as the Southern Shore of Pugets Sound has been visited occasionally but in consequence of a serious affray which took place with the natives some years ago and not yet amicably settled our intercourse with that quarter has since then been limited.' He lamented the poor quality of maps and charts of the coast, the most recent of which were done by Vancouver thirty years earlier, and which omitted such important features as the Fraser River. 'Frazer's River we knew little about until this season as neither Cook Vancouver nor any of the Traders on this Coast take any notice thereof.' Simpson thought this lack of knowledge 'a disgrace to the whole concern.' A few days after his arrival at Fort George, he sent a party under James McMillan, who had accompanied him across the continent, to gain a knowledge of Fraser River and the adjacent country.[18]

This voyage of exploration was the first attempt to assert the company's commercial presence on the coast of what is now British Columbia, and the first visit by land-based traders since Fraser's in 1808. McMillan left Fort George on 19 November 1824 with forty-two men and a copy of Vancouver's chart. Fittingly, one of McMillan's men had been with Simon Fraser on his descent of the river. McMillan travelled up the eastern shore of Puget Sound with the San Juan, Gulf, and Vancouver islands in the distance. Simpson reported their main findings to the G&C. 'The channel which divides Vancouver's Island from the main land they found studded with Islands,' he wrote. Vancouver had missed the Fraser, Simpson said, because its entrance to the Gulf of Georgia is 'covered with high Grass and Willows which gives it the appearance of an extended Marsh or Swamp ... the only indication of

a large River emptying itself at this place is the freshness of the Water
and the numerous trunks and Roots of Trees strewed along and stick-
ing on this Shoal.' Vancouver's charts were their guide to the coast itself.
One of the explorers, John Work, identified a promontory as 'Vancouver's Point Roberts ... where we are now encamped is the Birch Bay of
Vancouver.'[19]

McMillan learned that the Native name for the river was 'Cowitchen.'
He and his party kept an eye open for provisions and cultivable land.
'The soil appeared to be rich and fertile' and the explorers found 'good
situations for the site of an Establishment in every reach and many
beautiful clear spots adapted for agricultural purposes.' They learned 'that
the Country abounded with Deer and that Beaver were numerous.' The
Natives of the Fraser River spoke of the Kamloops Indians as their
neighbours, Simpson said, and they told McMillan, quite erroneously,
that all the way to Kamloops the Fraser was 'a fine large bold stream
and not barred by dangerous Rapids or falls.'[20]

Simpson considered this exploration 'most flattering & satisfactory.'
He was convinced that the Fraser would prove to be a superior northern version of the Columbia, free of the threat of American overland
competition. 'In short Frazer's River appears to be the grand Communication from the Coast with all the Establishments on this side of the
Mountain.' No time, he said, should be lost in making the Fraser the
main route between the coast and New Caledonia. New Caledonia and
'Thompson's River, Spokane, Fort Nez Perces, Flat Head, and Coute-
nais, also Fort George,' could be outfitted from a post on the lower
Fraser. Such a post could become, owing to its central location and easy
access to the interior, the principal depot for the whole department. He
concluded that the trade of the North West Coast held out advantageous prospects if 'conducted with enterprise spirit and activity from
Fraser River,' and that important savings and gains would result from
forming a single department west of the Rockies that could be outfitted from this safe, central location.[21]

McMillan's explorations convinced Simpson that the North West Coast
was worth keeping and integrating into the HBC's larger operations:

The riches of this Coast, and its interior Country, are unquestionably worth
contending for, and if the British Government does take that interest in the

Fur Trade which it is wonted to do in every other branch of its widely extended Commerce it must as a matter of course fall into the hands of the Honble Company and if the business is properly managed, and sufficiently extended I make bold to say that it can not only be made to rival but to yield double the profit that any other part of North America does for the Amount of Capital employed therein; but in order to turn it to the best advantage New Caledonia must be tacked to this Department, and the Coasting Trade must be carried on in conjunction with the inland business.[22]

Simpson conceived that a new Pacific commerce could be based at a post on the navigable Fraser River. He revived the NWC's old idea of sending ships from England to the coast and thence directly to China with fur, the idea that the G&C had, in 1822-3, considered and rejected. Simpson saw the Fraser River depot as a place 'from whence a Vessel for China would sail annually with the returns.' Without acknowledging the source, perhaps because it was so current, he resurrected the China trade envisaged by Dalrymple, Mackenzie, the NWC, Peter Corney, and others, even to the extent of hoping for a licence from the East India Company. He considered that a London-Columbia River-Canton-Lima trading circuit would benefit the company and also 'become an important branch of Commerce in a National point of view.'[23]

His plan worked as follows. The company would send its Columbia furs directly from the lower Fraser to Canton on its own vessel every two years. After depositing the furs with an East India Company agent in Canton, the captain would buy a cargo of China produce. Meanwhile, the G&C would send a cargo of British goods directly from London to Lima or Acapulco. The Canton vessel would then proceed to Lima with its Chinese goods. After selling these to the Spanish, and collecting the trade goods sent from London, the vessel would return to the Fraser River, trading in Mexico and California on the way. Thus, the company needed a licence from the East India Company and two ocean-going vessels: one to commute between London and Lima, the other to perform a circuit through the Pacific Ocean. Simpson thought a vessel of 150 tons suitable for the Pacific trade.[24]

A smaller vessel would do for the coasting trade. And, betraying a knowledge of the habits of the maritime fur traders, Simpson stated that salmon and spars could be sent with the furs to Canton; Native labour was so inexpensive that he had bought thirty-five salmon at Fort George for the equivalent of seven pence. Farm produce might also become 'an article of Trade from this Coast if a market could be found.' 'Your Honors will see the propriety of conducting the business on a more enlarged scale.' He thought that this extended scheme would cost £10,000, principally in salaries, freight, and charter and purchase of vessels, but would be worthwhile because 'settling a new country' required money. Enterprising men were needed for the task; the rest, he said, could go back over the Rockies.[25]

At the very least, Simpson believed that the Columbia Department would yield an annual profit of about £5,000 if the Columbia District posts were maintained, if New Caledonia were attached to the Columbia, and if the company entered the coasting trade and built coastal posts north of the Columbia. 'Whether we are assailed by opposition or not I think there is a Field for Commerce on this side the Mountain which has been much neglected and which if properly cultivated would become an object of the first importance to the Honble Hudson's Bay Company.'[26]

Simpson's plan served many ends. Furs would reach Canton eighteen to twenty-four months sooner than if sent to London and then overland through Russia. He was so confident of success that he offered to trade his salary for an interest in the China trade scheme. He proposed to spend one or two winters on the Columbia and the whole of the winter of 1826-7 conducting the plan. He asked the G&C to send a vessel out immediately so that he could accompany it to Canton and South America, but it would be at least a year before he would hear the G&C's response to his proposal.[27]

On his departure in March 1825, Simpson left John McLoughlin in charge of the Columbia Department. Absent in name from Simpson's 1824-5 despatches, McLoughlin was charged with implementing the full range of Simpson's reforms and policies west of the Rockies. A former Northwester, he was well aware of the importance of his mandate; indeed, he carried over the Rockies Sir Alexander Mackenzie's gun, which he coveted.[28]

On Simpson's journey back across the continent, he removed Spokane House to a new location on the Columbia River, just above the Kettle Falls Portage. A local chief made a 'formal session' of the soil to him. 'We selected a beautiful point on the south side,' he wrote in April 1825, 'an excellent Farm can be made at this place where as much Grain and potatoes may be raised as well would feed all the Natives of the Columbia and sufficient number of Cattle and Hogs to supply his Majesty's Navy with Beef and Pork.'[29] He named the new post Fort Colvile after Andrew Colvile, a member of the London committee. This post later supplied foodstuffs over a wide region – the Snake Country, the Columbia River brigades, Kamloops, and New Caledonia – and eventually supplied Fort Edmonton with seed-wheat.[30]

Simpson's visit had a galvanizing effect on the region. Between his departure and his return in the fall of 1828, company officials completed the new depot at Fort Vancouver, started farms, attached New Caledonia to the Columbia Department, embarked on the coastal fur trade, opened a post on the Fraser River, extended the fur trade south of the Columbia, visited California, explored to the west and north of New Caledonia to forestall Russian expansion toward the interior, and negotiated with the East India Company for direct access to the Canton market. Simpson had the entire backing of the G&C for his Columbia

FIGURE 2 Built in 1825, Fort Colvile, on the Columbia River near Kettle Falls, possessed a fine farm that provided foodstuffs to much of the interior fur trade. [Henry Warre, *Fort Colvile in August 1844*, American Antiquarian Society, No. 68]

plans.[31] The only aspects of the plan out of Simpson's control were the tantalizing China adventure and the navigability of the Fraser.

The G&C responded with interest to Simpson's request to open a direct trade with Canton. In 1824 they opened discussions with the East India Company to transport and sell Columbia furs in Canton and Singapore; in the same year, the East India Company agreed to carry a test shipment of Columbia pelts from London to Canton, bypassing the overland route through Russia. Simpson approved of the arrangement with 'that powerful and highly respectable body' because he still considered that 'the China Market appears to us to present an outlet for the Compys Trade on the North West Coast.' Moreover, he was anxious not to continue the NWC's use of Perkins and Company owing to their high freight and commission charges. Five months later, the G&C reported that the Chinese shipment had failed owing to the great variety of pelts, which had not found a willing buyer in Canton. Because of the failure, they decided not to send a vessel directly to Fort Vancouver and Canton, 'more especially,' they wrote, 'as there is no probability that the East India Company would allow us to take a return Cargo from thence. They seem to be liberally and well disposed to the British Fur Trade, but are tenacious and jealous of their exclusive right to the China trade.'[32]

The next year, however, the G&C again contracted with the East India Company to market fur in Canton and Singapore. Again, the shipment lost money. They told Simpson that 'it will be better for the Company to sell their Furs here [London], to those who can carry on such a Trade with the Chinese.'[33] On hearing this news, Simpson had no choice but to concur:

> We are sorry to learn that the consignment to Singapore has not answered expectations, and are of opinion, from the result of the late shipments to China, that the Hon'ble Company are likely to do better by desposing of the returns at home to manufacturers, and shippers, than exporting on their own account, and we fear that the last contract which the East India Company had, was so unprofitable, that they are not likely to renew it.[34]

This news, in July 1828, marked the end of Simpson's China scheme, and the end of Dalrymple's older hope of forging a direct Pacific link between the Hudson's Bay and East India companies.[35] Like the Northwesters' version of the plan, Simpson's ambitious Canton adventure failed owing to the unsuitability of Columbia furs in Canton and Singapore and to the East India Company's refusal to allow the HBC to carry a return cargo from China. While the Canton trade never materialized, Simpson's scheme bore indirect fruit: in January 1829, the company appointed an agent at the Sandwich Islands, and in 1833, they established an agency there that effectively took the place of Canton in the trans-Pacific ambitions of the British fur trade.

Disappointed at the collapse of his elaborate China scheme,[36] Simpson pinned his faith on the company's extension to the North West Coast where he believed sea otter were numerous, but here again he would be disappointed. In 1827, he wrote hopefully that 'Now that the Trade of the Coast is becoming more extended, we shall be able to furnish a considerable quantity of Sea Otter Skins, an article, which we understand was some years ago in great demand in the Northern parts of China.'[37]

The company possessed the exclusive British licence to the trade of the 'continental shore' of the North West Coast, which meant it could build posts on land without the threat of British competition; this situation did not, of course, extend to American trading competition. Americans, mainly from Boston, traded at sea and at three main harbours on the long coast: Neah Bay (inside Cape Flattery), Nawitti (on Shushartie Bay), and Kaigani (within Dixon Entrance) (see Map 4). Increasingly, they traded for fur that originated in New Caledonia and elsewhere in the interior, and they chased a rapidly dwindling number of sea otter pelts. Competition, Alexander Ross wrote, had 'almost ruined the coast trade, and completely spoiled the Indians,' by which he meant that the great number of American vessels and dwindling number of sea otters had created a seller's market. Since the 1790s the Americans had promoted the use of spirituous liquors, mainly rum, in their North West Coast trade.[38] They had also diversified into the sandalwood trade of the Sandwich Islands, and increasingly they supplied the Russians and Spanish with provisions in Alaska and California. They also took the odd deckload of spars from the North West Coast to Oahu. Simpson accurately described their seasonal rounds in 1828:

> They are Chiefly outfitted from the United States, prepared for a three years cruise, and loaded with Trading Goods; at the Sandwich Islands they leave

what is not required for the Trade of the first season, there get supplied with Provisions, proceed to the Coast and return at the close of the season with what they may have collected, such part of their returns as is adapted for the China Market is forwarded by any vessel going thither, consigned to their Agent at Canton, and such as is likely to meet a better market in the States is sent thither in like manner; this is repeated the second year and the third they proceed to China filling up with Sandal wood; then return either to the States with a cargo of China produce, or to the Spanish or Russian Settlements, with Goods, which they barter either with the residents at the Settlements or with the shipping frequenting those Ports and such supplies for the Fur Trade, as cannot be obtained in this manner, are sent on freight from the United States either to the Sandwich Islands or to the Spanish Settlements as may be agreed on, where they are deposited until called for.[39]

The North West Coast fur trade, judging from the Americans' continuing interest, appeared profitable.

Before extending their own reach, the HBC had to put vessels on the coast to learn the tricks of the trade. In July 1824, the G&C sent the *William & Ann* from London on a coastal reconnaissance. 'Our object in dispatching the *William & Ann* thus early, is, that as soon as she has delivered her outward bound cargo she should proceed to the Northward to ascertain if there are good harbours on the coast, and whether a beneficial trade may not be carried on with the Natives. The principal point to which we have directed Capt. Hanwells attention is the Portland Canal.'[40]

The *William & Ann*'s 1825 voyage to the North West Coast was an initial reconnaissance of a region that was still almost entirely unknown to the land-based British fur trade. John Scouler, the naturalist on board, made a series of observations that indicate how recently and strongly Captain Vancouver's presence had been felt. 'The Indians [at Observatory Inlet] appeared to have some traditions of C. Vancouver,' wrote Scouler, who had a copy of Vancouver's *Voyages* with him. 'They were at some pains to make us understand that a great many snows ago two vessels had anchored in the place where we are now.'[41] Putting back to sea, the *William & Ann* visited Nootka in July and entertained Chief Maquinna:

Before venturing on board the old man inquired from what country we had come, & on being informed that we were English, he & his people clapped

their hands & seemed highly delighted. On showing him a portrait of Mr
Mears he soon recognised his old friend, & had not forgot the Spaniards or
C. Vancouver. When we showed him the portraits of himself & Calleum, he
easily found out the unfortunate chief & told us that Komkela was dead for
many years. In the evening he & his people left us, much pleased with the
reception they had experienced.[42]

'His tribe indeed is now seldom visited by traders, on account of the
hostile character he acquired, and the poverty of the place, yielding very
few furs.'[43]

Simpson was not pleased with Captain Henry Hanwell, who had done
little trading and avoided much of the coast. Simpson stormed that the
company still knew nothing of 'either Harbours, Rivers, Trade or Country.' Hanwell had 'rarely ventured within a sufficient distance of the land.'
'Prudence in moderation is commendable but is an evil when carried to
an extreme and we certainly think that Captn. Hanwell's prudence on
that voyage amounted to pusillanimity.'[44]

In the spring of 1826, McLoughlin gave Hanwell a second chance; he
provided a wide assortment of trade goods 'so as to discover those best
adapted for the trade,' and he instructed the vessel's Indian Trader (the
person in charge of the trade in fur), Alexander Mackenzie, to undersell any trader he met on the coast. He gave Hanwell a list of places
frequented by traders, with orders to visit them 'so as to spread among
the Coasters the news of our Entering the Trade ... we can afford to
undersell them by carrying on this business in conjunction with an
Extensive Inland Trade.' Meanwhile, echoing Simpson, McLoughlin recommended that officers in charge of New Caledonia send people down
the rivers to the coast to obtain a complementary knowledge of the
region.[45]

As a result of Hanwell's poor performance, the company hired Simpson's capable cousin, Aemilius Simpson, to conduct the coasting trade.[46]
Formerly a lieutenant in the Royal Navy, Simpson was sent to the coast
in 1826, and the following spring took command of the brigantine *Cadboro*, which had just arrived from England. Before his death in 1831, he
was closely involved with the North West Coast trade and the opening
of the California trade. His first job was to establish Fort Langley. After
picking up a land party in Puget Sound, including James McMillan,
George Barnston, and Francis Annance, Captain Simpson guided the

Cadboro up the Fraser River on 22 June 1827, the first European vessel to enter the river. The men went ashore on the last day of July and started building a post on the river's thickly wooded banks. The post was named after Thomas Langley, a member of the company's London committee.[47] George Simpson instructed that after lending the fort protection for three weeks, the vessel was to 'proceed to the northward touching at all the Ports and villages between that and Norfolk Sound, likewise touching at the Russian Establishments.' Such a trip was commenced: in September 1827, Captain Simpson and Alexander McLeod explored northward as far as Johnstone Strait only to discover that American traders had 'scoured' the coast before their arrival. In future, McLoughlin wrote, the coasting vessel had better leave Fort Vancouver early every spring to forestall the Americans.[48]

George Simpson, who still hoped that the Fraser River would be navigable between the coast and New Caledonia, formed Fort Langley to replace Fort Vancouver as the new depot (he feared that serious American competition on the Columbia 'would be attended with a ruinous sacrifice of money'), and because he needed a central fort to carry the trading war to the Americans on the coast.[49] However, Simon Fraser's 1808 findings made Simpson cautious, and in 1826 he wrote that until the navigation of the Fraser River between the coast and New Caledonia was thoroughly known, he would not venture to make Fort Langley the principal depot on the coast.[50]

Simpson returned to the Columbia Department in 1828 largely, Margaret Ormsby writes, to examine Fort Langley and 'ascertain its suitability as the main Pacific depot and determine positively whether or not the Fraser River was navigable throughout its length.' Simpson descended the lower Fraser River in October 1828. Twenty years earlier, Simon Fraser had described how 'navigation was absolutely impracticable' in the Fraser Canyon: 'We had to pass where no human being should venture.'[51] Simpson had to learn for himself, and his own description of his perilous descent is practically a paraphrase of Fraser's. The river was not navigable above the falls, he said – 'I should consider the passage down, to be certain Death, in nine attempts out of Ten. I shall therefore no longer talk of it as a navigable stream' – and the trip finally convinced him that Fort Langley could never replace Fort Vancouver as depot. 'Frazer's River, can no longer be thought of as a practicable communication with the interior,' he wrote.[52] Whereas portages allowed the company's boats and brigades to bypass the cascades and Dalles of the Columbia, the sheer walls of the Fraser allowed no such traffic, and Simpson and his entourage, including James Yale, were swept through the canyon at an alarming rate. They were the first Europeans to cross the Coast Mountains in twenty years.

After determining the post was unsuited as depot, Simpson ordered Fort Langley to be reduced in size and maintained for the fur trade and for coastal transport. The fishery and farm also showed potential, and Fort Langley's access to the Straits, the Gulf, and the Sound convinced Simpson that the post 'will become a valuable acquisition to the Business, and that in co-operation with the Vessel to be employed in transporting its outfits and returns, will secure the Trade of the Straits of St. Jean de Fucca and inland of Vancouver Island.'[53]

The new post was the centre of a large Native trade. In 1830, Archibald McDonald estimated the 'number of men' inhabiting Fort Langley District, which included all of Puget Sound, the Gulf of Georgia, the Fraser River and the Fraser canyon, at 4,160. This number might be considered incredible, he said, if he had not repeatedly quizzed chiefs trading at the post.[54]

North of Langley, Simpson sought to undersell the Americans and prevent them from obtaining interior furs. 'The Country situated to the Northward of Frasers River, up to Lat. 54, is beyond all doubt valuable from the number of land Skins that find their way to the coast,' he wrote in March 1829. 'The greater part of the Land Furs, is got at the Port of Nass, entrance of Simpson's [Nass] River, and they find their way from the unexplored parts of New Caledonia.'[55] With this is mind, he decided to establish a centrally located post at 'Port of Nass' on Portland Inlet. Simpson outlined the strategic and commercial importance of this location:

A strong establishment at this point would collect the Land Furs that come down from the Northern parts of New Caledonia which forms the principal returns made by the Americans on this coast, it would likewise enable us to settle the Country to the eastward of the Russian Boundary Line running parallel with the Coast which is now drained by their Establishment at Norfolk Sound, and in co-operation with our Shipping would in the course of 2 or 3 Years compel the Americans to relinquish the contest.[56]

'From all I am able to collect,' Simpson wrote, 'it appears that the Fur Trade of this coast, is by no means so extended as we were led to suppose; the average Annual returns of the Americans for some years past, not exceeding 600 Sea Otters, and also about 6000 Beaver and Land Otters.' And, he continued, 'Altho' the Fur Trade of this coast, is not so extensive as it has been represented, it would nevertheless be of great value to the Honble. Compy., if unrestricted by Opposition; indeed it is the Land Skins of our interior Country, that renders it all worth following, as the Marine Furs, form a very small proportion of the returns.'[57]

By 1829, then, the company's plan for the North West Coast trade was in place, though Fort Simpson would not be built for another two years. Measures aimed at combatting American traders were complemented in 1825 when the British and Russian governments signed a convention giving the British the right of access to the north Pacific coast east of 139° longitude, from the interior of British territory via the rivers flowing to the coast. This convention, advantageous to the HBC, enabled the company to operate in the whole of the panhandle.[58]

In the interior, Simpson proceeded in 1825 with his plans to outfit New Caledonia from the coast by means of the Brigade Trail from the lower Columbia to the upper Fraser, and to unite the New Caledonia and Columbia districts. From 1820 to 1822, New Caledonia had been outfitted from the coast and, until 1825, from York Factory via Norway House, a much longer route. During these years, the G&C considered the York Factory route the more secure of the two in the event of American competition on the Columbia, but old Northwester John Stuart, in charge of New Caledonia, argued repeatedly that the Columbia route was fully fifty per cent cheaper than York Factory.[59] Ultimately this economic argument, combined with the company's entrenched position on the lower Columbia after Simpson's first visit, prevailed. As Simpson wrote in 1825, 'There is a great Field for extension of Trade in this part of the Country but while it continued to be outfitted from York Depot it was impossible for us to reap the fruits thereof as nearly the whole year round was occupied in transport.' The route was reopened in May 1825; the decision to annex New Caledonia to the Columbia was approved in June, and by August 1826, New Caledonia District was part of the

Columbia Department for the purposes of supply and transport. In 1828, New Caledonia and Columbia accounts were merged into 'one complete set' for transmission to York Factory.[60]

Transport took on a variety of forms. Communication, Joe McKay recalled,

> was carried on by means of boats, horses, dog sleighs, and on foot. When Vancouver was the depot, the interior was furnished by flotillas of boats, called by the French Canadians brigades, each district having its separate brigade. The districts situate north of the Columbia landed their outfits at the mouth of the Okanagan, and packed them on horses thence to their destinations ... goods for the Upper Columbia and Kootenay were landed at Fort Colville (Kettle Falls); those for the Snake River were landed at Walla Walla.

The HBC kept 200 horses at Fort Alexandria, and between 500 and 600 at Kamloops.[61] Goods were portaged around the dangerous rapids on the Columbia. Birchback canoes, introduced briefly by the Northwesters, were replaced in coastal areas by Native dugout canoes, and everywhere by boats and *bateaux*, which, Dunn recorded, 'are made of quarter-inch pine boards, and are thirty-two feet long, and six and a half feet wide in midships, with both ends sharp, and without a keel – worked, according to the circumstances of the navigation, with paddles, or with oars. These boats are found to be better adapted to the lakes and rivers there, than the canoe of the north.'[62]

The brigade between York Factory and Fort Vancouver, via the Athabasca Pass and Fort Edmonton, remained the department's main link with the outside world. This was not a fur but an express brigade, carrying departmental accounts and letters, and attended (in 1825) by forty men and two boats.[63] It was based directly on the NWC's old spring and fall express linking Fort George on the lower Columbia with Fort William on Lake Superior. Known as the York Factory Express on its spring/eastern journey, and the Columbia or Autumn Express on its fall/westward journey, the brigade set out every spring from Fort Vancouver on a breakneck journey to Hudson Bay, returning in early winter. Usually two expresses were in use, leaving from opposite sides of the continent in spring and passing in the middle of the continent. 'The communication to Hudson's Bay in the March and September journey usually occupies three months and ten days,' wrote visiting naval officer

FIGURE 3 By 1846 the treacherous waters of the Columbia River had claimed the lives of sixty-eight HBC employees, their families, and visitors. *Going through Rapids,* a vivid watercolour by Henry Warre, shows a Columbia River boat towing a birch-bark canoe through rapids on the Columbia. [BC Archives, PDP 47]

Edward Belcher in 1839.[64] The express was usually in charge of an able clerk, for example, Edward Ermatinger or James Douglas.

To the south of Fort Vancouver, McLoughlin continued the NWC's policy of extending the fur trade on the Columbia and its tributaries. To offset the scarcity of furs on the lower Columbia and to keep American trappers to the east, he mounted a fur hunting offensive in the Snake Country, defined by Ogden in 1826 as the large region 'bounded on the North by the Columbia Waters on the South by the Missourie, on the West by the Spanish Territo[ries] and the East by the Saskatchewan Tribes.' American trappers worked to the east of this frontier. To the HBC, a frontier was a region on the outer edges of the Indian Country where the fur trade ended and competition or settlement started, where aggressive policies of price inflation and overhunting were practised. 'It must not be forgotten that this is a frontier and may be made a cover and protection to our own proper Country,' Simpson wrote of one such place.[65] The department's frontiers would be the

FIGURE 4 The HBC's overland express route between the Columbia River and Hudson Bay followed Athabasca Pass, located by David Thompson in 1811. This watercolour by Henry Warre, entitled *Ascending the Rocky Mountains*, shows the York Factory Express approaching Athabasca Pass on 3 May 1846. [American Antiquarian Society]

Snake Country, northern California, the North West Coast, and occasionally the lower Columbia.

The company monopolized the Snake Country fur trade as quickly as possible with the aim of trapping it out. As Simpson said, 'An exhausted frontier is the best protection we have against the encroachments of rival traders.' The Snake, he wrote in 1825, was 'a rich preserve of Beaver and which for political reasons we shall endeavour to destroy as fast as possible.'[66] McLoughlin and former Northwesters Alexander Ross, Peter Ogden, Finan McDonald, François Payette, John McLeod, and Thomas McKay took up Simpson's orders with a fanatical zeal, declaring war on fur-bearing animals south of the Columbia. Between 1823 and 1829, the Snake hunts were in the charge of Ogden, who on several occasions strayed with his trappers into American territory east of the continental divide, and across the Mexican frontier near Great Salt Lake. The company's Iroquois hunters and independent freemen were, Simpson said, 'the most unruly and troublesome gang to deal with in this or perhaps any other part of the World.' With this in mind, Simpson continued the NWC's strategy of employing Iroquois on the Columbia frontier.[67]

The early Snake River journals and correspondence read like battle reports. 'And in concluding remember Gentlemen we ought to get all we can from the south side of the Columbia while it is in our power,' Simpson wrote in 1825, and two years later he urged McLoughlin that

> the greatest and best protection we can have from opposition is keeping the country closely hunted as the first step that the American Government will take towards Colonization is through their Indian Traders and if the country becomes exhausted in Fur bearing animals they can have no inducement to proceed thither. We therefore entreat that no exertions be spared to Trap every part of the country ... the Snake Expedition we look to as a very prominent branch of our business and we wish by all means that it be kept constantly employed; even under all the disadvantages and misfortunes that have befallen it, the profits are most respectable, it moreover does much good in over-running and destroying that extended country south of the Columbia which is the greatest temptation to our opponents.[68]

The Americans could not compete with such a policy. After 1825, Galbraith writes, American competition from the east was insignificant.[69]

Some traders who operated unsuccessfully against the company on the upper Snake, headwaters of the Missouri, and Rocky Mountains before 1829 were General William Ashley of the American Fur Company, William Johnson Gardner, Jedediah Smith, David Jackson, William Sublette (of the firm Smith, Jackson, and Sublette), Thomas Fitzpatrick, and Joshua Pilcher of the Missouri Fur Company.[70] One or two got through to Fort Vancouver in an emaciated state, but increasingly the company forced them to stay in the Rockies: hence their appellation 'Mountain Men.' In the Rockies, far from the Pacific, landlocked and isolated, the Americans retained their connections with St. Louis throughout the 1820s and 1830s, and their main explorations were restricted to the eastern and southern edges of the Columbia Department. In 1823, for example, Irishman Thomas Fitzpatrick of the Rocky Mountain Fur Company relocated Robert Stuart's 1812 route through South Pass, 'an easy entrance into the valley of the Green River, a region rich in beaver.'[71]

The most ambitious American fur trader of the 1820s was Jedediah Smith who, after reaching California via the Colorado River system and the San Joaquin River,[72] was attacked by Native people on the Umpqua River in the summer of 1828. His expedition was a catastrophe: fifteen of his nineteen men were killed by the Umpqua people. Simpson, who happened to be at Fort Vancouver, sympathized with Smith but chastised him for his 'harsh treatment on the part of your people towards the Indians who visited your Camp some of whom they said you had beaten, and one of them bound hand and feet for some slight offence.' In September 1828, Simpson sent Alexander McLeod out to rescue the remnants of the Smith party and its effects; McLeod retrieved 700 beaver skins and 39 horses all in very bad condition, for which McLoughlin paid Smith $2,600.[73]

By 1828, Snake Country returns exceeded those of the lower Columbia; the approach from the east had been rendered uninviting, and the company had acquired effective control over the vast region. 'I am of opinion,' McLoughlin wrote in 1829, 'we have little to apprehend from Settlers in that Quarter, and from Indian Traders nothing; as none, except large capitalists could attempt it, and this attempt would cost a heavy Sum of Money, of which they could never recover much.'[74]

The company found other fur regions south of the Columbia. Mexican territory extended nominally from California to the forty-second parallel, but the Mexicans were unfamiliar with the interior and the HBC's trappers ranged southern regions at will. Finan McDonald and Thomas McKay explored south of the Columbia River in 1825. In the summer of 1826, Alexander McLeod and Donald Manson led a trapping party to the Umpqua River (see Map 4); between September and November 1826, McLeod, Manson, David Douglas, and thirty men trapped and explored 'to that country south of the Columbia and the Multomah [Willamette] and towards the Umpqua River.' Douglas called it 'preparing for a journey to Northern California.'[75] Between September 1826 and March 1827, McLeod reached the Klamath River via the Umpqua and Siuslaw rivers. McLeod and his party were the first Europeans to venture into this interior realm: Douglas reported that 'All the natives [at the Siuslaw River] like those here [Umpqua] had never before seen such people as we are, and received him [McLeod] narrowly and with much curiousity; but hospitable and kind in the extreme. Kindled his fire, assisted in making his encampment, glad and pleased beyond measure on receiving a bead, ring, button, in fact the smallest trifle of European manufacture for their services.'[76] Between September and December 1828, McLeod explored the Sacramento River, and in 1829, he led the company's first trapping expedition into the Sacramento Valley as far as present-day Stockton. McLeod established an inland route, probably based on existing Native trails, between Fort Vancouver and the Sacramento; the route became known as the California Brigade or Southern Party route, following the Willamette, Umpqua, and Rogue ('Rouge') rivers, the Siskiyou Mountains, Klamath River, and the Sacramento Valley.[77] It was known as the Siskiyou Trail after 1828, when McLeod lost a 'Siskiyou' (a Cree word for bob-tailed horse) at Siskiyou Pass.[78]

At the same time, company vessels began to locate sources of trade on the coast south of the Columbia. In 1828, the *Cadboro* visited the 'Spanish settlement of Monterrey' for supplies of beef and salt when Fort Vancouver was in short supply. George Simpson reported the trip to the G&C. 'Lieut. Simpson seems to think that a profitable branch of trade might be opened with the Spanish Settlements in Salmon and Timber, which will be fully considered when I get to the Columbia.'[79] This, however, came later.

To provision its fur trading expeditions and brigades, McLoughlin created an agricultural oasis at Fort Vancouver. The success of the farm led Simpson to congratulate himself in 1829 that 'never did a change of system, and a change of management, produce such obvious advantages in any part of the Indian country, as those which the present state of this Establishment in particular, and of the Columbia Department as a whole, at this moment exhibits.' Fort Vancouver's own district, however, exhibited 'a gradual decline of the Fur bearing race; which in our immediate neighbourhood amounts to extinction,' Simpson wrote,[80] which encouraged the HBC to consider other export trades on the lower Columbia.

Simpson hoped to establish a Pacific commerce in the 1820s, but his energies, of necessity, were largely devoted to extending the fur trade over the vast spaces of the department and establishing a bulwark against American competitors. Although pelts remained the only export, the fur trade was in sharp decline in some places; in others, Native people had little need to hunt, and salmon was the staple food everywhere on the coast. Despite the riches of the Snake Country and New Caledonia, Columbia Department fur was of a variable quality; in some mild coastal regions, fur returns were negligible. Even the sea otter trade, still dominated by Americans, did not seem as promising as anticipated. Simpson remained hopeful: in 1826, he thought that in the long run it 'cannot fail to do well and our views and plans connected therewith remain unaltered.' And a year later, he complained that 'The Columbia Department does not improve so rapidly as I could wish altho' great exertions are making to extend the Trade, and every encouragement held out to induce the natives to shake off their indolent habits and devote more of their time and attention to the chase.'[81]

It would be many years' work to make the region very profitable. In 1826, Simpson was asked 'What, on a rough calculation are the annual profits of Trade in the district of Columbia and do they arise from the Northern or Southern portion of that district principally?' 'The Trade,' he responded, 'of the Columbia district is yet in its infancy and the Countries to the Northward and Southward [of the Columbia] produce an equal quantity of furs amounting together in value to between 30 and £40,000 p. annum.' The accuracy of Simpson's statement is borne out by the figures: between 1821 and 1825, furs from the Columbia Department were valued at an average of £32,209.[82] Owing to high expenses, profits were considerably less: £13,907 in 1830 (Table 7).

A valuable fur trade and potential new exports lay in the background to the policies formulated by Simpson in 1828-9. The Columbia would yet repay the money invested in the extension of trade, building of new posts, exploration, hiring and purchase of vessels. 'I still conceive it presents a wide and valuable field for the exercise of activity, and enterprise, and when all the branches of Trade are brought into full and regular operation, I feel satisfied it will realise the hopes and expectations that were a few years ago entertained of it, unless we are disturbed by opposition.'[83]

In his 1829 dispatch, sent just before returning to the east, Simpson outlined his achievements. He asked the people east of the mountains, who were already distrustful of developments on the Pacific coast, to show some patience about the expenses involved in the Columbia trade. On the coast, he stated, shipping and commerce – not the extension of the fur trade itself – held the most promise. Now that the transportation infrastructure was in place, Simpson suggested the company was ready to embark on the export of salmon and timber from forts Vancouver and Langley in the dead season. He also reported that Richard Charlton, the British consul-general in the Pacific, had been appointed the company's agent in the Sandwich Islands (January 1829), and that Aemilius Simpson had placed a first load of timber and other exports in Charlton's hands. In most other parts of the continent, George Simpson had only the fur trade to cultivate. But in the Columbia, he wrote in March 1829, 'new and extensive fields present themselves, which to yield rich harvests, only require a spirit of Enterprize, with steady and active management; but which none can cultivate to advantage except ourselves.'[84]

CHAPTER 4

Nature Here
Demands Attention

From the Chutes down to Vancouver the country assumes a different
character ... the eye can fix on no one object which is not directly the
reverse of any thing to which it has been accustomed even on the east side
the mountains. The trees birds insects & flowers all wear a foreign aspect.
By its overpowering abundance all nature here demands attention.

— DUNCAN FINLAYSON, FORT VANCOUVER, 1831[1]

The Pacific coast was suited to the application of a broad commercial scheme such as George Simpson's. The region's resources and commercial potential were out of the ordinary and unmatched elsewhere in British fur trade territory. The area possessed a temperate climate, cultivable land, long growing seasons, accessible markets, abundant Native provisions, and a large Native population willing to trade and labour. Indeed, almost from the start, from Mackenzie and Thompson onwards, the Northwesters had thought the region better suited to colonization than anywhere in fur trade territory.

The terrain over which the Hudson's Bay Company operated in the nineteenth century varied greatly in environment and economic potential, and the British fur traders adapted to new circumstances wherever they went. This chapter considers the ideal environmental conditions that supported the company's ambitious commercial plans. The HBC, under Simpson's direction, translated natural abundance into a diverse and viable economy after 1821. Environmental constraints and limitations in overland transport made it impossible for fur traders to export anything but lightweight and valuable fur from most regions east of the Rockies and from the mountainous and landlocked interior.[2] The isolated fur-producing regions east of the Rockies, in New Caledonia, and in the southern interior of the Columbia Department provided no immediate potential. While mere survival and subsistence were para-mount in Rupert's Land, fur traders on the Pacific coast took subsis-tence almost for granted and introduced a general commerce.

The company regarded the Columbia Department as a single admin-istrative unit, isolated in the east by a major mountain range and in the west by an ocean (Map 6). The department was intersected by major salmon rivers, which drained southward and westward through perpet-ually mountainous country to the Pacific Ocean. The Columbia and Fraser watersheds occupied much of the central and northern reaches of the department. 'The natural limits of this extensive and important region, are strictly defined by nature,' Dunn wrote in 1844. The depart-ment extended, officially, from the northern frontier of Mexico at the forty-second parallel to Russian America, and from the Rocky Moun-tains to the Pacific Ocean. Within the department, traders identified two major regions, coast and interior, separated from each other by the Coast Mountains in the north and the Cascade and Coast ranges farther south.[3]

The North West Company had recognized two districts west of the Rockies: New Caledonia in the northern interior, and the Columbia Dis-trict in the southern interior and lower Columbia. At first, each district had its own transport, supply, administrative arrangements, and reputa-tion in fur trade circles. The HBC merged them in 1827, and although the name New Caledonia persisted, the Columbia eventually gave its name to the entire department. Coast and interior differed widely in natural and cultural terms, in their commercial potential, and within themselves. The interior was known mainly for its fur and the coast for its varied resources that invited a general commerce.

Fur trade divisions, like the major ethnographic ones, tended to be based on major physical obstacles like mountain ranges, oceans, and rivers, rather than on the straight survey lines characteristic of colonial politi-cal divisions. Modern scientific and cultural definitions provide different names for the fur traders' divisions without, of course, altering their nat-ural foundations. For example, the fur traders' North West Coast is now contained within the Pacific Maritime Ecological Region, a region lying west of the Coast Mountains and characterized by heavy rainfall, mild temperature, and abundant vegetation (Map 7). British Columbia's Pacific Forest, identified by paleobotanists and glacial geologists, and

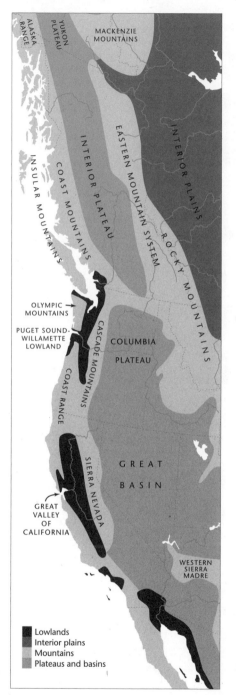

MAP 6 Physiographic regions of western North America

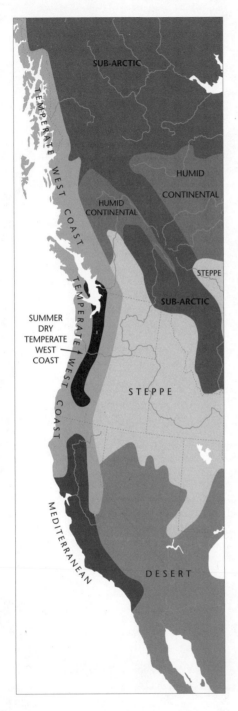

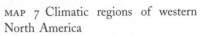

MAP 7 Climatic regions of western North America

characterized by Douglas fir, cedar, hemlock, spruce, and pine, covers much of the region. Major salmon streams intersect the entire area. There is a close match between ecoregions and west coast culture areas, a term defined by the anthropologist A.L. Kroeber as 'geographical units of cultures' (Map 8). The fur trade of the enormous Columbia Department embraced all or part of no less than five culture areas of North America and dozens of separate language families (Map 9). The department's coastal operations mirrored the Northwest Coast culture area; indeed, this region corresponds almost exactly with the maritime ecoregion and with the west coast archaeological region. The Northwest Coast culture area begins on what is now the Alaska Panhandle, in Tlingit territory, and extended into northern California. To the east, south, and north, the Fort Vancouver-based fur trade extended over the Plateau, Subarctic, Great Basin, California, and Southwest culture areas.[4]

The narratives and correspondence of the British fur traders contain striking references to the variety and diversity of the Pacific Coast. Newcomers like Alexander Mackenzie and Duncan Finlayson were accustomed to winters on Hudson Bay and in Rupert's Land, and they appreciated the coast's novelty. They responded to the coast with an enthusiasm uncharacteristic of the more mundane commercial records of the continental fur trade. The environment and the Native people needed to be described in terms that would have been inappropriate farther east.

The first people to identify these broad environmental and cultural patterns were the Scottish botanists David Douglas and John Scouler, in 1824. Scouler was hired by the HBC 'to make collections in the various branches of natural history.' The company was anxious, he wrote, 'to advance the knowledge of these exhaustive regions which are within the sphere of their commercial exertions.' Douglas was hired by the Royal Horticultural Society to make known 'the vegetable treasures of those widely extended and diversified countries' over which the company operated, and he too operated under the company's aegis. Scouler and Douglas left London at the end of July 1824 on the *William & Ann*, on a reconnaissance of a region that was still little known to the HBC. They began their botanical and ethnographic observations as soon as they entered the Columbia early in 1825.[5] Scouler would concentrate on the coast region and Douglas on the interior. In his articles, Scouler drew

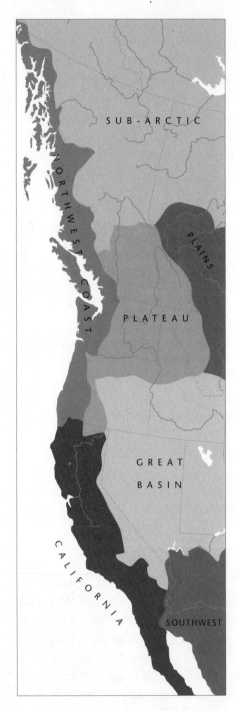

MAP 8 Culture areas of western North America

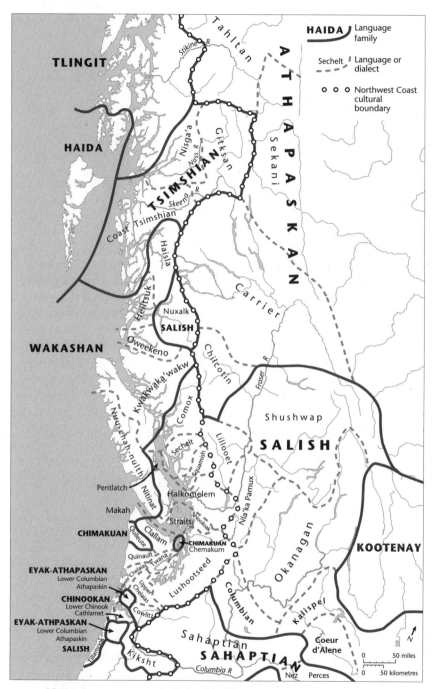

MAP 9 Native language groups, Columbia Department

attention to the mildness of the coast compared to eastern North America:

> Every traveller who has visited the N.W. Coast of America has remarked on the uncommon mildness of its climate when compared with that of the eastern side of the continent in the same parallel of latitude. While the inhabitants of Quebec are subjected, during the winter months, to all the severity of the most intense cold, the natives of the Columbia, in nearly the same latitude, are almost strangers to the phenomena of frost and snow, and go about during the coldest season of the year in state little different from nudity.[6]

He also described the magnificent salmon streams of the Pacific, which afforded the inhabitants their primary provision:

> Several causes contribute to produce this remarkable difference between the tribes on the eastern and western sides of the mountains. The most abundant supply of game in N. America is that afforded by the buffalo, and this animal has never penetrated to the N.W. coast; at the same time, the Columbia River, Fraser's River, and the other streams on the W. side of the Mountains, abound in salmon almost to their source. The inland tribes of the N.W. regions reside chiefly on the margins of the rivers, where they live on salmon during the summer, and prepare greater quantities of the same fish for their winter supply. The produce of the chase is, therefore, with them a secondary consideration.[7]

He explained cultural developments in terms of the environment:

> It is, at least in part, owing to these peculiarities of their physical condition that the habits and social arrangements of the Indians on the opposite side of the mountains present such a remarkable contrast. The N.W. Indians, especially the coast-tribes, have made considerable progress in the rude arts of savage life. Their canoes are constructed with much skill; their houses, being for permanent residence, have been erected with some forethought and attention to comfort; and their fishing apparatus and articles of domestic economy are far more numerous and elaborate than can be found in the temporary lodges of hunting tribes. From this settled mode of life, they are more accustomed to continuous labour, and even show considerable aptitude for passing into an agricultural state ...[8]

Scouler, Douglas, and other European visitors also noticed a basic distinction within the coast region itself. The northern and outer parts of the coast were exposed to the sea; they were rainier, colder, and generally possessed a less bounteous resource base than the south. This outer, inhospitable, northerly region had been named the 'North West Coast' by explorers and maritime fur traders (not to be confused with the ethnographic term Northwest Coast). On the outer coast, the region began at Cape Flattery; on the inside coast, it began at Cape Mudge and extended far into Russian territory to the north. Early British and American visitors characterized winters on the North West Coast as 'dreary,' 'inhospitable,' 'wretched,' 'savage,' 'one vast wilderness and unbroken solitude.'[9] 'The coast from Cape Flattery ... is what the seamen call a *straight iron bound shore*,' wrote an American visitor in 1822.[10] A meteorological register kept from 1833 to 1835 by William Tolmie at Fort McLoughlin, in the heart of the North West Coast, showed that some winter months got as many as twenty-seven days of rain, though the mean annual temperature was a mild fifty degrees Fahrenheit (Map 10).[11] In 1841, Simpson described the North West Coast inlets as follows:

> Moreover, this land of rocks is as difficult of access, excepting on the immediate region of the sea, as it is impracticable in itself. Most of the streams to the northward of Frazer's River are mere torrents, which, being fed in summer by the melting of snows, and in winter by the untiring deluges of this dismal climate, plunge headlong in deep gulleys between the contiguous bases of precipitous heights of every form and magnitude.[12]

To the south were the mild, protected regions of the inside coast: the Gulf of Georgia, the lower Fraser delta, the Strait of Juan de Fuca, Puget Sound, and farther south, the lower Columbia River. The HBC's new export trades emerged in these southerly, sheltered regions, distant from the pounding and hostile surf of the North West Coast. A trader who passed the winter of 1795-96 in the mouth of the Columbia found the climate warmer than the south of England, and a meteorological register kept by botanist Meredith Gairdner at Fort Vancouver from 1833 to 1834 showed a mild climate, with a good deal less rain and higher summer temperatures than Fort McLoughlin.[13]

The resources of the Gulf of Georgia-Puget Sound region were especially abundant, as Scouler noted in 1825 in the Strait of Juan de Fuca:

> When we consider the abundance of provisions this beautiful country affords, we shall not be surprised at the great population it maintains; and, probably,

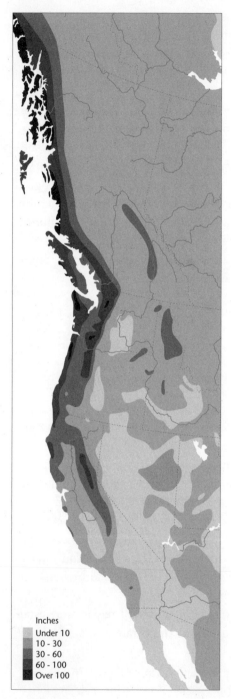

Inches
Under 10
10 - 30
30 - 60
60 - 100
Over 100

MAP 10 Average annual precipitation of western North America

no Indians in North America have less difficulty in procuring their food than the tribes from the Gulf of Georgia to the Columbia River; the sea yields an abundant supply of fishes of the most delicious kinds, as various species of mullet, turbot, and cod; every rivulet teems with myriads of salmon; and the meadows and forests produce an endless variety of berries and esculent roots. The collection of the latter forms the occupation of the women and children, while the men are occupied in procuring the former, and both are carefully dried for winter stores.[14]

The coastal abundance described by the fur traders was of very long standing. Archaeologists believe that at the end of the last ice age, a mobile, seafaring people came down the coast from Asia or up the coast from unglaciated regions hunting, fishing, and generally exploiting the rich marine habitat. From them were descended the Native inhabitants encountered by the fur traders.[15]

The whole coast shared certain characteristics. By the 1820s, its richest and most glamorous commodity, the sea otter, was nearly extinct. Native populations were generally high due to the varied marine abundance, especially the copious salmon migrations. Salmon frequented every major river drainage from Russian America to California (Map 11). 'The salmon is to the north-west Indians what the *cerealia* are to us, the fishing season being their harvest,' Scouler wrote.[16] Local and seasonal variations in available resources, identified by anthropologist Wayne Suttles, did not lessen a general impression of abundance.[17] The peoples of the coast, despite the recent disappearance of sea otters, retained control, access, and ownership of a range of commodities. They lived in a mild region noted not for fur-bearing land mammals but for an abundant marine and land provision base, most notably salmon, shellfish, and camas. European fur traders, obsessed with hunting, would condemn these people for what they saw as apathy and 'indolence.' To the traders, abundance demanded attention through resource development, and they could not respect cultures that let such opportunities pass. Judgments about 'indolent' Native people indicate that the fur traders had entered a distinctive region where Indians did not always have to kill mammals for protein or to obtain pelts for trading purposes. Salmon and other marine resources could serve both ends.

Simpson, for example, acknowledged the natural abundance available

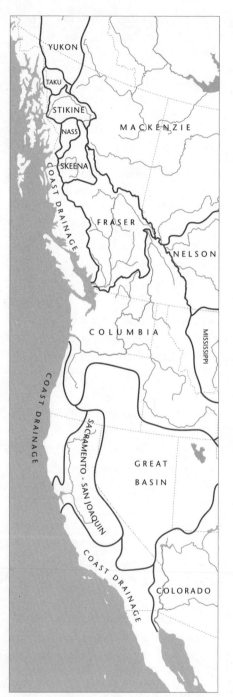

MAP 11 Major drainage basins of western North America

to the people of the coast, but still condemned Native people for their 'constitutional indolence.' He and his colleagues possessed a bias in favour of hunting that was natural to their profession, and they tried to convert the 'indolent fishing Indians' of the coast into the 'manly hunting Indians' of the interior. A.C. Anderson contrasted the 'wretched fish eaters of the Columbia and its neighbouring coast' who procured an 'abundant livlihood with little exertion,' with the interior hunters, 'nerves and sinews braced by exercise, and minds comparatively ennobled by frequent excitement.'[18]

Overland fur traders' perceptions of coastal people were influenced largely by their experience of the Chinook people of the lower Columbia River. Their negative views of Chinook industry changed little between the 1790s and the 1840s. The Native people were judged to be 'self-indulgent' and 'lazy' for their dependence on fishing, and for their refusal to hunt or farm. Franchère noted that salmon was their staple food, and that 'not being hunters, they rarely eat meat, though they like the taste of it.'[19] 'The Chinooks among whom we are resident do not exert themselves in hunting and rarely employ their Slaves in that way,' Simpson wrote in 1825. He continued:

> I do not know any part of North America where the natives could be civilized and instructed in morality, and religion at such a moderate expense and with so much facility as on the banks of the Columbia and Frazers River. On the East side the Mountain it does not appear to me practicable on account of the erratick life the Indians lead changing their Encampments almost Daily and the great difficulty nay utter impossibility of procuring the means of subsistence for any Considerable body of people until Cultivation becomes a principal object of attention among them! but in many parts of this Country they are settled in villages, the waters afford ample Provision, the earth yields spontaneously nutricious Roots and Fruits, and all descriptions of Game are abundant.[20]

Later, Paul Kane noted the combination of natural abundance and Native 'indolence' on southern Vancouver Island: 'All the tribes about here subsist almost entirely upon fish, which they obtain with so little trouble during all seasons of the year, that they are probably the laziest race of people in the world.' The copious harvest of the sea prevailed on the whole of the ethnographic Northwest Coast. In 1839, Ferdinand Wrangell of the Russian American Company observed a universal reliance on the sea for sustenance: 'The natives of this coastal strip and those of the neighbouring islands are ... completely dependent on the sea for sustenance. Fish and other sea creatures are their chief, and sometimes their only, source of food. In this regard, the natives' way of life cannot be altered.'[21]

The coastal people, therefore, were not known as hunters but as fishers and traders. Fur-bearing animals had adapted to the mild coastal climate and lost the dense (and valuable) pelts of animals in the interior and northern regions. These basic environmental and cultural distinctions contributed to the readiness with which the HBC broadened its commercial base on the Pacific after 1821.

The major natural cleavage within the department lay between coast and interior. Travellers found a great natural and cultural divide, for example, in the Coast Mountains separating the Chilcotin Plateau from Dean Channel, in the Fraser canyon, and in the Cascades at the Dalles of the Columbia. In 1793, Mackenzie found a wooden house containing three doors and hearths, the only 'Indian habitation of this kind I have seen this side of Michilemakina.' Impressed, he measured the house, finding it thirty by twenty feet.[22] Simon Fraser, between Spuzzum and Yale in 1808, found a people whose language was quite different from those he had passed. He was surprised to find large villages and tombs 'superior to any thing of the kind I ever saw among the savages.' Like Mackenzie, he measured a house, finding it forty-six by twenty-three feet and 'constructed like American frame houses.' Near Yale Fraser observed that Indians had 'scarcely any leather, so that large animals must be scarce.'[23]

On the Fraser River, the great divide between coast and interior started some 110 miles inland from the Gulf of Georgia. Anderson described the Fraser canyon:

> The series of rapids called the 'Falls' is about three miles in length. There is no such abrupt descent as the name implies. At the low water these rapids may be ascended with light craft, by making portages; but at the higher stages of the water they present a difficulty almost insurmountable. During the summer season, the rocky shores of the 'Falls' are thronged with Indians from the lower country, who resort thither for the salmon fishery. A ceaseless feud, I might here mention, prevails between the Couteau and the lower Indians, who differ from each other widely in many respects.[24]

In ascending the Fraser the coast climate may be said to extend some miles above Yale, where the river emerges from a deep mountainous gorge. Proceeding upwards the evidences of a drier climate begin to appear; the nature of the vegetation changes; and on reaching the junction of Thompson's River with the Fraser at Lytton, some 55 miles beyond Yale, all the evidences of a hot and dry summer-climate are perceptible.[25]

The Fraser canyon, Anderson wrote, prevented large-scale contact between coast and interior, though trade took place at a number of places. 'Nature it would hence appear, herself places a barrier which alike checks the future extension of the interior nations seaward, and prevents invasion of the coast tribes beyond the limits easily accessible with the canoes.'[26]

The Columbia River passes through similar climatic zones in its final stages. Many accounts have survived of the marked physical differences on either side of the Cascades and of the river's final tumultuous descent. Part way down was the Grande Coulee, described by Simpson as 'a dry channel, – apparently the ancient bed of the river.'[27] Duncan Finlayson, on his 1831 descent of the Columbia between Fort Nez Perces and the Dalles, wrote that

here & there along this River a monumental cross marks the spot of some fatal catastrophe. The country from Walla Walla to the Chutes consists of high steep masses black rocks & Stones resembling lava – it presents a picturesque but desolate and sterile landscape amidst which the eye seeks in vain for some spot capable of producing vegetation – not a solitary tree to be seen. We even had [to] purchase pieces of drift wood from the natives to supply our daily wants.[28]

A weather table kept at Fort Nez Perces in 1822 revealed a hot and dry summer followed by a clear and cold winter.[29]

Similarly, David Douglas encountered 'the vast change of climate and soil experienced between the western and eastern base' of the Cascade Range. 'As far as the eye can stretch is one dreary waste of barren soil thinly clothed with herbage,' he wrote in June 1825 between the Grand Rapids and Great Falls (the Chutes) of the Columbia. He found 'Nothing but extensive plains and barren hills, with the greater part of the herbage scorched and dead by the intensive heat.' However sterile the land around, the river itself yielded a rich salmon run. 'Along the shore,' De Smet wrote, 'on every projecting point, the Indian fisherman takes

FIGURE 5 The Columbia River cut through a barren but monumental landscape in the final stages of its descent from the Rockies to the Pacific. [Henry Warre, *Mount Hood from Les Dalles*, 24 August 1845, National Archives of Canada, C-26344]

his stand, spreading in the eddies his ingeniously worked net, and in a short time procures for himself an abundant supply of fine fish.' This desert country ended on the west side of the Dalles, the fourteen-mile-long rapids, consisting of the Dalles, the Little Dalles, and Celilo Falls. Thirty miles below the Dalles were the Cascades, the site of a portage to the west of which, suddenly, was the inland tidal estuary of the Columbia River, 120 miles from the sea.[30]

All this was breathtakingly different terrain for the overland fur traders from Montreal or York Factory. In 1811, David Thompson noted log houses west of the Cascades and remarked on the presence of slavery on the lower Columbia. In the same year, Franchère described many of the standard elements of the Northwest Coast: abundant salmon, sturgeon, camas, and *haiqua* shells. He noted Native salmon fishing methods and technology, and that the Chinook people would not allow fur traders to cut salmon crosswise.[31]

New Caledonia, by contrast, gained a reputation for harshness, poverty, and a fine fur trade.[32] Cut off from Rupert's Land and the Pacific by mountains, this district between the northern Rockies and the North

West Coast was completely inaccessible to ocean-borne commerce, and provisions were a perennial problem. Fur traders lived largely on salmon that ascended the Fraser and its tributaries in prodigious quantity, but in variable quality and regularity. The fish were wasted after the long journey from the ocean, and their non-appearance could spell starvation in Native and fort communities alike. Such a provision could not support a large Native population, and the 747 people trading at Fort Alexandria in the 1830s constituted the largest population attached to any post in New Caledonia.[33]

The periodic failure of salmon prompted Daniel Harmon's venture into agriculture in New Caledonia between 1811 and 1818. Although permafrost was absent west of the Rockies, summer frosts made horticulture a problem, and, despite great efforts, only turnips could be grown at Stuart Lake in 1836. Sometimes, even potatoes failed throughout New Caledonia. In 1842, the missionary Modeste Demers described New Caledonia as 'a sterile country with a vigorous climate. With the exception of some localities exploited by the Company, the soil is untillable; the winters are long and hard; frosts are felt until the month of June and destroy now and then entirely the harvests of the Company.'[34]

New Caledonia made a poor impression in fur trade circles. Moose (*Alces alces*) were scarce in New Caledonia in the early nineteenth century.[35] David Douglas, preparing to visit in 1833, was told that 'The country is certainly frightful; nothing but prodigious mountains to be seen: not a deer comes, say the Indians, save once in a hundred years – the poor natives subsist on a few roots.' John McLean, who arrived the same year, recalled that the menu at Stuart Lake was 'scarcely fit for dogs.' From as early as 1806, the NWC awarded more generous salaries and allowances to men stationed there, and after 1827, labourers in New Caledonia got £2 a year more than their counterparts elsewhere in the Columbia Department.[36] Even the hard-nosed Simpson could not hide his opinion. 'The situation of our New Caledonia Friends in regard to the good things of this Life, is anything but enviable,' he wrote in 1828, and continued:

In regard to the means of living, McLeods Lake is the most wretched place in the Indian Country; it possesses few or no resources within itself, depending almost entirely on a few dried Salmon taken across from Stuarts Lake, and when the Fishery there fails, or when any thing else occurs to prevent this supply being furnished, the situation of the Post is cheerless indeed. Its

complement of people, is a Clerk and two Men whom we found starving, having had nothing to eat for several Weeks but berries, and whose countenances
were so pale and emaciated that it was with difficulty I recognised them.[37]

What was bad for company employees was nevertheless good for company finances. New Caledonia's numerous rivers and lakes, rolling hills,
and often bitter winters favoured animals with fine pelts, and the district was known as the nursery of the Columbia Department fur trade.
It may have been the crucible of the transmontane fur trade, but New
Caledonia's isolation prevented the export of other commodities. As early
as 1828, the district's fur returns had peaked. Simpson doubted that the
district's profits could ever exceed £10,000 to £12,000 a year, beyond
which, he wrote, 'it cannot materially rise, as its Trade does not appear
to me, capable, of further extension.'[38]

To the south were several large, interior districts: Thompson's River
District, Okanagan, the upper Columbia districts, and the Snake
Country. Great regional variations existed, but all were milder than New
Caledonia and generally possessed rich fisheries and farming potential
in their valley bottoms and lower benchlands; like New Caledonia, however, none could consider non-fur exports under the prevailing transport
conditions. Fraser and Columbia river salmon provided principal provisions throughout; midway between New Caledonia and Kamloops was
Fort Alexandria, a transport post where, in 1827, seventeen people consumed 10,000 salmon.[39] When salmon failed, Native people were without a provision to sustain their winter hunts. As John Tod recalled, '"No
salmon, no furs" was a pithy, true saying to the westward of the Rocky
Mountains.'[40]

In 1827, Archibald McDonald drew a map of Thompson's River
District – the first map of what is now the southern interior of British
Columbia (Map 12). He showed the district's tenuous, but known, connection with the Pacific via the Fraser River and the important central
location of Kamloops in the line of communication between the
Columbia River and New Caledonia. He also recorded the main ethnographic divisions of the Natives of the interior plateau. This entire region
was fed by the great salmon runs of the Fraser and Columbia rivers.

Most years, salmon gave Native peoples a protein-rich provision that
spared them from an absolute dependence on hunting. Simpson wanted

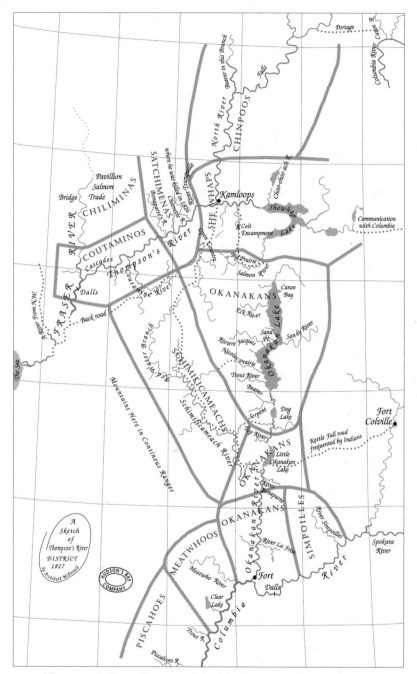

MAP 12 Thompson's River District of the Hudson's Bay Company (redrawn from Archibald McDonald map, 1827)

to abandon Kamloops in 1824 because '1700 Beaver will do little more than cover the Interest on the Capital employed, whereas in many other parts of the Country it can be turned to much greater advantage.' He believed this was less a result of a natural scarcity of fur-bearing animals than of Native 'indolence,' but he maintained the post as a provision centre on the main New Caledonia-Fort Vancouver brigade.[41] Fort Okanagan was little better: Joseph McGillivray of the NWC remarked in 1814 that the Okanagan Indians were 'incontestably the most indolent rascals I have ever met,' and the HBC maintained the post only as an entrepôt for Kamloops. Okanagan, Simpson wrote in 1841, was 'an outpost from the establishment of Thompson's River, maintained more for the purpose of facilitating the transport business of the post and New Caledonia than for trade, as there are few or no fur bearing animals in the surrounding country.' Beaver returns from Kamloops and Okanagan declined from 2,946 pelts in 1822 to 1,051 in 1826, causing Archibald McDonald to write in 1827 that 'the Beaver run on the verge of extermination, which the Natives themselves observe.' 'A person can walk for days together without seeing the smallest quadruped, the little brown squirrel excepted,' McDonald repeated two years later. The HBC urged Native hunters at Kamloops to procure marten skins in the face of the beaver shortage.[42]

The fur trade rarely satisfied officials who, typically, blamed the situation on Native hunters. 'Many Indians Hunt furs (In the Interior) merely to please us,' McLoughlin observed in 1826. Northwester Donald McKenzie complained that Nez Perces men, accustomed to a roving life of buffalo hunting and warfare, refused to submit 'to the drudgery of killing beavers. They spurned the idea of crawling about in search of fur,' McKenzie told Alexander Ross. 'Such a life,' they said, 'was fit only for women and slaves.' To the northeast, in the Kootenay region, A.C. Anderson blamed the scarcity of furs on the 'negligent' hunting habits of the Kootenay Indians.[43] Company officials in such places were unable to consider exploiting other resources, which at any rate remained landlocked until the railway era.

In the 1820s and 1830s, the activities of the Columbia Department stretched, seemingly without end, to the south and southeast, where traders operated beyond the headwaters of the Snake, beyond the continental divide and in the western headwaters of the rivers that ran into the Missouri River. They worked the eastern slope of the Rocky Mountains, and at Green River, the Humboldt, the Sacramento, San Joaquin, and Colorado rivers. Their enormous range included four of Kroeber's culture areas. They traded as far east as the territory of the Crow Indians in the Rocky Mountains. The cultural and environmental diversity of this enormous territory is suggested in an observation of Crow chief Arapoosh, quoted by fur trader Robert Campbell:

> If you go to the south, there you have to wander over great barren plains; the water is warm and bad, or you meet the fever and ague.
> To the north it is cold; the winters are long and bitter, with no grass; you cannot keep horses there, but must travel with dogs. What is a country without horses!
> On the Columbia they are poor and dirty, paddle about in canoes, and eat fish. Their teeth are worn out; they are always taking fish bones out of their mouths. Fish is poor food.
> To the east, they dwell in villages; they live well; but they drink the muddy water of the Missouri – that is bad. A Crow's dog would not drink such water.[44]

Overland fur traders had been nurtured in conditions that prepared them to recognize the novelty of the Pacific coast. Animal hunting provided the major provision to Native people and fur traders alike in the vast northern boreal forest. The Columbia Department, by contrast, offered a unique emphasis on fishing (Map 13). To the east of the Rockies, and north of the forty-ninth parallel, was the Northern Department of the HBC, the vast and desolate heartland of the North American fur trade. Contemporary impressions reveal a frustration with the environment of this region, which resembled New Caledonia more than the lower Columbia or the North West Coast. Even simple subsistence was difficult on Hudson Bay, which was ice-free only a month or two annually, making year-round export impossible, and where permafrost prevented the cultivation of all but potatoes and a few vegetable crops. The most basic provisioning needs could not be met locally, and the bay was, an early fur trader wrote, 'a Very uncertain place for the English mens living.'[45] English food and Native provisions were always required; a seventeenth-century attempt to grow Virginian corn failed, and wheat would not survive owing to low summer temperatures. To avoid scurvy, traders grew vegetables, cereal crops, greens, and even English dande-

MAP 13 Major provisions, British fur trade territories

lions in the short summer months. Anti-scorbutic spruce beer, made by boiling the green leaf buds of fir trees, and native berries like cranberries remained vital to the fur traders' health.[46]

The unusually severe winter of 1715-16 forced the company to locate local provisions, especially the 'perdigious Variety of fowls' on the bay, which a fur trader described in 1749 as 'Extrodinary good Eating fresh or Salt ... the chief of our Diet.' Large-scale shoots took place every spring and fall at Churchill, Albany, and York (Map 1), when tens of thousands of geese, partridges, and swans (trumpeters and whistlers) were preserved for winter use. As many as 90,000 partridge were eaten at a single post in a winter. Productive fisheries were also established at most bayside posts. By the 1750s, an internal provisioning scheme was supplying the barren Eastmain posts with local fowl and fish and with English provisions such as flour, transported from the west-side posts and from those at the bottom of the bay.[47]

Fur traders had no illusions about the harshness of Hudson Bay winters. The export of timber and minerals was barely feasible in such a remote and barren place. Governor Simpson defended the company's neglect of the mineral resources of the Eastmain coast on the grounds that insuperable obstacles prevented the working of mines 'in that remote and hyperborean region.' 'If mining attempts in Canada had failed, what, then, would be the prospect of a mine on the East Main Coast, in the midst of a sterile and uninhabited region, with a winter of eight months duration and accessible only through Hudsons Straits, which are seldom navigable for more than two months out of the year, and never free from icebergs and floe ice at any season?'[48]

The HBC's provisions of fish and fowl allowed it to extend trade inland from the bay in the late eighteenth century, but these provisions did not match the pemmican obtained by the Montreal-based fur traders to the south and east. In 1811, the HBC promoted the formation of the Selkirk Colony at Red River to provide foodstuffs and pemmican for the inland fur trade.[49] Red River's difficulties would be many, as a group of incredulous Northwesters prophesied in 1815:

> That the communications by Canada and Hudson's Bay are impracticable for the purposes of commerce;
> That there is no market for grain or provisions of any sort;
> That only one article, viz., wool, can be pointed out capable of paying transport;
> That this article may not succeed, on account of the wolves, the soil, and climate;
> That the difficulty of communication will prevent the colonists from receiving any supplies, unless at enormous expense.[50]

Early farming experiments at the Red River colony were hindered by malnutrition, spear-grass, needle-grass, and blowfly infections in livestock, as well as rattlesnake bites, wounds caused by lameness, severe cold, floods, weeds, mosquitoes, grasshoppers, horseflies ('bull-dogs'), and flocks of birds that destroyed crops and harassed livestock. Wolves preyed on unfenced cattle and sheep. The HBC G&C sent the colony two ounces of strychnine, considered 'the most powerful agent for destroying wild animals (it is used in the East Indies for killing Tigers and Leopards).' Alexander Macdonell was known as the 'Grasshopper Governor' after the insects that attacked wheat, barley, and potatoes. Alexander Ross summarized the results of the 1819 'locust' swarm as follows: 'Along the river they were to be found in heaps, like sea-weed, and might be shovelled with a spade. It is impossible to describe, adequately, the desolation thus caused. Every vegetable substance was either eaten up or stripped to the bare stalk; the leaves of the bushes, the bark of the trees, shared the same fate; and the grain vanished as fast as it appeared above ground, leaving no hope either of "seed to the sower, or bread to the eater."'[51]

Red River was like a 'Lybian tyger,' Simpson lamented. 'The more we try to tame it, the more savage it becomes; so it is with Red River; for every step I try to bring it forward disappointment drives it back two.' Although agricultural crops and pemmican supplied the colony's internal needs and its expanding provision and transport networks by the 1820s, the colony was not yet self-sufficient. 'Our readers are aware,' an American newspaper editorialized in 1847,

> that there is an isolated settlement of several thousand inhabitants in a high latitude of British North America, known as the 'Selkirk Settlement.' Cut off from the commerce of the world, they rely entirely upon their own resources, their farms, their flocks and fishing for support – being a community, so to speak, of Robinson Crusoes. Their crops having failed the last two seasons, they have been forced to break out of the wilds again, and seek food in the Markets of the great brawling world.'[52]

Rupert's Land ended at the Rocky Mountains, which provided the principal natural divide in fur trade territory; the Columbia Department was sometimes informally referred to as 'Beyond the Mountains.' Travellers familiar with the Pacific coast often found the prairies monotonous. 'Here all is dwarfish and stunted,' commented Northwester Ross Cox near Rocky Mountain House in 1817, 'while on the Columbia the vegetable world is seen in its richest and most magnificent forms – including all the varieties from a luxuriant growth of blackberry or wild-cherry, to the stately pine, and majestic cedar.' Botanist David Douglas, who accompanied the York Factory Express from the Pacific ten years later, complained that the Assiniboine River 'admits of no variety, seeing one mile gives an idea of the whole.' He wrote that, between Jasper House and Fort Assiniboine, 'this uninteresting wretched Country' afforded him no plants. A travelling companion recalled that Douglas's spirits flagged on the Saskatchewan River: 'The sameness of scenery for hundreds of

miles, and absence of variety in the vegetable kingdom damped his energies, and he floated down the stream apparently as unconscious of the
magnificent scenery ... as the boat in which he rode.'[53]

These regions sustained only a small, dispersed Native population
characteristic of hunting-gathering societies relying on a seasonal food
supply. 'For the great duration of the winter,' wrote Alexander Ross, 'the
means of subsistence are scanty and the natives are thereby scattered over
a wide extent of country.' In 1808, Northwester Duncan McGillivray
estimated the total Native population between Labrador and the Rocky
Mountains at 15,000. David Thompson noted that in 'Muskrat Country,' ninety-two families hunted over 22,816 miles, giving each family a
hunting territory of 248 square miles. In 1843, the population of the
Norway House District, north of Red River (Map 1), was between 760
and 780, allowing Donald Ross to calculate that 'each individual may be
said to occupy a tract of land equal to *one hundred* Square Miles.' The
district contained about 78,780 square miles.[54]

An abundant environment, then, set the Pacific coast apart from the
interior of the continent from an early date. The bountiful sea had long
supported the rich material cultures of the ethnographic Northwest
Coast; the abundance evident in coastal middens was later turned to
good account by fur traders and eventually found its way to Pacific markets in the holds of HBC vessels. The commercial potential of the Pacific
was irresistible to these entrepreneurial fur traders steeped in the broad
commercial ambitions of Alexander Mackenzie. Northwesters familiar
with the lower Columbia, like David Thompson, were ecstatic about its
larger potential. 'The whole of this River [the Willamette] is a very
beautiful and rich Country and happy Climate,' Thompson inscribed on
one of his maps. Ogden went a step further and envisioned a colony. 'I
started this morning to Fort Vancouver,' he wrote on his return from the
Snake Country in 1825, 'no doubt ere many years a Colony will be formed
on this Stream and I am of opinion it will with little care flourish and
Settlers by having a sea post so near them with industry might add
greatly to their comforts and probably to their happiness.' Similarly, in
1831 Finlayson observed on his arrival at Fort Vancouver from Red River
that 'It has hither to been the fate of this part of the country, like modest minds to remain unnoticed; but [we] will do it justice; towns & cities

will hereafter flourish where all is now desert; the waters over which scarcely a solitary boat is yet seen to glide will reflect the flags of all nations & a happy people will dispense what nature here bestows so freely to every port of the world.'[55] Yet Ogden and Finlayson knew that the trade in fur could never produce such changes.

With such abiding impressions of abundance, it was natural that the Pacific coast was the only fur trade territory in British North America considered highly suitable for colonization. In 1809, Alexander Mackenzie proposed that the British government form a commercial colony on the North West Coast; and in 1812, when Northwester George Nelson heard of the arrival of the Red River settlers, he wrote that 'if the English were so keen on planting colonies they should consider the Columbia region.' David Thompson had told him that there was 'a country & climate ... not inferior to many of the Spanish provinces of America,' where colonists could reap 'much more benefit than they will ever be able in my humble opinion to do in Red River.' Thirty years later, in 1842, fur trader George Gladman echoed these thoughts: 'Red River has I suspect seen the acme of its prosperous days – its position in the heart of the Country is so decidedly against its advancement, that there can be little doubt that many of its present inhabitants will migrate annually to Columbia.' Clearly, a natural abundance underlay an impressive commercial potential and influenced the HBC's policies on the Pacific.[56]

CHAPTER 5

From Fort Vancouver to the Vermilion Sea

In short, being appointed to this side of the mountains is reckoned by the Sanguine as a sure step to their promotion, in as much as it is thought to be the only field where a young man can exert himself.

— FRANCIS ERMATINGER,
KAMLOOPS (THOMPSON'S RIVER POST), 1826[1]

The Hudson's Bay Company's invasion of the vast and environmentally diverse region west of the Rockies was an impressive feat by any standards. In 1821, the Northwesters had controlled the fur trades only of central New Caledonia and of the lower and middle Columbia River drainage; twenty years later, the HBC controlled or dominated the fur trade of most of the Columbia watershed, the watersheds of the Umpqua, Klamath, Willamette, Columbia, Snake, Fraser, Thompson, Skeena, Nass, Stikine, and Taku rivers, dozens of minor rivers, Puget Sound, the Gulf of Georgia, Vancouver Island, the North West Coast, the Queen Charlotte Islands, as well as the interior fur trades of the entire continent west of the continental divide, excluding Russian and Californian coastal settlements. HBC traders had followed the Colorado River to the Gulf of California (the Vermilion Sea) in present-day Mexico, and trapped regularly in the Sacramento and San Joaquin rivers. Boston traders had abandoned the coast, and the Missouri traders were never securely established west of the Rockies. Although they enjoyed equal access and legal status in the region, American merchants were no match for the expertise, capital, and range of the British fur traders. 'The Americans do not possess an atom of land on the Columbia!' wrote surprised Royal Navy officer Edward Belcher in 1839.[2]

Between George Simpson's departure in the spring of 1829 and his return in the fall of 1841, company officials extended and consolidated their control over the three largest regions of the Columbia Department: the Columbia River and its inland tributaries, the North West Coast, and New Caledonia. HBC transport systems connected these regions with each other and with the outside world (see Map 14). Throughout the entire Columbia Department, the company employed a uniform set of policies against American fur traders. This chapter deals with the competitive fur trade policies that made monopoly possible on the Columbia River and to the south; the following chapter considers the application of the same policies on the North West Coast.

West of the Rockies, the interior offered a fur trade and the coast offered a general commerce. HBC policy in the southern interior was aimed at creating a 'fur desert' to discourage American overland commercial interest and to prevent Native traders from taking or sending furs to the coast where competitors were sometimes present and prices were high. The Columbia River led to regions where American fur traders operated and to the Missouri traders' annual 'Rendezvous' in the southern Rockies. From its Fort Vancouver headquarters, the HBC sent hunting, trapping, and trading brigades to the southern and eastern frontiers of the Columbia Department.

Fort Vancouver was the emporium – the centre – of the company's extensive fur trading operations everywhere west of the Rockies. It inherited this role from Fort George in 1825. As Dunn noted, it was the place where British trade goods were unloaded and furs were loaded onto the annual ship from London:

> Fort Vancouver is then the grand mart, and rendezvous for the company's trade and servants on the Pacific. Thither all the furs and other articles of trade collected west of the Rocky Mountains from California to the Rocky Mountains, are brought from the several other forts and stations: and from thence they are shipped to England ... in a word, Fort Vancouver is the grand emporium of the Company's trade, west of the Rocky Mountains; as well as within the Oregon territory, as beyond it, from California to Kamschatka.[3]

The fort was substantially built, surrounded by the habitations of Kanakas and Iroquois, including their wives and families. An early visitor wrote that the fort buildings were wood, 'generally hewn logs, like

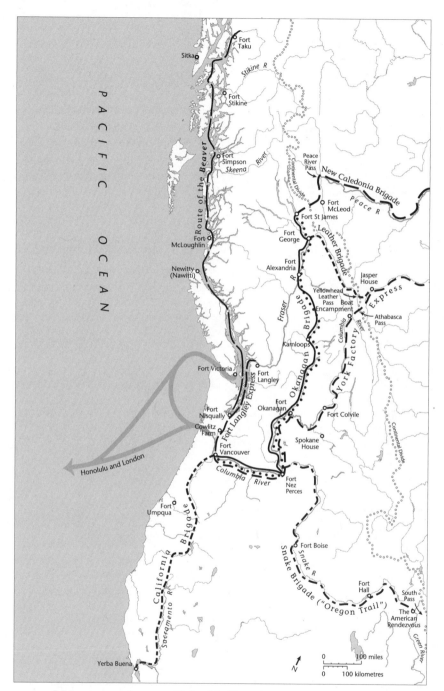

MAP 14 Major transport routes, Columbia Department, 1843

the universal log House of Canada.'[4] On his arrival there in September 1834, the American naturalist John Townsend wrote that

> Fort Vancouver is situated on the north bank of the Columbia on a large level plain, about a quarter of a mile from the shore. The space comprised within the stoccades is an oblong square, of about one hundred, by two hundred and fifty feet. The houses built of logs and frame-work, to the number of ten or twelve, are ranged around in a quadrangular form, the one occupied by the doctor [McLoughlin] being in the middle. In front, and enclosed on three sides by the buildings, is a large open space, where all the in-door work of the establishment is done. Here the Indians assemble with their multifarious articles of trade ...[5]

The HBC tried hard to discourage Americans from coming by land or sea to trade furs on the lower Columbia. There was a 'just apprehension,' John McLean wrote, 'that if once a footing were obtained on

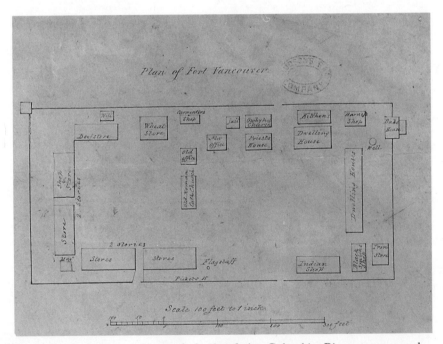

FIGURE 6 Situated on the north bank of the Columbia River at present-day Vancouver, Washington, Fort Vancouver was the Columbia Department depot for twenty years after its construction in 1825. [Mervyn Vavasour, *Plan of Fort Vancouver*, 1845, HBC Archives, Provincial Archives of Manitoba, N11131]

the coast, an equal eagerness might be manifested for extending their locations into the interior.'[6] At first this was a simple matter: between the visit of the *Arab* in 1819 and the *Owhyhee* in 1827, not a single American vessel visited the Columbia River for the purpose of trade.[7] In 1827, the *Owhyhee*, under Captain John Dominis, traded furs and cut spars at the mouth of the Columbia; in 1829 and 1830 Dominis returned on the *Owhyhee* along with Captain D.W. Thompson of the *Convoy*. Both vessels were owned by Bryant & Sturgis of Boston. They entered the river, a crewmember recalled, 'to trade with the Indians,' but left in the summer of 1830, having salted fifty barrels of salmon, and never returned. Their captains were disillusioned by the shortage of furs and the HBC's fierce competition. 'The English Company here have a great advantage over us,' Captain Thompson told a Boston merchant in 1829, 'knowing the language well and the best hunting grounds. The greater part of their collection of skins they trap themselves, and they are determined to drive us from the river.' The resident Chinook people were convinced the Americans had introduced a fever to the region.[8] Between 1830 and 1840, only one American trading vessel entered the Columbia River: Nathaniel Wyeth's *Mary Dacre*, in 1834.

Wyeth's company, the Columbia River Fishing and Trading Company, was founded by New York and Boston merchants in 1834, two years after Wyeth had come to Fort Vancouver on a fur trading expedition. He had been so impressed with the HBC's operations that he capitalized the new company on his return to the United States.[9] He planned to establish a fort and fishery on the Willamette in competition with Fort Vancouver; indeed, Wyeth's plan was an American version of the HBC's Columbia River operations, with Boston substituted for London. Astor and his Pacific Fur Company had been gone from the Columbia River for twenty years by this time, and the HBC, which had developed a successful salmon fishery on the river, provided the commercial precedent, as Dunn recalled:

A fortified trading post was to be established on the Columbia, to carry on a trade with the natives for salmon and peltries, and to fish and trap on their own account. Once a year, a ship was to come from the United States, to bring out goods for the interior trade, and to take home the salmon and furs which had been collected. Part of the goods, thus brought out, were to be despatched to the mountains, to supply the trapping companies and the Indian tribes, in exchange for their furs; which were to be brought down to the Columbia, to be sent home in the next annual ship: and thus an annual round was to be kept up. The profits on the salmon, it was expected, would cover all the expenses of the ship so that the goods brought out, and the goods carried home, would cost nothing as freight.[10]

The *Mary Dacre* (Captain Lambert) reached the lower Columbia River in 1834 and rendezvoused with a party of fur traders and naturalists who had come overland to meet them, including Wyeth and Townsend. In November, Wyeth's men commenced building 'a large and permanent dwelling of logs' on Sauvie Island, near Fort Vancouver on the Willamette – 'the accent being upon the second syllable' – River. The settlement was known as Fort William. Within a year, the ambitious enterprise had failed, owing in large part to the Americans' inexperience in the salmon fishery and to their inability to trade many furs on the lower Columbia. John Ball, who came overland with Wyeth, recalled that they were no match for the British: 'The fur trade was their business, and if an American vessel came up the river, or coast, they would bid up the price on furs, and if necessary a price ten to one above their usual prices. So American traders soon got entirely discouraged.' Fort Vancouver was known in the Chinook jargon, Townsend recorded, simply as 'King George.'[11] Dominis, Wyeth, and others spread word around Boston and New York of the company's keen competition, and this did much to keep American fur traders out of the lower Columbia. Upon Wyeth's departure, McLoughlin ordered the demolition of Fort William and the construction of a dairy farm on Sauvie Island.[12]

Unknown to American visitors, the HBC itself was by no means happy with the lower Columbia fur trade. By the 1820s it was moribund. David Douglas, at Willamette Falls in August 1825, wrote that 'This at one time was looked on as the finest place for hunting west of the Rocky Mountains. The beaver now is scarce; none alive came under my notice. I was much gratified in viewing the deserted lodges and dams of that wise economist.' The fur returns of Fort George had remained constant throughout the North West Company's tenure,[13] and the stagnant Fort Vancouver fur trade paled in comparison to that of other districts within the department. Although the lower Columbia region contained a great many species of fur-bearing mammals, the Chinook people had a reputation for being abysmal hunters. In 1812 Robert Stuart found the

Cowlitz Indians 'totally ignorant of the mode of taking' beaver. He also attributed the poor fur returns of the lower Columbia to the impenetrable undergrowth, poor visibility, and unceasing winter rains. 'The fact is,' John McLoughlin wrote in 1825, 'the Indians hereabouts are poor animal hunters though animals are numerous.' He complained a year later that furs procured at the new post passed through so many hands that it was impossible to obtain properly dressed skins for the London market. In 1827, Simpson observed that Fort Vancouver commanded 'nearly the same Trade that Fort George did and as the Indians in that neighbourhood become more accustomed to the use of European supplies they will devote more of their time & attention to the chase in order to procure the means of obtaining them.'[14] This would not be the case; even fewer furs were traded at Fort Vancouver than at Fort George, and the new headquarters competed with the coastal fur trade still tapped by Fort George. Moreover, the new northern posts, Fort Langley (1827) and Fort Nisqually (1833), diverted furs that previously had gone south to Fort Vancouver.

European fur traders, characteristically, accused the Chinook of indolence for their lack of interest in hunting. 'They are too free and indolent to submit to the drudgery of collecting the means of traffic,' wrote Alexander Ross. In 1838 the 'growing indolence and inactive habits of the Chinook population' led James Douglas to pen this observation about commercial economy:

> We know the natural indolence and improvidence of the Columbia Indn. He must be urged [to] exertion by the most pressing wants. A few Beaver Skins appear to him wealth inexhaustible, and he remains inactive, until he finds a purchaser. This effect is not uncommon, neither is it peculiar to the Native American. It may be observed in a modified form even among the members of civilised and industrious communities, when disappointed of a market, for produce which has been with much pains & labour accumulated.[15]

Finally, fur from the lower Columbia region came less frequently from the Chinook and increasingly from 'Columbia freemen,' that is, French Canadian, Iroquois, and Metis employees (trappers, hunters, and guides) who had retired from the company to farm or pursue their previous occupations in the Willamette and elsewhere. After about 1818, Columbia freemen had settled in the Willamette, the 'garden of the Columbia,' where they constituted a growing seasonal and part-time labour pool for the HBC. They trapped and traded fur to the company at Fort Vancouver.[16]

One of these freemen was Alex-see, a Mohican-Iroquois originally from Montreal, who arrived at Fort Vancouver in about 1824. Interviewed on northern Vancouver Island in 1882, Alex-see stated that he and his partner were assured of work because 'the natives on this river were so well supplied with food they only trapped in order to trade for things they needed in the chase.' He continued:

> So it came about that we both worked to clear the ground for what would later be Fort Vancouver, and so we followed the traps. These people caught many furs, but were not real trappers. They did not go back where the martin and inland beaver were, but trapped the beaches and rivers. When I came in with my furs, they were well fleshed, caught where the winter's cold had set well the color. I had to return three times to bring in my catch, and received a compliment from the factor who seldom did a thing like that.[17]

The lower Columbia fur trade dwindled as the company diversified and, by the early 1840s, other political and commercial topics dominated the voluminous correspondence generated at Fort Vancouver. 'The Indian trade, however, is but a very small branch of the business at Fort Vancouver,' Simpson noted in 1841, 'the operations of which are varied and extensive.' By the end of the decade, Fort George's fur returns had declined by 95 per cent over earlier years.[18]

Fort Vancouver was, in spite of this, the depot for an extensive and profitable inland fur trade inherited from the NWC and expanded in the 1820s. The company annually sent out from Fort Vancouver two well-equipped hunting and trapping parties, usually numbering between fifty and one hundred men and women (French Canadian, Native, and Metis) and led by a single seasoned officer, often an old Northwester. The first party (the Snake Party) went up the Columbia and southeast down the Snake as far as the continental divide; the second party (the Southern Party) went up the Willamette and overland to San Francisco Bay. The Americans could field nothing to equal these professional trappers, agents of a commercial policy whose purpose, as always, was to create a fireguard against American fur traders outfitted from east of the

Rockies. This policy was so successful that, between 1821 and 1843, only three American fur traders managed to reach the lower Columbia: Jedediah Smith in 1826 and 1828-9, Nathaniel Wyeth and his party in 1832 and 1834, and Hall Kelley in 1834. The Smith and Kelley parties came up from California, seeking the HBC's protection after alienating or battling the Californian authorities and Native traders en route.[19]

British fur trade strategies were so effective that American overlanders were convinced that the HBC kept a special fund at Fort Vancouver to defeat competition by land or sea. Missionaries Daniel Lee and John Frost asserted that the company possessed 'a sinking fund' of two million pounds, and John Townsend wrote in 1843 that 'The company has a sum of money amounting to several thousand pounds sterling, laid aside at Vancouver for the sole purpose of opposing all who may come to interfere with its monopoly, by purchasing at exorbitant prices all the furs in the possession of the Indians.'[20]

The range and success of the Snake and Southern brigades made these statements possible. Edward Belcher, who visited Fort Vancouver in August 1839, wrote that 'The hunters are equipped with hunting instruments, firearms, traps, &c., each outfit amounting to between £40 and £50 per man.' Farnham, who was at Fort Vancouver for most of 1840, observed that 'They also have two migratory trading and trapping establishments of fifty or sixty men each. The one traps and trades in Upper California; the other in the country lying west, south, and east of Fort Hall.' These parties were based at and outfitted from Fort Vancouver; as Dunn recorded, 'Though a party may be obliged, from a variety of circumstances, to winter in the plains, or in the recesses of the mountains; on the borders of the lakes or rivers, some numbers of it return to the fort [Fort Vancouver] at the fall, with the produce of the season's hunt, and report progress; and return to the camp with a reinforcement of necessary supplies.' Before 1843, these two parties often comprised the only European presence in much of what is now the western United States.[21]

The Snake was the richest of the two hunts. As in the 1820s, the hunt had both a strategic and a commercial motive. John McLean, in New Caledonia in the mid-1830s, wrote that 'Strong parties of hunters are also constantly employed along the southern frontier for the purpose of destroying the fur-bearing animals in that quarter; the end in view being to secure the interior from the encroachments of foreign interlopers.'

Belcher wrote that the Snake River brigade hunted as far as the headwaters of the Sacramento River; Tolmie recalled that it went as far as a 'point called the Rendezvous in the Rocky Mtns where American trappers had at a certain period of the year to congregate and sell their furs to the highest bidder.' Between 1824 and 1846 the Snake expeditions produced what historian Frederick Merk called a 'steady, if not handsome profit' of about £30,000 altogether.[22]

The Snake Country hunts originated in what is now Washington State and operated in present-day Oregon, Idaho, and Wyoming. Parties connected with the hunt travelled over parts of present-day Arizona, Nevada, and California. From 1823 to 1829, the Snake River brigade was in charge of Peter Ogden, who ranged widely to the south and east. In 1827 McLoughlin instructed him to 'hunt all the head branches of the Missouries,' and in 1829-30 Ogden took his French Canadian and Iroquois trappers on an extraordinary exploration through modern Utah, Arizona, Mexico, California, and Nevada (Map 15). The brigade reached the mouth of the Colorado River in the Gulf of California, the 'Vermilion Sea,' in present-day Mexico, where Ogden found beaver scarce. He went overland and west to the San Joaquin and Sacramento rivers, and then east to Great Salt Lake and back to Fort Nez Perces. He left his name on several places on the map (e.g., Ogden, Utah, and Ogden's River in Nevada, now known as Humboldt River). On Ogden's return, unfortunately, the maps and journals of his expedition were lost in a whirlpool of the Columbia River.[23]

Fort Nez Perces was the original western base of the Snake Brigade. Built by the Northwesters in 1818 near the confluence of the Columbia and Snake, the fort was named after the local Indians, so called by the Montreal traders for their pierced noses. Irving wrote in 1837 that 'We should observe that this tribe is universally called by its French name, which is pronounced by the trappers, Nepercy.' The post was in charge of Pierre Pambrun when Townsend visited in September 1834:

> The fort is built of drift logs, and surrounded by a stoccade of the same, with two bastions, and a gallery around the inside. It stands about a hundred yards from the river, on the south bank, in a bleak and unprotected situation, surrounded on every side by a great, sandy plain, which supports little vegetation, except the wormwood and thorn bushes. On the banks of the little river, however, there are narrow strips of rich soil, and here Mr. Pambrun raises the

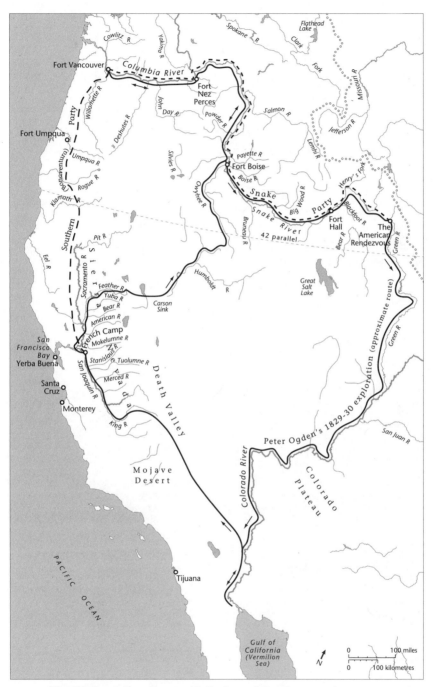

MAP 15 The Hudson's Bay Company's Snake and Southern parties

few garden vegetables necessary for the support of his family. Potatoes, turnips, carrots, &c., thrive well, and Indian corn produces eighty bushels to the acre.[24]

The post burned down in 1841 and was rebuilt in 'adobe, or unbaked bricks' by Archibald McKinlay.[25]

Far down the Snake was Fort Hall, built in 1834 nine miles above the Portneuf River by Nathaniel Wyeth, the HBC's only serious competition for the fur trade west of the Rockies before 1843. Prior to leaving Boston in 1833, Wyeth decided the Snake Country offered American fur traders the best opportunity anywhere west of the Rockies to compete against 'the English.' McLoughlin, however, deployed a strategy he had learned with the NWC during their pre-1821 contest against the HBC traders: he established Fort Boise on the Snake, midway between Fort Nez Perces and Fort Hall, as a rival post. Fort Boise ('Boisais' or 'Boisee' to British and American travellers) was so successful that, in 1836-7, Wyeth vacated the Snake Country and McLoughlin bought his entire

FIGURE 7 The Snake River navigated a forbidding arid landscape that for many years rendered the westward journey from South Pass uninviting to American over-landers. [Henry Warre, *Sandstone and Basaltic Rocks on the Snake River*, American Antiquarian Society, no. 41]

fur trading operations west of the Rockies. He was unable to comply with Wyeth's offer to 'place himself in the service of the Hudson's Bay Company.'[26] Just as the NWC had absorbed the Pacific Fur Company and its personnel in 1813, so McLoughlin bought the Columbia River Fishing and Trading Company, hired one of Wyeth's men, Courtney Walker, and put him in charge of Fort Hall in 1838-9. The company rebuilt Fort Hall in adobe and added it to its Snake River operations. The post, Dunn said, 'commands a wide range of trading operations.'[27]

The history of the Snake brigade is one of gradual eastward and south-eastward extension from Fort Nez Perces to combat the American fur trade. By the early 1830s, the trade among the Flathead Indians, conducted by the Snake parties and from Fort Colvile and Flathead Post, was depleted through competition between the company and American trappers, who had worked overland from the northern tributaries of the Missouri into the Flathead region as early as 1823. Snake Country returns declined in the 1830s as the company turned the Flathead and lower Snake River regions into fur deserts. The HBC's 'scorched-earth' policy on the American frontier of the Columbia Department was so successful that fur returns from the Snake brigades declined from 2,099 large beaver pelts (1826) to 800 (1836), in the process rendering the region barren to American traders trapping from the east.[28] The company adapted to the shortage of furs on the Snake by moving directly into the heart of American fur trading operations in the Rocky Mountains, a policy that ensured that American competition remained distant and negligible.

Between 1823 and 1840, the American Rendezvous was the great destination and the romantic location of the western American fur trade, immortalized by Washington Irving and American frontier artists. The Rendezvous was usually held at Horse Creek on the Green River,[29] a tributary of the Colorado, southeast of the headwaters of the Snake, among the western foothills of the Rockies and in the territory of the Crow Indians. 'The American fur companies keep no established posts beyond the mountains,' Irving wrote in 1837. 'In the months of June and July, when there is an interval between the hunting seasons, a general rendezvous is held, at some designated place in the mountains ... To this rendezvous repair the various brigades of trappers from their widely separated hunting grounds, bringing in the products of their year's campaign ... To this rendezvous the [American Fur] company sends annually a convoy of supplies from its establishment on the Atlantic frontier.'[30] In the mid-1830s the Rendezvous attracted 450-500 men – the entire component of freemen and trappers attached to the American fur trade companies in the Rocky Mountains and the tributaries of the upper Platte and Missouri rivers. The Rendezvous was also a meeting place for a great many Native people. In July 1835 an American missionary encountered 2,000 'Shoshoni or Snake Indians, and forty lodges of Flathead & Napiersas, and a few Utaws.'[31]

In the early 1830s the HBC, securely ensconced on the lower Columbia, decided to crash the Americans' annual party at the Rendezvous. In 1833-4 Francis Ermatinger transformed the HBC's Snake Party from an active hunting and trapping party into a trading party. As McLoughlin told Edward Ermatinger in 1834, 'Your brother is out in the Snake Country but more properly on a trading Exped. than hunting. It is a plan mostly of his own and I hope it will (on his Account) turn out well.' This transformation allowed the HBC to visit the American Rendezvous in search of fur for the first time in 1834; in the late 1830s, the Snake parties were also called the 'Rocky Mountain' parties.[32] Before 1840 the HBC disabled the far western American fur trade by sending Ermatinger and John McLeod to the Rendezvous with pack horses loaded with the same British goods that the Americans had to transport 1,400 miles inland from St. Louis. An American visitor wrote that McLeod 'could well afford to undersell the American fur traders on his own ground.' A Scottish traveller, Captain William Drummond Stewart, met the same representative of the 'colossal mercantile power' at the Rendezvous in the summer of 1837. Stewart, who had come overland with an American Fur Company brigade, noted that McLeod collected debts, 'and by the superior excellence and lower prices of his commodities,' disparaged those of the American traders and entered into open competition.[33]

With American trappers absent from the Snake River and most of the Columbia watershed, Ermatinger and McLeod exchanged English trade goods at the Rendezvous for the Americans' pelts. This change in policy had a devastating effect on the American fur trade companies, as the HBC could supply the companies and mountain men with English trade goods from Fort Vancouver at a lower price than the same goods

FIGURE 8 Scottish aristocrat William Drummond Stewart at the Rendezvous in the summer of 1837, located at Green River in present-day Wyoming. The HBC's Snake Party visited the American Rendezvous to buy furs from mountain men and Native hunters. This romanticized painting by Alfred Miller shows Stewart accepting a pipe above the general gathering, with the southern Rockies in the distance. [*The Rendezvous near Green River ... Final Destination of the American Fur Company Caravan*, National Archives of Canada, C-439]

from the eastern seaboard via the Missouri system. The Americans were suffering from the same problem that had beset the NWC: long-distance supply from the Atlantic seaboard. The British company's great advantage was its Fort Vancouver headquarters, where it received goods directly from England and where, by the late 1820s, it had established a secure provision base. In 1838 an American newspaper observed that the HBC sold its goods at the Rendezvous for less than a quarter the price charged by the Americans. 'The American Fur Company will soon abandon the mountains,' wrote the *Oregonian and Indians' Advocate*; 'The trade is unprofitable and the men are becoming dissatisfied, besides the Hudson's Bay Company will break down all opposition. Their resources are boundless and they stop at no expense.' The following year, the American Fur Company could only afford to pay alcohol to its employees at Green River.[34]

By the Anglo-American Convention of 1818, joint occupancy was limited to the region west of the continental divide but Ermatinger, like Ogden in the previous decade, blithely ignored this and trapped in American territory to the east. In the summer of 1835, operating out of Fort Colvile, Ermatinger trapped beyond the Rocky Mountains, near the forks of the Beaverhead and Jefferson rivers, tributaries of the Missouri. Osborne Russell, an American trapper, wrote in his journal that 'Here we found a trading party belonging to the Hudson's Bay Co. They were under the direction of Mr Francis Ermatinger who was endeavouring to trade every Beaver skin as fast as they were taken from the water by the Indians.' Here, among the Blackfoot, Ermatinger encountered mountain men (free trappers) like Kit Carson.[35]

By 1841, this policy had triumphed. As Simpson wrote, 'The Snake Country and its affairs, which until they fell under the direction of Chief Factor McLoughlin were in a very disorganized state, have for several years past been managed with so much judgement and address that they have been a source of profit, while in very many instances they have been ruinous to the United States adventurers.' So effective was the company's opposition that the American Rendezvous was held for the last time in 1840.[36] The company's Snake River brigade trail via forts Hall, Boise, and Nez Perces was adopted at this time by American overland immigrants, who incorporated it into the Oregon Trail. Until the 1840s American overlanders received a guided tour to the promised land of

Oregon. Missionary Henry Spalding, for example, in 1836 at the Rendezvous 'fell into Capt. McLeod's camp, a British fur trader, whom it would seem the Lord has sent up from Vancouver, on purpose to carry me on down.'[37]

'Prior to 1834,' wrote American historian James Gilbert, 'as many as eleven different [American] fur companies had tried to gain a foothold in the territory, but all were forced by ruinous competition to ply their trade in regions further south, to sell out to the Hudson's Bay Company and enter its service or to quit the fur trade altogether and seek a livlihood elsewhere.' By 1841, the American Fur Company and the Rocky Mountain Fur Company were ruined by a decade of great competition.[38] In 1846, only about fifty American trappers and mountain men remained in the Snake Country to the west of the Rockies, down from five or six hundred in 1826.[39]

So complete was the British fur traders' victory that Irving stated in 1837 that the company maintained 'an unrivalled sway over the whole country washed by the Columbia and its tributaries.' The few American travellers to reach the lower Columbia paid nostalgic visits to what remained of Fort Astoria, a chimney in the bush near Fort George, which Townsend called 'a melancholy monument of American enterprise.'[40]

American fur traders and travellers left convincing testimony of the HBC's strength. In 1839, Wyeth described, with knowledge and respect, the company's advantages to an American congressional committee:

I will observe that the measures of the Hudson's Bay Company have been conceived with wisdom, steadily pursued and have been well seconded by their government, and their success has been complete without any gross violation of existing treaties. Experience has satisfied me that the entire weight of the company will be made to bear on any trader who shall attempt to prosecute his business within its reach, in proof of which is the establishment at Fort Boise after Fort Hall had been set up, and the fact that a party was kept within the vicinity of Fort Hall with an especial view to injure its trade. No sooner does an American concern start in these regions than one of these trading parties is put in motion, headed by a clerk of the company whose zeal is stimulated by the prospect of an election to a partnership in it. He is fitted out with the best assorted goods from their ample stores and given men who have long been in the service of the company and whose wages are in its hands as security for fidelity. Under these circumstances we come in contact. If there are furs in the hands of the Indians, their superior assortment of goods will obtain them.[41]

The British fur traders, then, held many advantages over the Americans. With commercial control of the lower Columbia, they could gauge the demands of the interior Indians better than ambitious newcomers who were unfamiliar with local conditions. Wyeth found, for example, that 'a great deal of goods he had brought with him were unfitted for the Indian trade.' American fur traders were also, according to Irving, chronically short of capital,[42] and they had to import British trade goods on the eastern seaboard and ship them overland to the Rockies. They could have sent the goods around to the mouth of the Columbia, as Wyeth did, where neither the British nor the Americans paid duty; but they would still have had to pay duty at Boston, and then somehow transport their goods inland to the Snake, through regions unknown to them and among Native people used to the HBC's products, policies, and prices. 'It will be seen at once that no Enterprise, talent, or industry can successfully compete in this Trade,' wrote American general William Clark, formerly of the Lewis and Clark expedition, in 1830.[43]

According to travellers, the company's brigades were orderly, well organized, and cohesive. Central to them were French Canadians. Captain William Drummond Stewart, who visited the Rendezvous in 1837, spoke admiringly of the 'hereditary *voyageurs* among the French; who, of Canadian origin, have emerged from the seigneuries and snows of the North, to a less rigorous climate, if not milder laws.'[44] Stewart also wrote, interestingly, that the HBC was still known to American fur traders in the Rockies as the 'North West Company.' Townsend reported that Thomas McKay's party at Fort Hall in 1834 consisted of thirty men: seventeen French Canadians and 'half-breeds' and thirteen Indians (Nez Perces, Chinook, and Kayoose). 'But above all,' Townsend wrote, 'I admire the order, decorum, and strict subordination which exists among his men, so different from which I have been accustomed to see in parties composed of Americans.'[45] As Father de Smet noted, Americans, but not the company, traded whiskey to Indians on the Snake:

> The [beaver] skin is sold for nine or ten dollars' worth of provisions or merchandise, the value of which does not amount to a single silver dollar. For a gill of whiskey, which has not cost the trader more than three or four cents, is sometimes sold for three or four dollars, though the chief virtue which it possesses is to kill the body and soul of the buyer ... The Honourable

> Hudson's Bay Company does not belong to this class of traders. By them the
> sale of all sorts of liquors is strictly forbidden.[46]

Moreover, an integral part of the company's success against American traders was a superior 'Indian policy.' This policy was widely regarded, by British and American commentators alike, as a central part of the HBC's commercial success in the Columbia Department. In 1831, for example, General William Clark, Superintendent of Indian Affairs at St. Louis, wrote that the main disadvantage of the American fur trade was 'the preference which the Indians themselves have always Shewn, and still continue to Shew, the English.' 'Instances are within the recollections of persons yet living, of the most vigorous measures pursued by the British government against Traders of their own Nation, whose intercourse has been marked by improper conduct towards the Indians.' The American fur trade abounded with examples of habitual brutality and even genocidal tendencies. For example, in 1834 in California, Hall Kelley encountered Joseph Walker of the American Fur Company. 'Walker's chief object has been,' Kelley reported, 'for more than a year, to hunt and destroy Indians.' In 1835, Townsend blamed the failure of the Columbia River Fishing and Trading Company partly on its inexperienced Indian policy, and Dunn referred to the Americans' want of 'liberality of dealing,' their lack of 'integrity in their dealings with the natives.' In January 1841, James Douglas referred to the mountain men who reached California as 'the banditti of the mountains' who committed 'ruffianly outrages ... on the frontiers,' and Simpson referred to 'cowardly atrocities' committed by American trappers.[47]

The second trapping party from Fort Vancouver was known both as the Southern Party and the 'Bonaventura Expedition,' after the earlier name of the Sacramento River.[48] Tolmie wrote that, from the fort's headquarters, the brigade 'went south thro' Oregon and Northern California to certain parts of San Francisco Bay, where Beaver, then very high priced, greatly abounded.' The mouth of the Sacramento was the chief place for beaver. A London official wrote that the Southern Party went to 'the Head Waters of the Rivers falling into the Bay of San Francisco.'[49] At first outfitted from Fort Vancouver, after 1841 the party was also connected to the company's short-lived commercial agency at Yerba Buena on San Francisco Bay. California was a province of Mexico from 1821 until 1848, when the United States took it over.

The Southern Party was led by Alexander Roderick McLeod, Thomas Mckay, Peter Ogden, Michel Laframboise, John Work, Francis Ermatinger, and others between 1828 and 1844:

1828-9	McLeod to the San Joaquin River
1829-30	Ogden to the San Joaquin via the Colorado
1832-3	Work to the Pit River
1834-5	Laframboise to the Sacramento
1836	McKay to the Pit
1836	Laframboise to the Sacramento
1836-7	Laframboise
1838-9	Laframboise
1840-1	McKay and Laframboise
1841-2	Francis Ermatinger
1842	Laframboise
1843	Ermatinger
1844	Abandoned[50]

The Southern Party was modelled after the Snake Party in organization and rationale. It had its origins in the 1825-9 explorations south of the Willamette conducted by Alexander McLeod, Manson, Thomas McKay, and Ogden, journeys of reconnaissance, exploration, and trade, and it incorporated, as well, Jedediah Smith's 1828 route from the Sacramento and Umpqua. The company's early explorations of the Umpqua, Klamath, Pit, Sacramento, and San Joaquin rivers defined the brigade's normal spatial limits, and Ogden's extraordinary journey to the Vermilion Sea in 1829-30 provided the party with a distant southern frontier. Mexican settlement was restricted to the southern and coastal regions of California, and for almost twenty years, between 1826 and 1845, the company's fur brigades almost exclusively exploited northern California.[51] Apart from the brief visit by Americans Smith and Kelley, northern California was dominated by fur traders out of Fort Vancouver. During this time, HBC employees named prominent features of the land, including Umpqua, Siuslaw, Klamath, and Shasta, after the Native peoples of those localities. Eastern California was also visited by American trappers working westward from the Rockies or inland from the coast.[52]

The trail to the south of Fort Vancouver followed the Willamette, which Townsend noted was navigable for large vessels to the distance of twenty-five miles. (In 1832 Simpson had advocated, without success, a post on the Willamette River in part for the 'Willamette River fur trade.') Eight or nine days' journey overland from Fort Vancouver was the Umpqua, the first major river south of the Columbia, located by McLeod and Manson in 1826.[53] Dunn described the river:

> The Umpqua runs into the Pacific in nearly a westerly direction, from its source in the President's [Cascade] range; and is lined for about 100 miles by precipitous and rocky banks, covered with woods. It is nearly a mile wide at its mouth; and about three fathoms deep. The tide runs up about thirty miles; and is then checked by rapids and cataracts, which are to be found, even when the lower cataracts are passed, up the course of the river to its mountain source. Its entire length is about 170 miles.[54]

The river had, de Mofras wrote, an adequate entrance only for vessels with draughts of less than ten feet. In the 1830s, the company 'made a careful survey of all streams where beaver were abundant,' including the Umpqua, and Fort Umpqua was opened around 1838, some fifteen miles from the river mouth. Situated north of the forty-second parallel, Fort Umpqua was within the territory held by the 1818 convention; it was intended to serve for the fur trade of the Umpqua, Rogue, and Klamath rivers, all of which possessed bars impassable to ocean-going vessels. It was the company's post closest to the California frontier. The fort's garden was known for its magnificent turnips weighing five pounds apiece.[55]

About 50 miles south was the Klamath, with a course of about 150 miles. 'This is the most southerly river of any note in the whole region,' Dunn wrote, 'and one that may be called the natural inland water-boundary, on the south-west, between Oregon and California.'[56] The Klamath's mouth was

> blocked by a bar over which large ships cannot pass. For this reason the Hudson's Bay Company uses small sloops, drawing 7 or 8 feet of water, on the river. The stream was carefully explored in 1836 by the schooner *Cadborough*, Captain Brotchie, who inspected various points along the coast for this company and who has supplied much valuable information. Klamath is navigable by small boats for 20 or 25 leagues.[57]

Not far south of the Klamath River was Trinidad Bay on the coast, where the company contemplated establishing an entrepôt for the Southern Party. 'Trinidad Bay was to be used as an assembly point where Hudson's Bay Company's "southern trappers" could be met by the *Cadboro*, carrying goods and traps, to enable Laframboise's men to make a fresh hunt before coming back to Fort Vancouver; the plan fell through in 1838,' wrote historian Anson Blake.[58]

The California Brigade trail joined the Sacramento River valley near the McLoud River, named (or rather, misnamed) after Alexander McLeod. For the whole length of the trail, the Coast ranges of present-day Oregon and California were to the west, and the Cascade and Sierra Nevada ranges were to the east. At the south end of the Cascades, Ogden named Mount Shasta after the Shasty Indians. French Canadian trappers, ignorant of the Spanish names for the tributaries of the Sacramento and San Joaquin, gave French names to many rivers. These names would be replaced, in turn, by English names when California became American in 1848, by which time the Southern Party had been abandoned. One of the few 'French' names remaining is French Camp, on the San Joaquin near the present city of Stockton, where Laframboise wintered several times in the 1830s (Map 15). 'This was the southernmost regular camp site of the trappers after La Framboise had established his headquarters here in 1832,' wrote Erwin Gudde; 'By the Spanish Californians it was called Camp de los Franceses, a name preserved in the land grant of January 13 1844.'[59]

The Southern Party passed into Mexican territory at the forty-second parallel, near the Klamath River. Generally, the company's brigades operated inland and east of Mexican coastal settlements, in what the Californian authorities regarded as their frontier. In 1833, Duncan Finlayson received permission from the Mexican authorities to hunt, free of charge, in the Sacramento Valley; thereafter, the HBC's brigades trapped among and to the east of what Douglas called the 'frontier Indians,' along the many rivers that drained the Sierra Nevada Mountains into the Sacramento and San Joaquin.[60] The brigade earned a furtive reputation for staying among the Indians on the frontiers of California and avoiding Californians and European visitors alike.[61] Their competitors in these eastern regions were American mountain men who, by the late 1830s, had extended their trade westward from the southern Rockies.

Despite its southerly location, California contained rich, and vulnerable, beaver habitat. In 1839, the British resident Alexander Forbes remarked that 'The otter and beaver are still to be found on all the rivers, lakes, and bays; but their numbers have greatly decreased since the country has been settled.'[62] The richest beaver regions of California were on the lower stretches of the Sacramento (Bonaventura), San Joaquin ('Valley of Tulares,' 'South Branch,' or 'Smith's River'),[63] and Colorado rivers. Throughout these southern regions, beaver had adapted to the warm climate by living year-round in pools and marshes where they were easy prey for hunters armed with traps and rifles. As de Mofras observed in 1841-2:

In New France and the colder regions of North America where lakes and rivers freeze, beaver are forced to congregate to build winter quarters. Their dams and bars are built in rivers which are in danger of overflowing, and provide a way to catch fish. In the warmer countries, lying south and west of the Rocky Mountains, however, these amphibians do not need to erect these remarkable hydraulic works that are found in the lakes of Canada. As the rivers here do not freeze and the ground is never covered with snow, as a result beaver live in isolated spots, feeding principally on roots and bark. Usually they make their homes in holes dug along waterways or in lagoons. When floods occur, they withdraw to dry localities where new dwellings are then erected.

Naturally, their nomadic habits make these animals more difficult to hunt. However, since one man can watch a number of traps, they are rapidly caught. Traps are of iron, like those used for obnoxious animals in France. Bait, called medicine, is placed in the centre. The trap, attached to an iron chain, is held down by two small weights of the same metal, for if wood and hemp were used, by means of his teeth the beaver would soon regain his liberty. Frequently hunters hide, and, without setting traps, shoot the creatures. Their skins are so heavy that one man cannot carry more than ten or twelve. Each trapper is invariably accompanied by an Indian or a horse to transport his skins.

Beavers caught in traps usually have a nose or a paw broken, and are at once despatched with a knife. The skin, stretched on a board, is then hung in the sun.[64]

Native people from a huge area hunted for the company. In the 1830s, Laframboise made a list of some of the principal groups between the Columbia and Umpqua. De Mofras wrote that around Mount Shasta

and at Klamath Lake, near the headwaters of the Sacramento and Klamath rivers, was a region 'inhabited by many Indian tribes who live by
fishing and selling furs to the trappers.'[65] In 1840, the population of Mexican California alone was roughly 9,140 Native people and 5,780 *gente de
razon*.[66] During this time, much of the California interior was inhabited, de Mofras wrote, 'only by the Indians but often visited by French
Canadians or pack-trains from the United States and Mexico.' The
Amagagua Indians, he continued, hunted 'Beaver, selling the skins to
American trappers from the United States, or to Canadians sent down
by the Hudson's Bay Company from the Columbia River as far south
as the mouth of the Colorado River.'[67]

The Southern Party was often away from Fort Vancouver for two years
at a time, wintering at Camp de los Franceses, and travelling among the
Native peoples of the Californian interior, without interference. According to de Mofras:

> Notwithstanding the numerous Indian settlements scattered at various points
> throughout the valleys, these expeditions, though generally uncomfortable
> because of fatigue and privations of every kind, are not exposed to serious
> dangers except when travelling off the main route, or in small groups, since
> savages never attack trains of 60 or 70 white men armed with carabines.[68]

The Southern Party consisted of between fifty and seventy people. As
with all the HBC's labour force, French was their common language. Like
the Snake Party, it was a socially heterogeneous group, including freemen,
trappers, slaves, and their offspring. In 1832, John Work stated that 'I am
going to start with my ragamuffin free men to the southward towards the
Spanish settlements with what success I cannot say.' Some were less char-
itable. 'This brigade,' Blanchet wrote in 1841, 'is a hideous assemblage of
persons of both sexes, devoid of principles and morals.'[69] Expedition leader,
Montreal-born Michel Laframboise (circa 1790 and 1861), claimed to have
a wife in every Native 'tribe' between Fort Vancouver and California before
he settled down at French Prairie in 1838. 'It was his boast that having a
wife in every tribe insured him safe conduct.'[70]

Before it was famous for gold, the Sacramento River was known for
beaver. It took the HBC, and American trappers working from the east,
about fifteen years (1829-43) to exhaust this resource. 'The [sea] otter
and beaver which abounded in California,' General Vallejo complained

in 1838, 'have been exterminated, the first by the Russians, and the latter by the Columbians who still continue to trap them to the point of extinguishing the species, as the Russians have done the otter.' Belcher wrote in 1837 that the Sacramento was once famed for its beaver and land-otter, but even in 1838, the river and its tributary, the Feather, were the subject of Laframboise's 'particular attention.'[71] The fur traders did not notice the gold in the river; nor, until 1848, did the company's main competitor in the Sacramento fur trade, the Swiss adventurer Captain John Sutter, who had leased a place from the Mexican authorities 115 miles up river from San Francisco. Sutter recalled that the HBC's Southern Party used to come and go in large crowds, and 'when they pitched their tents it was like a village.'[72]

The San Joaquin Valley joined the Sacramento near San Francisco Bay, but the lower valleys of both rivers, Douglas noted during his 1841 visit, were 'originally marshland where bulrushes and similar reeds ... provided a breeding ground for beaver.' In the same year, Farnham wrote that

> near and about the mouth of the Sacramento, as before observed, lies a wide extent of low land overflowed by the tide, and including some hundreds of small islands, covered with an enormous growth of rushes. There is probably no spot of equal extent on the whole continent of America, which contains so many of these much sought for animals. For the last fifteen years the Hudson's Bay Company have annually sent hither a company of from fifty to one hundred trappers ...
>
> It is said by hunters well acquainted with the Rocky Mountain region, that they have never seen anywhere such large and fat beavers. On account of the scarcity of the timber of which their huts are generally constructed, the beavers, like true philosophers, have here accommodated themselves to circumstances, and build their habitations of rushes, curiously and skilfully interwoven.[73]

About 600 miles southeast of San Francisco Bay, in Mexico proper, was the entrance to the Gulf of California, known also as the Vermilion Sea and Red Bay. Ogden had been there in 1830, and the HBC retained an interest in its fur wealth. In 1838, McLoughlin instructed Laframboise 'to explore the entrance to the Colorado in the Gulf of California which is said to abound in Beaver'; the following year, Douglas reported that the Colorado River was rich in beaver, 'particularly near its discharge into the Gulf of California.' McLoughlin, at about the same time, wanted to send a party 'to hunt the entrance of the Rio Calorado, known by the name of Red Bay by the Calefornians where Beaver is said to be more abundant than I ever heard mentioned in any place of the same extent on the East side of the Mountains.'[74]

While McLoughlin and Douglas planned simply to extract and extinguish the beaver population of the lower Colorado, they took a broader interest in San Francisco Bay. In 1841, they established an agency at Yerba Buena (San Francisco) for the sale of British retail goods. Douglas had obtained a licence from General Mariano Vallejo in the spring of 1840 for 'permission to trade and hunt furs in any part of the Mexican territories, paying a duty of half a dollar per skin on our returns.' Later that year, McLoughlin instructed Douglas to secure 'an exclusive right to hunt the Bay of St. Francisco and the Gulph of California' and, like Sutter, 'a tract of Country some distance from St. Francisco where we might establish a Rendezvous for our people.'[75]

In January 1841, Douglas visited Monterey to ask for Alvarado's cooperation with the HBC's projected commercial enterprises in California. The first topic introduced, Douglas recorded, 'was a delicate one, relating to our party under Laframboise who have been for several years trapping in the Valley of Tulares.' Alvarado wanted the company's San Joaquin party withdrawn, as Mexican settlements now extended to the HBC's hunting grounds. After a week's negotiation, however, Alvarado allowed the company to send a party of thirty beaver hunters to California 'in order to extend their hunting operations into every part of the country.'[76] Douglas reported to McLoughlin that, while Alvarado had sanctioned the opening of an agency at Yerba Buena, 'We would of course at the same time, turn attention to our own peculiar avocation of Beaver Hunting and test the reputed fur wealth of Red Bay.' Douglas recorded that Alvarado promised all his help to the company

provided we submit to the formalities required by the Laws of Mexico. This is to say, on these terms, the whole trade of the country will be open to us; a free grant of land for the erection of warehouses with other privileges will be conceded to the Company in their own name and right, within the harbour of San Francisco. Parties of Beaver hunters may be introduced through the regular Port of Entry, who will receive Passports, and be licensed to hunt in all parts of the uncultivated frontier, every such person being compelled by the authorities to execute fully the conditions of their agreement with the Company.[77]

Perhaps George Simpson blanched at the idea of his beaver hunters carrying passports. At any rate, he took a dim view of the declining Sacramento fur trade and of California's larger commercial potential. The Southern Party had never made great profits (in 1837, £831; in 1842, £32; in 1843, £425).[78] Francis Ermatinger had reported on the poor prospects, and in March 1842, Simpson proposed that the HBC close its operations 'south of the Umpqua,' or 'South of the Shasty Mountains.'[79] In 1843, the Southern Party 'made out miserably,' having procured fewer than 650 otter and beaver skins. The 1844 Southern Party was to hunt around the Umpqua River, but in 1845 it was not re-equipped, Simpson said, 'as the last collection of furs barely covered the expenses, from which it would appear that, the Country is exhausted.'[80] By this time, the company had obtained at least 17,000 beaver and land otter skins in California.[81]

American traders and visitors – Wyeth, Captain Bonneville, Townsend, Dominis, General Clark, Rocky Mountain Fur and American Fur company traders – knew the HBC had earned its monopoly in a region where they had equal rights of access and trade. They were quick to acknowledge the company's advantages in personnel, policy, prices, trade goods, financial resources, and knowledge of the land and its inhabitants. 'That huge monopoly,' Irving summarized in 1837, 'centres within itself not merely its own hereditary and long established power and influence; but also those of its ancient rival, but now integral part, the famous Northwest Company. It has thus its races of traders, trappers, hunters, and voyageurs, born and brought up in its service, and inheriting from preceding generations a knowledge and aptitude in every thing connected with Indian life, and Indian traffic.' Only a diplomatic agreement favouring the United States and ending the joint British-American occupancy of Oregon Territory could possibly destroy the HBC's commercial hegemony south and east of the Columbia River, as Irving realized. American traders, he asserted, would never 'be able to maintain any footing in the land, until the question of territorial right is adjusted between the two countries.'[82] In 1846, the Oregon Treaty vanquished the hope of British title south of the forty-ninth parallel, and gradually the HBC withdrew from the whole of what is now the western United States.

The company's frontier policies succeeded for the 1820s, 1830s, and for the first few years of the 1840s – in fact, for as long as the region remained under joint British-American occupancy. 'At present,' Wyeth observed in 1839, 'the United Sates, as a nation, are unknown west of the mountains.' American fur traders were, for the most part, kept away from the lower Columbia and from much of the watershed of the Columbia River and the Pacific coast north of California. 'The country is quiet and undisturbed by American opposition,' Simpson wrote in 1841; 'indeed it is highly gratifying to be enabled to say that all opposition from citizens of the United States is now at an end.'[83]

These southern regions provided the company with experience and precedent. HBC fur traders learned valuable tactics in the Snake and Southern parties, tactics they would transfer to the north in the late 1820s and early 1830s. Ogden and Work, Snake Country specialists, would figure prominently on the North West Coast – a region adjacent to New Caledonia, the nursery of the Columbia Department fur trade – where the need to keep American fur traders at bay was just as great as on the Columbia.

CHAPTER 6

The
North West Coast

*I entertain sanguine hopes that before the expiration of 5 years
there will not be an American on the Coast.*

— GEORGE SIMPSON, 1830[1]

Between 1829 and 1843, in a virtuoso display of commercial prowess, the Hudson's Bay Company virtually eliminated American competition in the Columbia Department fur trade. 'When the Company first went into the disputed territory of Oregon,' Edward Ermatinger wrote in 1857, 'they found the trade in the hands of the Americans & Russians; they contested it with them & drove both Russians and Americans from the field in every part of the continent that belonged to or was claimed by Great Britain.'[2] By 1843, the Columbia Department fur trade had reached its greatest territorial extent, with the company operating from San Francisco Bay to the Taku River valley. The HBC also pushed the fur trade as far north as Lynn Canal at the fifty-ninth parallel.

Historians generally refer to the sea otter trade of the north Pacific coast between 1780-1840 as the 'Maritime Fur Trade.' This was not a contemporary term, however, but one coined by historians to distinguish the Pacific coast trade from the continental fur trade. Contemporaries called it the 'North West Coast trade,' which was rarely spelled with one word, as in 'Northwest.'[3] The definition of the North West Coast changed between 1821 and 1843, reflecting the company's increased use and understanding of the Pacific coast of North America. At first, the maritime fur traders defined the North West Coast as the entire coast north of the Columbia River, including Cape Flattery, Vancouver Island, the Queen Charlotte Islands, the southern part of Russian America, and the contiguous inside waters. This was the region, roughly, where sea otter were originally most abundant; but the North West Coast moved northward and shrank in size with the extermination of the sea otter and with the concentration of the company's activities on the lower Columbia, Puget Sound, Gulf of Georgia, and lower Fraser. By the 1840s, the HBC rarely regarded these places as part of the North West Coast. The new North West Coast included the west coast of Vancouver Island, the inside coast north of Cape Mudge, the whole of the Queen Charlotte Islands, and the southerly regions of the Russian territories. This chapter defines the North West Coast in the company's 1840s sense: as the outer coast north of Cape Flattery and the inner coast and islands north of Cape Mudge.[4]

In 1821, the HBC knew almost nothing about this coastal region. Alarmingly, the area was dominated by American fur traders who showed an increasing interest in the continental fur trade of the adjacent inlets and rivers. The Americans arrived in Boston-based vessels; land-based fur traders from the Columbia River had avoided the coast since the destruction of the *Tonquin* on the west coast of Vancouver Island in 1811. 'The fur trade [of the North West Coast] is now totally in the power of the Americans,' Northwester Peter Corney wrote in 1821. With the gradual decline in the sea otter trade after 1800 or 1810, the Boston traders had moved eastward, toward the inside coast, in search of land furs, especially beaver and land otter.[5]

At stake was the core of the Columbia Department fur trade, New Caledonia, which enjoyed consistently high profits of about £8,000 a year, in part due to the absence of competition in the northern interior. McLean called it 'One of the richest districts in the Company's domain' with about 8,000 beaver traded annually.[6] This wealthy region had to be protected by securing the Pacific coast. Since the North West Company era, traders in New Caledonia had encountered Russian and American metal goods traded from the coast, so they knew that effective and extensive Native trade took place up the main rivers – the Skeena, Nass, and Stikine. Alexander Mackenzie and Simon Fraser, for example, had found the Sekanni and Carrier in possession of iron tools and implements. 'North of Vancouver Island,' Charles Ermatinger recalled, 'the natives were accustomed to bring their peltries to the ocean to be bartered on the decks of the trading vessels ... or to exchange them in the interior with the tribes nearer the coast, who sometimes acted as middlemen.' Ogden, for example, recalled that the 'Chyniseyans' (Coast Tsimshian) traded with the Carrier 'upon a scale of magnificence.'[7]

On the coast, the Americans paid more for beaver and land otter than the HBC offered in New Caledonia, resulting in a haemorrhage of pelts from the interior to the coast via Native trade routes. This trade was substantial. Between 1815 and 1818, American traders alone took 3,000 to 5,000 beaver skins annually from the North West Coast to Canton;[8] in March 1832, Duncan Finlayson was 'creditably informed that from 8 to 19 thousand Beaver Skins can be collected annually on the coast, this is worth a struggle & from the steady & well regulated opposition now carried on by us, we have every reason to expect our efforts will be ultimately crowned with success.' Later that year, he revised the figure down to 10,000 beaver skins after making inquiries at the Sandwich Islands; George Simpson later estimated that the trade of the North West Coast amounted to about ten thousand beaver and land otter skins a year. This was worth fighting for.[9]

Control of the North West Coast was, therefore, critical to the security of the Columbia Department as a whole and indirectly to British interests in western North America. There was nothing stopping American traders from building forts on any part of the North West Coast south of Russian territory. As Simpson wrote in 1830, he wanted to put the HBC in the 'undisturbed possession of a branch of Trade ... the value of which will be greatly enhanced in our estimation from the circumstance of its being wrested out of the hands of Foreigners, by whom it has been so long, so insultingly, and so unjustly monopolized.'[10] He sought to engross the entire coastal fur trade by intercepting interior furs before they reached the Pacific. This required the construction of posts on strategic locations of the North West Coast itself, posts that could offer better prices and merchandise than the American coasters, and that could work with interior posts to establish uniform prices. The first of these posts were Fort Simpson at the mouth of the Nass (1831) and Fort McLoughlin on Campbell Island (1833). To service them and to trade at the principal Native trading stations, the company put vessels on the coast, manned by experienced and knowledgeable employees and forming a competitive, aggressive marine department, known colloquially as the 'coasting trade.' It was the charge successively of Aemilius Simpson (to 1831), Peter Ogden (1832-4), and John Work (1834-52).[11] In 1832, the HBC hired the experienced Boston trader W.H. McNeill, and placed the steamer *Beaver* on the coast four years later. By 1837, American competition on the North West Coast was effectively over, and the maritime fur trade was once again controlled by London-based capitalists, as it had been in the 1780s.[12]

In the 1820s, the company had sent the *William & Ann* on a reconnaissance of the North West Coast, dispatched an expedition to the Fraser River in 1824, initiated a new provision base at Fort Vancouver in 1825, established Fort Langley in 1827, and sent the *Cadboro* to trade on the southern edges of the North West Coast. Despite these measures, in 1829 the coast remained in the control of American fur traders.

American competition on the North West Coast was more pressing than Russian competition. The Russians posed little threat, either to the American coasters or to the HBC's coastal ambitions. This was because in 1824-5, the British, Russian, and American governments had signed treaties placing the southern boundary of Russian territory at 54°40′ north latitude, in the process defining the coastal boundary between the jointly occupied Anglo-American Oregon Territory and the Russian possessions to the north.[13] The Russians traded extensively on the coastal strip that later became the Alaska Panhandle, though their operations extended far to the north, as Aemilius Simpson learned in 1831:

> I have once visited their establishment at Sitka Norfolk Sound & am told they have some others to the North of it on the Continent as well as on the Aleutian, Analaska, & Kodiac Islands, but I have no idea as to the extent of their business however if I may judge from the establishments & the number of Vessels they employ I should infer the trade carried on by the Russian Fur Company in these seas as very extensive.[14]

The Americans were another matter altogether. Masters of North Pacific maritime commerce, they came annually from Boston and Honolulu in vessels known to the company as 'Coasters' or 'N.W. Coasters,' and they traded at such places as Neah Bay, Nawitti, Nass, and Kaigani (Map 4). In 1831, Aemilius Simpson, HBC superintendent of the marine department, wrote that the Americans 'have not formed any fixed trading Establishments on the Coast but carry on their trade in Vessels, whose number vary from two to six annually in which they visit the different Harbours from the Northern extremes of Quadra & Vancouver Island to the northern part of Chathams Strait.' The Americans were experts in the coastal trade and knew the Honolulu, Sitka, and Canton markets as well. 'Every Channel of speculation appears to be entirely glutted by the unusual number of Amn Vessels resorting to these seas,' Duncan Finlayson wrote in his 1831 journal. 'The American Coasters,' he wrote, 'are masters & part owners of their Vessels & cargoes filled out on the most oeconomical & cheapest manner & who moreover enjoy facilities & privileges in his Canton Dealings of which British subjects are deprived.' And he continued: 'No means exist by Statute or by treaty to check the Americans on the coast – they are more accustomed to the trade and better acquainted with the natives & have other facilities of which we are not possessed our only plan therefore is to oppose them with a well regulated steady opposition.'[15]

The surest way to intercept the Native trade of pelts to the coast and hence deter the American coasters was to build coastal forts, which could be supplied regularly from the company's marine department based at Fort Vancouver. In 1829 Simpson informed the Russian American Company of his plan to establish 'a house near the northern frontier,' and in July of the next year Aemilius Simpson of the *Cadboro* visited the mouth of the Nass River, which he reported had long been spoken of by Russian, American, and Sandwich Islands traders as 'the grand mart of the Coast.' He obtained 100 very fine beaver that, from the manner they were stretched and dressed, he concluded had originated in New Caledonia. An HBC post at the Nass would stop these interior pelts from going to the Americans and also reduce the role of Native middlemen. The Native people at the Nass River were not primarily hunters, but fishers and traders; they fished oolichan at the mouth of the Nass and rendered it into oil, which, George Simpson wrote in 1831, 'forms a principal Article of Barter with the Natives of the Interior.'[16]

The establishment at Nass was to have commenced in the fall of 1830, but an infectious fever among the ship's crew postponed the voyage. Aemilius Simpson and Ogden finally embarked from Fort Vancouver in March 1831, and in April established a post at the mouth of the Nass.

FIGURE 9 Secure on the Columbia River, the HBC extended its trade to the North West Coast in the late 1820s to compete with American sea otter traders. This undated map shows the Queen Charlotte Islands (then thought to be a single island) and the adjacent coast, where the company would establish the first Fort Simpson in 1831. ['North West Coast of America from Lat. 52° to Lat. 57°30′,' Hudson's Bay Company Archives, Provincial Archives of Manitoba, N4466]

'There is a grand ado preparatory to an expedition under Mr. Ogden to extend the trade far north of Frazer's River,' Francis Ermatinger noted.[17] A good deal of apprehension surrounded the establishment of this post in the crucible of the North West Coast, 500 miles north of Fort Langley, and it is significant that Ogden and Work, seasoned veterans of the Snake and Southern campaigns, were chosen. Clerks Donald Manson and John Kennedy were also selected for the new post.

James Douglas, then a twenty-eight-year-old clerk recently arrived at Fort Vancouver from New Caledonia, reported on the Native reaction to the Nass Party:

To their great surprise and not a little to their satisfaction, the natives received them in the most friendly manner, nor have they as yet displayed any

symptoms of a hostile or turbulent disposition. They are nevertheless keen
hands at a bargain and make the most of the competition among the traders.
If they cannot do business with one party they make no ceremony in trying
what can be done with the other.[18]

Aemilius Simpson and Ogden spent the summer trading at the new
post and at the Queen Charlotte Islands, but Simpson died in September 1831 and the post was named after him. When McLoughlin heard
of his death he wrote that 'The best that we can now do in my opinion is to attach the coasting Trade to Fort Simpson & give Mr C-T
[Chief Trader] Ogden charge of the two.' 'Mr Ogden writes the Post of
Fort Simpson has no direct Water communication with the Interior no
Ground about it to make a Garden and that very little Provisions can
be procured from the Natives.' Although provisions had to be imported
from forts Vancouver and Langley, Fort Simpson did what it was meant
to do. By November 1831, George Simpson wrote, 'the furs collected by
the Shipping and establishment [Nass] amounted to upwards of £4000
in value.' This was despite the competition of the American brig *Lama*,
captained by W.H. McNeill. Word had spread quickly among American coasters that the company, already evicting American traders on the
Columbia system, was building this land post on the North West Coast.[19]

Partly as a result of Manson's 1832 exploration of the Nass and Skeena
rivers, Fort Simpson was moved in August 1834 to a more favourable
trading location on the Tsimpsean peninsula, equidistant from both river
mouths (Figure 10).[20] Here, the fort became the headquarters of the
coasting and land-based trade of the entire North West Coast and the
'grand mart' for Native traders from the densely populated north coast.
In 1841, Fort Simpson was visited by about fourteen thousand people, of
whom about eight hundred were the Tsimshian homeguard. The
Tsimshian obtained fur from many north coast groups including the
Tongass, Haida, and Kaigani, and also from the Carrier in the interior.[21]
In 1836, Finlayson described the post's trade and Native customers:

The best hunters and traders who are in the habit of selling their furs at this
place, and from whom the Returns are chiefly collected, may be estimated in
the following order, in which they are classed – The Pearl Harbor and Skeenah
Indians called the Chimmesyan tribe – The Nass, the Stikine, Tongass, Sebassa,

and the Queen Charlotte Island tribes: and it is now confidently expected that the Kygarnie Indians who have commenced to negotiate a treaty of peace with the natives of this place, will, if it be concluded, occasionally trade here; so that the objects which were anticipated by the removal of the settlement from Nass hither will thereby be gained – as all the surrounding tribes some of whom inhabit Russian territory will give us some portion of their Furs – So that the present situation possesses many advantages over the former – such as being more centrical for the trade – affording better facilities for the shipping, better resources in the way of living – and better means of guarding our frontiers from the encroachments of our enterprising opponents.[22]

John Dunn described a trading scene at Fort Simpson during the 1830s:

The Indians coming from distant parts to this fort, have large canoes, from thirty to fifty feet long ... Besides containing numerous Indians, their canoes

FIGURE 10 Fort Simpson, the HBC's post between Portland Inlet and the Skeena River, became the 'grand mart' of the fur trade of the North West Coast in the 1830s. The houses of the Tsimshian 'homeguard' surround the post, built on this location in 1834. [Undated painting by an unknown artist, Hudson's Bay Company Archives, Provincial Archives of Manitoba, 1987/363-P-26/1]

are piled up with goods for barter. They remain mustered here for some weeks, making the fort a complete fair. It requires strict and good management, at this time, by the companies of officers, to protect the fort. On landing at the fort, their canoes are piled up in large heaps, covered over with mats, to keep the sun from cracking them. They bring provisions with them, to last during their stay and journey home. Feasts are given by the chiefs; and invitations sent regularly round to the different guests. Should any of the officers of the fort be invited, stools are placed by the side of the fire, covered over with cloth and fine calico; and they are introduced with great ceremony – the chiefs standing to receive them. Skins are given, as presents, to the officers; and in the course of a day or two, the trader returns the compliment, by making them presents of British manufactured clothing.

After the various tribes have finished their trading speculations; and paid their various visits of friendship to one another, and the officers; they launch their canoes, laden with the return goods …[23]

Fort Simpson's fur returns increased steadily until they surpassed those of any post on the Pacific coast of the Columbia Department. Douglas reported in 1838 that the fort's returns 'exhibit a uniform and rapidly progressive improvement which has not I hope attained its extreme limit.' Work wrote in 1840 that 'Our trade this Year is Good,' with returns valuing £6,964, but costing only £2,162. A year later, Simpson reported that the post's returns were from 3,000 to 4,000 beaver and otter and a large quantity of small furs, the gross amount being about £6,000, of which about £3,000 was profit.[24]

The fort's provision problem was solved by the Indian trade. In 1836, Finlayson wrote that the supply of Native provisions was usually quite ample for the maintenance of the fort. 'The resources in the way of living which Fort Simpson affords, are Deer, Halibut, and Salmon, which, however may be considered as precarious while our dependence is placed on the natives for providing them.' The fort, he continued, could only be maintained with safety with a six month stock of provisions, and its garden already produced up to 200 bushels of potatoes a year. By 1841, the means of living were abundant, consisting principally of fish, venison and potatoes.[25]

Fort Simpson was intended as the most northerly in a chain of coastal ports starting at Fort Langley. As Finlayson noted in 1832, 'we have it in view to extend our settlements along the coast, being the best & most judicious plan, we can adopt for the purpose of wresting the trade from the grasp of the Americans, who have so far monopolized it & no doubt derived considerable gains therefrom.'[26] Fort McLoughlin was built in May or June 1833, on Finlayson's order, 200 miles south of Fort Simpson on a protected bay on Campbell Island, at Lama Passage in Fitzhugh Sound (Map 14).[27] The post was placed in charge of Dunn, who recalled that

> My instructions were to lower the price of skins; give in payment useful, substantial, and lasting articles; and endeavour to do away, if possible, with the injurious and degrading article of spirits, as a medium of barter: as the American vessels had previously been here, and had given immense prices, and sold spirits, so that the company's vessels should be debarred from the whole trade.[28]

Known at first simply as 'Milbank Sound' after its seaward access, the post was strategically situated to catch both coastal and interior furs. 'The country is unquestionably rich in Beaver and otters,' Simpson wrote in 1834, 'as the skins are frequently brought to the Establishment fresh, which is proof that they are taken in the immediate neighbourhood.'[29]

The post was built in the thick of a Native world. Near the fort, Simpson wrote, was a village of about five hundred 'Ballabollas.' Tolmie's 1834-5 diaries show the 'Quaghcuils,' 'Kitamats,' and 'Chimnseyans' trading at Fort McLoughlin, though the Bella Coola furnished more beaver than any people visiting the post.[30] Finlayson, on the *Beaver* in 1836, likewise found that 'the greatest part of the Furs sold at Mill bank' were collected on Dean Channel and Bentinck Arm. He wrote that

> the Bela hoola tribe inhabiting Deans Canal and Bentincks Arms trade the greatest number of skins at this post. The Wacash tribe of Milbank Sound who procure theirs chiefly from the neighbouring tribes, are the next in importance. The Oyalla tribe who procure theirs in like manner as the former may be classed after them, and the Chichysh who are considered the best beaver hunters in the Sound, hunting themselves all the Furs they trade at the Fort are the next.[31]

Charles Ross, Manson's successor in charge of the post in 1842, estimated the 'Billbillah' population at 1,500 and the 'Bellwhoola' population at 650 individuals of every age and sex.[32]

Pelts came overland along the Native grease trails in exchange for

oolichan oil and other coastal products; Mackenzie had followed one
such trail from the Chilcotin Plateau in 1793. Scouler, in 1825, had
recorded that the memory of the explorer was still alive: 'It was on this
part of the coast, inhabited by the Billechoola, that Sir A. McKenzie
first reached the Pacific; and some of the old men of the tribe still
remember his visit.'[33]

Fur prices were lower inland than on the competitive coast, so interior people preferred to sell their furs on the coast. In 1836, for example, Manson of Fort McLoughlin sent a letter eastward via the Native
trade to the 'Gentlemen of New Caledonia.' He complained that 'some
of the New Caledonia Indians have found their way to Mill Bank Sound,'
a practice that would injure New Caledonia's trade. Similarly, Douglas
complained in 1838 that Fort McLoughlin continued to draw New Caledonia furs to the coast and insisted that Manson adhere to the lower
prices recently fixed for the coast. He asked him to trade as much as
possible with 'the maritime Tribes and guard with the utmost care against
interference with the interior Districts':

> The Coast establishments should not become the instruments of drawing the
> furs from the Inland Districts, where the cost is moderate, into the very focus
> of opposition without any security whatever, of their finally falling into our
> hands, even at the extravagant prices paid for them. New Caledonia extends
> westward to the marine range of Mountains and sweeps along their base, from
> the 52nd to the 50th degree of North Latitude embracing the whole extent of
> our Coast possessions, and no attempt can be made to abstract the trade from
> the east side of that range of mountains, without signal mischief to the Com-
> pany's best interests.[34]

In short, monopoly control of the coastal fur trade allowed the HBC to
impose a uniform tariff on both sides of the Coast Mountains.

Local provisions at Fort McLoughlin, built on a rocky island without
good land, were scarce. Between 500 and 600 bushels of potatoes were
required annually from forts Langley, Nisqually, and Simpson. In 1836,
Finlayson recommended that enough venison and salmon be salted at
McLoughlin to supplement provisions 'procured in plentiful seasons from
the natives,' but within a few years Charles Ross had fertilized Donald
Manson's three-acre garden with a soil principally formed of seaweed,
which produced cabbages, potatoes, turnips, carrots, and other vegeta-

bles. The post, Simpson wrote in 1841, was visited by about fifty-two hundred Indians, the Natives of seven main villages. Its furs were worth from £2,500 to £3,000, annual costs were about £1,400, and net profits about £1,200. Ross concurred with Simpson: 'The trade, too, is pretty fairish – realizing about £1500 a year – which if a body were permitted to put in his own Pocket he aught indeed to be truly thankful.'[35]

Forts Simpson and McLoughlin served as the northern and central anchors of the North West Coast fur trade, but could not serve the whole coast. Trade could best be extended to the principal Native trading locations by adopting the seafaring methods of the Americans themselves, and in 1828-9 Simpson and McLoughlin devised a plan for the operation of the coasting trade. The company should have two vessels, McLoughlin said: one based on the North West Coast that would, when time permitted, take a cargo of salmon or lumber to the Sandwich Islands or to California; the other stationed at Fort Langley 'constantly going between that place and De Fuca Straights.' The plan took a few years to mature. Vessels destined for the North West Coast trade had to arrive in time to intercept the spring hunts and forestall the American competitors. This meant, in turn, that trade goods had to arrive at Fort Vancouver from England in time to be sent to the coast. Until 1832, McLoughlin lacked the vessels or personnel to put the plan into effect.[36]

Duncan Finlayson's recruitment of William Henry McNeill in 1832 provided the solution. McNeill was an experienced Boston trader who had first been on the coast in 1816.[37] A former shipmate of the HBC's nemesis Captain John Dominis, McNeill had been employed in the 1820s by Bryant & Sturgis of Boston as captain of their ship *Lama*,[38] and he now joined the HBC through the back door. The company's new brig *Isabella* had been wrecked on the Columbia bar in 1831, and Finlayson went to the Sandwich Islands to buy a vessel for the coasting trade. Suitable ships could be bought there for between $5,000 and $7,000. 'You ought to endeavour to get McNeill for the Coast,' McLoughlin advised Finlayson in July 1832, 'as he is well acquainted with that business ... the man's superior knowledge of the business in comparison to any of our Sea Officers, renders his services more valuable, & his knowledge is worth something.'[39] In giving this instruction, McLoughlin followed an old strategy of the British fur trade on the Pacific: hiring traders from the ranks of struggling or vanquished opponents. McNeill, the Boston Yankee, now joined old members of Astor's and Wyeth's overland schemes as employees of the British company.

Finlayson recalled the voyage:

> I made a cruise to the Sandwich Islands, for the purpose of purchasing a vessel & collecting information relative to the trade of the NW Coast ... I remained behind at the Islands to prosecute the object of my voyage & was fortunate enough to purchase a fine new Brig [the *Lama*] of about 150 tons, for £1250 ... I also engaged her captain ... to continue in the command of her, as his experience on the NW Coast, from cruising theron for the space of 12 years, will give our people an insight into the nature of the trade & a knowledge of the Bays, Inlets, Harbours & trading stations of that Coast, hitherto unknown to us & which cannot fail to give us a footing & promote our interest in that quarter.[40]

Finlayson hired McNeill and his two mates, he said, because 'We have seen, since we entered the field with the Americans on the N.W. Coast, the advantage their experience gave them over us, & from the inefficient state of our Naval Force, during the last Summer ... it became the more necessary to oppose them with their own weapons.' McLoughlin naturally agreed. 'These gentlemen are perfectly acquainted with the Coast, & with the Trade with the Natives,' he wrote, adding that the company's own men were deficient in such knowledge.[41]

The G&C were startled when they read, six months later, that McLoughlin had engaged three Americans in the 'principal situation of our Naval force.' McNeill would be seized if he went to England because foreigners were ineligible to command British vessels. The G&C may have been surprised at the hiring of Americans when their whole policy, and whole expense, had been to get rid of them. McLoughlin defended his actions by citing Simpson's 1829 plans for the coasting trade, which required someone of McNeill's stature: 'If when we had began the business we had in command of the Company's Vessels persons equally well acquainted with the coast and with the manner of dealing with the natives it would have saved the Company a good deal of money and me an immensity of trouble ... our Naval Gentlemen [Hanwell and Aemilius Simpson] were unacquainted with the coast and had never seen an Indian till they came here.'[42]

McNeill gave the marine department just the advantage it needed. He did a fine job watching and keeping in company with the American vessels on the coast, Finlayson wrote, 'and the manner in which he has performed this duty reflects much credit upon him; having from his intimate knowledge of the harbours, and trading stations on the coast, on many occasions given them the slip and secured the skins before their appearance at such harbours and when they happened to be together the Lama generally collected the best share of what ever was to be gleaned.'[43]

A few years later, McNeill's coastal knowledge from the maritime fur trade would be wed with industrial technology. Simpson had mooted the need for a steam vessel in 1832. The combination of permanent establishments and coastal vessels gave the company a decided advantage over American traders, and Simpson thought that the addition of a steam vessel would strengthen this combination. Sailing vessels took as long as two months to get in and out of Fort Vancouver, he told the G&C, and 'The saving of time in ascending and descending the Columbia and Fraser's Rivers, of itself, would be a very important object.' A steamer would also provide regularity on the coast. 'A steam Vessel would afford us incalculable advantages over the Americans, we could look into every Creek and cove ... we could ascend every stream of consequence upon the coast, we could visit our establishments at stated periods.'[44]

The G&C also favoured the idea because a steamer would allow the company's other vessels to enter the export trades. A steam vessel would 'perform the service of four of the Saling Vessels now employed on the Coast,' they said. 'We think there is a prospect of combining with the Coasting Trade a promising branch of business with the Sandwich Islands and the Spanish American Coast in the articles of Timber, Cured Salmon, Grain and other supplies.'[45] Steam would be used where it was really needed, on the coast, while sail would be used on the open ocean in establishing new export trades in lumber and salmon.

Launched in 1835, the SS *Beaver* reached Fort Vancouver under its own sail the following spring, with side paddles in its hold. A very precocious arrival, it was the first steamship in the Pacific Ocean. Known in the Chinook trade jargon as a '*Skokum* ship,' the *Beaver* caused a spatial revolution in the coasting trade by visiting the heads of inlets inaccessible by sail, where Native furs first reached the coast. The vessel, against which, Simpson wrote, 'neither calms nor contending winds were any security,' made the coast even more unwelcome to visiting fur traders.[46]

The vessel's inaugural voyage is well documented, a voyage, Dunn wrote, to 'reconnoitre the coast.' In June 1836, McLoughlin wrote ahead to Kittson at Fort Nisqually to prepare fifty cords of firewood 'cut into pieces of the length of three feet and piled in a convenient place on the beach for the use of the steamer,' and he instructed Yale at Fort Langley to prepare fifty cords of '*pine* wood' [Douglas fir] and store it on the bank of the Fraser River.[47] This job of preparing the *Beaver*'s cordwood, Tolmie recalled, was given to Native people. The results were very satisfactory. 'The result of the trials is that she can stow enough of wood to take her from one Fort to another, through the canals where the water is smooth, or from 2 to 230 miles,' Finlayson wrote.[48]

John Work, in charge of the coasting trade, and John Dunn, trader and interpreter, were on the *Beaver*'s first voyage. The ship got a late start from Fort Vancouver on 18 June, and travelled down the Columbia to the Pacific, then north to Cape Flattery, Puget Sound, and Fort Langley. From there the vessel made its way to Fort McLoughlin – where it took on twenty-six cords of firewood, enough for three or four days – Dean Channel, Bella Coola (North Bentinck Arm, the Salmon River of Mackenzie), Knight Inlet, Fitzhugh Sound, Fort McLoughlin again, Cape Swain, Point Day, Canals de Larado and Delprincipe (Sebassa area), and eventually Sitka. Dunn recalled that

> it was the intention of Mr. Finlayson, under whose instructions all our scheme of proceeding was to be conducted, to push along the numerous and intricate inlets (that interlace the whole country) as far as possible inland, in order to come as much within reach of the interior tribes as possible. Therefore we ran into their uttermost extremities, along almost the whole of the labyrinth; stopping sometimes to trade, and ascertain the capabilities of the country, and the character of the natives, who had never seen a large vessel (and especially a steamer) or a white man before.[49]

Work had orders from McLoughlin to accompany the *Beaver* to Queen Charlotte Sound, 'and after clearing these Indians of all their skins you will hurry on to the residence of the Sabasus Tribe' before the Americans arrived.[50]

Finlayson, who was on board, wrote that the navigation of the coastal inlets 'for steam, is very favourable – not a rock to be seen in mid Channel':

> In the canals we do not find it safe to run at night, owing to the quantity of drift timber which the tide carries along; and which if it came in contact with the Paddles, would break them to pieces, and perhaps cause some serious injury to the vessel and the engine. On the whole she will give the most effectual blow to the opposition which they have ever met with on the Coast, and will also lessen in a great measure the traffic carried on amongst the natives themselves.

The trip was a success. In September 1836, Finlayson reported 'a considerable increase' in the general returns of the coast.[51] The vessel's *modus operandi* consisted of visiting, in the spring and early summer, the main trading stations on the coast.[52] One such place was McNeill Harbour, which George Simpson visited on the *Beaver* in September 1841, and where he observed McNeill at work: 'The standard of prices being fixed after two hours of haggling, the business then went on briskly. Stationing himself at the steerage hatchway, Captain McNeill threw down each skin, as he examined it, with its price chalked on it – the equivalents being handed up from below by the two or three men that were in charge of the store.'[53]

The *Beaver* gave sailors in the HBC's marine department a sensitivity to the requirements of the coastal fur trade. In December 1836, McLoughlin urged Work to 'commence plying as early as in February or March as possible, so as to collect the Spring Hunts before the appearance of any opposition.' He was to observe the different fur tariffs established by the company: to pay high prices on the competitive North West Coast and low prices on the south coast in the absence of competition. Nisqually and Langley fur prices were to apply at all trading stations to the south of Johnstone Strait. In 1837, McNeill was to trade at the usual stations without actually going up the inlets, as this would interfere with the trade of New Caledonia.[54] In the absence of American competition, Native people were boxed in. They could only dispose of fur overland to New Caledonia, to coastal posts, or to the steamer – all of which offered the HBC's uniformly low prices (Map 14). The success of the *Beaver* is indicated by the aggregate figures: between 1825 and 1849, the vessel traded a total of 109,389 pelts, a number surpassed on the coast only by Fort Simpson, where 173,452 pelts were obtained. And the *Beaver* also succeeded against the American coasters. Tolmie recalled that the vessel simply 'made it unprofitable for traders in sailing vessels to visit the coast' after 1836-7.[55]

George Simpson toured the coast on the *Beaver* in September and October 1841, ecstatic about its superiority over sail, and full of praise for Captain Vancouver's surveys:

> Still, on the whole, the paddle is far preferable to canvass in these inland waters, which extend from Puget's Sound to Cross Sound, by reason of the strength of the currents, the variableness of the winds, the narrowness of the channels, and the intricacy and ruggedness of the line of coast. We found Vancouver's charts so minute and accurate, that, amid all our difficulties, we never had to struggle ...
>
> Thus had I traversed the most extraordinary course of inland navigation in the world. According to the tenour of my journal, this labyrinth of waters is peculiarly adapted for the powers of steam. In the case of a sailing vessel, our delays and dangers would have been tripled and quadrupled – a circumstance which raised my estimate of Vancouver's skill and perseverance at every step of my progress.[56]

The *Beaver*, however, was neither needed nor suitable for the entire North West Coast. With American fur traders gone, the few furs from the rugged outer coastline of Vancouver Island found their way north to Nawitti or south to Cape Flattery, and thence into the HBC's trading system at no additional expense to the company. As a result, the west coast of Vancouver Island never entered the HBC's immediate range, and the company never built a post there. The company's sailing vessels bound for Fort Simpson kept well out at sea. In July 1825, Scouler had visited Nootka on the *William & Ann*, reporting that the sea otter trade was nearly extinct.[57] No more thought was given to Nootka until 1838, when Douglas considered using the *Beaver* to explore the island's west coast. He decided against it owing to the hazards involved and because the company already indirectly controlled the fur trade of the region.[58]

Douglas was, however, anxious to build a post in the Queen Charlotte Sound region on the northeast end of Vancouver Island. A post in the sound would attract the fur trade of the island's west coast and of the 'continental shore' to the east. He was also anxious, he wrote in June

1838, 'to form a more intimate acquaintance with its inhabitants and commercial resources. The Coquilt Tribe, in their trading excursions in that quarter, gather a considerable number of Skins.'[59] Douglas instructed the *Beaver* to visit the canals and inlets of Queen Charlotte Sound between 50° and 52° north latitude. The results of this survey convinced Douglas that a post was needed at 'Shushady or Neweety,' which he described as 'a commodious harbour at the north end of Vancouver's Island, accessible to shipping at all seasons, and almost directly in the centre of the native population.' A post near Nawitti, Simpson noted, had the added advantage of being 'near the site of the coal mine' recently located on northern Vancouver Island. The post was never built.[60]

The *Beaver* was also employed in the company's move to the far North West Coast in the 1830s, a northern expansion that had its origins in the 1825 convention between the British and Russian governments. The agreement set the coastal boundary at 54°40′ north latitude, and gave the British rights of navigation to the long, narrow strip later known as the Alaska Panhandle, stretching thirty miles back from the coast.[61] In 1833, Ogden went up the Stikine on a reconnaissance and found the river too shallow for the company's sailing vessels.[62] The next year, he returned on the *Dryad* to establish a post on the banks of the Stikine that, like forts Simpson and McLoughlin, would intercept the Native trade in interior furs to the coast and that would also, Work wrote, 'enable us to Extend our trade in the country north of New Caledonia.' The Russians, despite the 1825 agreement, prevented Ogden from building the post in 1834. McLoughlin considered that the company's 'rights of territory' on the panhandle had been violated, and that the Russian action had lost the HBC £22,150. High-level negotiations between the Russian and British governments ensued, resulting in part in the liberal lease of 1839.[63]

This ten-year lease gave the HBC the right to build posts, hunt, and trade furs along the 400-mile-long coastline between Fort Simpson and the head of Lynn Canal. In return, the company agreed to furnish the Russian American Company with provisions. Unable to grow much food, the Russians had traditionally obtained their provisions from Boston merchants who had, since 1832, supplied liquor to the Native peoples of the North West Coast to the detriment of the Russian and British trades.

The 1839 'Provision Contract' between the British and Russian companies required the HBC to assume the role of foodstuffs suppliers in exchange for the lease of the coast and interior country between Cape Spencer and 54°40' north latitude, roughly the Alaska Panhandle. The agreement worked to both companies' interest: it rid the North West Coast of American suppliers who interfered with their fur trades, thus allowing the British and Russians to ban the distribution of liquor in the region.[64]

In 1839, Douglas was instructed to establish posts at Taku and Stikine, and in June 1840 he left in the *Beaver* to take possession of what he called the company's 'newly acquired territory at the coast.'[65] Douglas's trip is one of the most extraordinary in the history of the fur trade, comparable to Ogden's trek to the Vermilion Sea. In the space of one summer, the HBC extended its trade some 400 miles to the fifty-eighth parallel and into the far northern reaches of the coast (Map 14).[66] Douglas explored the lower thirty-five miles of the Taku River, which he learned led to an 'inland mart' 200 miles away where the Taku Indians traded their furs; between June and August, he built Fort Taku (also known as Fort Durham) on the coast, fifteen miles south of the river. Douglas described the site: 'The situation is in every respect favourable, being well supplied with fresh water, having abundance of good Timber while it is directly in the highway of trade, at a convenient distance for the people of Chilcat and Cross Sound; and should it be hereafter desirable, we can push into the interior, with as much facility from it, as from any point nearer the river.'[67]

Cheap and plentiful venison was the major provision at the post. Simpson noted in the fall of 1841 that 1,200 deer skins from Taku were sold at a profit in London:

> The fort, though it was only a year old, was yet very complete with good houses, lofty pickets, and strong bastions. The establishment was maintained chiefly on the flesh of the chevreuil, which is very fat, and has an excellent flavour. Some of these deer weigh as much as one hundred and fifty pounds each; and they are so numerous, that Taco has this year sent to market twelve hundred of their skins, being the handsome average of a deer a week for every inmate of the place. But extravagance in the eating of venison is here a very lucrative business, for the hide, after paying the freight and charges, yields in London a profit on the prime cost of the whole animal.[68]

In August 1840, with a copy of Vancouver's voyages in hand, Douglas explored farther north on the *Beaver*, from Taku to Cross Sound and Kucknaoo. At the head of Lynn Canal, he received the principal chiefs of a Chilcat village on board the *Beaver*, who told him that forty-five of their people had been killed by the crew of an American trading vessel. In his diary Douglas described the Chilcat 'circle of life' (seasonal round), and learned that they traded far into the interior. They asked him to establish a post in their territory, which he was unable to do.[69]

At the end of August, Douglas and his party left to take possession of Fort Wrangell, the Russian post at the mouth of the Stikine River on Wrangell Island, which the Russians had agreed to transfer to the HBC under the 1839 treaty. Douglas renamed the post Fort Stikine after the river and the Stikine people. Fort Stikine was situated on a peninsula barely large enough for the necessary buildings, 'next to mud flats which oppressed the atmosphere with a most nauseous perfume.'[70] Prospects for provisions at Fort Stikine looked good. 'The provision resources of this Post, are more than equal to meet the wants of its establishment,' Douglas wrote, 'in fact the waters abound with salmon and the forests with deer, which the Natives sell cheerfully, at a moderate price. On one occasion 300 carcasses of Deer, were traded in 15 days, by the late Russian Commandant.'[71]

On this voyage, Douglas considered the possibility of extending the trade up the Taku and Stikine rivers, but decided against it: the HBC already controlled the interior trade, and an extension might have interfered with the trade of the Mackenzie and Liard river posts. Instead, he ordered the Stikine explored from the coast inland. Douglas observed that the absence of navigable tributaries was the 'one great difficulty incident to all rivers on the North West Coast,' an impediment that led him to suggest the direct employment of Native hunters on their own trade routes.[72]

In the late 1830s, the company was in a position to take the offensive in the coastal fur trade. Fort Simpson, especially, was the base for the company's extraordinary 'Sea otter Adventure' of 1837-9, a hunt designed to mop up the remnants of the sea otter trade of the west coast of North America between Russian America and California. Traditionally, North West Coast sea otters had been obtained by Native hunters, traded to

Americans or Russians, and sold in the Sandwich Islands or Canton.[73] The sea otter trade had figured prominently in Dalrymple and Mackenzie's plans, but by the third decade of the nineteenth century it was on the decline, and the indifferent quality of Columbia Department fur contributed to the failure of the NWC's and Simpson's China ventures.

At first, Simpson hoped an extended coastal trade would bring in many sea otters, but in 1829 he learned that the annual American catch in the region 'for some years past' had not exceeded 600 pelts, down from 15,000 in 1802. Yet in the 1830s, sea otter were still available, and as late as 1835 and 1836 the company obtained a total of 404 pelts from the Pacific coast. These were not the huge numbers of preceding decades, but they constituted a valuable trade. In some coastal areas, sea otter had been exterminated through overhunting. Scouler and Dunn had found the people at Nootka with only a few sea otter to dispose of, and in 1831 Aemilius Simpson reported that few could be acquired in the Gulf of Georgia and lower Columbia trades.[74] The animals persisted on the open Pacific shore between Cape Disappointment and Cape Flattery, but they had never inhabited inland waters, such as the Gulf of Georgia, Puget Sound, or the Columbia River. Corney noted in 1821 that 'The sea otters are taken on the coast, but never enter the river.'[75]

Dunn, who was in charge of Fort George in the 1830s, wrote that sea otters were still numerous at Cape Flattery, where the company obtained pelts in the normal course of its coastal operations. Dunn described a hunt there:

> The sea otter is plentiful about these parts. The mode usually adopted in killing it is this: the natives, or the half-breeds, who now adopt all the customs of the natives, row out to the parts frequented by this animal, whose habits resemble those of the seal. Two men manage the canoe, while a third stands ready; and the moment the otter rises to the surface he is unerringly shot. When he feels himself hit he dives, and the boatmen dart after him, well aware of the direction he will take; and keep pace with him until he rises again. Then, unless he floats a dead carcass, he is a second time shot, and the chase is renewed, until he is at last killed. He is then hauled into the boat. Sometimes a sort of screen is erected on the shore, behind which the marksman lurks, and, when the animal comes to bask on the sands or the rocks, he is shot.[76]

Farther south, on the coast of California, Russian and American traders obtained a different, slightly less valuable species of sea otter than the northern variety. For years, McLoughlin had hoped to secure these pelts for the company. In 1825, he planned to send a vessel from Fort Vancouver to hunt or trade sea otters at San Francisco and Monterey.[77] The Russians held a legal right to hunt sea otter in California from their base at Fort Ross in San Francisco Bay; American vessels, General Figueroa told Duncan Finlayson in 1833, 'without any permission are constantly hovering about the Californian Coast, for the purpose of hunting the otter.'[78]

The American sea otter traders had, however, started employing experienced Native hunters from Kaigani, in Russian America, for the California hunt. In January 1834, Finlayson, while at Honolulu, learned that an American vessel with twenty-five 'Kyganni indian hunters on board' had taken 650 sea otters the previous summer, and that at least 900 more had been collected by other American vessels in California. He also learned that an American ship had recently arrived from Kaigani with a Native crew, and that they too were bound for the coast of California.[79]

Hiring Native hunters from the North West Coast for the California offshore sea otter hunt appealed to McLoughlin, who devised a plan with John Work in 1836 to send the *Nereide* out from Fort Simpson 'with Indians to hunt the sea otter,' but they decided instead to send the *Nereide* to Honolulu with a load of lumber. Then, in January 1837, the American brig *Loriat*, captained by John Bancroft, arrived at Fort Vancouver with sea otters for sale. McLoughlin was impressed that Bancroft was an Englishman and that he had 'been frequently engaged in hunting the sea otter on the Coast of California for the Americans.' They struck a deal: Bancroft would buy the company's surplus vessel *Lama* for $5,500 if McLoughlin would grubstake him with goods for the sea otter trade; but because Bancroft did not have this much cash, McLoughlin agreed to accept part of the potential sea otter catch as payment. The *Lama* was an English ship, and Bancroft an Englishman, so all seemed well.[80]

Bancroft was to collect part of his outfit at Fort Vancouver and part at Fort Simpson, and he was to hunt sea otter on the North West Coast or in California and to deliver his catch to Fort Simpson or to the company's Oahu agency. (The company would then ship the furs directly to London on its regular vessel, rather than to Canton because, as McLoughlin told Honolulu agent George Pelly in 1836, 'We are not authorized to send Furs to any other but the English market.') The arrangement was not unlike Bancroft's earlier deals; he simply changed from an American to an English vessel and worked with British, rather than American, fur traders. In March 1838, Bancroft was at 'Kygarney' hunting sea otters, and the arrangement was extended for the winter of 1838-9. Douglas forwarded supplies to Fort Simpson, and he instructed Pelly at Oahu to pay Bancroft $35 for a large prime sea otter, $20 for a middling prime, $12 for a small prime, and $1 for pups.[81] Bancroft, his Hawaiian wife, and his crew were next heard of in April 1839, when Pelly notified the HBC Governor and Committee that

> the NW Indians employed in your former Brig the Lama hunting for Sea Otters on the Coast of California mutinied and shot Capt Bancroft and his wife who was with him Capt. Bancroft was killed and his wife lingered until her arrival here she is since dead, the Pirates then compelled the Mate to take them back in the Lama to Kygarnee on the NWst Coast and having then plundered the Brig of everything of value they then very unexpectedly permitted her to return here.[82]

After this remarkable episode, the company reverted to obtaining sea otter in its regular coastal trade and at Honolulu, where sporadic purchases continued into the 1840s. By this time, pelts had become very scarce. In 1839, Alexander Forbes, a British resident of California, wrote that the California sea otter catch had 'dwindled into insignificance' as a result of Russian overhunting.[83]

These policies, posts, and vessels brought an increasing number of pelts to the HBC's stores, making the coast uninteresting to American traders. By the mid-1830s, the North West Coast had become a major fur region within the company's North American territories. In 1839, Simpson spoke proudly of the company's measures of protection as 'amounting to a strict Coast Guard,' and two years later he reflected on the company's entrance into the North West Coast fur trade. 'Though, from 1780 to 1795, the British shared in the fur-trade which their countrymen had opened, yet, from the latter date to 1828, the Russians and Americans between them monopolized nearly the whole of it. Since 1828, however, the Hudson's Bay Company came with energy to the coast; and now, while the Russians confine themselves to their own territory, not a single American is engaged in the branch of commerce in question.'[84]

American fur traders felt this competition and left the coast. When Captain John Dominis of the *Owhyhee* returned to New York in 1832 after two years trading on the lower Columbia, Gulf of Georgia, and Puget Sound, he told a newspaper that the country was 'delightful, but that the Hudson's Bay Coy. are too well established for citizens of the United States to make any thing in the way of Fur Trade.'[85] Similarly, the Boston merchant Nathaniel Wyeth in 1832 lamented the company's control of the coast trade. He spoke admiringly of the 'the more economical methods of the British' that, prophetically, he thought could only be defeated by diplomatic manoeuvres. He condemned the 'peculiar state of the trade in the country in question' resulting from the 1828 convention:

> I think this convention will not be renewed because it virtually destroys our trade there by opening it to the competition of the British Co. whose capital and facilities are so great that [American] vessells cannot trade to a profit on that coast they being subject to a long delay on the coast whereas the British trade is effected by posts and their vessells have nothing to do but to discharge and re-load.[86]

A year later, in 1833, Wyeth wrote that the risk of bringing a vessel out from Boston to the coast was too great: 'The whole coast as far as furs are concerned is taken up by the H.B.Co.' And to a different merchant house in Boston, he stated in the same year: 'I tell you plainly that my prospects of doing any thing on the coast with no more means than I have still left of my own are at an end. I have traversed the country in many directions and found all those places which [are] accessible to shipping occupied or about to be by the H.B.Co. who are efficient opponents.' 'I will in conclusion observe that I consider all the coast & country North of the Columbia completely occupied by the English.' The American Thomas Farnham, who visited in 1839, remarked that 'the HBC employ their incomparable ingenuity and immense wealth in driving every American trader from the coasts of the Pacific.'[87]

Other Americans did not accept the company's commercial success as well as Wyeth and Farnham did. 'This Northwest fur trade,' James Swan wrote, 'has been gradually taken from the Americans by that grasping monopoly and incubus on all attempts at American enterprise.'[88] That the company had achieved a monopoly on the fur trade of the North

West Coast through the scale and efficiency of its trade was lost on commentators like Swan. In fact, the company possessed no *de jure* trading monopoly against American merchants anywhere in the Columbia Department; the Americans had equal rights and access, yet failed to build a post anywhere on the coasts of what became Oregon, Washington, Alaska, and British Columbia.

The company's own sources document the gradual disappearance of American fur traders from the North West Coast south of Russian territory.[89] 'Five [American] Vessels, well officered, manned & equipped in every respect' were on the coast in the summer of 1831, according to Finlayson. Despite this the HBC's total returns amounted to 3,000 beaver skins worth £1,613 – the 'first gains ever realized from it.'[90] In the spring of 1832, McLoughlin wrote that, having 'nothing to interrupt our proceedings – we intend to give it the first fair Trial it has had,' and Finlayson reported that 'The coasting trade, which has suffered much in the loss of the late Captain [Aemilius] Simpson ... is not as yet, on as firm a footing, as to realise anything handsome. The natives, sagacious enough to pursue their own interest with persevering industry, are owing to the Yankee opposition most extravagant in their demands.'[91] The Americans returned in force in the summer of 1832. 'Ogden was getting a few Beaver,' John Work reported, 'but was paying very dear for them as there was no less than six Yankee ships opposing him.'[92]

The year 1833 was the watershed in the history of the North West Coast fur trade. Ogden worked without competition.[93] For the first time in about forty years, not a single American vessel traded on the coast, south of Russian territory, and the HBC traded fur on the North West Coast worth at least £13,000, including pelts from New Caledonia and other interior regions brought to the coast via Native trade routes.[94] Late in 1833, Finlayson made a special trip to Oahu to buy trading goods and provisions such as leaf tobacco, rice, and beef – commodities the Americans had provided for years. These were 'absolutely necessary' for the company's coastal trade, he said, 'as the departure of the opposition therefrom has thrown a greater demand of these articles upon us than we anticipated.'[95] Finlayson's purchase commenced a new era in North West Coast fur trade history: thereafter, the Native demand for European goods was met not by Boston traders but by the HBC.

In 1835, two American vessels returned to the North West Coast, and the next year at least one, but Dunn stated that by 1836 the opposition was gone. During the next two years, there were no Americans present,[96] and the HBC's shipping department engrossed the coast in a web of scheduled activity.[97] In 1838, Douglas stated that the *Beaver* and forts McLoughlin and Simpson were 'fully adequate to the protection of the Trade' on the coast. 'Our Trade now embraces almost every accessible portion of the Coast as far as the Russian Line of Demarcation,' he wrote.[98] When an American vessel did venture south of Russian territory in August 1839, the company was prepared. 'The trade of the coast received a rude shock,' Douglas said, 'from the arrival, in August, of an American vessel, the Thomas Perkins of New York, she was vigorously opposed in the Fur market and left the coast, after a stay of three weeks at Fort Simpson, without visiting any other harbour.' And he told James Hargrave that

> an American vessel made her appearance in August at Fort Simpson; but met with no encouragement: furs were scarce and we were constantly at their elbow to buy up the few that were in circulation; such treatment they no doubt considered harsh; it however answered our object and had the effect of shortening their stay, at a place where they were neither welcome, nor their presence much coveted.[99]

So effective was the company's policy that the next non-British vessels to trade on the coast were not North West Coasters from Boston in search of land furs, or whatever sea otter remained, but commercial whalers. A French whaler visited the west coast in the summer of 1841, and two American whalers visited Nawitti the following year, and another two in October 1843. One of these last two vessels, encountered by the *Beaver* 'lying at Newitte,' carried an assortment of trade goods, but of such an inferior quality that they could only procure seventy skins. Yet Douglas considered this 'an ominous visitation.' 'If whales are found in the Sounds and Bays of the Coast, the circumstance, when known, will attract so many vessels to these shores as to endanger the security of our trade.'[100] The company afterwards kept a close eye on whaling activity, but Douglas's alarm was unfounded: whalers did not return once they found that whales did not breed in the canals and inlets of the coast.

The company's investment in the North West Coast, in terms of personnel, transport, and trade goods, did not yield immediate profit.

Coastal extension had entailed high expenditures on competition, provision, and transport. The region lay on the company's far outer frontier, accessible not overland from New Caledonia, but at first circuitously
from the mouth of the Columbia. It lay beyond the company's established continental, river-based transport systems, and the company had
to pay more for coastal pelts when American traders were present.
McLoughlin estimated that costs of competition and shipping made it
ten times more expensive to obtain furs on the coast than in New Caledonia.[101] Until the North West Coast trade turned a profit in the early
1830s, the rich interior fur trades of New Caledonia and the Snake Country compensated for capital outlay on the coast. But by 1840, between a
quarter and a third of the department's total fur returns came from the
coast,[102] and the coastal fur trade was able to absorb costs involved in
the construction of forts Taku and Stikine. 'The Company's business in
this quarter is going on prosperously,' Douglas told Hargrave in 1840,
that 'the result of the outfit will not fall short of last year's even tho' it
is saddled with the heavy expenses of the new settlements on the coast.'[103]

The HBC's aggressive policies were directly responsible for the departure of American vessels in the 1830s from the North West Coast, a
region where the Americans had a clear legal right to trade and where
the fur trade was still valuable. In a 1992 book, James Gibson states that
the Americans voluntarily 'abandoned,' 'quit,' or 'withdrew' on their own
accord in about 1840, when sea otter disappeared and the fur trade of
the North West Coast dwindled to 'insignificance.'[104] It is true that by
1840 both the sea otter and the Americans had left the coast, but American traders had long since (circa 1800-10) diversified their North West
Coast trade to include beaver and land otter,[105] and falling sea otter
returns did not constitute a good enough reason for their departure. Land
furs available on the North West Coast did not diminish in quantity or
quality for many years; in 1841, 10,000 beaver and land otter were still
available annually on the North West Coast, a valuable harvest.[106]
Combined profits of Fort Simpson and the *Beaver* after 1842 were £3,721
in 1843, £4,285 in 1844, £6,696 in 1845, £6,428 in 1846, and £8,176 in 1847.[107]
These were not insignificant figures.

The pelts found their way not to Canton in the holds of American
vessels, but to London in the holds of HBC vessels; and profits went to
British capitalists and company shareholders, not to Boston merchants.

Concurrently, American exports of fur to Canton declined from $480,000 in 1821 to $200,000 in 1832 to $56,000 in 1839.[108] Gibson's assertion that the 'complacent and conservative' HBC falsely 'claimed to have driven off the "Boston pedlars" from the coast' is not supported by the spirit or content of the documentary sources.[109] American traders were indeed outcompeted for the valuable peltries of the North West Coast – by a combination of extensive capital resources, assertive shipping, and experienced personnel based on the *Beaver* and at posts such as Fort Simpson.[110]

British fur traders on the coast, like observers in the Snake Country, attributed the Americans' failure to their lack of capital, their individualistic and destructive competition with one another, and their shortsighted trade in alcohol. American coasters were, McLoughlin stated, 'mere Adventurers without capital,' no match for the company's skill and resources.[111] He believed that the HBC had 'Defeated American traders in fair opposition,' 'in fair Dealing and Honorable Conduct.' 'The Americans were not so much rivals of the company as they were of one another,' Dunn wrote; 'indeed they could never be said to be, in the strict sense of the word, rivals of the company, for they had not the power, either as to capital, union, or sound notions of trade. I had many opportunities of witnessing this, when I was stationed on the northern posts, or employed in the company's trading ships on that coast.'[112]

The HBC's entry to the North West Coast had several important results. Spatially and politically, it gave the company *carte blanche* to an important and valuable new region where American merchants could legally have built posts at any time. It enabled the company to lower fur tariffs and to gain complete access to Native trading networks, resources, and labour. Control of the coast also allowed the HBC to contemplate, safe from American competition, the formation of provision and export trades and agricultural establishments to supply the Russians with foodstuffs. Finally, control of the coast gave the British, at the end of the 1840s, a solid economic base upon which to initiate the formal colonization of Vancouver Island. The extended fur economy of the coast was distinct, however, from the evolving regional non-fur economy of the same region – a new economy that required its own shipping, expertise, and markets.

CHAPTER 7

New Markets
for New Exports

The company's ship Vancouver is lying in this port.
She brought more than one hundred thousand feet of
Columbia River lumber.

— THOMAS FARNHAM,
HONOLULU, JANUARY 1840[1]

By the early 1830s, the Hudson's Bay Company had made substantial inroads into American trading activity on the North West Coast, the Snake Country, and on the lower Columbia River itself. The American retreat gave the company the freedom to experiment with new exports from the Columbia and Fraser rivers and to locate new markets on the Pacific. Three aspects of the company's mastery of the fur trade promoted the rise of export trades: the provision trades underpinning the fur trade could just as well support, or even *become* new export trades; ships purchased for the coastal fur trade could just as well service Pacific markets in the dead season; and, similarly, fur trade personnel could be put to work in other activities.

Nothing was done in the fur trade without food. At every fort ever built by the British fur traders in North America, Native provisions were procured and European horticulture or agriculture were practised. Wherever possible, farming was the favoured means of obtaining food because it lessened a dependence on Native food supplies. Agricultural self-sufficiency was a desired prerequisite to all exports, including fur. As George Simpson wrote in 1824, 'It has been said that Farming is no branch of the Fur Trade but I consider that every pursuit tending to lighten the Expense of the Trade is a Branch thereof.'[2]

The Northwesters, like the maritime fur traders, had obtained staples such as grain and preserved meats in California and Honolulu, but Simpson would have none of this. The Northwesters' Fort George was built on rocky, uneven land, but its replacement, Fort Vancouver, possessed the finest farm anywhere in British fur trade territory. Simpson had selected the site late in 1824 with self-sufficiency and economy in mind. 'He considers the soil and Climate of this Place,' HBC governor, John Pelly, wrote in December 1825, 'to be so well adapted for Agricultural pursuits, that in the course of two or three years it may be made to produce sufficient Grain and Animal Provisions to meet not only the demands of our own Trade but to almost any extent that may be required for other purposes.'[3]

For this subsistence program Simpson relied on Dr. John McLoughlin, who was, Rich noted, 'a far-sighted and competent agriculturalist.'

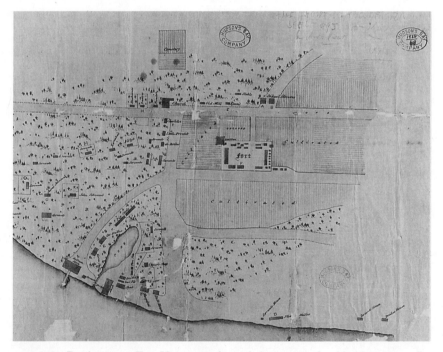

FIGURE 11 By the 1840s, Fort Vancouver formed the centre of a sizeable community of European, French Canadian, Iroquois, and Kanaka settlers and their Native or Metis wives and families. This plan of Fort Vancouver is based on Richard Covington's *Fort Vancouver and Village in 1846*. On the Columbia River are the HBC's wharf, salmon house, salt house, and stables. [Hudson's Bay Company Archives, Provincial Archives of Manitoba, N4165]

Son of a farmer and raised on his French Canadian grandfather's seigneury on the St. Lawrence, McLoughlin may have inherited his passion for farming on the north shore of a great river. He recalled that 'Had it not been for the great expense of importing Flour from Europe, the serious injury it received on the voyage, and the absolute necessity of being independent of Indians for provisions, I never would have encouraged farming in this Country.'[4]

The Columbia offered a longer growing season than Hudson Bay or Red River, and by 1829 Fort Vancouver was independent of imports of English or Hawaiian food. 'The main object in view has been attained,' Simpson wrote, 'that of rendering ourselves independent of Foreign aid in regard to the means of subsistence, which is here, perhaps more than anywhere else, the Main Spring of the business.' The HBC Governor and Committee responded with delight: 'We notice with much satisfaction the success which has attended your exertions in Agricultural pursuits and raising Stock, and trust you will continue to prosecute these objects, indeed your whole management is marked by a degree of energy zeal and activity highly creditable to yourself, important to the interests of the Service and meeting our warmest Commendations.'[5]

The figures were impressive. Wheat production increased from 12 to 3,000 bushels between 1826 and 1832, and potato production from 600 to 6,000 bushels. Fort George had a herd of 17 cows in 1824; Fort Vancouver's herd stood at between 400 and 450 seven years later. Ball, who came with Wyeth in 1832, recalled that 'The voyage around Cape Horn was so long to take supplies, that the company bought a bull and cows from California, and in seven years they had raised from this start four hundred head of cattle.' By the late 1820s, Fort Vancouver was able to provide provisions for the company's extended coastal operations on land, for its growing marine service, and for the Snake and Southern parties. An agricultural oasis, Fort Vancouver provided a surplus of provisions – a rarity in the fur trade. For example, when salmon were scarce at Kamloops in 1829, seven men were simply sent down to Fort Vancouver for the winter. It was cheaper to send men to the coast than to send food to the interior. 'We often had a bountiful table in those days,' recalled HBC clerk George Roberts, who arrived in 1831, '& how often I've heard the Dr. say "it's all the produce of the country, Gentlemen."'[6]

The orchard at Fort Vancouver contributed to its reputation as an oasis. The story goes that Captain Aemilius Simpson, prior to leaving England in 1826, attended a dinner party at which a woman slipped some apple seeds into his waistcoat pocket, 'and told him to carry them out to his far off destination and then plant them.' He forgot about the pips until he reached Fort Vancouver, when he next wore the waistcoat, and when planted they produced apple trees. 'And what a delightful place this is,' wrote the American missionary Narcissa Whitman on her arrival in 1836; 'What a contrast to the barren sand plains through which we had so recently passed. Here we find fruit of every description.'[7]

Rival American fur traders on the North West Coast and on the Columbia, outfitted from Boston or St. Louis, acknowledged the advantages lent by Fort Vancouver's farm to HBC operations everywhere west of the Rockies. In 1834, Simpson reminded the G&C that

> the Farm at this place is an object of vital importance to the interests of the business on the west side the Mountains, generally, as it has enabled us to dispense with imported provisions, for the maintenance of our shipping and establishments, whereas, without the farm, it would have been necessary to import such provisions, at an expense that the trade could not afford. The Farm was unusually productive last year, yielding upwards of 10,000 Bushels Grain of all Kinds, and we are beginning to dispose of some of our surplus produce at the Sandwich Islands to advantage.[8]

A year later, Simpson reported a situation that had never arisen, and would never arise, on Hudson Bay. It would no longer be necessary, he wrote, 'to provision the Ships from England for the homeward voyage, as an abundant supply may be depended on from Vancouver.'[9]

Having achieved self-sufficiency in foodstuffs, Simpson was at liberty to export salmon, lumber, and eventually flour from Fort Vancouver. Transport, market, and labour conditions favoured the rise of export trades on the west coast, and the company took advantage of the Pacific position it inherited from the North West Company. The Kingdom of Hawaii, Mexican settlements in California, and the Russian American Company's base at Sitka emerged in the 1830s as major markets for Columbia produce. Importantly, none of these markets was yet American; the Americans would not have a foothold on the Pacific until they obtained Oregon and California in 1846 and 1848 respectively. Until then, the closest American ports, markets, and centres of production were on the eastern seaboard, a long and tedious voyage around Cape Horn. The HBC's general commercial business at Oahu (Honolulu) and Yerba Buena (San Francisco) would at first be conducted through agents, and later through company stores. From these locations, transshipments of Columbia produce would reach such places as Valparaiso, the Seeward Islands, Manila, China, London, and Boston.

Always in the back of the British fur traders' minds was a desire to establish a commerce linking the Pacific coast with Pacific markets. Mackenzie and Dalrymple had advocated this, the maritime fur traders had initiated trade between the North West Coast and Canton, and the Northwesters had exported Columbia furs to China. In 1824-5, Simpson resurrected a plan to ship furs directly to Canton from the lower Fraser, then rumoured to be navigable as far as the interior, or from the lower Columbia. In the same period, the G&C sent furs from London to China on East India Company vessels, but the experiment had been unprofitable. Still, Simpson and McLoughlin hoped to establish a Pacific commerce independent of the East India Company's trade.

On his 1824-5 visit, Simpson suggested that the company's vessels could be trading to Canton and South America during the dead months of winter. He need not have looked so far abroad. Hawaii became the company's dominant market on the Pacific, the answer to Simpson's 1825 scheme, and, after the relaxation of the East India Company's monopoly in 1833, the answer to Dalrymple and Mackenzie before him.[10]

In 1821, the Sandwich Islands promised to occupy a pivotal place in North Pacific trade. Since Cook's visit in 1778, the islands had increased in trading importance; they were, geographer Sheila Robinson writes, at one end of a quadrilateral circuit in the maritime fur trade, which also comprised the coast, Canton, and Boston. The islands 'not only furnished supplies, but eventually furnished several opportunities for the maritime fur traders to increase their profits.' Fur traders diversified into the sandalwood trade at the islands, and Oahu became the base of the north Pacific whaling fleet.[11]

The NWC had patronized the islands as a provision centre and supply entrepôt, both for its own vessels and for American vessels chartered to take furs from the Columbia River to Canton. The Northwesters had

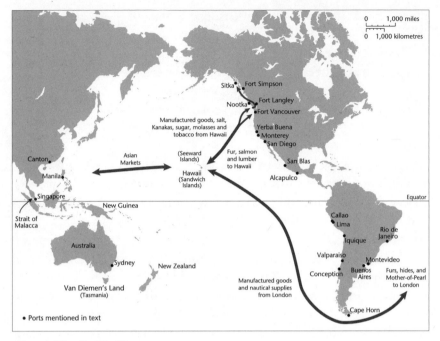

MAP 16 The Pacific Rim

established good relationships. In January 1815, the king of Hawaii had given Duncan McDougall permission to 'stop in his dominions as long as he pleased,' an invitation that was later extended to the fur traders from Hudson Bay.[12]

The islands were centrally located between the Orient, the south and central Pacific, the Columbia River, and the North West Coast. 'For all practical purposes,' Simpson wrote in 1842, 'the Sandwich Islands are on the direct route from Cape Horn to all the coasts of the Northern Pacific.' The islands were a place resorted to by whalers 'for refuge and refreshment, while they have gradually come to be frequented for ordinary repairs, and also for stores and equipments of every description.' In 1835-6, the largely Native population of the archipelago was 107,954, forming a substantial market.[13]

The British, Americans, and French all hoped to acquire the islands in the early nineteenth century, but they somehow remained independent until annexed by the United States in 1898. Corney emphasized the crucial position of the islands in 1821; indeed, he began his book with a plea to British merchants: 'The only object the author of this book has in making his observations on the trade between the north-west coast of America and the Sandwich Islands and China, is, to point out to the merchants in this country the vast trade that is carried on between those places by the Americans and the Russians while an English flag is rarely to be seen.' Corney wanted Great Britain to consider the possibility of acquiring the Sandwich Islands, owing to their 'vast importance,' and other British merchants were to echo Corney's sentiments.[14]

The islands were also the closest overseas market to the Columbia River, and later to Vancouver Island. On average, they were a three-week trip from the coast, but they could be reached in as few as ten days from the mouth of the Columbia. London, by contrast, was a five month voyage from Honolulu.[15]

The HBC's long involvement there began in November 1827, when McLoughlin asked Aemilius Simpson of the *Cadboro* to report on the timber market in the 'Owhyhee Islands.' Simpson reached Oahu in January 1829 with a cargo of lumber from the company's new sawmill near Fort Vancouver; the lumber got a good price.[16] While there, he recruited Captain Richard Charlton of Oahu as the company's agent. Since 1824, Charlton had been British consul for the Sandwich, Society, and Friendly Islands, an appointment aimed at furthering trade between the islands and British manufacturers. Charlton's job was to find buyers for salmon and timber shipped from forts Vancouver and Langley, and to buy staple commodities such as salt, sugar, rice, and molasses needed on the coast. His appointment came only months after the failure of the East India Company's final shipment of Columbia Department furs from London to Canton.[17]

George Simpson was enthusiastic about the new market, which was, after all, a nearer and more practical version of his Canton export proposal of 1824-5. In March 1829, during his second visit to the Columbia region, he and McLoughlin advanced their new scheme to locate Pacific markets for Columbia produce. They convinced the G&C that exports of timber and salmon when 'united with the Fur Trade' of the coast would become a 'very profitable branch of business.' 'During the dead Season of the Year, say from October until March, when little can be done on the coast, we purpose employing the Vessels in carrying Timber, either to the South Coast wherever a market can be found for it,

FIGURE 12 In 1833 the HBC opened a store in Honolulu for the sale of salmon, lumber, potatoes, and flour from forts Vancouver and Langley to native Hawaiians and the Pacific whaling fleet. This watercolour of Honolulu by a French admiral shows what was already the major settlement in the Hawaiian archipelago. [François Edmund, *Iles Hawaii, Honorourou capitale de'Oauahou Vu de Mouillage,* 1839, Bishop Museum Archives, CP 117,126 - XC 114,288]

or to the Sandwich Islands, which yield a very handsome profit.' The scheme called for the appointment of agents 'so that we may have merely to deliver our Cargoes, and return in time for the Fur Trade to the Northward.' So confident was Simpson that he embarked on the project without waiting for the G&C's approval:

> We are therefore satisfied, that your Honors will see the expediency of connecting this branch of business with the Fur Trade, and as much valuable time (3 years at least) would be lost by transmitting the information we have collected to England, and waiting for your instructions thereon, we trust you will not consider that we are exceeding the limits of authority invested in us, by anticipating your approval of our design, and by our acting accordingly.[18]

Presented with a fait accompli, the G&C could only acquiesce. In the fall of 1829, with two American vessels then trading fur, salmon, and spars in the Columbia, McLoughlin stressed the need to open a timber

trade with Oahu in the winter months, and added a compelling competitive reason. 'We must avail ourselves of all the resources of this
Country if we have to compete for the trade of it with the Americans
as we may depend they will turn every thing they possibly can to
account.' As it happened, the threat of American commercial competition was much more serious at Oahu than on the Columbia River.[19]

Other commodities soon joined timber as Columbia exports. Charlton sold the lumber immediately, prompting McLoughlin to write that
'Salmon also might be made an Article of trade – this would require an
Increased Establishment.' By 1832, when Finlayson visited the islands,
he found that Columbia and Fraser river salmon were selling much better than timber and, he told McLoughlin, the market was better suited
to provisions than to timber: 'In the months of March & October, the
period at which the Whalers visit this place, 400 Bushels of potatoes
would command a dollar each – 200 Barrels of Flour of about 196 lbs
each, would sell at not less than 9 dollars pr Bbl, & from 20 to 30 firkins
Butter at about 30 @ 35 cents pr lb. These are all the productions of the
Columbia I could discover likely to command a market here.'[20] So substantial were the HBC's sales of Columbia produce in 1832 that Finlayson bought Captain McNeill's brig *Lama* for the coasting trade. The
vessel was principally paid for, he wrote, from the proceeds of timber
and salmon sent to the islands.[21]

In 1833, Simpson dismissed Charlton as company agent when he
learned that he was engaged in the fur trade of the North West Coast.
Charlton, who may have been buying furs from Boston traders and selling them to Canton merchants, defended himself by pointing to the
patriotic reasons that had motivated him to accept the agency:

> I beg to state that I never solicited the Agency for the Company – when Cap-
> tain Simpson first asked me I refused, but afterwards upon asking me again
> I considered that I might benefit the Commerce of my Countrymen by accept-
> ing it, though the Company in London (it appears by a letter I have lately
> received) have stated I was never an agent for the Hudson's bay Company. I
> therefore enclose a copy of Captain Simpson's letter a duplicate of which Cap-
> tain Simpson forwarded to London.[22]

News of Finlayson's transactions in this ideal new market reached
London in 1833, just as the British government modified the charter of

the East India Company to allow other British companies to formally operate in what had been its monopoly territory. In October 1833, Simpson and the G&C decided that, with Charlton gone, it was 'essential the Company should have an Agent at Wohao,' and they selected John Pelly's cousin George Pelly, at a yearly salary of £300. Formerly a captain in the East India Company, Pelly became acting British Consul at Oahu in the 1830s (as well as Hawaiian agent for Lloyd's of London), and he remained in sole charge of the HBC agency until 1841. His mandate was to superintend the company's Oahu affairs, selling and finding markets for 'Timber Salmon and other articles ... [and] providing freight to fill up the Company's Ships on their Return Voyages to England.'[23]

The Hawaiian agency was attached to the Columbia Department from its opening in 1834 until 1844, nominally under McLoughlin's direct supervision. One of seven leading business houses at the Sandwich Islands, the company's store was located, until 1846, on the corner of King and Nuuanu streets in a two-storey building. According to W.F. Tolmie, who visited in 1833, Oahu was 'a scattered village built without any apparent order,' possessing twenty-one 'grog shops.'[24]

The founding of this agency marked a satisfactory conclusion to the direct China trade scheme that had intrigued British fur traders for fifty years. While Simpson's hope of a direct link between the coast and Canton had to be abandoned, the Oahu agency marked the beginning of a more realistic commercial strategy. This convenient mid-Pacific entrepôt would serve as a destination for Columbia produce, a market for all the staple and exotic commodities of the Pacific and Orient, and a convenient refuelling and provisioning station for the company's vessels bound to and from London.[25] Moreover, the demise of the East India Company's monopoly led to a general increase in British mercantile activity in the Pacific, and by 1840 George Pelly would have various dealings with Jardine Matheson & Company, major Canton merchants.

The G&C, fully aware of the commercial and political value of the islands and pleased that the East India Company had finally relaxed their charter, instructed McLoughlin in December 1833 to spare no exertions in exporting Columbia produce to Oahu and to the California settlements:

The growing state of importance of the Sandwich Islands as a place of resort and refreshment for shipping engaged in the Whale and Pearl Fisheries of the South Seas, and in the New Zealand, Spanish Main and North West Coast Trades, likewise that of China, arising from the late changes, which have been made with regard to the East India Company's Charter, leads to the hope that it may become a favourable outlet for timber, cured Salmon and other articles which may be provided for these markets at our Establishments on the North West Coast ...

Timber and cure salmon can be provided from the Honble Companys Establishments on the North West Coast to any extent for which an outlet at a remunerating price is likely to be found and as the Sandwich Islands produce no Timber, and the population of the Spanish American Coast are unaccustomed to the severe labour of hewing and rafting, all that is used in these Islands, and the greater part of what is required on that Coast are imported from the United States and New Zealand, but the facilities which the Honble Company possess for preparing the Timber at their Establishments, and sending it to market on their shipping at a Season of the year when they can not be employed in the Fur Trade or in any other useful service, afford the Company such a decided advantage over these People in that branch of business, that if well conducted there is every probability of its following entirely into the Company's hands: and the Towns and Settlements on the Spanish American Coast being chiefly by Catholics, and the Waters of those Countries being unproductive in Fish, it is thought that, an extended trade if judiciously pushed, may in the article of cured salmon be opened in that quarter.

You will therefore be pleased, to direct your attention particularly to the opening of a Trade in those Articles.[26]

It took several years to make shipments of Columbia produce profitable. In June 1835, Simpson admitted that the newer export trades in timber were still in their infancy and had 'not hitherto been productive,' but later that year, the G&C urged McLoughlin to send all varieties of Columbia produce to Oahu, and added a political reason for wanting to push this trade:

With regard to the Sandwich Islands Timber trade ... we think that a large stock, say a year's consumption, should be always kept up in the hands of Mr George Pelly which would very soon put a stop to the further importation of Timber by the Americans, a large stock of Salmon for the Spanish market should likewise be kept on hand there, likewise Flour, Malt Cheese Butter Beef Pork Potatoes and other farm produce, in short anything that will sell and pay the expenses should be sent, whether the trade yields a profit or not, as it enables us to maintain a large Establishment of People [Fort Vancouver] which on particular occasions might be of the utmost importance to our interest, and would always command respect both in the eyes of Strangers & the Natives.[27]

The *Beaver*'s arrival on the North West Coast liberated a ship or two, and in 1836 McLoughlin had a vessel constantly employed in taking valuable shipments of Columbia produce to Oahu. Pelly built a lumber shed that year, and asked the company's London secretary if he could keep a small assortment of goods on hand 'as a medium of payment for the stores I may be required to procure for the service of the Columbia Department and your shipping.' Approval was granted, and Pelly embarked on the retail trade in 1837, with James Sangster in charge of the store.[28]

Trade, naturally, worked in both directions. The Sandwich Islands' most lasting 'export' to the west coast were its young men, the 'Kanakas,' the hiring of whom solved one of the HBC's labour problems in the 1820s and 1830s.[29] Among Simpson's drastic economy measures of the 1820s was the reduction of personnel to a bare minimum throughout fur trade territory. Some men returned to Scotland or to Lower Canada, many retired to Red River, and others settled in the Willamette Valley. No sooner had they done so than the extension of the fur trade north and south of the Columbia and the opening of new posts required new men. 'In consequence of the extension of trade on the other side of the Mountains,' Simpson wrote in 1827 regarding the Columbia Department, 'there is a constant demand upon us for men which we cannot meet without serious inconvenience to the districts on this side as our Complement at every Establishment has been reduced to what is absolutely required for the transport of Outfits and Returns.'[30] Hawaii was a nearer and cheaper source of labour than Lower Canada or Scotland, and the hiring of Kanakas was encouraged by Simpson.

Kanakas had been employed as crewmen by the maritime fur traders, the Pacific Fur Company, and the NWC. Twelve Kanakas were killed on the *Tonquin* at Clayoquot Sound, and in 1817 Corney hired sixty of them at Oahu for the NWC's coastal operations. Pelly extended and enlarged upon this precedent; in 1840, he sent 'Seventy Natives they are fine young athletic men and engaged to serve the Company for three years.'[31] Father Bolduc stated in 1842 that more than 500 Sandwich Islanders were on the Columbia River in the company's service, and a

Hawaiian newspaper put the number at 300 to 400 on the coast in 1844.[32] These figures must have referred to the total number of Kanakas ever sent to the coast by the company, because that many Kanakas were not in the HBC's employ in the mid-1840s; some had died, others had migrated to the Native community, and others had returned home. Many stayed on the coast and gave their name to such places as 'Kanaka Row' (Humboldt Street) in Victoria, Kanaka Bar on the Fraser, and Kanaka Creek near Fort Langley.[33]

At Oahu, vessels exchanged salmon and lumber for commodities needed on the coast and in the Indian trade, principally salt, molasses, tobacco, and rice – known at the company's agency as 'Island Produce.' Material exports from Oahu to the coast were also of Chinese, Malaysian, Caribbean, and Indian Ocean origin.[34]

Salt, the most important commodity, was needed in the pre-refrigeration era for preserving or flavouring salmon, beef, pork, and butter. As early as 1825, McLoughlin, low on English salt, turned to Oahu and bought up to 300 bushels annually from the Sandwich Islands. In 1828, Simpson asked the G&C to fill up the ship from London with salt, which he called 'a very necessary article, of which, we cannot have too much as what may not be required for our own consumption can be well applied in curing Salmon for the Spanish Settlements.' Salt springs were found on the Willamette River, and salt could be made at Fort Vancouver, but McLoughlin stated that 'to make it here will cost 20/-pr. Bushel and we cannot ever make the quantity we require.'[35]

Excellent sources of salt existed on Oahu. 'Salt is gathered,' Simpson wrote, 'in a crystallized form, from the surface of a small lake about four miles to the west of Honolulu, situated within an old crater about a mile from the sea.' 'In the course of one year, as much as 30,000 barrels have been procured from the spot.'[36] After 1829, the islands replaced England as the main source of salt. Increasing quantities were needed for the coastal trades, especially the salmon fisheries. In 1832, Fort Langley received 620 bushels direct from Oahu, and two years later McLoughlin asked Pelly to fill with salt every ship bound for the coast. This was easier said than done. In March 1835, Pelly wrote that 'There is much difficulty in procuring Salt here, the King and Chiefs having determined not to allow it to be sold under two dollars per Barrel.' Pelly had, however, secured 800 barrels for $1.25 a barrel just before this restriction was enforced. In 1835, the Columbia and Fraser fisheries each received 1,000 bushels, and in 1838 McLoughlin estimated this quantity should be the 'annual supply.' Shipments increased enormously in the 1840s with the expansion of the company's salted salmon and salted beef trade on the coast.[37]

'Tobacco, cotton, coffee, arrow-root, indigo, rice, and ginger thrive luxuriantly throughout the group,' Simpson noted. Indigo cotton of an indifferent quality was grown on the islands, and Ladd & Co. of Honolulu produced sugar from locally grown sugar cane. Simpson considered the islands' arrowroot (a starch) to be 'of a fine quality; but so negligent are the manufacturers in washing and drying the article, that a small parcel lately sent to England by the Hudson's Bay Company did not cover cost and charges.' Silk from mulberry bushes was also produced on the islands.[38]

It is hard to distinguish between goods obtained at Oahu that were destined for the Indian trade and those destined for the company's own workforce. Some island staples, notably tobacco, tea, rice, and molasses, were intended for both.[39] Significantly, the company filled a void caused by the withdrawal of the Americans from the coast. Starting in 1830, Charlton bought tobacco (leaf and plug) and rice; two years later, Finlayson purchased from 11,000 to 12,000 pounds of rice, 6,000 pounds of molasses, and from 1,000 to 1,500 pounds of plug tobacco at Oahu, some from South American merchants. In 1833, Finlayson bought from American merchants in Oahu 30,000 pounds of rice, 50 tuns of rum, 50 tuns of molasses, 200 pounds of vermilion, 20,000 yards of American domestic bleached sheetings, and 50 pairs of black American handkerchiefs – goods required for the coastal Indian trade in the absence of American competition there. In January 1838, McLoughlin estimated the annual supply needed at the islands as 1,800 pounds of coffee and 100 pounds vermilion.[40]

The victory over American traders on the coast threw other business into Pelly's hands. In 1835, he entered into a contract with American merchant William French, of French and Company of Honolulu, for salt, molasses, tea, paint oil, treacle, cocoa, cordage, soap, rum, black camlet, linseed oil, claret, and prayer books; a year later, French provided Congo, Hyson, and Twankey tea from China, and Chinese sugar.[41] Pelly also obtained American leaf and plug tobacco at the islands, and by the early 1840s, Chinese tea and rice and American tobacco were staple demands of the Columbia trade, in addition to molasses, sugar, and salt. In 1831, McLoughlin had even put in a request for quinine (Peruvian bark), presumably for medicinal purposes.[42]

Among the more exotic trade items obtained at the islands were 'China Boxes,' boxes made of sandalwood or camphor wood that were popular as feast or potlatch goods on the coast. Artist Paul Kane, who attended a potlatch near Fort Victoria in the 1840s, noted the 'numerous beautiful Chinese boxes, which find their way here from the Sandwich Islands.' And Japanese sailors, survivors of a junk driven ashore on the coast south of Cape Flattery in 1834, were also recorded in the company's accounting system.[43]

Among other unusual exports to the Columbia Department was coral, burned to make lime for fertilizer, whitewash, and also used in mortar in the foundations of buildings and chimneys. Finlayson sent a batch of coral to Fort Vancouver in 1832, with the following instructions to McLoughlin: 'The coral shipped on board the Eagle is sufficient to make 300 Bbls of Lime. The larger the kiln, the smaller it is pounded or broke down, & the sooner it is burnt after being landed, the more productive it is. It must not be exposed to Rain before burning it, as in that case it is very perishable. It does not require so much firewood as the common limestone, but in every other respect the same process is used in burning it.' Limestone was found on the Willamette River, but did not replace coral. In 1835, McLoughlin asked Pelly to load the *Ganymede* with coral as ballast 'by every trip she in future makes, till we have the quantity we require.' Pelly replied, 'I have only sent 12 fathoms of Coral ... the Chiefs demand an unreasonable high price for it, but at such prices as they choose to dictate.' Vessels were ballasted with coral in 1837 and 1838.[44]

The Oahu agency also had a commercial life of its own in the Pacific economy. Over 200 ships from the north Pacific whaling fleet, as well as British, French, Russian, and American men-of-war, stopped there for refit or repair.[45] Between 1836 and 1839, 369 vessels arrived at Honolulu, 255 of them whalers. Simpson estimated that whalers accounted, in various ways, for nearly half of all local consumption. They required specialized naval stores and hardware that the company, trading directly with London, was in an ideal position to supply. The company's annual vessel bound from London to Fort Vancouver arrived at Honolulu every spring after a voyage of 135 to 160 days[46] carrying special cargoes of 'European Manufactures' or 'Imported Goods' in return for furs from the coast and island produce like mother-of-pearl shell and whalebone. The London-Oahu trade in naval stores and other commodities had little to do with the Columbia Department fur trade or with shipments of Columbia produce; rather, it was the result of a desire to capitalize on an unexpected, new commercial opportunity.

British industrial goods were sold in large quantities after 1837, when Pelly opened a retail store and stocked it with naval stores for visiting men-of-war and especially the whaling fleet. 'So much depends on time in this limited and fluctuating market,' he wrote, 'our Sales are much influenced by the arrival of the Ships in May and Novr, particularly the Novr Fleet, which generally refit here and take in their supplies for their next cruise.' In 1838, the demand for sheet copper and sheathing nails was very great: 'Thirty or forty crates would meet a ready sale at all times from thirty eight to forty four cts. per Pound,' Pelly wrote, and the next year he requested 'Staple articles [that] … would return the Company a handsome profit,' namely anchors, anchor chains, copper sheathing, rolls of canvas, and Stockholm tar. Black and white paint, he said, 'would always sell to good advantage.' In 1840, Pelly ordered sheet copper, ship's paint (black, white and fancy colours), brown canvas, tar, pitch, varnish, paint brushes, iron hoops, copper bolts, and rivets for hoops. He thought that English salted pork and beef would sell well to the whalers, and that arrowroot would obtain a high price at the islands.[47] Pelly also imported Arrowsmith's Pacific charts and English nautical almanacks ('2 Setts of Arrowsmith's Charts of the Pacific Ocean & Islands including the China Seas and Straits of Sunda and Malacca'), and kept up an active commercial correspondence with McLoughlin concerning items required by the whalers. 'Do you manufacture Tar,' he asked in 1835, 'as it is always an article in demand here.'[48]

There was little point in sending vessels to London with light, albeit valuable, continental cargoes of fur if space remained on the ship, so Pelly found local supplementary or ballast cargoes. After 1840, he traded small quantities of whalebone from American whalers (1,347 pounds in 1842). Whalebone had a number of industrial uses, including the manufacture of women's corsets. The HBC's London secretary, Archibald Barclay, made some inquiries in the London market and reported to Pelly and his assistant George Allan that 'Good whalebone is a saleable article here. Columbia 1843 realised £15 per Cwt. Tortoiseshell is worth 23/- to 24/- per lb, Mother of Pearl Shells also sell well say £20 per ton for unpicked, in that state therefore they may be purchased pretty freely if an opportunity offers.' Pelly and Allan replied that 'Whale bone is principally American caught and they prefer sending it to the United States.'[49]

Even more incongruous than the trade in naval supplies and whalebone was the trade in mother-of-pearl shell, used in the manufacture of buttons and furniture inlay. These bivalves, found in the sea and in tidal lakes near Oahu, were caught for their oysters, but their shells also had market value. In 1838, Pelly sent the *Columbia* to London with a cargo containing 27,514 pounds of mother-of-pearl shell (worth £4 a ton) as ballast, as well as furs, slush (waste fat), tallow, and bullock hides and horns.[50]

McLoughlin went to Europe on furlough in 1838-9, leaving Douglas in charge of the Columbia Department. With his usual enthusiasm for commerce, Douglas assured the G&C that he was forcing out competitors for salmon and timber at Oahu by undercutting them, and that he would raise prices once they had gone. Also, he wrote that 'I will not fail to pour in supplies, of Columbia produce, by every opportunity, and endeavour, by that means, to confirm, the impression already produced.' By 1839, the HBC's trade had become so extensive that Simpson enlarged its retail function and provided a colleague for Pelly – his cousin, Alexander Simpson of Moose Factory. Governor Simpson met with the Northern Council of Rupert's Land and decided that 'a commercial establishment on a more extended scale than any that has yet been formed there, would be successful in commanding all good business in that quarter ... those Islands now present a good field for mercantile enterprize.' Alexander Simpson and George Traill Allan arrived in 1841.[51]

The Oahu agency served a larger financial purpose in the islands. Sir John Pelly served simultaneously in the 1840s as Governor of the Bank of England and of the HBC; with his cousin George Pelly in charge of the Oahu agency, the well-capitalized company acted as banker to the Hawaiian kingdom. In 1842, the HBC possessed ties in the City of

London to finance a £10,000 loan to the Hawaiian government. 'Knowledge of markets, shipping practices, and foreign finance were matters of daily routine,' historian Alfred Lomax writes.[52]

Simpson was impressed by the agency. 'This port,' he wrote on his March 1842 visit, 'is more over becoming an entrepot for a portion of the South America, California, Manilla and China markets.' 'For country produce from the Columbia and North West Coast, such as timber, salmon, flour, &c, and a few other articles, there will always be a demand, as we can furnish most of those supplies at a cheaper rate than they can be obtained from elsewhere.' George Pelly, Simpson continued, was not known for his 'business like finish or neatness, but I consider ... that great zeal has been manifested throughout this Agency.' The 1841 requisition was for about £2,500 worth of British goods, though Simpson estimated that future requisitions should amount to between £4,000 and £5,000 a year; Alexander Simpson later recommended the import of British goods valued at 'upwards of ten thousand pounds.'[53]

George Simpson noted that the company rented its premises from King Tuanoa himself, and that a retail store had been commenced 'for the convenience and accommodation of the public.' Always on the lookout for a new way to make money, George Simpson investigated the possibility of opening a trade between the islands and London in 'Kukui, or Candle Tree Oil.' 'The Kukui oil is an article of rising importance. It is extracted from the nut of the *kukui*, or light-tree, which are so unctuous, that, when strung on a twig, they serve the natives as candles ... one of the foreign residents has lately erected a mill for breaking and pressing them so as to separate the juice from the husks.' More than 1,000 barrels of the oil were sent annually to Lima.[54]

Some very substantial cargoes made their way to Oahu from the Columbia and Fraser rivers. The *Dryad* landed a cargo worth $5,000 in December 1835, and the *Ganymede* arrived a month later with $4,900 worth of salmon and lumber. In the first months of 1836, Pelly sold $7,000 worth of Columbia produce; later that year, McLoughlin sent an accountant, Robert Cowie, to instruct Pelly in accounting and to examine his records. In August 1843, Pelly and Allan had on hand Columbia produce valued at £3,907 (or $19,535, at an exchange rate of 5:1).[55] A detailed account of agency sales from July 1843 to February 1844 survived.

TABLE 2 Oahu sales of country produce and imported goods ($), 1843-4

Month	Columbia produce	Imported goods	Total
1843			
July	663.39	518.42	1,181.82
August	1,150.75	292.97	1,443.73
September	881.03	434.75	1,315.78
October	194.10	5.12	199.22
November	1,353.62	248.00	1,601.62
December	693.06	433.52	1,126.58
1844			
January	735.96	1,068.90	1,804.86
February	701.13	328.22	1,029.36

These figures support Pelly's observation in 1839 that business revolved around the arrival of the whaling fleets in May and November.[56]

By 1843, even the hidebound accountants on Hudson Bay were impressed by the rapid creation of a Pacific outlet for the company's goods, and by the trade in ships' anchors, barrelled salmon, coral, mother of pearl, Kukui oil, and Twankey tea. As Dugald Mactavish wrote in April 1842:

> A handsome profit appears to have been made upon the transactions at the Islands for [Outfit] 1841 – of that Amount however there is about £800 merely nominal, the rest is good. We do not have sufficient time to examine particularly the Accounts received from the Islands – or rather their Accounts do not sufficiently explain – upon what the profit has been made – but I strongly suspect it has been principally upon the Timber & other Country produce sent there from the Columbia.[57]

The HBC's agency was a permanent commercial fixture in the island economy and turned an annual profit of £2,000 in the early 1840s. The American whalers' visits were seasonal and ultimately less enduring than the company's permanent business, which saw vessels arriving at all times of year. 'At the Sandwich Islands they [the HBC] have a large trading establishment,' wrote a visiting American captain in 1842, displaying the usual American fears, 'and have commenced engaging the commerce of the country, with evident designs to monopolize it.' Hawaiians and visitors alike grew to depend on the company's high-quality and regular imports of Columbia produce and British naval stores. The HBC agency, a Honolulu newspaper reflected, 'was for years a sort of commercial moderator, a mercantile balance wheel when fluctuations seized on others.' This stemmed from the agency's financial stability, the regularity of its imports, and its proximity to the coast. 'The Company's control of its own shipping,' Alexander Spoehr wrote, 'meant that the Agency could depend on a fairly regular shipping schedule. This gave a competitive advantage to the Agency and benefitted the community through the dependable arrival of imports.'[58]

Indeed, a large transport system was needed to carry on the trade with the islands. Edward Belcher, who arrived at Fort Vancouver in August 1839, noted that the company employed four sailing vessels and one steamer (Table 3).

TABLE 3 Columbia Department shipping, 1839

Vessel	Tonnage	Armament	Crew
Barque *Columbia*	300 tons	6 guns	24 men
Barque *Vancouver*	324 tons	6 guns	24 men
Ship *Nereide*	283 tons	10 guns	26 men
Schooner *Cadboro*	71 tons	4 guns	12 men
Steamer *Beaver*	109 tons	5 guns	26 men

Source: Edward Belcher, *Narrative of a Voyage Round the World, Performed in Her Majesty's Ship Sulphur, During the Years 1836-1842 ... Vol. 1 (London: Henry Colburn 1843), 301*

'One of these sailing ships arrives at Fort Vancouver [from London] in the spring of each year,' Farnham wrote, 'laden with coarse woolens, cloths, baizes, and blankets; hardware and cutlery.' French traveller Duflot de Mofras observed that the HBC's ships were identical, so that rigging and other equipment could be used interchangeably. 'In addition to the English flag that floats aloft, the bowsprit carries the Union Jack. From the mainmast flies the Insignia by which they are always recognized – a pennant consisting of a blue background on which are traced in white the three letters H.B.C.'[59]

These vessels also traded in California, the company's second Pacific market. Mexico had achieved independence from Spain in 1821, and California remained a Mexican province until 1848, when the United States took it over. Before then, California's main exports were cattle hides and tallow (hides produced leather and leather goods; tallow produced soaps, candles, and axle grease). Since 1822, British and American merchants had been active in the hide and tallow trade. In 1826, for example, Captain Beechey of the Royal Navy noted that 'Hides and tallow constitute the principal riches of the missions and the staple commodity of the commerce of the country.'[60]

In 1821, the HBC knew little about California except that its residents owed them money: the NWC had never been paid for some of its commercial transactions there, and the company assumed their debt. By the end of the decade, however, California had emerged, after Oahu, as a natural market for Columbia produce. After initial attempts to sell Columbia lumber and salmon there, the company entered the hide and tallow trade in 1833, and in 1841 established an agency to barter British goods for hides and tallow in the cashless local economy.

California's pastoral economy was based on exports of hides, tallow, and grain, in that order. Wheat from California missions had been traded, on a small scale, to maritime fur traders and to the Russian American Company, and the province also supplied livestock, particularly sheep and cattle, to the company's coastal farms. Horses of an 'inferior breed' abounded on coastal California; Simpson noted that at San Francisco, horses were 'nearly as plentiful as bulrushes.' Yet the California market was limited, and ordinary calico cloth was the principal import.[61]

British travellers were struck by the Californians' dependence on the hide and tallow trade. They saw it as a hindrance to a more extended commerce and a cause of apathy and indolence. The trade attracted neither industry nor a large population, and Californians acquired a reputation for indolence and commercial backwardness in the eyes of the pushy traders from the Columbia. The hide and tallow trade was on the decline: in 1831, there were more than 215,000 cattle and 150,000 sheep in California, but between 1838 and 1844 the number of hides exported fell from 200,000 to 100,000.[62]

British observers of the 1820s and 1830s made a connection between 'pasturage' and 'indolence.' Captain Beechey thought the ease with which the hide and tallow trade was conducted contributed to a 'want of commercial enterprise,' while resident J.A. Forbes wrote that 'Pasturage is ... the principal object pursued in California as in all the Spanish settlements of America. The immense tracts of country possessed by them in proportion to the population, added to the indolent and unenterprising habits of this race of men, renders the pastoral state the most congenial to their situation and disposition.'[63]

The American side of the California hide and tallow trade was recorded by Richard Dana, a student at Harvard College who dropped out and signed on as a crew member of a Boston hide and tallow ship, the *Pilgrim*, owned by Bryant & Sturgis. In 1835-6, he collected and cured bullock hides in California, as described in his book *Two Years Before the Mast*. Dana did not record meeting his rivals from the Columbia, but he did share the Anglo-American view that Californians were 'an idle, thriftless people, and can make nothing for themselves. The country abounds in grapes, yet they buy, at a great price, bad wine made in Boston and brought round by us, and retail it among themselves at a real (12 ½ cents) by the small wine-glass. Their hides, too, which they value at two dollars in money, they barter for something which costs seventy-five cents in Boston.'[64]

The Columbians echoed and enlarged Dana's views. Douglas, in 1841, wrote that 'There indeed appears to be a total overthrow of public morals among this degenerate people, even from the Priest downwards. The Calefornian is proud, lazy and passionate; but kind and hospitable; the vices and virtues of a badly regulated but generous mind.' Simpson went even further, writing that time was 'a perfect glut in a community of loungers.' To Simpson, this was a result of cultural pressures: 'But the population of California in particular has been drawn from the most indolent variety of an indolent species, being composed of superannuated troopers and retired office-holders and their descendants.'[65]

Visitors, nonetheless, appreciated California's climate and commercial potential. In 1837, Commander Belcher of the Royal Navy noted that, 'Taking into consideration the whole port of San Francisco, the Sacramento, and minor streams, there is immense field for capital, if the [Mexican] government could protect its citizens or those inclined to reside.' Forbes thought it presented an inexhaustible field for traffic, an ideal subject for British annexation and colonization, while Douglas thought that no country had 'more attractions than Calefornia' on account of its fertility and agricultural potential. Francis Ermatinger of the Snake Country, who slept between sheets for the first time in twenty-four years while at Yerba Buena in 1843, was decidedly impressed: 'It is a country I like – the people all live and have plenty – yet there is scarcely a dollar in it. A man kills his bullock, eats the beef, and gets what he wants for the skin.' Dugald Mactavish, who spent two months in Monterey in 1846 during its seizure by the United States, wrote that 'The Country is a beautiful one and most fertile – but nothing has been done for its improvement by the late possessors of it, who were altogether too indolent & proud to turn their attention to any thing but killing Cattle and living upon what the hides & tallow would produce in the market.'[66]

Although McLoughlin first mentioned hides as a possible export in 1826, the company's initial foray into California occurred in December 1830, when McLoughlin sent Aemilius Simpson south with a cargo of deals (lumber) and salmon. 'The object of my present visit to this place,' McLoughlin told a Monterey merchant, 'is to endeavour to find a market for Deals & Salt Salmon as it is the intention of the HBCo to encourage the fisheries at their establishments on the Coast & to erect Saw Mills to saw Deals if these commodities will pay. In Upper California I find the demand is very limited for these articles.' George Simpson noted that his cousin's trip had been a disappointment. Lumber and salmon were not in great demand, coin was scarce, and hides and tallow were the sole medium of exchange (a limited one at that), and the Californians did not eat fish. 'It does not appear that any profitable branch of business can be opened in that quarter,' wrote Simpson. He did think, however, that the company might profitably enter the coastal barter trade in hides and tallow.[67]

McLoughlin wanted to examine the markets even farther south, and made plans in 1831 to send Aemilius Simpson the next winter to the coast of Mexico or Peru with a cargo of salmon and deals. Captain Simpson's death, however, destroyed the plan, and it was not until October 1833 that Finlayson left Fort Vancouver with a cargo of deals and salmon bound for 'the California and Wahoo Markets.' He was unable to sell any of the lumber or salmon, and was forced to pay cash for some 15,500 pounds of tallow required in the company's own trade.[68] Finlayson did, however, recruit James Alexander Forbes as the company's very useful agent. Born in Scotland in 1804, Forbes went to California in about 1830 via South America, converted to Roman Catholicism, and married a Californian woman in 1834. During the period 1843-51, he was British vice-consul for California. Forbes owned a large ranch – El Potrero de Santa Clara, two leagues from the San Jose mission – where he farmed and traded. Fluent in Spanish, he was known to the Californians as Don Diego Forbes; de Mofras described him later as the company's 'intelligent agent.' 'Forbes is an active and energetic young man, and an ideal type to further the ambitious plans of the company.'[69]

George Simpson summarized the findings of Finlayson's voyage in July 1834, showing an early caution about extending the HBC's trade too extensively on the shores of the Pacific:

> The object of Chief Factor Finlayson's voyage to California and the Sandwich Islands, was, to ascertain if any advantageous branch of trade could be opened at the former place; and to dispose of timber and other country produce ... Chief Factors McLoughlin and Finlayson seem to think that sufficient Tallow and hides, to fill up the annual ship for England, might be purchased on advantageous terms there ... but I am of opinion that we have quite enough of business on our hands at present on the shores of the Pacific, and am therefore averse to entering on any fresh branch of trade, until our affairs are put on a more regular and uniform footing than they at present appear to be.[70]

McLoughlin did not propose to give up so easily. In May 1834, he sent Captain Langtry with a cargo of deals and spars on an adventure to the ports of California or South America. Langtry's assignment was to sell his cargo by private sale or public auction, to announce that the company would make three voyages a year, and to see if lumber would sell in San Diego. 'You will please to observe that if the timber pays we intend to make a regular business of it – and in course of time would undertake to supply any quantity which might be required from us.' Langtry was to invest the proceeds in a cargo of hides and tallow.[71]

McLoughlin was aware that the company's hide and tallow adventures should not interfere with vessels required in the important fur trade of the North West Coast. He told the G&C that the 1829 plan to export lumber and salmon as far south as Valparaiso and Lima 'may be superfluous' because 'we have been so constantly employed with the coast (which required our first attention) that we have never been able to send to those places till now.' Nonetheless, he hoped to send the *Eagle* in the fall of 1834 to 'some port to the south of this' with spars and salmon, and the *Lama* (Captain McNeill) to San Francisco for a cargo of tallow, for the London market and for making candles and other products at Fort Vancouver.[72]

Accordingly, in July 1834, McLoughlin sent McNeill to San Francisco or Monterey to salt eighty barrels of beef and to barter spars and salmon for tallow. He recommended that McNeill hire Don Diego Forbes to manage his sales at San Francisco in return for a commission of 5 per cent on all sales. McNeill's adventure turned out very well. At San Francisco, he procured twenty casks of tallow and 586 bullock hides, all of which McLoughlin shipped directly to London along with a requisition of goods suitable to the California market. The G&C approved of McNeill's adventure. The California trade, they told McLoughlin, 'should be pushed if it pays at all, as it will afford a freight to our Country Vessels, and a filling up freight in the article of Tallow to the Homeward Ship of the season.' In 1834, the California hide and tallow trade looked promising and enjoyed the active support of the London committee.[73]

Trading adventures continued. Over the winter of 1836-7, the *Lama* collected hides and tallow on the coast of California, but returned from San Francisco with only 3,000 pounds; it was not the tallow season. In August 1837, McLoughlin sent his son-in-law William Glen Rae to California on the *Cadboro*. 'As you know the object of your voyage is to procure Tallow, of which we require about 12 M lbs.' Rae was to go to Monterey if he could not get enough in San Francisco. 'If you find you could trade more Tallow and Hides than the Cadboro could bring, and that you could send your purchases to Oahu, you will do so.' Rae succeeded in this task. In December 1838, the company shipped 979 bullock hides, 4,209 bullock horns, and eight barrels of tallow (1,840 pounds) to England, and in 1840 the *Vancouver* left for England with nearly 16,000 pounds of tallow.[74]

In 1839, Forbes summarized the company's California trading activities in his book *California: A History of Upper and Lower California from their first Discovery to the Present Time.* 'The North-American traders, who are always the first to take advantage of new and remote markets, also turned their attention to California,' he wrote. The company had sent several vessels to California, he said, but trade had not increased for them with hides and tallow as the province's only products, and they had abandoned the effort.[75]

In 1841, however, the HBC opened an agency in California modelled after that at Oahu. It was to offer British manufactures in exchange for hides and tallow, and to serve as a base for the company's fur expeditions up the Sacramento and San Joaquin rivers. Four company officers visited California between 1840 and 1842: Alexander Simpson, James Douglas, William Glen Rae, and George Simpson. Alexander Simpson and Douglas recommended the construction of a post at San Francisco, Rae established the post, and George Simpson surprised them all by shutting it down.[76]

In June 1839, Simpson and the Northern Council instructed an officer to go to California to investigate 'the Commercial operations of that Coast with a view of enabling us to form a Commercial Establishment there hereafter.' Alexander Simpson was selected, and in October 1840 he recommended the formation of an establishment at Yerba Buena. The entire coasting fleet of California consisted of only eleven vessels, mainly British and American, but their owners were opposed to the company's entry into the trade. 'A strong desire is expressed by all,' Simpson wrote, 'except those engaged in the [coasting] Trade, that the company or some other Body of Weight and respectability should engage in the Commerce of the Coast and thus reduce the present exorbitant price of Goods.' He recommended an outfit of £4,000 in British imports, chiefly in cottons.[77]

Simpson found that more than half the exports of California were collected at a little village on San Francisco harbour named Yerba Buena where, he found to his satisfaction, only one small retail shop existed. Two months after Alexander Simpson's visit, in December 1840-January 1841, James Douglas returned on the *Columbia* with an outfit suitable to establish a trading post at Yerba Buena, which he called 'the most favourable point for a mercantile house.' According to Forbes, San Francisco harbour was the largest and safest [port] on the whole western coast of America. About two miles from the entrance to the bay was Yerba Buena, translated variously as 'good herbs' and 'the village of mint.' 'On the south side of the promontory on which stands the fort, Castillo

FIGURE 13 This sketch by an unknown artist, circa 1842, is entitled *The Sea Town and Port Yerba Buena in St. Francisco Bay in California*. The HBC store, purchased in 1841, is the large building marked '1' at the water's edge in the centre of the image. This is now the downtown financial district of San Francisco. [Bancroft Library, Berkeley]

de San Francisco,' Farnham wrote, 'is a little village called Yerba Buena.' In 1843, the village had a population of about 200, consisting of Spanish Mexicans, Indians and a few foreigners.[78]

Douglas kept a journal of his trip to California. 'We have also other objects of a political nature in view,' he wrote on his arrival. He was to buy sheep and cattle for the Puget's Sound Agricultural Company, to secure permission for deployment of the Southern Party; and to buy a building lot or a suitable building for a trading post at San Francisco. Alternately, he was to buy Bodega (Fort Ross) from the Russians, but the Swiss adventurer Captain John Sutter bought it in 1841. 'We ought at all events to start as wholesale dealers,' Douglas wrote, 'and as we aquire experience in the trade, and qualified [Spanish-speaking] agents to manage it, we may find it proper to enter into the minuter ramifications of the business.'[79]

At Monterey, Douglas met General Alvarado, with Forbes interpreting, to work out an agreement concerning the company's projected commercial enterprises in California. The company, Douglas wrote, intended to embark in the general commerce of the country, to sail one or more coasting vessels under the Mexican flag, and to buy a building lot in a convenient position for shipping and receiving goods at Yerba Buena, where the HBC proposed to exchange hides and tallow for British manufactures. As wholesale dealers, he wrote in his journal, the company could supply the country merchants with goods, and receive payment in hides, tallow and grain. 'By pursuing this plan, we would be secure from great risks.'

Douglas's negotiations were an unqualified success. Alvarado told him 'that we might carry on any business we thought proper in the Californias, with the express sanction of Government.' Douglas also met General Vallejo's brother-in-law Jacob Primer Leese, who offered to sell his waterfront lot and store at Yerba Buena for $4,000.[80] As noted in Chapter 5, Alvarado also gave permission to send beaver hunters to the interior of California. Douglas referred to 'these not illiberal concessions': 'By taking advantage of them, we may found a permanent business of considerable value, which will yield an immediate return for capital.'[81]

In August 1841, William Glen Rae (brother of the Arctic explorer) and clerk Robert Birnie returned to establish the Yerba Buena agency. For $4,600, Rae bought Leese's waterfront store, built in 1837, in what is now the downtown business district of San Francisco. 'If it be the Companys wish to drive a profitable business here,' Rae told McLoughlin in October, 'and put down competition, they must embark more extensively in the Trade than at present.' With more trade goods, a vessel for the coastal trade, and between $20,000 and $30,000 in cash annually, Rae believed, the trade could be entirely engrossed. He enlisted Forbes to act as agent for the sale of goods and purchase of hides throughout the bay and along the coast. Originally on the waterfront, the company's premises were located in what is now the block bounded by Montgomery, Sacramento, Clay, and Kearney streets in present-day San Francisco. De Mofras called the company's 'the largest and finest house' at Yerba Buena, and a visitor in November 1841 observed that the company's store was the best of half a dozen houses in Yerba Buena. 'It is built of wood, shingled, &c., and of the old-fashioned Dutch form.' It was the first two-storey wooden house in San Francisco.[82]

Great expectations were held out for this establishment, both for its wider commercial possibilities and for its utility to the Southern Party trappers. 'At California,' Dugald Mactavish told Hargrave in April 1842, 'handsome returns are expected in the way of Hides which are as valuable as Beaver in the London Market.' By November 1842, Rae had collected 20,000 pounds of tallow, 5,000 bullock hides, 3,000 *fanegas* of wheat, 445 otter skins, 254 beaver skins, and some sea otter skins.[83] Rae also accepted Bills of Exchange, as did Pelly at Oahu.

The French traveller de Mofras, who visited Yerba Buena in 1842, described some of these activities. With considerable exaggeration, he wrote that the HBC 'maintains its principal depot at San Francisco; another is close to San Jose, and a third near Monterey. The company intends to establish additional posts at Santa Barbara and Los Angeles, and to use light vessels to carry merchandise and take hides and tallow.' He noted that the company had established a 'factory' at San Francisco to prepare their own hides, and had investigated the harbours of the Mission of Santo Domingo and San Francisco with the idea of extracting some of the extensive salt deposits as yet unexploited that existed in both places.[84]

American visitors, characteristically, were suspicious of Rae's rapidly extended operations, and described the company's plans with their usual combination of admiration and exaggeration. In May 1842, Henry Price, an American sea captain lately returned from California, wrote that

> at San Francisco they purchased a large establishment and depot for merchandise; and they intend this year to have a place of the same kind at each of the principal ports of Upper California. Two vessels are building in London, intended for the same trade – that is, for the coasting trade; and after collecting their cargoes, to carry them to England. These things, with others, give every indication that it is the purpose of the Hudson's Bay Company to monopolize the whole hide and tallow trade of California, a trade which now employs more than half a million of American capital.[85]

In the fall of 1843, American overlander Lansford Hastings described Yerba Buena:

> This is a delightful site for a town ... The Hudson's Bay Company having seen, the superior importance, of that section of country, located at that place, at an early day, where it now has an extensive trading establishment, at which,

a very extensive trade, is now carried on, both with the Mexicans and the foreigners. The gentleman in charge of that establishment is Mr. Raye, who is not only a very intelligent business man, but also an honourable, kind and hospitable gentleman. He receives and entertains foreigners with the utmost kindness and attention and without regard to their national origin ...[86]

Simpson, however, got cold feet on his January 1842 visit, and he ordered the post's closure as part of his plan to reorganize the company's Pacific business toward the north. He was aware of California's commercial potential, but scared by its government and personality: 'English, in some sense or other of the word, the richest portions of California must become: either Great Britain will introduce her well regulated freedom of all classes and colours, or the people of the United States will inundate the country with their own particular mixture of helpless bondage and lawless insubordination.'[87]

He described Yerba Buena as a settlement destined, 'under better auspices, to be the site of a flourishing town, though at present they contain only eight or nine houses, in addition to the Hudson's Bay Company's establishment.' The G&C supported Simpson's plan because sales of the company's hides in London had not been favourable. McLoughlin, unaware of their decision, instructed Rae to keep trading tallow, and eventually Rae got caught in a bitter struggle between Simpson and McLoughlin over the agency's worth. Tragically, he committed suicide in 1845.[88]

Dugald Mactavish sold the store property in 1846 for $5,000. Two years later, gold was discovered on the Sacramento River on Captain Sutter's property, and Yerba Buena became the major city on the west coast of North America. 'To think how such a place could have sprung up in so short a space of time,' one fur trader wrote, 'and what a contrast it now presents to its appearance a few years ago – when nothing but the hide and tallow trade was carried on.'[89]

Sitka, the Russian American Company's settlement in Norfolk Sound, was the third market developed by the HBC. The company was concerned not so much by Russian competition as by that of American merchants, who supplied the Russians with provisions and foodstuffs and traded for furs on the North West Coast. The HBC's strategy, therefore, was to replace the Americans as provision suppliers, for this would provide a local market for Columbia produce and discourage American traders from visiting the coast for any reason. Aemilius Simpson offered to supply the Russians with Columbia produce as early as 1829, and in 1832 Ogden met with Baron Wrangell at Sitka; he proposed to supply the Russians with food and merchandise as a way of forcing out American suppliers. Wrangell declined the offer. Four years later, following the *Dryad* affair, Finlayson returned to Russian America for general discussions. He knew that the Russians faced provisioning problems: they were unable to grow more than garden vegetables at Sitka, and their wheat supply from Fort Ross in California was precarious.[90]

The two companies were united by a desire to rid the North West Coast of American traders who traded alcohol to Native people to the detriment of the Russian and British trades at Sitka, Fort Wrangell, and Fort Simpson. Finlayson suggested that the HBC's farms on the Columbia were now advanced enough to supply the Russians for less than American traders based at Honolulu and Boston. Provisions could be taken up the coast on the *Beaver,* and stored at Fort Simpson if necessary. In September 1836, Finlayson wrote that the governor of Sitka 'fully agreed with me that an understanding of this nature between the two companies would be beneficial to both,' and furthermore that 'It will show the American adventurers that we have entered the Sitka market.'[91]

Thus, a union of Russian and British commercial interests was planned. In 1838, Douglas reported that while the Russians appeared content to receive their supplies from a merchant house in Boston, 'It would be very satisfactory to furnish supplies on terms mutually beneficial.' An agreement with the Russians would rid the Russian coast of American vessels engaged in the supply trade, just as the company's trade extension had rid the rest of the coast of American fur traders. Meanwhile, Simpson was in Hamburg negotiating with Baron Wrangell of the Russian American Company over the Russians' future grain supplies. In their extensive bargaining sessions, Wrangell said he could get the grain from Chile; Simpson insisted that he could provide Columbia grain for less.[92]

There is no more impressive indication of the success of the company's farms than the agreement Simpson reached with Wrangell in Hamburg in February 1839. The HBC was to supply the Russian

FIGURE 14 Sitka, the Russian depot on Baronof Island in the north Pacific, was the third offshore market tapped by the HBC in the 1830s. In 1839, George Simpson entered into a contract to supply this colonial settlement of the Russian American Company with foodstuffs. [*The Russian American Company Headquarters at Sitka*, undated sketch by an unknown artist, Hudson's Bay Company Archives, Provincial Archives of Manitoba, N5380]

American Company with Columbia produce and peltries for a period of ten years in exchange for a lease of the coast and the interior country between Cape Spencer and 54°40' north latitude. In exchange, Simpson agreed to provide 2,000 sea otter skins from west of the mountains and 3,000 land otter skins from east of the mountains, or their equivalent value. In addition, he agreed to sell the Russians 2,000 *fenagas* (126 tons) of wheat in 1840 and 4,000 *fenagas* annually thereafter, as well as 300 cwt. salted beef, 160 cwt. wheat flour, 160 cwt. salted butter, 130 cwt. peas, 130 cwt. grits and hulled pot barley, and 30 cwt. pork hams.[93] Such exports, ten years before, would have been unthinkable. The companies also agreed to ban the sale or trade of liquor on the entire coastline.

Douglas visited Sitka in May 1840 to hammer out the specifics of the lease and provision contract. He showed the HBC's customary disappointment with the commercial ability of traders of other nationalities. He met men at Sitka 'most unqualified to manage commercial undertakings.' 'The business of the Russian American Company does not appear to be conducted with system or that degree of well-judged economy, so necessary in extensive concerns.' The contract subsequently earned the HBC an annual profit of $8,000-10,000, forced American suppliers out of the provision and fur trades, and opened a new market to the HBC.[94]

By 1843, the company had capitalized on its Pacific presence by locating three offshore markets for its produce. Although Simpson had to abandon the goal, first expressed by Dalrymple and Mackenzie, of marketing Columbia Department furs in China, he did find an outlet for new west coast exports at Oahu. All pelts from the department continued to be sent annually by ship to London for auction, in a transport regime modelled on the company's much older trade on Hudson Bay. A new regional export economy appeared in the 1830s in the path of the company's fur trade extension through the Columbia. The company's success at Oahu, Yerba Buena, and Sitka resulted in part from the abundant resources and favourable conditions on the lower Columbia and Fraser rivers.

CHAPTER 8

Columbia
Country Produce

*Deal boards are now as much thought of as Beaver
and a transport of them has already been made to the
Sandwich Islands.*

— FRANCIS ERMATINGER,
THOMPSON'S RIVER, 1830[1]

In contrast to the harsh interior districts, the west coast fur trade unfolded in a region with abundant resources, and where mild, sedentary winters promoted the development of a complex social realm. 'The climate is softened by the influence of the Pacific,' Thomas Simpson wrote regarding the lower Columbia, 'food is abundant; the numerous natives do not lead the same solitary wandering lives as the eastern tribes, but dwell together in villages.'[2] This abundance supported a dense Native population, far in excess of that of the interior. In 1826 McLoughlin estimated that 2,000 people lived between the Dalles and the Pacific, though European diseases had already ravaged the coast.[3] The Hudson's Bay Company established its headquarters in the midst of this Native world, and responded and adapted to the natural abundance of the lower Columbia by building a new depot featuring extensive provision trades, as well as export trades in salmon, lumber, and agricultural produce.

Visitors from the other side of the mountains were impressed by Fort Vancouver. Dugald Mactavish, on his arrival in 1839 from east of the mountains, wrote to his brother that 'The Company have got an extensive farm here and a large complement of men is required, so that the business may be properly carried on. The Fort is so very large that on first arriving a stranger is almost apt to imagine himself in the civilised

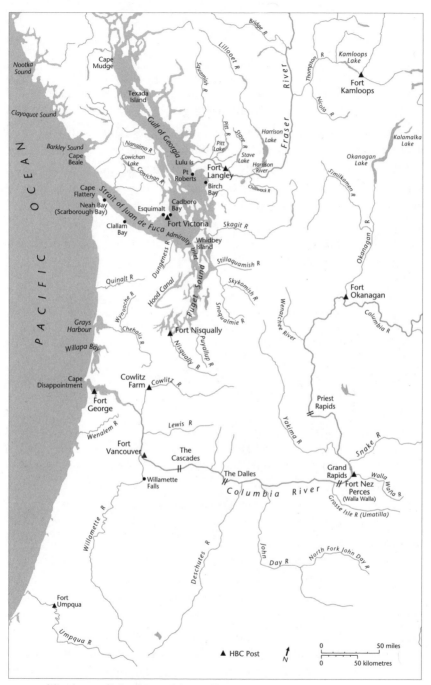

MAP 17 The lower Columbia and lower Fraser regions, 1843

world.' The fort itself, Belcher wrote, was 'a picketed enclosure three hundred yards square, the pickets being eighteen feet high, composed of roughly-split pine [cedar] logs.'[4]

The fort possessed storage facilities on a large scale, including a wheat store, a beef store, and four others, tanneries, a pharmacy, a Catholic church that doubled as a school, a blacksmith shop, cooper shop, carpenter shop, tinsmith shop, a 'Sale Shop' for Willamette farmers and visitors and an 'Indian Shop' for the fur trade and other Indian Trades. 'They raise their own foodstuffs,' wrote an American missionary in 1829, 'cultivate barley, malt it and make beer which they will soon be able to export in small quantity.' The Fort Vancouver distillery was dismantled in the early 1830s due to its bad effects after producing only 300 gallons.[5] The fort was the scene of prodigious activity, as Lansford Hastings observed:

> Within this fort, you see nothing but stirring activity, and the most persevering industry; officers, clerks, mechanics and servants, are always to be seen constantly passing and re-passing, each intent upon the prompt and efficient discharge, of his individual duty; which, together with the diligent and incessant plying of the hammer, sledges and axes, and the confused tolling and ringing of bells, present all the impetuous commotion, rustling, tumultuous din of a city life, in the oriental world.[6]

The annual supply ship ('London Packet' or 'English vessel') arrived every spring; Ogden recalled that for weeks before its arrival it was the only topic of conversation at Fort Vancouver. Paperwork was done by clerks who worked very long hours. Fifteen clerks, de Mofras asserted, 'spend their time trading with the Indians, selling goods, or keeping books. They arrive at their offices punctually at seven o'clock and work until nine at night.' The depot, he decided, was 'in reality nothing more than a supply and accounting house for the city of London.' Joe McKay recalled that the actual Indian Trade was conducted by clerks and interpreters: 'Most of the intercourse with the Indians was carried on through the interpreters, who were under the control of the clerks or other officers who might have charge of the trade department for the time being, each officer having his special charge, for the good conduct of which he was responsible to the Chief Factor.'[7] In 1840, Farnham took the reader on a tour of the depot:

We will now enter the fort. The blacksmith is preparing ploughshares, har-
row teeth, chains and mill irons; the tinman is making cups for the Indians,
and soup-kettles, &c; the wheelright is making waggons; and the wood parts
of ploughs and harrows; the carpenter is repairing houses and building new
ones; the cooper is making barrels for pickling salmon and packing furs; the
clerks are posting books, and preparing for the annual returns to the board in
London; the salesmen are receiving beaver and dealing out goods.[8]

FIGURE 15 This sketch by Paul Kane shows Fort Vancouver from an unusual inland
angle, with HBC fields in the foreground and a company ship docked at the wharf
on the Columbia River in front of the fort. [*View of Fort Vancouver, Looking South,*
1846 or 1847, Royal Ontario Museum, 946.15.211]

The fort and its industries required a large complement of clerks,
tradesmen, and labourers. By 1838, seventy-four tradesmen worked at the
fort, namely 'Saw Mill 26 Forge 9 Coopers 4 Millers 2 Cattle & Dairy
7 Swine Herds 3 Shepherd 1 Farm labourers 10 Hospital 1 Bakers 3
Carpenters 3 Stores 1 Domestics 4.' There were, Simpson wrote three
years later, between 130 and 200 people at Fort Vancouver according to
the season of the year, including 'agriculturalists, voyageurs, blacksmiths,
tinsmiths, carpenters, masons, tailors, shoemakers, &c &c.' In 1840, sev-
enty-six of these were French Canadian. Labourers worked, according
to Simpson, 'the regular hours, say from 6 to 6.'[9]

In 1835, McLoughlin defended himself against an accusation that Fort
Vancouver was overstaffed:

I am told a Gentleman on the other side said, the work of this place might be done with twenty five men. The Saw mill alone requires twenty, and besides, we have the farm, the Indian trade, the Salmon fishery, to load and unload vessels, to reinforce when required other places, the drawback caused by the fever, and to keep a set of tradesmen constantly employed such as Blacksmiths, Coopers and Carpenters, and it is certain, that whoever is the person that said that twenty five men would suffice for the work of this place proves by his asserting this, that he is ignorant of what is done here.[10]

The river at Fort Vancouver was a mile wide, and wharves on the shore permitted the moorage of vessels. Hastings, who visited in 1842-3, wrote that the company's vessels measured from 200 to 700 tons:

They are all engaged, the greater part of the year, in importing goods from England, and exporting wheat, furs, fish and timber in return. One of these ships arrives every spring, with a stock of goods, which having been disposed of in that manner, a cargo of lumber is taken to the Sandwich Islands, or a cargo of goods and flour to Sitka or Kamschatka. Having disposed of their freight, at the prices last mentioned, these vessels return to Vancouver, in the latter part of the summer, where the furs, collected during the previous year, are shipped to England.[11]

From the satellite fishery and sawmill, the company exported salmon and lumber, as Belcher explained in 1839: 'In the neighbourhood about two miles down the river, they have a very extensive dairy, numerous cattle, sheep, pigs, goats, &c.; and about three or four miles up the stream, water-mills, for grinding, sawing planks, and an establishment for curing salmon – the two latter objects forming the principal export to the Sandwich Islands.'[12]

McLoughlin found it difficult to manage this extensive post on his own. In 1837, when he wanted to go on leave, he argued in favour of two chief factors for Fort Vancouver. 'Mr Finlayson ought to have remained,' he told the HBC Governor and Committee, 'as the business of the place is became so extensive, and I may say so complicated that there ought always to be two Commissioned Gentlemen attached to this place, intimately acquainted with the business – that in case of accident to one the business would still go on.' Nonetheless, the G&C appointed Douglas to the sole interim management not just of Fort Vancouver, but of the whole Columbia Department. Before his departure in 1838,

McLoughlin reminded Douglas that 'As you well know the Business of the Place may be classed under four heads the Farm, the Depot, the Indian Trade and the saw mill.' The farm, McLoughlin continued, was the most important: 'I have always considered the farm as an object of primary consideration as without provisions the different Branches of the Business cannot be carried on.'[13]

Salmon and potatoes were the common fare, the main rations included in labourers' and tradesmen's contracts. 'Their weekly rations,' Simpson stated in 1841, 'are usually twenty-one pounds of salted salmon and one bushel of potatoes for each man; and in addition to fish, there are also venison and wild fowl, with occasionally a little beef and pork.' Fort Vancouver's example was emulated elsewhere, and employees received, ideally, this balance of Native provisions (usually salmon or venison), cereals, and vegetables. 'There were never better fed working men in any country,' McKinlay claimed, 'they had graham flour, sometimes horse-meat, potatoes, turnips, dried salmon, fresh salmon, bear meat, grease, ducks, and all other kinds of game, usually unbolted flour, never tea, coffee, or sugar. They had milk and butter.'[14]

The abundant resources of the lower Columbia provided the Chinook people with a variety of marine life, including sturgeon, oolichan, and their principal provision, salmon. Scouler and Douglas, on their arrival in the spring of 1825, reported that 'Everywhere the banks of the river were tolerably thickly inhabited by a people who never till the ground, and who subsist almost entirely by fishing.'[15] Indeed, Native people travelled up to 400 miles to fish for salmon at the mouth of the Columbia. Its price and nutritional value had made salmon the ideal provision for the maritime fur traders, and the staple food for the Pacific, North West, and Hudson's Bay companies, though the Northwesters seem to have been first to systematically exploit the fishery. In 1816, Corney wrote that the Chinook people around Fort George had 'not the least notion of tilling the ground; they trust to Providence for every thing, and derive their chief support from the river and sea.' Franchère noted that salmon were caught either in strong nets made of nettle fibres or with spears 'made of two small pieces of curved bone in the middle of which they put a small iron point about half an inch long.'[16]

Like fur, salmon was traded from Native people; the HBC did

FIGURE 16 A British naval officer was one of the few visitors to record what must have been a common sight. The Native people of the lower Columbia River provided the HBC with labour and fresh salmon, the raw ingredients of its provision and export trades. [Edward Belcher, *Canoe, Columbia River,* 1839, University of British Columbia, Special Collections Division]

not employ European fishermen. Dunn, in charge of Fort George in the mid-1830s, left an invaluable description of the lower Columbia fishery:

> The salmon season, of those tribes towards the mouth of the Columbia, commences in June: and its opening is an epoch looked forward to with much anxiety, and is attended with great formality. They have a public festival, and offer sacrifices. The first salmon caught is a consecrated thing; and is offered to the munificent Spirit, who is the giver of plenty. They have a superstitious scruple about the mode of cutting salmon; especially at the commencement of the season, before they have an assurance of a plentiful supply. To cut it crosswise, and to cast the heart into the water, they consider most unlucky, and likely to bring on a scarce season. Hence they are very reluctant to supply the traders at the stations with any until the season is advanced, and they can calculate on their probable stock; lest an unlucky cross cut by the whitemen may mar their prospects. Their mode is to cut it along the back; they take out the back bone, and most studiously avoid throwing the heart into the water. The heart they broil and eat; but will not eat it after sunset. So plentiful is the fish, that they can supply the white men in abundance.[17]

The fish were traded both fresh and dried. 'We had abundance of salmon brought to us by the native tribes, which was purchased cheap and which we found excellent,' David Douglas wrote on his arrival in 1825. 'This being the season of salmon-fishing, I had opportunities of seeing prodigious numbers taken, simply with a small hoop or scoop net fastened to the end of a pole. The salmon is excellent in quality, averaging 15 lb. in weight. The seine is resorted to as a means of taking salmon in the still parts of the stream with great success.' Corney wrote that 'the salmon they cure by splitting it up into four slices, and running splinters of wood across them ... These they also dry in the sun, and then hang them up in the houses, where they are soon smoked and laid by for use. They are cured without salt, which is never used.' After the abundance, the most appealing thing about Columbia salmon was the price. British and American visitors bought large fish for trade items worth between one and six pence.[18]

So prolific were Columbia salmon that seals from the Pacific followed them as far as the Dalles, 200 miles from the ocean. Below the Dalles,

FIGURE 17 On 25 August 1845, Henry Warre produced this fine watercolour wash and pencil sketch entitled *Salmon Net Fishing, Head of the Cascades on the Columbia River*. Native people provided the HBC with all the fish required for provision and export on the Columbia and Fraser rivers. [National Archives of Canada, C-047014]

Simpson counted seventeen hair seals at work among the salmon in 1841. 'These animals ascend the Columbia in great numbers in quest of the salmon; and certainly that fish is sometimes taken with a hair seal's mouthful out of its side.'[19] At the Dalles was a native fishery that David Douglas visited in June 1825. He observed 'an almost incredible number of salmon,' and bought two 35-pound fish 'for two inches of tobacco (½ oz.) value two pence, or one penny each. How little the value from that in England, where the same quality would cost £3 or £4 ...'[20]

The company traded salmon principally at the Cascades, Fort Vancouver, and Fort George. At the foot of the Cascades – 'the lowest of the three portages of the Cascades' – the HBC employed men to catch and cure salmon. The product of this fishery was sent by boat to Fort Vancouver, and some was also marketed in the late 1830s at Oahu as 'Cascade Salmon.' The Fort Vancouver fishery was located on the north side of the Columbia, opposite Sauvie Island, a few miles downstream from the fort. It was here that Tolmie hired young Klickitat Indians to seine salmon for the company in the 1830s. The company also salted salmon on the Cowlitz River, near its farm there, and occasionally at Willamette River or Falls.[21]

The main fishery was at Fort George, where patterns of procurement, storage, and transport emerged in the 1830s. The extended Fort George fishery originated during its days as a North West Company depot. Abandoned between 1825 and 1829, Fort George by 1835 was, Dunn wrote, 'now only a small outer depot, belonging to the company's head quarters at Fort Vancouver, and kept up for the convenience of the trade with the Indians towards the mouth of the river; and for the salmon fishery.' In charge of James Birnie, the post was busy during the salmon season and quiet at other times ('Birnie vegetates still at Fort George,' a friend wrote in 1833). In 1839, Belcher noted that nothing remained of the extensive depot of the Pacific and North West companies. 'A small house for Mr. Birnie, two or three sheds for the Canadians, about or eight in number, and a pine stick with a red ensign, now represented Fort George.'[22]

Pillar Rock, a seasonal fishing camp, was attached to Fort George for practical and accounting purposes, and in 1842 the company also had a smoke house for drying salmon at Oak Point, near Tongue Point, some miles upriver from Fort George. *Bateaux* connected the fishing stations to Fort Vancouver. 'They have likewise,' Dunn wrote, 'other craft, during the salmon season, for the conveyance of supplies to the fishing stations on the parts of the river unnavigable to the larger craft.'[23]

Native fishers brought salmon by canoe to Fort George and Pillar Rock, where they were exchanged for small trade goods rather than for blankets, which were reserved for the fur trade. At Fort George in 1825, McLoughlin explained that blankets would be devalued if they were used for the salmon trade:

> As to the Indians wanting Blankets for fish it is certainly true we might get more fish or meat for a Blanket than for the same value in any other kind of Goods But as Blankets is one of the few Articles held in Estimation by the Natives about this place and for which we will only take Furs – were we to take payment in fish for Blankets the value of the latter would be so reduced in the Eyes of the Natives, we would have some difficulty in getting furs from them.[24]

The fish were processed by Native women and then delivered to the company's coopers, who packed them in barrels, or in casks known as tierces (literally, a third part), in size between a barrel and a hogshead. Dunn managed the fishery in the mid-1830s, and left an eye-witness account:

> *Mode of Curing Salmon.* As soon as a cargo of Salmon is caught, the natives bring it to the trading post in their canoes. A number of Indian women are employed by the traders, seated on the beach, with knives, ready to cut up the fish. The salmon are counted from each Indian, for which a ticket is given for the quantity, large or small. After the whole of the salmon are landed, the Indians congregate round the trading shop for their payment, and receive ammunition, baize, tobacco, buttons, &c.
>
> The women employed by the trader commence cutting out the backbones, and cut off the heads of the salmon. They are then taken to the salter, and placed in a large hogshead, with a quantity of course salt. They remain there for several days, until they become quite firm. The pickle produced from these is boiled in a large copper kettle; and the blood, which floats by the boiling process to the top, is skimmed off, leaving the pickle perfectly clear. The salmon are then taken from the hogshead and packed in tierces, with a little more salt; the tierces are then headed up, and laid upon their bilge, or widest part, leaving the bung-hole open; the pickle is next poured in, until the tierce becomes full; a circle of clay, about four inches high, is then made round the bung-hole, into which the oil from the salmon rises. This oil is skimmed off; and, according as the salmon imbibes the pickle, more pickle is poured in, so

as to keep the liquid sufficiently on the surface, and afford facility for skimming off the oil. After the oil ceases to rise to the circle round the bung-hole, the salmon is then supposed to be sufficiently prepared; the clay circle is cleared away, and the hole is bunged up. Salmon, so cured, will keep good for three years.[25]

Salmon awaiting export or domestic use was stored at Fort George or Fort Vancouver. Prior to export, 'Fort George Salmon' was kept apart from 'Pillar Rock Salmon,' though in Oahu both were known as 'Columbia Salmon.' Salt was sent from Oahu, usually in the spring, and kept in barrels at forts George or Vancouver; salt destined for Fort Langley was also stored at Fort George, or taken there directly. Country-made barrels were supplied from Fort Vancouver, and Langley barrels undoubtedly found their way south. In this industry, salmon was abundant; salt and barrels were scarce. 'We must salt all the Salmon we can, & on the return of the Broughton she will be sent to you with a Load of empty Barrels, & so on till we have sent all we have,' McLoughlin told Birnie in July 1832.[26]

Columbia fishery records have survived for part of the 1830s. At the end of June 1835, McLoughlin sent Dunn and others to salt salmon at Pillar Rock. They remained active until August, when McLoughlin sent a vessel downstream to pick up all the salted salmon and empty barrels from Pillar Rock. These seasonal rounds continued. 'On arrival at Fort George,' Douglas told Captain Brotchie, who was on his way down the river on 4 June 1838, 'you will land a sufficiency of Salt to complete the summer curing, and be regulated by the same rule in passing at Pillar Rock.' In August, Douglas ordered an incoming vessel to collect the Pillar Rock salmon for Fort Vancouver.[27]

The strictest economy was observed. In June 1839, Douglas told Birnie that 'Our salmon casks are all full, and we are now filling all the old water casks about the place; and I must entreat you to follow the same plan, in order to secure every ounce of provisions that can be scraped together.' In August, Douglas asked for all the fish cured on the lower river and for any salt remaining at Fort George, and at the end of the season he ordered Birnie to send him 200 barrels of salt, as well as 'all the Pillar Rock Salmon, and as many Barrels of Fort George fish as she can conveniently receive. The "Vancouver" when she is passing at Fort

George will land 4 or 5 hundred Bushels of Salt for the fishery of next year.'[28]

Because barrels were scarce, Birnie made a 'salmon box' at Fort George in 1840 for the temporary bulk storage of salmon. In salmon season, Birnie filled the box with cured salmon, and returned empty barrels to Pillar Rock for refilling, so as to continue to salt salmon as long as possible. In August, McLoughlin urged Birnie to keep the pickle in the box until he could send some casks from Fort Vancouver. The box was later lined with sheet lead from England.[29]

An indication of how highly the HBC valued its fishery was given in August 1840, when Kenneth McKay and a Native youth were killed at Pillar Rock. In August, McLoughlin sent a circular letter to the missionaries in the valley and to the Willamette settlers stating that 'One of our men Kenneth McKay and an Indian boy have been murdered by the Indians at Pillar Rock.' McLoughlin, who referred to McKay's peaceful conduct, asked for, and received, the help of all non-Native people (including American missionaries, ships' captains and crews) in a punitive expedition, led by Tolmie and McLoughlin. On 26 August 1840 the outing achieved its object; Michel Laframboise shot one Native 'murderer' (a slave) through the chest and another Native man was hanged.[30] McLoughlin, wrote an American missionary, decided this man 'was worthy of the death penalty according to the laws of Great Britain & America. He was therefore, by orders of the Governor, hung by the neck until he was dead, at 1 o'clock p.m.' Similar expeditions occurred regularly over the next twenty years on the coast of the Columbia Department.

Such an abundant and inexpensive food was too good for the provision trade alone. 'Were a foreign market to present itself,' wrote Northwester Alexander Ross, 'the natives alone might furnish 1,000 tons annually.' As early as September 1826, McLoughlin proposed to export barrelled salmon to California if the G&C would send him salt by the next ship from England:

> We can purchase Salmon in the Columbia at an Average of 3½ to 5d. Each ... and thirty of these will fill a Barrell and I am given to understand it would sell well in New California – If you sent us Eight to Ten Barrels Salt for the purpose we might Salt forty of fifty Barrels, send them to Monterrey, Exchange them for all the Salt we want, sell the Remainder and see if any thing could

be done in this way ... the Experiment would not cost much. If the Business was well managed we might Salt a thousand Barrels p. Annum in the Columbia – I understand Salmon is more abundant in Frasers River than here.[31]

Over the winter of 1828-9, Aemilius Simpson learned that salmon would sell for twenty dollars a barrel in Monterey, and in November 1830 McLoughlin sent Simpson to California with lumber and sixty barrels of salmon. He had wanted to send the vessel 'to the South to Lima, touching on her way at California and perhaps at Acapulca with Salmon or Boards to ascertain the demand and prices of these articles,' but the vessel was needed to establish Fort Simpson the following spring, and was thus unable to visit Lima or Valparaiso. However, no one in Monterey wanted the salmon, and the company never found an opening for the fish in California. But a small sample of Langley salmon shipped to the Sandwich Islands at the same time met with instant success,[32] and Oahu became the principal destination.

HBC salmon quickly found a market in the Sandwich Islands. An 1831 consignment of thirty-three large barrels sold out, and Richard Charlton, the company's Oahu agent, sent samples to Manila and China with merchant Mr. French. The next summer, Finlayson reported that Mr Short, a 'Gentlemen of the Catholic Mission, exchanged a Barrel with the Captain of an English Whaler, which was sold in London for £4 Sterling, & was highly esteemed.' Sensing a good thing, in June 1832 McLoughlin sent another 180 barrels of salmon to Oahu (eighty barrels from the Columbia and 100 from the Fraser), and in July, Finlayson went there to market the fish and other produce. Columbia salmon had also been sent to the eastern seaboard of the United States by an American merchant, who told Finlayson it would fetch sixteen dollars a barrel there. Salmon from the 1832-4 shipments found went from Oahu to California, Lima, Valparaiso, Callao, Lintin, Manila, and London, both as a ship provision and a proper export.[33]

The G&C were delighted when they heard of these transactions, and they offered encouragement to McLoughlin, Finlayson, and Pelly. They urged Pelly to accept goods in barter, an important condition in an economy where trade items were first valued against, and then exchanged for goods of an equivalent value.[34]

TABLE 4 Columbia River salmon exports, 1830-43

Date	Vessel	Origin (River)	Market	Barrels/half-barrels/tierces	Value ($)
November 1830	*Dryad*	CR	California	60	
October 1831	*Ganymede*	CR	Oahu	33	20
June 1832	*Eagle*	FR, CR	Oahu	180	15
October 1833	*Dryad*	CR	Oahu	57/128 T	
May 1834	*Nereide*		California	108/66 H	
September 1835	*Dryad*	FR, CR	Oahu	252/115 H	6
November 1836	*Columbia*		Oahu	200	
1837	*Columbia*		Oahu	21	
February 1838	*Nereide*	FR, CR	Oahu	178/10 H	8-9
December 1838	*Nereide*		Oahu	200	
June 1839	*Vancouver*	CR, FR	Oahu	110	
November 1839	*Vancouver*	FR, CR	Oahu	170	8-11
May 1840	*Columbia*	CR	Oahu	10	
June 1840	unknown		Oahu	400	6
1842	*Vancouver*	CR	Oahu	695	4,170
1842	*Cowlitz*		London	200	1,250
January 1843	unknown		Canton	140	
January 1843	unknown		Boston	300	
Total				3,315 barrels	

Note: CR – Columbia River; FR – Fraser River
Sources: Most figures are from HBCA C.7/177, but see also York Factory Country Produce Account Book, 1828-36, HBCA 239/d/491, fo. 56; Pelly to Smith, 1 January 1837, HBCA A.11/61, fo. 20; Columbia District Country Produce Inventories Outfit 1837, HBCA B.223/d/106, fo. 8; June 1840: McLoughlin to Spalding, 19 June 1840, HBCA B.223/b/27, fo. 36; St. Clair, 'Beaver in Hawaii,' 41; Fort Vancouver Account Book, 1836-1860, HBCA B.223/d/212; Pelly and Allan to McLoughlin, 12 January 1843, HBCA B.223/b/30, fos. 18-19

At Oahu, the company's salted salmon entered the Native diet. Sockeye was the preferred species. 'They would slice it up into small bits, and with the addition of tomatoes, green onions, water and ice would serve up a tasty dish called *lami lami* salmon.' The Russians, incidentally, offered the company no competition, though they salted the equivalent of 1,500 barrels of salmon a year at Sitka. The Russian salmon were, Simpson noted in 1841, so inferior 'in richness and flavour, to such as are caught to the southward, that they are not adapted for exportation.'[35]

By the mid-1830s, the Pacific salmon trade was established, and about 200 barrels of salmon were sold annually in Oahu to merchants, Native islanders, and visiting whalers. The September 1835 shipment of 252 barrels was the largest yet to leave the coast: invoiced at six dollars a barrel, it was worth $2,082. In November, the *Columbia* left Fort Vancouver with another 200 barrels; the company also sent a large shipment in February 1838. In April that year, salmon was selling at eight or nine dollars a barrel, and by the end of May, only seventy-eight barrels of Langley salmon and twenty-two barrels of 'Cascade Salmon' remained.[36]

Douglas, who took over from McLoughlin in 1838-9, promoted the efficient production and marketing of salmon. In less than a year, he sent 480 barrels of Columbia and Fraser salmon to Oahu; by March 1840, it had all sold for ten to eleven dollars per barrel. Figures are missing for 1841, but in 1842 Douglas sent an imposing shipment of 695 barrels valued at $4,170. Soon there was a surplus, and McLoughlin started selling salmon wholesale to visiting American merchants on the Columbia. In June 1840, he sold 109 half barrels to Captain Spalding of the *Lausanne*, from New York, part of a large 'speculation' for 400 barrels that Spalding planned to sell in New York.[37]

As long as the international boundary was unsettled, the threat of American competition in the fishery itself remained. In 1826, when McLoughlin first considered a salmon export trade, he had argued that 'It is certain if the Americans come they will attempt something in this way.' Three years later, the North West Coast trader John Dominis, captain of the *Owhyhee*, fulfilled McLoughlin's prophecy. He spent the winter of 1829-30 on the Columbia River and in July 1830 left for Boston with 53 barrels of Columbia salmon. The fish, however, sold for only $14 a barrel, and 'proved of indifferent quality, and difficult to work off at retail.' Two years later, in 1832, Nathaniel Wyeth rekindled Dominis's plan for an American salmon trade, but at first he believed that the HBC's powerful opposition would ruin his plans: 'The Salmon alone without the fur I seem doubtfull.' He told his Boston backers that Native fishermen would take too long to get the fish to the traders: 'salmon would in this case be from 6 to 30 hours out of the water which is far too long in this warm climate.'[38] He decided that a profitable fishery could only emerge if the Indian fishery were bypassed. The salmon taken to Boston by Dominis were 'not in the best order,' which Wyeth believed resulted 'from their having been caught too long before they were salted.'[39] A dependence on Native fishers could be avoided, Wyeth believed, by importing Kanaka fishermen to the Columbia River.

Wyeth formed the Columbia Fishing and Trading Company and returned overland in 1834. He sent the *Mary Dacre* to the Columbia via Oahu, where the captain hired thirty Kanakas as fishers. As Townsend recorded in March 1835, 'We have had an accession to our crew of thirty Sandwich Islanders, who are to be engaged in the salmon fishing on the Columbia, and some of these have been allowed the unusual privilege of taking their wives with them.' Wyeth started a farm on Sauvie Island as a provision base, and by February 1835 he was prepared to cure salmon for New York. In May, the *Mary Dacre* arrived from Oahu with the Kanakas. They found the overland party busy with the fishery, and that fall McLoughlin learned that Wyeth had salted about 300 tierces of salmon, 'but this is so much less and they cost so much more than he expected, that I am told by some, that he is going to drop the business.' Wyeth's scheme collapsed in 1836 —'The Salmon fishing establishment by Wyeth has done the right about,' wrote W.G. Rae in March 1836 — and McLoughlin bought Wyeth's entire operations. McLoughlin later claimed that he opposed Wyeth 'so effectively as to prevent his getting even half a cargo, and which destroyed his opposition at once,'[40] while Dunn, the company's expert from Fort George, attributed Wyeth's failure to inappropriate technology and his use of Kanaka fishermen:

A Mr Wyeth, of Boston, having heard much of the salmon fishing in the Columbia, and thinking it would afford a profitable trading speculation, chartered a vessel, in 1835; and on his way took a number of the Sandwich Islanders as fishermen; supplying himself also with a cargo of fishing nets, and a great variety of other fishing apparatus, on the most approved principles. On arriving at the Columbia he set vigorously to work, dead sure of making a fortune. But his nets were totally unfit for the occupation; and his exotic fishermen, notoriously familiar as they are with the watery element, were no match for the natives, pursuing their natural occupation in almost their indigenous element, and so familiar with the seasons, the currents, the localities, and all the many other circumstances that ensure success.[41]

American merchants were unable to establish a successful Columbia River export fishery before 1846.[42]

The fishery was in a prosperous condition when Simpson took his final leave in 1842. He observed that with a view 'of affording freight for our shipping, and of benefitting by the demand in the Sandwich Islands, a quantity of salmon, according to the state of the fisheries, is cured here for the market, besides what is required for the use of the establishment.' De Mofras, who met Simpson, noted that the company exported annually to the Sandwich Islands and London about 600 barrels of salmon.[43]

After Simpson's departure, the company sent three large shipments, totalling 650 barrels, to London, Boston, and Canton to test new markets and remove some of its supplies. In May 1842, Simpson ordered the *Cowlitz* loaded with a return cargo of salmon and other produce for London, but the shipment of 200 barrels failed. The ship passed through a hot climate, and the fish, though heavily salted, deteriorated so much that they sold for only 22 shillings a barrel (about $5). Moreover, the G&C reported that too much blood was left around the backbone of the fish for the London palate, and that a tariff had recently been placed on foreign salmon. 'There is therefore no chance that this article will ever succeed here, and it must in future be reserved for markets more within reach.'[44]

At the same time, Pelly and Allan sent large consignments to China and the United States, as they explained in January 1843 to McLoughlin:

> As for the Salmon we are absolutely overwhelmed with that article ... and as the hot season is now fast approaching, we have been induced to act upon your advice, and consigned one hundred and fifty barrels to China on account of Vancouver Depot having most fortunately found a vessel here bound thence, we have also consigned three hundred barrels to the United States, and are sorry to say no very favourable results can be anticipated from either of these adventures ...[45]

These two consignments turned out poorly, due not to spoilage but to freight and commission fees charged by shippers and by the Canton and Boston merchants selling the salmon. The big advantage at Oahu was that such charges were absent; as middleman, the company controlled the fate of the fish from the time they were traded to the time they were sold.

The 300 barrels sent to Boston sold for $7.25 a barrel, which was, Pelly and Allan warned, 'a tolerably fair price but from that there remains to be deducted Freight, Charges, &c &c.' After expenses, the Boston consignment realized only four dollars a barrel which, they concluded, did not 'hold out any inducement to continue our consignments to that quarter.' The Canton shipment showed the company willing to take direct advantage of the 1833 relaxation of the East India Company's monopoly of the China trade. Pelly and Allan consigned 150 barrels to the Scottish merchant house Jardine Matheson & Co. of Canton, whose letters, however, 'do not prognosticate great things.' McLoughlin, meanwhile, hoped that the salmon would be exchanged in Canton for 'such of the Manufactures or productions of China as may sell to advantage' at Oahu or Fort Vancouver, and Jardine Matheson was asked 'to invest the proceeds of the fish in teas, an article which is always in great demand in the Columbia.' In March 1845, however, Pelly and Allan received bad news from Canton. 'We have just received the closing account of the consignment of 150 Barrels Salmon to China and are sorry to find that it has turned out very unsatisfactorily – the net proceeds being only an average of 3 dollars pr Barrel and which we have received in Tea for Columbia River.' The prospects for the sale of salmon in foreign parts, Pelly and Allan concluded, was not flattering, and thereafter they concentrated on Oahu, which by the end of the 1840s absorbed up to 2,000 barrels a year.[46]

The company's lower Columbia farms also yielded exports of flour, butter, and potatoes that piggy-backed on the salmon trade. References to Columbia wheat first appear in the early 1820s;[47] by 1830, Fort Vancouver provided flour for itself, the North West Coast, the country shipping, and the annual English ship. After about 1836, the agricultural opening of the Willamette Valley provided the company with an unexpected windfall in the form of wheat purchased from Canadian and, after about 1840, American settlers in this 'garden of the Columbia.' The Willamette possessed continuous ranges of fern-covered prairie. 'No felling of trees or grubbing is necessary here,' wrote a visiting American naval officer; 'A two-horse plough prostrates the rankest fern, and a fine crop of wheat the very next year succeeds it.'[48] The company stored the wheat in its granaries, as Douglas noted in March 1838:

The prosperity of the general business, is so intimately connected with the agricultural operations, and depends, so much upon the possession of an ample and regular supply of Provisions, that it long since became a desederatum with us to secure independently of the rising crop, a full years provisions, in advance, and it is now attained, as our barns contain a sufficient quantity of the more useful kinds of grain to meet the home and outward demand ... for the next eighteen months.[49]

Whalers wanted flour at Oahu. Finlayson reported in 1832 that 200 barrels of 196 pounds each would command a market during the March and October whaling visits. McLoughlin sent fifty barrels in 1834, which sold quickly, and the next year he sent another fifty valued at ten dollars each. These small shipments, he complained, resulted from the 'present inefficient state of our Grist mill' that, operated by an ox, furnished flour 'barely sufficient for our land and naval Establishments.' A better mill would permit larger exports.[50]

During Douglas's term in charge of the department, he displayed his usual energy for the wheat and flour trades. In October 1838, he announced that he was putting up 'a water power Grist Mill, adapted for two runs of 54 inch stone. A Barge of 40 tons burden, for River transport, is also in a state of considerable forwardness.' In 1839, he completed the Fort Vancouver mill, with a capacity of grinding between 80 and 100 bushels of wheat a day, and another granary near the fort, with a capacity to hold 18,000 bushels. As Farnham noted in January 1840: 'The HBC have erected during the past year at Fort Vancouver a very extensive granary and other edifices of a permanent character, and a grist-mill five miles above the fort ... This is in operation night and day, and grinds and bolts in forty-eight hours one hundred and twenty-five bushels of wheat.' Farnham continued: 'The grist mill is not idle. It must furnish bread stuff for all the posts, and the Russian market in the northwest. And its deep music is heard daily and nightly half the year.' Located on a stream known as Mill Creek, the grist mill was run by an Orkney man named John Stensgair (Stanger).[51]

The granary allowed the company to store wheat from its own farms and, increasingly, from the Canadian farmers in the Willamette. In 1836, Douglas bought about 1,000 bushels, their surplus produce, and in October 1838 he wrote that 'I am now buying up the crop of this season, to clear the market and leave nothing in store for casual visitors, a policy that ought not to be neglected.' In 1844, Demers noted that the HBC harvested 15,000-20,000 *minots* of grain on the lower Columbia, and bought the same quantity from Willamette and Cowlitz settlers. Flour, like everything else, became a bone of contention between Simpson and McLoughlin. In 1844, Simpson referred scathingly to McLoughlin's belief that a 'sufficient quantity of Grain should be sent to the Sandwich Islands to meet the demands of that market & of Sydney, & suggests that it might be found worth while to send flour to them (Sydney), some 7000 or 8000 miles distant! ... McLoughlin's views appear to us wild & speculative in the extreme.' By the mid-1840s, the company produced or traded large amounts of wheat, ground it at the new grist mill, and exported over 1,000 barrels a year to Oahu.[52]

The dairy farm on Sauvie Island produced surplus butter for export. Finlayson had reported in 1832 that the whaling vessels at Oahu would buy twenty to thirty firkins of butter regularly (a firkin is a small barrel containing nine gallons). 'Good butter is always an article in demand,' Pelly wrote, and in 1835 McLoughlin sent him twelve kegs, each containing eighty pounds of Columbia butter. In 1838, McLoughlin sent another twenty kegs to Oahu. The Sauvie Island dairy, which Simpson visited in 1841, was a substantial operation. 'At the dairy, we found a hundred milch cows,' wrote Simpson, 'which are said to yield, on an average, not more than sixty pounds of butter each in a year.' After 1839, Columbia butter was exported to Sitka to meet the company's provision contract with the Russians.[53]

In May 1811, Franchère had planted a dozen potatoes at what was then Fort Astoria; by 1820, the Fort George potato crop amounted to 1,000 bushels, and James Keith called potatoes 'our most valuable produce' along with salmon. The HBC introduced these tubers at all its Columbia posts, and Fort Vancouver produced 4,000 bushels a year by the late 1820s. Like all successful provisions, potatoes were soon considered for export. Finlayson reported in 1832 that every March and October, the company could dispose of 400 bushels to whalers at Oahu, and thirty barrels of potatoes were indeed sent there in 1838. Belcher, in his 1843 *Narrative*, wrote that potatoes had become a Columbia River export to the Sandwich Islands.[54]

Lumber was the other major non-fur export from Fort Vancouver. Newcomers, especially botanists like David Douglas, William Tolmie, and

Meredith Gairdner, were impressed by the magnificent timber on the lower Columbia. On his arrival in April 1825, Douglas wrote that 'The greater part of the whole country as far as the eye could reach is closely covered with pine of several species.' 'The trees which are interspersed in groups or standing solitary in dry upland ... are thickly clad to the very ground with widespread pendent branches, and from the gigantic size which they attain ... form one of the most striking and truly graceful objects of nature.' Finlayson noted the 'tall & stately timber' that threw 'their strongly defined shadows across the placid surface' of the mighty river, as did Tolmie and Gairdner on their canoe trip on the Columbia in 1833. Tolmie recorded the 'gigantic relics of the primaeval forest, which form a broad belt extending to the river's edge.'[55]

There was a world of difference between these romantic evocations of magnificent timber and serviceable lumber. The HBC entered the lumber trade knowing that everyone from Captains Cook and Meares to the American North West coasters had sent loads of spars and roughly sawn lumber to Oahu. However, these were sporadic, not systematic shipments, and the quality was poor, as Boston merchants Bryant & Sturgis noted in 1821: 'NW Coast vessels generally have a great deal ... of all such lumber & trash as is of no great value.'[56]

The company's lumber trade was conceived between 1825 and 1827, when the timber at the mouth of the Columbia attracted the notice of traders and Scottish botanists alike; species such as Douglas fir were identified and described at this time by company botanists. McLoughlin sent a cedar log to England for examination, only to have it identified as 'a species of soft Pine' of little value. In 1825, Simpson suggested that the company's ships be put to work during the dead months of the winter taking salmon and spars to Canton and South America, but his plan could only take effect with the North West Coast fur trade in operation. Far to the north, the American coasters continued their spar and rough lumber exports to Oahu; such exports, with the rapid decline in the sea otter trade, became more systematic and more valuable. Aemilius Simpson reported in 1828 that a great part of the crew of American coasters cut trees on shore and squared and sawed them into planks aboard ship, 'with which and Spars they fill up their vessels for the Sandwich Islands, where it commands a very high price.' Most of this activity took place at or near Russian ports like Kaigani, which the missionary Jonathan Green visited in May 1829. 'Kigani has always been much visited by traders,' he wrote. 'More or less boards are sawn on board ships during the season, and sold at the Sandwich Islands. At this place timber for this purpose and for masts has been obtained.'[57]

Late in 1827, Aemilius Simpson examined the lumber market in California and Oahu; he discovered that boards would sell in Monterey for forty or fifty dollars per thousand feet. 'If you visit the Owhyee Islands,' McLoughlin told him in November 1827, 'you will Enquire what price Deals will sell and the size most in Demand we are told they would bring sixty Dollars pr M feet.' McLoughlin had already started building a water-powered sawmill located on a 'never-failing stream of water' that fell into the Columbia about five miles upriver from Fort Vancouver.[58]

No detailed description or illustration of the Fort Vancouver saw mill, the first commercial logging operation on the west coast of North America, has survived, but fur traders' and travellers' accounts are available. 'We now have a Small Saw Mill a going,' McLoughlin announced in July 1828. When Francis Ermatinger visited a few months later, he found the mill 'knocking off from 70 to 100 deals per day and it was thought would do better in higher water.' In November 1829 Captain Dominis of the *Owhyhee* purchased a number of twelve-foot boards from 'Dr McLochlin.' The water-powered machine was, Simpson wrote, an experimental sawmill. At first, timber was dragged from the forest by two yoke of oxen, and the mill possessed a single saw operated by a primitive 'muley' system. The machinery was brought from England and installed by a millwright, William Frederick Crate, who came overland specially in 1828. He and an old Astorian, William Canning (or Cannon), managed the mill thereafter, and eight Kanaka labourers loaded lumber aboard company vessels moored in four fathoms of water at the river bank. In 1829, the mill's annual expense was about £150.[59]

Soon the mill was enlarged. In March 1835, James Douglas recorded in his journal that 'We landed at the Saw Mill, and remained there for nearly an hour. It works 12 saws, and cuts about 3500 feet of inch boards during the 24 hours.' In 1837, the mill employed ten yoke of oxen and twenty-eight men, and large stocks of lumber were dried at the mill for export. Beginning in 1835, McLoughlin wrote, he always had a spare cargo of lumber ready for shipment when a vessel was available, and in October 1837 he had 200,000 feet of sawn wood ready for export.[60]

TABLE 5 Columbia River lumber exports, 1828-43

Date	Vessel	Market	Quantity	Value ($)
1828	Eagle	Oahu	n/a	100.00 @ 1,000 ft.
1829	Cadboro	Oahu	15,501 sq. ft.	
August 1829	Ganymede	Oahu	63,305 sq. ft.	6,330.72
March 1830	Vancouver	Oahu	13,750 sq. ft.	
November 1830	Vancouver	Oahu	13,000 ft.	
November 1830	Dryad	Monterey	35,930 sq. ft.	
October 1831	Ganymede	Oahu	25,653	2,746.52
June 1832	Eagle	Oahu	43,408 sq. ft	5,531.68
May 1833	Eagle	Oahu	42,384 sq. ft.	4,775.64
October 1833	Dryad	Oahu	18,180 ft.	2,321.90
May 1834	Nereide	California	n/a	
July 1834	Lama	California	n/a	
November 1834	Eagle	Oahu	n/a	491.40
March 1835	Dryad	Oahu	41,562 ft.	2,334.48
September 1835	Dryad	Oahu	100,000 ft.	50.00 @ 1,000 ft.
October 1835	Ganymede	Oahu	121,842 ft.	
April 1836	Ganymede	Valparaiso	114,422 ft.	45.00 @ 1,000 ft.
June 1836	Columbia	Oahu	160,000 ft.	6,300.00
November 1836	Columbia	Oahu	34,230 sq. ft.	1,368.80
May 1837	Lama	Oahu	41,141 ft.	4,542.60
February 1838	Nereide	Oahu	147,785 ft.	
November 1838	Columbia	Oahu	58,000 ft.	
December 1838	Nereide	Oahu	59,000 ft.	
June 1839	Vancouver	Oahu	n/a	
November 1839	Vancouver	Oahu	100,000 ft.	
May 1840	Columbia	Oahu	n/a	
November 1840	Vancouver	Oahu	n/a	
[Nov] 1842	Vancouver	Oahu	n/a	307.20

Sources: Most of these references are from HBCA C.7/177. Others are from McLoughlin to McLeod, 1 February 1830, McLeod Papers, NAC; McLoughlin to G&C, 24 November 1830, HBRS 4, 95; York Factory, Country Produce Account Books, HBCA 239/d/491, fos. 44, 56, 67, 68, 80; McLoughlin to Governor, Chief Factors, Chief Traders, Northern Department, 29 August 1835, HBCA B.223/b/11, fo. 41; HBRS 4, 152 n. 1; McLoughlin to Simpson, Chief Factors, Chief Traders, 30 August 1837, HBCA B.223/b/17, fo. 32; Fort Vancouver, [Country produce list], HBCA B.223/d/94; McLoughlin to Simpson, 5 September 1836, HBCA B.223/b/15, fo. 66; 'Columbia District Country Produce Inventories Outfit 1837,' HBCA B.223/d/106, fo. 8; Pelly to Smith, 30 April 1839, HBCA A.11/61, fos. 51-2; Farnham to Poinsett, 4 January 1840, in Farnham, Correspondence Outward; St. Clair, 'Beaver in Hawaii,' 41

McLoughlin initiated a lumber trade in 1828. He hoped to market the lumber in California, but he was disappointed. In the 1830s, Oahu became the company's major lumber market, as well as an importer of Columbia River spars. Table 5 shows available lumber export statistics.

In July 1828, McLoughlin told the G&C that the sawmill had already produced a few planks. 'Would it be worth while to fill up the Vessel with deals of this kind? We can procure them with little additional labour.' Simpson arrived a few months later, and in March 1829 he and McLoughlin revived the idea that lumber and salmon exports could subsidize the costly North West Coast fur trade. During the dead season, from October until March, lumber could be sent to the south or to Oahu:

> Towards this object, a Saw Mill is already erected within Four Miles of Fort Vancouver which with only one Saw will give 300,000 feet of Deals p. Annum, and by removing it at an expense of about £100, twenty miles from hence, to the Falls of Wilhamet, where whole Forests of Timber can be floated into a very fine Mill Seat, which Dr. McLoughlin & myself have examined, Saws enough could be employed, to load the British Navy.[61]

He estimated that the cost of shipping deals was about ten shillings per thousand feet, and that if two vessels were engaged in the trade, a profit of about £5,000 a year could be expected after port dues, commissions, and all other 'Sacrafices and Expenses.' Simpson hoped that the lumber business, 'in which the shipping will be employed when the [fur] Trade of the coast is over, will I trust make up the loss we shall incur at the outset of the Opposition.'[62]

All Simpson needed was a market. He believed that the Californian and Spanish coasts offered the best potential, and proposed to employ agents in South America to save costs of marketing and distribution. The English house John Baggs & Co. of Lima seemed especially suitable for this purpose:

> This House, if found perfectly respectable, might be a good channel through which to transact our business, as they are very extensively connected all along the California, Mexican and Peruvian Coasts. Indeed, if we go into the business, it is necessary that your Honors should make the appointment of Agents, and the more extensively connected on the Coast, the better, so that we may

have merely to deliver our Cargoes, and return in time for the Fur Trade to
the Northward, as great inconveniences and delay, might be occasioned, by
hawking our Timber from Port to Port, along the coast.[63]

The G&C approved of the plan, and sent McLoughlin letters of introduction and credit to the English merchants Walford & Green of
Valparaiso and Conception (Concepción), and also to John Yates of
Lima, 'to whom you can consign any Timber, Salmon or other Produce
you may wish to send to those Markets ... These houses will in all probability find an outlet at other parts of the Coast.'[64]

The first Mexican shipment was in November 1830, when Aemiluis
Simpson took the *Dryad* to Monterey with about 36,000 feet of deals.
McLoughlin had wanted Simpson to take the vessel to South America,
but the *Dryad* was needed to establish Fort Simpson and could not go
farther south. The adventure was not a success: Captain Simpson traded
some lumber for hides at Monterey at a poor rate of exchange, and he
died on his return to the coast. McLoughlin's ambition to send another
cargo south in 1831 was postponed. At this time, California produced
enough lumber for its own use, and even exported a little to Oahu.[65]
This limited market was met by local producers, and the company looked
elsewhere.

Oahu became the HBC's closest market: the main destination for
Columbia produce, the principal entrepôt for vessels returning to England to obtain 'make-up' cargoes, and the source of staple foods needed
on the coast, like salt, sugar, molasses, and rice. The islands had been
stripped of sandalwood by American traders during the sea otter era; as
Manley Hopkins, Simpson's secretary, recalled, 'Sandal wood abounded
on the heights, but was lavishly cut down as an article of commerce, till
the tree was nearly exterminated.' Without sandalwood, the Sandwich
Islands lacked good building materials, and after the ravages of Pacific
storms the whalers needed spars and masts, which were provided by the
immense Douglas fir forests of the lower Columbia.[66]

The market was not exactly void of lumber, however. Competition in
Oahu came principally from Sitka, and also from New Zealand and the
eastern seaboard of the United States. In about 1834, the Russian American Company had built water-powered sawmills twenty miles south of
Sitka. As Belcher noted, 'Their most valuable wood is a very fine-grained

bright-yellow cypress, of which they build boats, and export the plank in payment of debts contracted for supplies from the Sandwich Islands, (principally China and other goods).'[67] Sporadic shipments, usually in the form of ballast or make-up cargo from the distant United States and New Zealand could not compete at Oahu, though they served to glut the market on occasion.

In the fall or early winter of 1828, the first export of sawn lumber from the Columbia River to Oahu took place, when Aemilius Simpson took a cargo on the *Eagle*. Right away, he and Charlton sold some boards for $100 per 1,000 feet. Charlton thought that 200,000 feet might be sold there at once. Shipments followed, and Charlton sent Columbia lumber to the Seeward Islands where, he wrote, 'there is a good deal of building going on.' Another two shipments followed in 1830, McLoughlin telling Charlton in November that 'The fall in the price of Deals is greater than we expected but as we intend to follow up the business and supply the Owhyhee Market with as many Deals as they will purchase providing the business pays, I send the schooner Vancouver with a small quantity as per accompanying invoice to ascertain.'[68] In January 1831, Charlton responded:

> In respect to the Lumber business from your River to these Islands I think it may be entered into to a considerable extent by having an assorted Cargo, say half boards, the remainder Oak plank logs and scantling: one fault found with the Columbia boards is their length, as they would be more saleable if they were longer say 20 feet: the scantling most saleable would be 3 by 4½ Inches … the immense quantity of Lumber brought into this market during the last two years has of course lowered the prices.[69]

In March 1831, McLoughlin reported this news to Simpson, adding that the Americans would drop the business when they learned of the HBC's Columbia exports. Simpson replied that by keeping the company's shipping 'constantly employed in this trade during the dead season on the Coast, we hope to glut the market so completely as to make the Lumber trade a losing business to the Americans, which would prevent their following it up and in due time give us the entire command thereof.' In October 1831, McLoughlin sent a cargo of plank, rafters, and oak logs, and a similar cargo in June 1832. 'The present is of the same description,' he wrote, 'except that there is no oak, which is scarce in this quarter; however in future we expect to be able to supply you with some.'[70]

Finlayson accompanied the *Ganymede* to Oahu in October 1831, and bought the *Lama* from sales of lumber and salmon. In August 1832 he reported that

> the market has been overstocked lately with timber, that it is now become a mere drag. Cargoes of it have been landed from New Zealand, Van Diemen's Land, & a number of Ships from the United States fill up their Spare room therewith. The N.W. Coasters land a considerable quantity, principally Spars, & the Whalers exchange it with the Natives for supplies & Provisions. From this overstock, it has been sold so low as 20 dollars pr M feet [but] ... it will again command from 45 @ 50 dollars per M feet, & the consumption at this place being according to the best information I can obtain, about 300,000 feet, you may readily perceive we could afford to compete for securing the market to ourselves, that our Lumber would pay, & yield a handsome profit.[71]

McLoughlin sent two large cargoes in 1833, but the market was depressed, and in 1834 he sent only a small shipment. Rafters that should have sold for two dollars went for only sixty-five cents, and McLoughlin was pessimistic. Prices unexpectedly improved, and in 1835 the doctor sent another three ships with pine boards, deals, rafters, and Fort George spars. These spars were probably aimed at New Zealand shipments and American imports from Russian America.[72] In his covering letter, McLoughlin wrote:

> Our saw mill is in full operation, and as we saw wood of any dimension required and I would request you would inform me, which size is most saleable, as our timber has sold so low of late at Woahoo we will only have about a cargo for the Dryad by the time she returns ... [so] give me your opinion of the quantity you think might be sold annually at Woahoo, and the price it wd. probably fetch.[73]

In Oahu, HBC agent George Pelly complained of imports from Sitka and New Zealand, and asked the company for ash logs for making cart shafts and spokes. 'If you could send 100,000 Shingles, about 18 Inches long and well made they would meet a Sale at $8 a thousand,' he wrote. 'I will send you a shingle by way of a specimen of those in demand here the Russians seem very desirous of engrossing the whole Lumber supplies to this place and by the great improvement and extent of their saw mill are likely to become formidable competitors.' American fur trader Hall Kelley, who accompanied the *Dryad* from Fort Vancouver to Oahu in March 1835, identified the HBC's exports as fir boards and other lumber, white oak ship timbers, spruce knees and spars, and white ash oars.[74]

The HBC agents devised transport and market arrangements for Columbia lumber. On one occasion in 1835, there was a dispute over quantity: the cargo of the *Dryad*, anchored at Honolulu, was loaded onto a raft, and a man on the beach counted the deals as they were taken ashore. From the beach, Pelly said, the lumber was 'taken in carts up to the Deal yards, not 40 yards from the Beach.' They were counted again before being offered for inspection and sale.[75]

Meanwhile, in 1834 McLoughlin had sent two cargoes to the south, perhaps because the Oahu market was glutted. The *Nereide*, sent in May, and the *Lama*, sent in July to Yerba Buena, Monterey, and South America, were to make 'a regular business' of the southern lumber trade. Their cargoes consisted of boards, rafters, squared and rough pine logs, and thirty spars, but low prices affected sales, and McLoughlin considered dropping the business if demand did not improve.[76]

In October 1835, McLoughlin suggested that Pelly sell lumber by retail. 'Deals have been sold latterly by wholesale,' he wrote, 'pray can none be sold by retail also, as it seems to me it would be the means of obtaining a better price for them.' Pelly took his advice, and the G&C, who had been watching with interest, suggested in December that McLoughlin flood the market and drive out the competition: 'With regard to the Sandwich Islands Timber trade, instead of feeding the market sparingly in order to keep up the price, thereby affording a good market for Timber brought from the United States and New Zealand, we think that a large stock, say a year's consumption, should be always kept up in the hands of Mr George Pelly which would very soon put a stop to the further importation of Timber by the Americans.'[77]

The success of the lumber venture caused the G&C to take an expensive sawmill out of mothballs at Moose Factory on James Bay. Made in 1811 in Aberdeen, the mill had been sent to Hudson Bay during the Napoleonic wars, when the French blockade had severed Britain from the Baltic timber and continental fur markets. Combined with a hope of providing a profitable return cargo for the Red River immigrant ships, the mill had prompted a timber adventure between 1809 and 1817. In 1809, the company sent a lumberman, Alexander Christie, to Moose Factory with a gang of men who erected the steam-powered sawmill on an island in the Moose River. Despite difficulties in erecting the mill, in cutting and preparing timber, and with unusually cold weather, Christie sent several shiploads to London in 1814 and 1815, by which time, however, the peace in Europe had led to the recovery of continental markets. The lumber export business, which had suffered from distance, mechanical problems, lack of suitable transport, and winter freeze-up, was abandoned. Attended with heavy expense, the project collapsed in about 1817, and the company returned for good to the fur trade on Hudson Bay.[78]

In March 1835, however, the G&C ordered that the old sawmill and steam engine be packed up and returned to England, 'as they will probably be required on the west side of the mountain.' The machinery was received in London in October 1835, and a few months later the G&C obtained drawings from the Aberdeen foundry to enable the mill to be resurrected on the Columbia. The mill would not arrive at Fort Vancouver until late 1836 or early 1837.[79]

By 1836, the company had a ship engaged full time in the Oahu lumber trade. In June, McLoughlin sent the *Columbia* with a cargo of 160,000 feet of pine boards, planks, and oak logs, the largest cargo of lumber ever to leave the west coast. McLoughlin remained optimistic about the company's exports because shipments from the United States, Sitka, and New Zealand remained casual and unsteady. By the beginning of September, Pelly had sold all his lumber except for a large cargo bought by the *Columbia*.[80] Two further lumber shipments of pine rafters, boards, and deals occurred in 1836-7. Pelly advertised the second shipment, received on the *Lama*, in the *Sandwich Islands Gazette* as consisting of boards, beams, and rafters of various dimensions. 'The above for sale, at wholesale and retail, in quantities to suit purchasers,' he noted.[81]

McLoughlin was still tempted by South America. In 1836, when business in Oahu was again slow, he sent William Eales of the *Ganymede* to England via South America with a large cargo of lumber consigned to R.F. Budge, an English merchant at Valparaiso, who had agreed to act as agent. McLoughlin wrote to Budge, asking him to sell the lumber immediately, to keep a commission for himself, and to buy a cargo of his choice at Valparaiso and send it, or the money earned from the sale, to London. He also gave him permission, if required, to buy a cargo at 'Mount Video, Bueno Ayres, or Rio de Ganeiro.' McLoughlin gave Captain Eales letters of introduction to English houses at all three ports.[82]

The *Ganymede* left Fort Vancouver in mid-April 1836 with 114,400 feet of pine boards and rafters. In August, Eales and Budge wrote from Valparaiso to say that they had sold the lumber for forty-five dollars per thousand feet, had paid a heavy duty, but had secured a freight home of copper ore valued at £1,350. On his way, Eales stopped in Iquique, a port in northern Chile, to take in some saltpeter for London. This circuitous Pacific adventure did not please the G&C because profits only slightly exceeded port and other expenses. They were also confounded by its sporadic and irregular nature: the G&C did not want their vessels tramping from port to port, buying and selling cargoes like any private adventurer. Oahu presented greater advantages in terms of proximity and regularity, and in February 1837 the G&C prohibited such adventures to South America: 'We have therefore to desire that none of our ships be allowed to touch there on their homeward passage in future but that they be dispatched from the Sandwich Islands, with no other cargo than the Furs or other returns that may be shipped from the Columbia for England, unless a good filling up freight can be procured at the Islands direct for London.' The company did not thereafter sell lumber from the Columbia Department on the Spanish-speaking coasts.[83]

In April 1838 Pelly reported that the company's lumber dominated the Oahu market. 'There was a large stock in the yards of several timber merchants,' Douglas wrote, 'chiefly of Columbia growth. Mr Pelly thinks that the competitors, in our line, are gradually withdrawing from the business.' The *Nereide* had recently arrived with a large cargo of pine plank, deals, boards, and rafters.[84] In July, Pelly reported that Columbia lumber was getting better prices owing to less competition:

> Formerly large quantities of Lumber were imported from the United States, New Zealand and Norfolk Sound and this small market was for a long time glutted now the Stock of Lumber is pretty well worked off and Norfolk Sound is now the only place were Lumber is brought to this market besides that from your Establishment at Fort Vancouver. The price now obtainable is from five to six Cents the running foot, one inch thick and Twelve inches wide; 60,000 feet has just arrived from Norfolk Sound in the Suffolk ...[85]

Two late lumber shipments occurred in 1838, and both had sold for good prices by April 1839, when Pelly told the company's secretary that the Oahu wood market was so dull and limited 'that a very small increase of import materially depresses prices. The low price of preceding years occasioned by a Glut of the market, has had one good effect that of checking inordinate imports from the US New Zealand and left you pretty well the exclusive market, and still the demand is scarcely equal to the supply.' Only rafters had not sold, owing, Pelly said, 'to the Natives supplying themselves and others from their own Forests at lower rates than I have hitherto submitted for those of the Company.'[86]

Meanwhile, the Moose Factory sawmill was being resurrected. Between February and October 1838, the mill was rebuilt on the Columbia, Douglas wrote, 'on a new construction, having a double gearing, lighter frames, diminished cranks, with a greatly accelerated stroke.' An inventory described it as '1 (one) substantially built sawmill, 91 × 30 feet, capable of working a gang of 11 saws with an overshot wheel 16 feet diameter.' In full operation, the mill could work from eight to ten saws and employ '25 men classed as Hewers, carters, fodderers Rafters sawyers, and one overseer.' There was also a forge at the mill.[87]

The labour force was made up of Kanakas, perhaps the same loggers who had cleared the Sandwich Islands' sandalwood forests for the maritime fur traders. Paid between £10 and £19 a year, the Kanakas were a cheap yet skilled source of labour. They cut the Douglas fir and dragged them to the mill using oxen and horses. 'The plant employs a score of workers,' de Mofras wrote, 'all men from the Sandwich Islands, and has horses, oxen, and carts in proportion.' In 1840, Farnham wrote that 'The saw mill, too, is a scene of constant toil. Thirty or forty Sandwich Islanders are felling the pines and dragging them to the mill; sets of hands are plying two gangs of saws by night and day; nine hundred thousand feet per annum; are constantly being shipped to foreign ports.' Charles Wilkes recorded that French Canadians were also employed, and Dunn added that the company kept 'scores of woodcutters, employed to fell timber, which is sawed up in large quantities – 3,000 feet a day, and regularly shipped for the Sandwich Islands, and other foreign parts.' The mill, Farnham continued, 'is in constant operation, and cuts from two thousand five hundred to three thousand feet every twenty-four hours. The lumber, exported to the Sandwich Islands and the coast of California, sells at sixty dollars per one thousand feet.'[88]

Production began in the middle of February 1839, when the sawmill employed twenty-six men. In four months, they had shipped 60,000 feet of one-inch boards to Oahu, which realized $2,400 – considerably more than the cost of production and shipment. Douglas thought the new mill could double the quantity of lumber sold annually at Oahu, and to prove his point, he sent three large cargoes in 1839 and 1840. Farnham wrote from Oahu in January 1840 that the *Vancouver* had brought more than 100,000 feet of Columbia River lumber.[89]

By March 1840, Pelly had sold most of his Columbia lumber, and the market was swollen by recent imports from the United States responding to the high prices he had obtained. He believed, however, that the Americans could not afford to sell their lumber for less than five-and-a-half cents a foot, so he lowered his price to five cents, 'and as the other holders cannot gain any profit at such a low figure I hope they will not make further shipments to these Islands.' The Americans had to pay high costs of freight, insurance, and other charges; 'the wood however is of superior quality to that from the Columbia and meets a readier sale in this market.' This American lumber was probably planed. Before the end of 1840, the Oahu market absorbed two more shipments of Columbia lumber, and prices improved despite American importations.[90]

Meanwhile, an 1842 experimental shipment to London, promoted by Simpson, was not a success. Spars and planks from the Columbia were, he said, procurable with little delay and at no cost, and he sent a shipload of them 'home' in 1842. The planks got a good price, but 'the spars, though pronounced of good quality fetched at public sale only 92/6 per load, their value being diminished by their length not being in due proportion to their thickness, which rendered them unfit for masts, and make it necessary to waste much of the best part of the timber in fitting it for other purposes.'[91]

Ominous signs appeared in the spring of 1843 when a shipment of boards, plank, and rafters arrived at Oahu from California. The shipment would interfere with HBC sales, Pelly and Allan wrote, 'as it is much superior to our Lumber ... Should Lumber continue to pour in from California, where we understand they have now got saw mills, we shall soon be obliged to reduce the price of ours.' There was also a growing threat from the Columbia region itself, where in 1843 American newcomers built two sawmills of similar design to the company's.[92] In October 1843, Pelly and Allan reported that a Dr. Babcock had arrived in Oahu, ostensibly for health, but really to market lumber from his sawmill at Willamette Falls:

> His real object in coming here is to form connexions and Procure an outlet for the sale of lumber. We have also learned from good authority that he in conjunction with his associates in business has ordered a Planing Machine for boards from the States with the view of underselling the Company's lumber at these Islands, – we would therefore strongly recommend that a Complete Planing Machine be sent us by first conveyance and so arranged as to work either by manual or Horse Power as independent of our wish to meet the Americans upon their own ground, we anticipate great advantages from it, because the labour of planing boards is the main objection to the Columbia River Lumber here.[93]

The G&C acceded to Pelly and Allan's request, and ordered a planing mill that went into operation on the Columbia in May 1845. The Fort Vancouver mill continued to produce until after the Oregon Treaty, when it was rented, in 1849, to an American. In the meantime, the company opened another sawmill at Fort Victoria, its new depot on Vancouver Island; this mill, too, would be manned by William Crate and workers from the Sandwich Islands.[94]

The company's exports of sawn, unplaned lumber were a success. Proximity to market, abundant supply, and cheap labour enabled Pelly to undercut distant lumber producers, and altogether perhaps 2,000,000 feet of lumber was sawn. Lumber was perhaps the principal source of profit for the Oahu agency: sales amounted to $16,943 in 1839. According to Mactavish, Sandwich Islands agency profits for 1841 had been made principally upon timber and other country produce sent there from the Columbia. At Fort Vancouver that year, Simpson noted that the sawmill provided all the wood required for the use of the Vancouver depot and the marine department, 'besides two or three cargoes a year for exportation to the Sandwich Islands, where the sales amount to about 10,000 dollars per annum. This branch of business affords a remunerating employment for the shipping, when not required for purposes more immediately connected with the fur trade.'[95]

Quietly and effectively, then, the HBC initiated the first phase of the great nineteenth-century assault on coastal forests. On the lower Columbia River, the emphasis in the 1830s was on the development and export of new commodities. Here, in a captive region of abundant resources and commercial opportunities, the company responded in ways that had been inconceivable on Hudson Bay or in Rupert's Land. The company's records show the seemingly incongruous spectacle of 'fur traders' sending salmon to Honolulu and Canton, and lumber to Valparaiso and Rio de Janeiro, in exchange for cargoes of copper ore and saltpeter destined for London. The company's records also show a stagnant fur trade on the lower Columbia. American visitors like Wilkes and Silas Holmes, in 1840, saw the new exports as a result of the decline in the fur trade. Fort Vancouver's fur returns declined steadily between 1833 and 1843 while those of the sale shop, where British goods were sold or traded for wheat, increased.[96]

Of equal importance was the precedent lent by such success. With these new exports underway, transport systems in place, and American settlers pouring into the lower Columbia valley, it was a straightforward matter to add new exports from more northerly coastal regions.

CHAPTER 9

Beyond the
Mere Traffic in Peltries

*Our Salmon, for all the Contempt entertained for any thing out of
the routaine of Beaver at York Factory, is close upon 300 Barrels, &
I have descended to Oil & Blubber too, tho not on your large Scale –
So that altogether, whatever others may think of Fraser's River,
I am much satisfied with its proceeds myself.*

– ARCHIBALD MCDONALD (FORT LANGLEY)
TO JOHN MCLEOD, JANUARY 1832[1]

Orth of the Columbia River was a mild and temperate coastal
region extending from Puget Sound to the Strait of Juan de Fuca and
the Gulf of Georgia, and bearing a generally poor fur trade. Posts in the
region were forts Langley (1827), Nisqually (1833), and Victoria (1843).
While the Columbia River was the principal source of new exports, this
northerly region also provided exports in the form of Fraser River salmon
and Puget Sound wool before 1843. Its protected inland waters offered
such an impressive potential for farming, livestock, fishing, lumbering,
and mining that it later became the heartland of British and American
settlement on the Pacific coast north of the Columbia. By the 1830s, the
Hudson's Bay Company had engrossed this region's fur trade in its fight
against American traders on the North West Coast, and in the process
had found that it possessed a fine, secure – and unrealized – commercial potential. By 1843, Langley was known more for its salmon than its
fur, and the Puget's Sound Agricultural Company's stock farms at
Nisqually promised real profit. Moreover, coal deposits had been located
on Vancouver Island in 1835, and James Douglas, five years later, had
reported favourably on central coast salmon and coal prospects. George
Simpson himself inspected these resources in October 1841, and his
examination resulted in his decision the following spring to move head-

quarters from vulnerable Fort Vancouver to Vancouver Island, and to exploit the broad range of resources available in the northerly region.

Underpinning all this was a modest fur trade. Native people of the lower Fraser, for example, exploited the resources of the river and ocean to provide for their needs, but the mountainous land around them lacked a large population of fur-bearing mammals. In 1828, James McMillan complained that 'they are very lazy and independent [because] the Sea and river Supply their wants plentifully'; in the same year, George Simpson observed that 'the ample means their country and Coast afford, in regard to the necessaries and comforts of life' had rendered the Native people 'perfectly independent of our supplies.'[2]

Fort Langley's construction in 1827 had brought with it hope of an extended and profitable fur trade. As many as three thousand Cowichan crossed the gulf every year to their summer fishing villages on the Fraser.[3] Company traders assumed that such people would yield a rich and sustainable fur trade. Simpson, for example, in 1829, urged the Indians of the lower mainland to hunt the beaver in their territory:

> There are a good many Beaver in the immediate vicinity of Fort Langley, and we have reason to believe that except in the very mountainous parts, the interior country is rich. Its permanent inhabitants, however, being few in number, are intimidated by the large and powerful bands that come to the River from Vancouver Island [and] the Coast, for the purpose of fishing, and as yet venture only to Steal a visit to us during the absence of their more warlike neighbours: they have begun, however, to supply themselves with our Traps, which they are surprised to find so much better adapted for taking Beaver than those of their own rude workmanship, and give us a few skins in exchange for Arms, Blankets, &c., so that as their wants increase, which they will soon do from an acquaintance with the use of our supplies, their Trade will become more valuable to us.[4]

Simpson surmised that the fur trade would improve over time, as did chief trader Archibald McDonald. McDonald wrote in 1830 that Fort Langley drew furs from a vast territory extending from the edges of the Chilcotin, Thompson's River, and New Caledonia districts; from the foot of Puget Sound to the end of the Gulf of Georgia, and from the inside coast of Vancouver Island to the lower Fraser. He wondered why, with such a large area, the fort's beaver and otter trade had increased by only 400 pelts over the two previous years: 'A superficial glance over this immense space ... naturally led to very high expectations.' McDonald blamed poor returns on recent American competition at sea and on 'the unproductive nature of much of the Country itself.' Beaver did not thrive in a mountainous country with tumultuous creeks and rivers. 'To the Northward of Barrard's Canal the face of the Country is still more Mountainous than hereabouts and of consequence yields but few returns.'[5]

McDonald's analysis was accurate. 'Fraser's River does not come up to original expectations,' he repeated a year later. Again, he blamed the terrain: explorations had revealed mountains, lakes, and rapid rivers. In 1827, from Kamloops, Francis Ermatinger had explored the Lilliwit (Lillooet) River; in 1829, McDonald examined the lower lengths of the Pitt and Silliwhite (Lillooet, i.e., Harrison) rivers, and Annance explored the Oussaak. McDonald named the Harrison after Benjamin Harrison, a member of the London committee. In 1830, he sent James Yale and eight men to the Harrison, which turned out to be an extension of the Lillooet (Map 17). Yale concluded that there was 'no prospect of drawing Beaver from a country so perfectly inaccessible with the mountains' as was the terrain between the Harrison and Thompson rivers.[6]

The post was intended as a base for the trading war against the Americans, who in the late 1820s ventured through the Strait of Juan de Fuca into Fort Langley's territory. In 1831, Aemilius Simpson noted that 'In the years 1829 & 1830 two vessels from Boston visited the Columbia & Gulf of Georgia but have now left the Coast, it had not for many years previous been the practice of American Traders to go there & I do not think it likely they will soon visit it again & from the Competition that has been carried on by vessels in different interests & the scarcity of Sea Otters. The profits of their Trade is I learn so small that I think it probable they will soon relinquish it.' The American ships were the *Owhyhee* and the *Convoy*. Commanded by captains Dominis and Thompson, these vessels felt the HBC's competition and abandoned the coast.[7]

The fort's returns gradually increased as the Boston traders forsook the coast. In January 1832, McDonald reported that the American absence since 1830 had caused a considerable increase of trade; Fort Langley was up from 1,400 to 2,500 beaver. Douglas told McLeod in the same year that 'Your friend Archy has been doing wonders at Fort Langley, he has collected about 2000 Beaver, and is not a little vain of his feat.'[8]

By the mid-1830s, however, Langley's fur trade had not grown as expected, even with the Americans gone. In some places the beaver population had been wiped out through overhunting. For example, in September 1841 on Texada Island in the Gulf of Georgia, Simpson 'found one object of interest in an old beaver-dam of great extent.' This was probably the remains of an isolated beaver population obliterated by the company's demand. Similarly, Chief Kakalatza of Somenos told naturalist Robert Brown in 1864 that his father used to hunt beaver at a small lake near the Cowichan River. 'The lake is full of [beaver dams], & Kakalatza tells me that his father used to hunt them long ago when the King Georges wore beaver hat and skin was worth trading at Fort Langley to Mr Yale – a very old story indeed.'[9] The coastal fur trade simply was not amenable to indefinite extension. Gradually, the HBC realized the futility of attempting to obtain fur from Native peoples who were not primarily hunters and whose limited fur resources had already been exploited.

The company's experience at Fort Langley set the pattern for the trajectory of development in the Gulf of Georgia-Puget Sound region in the mid-nineteenth century. A poor or modest fur trade drove the fur traders to exploit the varied resources of trade and labour available in the Native economy. Salmon was the most important of these. In 1841, Simpson observed that the Langley region had been 'closely wrought for many years, the returns in furs are gradually falling off; but the increasing marketable produce of the fisheries makes up for that deficiency.' In 1845 Yale wrote that the fort's fur returns were 'trifling to an extreme.'[10]

The salmon trade grew while the fur trade stagnated. Scouler had likened salmon to a staple cereal, and the colonial naturalist John Keast Lord called salmon 'one of the most prominent wonders of this region.'[11] Fraser River sockeye was the company's first non-fur export from what is now British Columbia – save perhaps isinglass, a valuable substance derived from the float bladder of the sturgeon and an important provision obtained in the Indian trade at Langley.[12] After proving the Fraser unnavigable in 1828, Simpson had maintained Langley as a branch of the coasting trade, and specifically for its fur trade, fishery, and farming potential. Thereafter, salmon followed fur as the post's major export[13] (Table 6).

TABLE 6 Salmon production and export, Fort Langley, 1828-43

Year	Total production	Exported to Oahu	Value at Oahu ($)
1828	16 tierces		
1829	85 tierces		
1830	220 barrels		
1831	300 barrels	100 barrels	10
1832	n/a		
1833	350 barrels		
1834	30 barrels		
	55 half barrels		
1835	605 barrels		6
	112 half barrels		
	25 tierces		
1836	200 barrels		
1837	450 barrels	350 barrels	8-9
1838	597 barrels		
1839	400 barrels	51 barrels	
1840	300 barrels		
1841	540 barrels		
1842	n/a		
1843	n/a		
Total	4,050 barrels (excluding tierces)		

Source: These figures are derived from the text and from Mary Cullen, *History of Fort Langley, 1827-96* (Ottawa: National Historic Parks and Sites 1979), 96

Native traders came from a number of places on the Gulf of Georgia and lower Fraser. Aurelia Manson, Yale's daughter, recalled that the 'old natives' of Point Roberts, New Westminster, Vancouver, Katzie, and Saint Mary's Mission could tell of Langley's 'work and doings.' Vancouver Island people fished at the river and had extensive summer villages there; indeed, in 1825 McMillan had recorded that the Native name for the Fraser was Cowichan. 'With the coming of the Sockeye in July,' ethnographer Homer Barnett wrote, 'all the able-bodied Cowichans left for the Fraser River for two months, where they camped on Lulu Island on the south arm of the river.' They dried their salmon there before returning to the island for the winter. In 1829, McDonald characterized the Nanaimo as the 'most forward' Indians trading at Langley: 'They also are a numerous tribe and live mostly on the Island – during the salmon season they occupy a large village they have about 3 miles below this on same side the river.'[14]

The HBC traded fresh fish at the fort, ran a fishing station or saltery at the mouth of the Chilliwack River, and may have traded salmon at Point Roberts. For Fraser River transport, the company introduced *bateaux*, modelled on Columbia River boats, of about three-tons burden in the 1840s.[15]

Fort Langley's records are full of references to the salmon fishery. 'I understand Salmon is more abundant in Frasers River than here,' McLoughlin wrote in 1826. Within forty-eight hours of the fort's founding, in August 1827, fresh salmon were obtained. The Fraser fishery, like that on the lower Columbia, relied directly on the Native trade, and indirectly on three fishing methods: hooks, spears, and nets.[16] The Native fishery centred on the production of dried salmon for winter use, and for the first two years McMillan traded dried salmon from the Cowichan on their return from the fishery at the canyon. Salmon was so abundant, he wrote, that he could obtain enough to feed all the people of Rupert's Land.[17]

McLoughlin, who had started curing salmon a year or two before on the Columbia, asked McMillan in the spring of 1828 to do the same at Langley. 'Will you please to Salt all the Salmon your means will permit, although if not required by you it will serve for us & to inform me what quantity you think you can Salt & the price a Barrel would cost,' he wrote. At the end of September 1828, McMillan wrote that 'our whole Trade this season is only 5000 pieces dry.' His salmon shed contained 3,000 dried salmon and sixteen tierces of salted salmon, each equivalent to forty-two wine gallons.[18]

Simpson descended the river a few weeks later and noted with pleasure that 'In regard to the means of living this Establishment may be said to be already independent: Salmon are so abundant, that besides the consumption of the Post a considerable quantity might be cured for Exportation if a market could be found.' By the spring of 1829, the men of the post were consuming their own salted salmon and potatoes, and McLoughlin asked Archibald McDonald (McMillan's successor) how many barrels he could salt at Langley for export and what help he would need.[19]

In August 1829, McDonald recorded the results of his salmon speculation. 'In case the salmon fishery at Fraser's River may hereafter become
an object of attention I here give a view of the season's trade.' In the
previous ten days, he had traded a total of 7,544 fish averaging six pounds
each for just under £14 ($70). This, he wrote with genuine understate-
ment, 'is in all conscience as cheap as provisions could anywhere be had.'
Axes, daggers, chisels, and knives changed hands, as did combs, rings,
mirrors, buttons, files, cod and 'Kirby' hooks, beads, vermilion, baize,
wrist bands, and tobacco. Nearly half the value of the trade goods was
made up of 640 country-made 'small chisels' or axes that, McDonald
wrote, were 'shabby little things got made here by ourselves.' As on the
lower Columbia, blankets were considered too good for the salmon trade:
'This Trade costs us very little, as vermilion, Rings, and other trifles are
the only Articles we allow for dried Salmon.'[20]

The Fraser fishery, like that on the Columbia, remained dependent
on Native procurement, as McDonald reported in 1831:

> I must inform that we made several attempts ourselves last Summer with the
> Seine & hand scoop net but our success by no means proved that we could
> do without Indian Trade, nor does even this appear to me a source of great
> disappointment as in years of scarcity the best regulated fishery of our own
> would miscarry, while in years of plenty such as the last the expense in trade
> would hardly exceed the very cost of Lines and Twine.[21]

In 1829, the post consumed 8,118 salted, 4,640 dried, 1,360 fresh, and 462
smoked salmon. McDonald asked for a helper from Fort Vancouver
because his men were inexperienced with curing.[22] The following year was
critical to the fishery. McDonald traded more than 15,000 fresh salmon
between 25 August and 15 September, enough, he wrote, to make up more
than 200 barrels. They cost £30 ($150) in trade goods. Salmon preserved
in Langley's own casks were, he feared, so poorly prepared that the first
cargo would not 'stand the test of a foreign market,' and he repeated his
request for a cooper who 'will know something of Fish curing.' At the end
of September, he sent 120 barrels and forty-five tierces of salmon to Fort
Vancouver, along with a small amount of kippered salmon; the *Vancouver*
was so laden with goods that another forty barrels of salmon had to be
left behind. McDonald's concern about the casks was well founded; they
very soon lost their pickle, and McLoughlin sent only a sample to Oahu.[23]

McDonald redoubled his efforts in 1831, when he built 'Wharves and other conveniences for the Salmon business.' In February he reported his progress to McLeod:

> Am now preparing from 2 to 300 Barrels to be at the Salmon immediately on the Commencement of the Season – they say a Cooper is come across [the Rocky Mountains] for me, but we saw nothing of him as yet. In consequence of my casks of last season losing the pickle, the Dr sent none of them to market but sent his own, & kept ours for home consumption. So the end is always assured, & perhaps this might at all times be the arrangement as the Columbia fish is acknowledged better than ours. Curious they are caught a week or two sooner at the Bridge than here – last season it was approaching the end of August before they appeared here.[24]

Oahu materialized as a foreign salmon market in 1831, when McLoughlin informed McDonald that 'Mr Charlton writes that at Woahoo your Salmon would sell at 10 dollars pr. Barrell you will therefore salt all the Salmon you can and on the return of the Dryad from the North she will call at your place for it.' McDonald threw himself into the work, and the fishery produced about 300 barrels to counteract the 'contempt' entertained for it by the company's accountants at York Factory. The result was the export on the *Eagle*, in 1832, of at least 100 barrels of Langley salmon, the first commercial salmon export from what is present-day British Columbia.[25]

The company's Oahu records give a view of the shipment's passage. Duncan Finlayson accompanied the *Eagle* to Oahu where, enthusiastically, he reported that the salmon trade was 'an object likely to become lucrative':

> A Gentleman by the name of Reid, lately of a respectable house in Lima, but now set up in business at this place, has purchased 100 Barrels of the Langley Salmon ... at 10$ each, for the Lima market, where, in his opinion it is highly esteemed, & will there command a remunerating price. He will hereafter enter into a contract to be furnished annually with a larger quantity at this place ...
>
> Under these circumstances, I may venture to assure you that the Salmon will at all times meet with a ready market, & command a good price, I have therefore sent pr the Eagle to Fort Langley about 380 Bushels of Salt, so that Mr McDonald may increase his quantity to 300 Barrels. It may however be

proper to remark that the Columbia Salmon is much more esteemed, & meets
with a much better market & price than that of Frazer's River; indeed, so
confident am I that the Salmon, if attended to, will become a profitable Branch
of our business, that I would not hesitate, if at liberty to do so, to embark all
my earnings in speculating thereon.[26]

To McDonald, Finlayson wrote on the same day that

> as 'tis probable the Fraser's River Salmon will command a remunerating Price,
> I have shipped on board the Eagle, 100 Barrels containing 380 Bushels Salt,
> which will enable you to cure about 300 Barrels of Salmon, & which I think
> can be disposed of to advantage ... The Kippered Salmon is highly esteemed
> at this place; samples of which are now making up for Valparaiso & Callao,
> & we will be informed, ensuing spring, the price it may fetch at those
> places.[27]

But the Langley coopers, as McDonald knew, were still perfecting
their art. When Reid discovered that most of the salmon was from the
new Fraser fishery, and not the established Columbia fishery, he complained to Charlton, who reported to McLoughlin that all but two of
the barrels were 'what the traders to the North West Coast call "Squag-
ging,"' that is, a less desirable northern species.[28] Complaints disappeared
as quality improved. The 1833 fishery was the best yet, yielding at least
350 barrels. On 12 September of that year Tolmie of Fort Nisqually noted
that 'In the evg. the Cadboro hove in sight [with] 280 barrels of salt
salmon on board,' much of which was supplied to forts Nisqually and
Vancouver as a provision. The catch was so abundant that Fort Vancouver remained a principal market for Langley salmon for a decade.[29]
In 1834 McLoughlin asked Yale for all the salt salmon he could spare,
and to send thirty barrels to Nisqually. McLoughlin called it 'as well
cured as any I ever saw.'[30] Yale grew to resent these provisioning demands
because salmon, if exported, would have produced greater revenue for
Langley. But Langley was a provision centre, subsidiary to the company's
larger business, and answerable to orders from headquarters.

The right variety and quality of wood was required for the hundreds
of barrels needed every year. In September 1829, McDonald sent four
men into the woods for barrel staves; he visited them twelve days later
and recorded that 'we now have about 1000 excellent staves.'[31] Stave Lake
and Stave River were named after one of the company's wood sources,

and by the 1840s four coopers worked at Langley. Historian Jamie Morton describes the process:

> Raw materials were required in advance. A crew split straight-grained, knot-free trees and split the logs to the right length. The flitches (slabs of timber from the tree trunk) were used for either staves or end. This wood was then seasoned at the fort ... Next the staves were worked into their final shape – smooth, curved and dressed by specialized knives and a stationary jointer's plane. Here the cooper's skill or 'eye' became paramount if all the staves were to join neatly with no leaky gaps and if the barrel were to have the proper 'bilge' or belly.[32]

The coopers produced salmon barrels in two sizes: full barrels, containing twenty-four gallons and with a capacity for 180 or 200 pounds, and half barrels, containing twelve gallons and holding 90 pounds. At first, they were bound with wooden hoops. By 1841, if not earlier, iron hoops were in use.[33]

In 1830, barrels were made of '*pin blanc*' (western white pine, *Pinus monticola*) from the vicinity of Langley. That year, McDonald sent men 'off to the pines, about 3 miles up river, where the one half will employ themselves rising staves.' Rising staves meant felling trees, bucking them into stave bolt length, and splitting the bolts into the required material. In 1835, McLoughlin asked Kittson of Nisqually to cut 8,000 barrel hoops for immediate shipment to Langley, and four years later, McLoughlin visited Langley and wrote that wood for salmon barrels was a pressing need. 'If possible we ought to get the wood for 1000 Barrels,' he told Yale. Yale, however, complained of the difficulty of finding the right stave wood. 'I observe what you state about the difficulty of getting white Pine Staves,' McLoughlin replied, 'but I think red Pine would answer the purpose, and even if we get a sufficiency of white pine we must try a few red Pine Barrels to see how it answers.' Red pine was Douglas fir (*Pseudotsuga menziesii* ssp. *menziesii*), eventually the preferred species. It was named Red pine on account of its orange tinge.[34]

Shipments grew steadily in the 1830s. In 1836, 800 bushels of salt were needed at Langley and on the North West Coast, and the 1837 fishery yielded 350 barrels of salmon for exportation besides the quantity required for fort use. In June 1839, a joint summer shipment of Columbia and Fraser River salmon took place, when the *Vancouver* left

Fort Vancouver for Oahu with '59 Barrels Columbia Salmon' and '51 Barrels Frazers River Salmon'; the thrifty Douglas probably rounded up salmon intended for winter use, but not consumed. Toward the end of the decade, he told Yale that 'The Salmon fishery is an object of much importance and merits the utmost attention; if you think its produce could be greatly increased, the means will be furnished of doing it ample justice.'[35]

McLoughlin, Douglas, and Yale conducted an experiment in the late 1830s. 'You will salt thirty Barrels or Casks salmon with the heads and back bones in the fish by way of experiment,' McLoughlin told Yale in 1836. Two years later Douglas told Pelly that 'Forty Barrels of the Salmon now forwarded, are cured with their heads and bones; if in that state they are found to keep well, and to suit the market better, we will introduce that mode of curing at all our fisheries.' The next spring, however, Douglas reported that 'Fish cured with the head and backbone are not found to answer the Sandwich Islands Market, you will therefore continue to cure in our old way.'[36]

All this activity came to a sudden end on 11 April 1840, when Fort Langley burned to the ground with the loss of 300 barrels of salmon worth £300. 'It broke out in the Forge,' Douglas wrote, 'consumed building after building with rapid and relentless fury, unquelled by the efforts made to arrest the course until the Fort lay a waste, reduced to a heap of smoking ruins.' Everything was lost in the fire except trade goods, a bundle of furs, and seven barrels of salmon. 'Staves and hoops ready prepared for seven hundred Barrels, Tubs for pickling salmon in and all went with the rest,' Yale wrote. The fire made it difficult for Pelly to meet his obligations in Oahu, and thirty barrels of Columbia salmon were used to provision the new post at Taku. Reconstruction began immediately. Empty barrels were supplied to Langley from Fort Vancouver, and McLoughlin urged Yale to make a 'large box or two,' like the salmon storage bin recently made at Fort George. These open vats were 'say 18 feet long 8 broad and 6 high the planks ought to be three inches thick the seams well caulked from the inside and well pitched but not tarred as ours are here which Capt. Scarborough can describe, I am sure they would hold a great deal of salmon.' The fire allowed Yale to rebuild on a new and larger scale. In October 1840, McLoughlin promised to send two extra men to help him extend his farming and

FIGURE 18 This 1858 sketch of the interior of Fort Langley shows the post at the beginning of its decline, at the onset of the Fraser River gold rush. Clearly visible is the HBC's post-and-sill or *pièce sur pièce* form of timber-frame house construction that flourished along the lower St. Lawrence River in the seventeenth century and reached the shores of the Pacific two centuries later. [Edward Mallandaine, *Interior of Fort Langley Yard Looking South Showing 'The Hall*,' 15 December 1858, British Columbia Archives, PDP 3395]

fishing operations. 'Make as many barrels for salmon as we can I wish you would make a thousand and fill them.'[37]

By November 1841, Langley's salmon trade was worth about a third as much as the post's fur trade, according to Simpson's analysis:

> The returns in furs amounting to about £2,500 and in salted salmon for mar-
> ket say about 400 barrels to about £800, the profit on the post being about
> £1600 per annum ... as the country has been closely wrought for many years,
> the returns in furs are gradually falling off; but the increasing marketable pro-
> duce of the fisheries makes up for that deficiency.[38]

'The exuberant fertility of the low delta lands of the Fraser is locally proverbial,' A.C. Anderson wrote. John Work, in 1824, noted the 'rich, black mould' at what became Langley Prairie, and ten years later Yale started a large farm there. In the spring of 1834, McLoughlin wrote that the Langley farm would protect Fort Vancouver in case 'we will be obliged to neglect perhaps our farm – and by having farm produce from you we will be able to do so without injury to our business.' Douglas, however, urged Yale not to cultivate the farm at the expense of the salmon fishery. 'Remember that the Salmon trade must not be sacrificed,' he wrote in 1838, 'as it will always yield, a more valuable return at less trou-ble risk & expense than the farm.' The farm possessed cattle, horses, pigs, poultry, and produced large crops of grains, peas, and potatoes from its two separate operations. It supplied the fort, the North West Coast posts, and coasting vessels, but did not provide foodstuffs for export until the 1840s, when it supplied provisions to the Russian American Company.[39]

Nor did Langley develop a lumber trade, despite the early enthusi-asm of Archibald McDonald, who proposed to build a sawmill on the Fraser. He did, however, produce boards and shingles for a short time for export to Oahu. 'Lieut. Simpson ascertained in his voyage to the Sandwich Islands that Boards of one inch thick and one foot broad sold in Retail for one hundred dollars per thousand feet,' McLoughlin told McDonald in June 1829; 'if you have no other employment for your men they would pay their wages by sawing boards.' McDonald promptly sent 300 hand-sawn, two-inch-thick planks to Fort Vancouver, but the export of lumber could not, he wrote, 'by mere manual strength ... be made a lucrative business.' On the other hand, shingles (also known as shakes: wooden roofing tiles split from rounds of cedar) presented little problem because they could be made locally and without a sawmill. 'I dare say few places are better adapted for shingles,' McDonald observed in September 1829, and by mid-October he had procured 10,000 shingles of 'excellent quality' together with a few thousand feet of plank.[40] These were probably obtained in the Native trade. In February 1830, he reported that

> among other returns that could be made from this place, last fall we had 3000 feet of Plank, and 10 M Cedar Shingles ready for Shipment: the latter I should suppose would answer well, but the Boards with mere manual force can hardly be made worth the trouble when Machinery is in competition, – should the demand for Timber continue we thought a Saw Mill here also an object of attention, but without exposing ourselves at too great a distance [from the fort], the improbability of finding a good Seat where Wood is in abundance is a great objection.[41]

Later that year, McDonald sent his 10,000 dressed cedar shingles to Oahu, where Charlton sold them for eighteen to twenty dollars per thousand. However, the Russian American Company seems to have engrossed the Hawaiian shingle market, and Langley shingles disappear from the record after the 1830 shipment,[42] and the fort's lumber export trade was moribund thereafter.

Originally, Fort Langley's territory extended north, west, and south of the Fraser delta to include the Gulf of Georgia, the Strait of Juan de Fuca, and Puget Sound. In the late 1820s, the critical spot in this territory was Cape Flattery (Neah Bay), an important trading station for American vessels in the maritime fur trade. Located between the Nuu-cha-nulth and Salish peoples, Cape Flattery was well situated to attract the Indian trades of Vancouver Island, the western parts of the Gulf of Georgia, Puget Sound, the Olympic Peninsula, and the coast between Cape Flattery and the Columbia River. Fur from within the Strait of Juan de Fuca was traded there in the same east-west, interior-coast, pattern that characterized the maritime and Columbia Department fur trades.

American coasters had congregated at Cape Flattery with the disappearance of sea otter at Nootka and with the company's fierce competition on the Columbia River. In the spring of 1829, for example, Captain Dominis of the *Owhyhee*, owned by Bryant & Sturgis of Boston, traded 300 beaver at Cape Flattery, and cured salmon there and at Port Discovery. In September the missionary Jonathon Green, who had talked to Aemilius Simpson as well as captains Dominis and Thompson, noted that Nootka Sound was 'formerly much visited by traders,' but had not been visited for several years owing to the scarcity of furs. Nootka was also located on the treacherous west coast of Vancouver Island, which was avoided by mariners. 'The straits Juan de Fuca,' on the other hand, were 'becoming a place of resort for the purpose of trade. They are easily entered, and the country about them is said to be an excellent one.'[43]

This was disturbing news to the HBC, which sought to discourage American traders on the Gulf of Georgia and Puget Sound as effectively as elsewhere on its frontiers. Continuing visits to Cape Flattery by American traders prompted McLoughlin in 1829 to propose that the company keep a vessel at Langley 'constantly going between that place and De Fuca Straights.' Archibald McDonald of Langley had tried to redirect this trade eastward and northward to the Fraser. He wrote that Captain Dominus had been active in Puget Sound in 1830 where the opposition was particularly felt. McDonald was distressed at his 'total inability' to annoy his rivals in Puget Sound and proposed to send a mobile trapping party there from Fort Langley. Yet this was a risky proposition: a five-man party under clerk Alexander Mackenzie had been killed by the Clallum people over the winter of 1827-8.[44]

McLoughlin's 1829 plan to patrol the Cape Flattery fur trade via a vessel from Fort Langley did not materialize because the company's growing business generated enough regular traffic in the straits to capture the trade and discourage American coasters. Captains Dominis and Thompson left the coast in 1830 and never returned. 'To state to you all the circumstances and difficulty in getting furs in Columbia River and Juan de Fuca it will be of no kind of use to you,' Dominis told his boss in June 1829. With the North West Coast trade firmly under HBC control, Cape Flattery maintained its earlier role as a trading station, the difference being that British traders replaced the Americans. Company vessels took to stopping regularly at Cape Flattery, which had a rich trade in sea otter, land pelts, fresh fish, oil, *haiqua*, and slaves, though only American traders dealt in the latter.[45]

To the company, the most important of these were oil and *haiqua*. 'Cape Flattery oil,' also known as lamp oil and whale oil, appears in the 1832 record when McDonald reported that he was trading 'Oil & Blubber' at Langley. Thereafter, the substance appeared in inventories of coastal forts and vessels, in quantities of up to 160 gallons.[46] It may also have included dogfish oil. *Haiqua* (dentalia shell) from the west coast of Vancouver Island was the principal form of currency in the Native economy of the entire ethnographic Northwest Coast and much of the interior. 'At Friendly Cove,' Scouler wrote, 'Maquinna came on board and ... gave us a present of those beautiful shells which the northwest Indians value so much as an ornament. The natives call them *hyaquass*, and they are not only the jewels, but the currency of the country; and with a sufficient supply of these shells we may purchase any thing the country affords.' With Nootka abandoned by traders, the HBC obtained the mollusc at Cape Flattery and Nawitti, and traded it throughout the department. The Koskeemo Indians, Douglas wrote, were known as the 'Hayquois People.' The distribution of *haiqua* mirrored the company's territorial expansion.[47] Simpson, among the Shushady Newettee in 1841, wrote that

> after our friends had disposed of their furs, they brought into the market a large number of hiaquays – white shells, found only on the west side of Vancouver's Island. These articles, thus practically corresponding to the cowries of the East Indies, are used as small change all along the coast and in many parts of the interior, and they are also applied to more fanciful purposes in the shape of necklaces, ornaments of the hair, and so forth, while occasionally a large hiaquay may be seen balancing itself through the cartilage of a pretty girl's nose.[48]

The HBC, George Roberts recalled, had some imitation *haiqua* made in London of ivory, 'but they didn't take.'[49]

Cape Flattery became a provisioning stop for company vessels. Aemilius Simpson obtained *haiqua* from the Cape Flattery Indians in 1830; eight years later, Douglas revived an old plan to have 'the Ship call at the Trading Ports in the Straigts.' Every means 'of encreasing our intimacy with the inhabitants of the coast are desirable,' he wrote, and he instructed Captain William Brotchie to stop at Cape Flattery on his way from the Columbia to forts Langley and Nisqually. 'Circumstances favouring, you may touch there for the purpose of trading Furs and Oil with the natives, both on the outward and return voyage.' In 1839, he ordered Captain Scarborough to trade furs, oil, and *haiqua* at Cape Flattery. So frequent were Scarborough's stops that Neah Bay was also known as Scarborough Bay.[50]

The construction of Fort Nisqually in 1833 provided a permanent base in Puget Sound, allowing forts Langley and Vancouver to concentrate on their respective districts. Pelts that previously found their way from the sound to Fort Vancouver were now traded at Nisqually, and the new fort also attracted fur from the northern sound and the Strait of Juan de Fuca that previously had gone to Langley. McLoughlin wrote in 1833 that Nisqually would 'relieve us at this place [Fort Vancouver] from the necessity of keeping a party constantly in that quarter at the same time it will serve for the trade of Fort Langley and if necessary as a Depot.'[51]

McLoughlin put Francis Heron in charge. The soil was poor, he told Heron in 1833, 'But you will recollect that the main object of the Establishment is not farming and that it is formed in consequence of the American Coasters of late years frequently visiting the Straights of De Fuca which obliged us to keep a party constantly in Puget Sound – and if by being stationary it can also attend a farm so much the better.'[52] A permanent establishment would deter American visits, deflect the vulnerable trades of Juan de Fuca Strait and Puget Sound southward into the company's hands, and prevent the need for risky trading expeditions from Vancouver and Langley.

Initial results were promising. In the eight and a half months before March 1834, Heron traded 1,800 beaver and otter, 'not a bad beginning.' But this could not be sustained: the Puget Sound fur trade was a limited affair. As Douglas observed, the people of Fort Nisqually and Puget Sound subsisted 'Chiefly on the Sea and Shell Fish, provided in the utmost profusion by the all bounteous hand of Nature.' Blanchet wrote that 'Shellfish are for them an ever replenished resource ... Women and children frequent the shores at low tide to pull the oysters out of the sands with the aid of a curved stick.' In 1838, the epigrammatic Douglas told William Kittson, who succeeded Heron, that 'You know the Fur Trade is all in all, and every minor object must yield to its requisitions,' and that Douglas would be disappointed 'if the supineness and inattention to the Indian Trade, which I have observed in other Posts of the

Columbia, be found also at Fort Nisqually.' In 1841, Simpson defined Nisqually's region: 'The fur trade of Nisqually extends along the coast and interior country to Cape Flattery, likewise the shores of Puget Sound, and north as far as the northern end of Whidbey's Island; the returns amounting to about £1500, the profit on which is about £700 per annum.'[53]

Nisqually's prospects went from bad to worse in the 1830s, when its farming potential was found to be as poor as its fur trade. McLoughlin had hoped that the fort could contribute provisions for the North West Coast posts, but in 1835 he decided that self-sufficiency was a more realistic goal. 'The soil of your part of the country seems to be very poor,' he told Kittson, 'but I am of your opinion that you are in the best situation for trade,' by which he referred specifically to the trade in *haiqua*.[54]

In fact, Nisqually was an ideal location for grazing and stock raising, and the post subsequently became headquarters of the Puget's Sound Agricultural Company under Tolmie, and the major provision centre McLoughlin had predicted. The agricultural company originated on the Columbia River and was inspired by similar projects in Rupert's Land. The project grew from an appreciation of the declining fur trade on the Columbia River, from a knowledge of the excellent pasturage available there and on Puget Sound, and from McLoughlin's knowledge of the hide and tallow trades of Red River and California. In the early 1830s, McLoughlin had developed a passion for stock raising. Tolmie noted this interest in his 1833 journal, only eight days after arriving from England:

> Rode out after dinner along Vancouver Plains ... During our ride the Dr unfolded to G. [Meredith Gairdner] & me his views regarding the breeding of cattle here. He thinks that when the trade in furs is knocked up which at no very distant day must happen, the servants of the Coy. may turn their attention to the rearing of cattle for the sake of the hides and tallow, in which he says business could be carried on to a greater amount, than that of the furs collected west of the Rocky Mountains.[55]

The year before, McLoughlin had drafted plans for a venture called the 'The Oragon Beef & Tallow Company.' The HBC was just beginning to dabble in California hides and tallow, and McLoughlin probably had in mind the precedents of the Assiniboia Wool Company and the Red River Tallow Company, formed by Simpson in 1829 and 1831 respectively (the latter 'for the purpose of breeding Cattle for their tallow and hides, as an article of export'). In the early 1830s, great expectations were still held for the success of these companies.[56]

Calling it a 'scheme brought forward by John McLoughlin Esq.,' in 1832 the Oragon Beef & Tallow Company had a projected capital of £3,000, payable in 300 shares of £10 each. The venture was to market 'Inside Fat or Candle Tallow,' as well as marrow, salted beef, hides, and cattle horns. A starting herd of 700 to 800 cattle was to be obtained in California and sustained on the plains around Fort Vancouver; the company was to be managed by a large stockholder and run at first by five or six 'hands.' McLoughlin estimated that 500,000 cattle could ultimately be kept at farms both north and south of the Columbia, and he proposed that the company, like those at Red River, would have some sort of connection with the HBC.[57]

It is possible that McLoughlin's bad feelings for Simpson were based partly on the governor's appropriation of this scheme. In 1834, Simpson reported that 'Several Gentlemen in the service appear disposed to form a Joint Stock Association, for purpose of rearing cattle on the banks of the Wilhamet, with a view to establish a branch of export trade to England and other countries, and in provisioning for the South American and Sandwich Island markets.' Simpson thought the company itself should form such a business. The soil and climate were exceedingly well adapted for such an export, he told the HBC Governor and Committee, perhaps reflecting on his recent difficulties with the Red River Tallow Company. If operated as 'a Branch of the Fur Trade,' such a venture would cost little and promised to become 'an extended and important branch of export trade.'[58] (Simpson here meant 'Fur Trade' in its broad sense as a euphemism for 'Hudson's Bay Company.') The G&C agreed, believing such an undertaking 'might be profitable if carried on by the Fur Trade, with all the Protection and facilities, which might be supplied by the Company's establishments.' They went a step further, however, by forbidding any employee from engaging in a project unconnected with their duties to the 'Fur Trade':

> We can not however sanction such an arrangement as we think it would be detrimental, if not dangerous to the Fur Trade, were such an establishment,

formed by Individuals and conducted as a separate concern: Besides we consider that the Fur Trade, has a right to the best exertions, and to the undivided time and attention [of HBC employees] … and that they must not engage in any Concern, which may injure or interfere with its Interests during the period they may enjoy the benefits of a retired share. We cannot therefore permit any Person, to engage in this project while connected with the Company …'[59]

McLoughlin was angry. 'I see nothing in the Deed Poll that deprives me of the Right of investing my means in any business I think proper, except in trading directly or indirectly with the Indians; and forming a hide & tallow Company is certainly distinct from the Fur Trade.' He also argued that if the hide and tallow business was launched under the company's aegis, its start-up costs could only come from the company's profits, thus in effect depriving chief factors and chief traders of a portion of their annual dividends. A separate company, on the other hand, would divorce all costs and profits from those of the HBC.[60]

The G&C countered that they were 'quite sure that the Fur Trade and farming pursuits, branches of the business so foreign to each other, will be done more justice to and be more likely to prosper under distinct managements and separately attended to, than if combined.' The G&C were also afraid of losing money on another hide, wool, and tallow company like those at Red River, for whose losses they were liable. 'It was said,' George Roberts of Nisqually recalled, 'that owing to the HBC's losses whenever outside their legitimate business that some members in London were averse to anything in the agricultural way & proposed that those who wished to do so should form a separate Co.' It was these considerations – fear of losses and the need for distinctive managements and accounts for fur trading and farming – that prompted the G&C to conceive the separate agricultural company. Galbraith argued that the agricultural company was formed because legal advisors feared the company 'might invalidate its charter if it was directly involved in a business unrelated to the fur trade.'[61] If this argument is accurate, however, it effectively negates the whole history and momentum of the HBC's commercial experience, not only on the Pacific after 1821 but also at Red River and Hudson Bay. In fact, it was not illegal to *diversify* within the HBC, but to *invest* the company's own capital in a subsidiary company. Thus, it was a problem of financial, not commercial practice.[62]

At any rate, McLoughlin could not prevent Simpson and the G&C from forming the company's hide, tallow, and wool affiliate in 1839. The purpose of the Puget's Sound Agricultural Company, Dunn wrote, was 'rearing sheep; and laying the commencement of an extensive foreign wool trade.' The decision to locate the new company on Puget Sound instead of in the Willamette resulted from uncertainty over a possible boundary settlement, and, Galbraith writes, from the hope that the company's farms, owing to their location, would serve as 'a possible British counter in the Oregon dispute.'[63] 'Here was an opportunity to provide an additional source of revenue with which to bolster the profits of the sagging fur trade on the Pacific coast,' Galbraith notes. Also in 1839, Simpson entered into his provision contract with the Russian American Company, and he intended that the Puget's Sound Agricultural Company would provide foodstuffs to the Russians. The *Beaver* could simply load up with provisions at Nisqually, its base, and take them up the coast to Sitka.

Perhaps as a way to placate McLoughlin, in February 1839 Simpson and the Northern Council resolved in council to 'compencate' him for his efforts and responsibilities as chief factor:

> The great extent of the Columbia District together with its growing importance arising from the recent arrangements entered into with the Russ. American Fur Company the projected operation of the Puget's Sound Agricultural Company and other commercial objects in contemplation involving a greater degree of responsibility ... It is resolved that the Chief Factor ... of that District shall in addition to the emoluments arising from his Chief Factorship be allowed a Salary of Five Hundred Pounds p Annum to commence on the 1st June next.[64]

The HBC had already prepared the ground for the agricultural company. By 1835, Fort Nisqually was recognized as ideally suited to stock raising: 'Its soil was found to be better suited for pasturage than tillage,' Simpson wrote.[65] A stock farm there could provide beef, mutton, and pork provisions, and perhaps produce enough for export. 'Several of the great folks,' Francis Ermatinger wrote from Flathead Post in June 1837, 'have already sent to the Spanish settlements for Cattle, in order, I believe, to commence a hide and tallow speculation.' In the summer of 1838, Captain Brotchie bought 800 sheep at Yerba Buena, and in July he and Douglas delivered the 634 surviving animals to Kittson's proposed pasture farm at Nisqually. Old Northwester Kittson, who eight years before had written 'I hate every thing that comes in the way of Beaver,' cannot have been too impressed.[66]

Sheep and cattle throve. In 1840, Fort Nisqually was transferred from the HBC to the Puget's Sound Agricultural Company. By this time, Simpson recalled, 'the fur trade was almost extinct in that quarter.'[67]

Cowlitz Farm, the HBC's other post in Puget Sound, was also transferred to the agricultural company. Located on the portage of the Cowlitz River about thirty miles north of the Columbia, and connected by trail and by *bateaux* with Fort Vancouver, Cowlitz was founded in 1838 by Charles Ross. McLoughlin informed Douglas that Fort Vancouver 'cannot support our cattle and we are directed to make a Cattle farm on the North side of the Columbia ... I am afraid Nisqually will not afford sufficient pasturage and you will consequently have to make it at the Cowlitz.' The farm produced 7,000 bushels of wheat in 1841.[68]

The company continued to supplement its livestock at Nisqually with far better results than at Red River. In the spring of 1841, Douglas bought 3,670 sheep and 661 cattle in California, of which 3,200 and 551 respectively made it safely to Nisqually. Within two years, these numbers had increased dramatically to 5,888 sheep and 1,501 horned cattle, as well as 179 horses and mules, and 80 swine. Thereafter, both Nisqually and Cowlitz exported agricultural produce to London and Sitka. 'The wool, which is good,' Paul Kane wrote, 'finds its way to the English market by the Company's ships, and the cattle are slaughtered and salted for the Sandwich Islands and the Russian dominions.' By 1848, the company annually exported 20,000 pounds of wool to London.[69]

Some fur traders were opposed to the agricultural company. George Gladman of York Factory wrote in 1842 that 'I cannot persuade myself it will ever prove a profitable speculation, until nearer markets are discovered for Wool and other exportable stuffs.' John Tod of Kamloops was equally unimpressed, as he told James Hargrave in March 1843: 'It is true we are told by a few sapient men, not to despair, that if the Fur Trade fails us we have yet bright prospects in the Agl Company, but I am greatly mistaken if this business does not prove a mere soap bubble.' But Puget Sound was not Red River, and Gladman was not considering the Russian contract. The exports to London paid off: the company issued its first dividend of 5 per cent in 1844, followed by dividends of either 5 or 10 per cent for ten straight years.[70]

Glimmerings of the commercial potential of Vancouver Island and the North West Coast first appear in the HBC's records in the 1830s. Northern resources had been noted by company traders during this decade; passengers on the *Beaver*, like Dunn and Simpson, were especially prone to recording items of interest. Coal, salmon, and lumber were examined for the first time in the 1830s, but none were yet developed owing to the priority given to extending the fur trade to the North West Coast and to developing provision and export trades on the Columbia and Fraser.

Nonetheless, the 1830s offered foreshadowings of later developments. Unknown minerals were found on the Queen Charlotte Islands in 1833 and were sent to London for analysis; the same year, poor-quality surface coal was found at the Jolifie and Cowlitz rivers. At an unknown date, the Native people of Dean Channel provided the company with molybdenum ore, which rendered a silvery-white powder used as a lubricant for pulleys on board ship in lieu of graphite.[71]

Most importantly, coal was found on northeast Vancouver Island in the summer of 1835. The company investigated immediately, thinking of its forges and the chance of a profitable new industry. According to Walbran:

> There is a tradition ... that coal was discovered at the north end of Vancouver Island through some Indians from that place recognizing ... the large black stones burning in the forge at Fort McLoughlin (Bella Bella) as the same sort of 'klale stone' to be found in large quantities where they resided. The information was investigated by the officers of the Hudson's Bay Company and found to be correct, but for several years what little coal was obtained was only worked by the Indians and purchased from them. 'Klale' is Chinook for 'black,' and 'klale stone' was the Indians' first Chinook name for coal.[72]

Tolmie sent a specimen from Fort McLoughlin to Fort Vancouver, where McLoughlin hoped it might be used to power the new steamship, the *Beaver*. In the fall of 1836, Finlayson, Dunn and others visited the coal site on the *Beaver*'s inaugural tour.[73] Dunn described the discovery:

> I may here mention, that on my next expedition to this coast ... at [McNeill's Harbour] we made a very important discovery − a rich mine of coal near the

surface. The cause of the discovery was as curious as the discovery itself was important. Some of the natives at Fort McLoughlin having, on coming to the fort for traffic, observed coal burning in the furnace of the blacksmiths; and in their natural spirit of curiosity made several enquiries about it; they were told it was the best kind of fuel; and that it was brought over the great salt lake – months' journey. They looked surprised; and, in spite of their habitual gravity, laughed and capered about. The servants of the fort were surprised at their unusual antics, and enquired the cause. The Indians explained, saying, that they had changed, in a great measure, their opinions of the white men, whom they thought endowed by the Great Spirit with the power of effecting great and useful objects; as it was evident they were not then influenced by his wisdom, in bringing such a vast distance and at so much cost that *black soft stone*, which was in such abundance in their country. They then pointed out where it could be found of the richest quality close by the surface, rising in hillocks, and requiring very little labour to dig it out. This intelligence having been repeated at Vancouver, we received instructions to make the necessary enquiries and explorations. Mr Finlayson with a part of the crew, went on shore, leaving me in the ship, to conduct the trade; and after some enquiries and a small distribution of reward, found, from the natives, that the original account given at Fort McLoughlin was true. The coal turned out to be of excellent quality, running in extensive fields, and even in clumpy mounds, and most easily worked all along that part of the country.[74]

In 1837, Finlayson and McLoughlin agreed 'To remove Fort McLoughlin to the Coal mine when it can conveniently be done.' This was not done; instead, Fort Rupert was built there in the summer of 1849. Vancouver Island coal was used, however, in the company's own forges: for example, in the spring of 1839 there were '15 Tons Vancs Island Coals' in Fort Simpson's Country Produce inventory.[75]

Douglas had the Vancouver Island coal discovery in mind on his long voyage to Russian America on the *Beaver* in 1840, though he seems to have been more immediately impressed with salmon than either coal or furs. He estimated the 'Quakeeolth' population at 10,000, and he spent two days examining the shores of 'Shushady' and its vicinity for a fort location. 'And should our views hereafter extend beyond the mere traffic of peltries we will have it in our power to cultivate the fisheries of these shores, which, judging from the abundance of excellent Salmon I saw there, will yield a large produce, and may become a valuable auxiliary business.' In May 1840, Douglas learned that a quantity of *haiqua* sufficient for the entire Columbia trade could be obtained at McNeill's harbour 'at all times.' After visiting the region in October 1841 on the *Beaver*, Simpson concurred with Douglas's high opinion:

> The northern end of Vancouver's Island would be an excellent position for the collecting and curing of salmon, which, being incredibly numerous in these waters, might be rendered one of the most important articles of trade in this country. The neighbouring Newettees, a brave and friendly tribe, would be valuable auxiliaries, not only in aiding the essential operations of the establishment, but also in furnishing supplies of venison.[76]

From the North West Coast came suggestions that timber might be exported. Masts and spars could be felled right into the water, company vessels often had spare deck space, and American coasters were in the habit of sending deckloads of spars to Oahu from Kaigani and elsewhere. The HBC had similar ambitions. In 1833, McLoughlin asked the officers at forts Simpson and McLoughlin to have their men cut a few spars and masts for the *Ganymede*.[77] Always anxious to find work for idle hands, Simpson proposed in 1842 to export timber from forts Simpson and Stikine: 'The people at the different establishments on the Coast, who have a great deal of leisure time on hand, might be usefully employed in preparing timber for shipment when they have no more pressing duties to perform.' In April 1842, at Fort Stikine, Simpson speculated that

> on the north-west coast, dense forests of pine reach the water's edge, both on the continent and the islands, where might be drawn masts and spars of the finest timber and largest dimensions; and such wood is peculiarly abundant about Stikine, where there is also a species of cypress, which, from its availability and lightness, is almost unequalled for boat-building. Little or no attention has hitherto been bestowed on the subject of turning this natural wealth to useful account; but I gave orders that a number of logs and spars, both of cypress and pine, should be prepared for shipment, so as to be always in readiness to be conveyed by any of our vessels, as opportunities might occur, to our depot at Vancouver.[78]

He obtained from Russian governor Adolf Etholine a memo on spar dimensions suitable for men-of-war.

Simpson also considered the export of oolichan oil from Fort Simpson to England: 'As this oil, by the by, was free from smell, it might be applied to many purposes in the civilised world; and I accordingly ordered a few jars of it to be sent to London by way of sample.' Farther north, on the leased territory on the Alaska Panhandle, there was the possibility of extending the HBC's trade. The Russians had developed provision trades in salmon and herring, but none of exportable quality. Always alert, Douglas had happy visions of cured salmon on his 1840 visit to Fort Stikine. The waters abounded with salmon that the Natives of the region sold 'cheerfully' at a moderate price. 'If Barrels could be provided 100 tierces of Salmon might be cured annually, at this place, for exportation,' he wrote.[79]

Thus, while the Columbia River was the principal arena for new export trades in salmon and timber before 1843, the company also formed provision and export trades on the Fraser River and Puget Sound in the 1830s, and located promising resources even farther north. The stagnant fur trade of the south coast, the success of forts Langley and Nisqually, the potential of northern resources, the uncertainty of the company's tenure on the Columbia River, and the increasing arrival of American overlanders were all on Simpson's mind in 1842, when he decided to move the HBC's centre of gravity north to the Strait of Juan de Fuca and Gulf of Georgia.

CHAPTER 10

Crisis in
the Fur Trade

*A Fur Trader is now certainly a heterogenous animal, at least
the Fur Trade is a most curious compound of professions – Miners,
Lumberers, Furriers and the d___l only knows what else besides.
By the powers of St. Patrick the Incongruity of the Fur Trade
beats an Irish Medley all hollow.*

– JOHN LEE LEWES, 1848[1]

In the 1830s, the Hudson's Bay Company's success in locating new markets for new Pacific exports was soon followed by a dramatic decline in the beaver trade of North America – and a subsequent decline in company profits. The company still depended on profits generated on the London fur market for its general health, and the decline was perceived as a crisis by fur trade officers. And they were justified: by far the greater part of company territory was still connected by charter, precedent, and necessity to the London fur market. Simpson and McLoughlin's Pacific commerce was a notable and lively exception to the general rule. Animal pelts, as Harold Innis pointed out, remained by far the most accessible and profitable commodity available in the land-locked Indian trade of the northern part of North America.[2] The general effect of the crisis in the fur trade, however, was a continued emphasis on a diverse regional economy on the Pacific.

The generally high profits of the 1830s ended suddenly in the early 1840s, causing concern in the upper ranks of the HBC. Officers above the rank of clerk, chief traders and chief factors, were paid not a wage, but a percentage of the company's total annual profits from all sources. This arrangement, adopted from the North West Company, had been designed to encourage and reward individual initiative. The company's overall profits fell sharply in the early 1840s when beaver numbers declined and silk hats displaced beaver on the London market. Columbia Department beaver production fell from about 20,000 pelts a year in the 1830s to about 15,000 a year in the early 1840s – from a peak of 21,746 in 1831 to a low of 12,958 in 1846. Department profits plummeted from £28,000 in 1839 to £13,000 three years later. The decline was not restricted to the Columbia Department. Overall company dividends fell between 1838 and 1843 from 25 per cent (a record high) to 10 per cent, causing alarm among officers.[3]

By 1842, the stagnant state of the fur trade on the Pacific coast and elsewhere was a matter of common knowledge and concern. Innis estimated the aboriginal beaver population of North America at ten million – a large resource in an enormous area, but a finite and diminishing resource all the same. As early as the seventeenth century, the HBC had sought to diversify away from beaver to include 'small fur,' but fur traders first noticed a decline in the number of beaver and other fine fur pelts in the NWC era. In 1812, for example, Alexander Mackenzie noted a decline in beaver numbers produced by ruthless competition between the North West and Hudson's Bay companies.[4] William Tolmie noted the decline on his first arrival in fur trade territory in 1833. McLoughlin told the new recruit that 'Furs are already becoming scarce & the present supply is obtained by an almost exterminating system of hunting. In 1792 the NW. Coy. sent more furs from a comparatively small space of country than is now sent to Britain from all the HBCoy's country & the Government post in Canada.'[5] Fur was also declining across the whole continent by the 1830s; in the mid-nineteenth century, Rich wrote, 'fur returns from the main areas of the Company's territories steadily declined.'[6]

On the coast, natural and cultural factors made the decline potentially more critical than in the protected interior districts. Fur traders had found that many continental species did not live on the coastal islands or adjacent mainland coast. A subspecies of *Castor canadensis* had colonized Vancouver Island, and the hardy animal had even migrated to most of the adjacent Gulf Islands. Mainland species, however, did not live on the island, including mountain beaver, muskrats, lemmings, red fox, fisher, grizzly bear, lynx, hares, rabbits, woodchucks, ground squirrels, chipmunks, pocket gophers, pack rat, bobcat, porcupine, coyote, mule deer, moose, caribou, mountain goat, bighorn sheep, and badger. Of course, not all of these creatures produced commercially viable pelts, but Vancouver Island subspecies of wolf, marten, and wolverine were generally smaller and with far less luxuriant pelts than the interior species. Thick pelts were not needed on the mild temperate coast, and animals had adapted to the environment to the extent that subspeciation had occurred. Subspecies on the adjacent mainland coast shared the same characteristics of diminished size and pelt. The wildlife of the Queen Charlotte Islands was even more scarce: no species of beaver, wolf, raccoon, mink, wolverine, or elk were indigenous to these islands.[7]

The people of this temperate region largely depended on salmon or other marine resources for their protein, and few had developed subsistence hunting traditions. They were encouraged to hunt and trap by the company, but overhunting sometimes led to a rapid decline in populations of fur-bearing animals. On the Snake River, the results had been disastrous for mammalian life, and George Simpson, David Douglas, and later visitors found deserted beaver dams at such places as the Willamette River, San Juan Island, and Texada Island – remnants of tenuous beaver populations.[8]

A combination of technological, market and natural factors contributed to the continental decline in the fur trade. Fur traders debated the possible causes and solutions. The four most obvious problems were overhunting, the introduction of steel traps, the sudden popularity in silk hats, and the failure of the country to 'recruit' after the competitive period ending in 1821. The decline in the fur trade in more southerly districts was caused, Innis concluded, by more effective trapping methods and a greater number of Native trappers. After 1821, Simpson applied a comprehensive set of conservation measures to the company's territories in an effort to increase the number of beaver, but the strategies met with limited success. His plan to establish a 'Beaver Park' at Oxford House in 1832 did not work.[9] He tried to 'nurse' the country back to health after the competitive period with such strategies as, he put it, 'killing only a limited number of such males as have attained their full growth,' replacing beaver with muskrat, marten, and other small furs, discontinuing the use of steel traps and castorum baits, imposing a quota system, and restricting trapping during the summer when pelts were poor.[10] Simpson's strategies worked best in regions where the HBC possessed a monopoly, but at Red River and in frontier areas the company faced constant competition from Canadian, Metis, and American traders, who undid the HBC's conservation efforts. Simpson, in fact, wanted it both ways: he advocated conservation strategies in protected areas, but on the company's frontiers he encouraged a deliberate policy of extermination.

Simpson also blamed overhunting on managerial resistance. He believed that HBC officers in monopoly areas were generally unwilling to impose conservation measures that would affect the short-term productivity of their posts and, hence, indirectly lower their dividends. In 1829, he stated that while competition in southern regions was inevitable, it would continue 'until the fur-bearing race becomes extinct, which must at no great distance of time be the case.' His nemesis John McLean argued that nothing could reverse the 'destruction of fur-bearing animals,' and that conservation measures amounted to 'shutting the stable door after the steed was stolen.'[11]

Natural factors contributed as well. Fur-bearing animals were subject to the cyclical peaks and troughs characteristic of predator-prey populations. Native people and traders were powerless to artificially increase the number of fur-bearing mammals above the upper limit of these peaks. They were constrained by factors of wildlife demography that were unexamined until the 1930s, and are still the subject of debate.[12] Moreover, the animals were a finite resource inhabiting a finite area; the fur trade frontier in British North America reached its outer limits in the late 1830s, when most regions were already incorporated into Simpson's continental economy. The trade was incapable of further expansion after reaching the Pacific and Arctic oceans, and the southern frontiers of Canada and the United States.

The introduction of silk hats in the European markets coincided with the decline of the beaver trade in North America. First produced in about 1824, silk hats began to replace beaver hats in the fashionable world in the 1830s. A decade later, as Hugh Grant writes, 'the Parisian silk hat had all but eliminated the English felt-hat industry and precipitated major changes in the demand for Canadian beaver.' In 1845, the HBC Governor and Committee noted that the best silk hats could be purchased at retail shops in London for about half the price of the best quality beaver hat.[13]

The market for beaver naturally suffered. John Tod and John Work blamed silk hats for the fall in the price of beaver. Lack of demand resulted in what the Northern Council called, in 1846, 'The present distressed state of the English market for Beaver.' Total profits had been tied closely to auction sales of beaver. In former days, Donald Ross recalled in 1851, 'people always calculated their prospective profits by the number of Beaver sent to market.'[14] In 1839, Tolmie wrote that the company's profits had decreased recently, 'owing in part, to the depreciation in Beaver, occasioned by improvements in the manufacture of Silk Hats; but chiefly, to diminished Returns; caused by the exterminating system of hunting pursued, which if not checked, will speedily eventuate in the destruction of the more valuable Fur-bearing animals.' A lower price for beaver promoted attempts at 'species mix,' an old strategy of diversification that could not, however, bring into the market a wholly new resource. Increases in marten returns from New Caledonia did, however, compensate for declining beaver pelts obtained elsewhere in the Columbia Department.[15]

In the 1830s and 1840s, Native depopulation also affected the fur supply, as Robert Galois notes. Malaria, tuberculosis, and other introduced diseases led to declining fur returns on the coast; for example, in 1844, Yale noted, the Indians at Fort Langley were in such a 'degenerate, sickly and depopulated state' that they abandoned their normal pursuits.[16]

These factors translated directly into decreased profits. In 1843, the G&C informed McLoughlin that Columbia Department fur had fetched only a 'tolerable price' in the August auction: 'In that Staple article there has been, we regret to say a further depression to a considerable extent. This continually decreasing price, when considered in connexion with a constantly decreasing supply, holds out no very cheering prospect for the future, unless the tides of fashion change, and the consumption of Beaver in the manufacture of hats become more general than it has been for some time past.'[17] James Douglas blamed low beaver prices and a declining fur trade for the poor dividends:

> The dividends of '40 and '41 fell much below the lowest estimates ever made, by the least sanguine of our friends, and gives no very exalted idea of Indian trade. Could the world believe that a business enjoying the industrial produce with the absolute possession of one large third of North America, is indesputably less productive than many a ten square mile province in Europe.

Yet it is a fact, which cannot be concealed, and if known to the world would have the effect of lowering the idea of high importance, attached to the fur trade.[18]

When Simpson saw the unusually low Columbia Department profits of 1840 and 1841, he wrote that 'We cannot indeed contemplate either the present or future prospects of the fur trade on the west side of the Mountains without Anxiety ... the trade has fallen off greatly for two successive years, marking, it is to be feared, a rapidly progressive diminution of the fur bearing animals.'[19]

The destruction of local beaver populations prompted perhaps the earliest proposal to form a park west of the Rockies. In 1841, Archibald McDonald suggested that a nature preserve be formed west of Puget Sound before the Puget's Sound Agricultural Company colonized the region. 'I move that the Clalum district in a line from Hood's Canal to the Pacific be barred up & appropriated to the preservation of the poor expiring Beaver race, still, leaving country for the ostensible objects of the Agricultural Company.' McDonald's proposal covered much the same territory as the present-day Olympic National Park.[20]

Declining dividends affected morale. The fur trade 'evidently is declining in all quarters,' Tod wrote in 1843. More philosophically, he added that 'This is a subject that no doubt admits of some grave commentary, but it is too gloomy to be dwelt upon, altho' at times I cannot avoid a furtive glance into futurity, and wonder what eventually is to become of many worthy men.' A few years later, Finlayson wrote that he was 'very seriously looking out for something else, to which I might turn my attention,' since the fur trade produced only falling profits. In 1848, Donald Ross privately recommended to Simpson that the company sell or relinquish to the British government all its territories and exclusive trade rights rather than 'continue to hold them on their present rather precarious footing'; in the same year, John Lee Lewes of Fort Edmonton referred to 'the funeral knell that has been tolling in the west regarding the fur trade.' 'The fur trade will only be a thing that was and is no more.'[21]

Despite these difficulties and gloomy predictions, the company did not lose money on its Columbia business between 1821 and 1843. Between

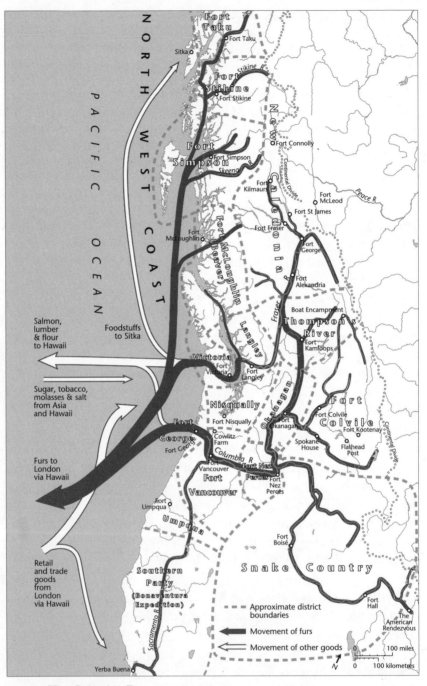

Salmon,
lumber
& flour
to Hawaii

Foodstuffs
to Sitka

Sugar, tobacco,
molasses & salt
from Asia
and Hawaii

Furs to
London
via Hawaii

Retail
and trade
goods
from
London
via Hawaii

Fort Taku
Fort Taku
Sitka
Stikine R.
Fort Stikine
Fort Stikine
New
Fort Connolly
Fort Simpson
Fort Simpson
Skeena R.
Caledonia
Fort Kilmaurs
Continental Divide
Fort McLeod
Peace R.
Fort St James
Fort Fraser
Fort McLoughlin
Fort McLoughlin
Fort McLoughlin (Beaver)
Fort George
Fort Alexandria
Fraser
Boat Encampment
Thompson's River
Langley
Fort Kamloops
Victoria
Fort Victoria
Fort Langley
Okanagan
Nisqually
Fort Nisqually
Fort Okanagan
Fort Colvile
Fort Colvile
Fort Kootenay
Cowlitz Farm
Spokane House
Flathead Post
Fort George
Fort George
Columbia R.
Continental Divide
Fort Vancouver
Fort Nez Percés
Fort Nez Percés
Fort Vancouver
Fort Umpqua
Umpqua
Fort Boisé
Southern Party
(Bonaventura Expedition)
Snake Country
Sacramento R.
Fort Hall
The American Rendezvous
Yerba Buena

— — — Approximate district
boundaries

Movement of furs

Movement of other goods

0   100 miles

0   100 kilometres

N

MAP 18 The Columbia Department, 1843

1830 and 1843, the HBC made a net profit of about £270,000, a profit that contributed substantially to the company's overall financial success during the period of a declining fur trade. After 1821 the bulk of the company's North American fur returns, E.E. Rich noted, 'was maintained by the Columbia trade and its satellites in the Snake Country and New Caledonia, and in part by Mackenzie River.' Despite the general decline, this was a successful company: between 1825 and 1863, the HBC paid dividends to its shareholders at a minimum rate of 10 per cent; for eight of those years, dividends were either 15 per cent or 20 per cent.[22]

Profit was based on the company's success in monopolizing the greater part of the North American fur trade. Fur traders, as Innis stressed, strove for monopoly control to reduce costs and increase profits. George Simpson and John McLoughlin had aimed to recreate a monopoly situation west of the Rockies, and they largely succeeded. But the costs were high: between 1827 and 1836, the HBC invested in trade goods, expensive ships, and experienced personnel; built a new depot at Fort Vancouver and new posts for the coastal fur trade; extended the interior fur trade into the Snake and Sacramento rivers; started new export trades on the Columbia and Fraser rivers; and opened new agencies at Oahu and Yerba Buena. Expenses in competitive regions like the North West Coast and the Snake Country were much higher than in monopoly areas like New Caledonia, Mackenzie River, and much of Rupert's Land. In 1845, Alexander Simpson stated that in 'protected territories,' the value of goods bartered for furs was only a fraction of the value of those furs in England. In the 1840s, Mackenzie District furs were worth ten times the district's total expenses, which included trade goods, supplies, and wages; and in mid-century Rupert's Land, where the company had little competition, furs were worth twenty times the value of the trade goods exchanged for them.[23]

Aggregate figures of value and profit for the Columbia Department as a whole have been located for the period 1821-43. The HBC's Columbia business fared strikingly better than the NWC's. The company made a continuous profit despite large expenses incurred in the extension of the fur trade, competition with American traders, and formation of export trades in this distant, vast, and initially competitive region. By the early 1830s, expenses were diminishing and returns increasing. In 1832, an accountant observed that the Columbia had improved its trade by about £6,000 and 'is now beginning to make up for the expences well laid out.' The next year, accountant Robert Miles wrote that the department was 'doing increasingly well & making amends for the outlay of former days'[24] (Table 7).

After the mid-1830s, annual departmental returns ran at about twice the value of annual profits. Returns were about £40,000, a figure that fur traders used to quickly calculate profits;[25] almost £20,000 were swal-

TABLE 7 Columbia Department, returns and profit (£), 1821-43

Year	Value of country produce	Total returns (value)	Total gain (profit)
1821		25,715	11,622
1822		31,726	
1823		32,720	
1824		40,952	
1825		30,431	
1826-9		n/a	
1830	50	30,014	13,907
1831	334	35,007	20,602
1832	1,116	34,951	18,170
1833	2,385	47,619	22,860
1834	1,646	36,013	18,313
1835	3,302	37,009	18,542
1836	4,330	41,014	24,347
1837	7,198	43,796	20,859
1838	8,003	45,622	20,020
1839			28,165
1840		38,982	16,345
1841		39,729	18,560
1842		34,793	13,116
1843		40,732	17,200

Sources: 1821-5 figures are from York Factory, Accounts Current 1821-26, HBCA B.239/d/286; 1830-9 figures (including country produce figures) are from York Factory, Abstract of Accounts Current, 1830-1839, HBCA B.239/d/547, fo. 18 (see also York Factory, Country Produce Account Book, 1828-1836, HBCA B.239/d/491); 1840-4 figures are from 'General Result of Trade Northern Department and Columbia pr Country Accounts,' Ross Papers, BCARS

lowed by substantial overhead expenses, especially shipping costs, insurance trade goods, and wages.[26] In 1842, French traveller de Mofras learned that the 'initial cost of European merchandise used in trade with the Indians does not exceed £8,000 or £10,000.' The department's annual requisition for British trade goods was £10,399 in 1834 and £13,300 in 1838. At first, the requisitions were mainly for Indian trade goods. After the opening of a sale shop at Fort Vancouver and agencies at Oahu and Yerba Buena, however, they included an increasing number of British goods destined for non-Native sale. Simpson estimated the value of the 'general cargo' required for the 1841 shipment at between £18,000 and £20,000.[27]

The company's accountants usually spent several years determining a post's final profits, owing to the long transport between London and the Columbia, and the time lapse between the furs' arrival and their sale. Requisitions had to be ordered years in advance and then subtracted from final gains; pelts might be auctioned in London a year or two after they were shipped; salmon and lumber were not always exported in the same year they were produced, and did not always sell immediately in Oahu; and transport and other departmental costs had to be subtracted from final auction and profits.

By 1843, sales of salmon, lumber, and British goods at Oahu, Yerba Buena, and to the settlers near Fort Vancouver contributed materially to departmental profit. Such sales contributed at least £4,000 annually to total departmental profits: about £2,000 came from Oahu, and another £2,000 from Vancouver and Yerba Buena. New exports possessed an unstoppable momentum. In 1849, for example, Douglas estimated the value of the company's exports to Sitka and the Sandwich Islands at £10,000 and £8,000 respectively.[28]

Departmental patterns emerged and changed with time. Table 8 shows returns of outfit year 1844 (the figures refer to values, not final profits). Snake Party and Fort Nez Perces returns, previously substantial, were in decline, a reflection of the company's scorched earth frontier policy and trade disruptions caused by American overlanders using the company's Snake Brigade route.[29] North West Coast returns (figures for Fort Simpson and the steamer *Beaver*) were considerably greater than those for the south coast (figures for forts Langley, Victoria, and Nisqually) – a reflection of the large, wealthy interior districts adjacent to the North West Coast, and of the milder climate and mountainous terrain in the south. Interior districts, especially New Caledonia and Colvile, generally offered a richer, more secure fur yield than did coastal districts. Indeed, once export trades and colonial economies had emerged on the south coast, the interior districts became known as 'the fur districts' or 'the fur countries' to distinguish them from the Pacific coast.[30]

TABLE 8 Columbia Department returns (£), 1844

District	Returns
New Caledonia	8,877
Steamer *Beaver*	6,176
Fort Simpson	4,678
Fort Colvile	3,773
Fort Stikine	3,480
California Establishment	2,747
Fort Vancouver Indian Trade	2,384
Snake Country	2,124
Thompson's River	1,873
Fort Langley	1,375
Fort Nez Perces	1,293
Fort Victoria	1,085
Fort Nisqually	572
Total	40,437

Note: Returns refer to values, not to final profits.
Source: '1846 Abstract of Returns Columbia Department, Outfit 1844,' in 'Fort Vancouver (Columbia District) District Fur Returns, 1844-1849,' HBCA B.223/h/1

The Columbia Department fur trade remained of primary importance even during the time of diversification. The HBC's control of the trade served to make the entire region and all its resources uninviting to distant American competitors. At the same time, the fur trade acted as the motor of the company's economic development: fur trade profits earned on the London market covered the initial expenses of the new export trades. Forms of labour and transport devised in the fur trade worked equally for new exports.

Nor could the fur trade have survived in this large, remote region without secure, local provisions. Provision trades, formed primarily on the lower Columbia and Fraser rivers to support this most distant region of the fur trade, grew steadily over these years, buttressed the company's extended operations, and helped maintain overall profit figures at about the same level. Columbia produce increased in value from a mere £50 to about £8,000 between 1830 and 1838 (Table 7); the cost of provisioning the department with imported foodstuffs would otherwise have been enormous. New export trades were based on the twin pillars of a visible market economy (hard cash earned from fur sales in London and from Columbia produce sold on the Pacific coast) and an almost invisible provision economy (an extensive local exchange of commodities in which specie was absent).

More than in the HBC's other territories, provision trades on the west coast tended to become marketable commodities. Having provided the means of subsistence that allowed fur trade posts to be self-supporting, provisions were then transformed into export commodities and shipped to Pacific markets on vessels that had been purchased with fur trade profits – which were also based on those same commodities in their original guise as provisions. New exports were grafted onto the exchange, provision, accounting, and transport systems developed for the fur trade. Exports of salmon and flour gained a momentum and importance of their own quite unrelated to the fur trade that had brought them into existence, and the agency at Oahu, intended for the sale of Columbia produce and the purchase of staples like salt and sugar, soon specialized in the sale of specialized British nautical goods and other supplies for the North Pacific whaling fleet.

The widespread decline in the fur trade made the need for a general commerce seem evident and inevitable to many fur traders, who from every corner of British North America transferred their profits out of the fur trade. The joint stock companies formed and promoted by Simpson at Red River failed, while the diverse experiments undertaken in the Columbia Department for the most part succeeded. A declining fur trade led Simpson and members of the London committee to set up Pelly, Simpson & Company, a Norwegian timber export company controlled by Simpson and the Pelly family. Fur traders on both sides of the Rockies entrusted their earnings to Simpson, who invested them in his timber company and in Canadian railway companies.[31]

In the early 1840s, almost every visitor to Fort Vancouver made a connection between the declining fur trade and the company's bold diversification program. De Mofras asserted that the Puget's Sound Agricultural Company was formed by HBC officials 'alarmed at the rapid decrease of fur-bearing animals'; Wilkes, in 1840, learned that the fur trade had declined by 50 per cent. The company's charter and trade licence allowed the production of new commodities, and exports of salmon, lumber, and farm produce proved successful in Pacific markets. Concerning the agricultural company, McDonald wrote in 1839 that 'The harvest is far more promising than the Beaver trade & will no doubt ere long become the grand consideration everywhere west side of the Rocky Mountains.' Holmes, who visited Fort Vancouver with the Wilkes expedition, ascribed the rise of export trades directly to the decline in the fur trade. He wrote that 'it is stated that the income of the H.B.C. from their fur trade is gradually diminishing; but that the deficit is more than supplied by their exports of flour, beef and agricultural products generally, with the lumber, of which they export a considerable quantity.'[32]

The large-scale settlement of American overlanders on the south bank of the Columbia after 1842 added to the company's woes. In 1844, Francis Ermatinger voiced what by then was common knowledge:

> The Columbia trade is getting from bad to worse, and upon the other side [south of the Columbia] it is not much better. The Americans are scattered all over the Country, from Fort George to the Cascades, and, as we may expect the emigration to increase, the fur trade must fall to nothing. Besides, the price of Beaver is falling, owing to the use of silk.[33]

A declining fur trade and new export opportunities were the background to Simpson's 1842 decision to realign the company's business to the resource-rich northern region.

CHAPTER II

Simpson's Reorganization

If they get the line of 49 our Columbia is dished,
what then will become of all the great doings of late years
on that side the Mountains.

– JOHN LEE LEWES, 1843[1]

That Lewes's seemingly imponderable problem could be solved within a few years is testament to the company's commercial achievement on the Pacific in general, and to the success of Governor Simpson's policy decisions of March 1842 in particular. Simpson's final visit to the Pacific coast heralded the beginning of a fresh commercial era on the British Columbia coast, and, simultaneously, the demise of the company's Pacific operations based at Fort Vancouver. Simpson's 1842 decision to phase out the Columbia Department depot at Fort Vancouver and to establish a new headquarters on Vancouver Island marked the beginning of a new British maritime commerce on the north Pacific. Fort Victoria, the new depot, was so well suited for a general, ocean-borne commerce that it remained the principal settlement on coastal British Columbia for fifty years.

Indeed, the 1840s witnessed the end of a thirty-year period during which the British fur traders effectively controlled the non-Native commerce of the coastal and interior districts between California and Russian America. There were two main reasons for Simpson's decision to move north. First, the Americans, whose attempts to establish a commercial presence had been thwarted by the Hudson's Bay Company everywhere west of the Rockies, finally staked their claim to the region through noncommercial means. Beginning annually in 1842, hundreds and then thousands of American settlers crossed overland on the old brigade route from South Pass and down the Snake (the Oregon trail) to the lower Columbia. Like most residents and visitors, they regarded the Columbia River as the unofficial border between British and American claims, and they generally settled on the south bank of the river, especially on the Willamette.[2] Inevitably, the Americans competed or interfered with the HBC's fur trade and other commercial operations, and Simpson was anxious to relocate to a secure northern location. Second, Simpson knew that a diplomatic end to the joint occupancy of Oregon Territory was imminent, and he was not convinced that the Columbia River would form the boundary. The 1844-6 negotiations ended with the Oregon Treaty, which saw the forty-ninth parallel extended from the Rockies to the Pacific Ocean, though the treaty awarded the whole of Vancouver Island to the British.

The Oregon Treaty did not, then, represent a craven capitulation to American interests. Lord Aberdeen, the British foreign secretary, wrote in 1844 that the American claim to the whole of Oregon Territory (as far north as 54°40′) was clearly unacceptable, as it would exclude Britain from Vancouver Island and the whole west coast. At the same time, Aberdeen was not committed to a border that followed more or less the course of the Columbia River. Rather, he believed that a border along the forty-ninth parallel, that also included the whole of Vancouver Island, would allow the British to form a perfectly viable colony. 'I believe,' Aberdeen told Prime Minister Sir Robert Peel in 1844, 'that if the line of the 49th degree were extended only to the water's edge, and should leave us possession of all of Vancouver's Island, with the northern side of the entrance to Puget's Sound [and the Gulf of Georgia] ... this would be in reality a most advantageous settlement.' British government emissaries (who happened to be Aberdeen's and Peel's sons) recommended that Britain retain possession of the whole of Vancouver Island in order to maintain a defensive position overlooking the Strait of Juan de Fuca. Moreover, Captain Gordon wrote, 'the northern channel round Vancouver's Island is not navigable for ships.'[3]

By 1841 Simpson was convinced of the need to construct a new northern depot and to withdraw sooner or later from the Columbia River. Seeing the writing on the wall, he decided to relocate the centre of the

HBC's operations. His new policy contrasted with an earlier one, in which he had encouraged the Fort Vancouver corps to hunt and trap as far south as the Vermilion Sea and to establish an agency in San Francisco Bay. But the Southern and Snake trapping parties had largely served their purpose by 1842: they were intended to create a 'fur desert' between the Columbia River and the American western frontier at the Rocky Mountains, a no-man's land designed to discourage potential American attempts at overland colonization. Simpson's frontier policies had worked well for twenty years, and though the Snake Country was still profitable in 1842, the HBC could no longer prevent Americans from entering the Oregon country. Indeed, company employees spent much valuable time escorting American overlanders down the Columbia River.[4]

In 1842, Simpson ordered the total closure and withdrawal of the company's retail business and trapping parties in California. He maintained the profitable Snake Brigade for the time being, but he refused to recognize the legitimacy of the French Canadian settlement on the Willamette River. Instead, Simpson ordered the development of new resources on southern Vancouver Island. He sought to centralize the company's activities on what was likely to become a British part of the coast, and to relocate to a region rich in natural resources and opportunities for export. Southern Vancouver Island, not the lower Columbia, would be the British Pacific commercial centre envisioned by Dalrymple, Mackenzie, and the Northwesters.

Simpson was also pleased with the Oahu agency's profits from the sale of Columbia produce and British goods, and he intended to maintain a high level of exports to the Sandwich Islands from the country within the Strait of Juan de Fuca. Thus, while preparing for the worst political result, Simpson also contemplated a broad new commercial undertaking in the sheltered inside waters accessible from the North West Coast.[5] His voluminous correspondence of 1841-2 contains barely a mention of the fur trades of the lower Columbia, Puget Sound, and Gulf of Georgia, an indication of the extent to which the HBC had become a general trading company on the Pacific.

The proposed new depot on Vancouver Island, named Fort Victoria in 1843, was Simpson's inspiration, just as Fort Vancouver had been. While Fort Vancouver reflected Simpson's 1824-5 plans for the department, Fort Victoria mirrored the experience of the intervening two decades and his new plans. The fur trades of the Columbia and Fraser drainages figured prominently in the 1820s. Terminus of the York Factory Express and the interior fur brigades, Fort Vancouver was built near the end of the transcontinental trade route located by the Northwesters. It was built on fertile land in order to provide provisions for much of the department's coastal and interior operations, most of which, in 1825, were accessible from the lower Columbia.

Fort Victoria, on the other hand, was a Pacific depot, accessible to the company's new deep-sea commerce from Oahu, Sitka, and San Francisco, as well as from London. Access to the Pacific was immediate: there was no hazardous and time-consuming river bar to cross. The new post was to be the base of an ocean-borne commerce with Pacific markets. Simpson planned to transfer the HBC's skills and ambitions to a region where natural resources were often more abundant and, owing to the extensive coastline and clear inland navigation, generally more accessible than on the Columbia. Furs would continue to be taken from interior districts, then gathered at the new depot for export to London. Like Fort Vancouver, Fort Victoria's farms would provision the coastal posts,

FIGURE 19 Getting to the new depot on Vancouver Island was not always easy. The British fur trade ended, paradoxically, on a Pacific island known for its temperate climate, abysmal fur trade, and sometimes heavy seas. This 1847 watercolour by Paul Kane, *Crossing the Straits of Juan de Fuca*, shows an express canoe from Nisqually approaching Fort Victoria. [Stark Museum of Art, 31.78/70, WWC 70]

though the farms at forts Langley and Nisqually lessened the need for the new post to be self-sufficient, or even to provide an agricultural surplus.

The founding of Fort Victoria permitted the formation of a new regional economy based on the Gulf of Georgia and Strait of Juan de Fuca. Such a new spatial emphasis did not, however, require any break with commercial precedent. As with the 1825 founding of Fort Vancouver, the company brought to bear a flexible and transferable set of commercial strategies developed by the fur trade to the east of the Rockies – for example, extension of trade, monopoly control, a search for local provisions and possible exports – plus some commercial practices inherited from North West Company operations in the region. On the Pacific coast, these strategies were united with those borrowed from the maritime fur traders (the marketing of deckloads of spars and masts at Oahu), with the personnel and expertise of vanquished maritime opponents (Captain McNeill, formerly of Bryant & Sturgis), and with strategies obtained indirectly from the British industrial revolution (the use of the steamship *Beaver*). The fur trade's eastern origins were still apparent – for example, in the fundamentals of its corporate culture and the demography of its workforce.[6] Together, these strategies made for a strong and durable commercial presence – a healthy capitalism adapted to local conditions – that blunted the sharp edges of political surrender involved in the Oregon Treaty.

In 1843, however, the HBC generated mainly furs in the vast coastal region north of the Fraser. Only at Fort Langley had the company developed new exports. The company had captured the coastal fur trade from the Americans and Russians, a feat of territorial extension that was to be a prelude to heightened economic and political activity. On the coast, the fur trade had acted as catalyst for later, diversified commercial activity. During routine company business, the HBC had located new sources of salmon, timber, agricultural land, and coal. Between 1840 and 1842, Douglas and Simpson toured the region with an eye to its commercial potential. These two men would also create the policies and direct the changes of the 1840s and 1850s.

Plans for a new northern depot dated as far back as 1821, when the company realized that the territory south of the Columbia River was almost certain, as John S. Galbraith wrote, 'to be awarded to the United States in any boundary agreement.' Fort George (formerly Fort Astoria), on the south bank of the Columbia, had been formally returned to the United States as a result of a contentious clause in the Treaty of Ghent. If Americans were to occupy Fort George, the company would face American competition from directly across the river, whereas a northern depot would avoid such competition. British hopes of a Columbia River boundary faded in the 1820s with the failure of the Huskisson-Rush and Addington-Gallatin negotiations and with the decision to prolong indefinitely the joint occupancy provisions of the 1818 convention. In 1828 the Governor and Committee instructed Simpson 'to acquire as ample an occupation of the Country and Trade as possible, on the North as well as the South side of the Columbia.'[7] At this time, they believed, wrongly as it turned out, that Britain's chances of the Columbia River becoming the border would be increased if they could demonstrate occupancy of the region north of the river. Simpson's plan to establish a departmental depot on the lower Fraser was dashed with his descent of the river's treacherous canyon in 1828, but even after proving its impassability, Simpson retained a belief that Fort Langley would, as he wrote in 1829, 'answer the purpose of a Depot, in the event of our being under the necessity of withdrawing from Fort Vancouver.' Serious American competition on the Columbia River 'would be attended with a ruinous sacrifice of money.'[8] This competition did not appear until the early 1840s. McLoughlin developed flourishing export trades on the Columbia in the meantime, but the political reasons favouring a northern move grew steadily more urgent.[9]

In the 1830s, American popular and political interest surpassed British official interest in Oregon Territory. Ever since the Northwesters' purchase of Astor's Pacific Fur Company in 1813, American politicians and fur traders had been anxious to re-establish a presence beyond the mountains. American visitors and commentators were united in a belief that the lower Columbia, with its Pacific access, was rightly part of the United States.[10] Between 1819 and 1839, Senator Thomas Benton, General John Floyd, President James Monroe, and Senator Lewis Linn, to name a few, recommended the termination of the joint occupancy agreements, the military occupation of Oregon, the construction of a line of military and fur trade posts across the continent, and the annexation of Oregon. Access to Pacific markets always figured in their plans. In 1839, for example, American government agent William Slacum drafted a memorial on behalf of the handful of American settlers in Willamette. 'We need hardly allude to the commercial advantages of the territory. Its happy position for trade with China, India, and the western coast of America will be readily recognized,' he wrote. Such sentiments, Galbraith notes, caused 'deep concern' to the G&C and Simpson.[11]

On his 1841-2 visit, Simpson met American travellers like Charles Wilkes and Horatio Hale, whose proprietary views about Oregon vexed him,[12] as did contemporary American writers like Hall Kelley, Washington Irving, and Thomas Farnham, who advocated a powerful political imperialism. Invoking the days when Astor apparently controlled the fur trade of Oregon Territory, these men rightly saw the HBC's commercial achievement as the main barrier to the fulfilment of manifest destiny in the region. Farnham, who spent a year as a guest at Fort Vancouver, advocated the old American plan of a fur trade connecting the Missouri with China. Indeed, notions of America on the Pacific remained virtually unchanged between Lewis and Clark and the migrations of the 1840s. Kelley's 1830 book, for example, is a detailed manifesto for American commercial expansion, ending with a plan to connect continental United States with China.[13] Between 1844 and 1846, the British government surrendered to this continentalist ideology, even though the HBC had defeated the Americans' commercial aspirations. Perhaps Simpson sensed that these American visitors would exert great political pressure on the diplomats deciding the fate of Oregon. Indeed, it is clear that while the company had superior commercial strategies on the ground, the Americans had superior political and organizational strategies both locally (for example, in the formation of the Oregon provisional government in 1843) and at the diplomatic level.[14]

By the mid-1830s, the HBC had charted the commercial potential of the coast, and had identified practical and political considerations for establishing a depot within the Strait of Juan de Fuca. The company had a detailed knowledge of the local Native populations and the considerable coal, salmon, and timber resources. A depot in the region would service the operations of the Puget's Sound Agricultural Company and

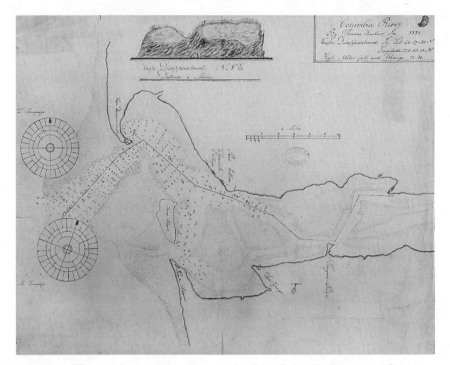

FIGURE 20 The treacherous bar at the mouth of the Columbia River gave Governor
Simpson a very good reason for establishing a new northern depot on Vancouver
Island in 1843. The mouth of the Columbia was notorious for its riptides, shifting
sands, and submerged sandbanks, between which a precise course had to be navigated. ['Columbia River, by Thomas Sinclair in 1831. Cape Disappointment in Lat.
46.17.30 N. Longitude 123.53.00 W.' Hudson's Bay Company Archives, Provincial
Archives of Manitoba, N4474]

the fur trades of the North West Coast and Fort Langley. Moreover, the
treacherous bar at the mouth of the Columbia, which had claimed three
company vessels, and the 'intermittent fever' at Fort Vancouver (malaria,
possibly aggravated by typhus) posed serious inconveniences to the
company's Columbia River business. Before 1846, the HBC had also lost
sixty-eight men and women, drowned in canoes in the dangerous
canyons and whirlpools of the Columbia River.[15]

Between 1832 and 1836, the company had considered several sites for
a new northern depot, including Cowlitz, Dungeness, Whidbey Island,
Lulu Island, Birch Bay, and Fort Langley. At first, they hoped for a depot
on Puget Sound, but by 1836 they decided that southern Vancouver Island

offered a safer political alternative. In 1832, Simpson proposed to establish a post at the Cowlitz portage to serve as the 'Grand Depot of the Department,' because Fort Vancouver was too sickly with fever.[16] In August 1833, Francis Heron of Fort Nisqually actively explored Dungeness and Whidbey Island for a depot location, to be operated in conjunction with the proposed stock farm. Tolmie reported that Heron found at Dungeness 'a plain of 400 acres, tolerable soil with an excellent mill stream, large extent of saltmarsh.' Heron considered Whidbey Island even more promising. 'On a voyage of discovery in the Cadboro' last summer,' he told Hargrave, 'I however found out a most eligible spot, on Whidbey's Island, which is most advantageously situated, between the Gulf of Georgia, Admiralty Inlet, and the Straits of Juan de Fuca – This place, if not chosen for the Grand Depot, is, at all events to answer for this post [Fort Nisqually] and Fort Langley.' The plan floundered, partly because Yale objected: a post on Whidbey Island would have cut into Fort Langley's territory and, Yale wrote, have 'so injurious an influence on the salmon and fur trade.' The main hindrance, however, was John McLoughlin, who was opposed to the idea of a new northern depot and ignored repeated requests to establish one.[17]

In London there was a greater sense of urgency. Throughout the 1830s, W. Kaye Lamb notes, the G&C and Simpson displayed a 'continual anxiety' about the joint occupancy of Oregon Territory, and became increasingly convinced of the need for a new northern depot. In the spring of 1834, the G&C told Simpson that

the unhealthy state of Vancouver for several years past, and the distance at which it is situated from the Sea, renders it by no means so well adapted for the sole depot on the West side of the Mountains, now that the Trade is extended to the Coast: we therefore think that a Depot should be situated on the shore of Puget Sound, where there are many places highly favourable for a Seaside Depot.[18]

McLoughlin visited Puget Sound in 1835, but could find no suitable place. Following repeated requests from Simpson and the G&C, McLoughlin finally instructed Captain McNeill of the *Beaver* to examine, in the summer of 1837, the 'south end of Vancouver's Island for the purpose of selecting a convenient situation for an Establishment on a large scale, possessing all the requisites for farming, rearing of Cattle together with a good harbor and abundance of timber, in short combining every advantage which is desirable such a situation should furnish.'[19] McNeill examined three harbours – Sooke, Esquimalt, and Victoria – and selected Victoria as the most promising. McLoughlin and Douglas visited the site in 1837. 'I am pursuaded,' Douglas reported to Simpson, 'that no part of this Sterile & Rock bound Coast will be found better adapted for the site of the proposed Depot or to combine, in a high degree, the desired requisites, of a secure harbour accessible to shipping at every season, of good pasture, and, to a certain extent, of improvable tillage land.' McLoughlin, however, continued to stall, arguing that the Columbia remained the only practicable route to the interior, that the loss of the company's ships on the Columbia bar was due to the captains' negligence, and that the new depot would be too costly.[20]

Meanwhile, in 1836-7, the G&C entered into negotiations with the British government regarding an extension of the HBC's 1821 licence for exclusive trade west of Rupert's Land, which was up for renewal. The company sought renewal, Rich wrote, 'not only with the old arguments put forward in 1821, that competition in the fur trade meant ruin and debauchery for the Indians, but also on the ground that the Company intended to develop an agricultural colony ... An agricultural settlement could always find support in the Colonial Office.' The agricultural settlements were Nisqually and Cowlitz, soon to be transferred to the Puget's Sound Agricultural Company. The G&C wanted to demonstrate an interest in the valuable region immediately north of the Columbia, so as to strengthen the British claim. The company's negotiations with the Colonial Office were successful. In May 1838, the government awarded the company a further twenty-one years' exclusive access to the Indian trade west of the Rockies.[21]

Simpson provided the G&C with much of the information they presented to the Colonial Office, and his arguments reveal a knowledge of the commercial potential of the Gulf of Georgia and Puget Sound. He already feared an unfavourable boundary settlement and advocated the prompt establishment of a new northern depot. In February 1837, Simpson summarized the HBC's commercial achievement on the Pacific:

The fur trade is the principal branch of business at present in the country situated between the Rocky Mtns and the Pacific Ocean. On the banks of the

Columbia River, however, where the soil and climate are favourable to cultivation, we are directing our attention to agriculture on a large scale, and there
is every prospect that we shall soon be able to establish important branches
of export trade from thence in the articles of wool, tallow, hides, tobacco, and
grain of various kinds.[22]

The Country situated between the Northern Bank of the Columbia River,
which empties itself into the Pacific in Latitude 46°20', and the Southern bank
of Frazer's River, which empties itself into the Gulph of Georgia in Latitude
49° is remarkable for the salubrity of its climate, and the excellence of its soil,
and possesses within the Straits of De Fuca some of the finest harbours in
the world, being protected from the weight of the Pacific by Vancouver's Island
and other Islands ... The possession of that Country by Great Britain may
become an object of very great importance, and we are strengthening our
claims to it (independent of the claims of prior discovery and occupation for
the purpose of Indian trade) by forming the nucleus of a Colony thru' the
establishment of farms and settlement of some of our retiring officers and
servants as agriculturalists.[23]

In the same month, the G&C recognized the two distinct sections of
the company's business by proposing to divide the Columbia Department operations in half, immediately, and to create a new depot within
the Straits of Juan de Fuca or Puget Sound, owing in part to the hazardous Columbia River bar. 'Besides this principal Depot,' they wrote,
'we intend that Fort Vancouver should be maintained as a Depot for the
business of the Columbia River, New Caledonia, and the Trapping Expeditions, likewise for the business with the Sandwich Islands, and as an
Agricultural and Grazing Establishment on a large scale, but to be supplied with Goods from the New Depot, which is to be named Fort
Adelaide.' The HBC's frontier policies on the lower Columbia, Snake
River, and the North West Coast meant that in 1841-2 Vancouver Island
was entirely beyond the reach of American commerce or influence. The
south end of Vancouver Island was very likely to remain British even in
the event of an unfavourable boundary settlement; it contained harbours
ideal for the trades of the Pacific, North West Coast, and Gulf of
Georgia, and the department's furs could be sent directly to England
without having to navigate the Columbia bar. Simpson was also worried
about having 'the whole of our valuable property warehoused at one
depot' on the volatile lower Columbia.[24]

The G&C, in December 1839, finally authorized Simpson to investigate McLoughlin's objections to a northern depot and to recommend the most suitable site. Simpson decided to ignore McLoughlin's concerns and build a new depot on Vancouver Island. Indeed, he planned a total restructuring of the company's business on the Pacific, what Douglas called the 'concentration of the trade on the Coast'; namely, the centralization of the company's business in the regions reached through the Strait of Juan de Fuca.[25] This concentration involved phasing out the Vancouver depot, closing the HBC's operations in California, abandoning the posts in Russian America, building a new depot on Vancouver Island, and developing a broad range of resources in the Gulf of Georgia and Strait of Juan de Fuca. The company's centre of gravity would shift north.

In 1842, Simpson prepared for the abandonment of the Columbia River itself. He rightly feared that the new international boundary would be drawn in a line westward to a point on Puget Sound, or even along the forty-ninth parallel, though publicly he stated (as late as 1843) that the boundary was likely to follow the Columbia, Snake, and Clearwater rivers to the continental divide.[26]

Simpson also did not share the Columbians' optimism about the commercial prospects of California. In November 1841, he pointed out that the most recent Southern Party had 'made indifferent hunts, principally within the tide-range from the Bay of Yerba Buena; on the outlets of the Buenaventura & other streams falling into that Bay; bringing out about 1200 Beaver & Otter,' but that the profits on the year's operations were only about £350. This was a very small return in the company's scheme of things. Early in 1842, Simpson visited San Francisco and Monterey and found the fur trade of the Sacramento River and surrounding country exhausted. Francis Ermatinger told him that beaver on all the rivers falling into San Francisco Bay were becoming scarce, and that there would not be 'remunerating occupation for a trapping party in that quarter another year.' Bands of American trappers, Simpson learned, working from the east, had rendered the Rio Colorado 'totally destitute of fur bearing animals.'[27]

Although Douglas and Rae in 1840-41 had negotiated concessions from the Mexican government, bought property, and set up an agency at Yerba Buena, Simpson had no hesitation in abandoning California on account of the scarcity of hides and poor commercial prospects. In November 1841, he reported privately to Donald Ross on his California plans:

The consignment sent to ... California, has commanded higher prices, but upon Credit, & from the rapid decline of the hide trade in that quarter, owing to the greatly reduced Stock of Cattle, I am very doubtful, notwithstanding the flattering reports of prospects, that our operations there will not turn out so profitably as could be wished; of this however, I shall be a better judge on my return. The Doctor & Douglas are very sanguine of great results ... I am not however, so much so, & should be very agreeably surprised if we benefit much by those new branches of trade.[28]

Ermatinger repeated to Simpson that the southern fur trade was in serious decline; 'there was no field south of the Umpqua, where a party of more than 10 or 12 trappers in number can be employed to advantage.' In March, Simpson wrote to McLoughlin:

From Mr Ermatinger's report of the country both on the Sacramento and other rivers falling into the Bay of San Francisco, and that of the Rio Colorado, about Red Bay, it is quite evident that no good can arise from persecuting the Fur trade or maintaining the trapping parties in those districts of country; and after the operations of the present season are over, instead of sending an Expedition back to California, or forming a trading establishment at Pelican or Trinidad Bay, as was contemplated, or any other part of the coast or interior country, South of the Shasty Mountains, I have to beg that the Expedition be broken up ... in short, the sooner we break off all communications, either directly or indirectly with California, the better.[29]

McLoughlin, however, ignored Simpson, and authorized the departure of the Southern Party for another two years.

Simpson had little faith in the Yerba Buena agency. He believed that McLoughlin had gone into business there precipitately, and he did 'not see that any good can arise from you or Mr Douglas revisiting California.' Simpson learned that California's whole exports or marketable produce consisted annually of only 50,000 to 60,000 ox and cow hides and 25,000 to 30,000 quintals of tallow. 'The only source of commerce that this country at present possesses arises from its numerous herds of black cattle.' This was a pathetic output for such a fine country, and Simpson ordered the closure of the agency.[30]

He applied an equally sharp knife to the northern posts. Since the *Beaver* was doing such a fine job of collecting coastal pelts, forts Taku, Stikine, and McLoughlin could be closed despite their productive fur trades. The steamship's regular visits were enough to engross the coastal fur trade and keep the Americans at bay. Fort Simpson, however, would be maintained as the anchor of the North West Coast trade and the only post north of Fort Langley. The company, with no competition in the interior, could still intercept furs that made their way to the coast. For example, a portion of Fort Stikine's returns came from 'the Nahanis' in the interior. 'Nearly all the furs collected at this post,' Simpson wrote in November 1841, 'which are appropriated by us, are brought from the British interior territory.'[31] Through its regular coastal visits, the *Beaver* could collect such pelts.

The closure of the posts and their substitution with the *Beaver* would save £4,000 a year; the steamship would collect the 10,000 otter and beaver skins available annually on the North West Coast. 'The trade of the coast,' Simpson wrote, 'cannot with any hope of making it a profitable business, afford the maintenance of so many establishments as are now occupied for its protection.' The posts fell victim to the industrial revolution: the *Beaver* could visit the coast six times a year, at 'stated periods' that, Simpson argued, 'would be conveniently often for the purpose of collecting the trade, and of supplying the Indians.'[32] The *Beaver* was then based at Nisqually. If the vessel were kept in constant operation, Simpson told McLoughlin, '& if actively employed, she will be found quite equal to all the inland transport work from the depot in the Straits of De Fuca, including Puget Sound and Frasers River, up to Cape Spencer, so that no sailing vessel need ever enter that inland navigation.'[33]

The *Beaver*'s success in navigating coastal inlets had also cut into Fort McLoughlin's returns, and Simpson declared the post redundant. The fort had been formed for the protection of the fur trade 'while American opposition existed on the coast,' but it 'may now with others be abandoned without either loss or inconvenience to the business.' It was, the G&C tried to convince McLoughlin, a measure of economy. Forts McLoughlin and Taku were closed in 1843, and Stikine was finally closed in 1849 and its operations relocated to the coal deposits on Vancouver Island.[34]

Local officers were upset with Simpson's economies and his supreme faith in the *Beaver*'s ability to manage the coastal fur trade. McLoughlin, as Simpson told company Governor Andrew Colvile privately in November 1841, was one. 'The doctor is as much opposed to the abandonment of the posts on the N.W. Coast noticed in the general despatch, as he has all along been to the Steamer, & for no other reason that I can discover, than that the measure did not originate with himself.' A few months later, Tod wrote that 'the whole chain of Forts on the Nor. West Coast, which cost such immense sums to establish, but which now may be maintained at a comparatively small expense, are to be abandoned, and the trade there in future carried on by means of a steamer.'[35]

Simpson was pleased with the new export trades, the performance of the HBC marine department, and the profit of the Oahu agency. On his visit to the Sandwich Islands in March 1842, he was overwhelmed by geographical metaphors. He wrote that the island group 'naturally connects the east and the west, as the south and north,' and that it 'may, without involving any inadequate sacrifice, be regarded as a stepping-stone from the whole of the American coast to the Celestial Empire.' 'In effect, the group is a kind of station-house, where two railroads cross one another, each with parallel lines for opposite trains.' In these statements, one can detect faint echoes of Simpson's proposed Canton adventure of the 1820s, and of Mackenzie and Dalrymple's schemes before him. Simpson ordered the Oahu agency maintained and expanded.[36]

He also proposed a new arrangement, in which the two ships sent annually by the company to North America – one to York Factory, the other to Fort Vancouver – would be supplemented by a third vessel that would make a Pacific voyage every two years. Two vessels would go to Fort Vancouver in 1842, one in 1843, two in 1844, and so on. They would carry British manufactured goods for the company's Oahu agency and for the coastal trades. Each should 'stow away a great many goods, I think little short of £18,000 to £20,000 worth of general cargo,' and all ships bound for the Columbia would visit Oahu. The demand for the third ship, Simpson realized, was greater on the Pacific than on Hudson Bay. 'The extra ship will find full occupation by coming here [Fort Vancouver] again,' he wrote, 'as I think from the increasing demands of the Russ. Am. Coy, we shall in future require one ship entirely for that concern.' Simpson's proposal indicates just how active the company's business was becoming on the north Pacific coast. On a more mundane and equally characteristic level, he asked the G&C to send a person out from England to Oahu qualified to tin meat, fish, and soups derived from Columbia produce. Simpson proposed that these tinned preserves be sold among 'the shipping frequenting these islands,' and sent to the 'China market.'[37]

Simpson found good reasons – commercial, political, and strategic – for proposing to phase out the Columbia River depot, and he found equally good reasons for relocating the depot to Vancouver Island. He was disgusted with his enforced three-week idleness at the mouth of the river in August 1841. The bar was time-consuming to cross and was also highly dangerous. It could take as long to get from Fort Vancouver to the open Pacific as from there to Oahu. Finally, the largest ships of the day – those drawing fifteen or more feet – could not cross the bar even in the most favourable conditions.[38]

At Oahu in March 1842, Simpson had galvanized his thoughts into a coherent new policy with immense implications, one in which the fur trade of the coast warranted scarcely a mention. He told the G&C that his long wait inside Cape Disappointment had reminded him 'very

FIGURE 21 Henry Warre spent two days in September 1845 sketching at the entrance of the Columbia River. This watercolour shows the HBC's barque *Vancouver* waiting off Cape Disappointment. 'The Vancouver failed in her efforts,' Warre wrote in his journal, '& was 31 days knocking about off the entrance to this dangerous River ... the tide sweeping across the Sands like a Sluice.' [*Cape Disappointment at the Mouth of the Columbia River,* American Antiquarian Society]

forcibly to the importance of a depot being formed for such portion of the Company's business as is more immediately connected with the foreign trade and shipping department, on some eligible part of the coast.' Simpson's important dispatch contains the blueprint for the company's business on the Pacific until 1858 and later:

> In measure as the natural resources and sources of commerce of the Northern Pacific and its shores and interior country develop themselves, in like measure does it become apparent that we cannot avail ourselves of them advantageously, while entirely dependent on Fort Vancouver as the principal depot; as independent of the dangers of the [river] bar, the time lost in watching opportunities either to get out or in (frequently from a month to six weeks, while three weeks more are often consumed after crossing the bar, in getting from Cape Disappointment up to Fort Vancouver) renders it impossible to calculate with any degree of certainty on the quantum of work that ought to be performed by the shipping, deranging the best laid plans, burdening the different branches of the business with very heavy shipping charges, and depriving us of the means of embarking in other branches of commerce, which might be carried on with great advantage, had we a depot eligibly situated on the coast.
>
> The southern end of Vancouver's Island, forming the northern side of the Straits of de Fuca, appears to me the best situation for such an establishment as is required. From the very superficial examination that has been made, it is ascertained that there are several good harbours in that neighbourhood: no place, however, has yet been found, combining all the advantages required, the most important of which are, a safe and accessible harbour, well situated for defence, with waterpower for grist and saw mills; abundance of timber for house construction and exportation; and the adjacent country well adapted for tillage and pasture farms on an extensive scale. I had not an opportunity of landing on the southern end of the island, but from the distant view we had of it in passing between Puget Sound and the Gulf of Georgia, and the report of Chief Factor McLoughlin and others who have been there, we have every reason to believe there will be no difficulty in finding an eligible situation in that quarter for the establishments in question.[39]

This plan, Simpson continued, would negate the worst possible outcome in the negotiations about to take place between the British and American governments:

> Independent of the reasons already given for establishing another depot, there are two which occur to me of much importance; the one is that the proximity

to Fort Vancouver of the Willamette Settlement, composed as the majority of its inhabitants is, of worthless and lawless characters of every description from the United States, is productive of well grounded alarm for the safety of the valuable property deposited there, rendering it highly expedient to lessen the risk by separating it between two depots. The other reason is, that in the final adjustment of the boundary question, it is more than probable that a line drawn through the Straits of de Fuca till it strikes the mainland south of Whidbey's Island, will become the coast boundary between Great Britain and the United States, in the Northern Pacific. I say so, because I am of opinion the Government of the United States will insist on having a port on the North West Coast, and that Great Britain will, for the sake of peace, accept the Straits of de Fuca as a boundary on the coast, and thereby give up Puget Sound and Hoods Canal, together with the country situated between those inlets and the lower parts of the Columbia. In that case, I presume the line would be continued from the southern end of Whidbey's Island, in an easterly direction, till it struck Lewis River, and following up that river till it struck the Rocky Mountains. It is exceedingly desirable, however, for the British interest in this quarter and for the national honour, that Her Majesty's Government should not submit to such degrading conditions; but I think it is nevertheless well to be prepared for the worst, and under all circumstances I am of opinion that another depot should be established with the least possible delay, and that on the southern end of Vancouver's Island, such establishment to be the depot of the coast, and Fort Vancouver that for the interior of the Columbia, including New Caledonia, and for any trapping parties it may be advisable to maintain.[40]

Simpson's new plan extended from the general to the specific. For details, the plan relied on his own observations and those of James Douglas, who was highly regarded by company management. It is hard not to see the chief factor's influence behind several of Simpson's specific recommendations. Douglas had spent from April to October of 1840 exploring the coast with its larger commercial potential in view, and he would be given the responsibility of initiating the new plan in 1843.[41]

There were two branches of trade, Simpson wrote, that could be carried on with great advantage from the proposed new depot: salmon fishing and whaling. 'Immense shoals of salmon and of very superior quality, are to be found periodically between the mainland and the shores of Vancouvers Island,' he wrote. The demand for salmon was increasing and promised to become very great; he regarded the salmon fisheries 'as a growing and almost inexhaustible source of trade.' Simpson devised an ambitious plan to tow a barge of 100 to 150 tons behind the *Beaver* up the coast from the new depot to Cape Spencer, stopping to trade salmon among the 'Comoucs, the Quakeeolths, the Newettees and other tribes who give their attention to fishery.' In this way, the fur and salmon trades of the coast could be secured in one fell swoop. The plan was abandoned owing to the lack of proper lumber for such a barge, the fear of ship-worm, and the expense of copper plating.[42]

He was also interested in the new depot's potential as a whaling centre. Whale oil, in its distilled form of benzene, was used in lighting London streets; the oil was dense, valuable, and easily stowed. Simpson learned of a visit to the coast by a French whaler, and in March 1842 he conceived an ambitious whaling plan. At first, he proposed to hire one Captain Hoyer, the master of a whaler based at Oahu, who was 'not unwilling' to enter the company's service. Hoyer believed that Right whales (*Balaena mysticetus*) bred 'somewhere in the bays along the North West Coast,' wrote Simpson. 'These bays, however, have not as yet been discovered, but in his opinion, they must be inside Vancouver's Island, or some of the inlets and channels in that vicinity.' Simpson thought that a post in the Straits of de Fuca would be admirably adapted for whaling, and he proposed that the company buy a fast and spacious sailing vessel. 'I think so well of this branch of business,' he concluded, 'that although perfectly sensible our engagements in this quarter are become so multifarious and complex as to be difficult of management, I cannot help recommending it.'[43]

A few months later, however, Simpson abandoned his scheme after learning that whales lived on the inside passage where sailing vessels could not navigate. He proposed instead that McLoughlin hire 'a few active experienced Harpooners and other Whale Fishers, to form part of the Crew of the Steamer' and of two fast whaleboats. A sufficient quantity of oil could always be collected in this way to fill up the English ship until other cargoes were available. Further, such a scheme would 'not involve any outlay of capital nor direct attention from the other important branches of business.' The scheme was never acted on, though whale oil from Cape Flattery and the west coast of Vancouver Island came to Fort Victoria in increasing quantities through the Native trade after 1843.[44]

Simpson also proposed that the HBC open a sawmill on Vancouver Island. In 1842, the G&C suggested that the grist and saw mills sent out by the *Vancouver* be erected 'near the new depot at Vancouver's Island' if a favourable location could be found, because the mills were more urgently required there than at Willamette Falls, their original destination. There was a good deal of valuable timber in the neighbourhood of Fort Victoria, Simpson reported. The sawmill in question was made in Aberdeen by Abernethy and Company in 1841 as a flour and barley mill for the Puget's Sound Agricultural Company, but it was transferred to the HBC in 1843. That year, Simpson ordered the mill sent to Victoria, but McLoughlin ignored him. In 1844, Simpson repeated that 'We understand from the report of Mr C.F. Douglas that there is a good situation for a tide mill at Camosun Arm, and if there be sufficient timber in the neighbourhood to form an export in that article, we think the mill in question ought to be erected there.' Simpson left it up to local management to move the mill to either forts Victoria, Nisqually, or even Simpson, and the mill was finally opened near Victoria in 1849.[45]

Simpson was aware that the general direction of his restructuring would not appeal to McLoughlin, who had devoted his life's work to the Columbia business. He had never been north of Vancouver Island. His private interests intersected increasingly with those of the incoming American settlers, and he still believed the Columbia might form the international border. Two of his children were in California. McLoughlin's outlook remained southerly even when Fort Vancouver was increasingly endangered by American settlement, and he fought tenaciously, but in vain, to convince the G&C to ignore Simpson's proposals.[46] Two days after writing officially to the G&C with his plans for the abandonment of California and the North West Coast posts, Simpson wrote privately to chief factor Donald Ross of Norway House, referring him to his dispatches to the G&C:

> From that correspondence you will see that some branches of the business promise well, while others which afforded great expectations, would if persevered in, been productive of more harm than good; & notwithstanding all my good feelings toward the Doctor, you will notice that I have not overlarded him or his management with praise. The fact is, I am not quite

clear that the business is managed in the best possible way, owing more to the want of system than a want of energy; and perhaps our engagements are rather too complicated & multifarious for the habits of business of our management.[47]

A draft of Ross's response of August 1842 has survived. In this revealing letter, he referred with admiration to the 'sweeping nature' of Simpson's retrenchment. 'As for the California business, I think it was a wise move to shut it up at once, even at a considerable sacrifice, – the Fur Trade is our proper business and I fear we shall never do much good in any other.' This is a curious statement, given Simpson's ideas for the Strait of Juan de Fuca region, and it suggests that Ross was unaware of the full range of his plans. It also reveals an outdated, hidebound belief in the ability of the fur trade to sustain the HBC through all its difficulties in all its regions. 'The Doctor [McLoughlin] is a proud and pompous man,' Ross continued, 'somewhat vain in his own parts as a man of business.' John Lee Lewes of Mackenzie River commented in April 1843 that 'We now see that we had too many Irons in the fire, some of which have been over heated, and rendered useless.'[48]

All the elements of the company's commercial and Indian policies were brought to bear on Fort Victoria, the first European settlement on Vancouver Island since the abandonment of the Spanish garrison at Nootka in the spring of 1795. The new depot was built at a place known to the Songhees people as Camosun or Camosack, or *Ku-sing-ay-lass*, which Joe McKay translated as 'the place of the strong fibre.' In what is now downtown Victoria grew willow trees, the inner bark of which, McKay wrote, was used for strapping stones for sinkers in deep-sea fishing.[49] On 16 March 1843, James Douglas recorded the fort's initial construction in his journal:

> The weather clear and warm. The gooseberry bushes growing in the woods beginning to bud.
>
> Put 6 men to dig a well and 6 others to square building timber. Spoke to the Samose [Songhees] today and informed them of our intention of building in this place which appeared to please them very much and they immediately offered their services in procuring pickets for the establishment, an offer which I gladly accepted, and promised to pay them a Blanket (2½) for every forty pickets of 22 feet by 36 inches which they bring.[50]

FIGURE 22 A pencil sketch by Henry Warre of Fort Victoria on 27 September 1845. 'I have little doubt that it will ere long eclipse Fort Vancouver and become the Head Quarters of the HBCo. West of the Rocky Mountains,' Warre wrote in his journal. [*Fort Victoria*, National Archives of Canada, C-058099]

Three days later, the Oblate missionary Father Jean-Baptiste Bolduc met 1,200 Native people 'from three large tribes, Kawitshens, Klalams and Tsamishes,' and shook hands with 600 of them in Douglas's presence on the fort site. After ten weeks, the pickets were up, the lumber prepared, and construction of the buildings underway. On 5 June 1843, Charles Ross, Roderick Finlayson, Thomas Lowe and a group of company labourers 'Commenced laying the foundation for the future Emporium of the Columbia.' 'The Fort is a quadrangle of 330 by 300 ft,' Ross wrote a few months later. 'The Buildings, exclusive of Bastions, are to be eight in number – of large dimensions, measuring 60 by 40 & 30 ft with 17 ft. Posts & Pavilion Roofs.' 'The Country is, so far as regards climate & scenery, the finest I have ever seen.'[51]

The fort was placed in the midst of the Natives' world. Victoria harbour was chosen as fort site over the superior harbour at Esquimalt because, McKay's daughter claimed, 'Camosun was more convenient for the Indians to beach their canoes.' It was to be a commercial establishment and the centre of extensive provision trades with the Native peoples. 'The natives of the surrounding country, known as the Songhies

FIGURE 23 A notebook sketch by Henry Warre of the south bastion and harbour of Fort Victoria on 27 September 1845 with the Sooke Hills and Olympic Mountains in the distance. 'The Country round the fort is very pretty – wide open prairies thinly scattered over with Fine Oak Trees.' [*The Bay of Fort Victoria*, National Archives of Canada, C-058097]

tribe, then resided at what is known as Cadboro Bay, but seeing the advantage of being near the white men they removed from their old home to the vicinity of the fort.'[52]

Fort Victoria was visited by many Native groups. In the spring of 1847, artist Paul Kane met the 'Clallums' (the local Indians), the 'Eus-a-nich,' 'Sinahomas,' and 'Cowitchans' (Saanich, Swinomish, and Cowichan), all of whom relied on the sea for much of their trade and sustenance; they had 'salmon, cod, sturgeon, and other excellent fish in great abundance.' A magnificent halibut bank lay off the entrance to the Strait of Juan de Fuca. The means of living at Victoria, Simpson wrote in 1844, were 'abundant, say fish, venison, domestic cattle & agricultural produce.'[53]

Victoria possessed other attractions. 'The place itself appears a perfect "Eden" in the midst of the dreary wilderness of the North west coast,' Douglas wrote in 1843, 'and so different is its general aspect from the wooded, rugged regions around, that one might be pardoned for supposing it had dropped from the clouds into its present position.'

FIGURE 24 Beneath its palisades, Fort Victoria attracted gatherings of Native people, company servants, and their families. Modern Wharf Street occupies the space portrayed by Henry Warre in September 1845. [*H.B.Co's. Settlement & Fort Victoria on Vancouvers Island, Straits Juan de Fuca*, American Antiquarian Society]

Simpson regarded it as 'a very Elysium in point of climate & scenery.' The southern end of the island, exposed to the Pacific Ocean, got less rain, fewer mosquitos, and more sunshine than the mountainous and cloud-locked mainland. Adam Dundas, a Royal Navy officer who visited Victoria a few years later, commented that 'Though fever and ague are very prevalent on the Main land yet from the absence of low and marshy ground they are unknown here.'[54]

Significantly, Simpson and other fur traders never regarded the island's fur trade as an object of notice. 'I do not expect,' Simpson wrote in 1842 regarding the proposed post, 'that any material benefit, as regards an increase of returns in the article of furs, will arise from this establishment.' The Natives around the new post, he reported two years later, were friendly 'but as yet, judging from the quantity of furs brought in, it does not appear they are very active either as hunters or traders, or that their country is rich in that way.' In Fort Victoria's first year of operation, only 400 beaver and land otter skins were collected. Charles

Ross wrote to a friend on Hudson Bay that 'We have got very few skins since our arrival, and it is not likely that this will ever become a lucrative Post in that ilk.' To his disgust, Yale of Fort Langley found his already disappointing fur returns drop after the opening of the new post, which attracted Native traders from Cape Flattery, Puget Sound, the Gulf of Georgia, and the west coast of Vancouver Island. At the end of the decade, Douglas observed that Fort Victoria was not very productive in furs.[55]

The climate made it possible for the Native peoples to wear woven cedar-bark clothing, rather than animal pelts, and to go barefoot year round. Kane, who spent two months at Victoria in the summer of 1847, wrote that Native men wore nothing at all in the summer, and only a cedar-bark shawl or an English blanket in the winter. 'The women wear only an apron of twisted cedar-bark shreds, tied round the waste and hanging down in front only, almost to the knees.' This was a far cry from Rupert's Land.[56]

The Victoria region contained more than enough agricultural land to maintain a fur trade post, though the fort's farm did not approach Fort Vancouver's in size or quality. Simpson wrote of a range of prairie between six and nine miles square 'extending as far as Port Gonzalo, well adapted for tillage & pasture.' The *Beaver* brought horses and cattle from Fort Nisqually to the new post in October 1843, and by the end of the year, five acres had been seeded to wheat.[57] Berthold Seemann, the naturalist on board the H.M.S. *Herald*, visited the post in July 1846:

> We were astonished at what we saw. About 160 acres are cultivated with oats, wheat, potatoes, turnips, carrots, and other vegetables, and every day more land is converted into fields. Barely three years had elapsed since the settlement was made, yet all the necessaries and most of the comforts of civilized life already existed in what was a wilderness. The company, when forming an establishment such as Victoria, provide the party with food for the first year and necessary seed for the forthcoming season; after that time it is expected that the settlements will provide completely for their future subsistence.[58]

· In the fall of 1844, the G&C instructed the captain of the HBC ship *Vancouver* to proceed from London directly to Fort Victoria instead of Fort Vancouver. This first supply vessel arrived at the new post in the spring of 1845, and the first shipment of the Columbia Department's fur returns from Victoria occurred in December 1846, when the *Vancouver* left for London.[59] Within a short time, Fort Victoria's commercial purpose would be fulfilled, and its business would became very extensive indeed. Peter Ogden remarked in 1852 that 'As a centre of operations for a general Commerce, such as we now carry on in the Pacific (and I presume there is no intention of abandoning all branches of business except the actual trade in Furs) Fort Victoria is better situated than any point with which I am acquainted.'[60]

In 1843, the centre of gravity of the HBC's operations began to shift. The new depot, together with the provision posts at Langley and Nisqually and with the shipping, formed the centre of a new regional economy based broadly on the extraction, trade, and export of varied natural resources. The region already exported salmon and foodstuffs, and the coastal fur trade had reached its limit. With the founding of Fort Victoria, the move of British commercial capital to the north started in earnest. The company's Columbia business may, as Lewes feared, have been 'dished' by the 1846 Oregon Treaty, but the rest of the coast, islands, and interior remained at the company's disposal. The HBC that undertook to colonize Vancouver Island in 1849 was not the mythical fur trade company of birchbark canoes, northern rivers, and beaver pelts, but a general resource company that had recognized an abundant new environment and a broad commercial opportunity.[61]

CHAPTER 12

The Native Foundation
of Trade and Labour

*The most certain means of retaining the trade in our
own hands is to aid and assist the Indians in working the
treasures of their own country.*

– JAMES DOUGLAS TO DONALD MCLEAN
(THOMPSON'S RIVER), 26 DECEMBER 1857[1]

The Hudson's Bay Company had certain advantages over Native traders in the Columbia Department. The company's brigades, express canoes, and steamships allowed the rapid movement of trade goods and transmission of information regarding Native trade demands. Its centralized administration, 'strategies of power,'[2] long experience in Indian trade, and monopoly of non-Native trade helped it to gauge the economic demands of linguistically and culturally distinct people occupying a vast area. By the early nineteenth century, HBC officials had been dealing, with varying degrees of success, with Native trade and trading competition east of the Rockies for 150 years. The company's activities created a growing demand for Native pelts for the London market, for Native provisions for the domestic and Pacific markets, and for Native labour.

In this chapter I assess the nature and scale of Native involvement in the HBC's Pacific economy. After 1821, the fur, provision, and export trades that made up the company's regional economy were grafted onto the established and thriving resources, trade, transport routes, and labour supplies of the coastal Native economies. The gradual extension of the company's business everywhere west of the Rockies resulted in the demise of Native forms of exchange like *haiqua* and slaves, and their gradual replacement by blankets and other British trade goods. The company's economy was, however, so intertwined with Native forms of trade and labour that slaves were prevalent in the HBC workforce before 1843. Their presence at Fort Vancouver, Nisqually, Cowlitz, the southern trapping parties, and the Willamette caused a scandal when British and American visitors learned of their existence in the late 1830s.

Contact between traders and Native people, and between local and more distant Native groups, involved an exchange of commodities. British trade goods included useful items for hunting, fishing, clothing, and ornament. 'The chief articles of trade,' Corney wrote in 1821, 'given in exchange to all the natives of the coast are muskets, blankets, powder, shot, red paint, (which they use to paint their faces,) tobacco, beads, buttons, thick brass wire, with which they make bracelets, rings, etc; ready-made clothes are in great demand; but, in fact, any trifling toys will please them.' In return, the maritime fur traders obtained sea otter pelts, slaves, salmon, *haiqua*, coppers, Native tobacco, oolichan, elk hides, and potatoes.[3]

At first, the principal medium of exchange along the lower Columbia was *haiqua*. The HBC obtained tens of thousands of these shells in the Gulf of Georgia and northern Vancouver Island and transported them cheaply on the *Beaver* to the entire coast and, via brigades, to places as distant as the Yukon River, where the shells were very valuable. In the 1820s and early 1830s, *haiqua* remained the 'currency of the country' for many Native groups throughout the Columbia Department; by the 1840s, however, 'Made Beaver' and blankets had replaced *haiqua* on much of the coast.[4]

The unit of exchange known as Made Beaver was the traditional currency of the continental and interior fur trades. Joe McKay recalled how it worked:

> No coin was necessary in dealing with the Indians. The unit of value was equal to that of a prime beaver skin weighing one pound. This unit was technically called a 'made beaver.' The value of other skins was regulated accordingly, each being either so many 'made beaver,' or so many aliquot parts of a 'made beaver.' The value of each article of merchandise given for the furs was regulated on the same principle, each article representing so many 'made beavers,' or so many fractions of a 'made beaver.'[5]

British fur traders introduced the Made Beaver to the regions west of the Rockies. It was known on the lower Columbia as 'Enna,' as Ross wrote,

> But of late, since the whites came among them, the beaver skin called enna, has been added to the currency, so that, by these two articles, [*haiqua* and *enna*] which form the medium of trade, all property is valued, and all exchange fixed and determined. An Indian, in buying an article, invariably asks the question, Queentshich hiqua? or, Queentshich enna? That is, how many hiqua? or, how many beaver skins is it?[6]

Blankets came into prominence in the last years of the maritime fur trade and early years of the land-based fur trade on the lower Columbia. Eventually they replaced both Made Beaver and *haiqua* exchange units. Made at Witney in Oxfordshire, the company's high-quality point blankets were introduced on Hudson Bay in 1779 and very quickly became important trade items; the NWC introduced similar blankets on the lower Columbia before 1821. 'The "points" were marks on the side of the blanket denoting its size and its value in beaver,' Edwin Rich wrote, 'a three point blanket being traded for three beaver, and so according to the number of points ... It was the quality of the blankets and the unfailing fairness with which the points were kept to standard measurements which made them so valuable an asset to the Hudson's Bay Company.'[7] By 1829, blankets had become the standard trade item on the lower Columbia, as at least one ill-equipped Boston trader discovered to his chagrin. 'There is no market for Cotton Goods here in Columbia River,' Captain Thompson of the *Convoy* informed his backer, 'nothing will buy Skins but Columbia River Blankets, Scarlet & Blue Cloths, Beads, Muskets, Duffil, Trunks, &c. These are the principal articles for Columbia River.'[8]

On the Pacific, the company adapted its exchange system to suit the local Native economies, in which beaver were scarce, trade prolific, and commodities numerous. Due to their quality, utility, and uniformity, blankets became the main unit of exchange, but they were usually exchanged only for large or valuable items such as beaver or sea otter skins, slaves, batches of haiqua, the ransoming of captives, and ultimately the purchase of land[9]; the company rarely exchanged blankets for occasional labour, salmon, or other provisions, for which beads, tobacco, and smaller, less valuable items were exchanged. Geologist George Dawson later noted that

The *blanket* is now ... the recognised currency, not only among the Haidas, but generally along the coast. It takes the place of the beaver-skin currency of the interior of British Columbia and the North-west Territory. The blankets used in trade are distinguishable by points, or marks on the edge, woven into their texture, the best being four-point, the smallest and poorest one-point. The acknowledged unit of value is a single two-and-a-half-point blanket, now worth a little over $1.50. Everything is referred to this unit, even a large four-point blanket is said to be worth so many *blankets*.[10]

On board the *Beaver* in 1841, Simpson noted that blankets were 'the grand equivalent' among the Quakeolths and Comoucs; later in the decade, Kane described the blanket as 'the standard by which the value of all articles on the north west coast is calculated.' They were the grandest of trade goods; at Fort Victoria, Kane heard of a potlatch where one man distributed twelve bales of blankets.[11] Blankets replaced dog-hair and mountain-goat blankets in the Gulf of Georgia region, as British naturalist Berthold Seemann found at Port Townsend in 1846: 'Since the Hudson's Bay Company have established themselves ... English blankets have been so much in request that the dog's hair manufacture has been rather at a discount, eight or ten blankets being given for one sea-otter skin.'[12]

The company's barter system, therefore, applied equally well to blankets as to Made Beaver and sea otter skins; there was little difference in the trading mechanism. Coin or specie did not enter the region until later. When furs were absent, which was increasingly the case, Native people found alternative ways of retaining access to the company's blankets and other trade goods. These alternatives consisted of identifying commodities required by the company, such as provisions and labour, and exchanging them for the same selection of British goods offered in the fur trade. Commodities proliferated in the presence of a flexible unit of exchange, an abundant resource base, and diverse Native trade. In terms of the HBC's exchange system, there was no practical difference between providing a beaver or marten pelt, a barrel of coal, a basket of potatoes, a pound of isinglass or whale oil, a brace of wild fowl, a canoe-load of salmon, or a day's agricultural labour to the company. Table 9 shows some Columbia Department points of exchange.[13]

A persistent demand for European commodities motivated the provision, fur, and export trades. Part of the HBC's commercial success was

TABLE 9 Selected rates of exchange, 1824-47

Date	Place	'Currency'	Native commodity
1824-5	Fort George	Goods worth 7 shillings	35 salmon
1825	Fraser River	1 blanket	10 beaver
1834	Snake River	1 awl and 1 fish hook	1 dried salmon
1834	Snake River	1 butcher knife	10 salmon
1834	Lower Columbia	10-12 blankets	1 slave
1834	Fort Vancouver	1 load powder and shot	1 duck
1834	Fort Vancouver	2 loads powder and shot	1 goose
1834	Fort Vancouver	4 loads powder and shot	1 swan
1834	Fort Vancouver	10 loads ammunition	1 deer
1835	Fort George	1 blanket	5 fathoms *haiqua*
1836	Cascades	1 twist tobacco	Carriage of boat
1837	NW Coast	8 blankets	1 sea otter skin
1837	Lower Columbia	10-15 blankets	1 slave
1840	Fort George	1 shirt	Canoe repair
1840	McNeill Harbour	1 blanket	1 beaver
1840	McNeill Harbour	1 blanket	400 *haiqua*
1840	McNeill Harbour	1 codhook	20 *haiqua*
1840	Fort Simpson	14 gallons oolichan oil	1 beaver
1840	Fort Vancouver	4 handkerchiefs	4 miles by canoe
1843	Fort Victoria	1 blanket	40 cedar pickets
1846	Fort George	1 shirt	10-15 salmon
1847	Fort Victoria	12 blankets	1 sea otter skin

its ability to adapt its exchange system from the trade in fur to the trade in provisions, then to the exchange of commodities destined for export, then to on-site labour, and finally to land itself. The trading mechanism remained the same. Mutual interest and trading opportunities drove the exchanges, as did the utility, quality, or novelty of British manufactures.

Native people were also willing to go to great lengths to retain access to HBC posts. A 'middleman' or homeguard trade appeared whenever the company opened a fort or traded regularly in a Native community or trading station. Posts, Anderson wrote, were 'the source of comparative affluence' because they gave local people a trading advantage over their neighbours. The homeguard provided provisions, security, and labour to company personnel.[14] They restricted access to a post's trade, profited by controlling transactions, and expanded their trading terri-

FIGURE 25 The depot at Fort Victoria and its mirror-image 'homeguard,' a Songhees village in adjacent Esquimalt. This 1847 watercolour by Paul Kane, sketched from the present-day location of the British Columbia parliament buildings, shows the proximity of trade and labour supply. [*Fort Victoria and an Indian Village*, Royal Ontario Museum, 946.15.212]

tories. Among the coastal middlemen groups were the Chinook of the lower Columbia, the Coast Tsimshian of the lower Skeena, and the Taku Indians. 'These Indians,' wrote Simpson at Fort Taku in 1841, 'were delighted to have us settled among them; and on this ground they viewed with much jealousy the visits of more distant savages, to whom they were desirous of acting as middlemen.'[15]

The application of British commercial capital to all regions of the Columbia Department required the productive power of Native peoples. Provisions and salmon obtained cheaply from the lower Columbia and lower Fraser allowed the company to ship profitably to overseas markets. While such exports were overseen by a select and competent workforce of tradesmen, and staffed by skilled European or Canadian labourers and Kanakas, they ultimately relied on the resources, provisions, or labour of Native people, especially the Chinook and Coast Salish. An immense creation and transfer of wealth occurred whereby commodities obtained from tens of thousands of Native people were converted in European and Pacific marketplaces into hard cash and

handsome dividends that went directly to a few dozen company shareholders, governors, and officers. The documents are full of gleeful, or at
least surprised, references to the absurd cheapness with which provisions,
export commodities, Native labour, and other services could be obtained
during the era of the company's monopoly. Tourists and occasional
visitors benefited from the low prices afforded by the absence of American competition.[16]

Native labour was both direct and indirect. Direct labour took the
form of work, while indirect labour took the form of trade. Hunting
itself was a form of off-site (indirect) labour, as was the work of the
Native people who guided, transported, and supplied the continental
explorers of the fur trade companies. Native labour underlay and, struc-
turally, united the company's trades: Indians hunted, trapped, traded,
travelled, fished, farmed, mined, and logged for the company. More than
the fur trade, the company's transport systems, provision trades, and new
export trades drew Native people into the HBC's Pacific labour force.
A trading imperative unified the Europeans and the indigenous peoples.
The west coast peoples were often characterized by Europeans as traders
rather than hunters,[17] and the HBC was in law and practice a trading
company with a broad interest in natural resources.

On the west coast, Native labour underpinned the company's operations during the years of intensified trapping, provision production, and
resource development. Non-Native labour was concentrated at the posts,
in transport, and in producing 'country-made trade goods.' The provision trades were perhaps the primary and most constant points of intersection between the Native communities and the fur trade economy:
subsistence was of more urgent importance to a post's survival than fur
acquisition. Provision supply required the active and varied involvement
of women as well as men. HBC standards of trade for 'country produce'
emerged in the nineteenth century alongside the better-known fur trade
standards.[18] In the absence of competition, a uniform value of country
produce, like that of pelts, could be established and maintained across
physical and cultural boundaries or between posts and districts, and the
provision exchange could be as closely monitored as the fur trade.

After salmon, potatoes were the most important Native provision
obtained by the traders throughout the Columbia Department. They

were introduced in the interior and on the coast by such traders as Harmon, Ross, Franchère, and Yale, and their cultivation was adopted by Native people, who impressed visitors with their apparent enthusiasm for this most basic 'European' food.

Potato cultivation spread rapidly through the Gulf of Georgia after the establishment of Fort Langley.[19] Visitors to the fort, already familiar with the harvesting of camas and other roots, introduced potatoes to their home communities. In the early 1830s, Yale encouraged the nearby Kwantlen 'to till the ground and raise potatoes,' and in 1839 Douglas informed the Governor and Committee of the general diffusion of the potato:

> I may be permitted to mention ... as a matter to interest the friends of our native population, and all who desire to trace the first dawn and early progress of civilization, that the Cowegians around Fort Langley, influenced by the counsel and example of the fort, are beginning to cultivate the soil, many of them having with great perseverance and industry cleared patches of forest land of sufficient extent to plant, each ten bushels of potatoes; the same spirit of enterprize extends, though less generally, to the Gulf of Georgia and de Fuca's straits, where the very novel sight of flourishing fields of potatoes satisfies the missionary visitors that the Honourable Company neither oppose, nor feel indifferent to, the march of improvement.[20]

These tubers became the standard accompaniment to salmon and replaced the common camas as a staple food in southern regions. Camas grew from the lower Columbia to Puget Sound and through the Gulf of Georgia; indeed, forts Vancouver, Nisqually, and Victoria and Cowlitz Farm were constructed on or near extensive camas plains. Native women were responsible for the bulbs' procurement. 'This root,' wrote English botanist Thomas Nuttall, 'which is wholesome to almost all palates, is collected by the aborigines in large quantities, and constitutes their greatest substitute for the *Cerealia* of civilised life.'[21]

Potatoes eventually superseded camas and other Native roots. Simpson, near Fort Colvile in 1841, was surprised to find potatoes being grown in place of camas. 'In one of their lodges,' he wrote, 'we were surprised to find several baskets of potatoes; and, in answer to our inquiries on the subject, we were shown two patches of ground where they had been produced, the seed and implements having been supplied from Fort Colvile.'[22]

The potato also made an appearance on the North West Coast, though its introduction between 1800 and 1815 predated the company's arrival. 'Some years since,' missionary Jonathan Green wrote in 1829, 'a trader left a few English potatoes at Queen Charlotte's Island, and instructed the natives in the cultivation of them. This is doubtless a benefit to the Indians, but not less so to the traders themselves. For years, at very little expense, they have been able to furnish [them] with most excellent potatoes.' Dunn visited the Charlottes in 1836 and found large potato gardens next to Haida houses. 'This vegetable was first given to them by an American captain; and is now grown in abundance, and traded by them to the vessels visiting their harbour, and to the traders at Fort Simpson. I have known from five to eight hundred bushels being traded in one season, from these Indians, at Fort Simpson.'[23]

The Haida, anxious to retain access to European goods, compensated for the disappearance of sea otter by trading potatoes to American coasters and later to the HBC.[24] Beaver and other valuable furs were absent in the Queen Charlotte Islands, and no local supply of land furs could replace the sea otter. On his visit to the Charlottes in 1825, Scouler noted potato cultivation, which, like Douglas on the Gulf of Georgia, he viewed as a moral advance as much as a useful introduction:

Around Skittegass, the potato is now pretty extensively cultivated, and they brought us plenty to sell. One cannot but rejoice at this symptom of commencing civilisation, which, if persevered in, will limit their wanderings, and give them better ideas of property, and teach them that more is to be gained by cultivating their fertile soil, than in following salmon up every creek, or spending days in the uncertain support of the chase.[25]

A.C. Anderson recalled that surplus potatoes produced by the Haida were used for 'bartering abroad for luxuries not otherwise available.' Native people even provided traders with their initial stocks of seed potatoes: in 1835, for example, Work obtained seed potatoes for Fort Simpson from the people of Laredo Sound, who appeared very poor. He noted that 'this formerly used to be one of the best places for sea otter on the Coast, but now scarcely any is found among them. They grow considerable of potatoes, they had several patches under cultivation about their village.' The potato trade provided major points of intersection between the HBC and Native economies. And the Haida transition from the sea otter trade to the potato trade suggests that Native people, like the Europeans, were quick to look beyond the fur trade.[26]

Two traditions of Native involvement in the fur trade economy met and merged on the Pacific coast after 1821: a regional tradition developed by the maritime fur traders on the west coast, and a Canadian and British land-based, continental tradition brought to the coast by the Pacific, North West, and Hudson's Bay companies. Both traditions operated against a backdrop of Native economies long noted for trading acumen. The HBC's employment of Native people, as with many other elements of its commercial practice, originated east of the Rockies as a measure of economy and expediency. The payment of Native people for their labour was an established custom in the Montreal- and London-based fur trades.[27]

In Rupert's Land, competition between the Hudson's Bay and North West companies brought more aboriginal workers into both the NWC and the HBC. In the early nineteenth century, part-time or seasonal Native labour became increasingly important as these companies extended their transport and provision systems toward the Rockies and beyond. Harold Innis, the first historian to assess Native involvement in the fur trade, provided numerous examples from Rupert's Land in the 1830s. Native people were hired as crew of freight boats; more than fifty Indians were employed at Norway House in the summer of 1832. Recent research supports Innis's early observations.[28] From the beginning, Native women's work was at least as important as men's in the provision trades that supported the continental fur trade. Native women, Sylvia Van Kirk notes, were an unofficial part of the labour force: 'They were servants who never received wages in any real sense and undoubtedly both companies profited by this source of cheap labour.' Numerous cases of Native women's provisioning work have been noted from Rupert's Land during Simpson's regime.[29] Women's work was also important in the Columbia Department. Ethnographic and archaeological sources indicate that women and men equally exploited the diverse maritime abundance of the region, and fur trade sources show, generally, continuity of precontact patterns.[30]

The British fur traders were not the only Europeans to exploit Native labour. An old and apparently harsh tradition of Native work existed in

California. In 1815, at Monterey, Northwester Corney wrote that the Spanish 'keep the Indians under great subjection, making them work very hard, chained two and two.' At Fort Ross, the Russians hired Natives for general labour and to hunt the sea otter, while Captain Sutter hired Indians by the hundreds and paid them in trade goods, HBC-style. In 1842 General Vallejo had 300 Indians in his employ at Yerba Buena, and Native people also worked at the missions.[31]

In the late 1820s, the HBC began hiring Indians in numbers on the lower Columbia and Fraser rivers. Previously, some Native people had been reluctant to work for the company because, Tolmie recalled, they considered labour the work of slaves:

> In the earlier years of the whiteman's presence ... [the] Tshinooks of the Lower Columbia and the Indians thence to Puget Sound would not work for the new-comers, any individual so-doing being reproached as placing himself on the level of a slave.
>
> The late, Canadian born, Mr. J.M. Yale, so long of the Hudson's Bay Co. at Langley, Fraser River, was perhaps the first to induce the natives to work. At Fort McLoughlin, Milbank Sound, they did day's work at extracting large stumps in 1834-35. Not long after 1836, when the 'Beaver' began to run, the Indians at various points prepared fuel for her in advance. At Vancouver, Columbia River, the young Kliketats, in 1836, and the following years, became ploughmen, carters, boatmen, and one year, six of them, acting with perfect honesty, seined salmon on shares with the company. In 1843-44 and the following years, the natives of the south-east of Vancouver [Island] and Puget Sound, became canoe-expressmen with mails or passengers, often both, between Victoria and Nisqually, ploughmen, carters, shepherds and sheep-shearers, the women doing as well as the men at the latter work.[32]

HBC officials encouraged Native people to trade and work for the company. 'Be Affable and kind to the Natives,' McLoughlin told Alexander Lattie of Fort George, 'that their Esteem may be secured in Short Encourage them in every way prudent, to Exertion and to do that [you] must Exert yourself.' Retired fur trader Joe McKay, who arrived on the lower Columbia in 1843, also attributed the origins of Native labour on the west coast to HBC policy. He recalled that 'Having been trained to work by the Company's people, they represent now a very important factor in the labour market.'[33]

The soundness of Tolmie's and McKay's recollections is borne out by contemporary evidence from the Columbia River, where Native people had provided the Pacific Fur and North West companies with provisions. In 1816 Corney had paid an Indian hunter one blanket to supply the *Isaac Todd* with ducks, geese, and swans. David Douglas hired a twelve-year-old girl in 1825 at Fort Vancouver to make him three hats made on the English fashion, for which he gave a blanket valued at seven shillings. Wyeth hired a Chinook girl in 1836 to make moccasins. At Fort George in 1846, Native women and men traded shellfish and cedar mats to the HBC. Such transactions were very common.[34]

The Columbia River provision trades relied on Native trade and labour. Wyeth's attempt to introduce Kanaka fishermen failed because the Sandwich Islanders knew nothing of the river or the habits of the fish. Indians were important in transport on the whole lower stretch of the Columbia. They took David Douglas by canoe from Fort George to Vancouver in 1825; farther upstream, they portaged and canoed Wyeth's overlanders around the Dalles. These were everyday occurrences. Tolmie recalled that while based at Vancouver in 1840-1, he hired Indians as boatmen and canoemen. Essential, too, was Native assistance in navigating the dangerous lower Columbia. In 1834 Captain McNeill recommended to Wyeth's party that a Cowlitz Indian named George pilot their ship from the mouth of the Willamette to Baker's Bay. And Townsend wrote that 'the navigation of this river is particularly difficult in consequence of numerous shoals and sand bars, and good pilots are scarce, the Indians alone officiating in that capacity.' Indians collected and sold firewood to travellers for their nightly campfires on the banks of the Columbia above the Cascades.[35]

In some places after 1821, the off-site Native labour implicit in the provision and fur trades metamorphosed into formal, explicit, working relationships based on the demands of the new provision and export trades. Previously, the fur trade, based on straightforward commodity exchange, required what to fur traders was a largely invisible labour within the Native economy; the new trades, however, increasingly required the actual, visible, formal employment of Native people at the company's forts, farms, and work camps. Indians found they could exchange their labour as easily as the fruits of their labour, and for the same trade goods.

Native workers were perhaps most common in farming. George Roberts, who arrived at Fort Vancouver from England in 1831, recalled that 'We employed a great many Indians at Vancouver often 8 to ten ploughs & as many harrows running with them – many of the Thlicatat tribe, those Indians were hunters and root diggers & were kept away from the fort by the river Indians until Dr Tolmie was trader & took a kindly interest in them. The Doctor was proud of having so many Indians employed & always held out to the missionaries that that was the way to civilize them to teach them to work.' Tolmie himself recalled much the same thing; in 1840-1, 'the various tribes known on the Columbia River as Klikatats had by this time so much changed their notions that the Company's large fields were mostly ploughed by Indians, who around Vancouver were friendly and useful in every way.' Farther down the river, at Fort George, Indians weeded and worked in the fort garden.[36]

The hiring of Native people as agricultural labourers on the Columbia River resulted in part from the difficulty and expense of hiring freemen, most of whom lived at the rapidly developing French Canadian and Metis community of Willamette. These settlers were busy with their own farms and harvests. As Douglas wrote in 1838, 'A grievous burden is, however, imposed on the agriculture of this portion of America, by the impossibility of finding labourers, exactly, at the season, they are wanted, with the option of dismissing them at pleasure.' Three years later, Simpson noted that the whole population of the Willamette amounted to about five hundred souls, 'besides about a thousand natives of all ages, who have been domesticated as agricultural servants.' F.X. Matthieu, a French Canadian farmer on the Willamette, recalled that 'For a blanket that cost $3 you could hire an Indian a month – or perhaps two months; and many of the Indians were good workers. They could handle an axe like a white man; and on the river they were the best boatmen. They could paddle all day in a canoe, or on a bateau, and want only a little meat and salmon skin.'[37]

British fur traders were also responsible for the spread of the pidgin language, Chinook, through the department from their Columbia River headquarters. Used to promote exchange and contact, this language originated in the 1780s and 1790s in the maritime fur trade on the west coast of Vancouver Island and was in use at the mouth of the Columbia by the first decade of the nineteenth century; the linguistic evidence strongly suggests a postcontact development of Chinook.[38] Historians Robie Reid and Frederick Howay reported that the Astorians and NWC found this ready-made pidgin 'waiting for them' at the mouth of the Columbia River in 1811. With use, many of the original Nuu-chah-nuulth words were supplanted by Chinook and French words. French was the working language of the British fur trade. 'I speak the Canadian french as fluently as I do English,' Londoner George Roberts recalled, 'when I came to this country little more than French was heard.' 'Siwash,' Chinook for Indian, was a corruption of *sauvage*. The populous French Canadian settlements at Fort Vancouver and the Willamette were the crucibles in which the mature pidgin formed. French traveller de Mofras in 1841-2 claimed that Chinook included 'innumerable French expressions. Many natives, especially the children, can understand our language [French] without difficulty.'[39]

Although usually regarded as a trade jargon, Chinook was increasingly a language of work. The language facilitated the exchange of furs, provisions, and labour. An early vocabulary, preserved in the back of the *Columbia*'s 1840 logbook, provided the Chinook words for the numbers one to ten and such items as blanket and barrel. Anderson, in another early vocabulary, gave instructions for hiring Native workers. He divided this vocabulary into such categories as 'Articles of food and clothing,' and 'Animals, birds, fish' – categories that gave immediate access to Native provisions.[40] To the north, Tolmie recalled, the company's eviction of American fur traders from the North West Coast in the 1830s resulted in the disappearance of the 'Kygani' trading jargon and its replacement by Chinook.[41]

Native labour began early on Puget Sound, too. 'Indians have been hired,' Tolmie wrote in July 1833 at Nisqually, 'to clear away the brushwood along the bank ... & for about 100 yards up from base.' The Puget's Sound Agricultural Company's operations, managed by Tolmie himself, saw an unprecedented emphasis on the hiring of Indian labour. In 1839 the G&C urged Douglas to hire 'a few docile native Indians, say emancipated Slaves,' as herdsmen, carters, and weeders. In the 1840s between one-half and two-thirds of the company's work at Nisqually was done by Indians. They were paid the equivalent of between £4 and £8 a year, compared to £35 a year paid to experienced British shepherds. When Simpson visited Nisqually in September 1841, he recorded that the 'Cowlitz, Checaylis, and 'Squally' people were 'now all quiet, inoffensive, and industrious people; and as a proof ... they do very well as agricultural servants.' Tolmie also hired Native people at Cowlitz, and in 1843 eleven of thirty-two men there were Native. The agricultural company's account books document numerous 'payments for Indian labour' at both farms.[42]

Years later, when Tolmie sought work as a Dominion Indian agent, he recalled that he had hired Native people at Nisqually to compensate for the destruction of camas beds by livestock grazing:

> The difficulties of Indian management at Nisqually had been greatly enhanced by the introduction of sheep and cattle in large numbers on the Plains, the Indians, themselves owners of horses, and considerably dependent on roots of native growth for subsistence [camas], found the innovation so much for the worse that discontent was often exhibited. General kind treatment, trifling payments for mischievous dogs shot, and the employment of Indians as shepherds, cattleherds, ploughmen &c &c gradually reconciled them to the new order of things.[43]

Farther north, Native people worked at the Fort Langley farm and fishery. Jamie Morton writes that the Native presence 'was not an ephemeral one; almost all the H.B.C. men were married to Native women and were raising mixed-blood families. There was also a long-established "home guard" Kwantlen village across the channel from the post, on McMillan Island.' In 1828, soon after the founding of the fort, Native women stored potatoes and salted salmon; the next year, ten or twelve Indians carried fence wood, and they loaded and unloaded the company's vessels and worked as farm labourers.[44] In May 1834 McLoughlin outlined to Yale the economic and moral consequences of hiring Indians at the new farm at Langley Plain:

> I am happy to find that you have anticipated my Views and so zealously begun your farming operations and I approve very much of your Employing Indians and paying them with the produce of your farm as this Labour costs you nothing and by accustoming and teaching them to work you are doing them the Greatest good you can and in course of time they may became as useful as most men we now a days get.[45]

Later, Native people were hired as milkers to Fort Langley's seventy or eighty cows. As on the Columbia, women prepared salmon for barrelling. When a new brigade route was sought in the 1840s, Indians helped pull the company's laden *bateaux* up the Fraser Canyon. This was a slow method, Anderson wrote, 'as the ascent can be effected only by warping along shore, with the aid of Indian canoes to pass the lines.'[46]

Native labour was important at Fort Victoria from the beginning. James Douglas recorded that in 1843 the Songhees immediately offered their services in cutting pickets in return for payment in blankets. They cut at least some of the fort pickets at Mount Douglas, hence its other name, 'Cedar Hill.' Their labour was also significant in farming and transport. Indians milked cows at the fort and guided the bullock-drawn ploughs, and the 1846-50 post journal records numerous other instances revealing a diversity of Native work.[47]

By the 1830s, a communication system – a mixture of HBC and Native forms of transport – spanned the coastal regions of the Columbia Department. Letters could be sent in weeks and sometimes days between contiguous posts and districts. The NWC had hired Indians to deliver letters in 1815 between the lower Columbia and the interior, and the HBC continued to send messages on existing Native trade routes. The company had no official route between the interior and the coast north of the Columbia River, but the immense coastal region south of the Russian territories was intersected by numerous east-west trading trails that followed river valleys and canyons, providing access to the interior. Letters were sent from the coast to the Chilcotin via such Native grease trails as the one Mackenzie followed. Letters were conveyed, Richard Mayne reported, 'by some such route, by Indian messengers, from the Hudson's Bay Company's steamer "Beaver" lying in the Bentinck Arm, to the officer in charge of Fort Alexandria, high up the Fraser River.'[48]

The use of Native transport on the coast was common, both before and after the coming of the *Beaver* in 1836. Vivid references to Native letter-carrying in the Gulf of Georgia region survive. Charles Ermatinger recalled how a letter was 'forwarded from tribe to tribe' between Langley and Fort Vancouver in 1828 after the bearer of the letter was killed. In 1831 McDonald of Langley noted that a packet of thirty-two private letters had reached him via Puget Sound 'after a March of 11 weeks thru the different tribes between Vancouver & this.' Three years later, Tolmie at Nisqually received a letter 'by indians' from James Yale reporting on the state of the fur and salmon trades at Langley. Letters were not the only items carried by such means: in September 1835 'a party of Indians' from Nisqually delivered two ploughshares to Fort Langley.[49]

After 1843, an express canoe system was established between Fort Victoria and Nisqually (see Figure 19); overland trails and the Cowlitz Portage connected Nisqually with Fort Vancouver. Paul Kane, who left Victoria for Puget Sound in the canoe of a Nisqually chief on 10 June 1847, recorded that

> he was very glad of my company, as my being the bearer of despatches would be a certain protection for the whole party from whatever Indians we might meet. I asked him how he had managed to escape coming down, and he showed me an old piece of newspaper, which he held up whenever he met with strange Indians, and that they, supposing it to be a letter from Fort Victoria, had allowed him to pass without molestation.
>
> The gentlemen in charge of the various posts have frequent occasion to send letters, sometimes for a considerable distance, when it is either inconvenient or impossible for them to fit out a canoe with their own men to carry it. In such cases the letter is given to an Indian, who carries it as far as suits his convenience and safety. He then sells the letter to another, who carries it until he finds an opportunity of selling it to advantage; it is thus passed on and sold until it arrives at its destination, gradually increasing in value according to the distance, and the last possessor receiving the reward for its safe delivery. In this manner letters are frequently sent with perfect security, and with much greater rapidity than could be done otherwise.[50]

Native employment occurred mainly in the Gulf of Georgia, Puget Sound, and the Columbia River because that was where most of the company's new resource trades developed. However, the 1830s also witnessed increased Native involvement in the company's extended northern commerce. Although a post was not established among them until 1849, the Kwakwaka'wakw provided coal and firewood for the *Beaver*. Indians at Beaver Harbour, Dunn wrote, provided coal to the steamship in 1836: 'The natives were anxious that we should employ them to work the coal; to this we consented, and agreed to give them a certain sum for every large box. The natives being so numerous, and labour so cheap, for us to attempt to work the coal would have been madness.' Later, the 'Quakeolths' and the Nawitte conveyed firewood to the steam vessel, and the Indians of Knight Inlet also provided cordwood in the summer of

1836. As Dunn wrote, 'We sent our wood-cutters on shore at this place, and renewed our stock of wood; the Indians assisting in carrying it to the beach, and bringing it alongside the vessel in their canoes; for which we gave them some tobacco.'[51]

At Fort Simpson, Native men and women entered the HBC's workforce in many capacities, and the Fort Stikine Indians carried wood and water to the *Beaver*. In the late 1830s, the company, in conjunction with Captain Bancroft, hired Kaigani Indians to hunt sea otter on the North West Coast and in California. Simpson, as ever concerned with 'system & economy,' wanted to hire Native sailors in 1842 for the company's marine department. He complained about useless English servants and asked McLoughlin to emulate the marine service of the Russian American Company, many of whose mates and half of whose seamen were 'natives of the country.' They had the advantage of being 'tractable, efficient and cheap servants.' 'It has for a length of time,' Simpson remonstrated, '& very frequently been strongly recommended, that you should get some of the natives apprenticed to the marine branch of the Service.'[52]

Between the 1820s and the 1840s, then, Native people worked as labourers at posts between the Columbia River and Fort Stikine. Their work was inexpensive compared to non-Native labour. They worked on a part-time, seasonal, or occasional basis, rather than as full-time employees. On his visit to Fort Vancouver in 1839, Captain Belcher learned that not more than ten Native Indians were permanently employed, out of a total of 550 Columbia Department employees.[53] The extent of full-time Native labour should not, then, be exaggerated. Increasing numbers of other workers, especially Kanakas, were needed in the company's extended coastal shipping and commerce, which existed largely in a Native world where Native access to and control of resources and trade had not yet been formally challenged. Aboriginal trade routes functioned everywhere in the Columbia Department, and Native trade remained more important to the company in 1843 than Native labour. In the mid-nineteenth century, Indians interacted with the HBC not primarily as labourers but as suppliers of provisions and recipients of British material goods acquired through trade. Nonetheless, all must have adapted in some degree to new forms of wealth and exchange.

Native slaves also worked for the company. Some of the workers mentioned above were undoubtedly slaves. At the point of contact, slavery was practised from the Aleutian Islands to northwestern California, and the proportion was estimated at between one-twentieth and one-third of the total population.[54]

Fur traders could do nothing to lessen the incidence of slavery anywhere in the densely populated regions of the ethnographic Northwest Coast. 'Pity that the Slavery Emancipation Act does not extend its influence to these remote shores,' Ogden noted at Fort Simpson in 1838. Given the urge to do so, it would have been impossible to abolish slavery in a culture where it was prevalent; indeed, in a pre-colonial era the company would have lacked the institutional and also the legal means to do so.[55]

Slaves originated in the south and were traded to the north. In 1836 Dunn wrote that the Bella Bella were the middlemen in the coastal slave trade. The northern tribes came down to Bella Bella to buy slaves obtained by the southern tribes, 'the original kidnappers.' 'A full-grown, athletic slave, who is a good hunter, will fetch nine blankets, a gun, a quantity of powder and ball, a couple of dressed elk skins, tobacco, vermilion paint, a flat file, and other little articles.' In 1834, Tolmie reported, the Tsimshian gave fifteen elk skins for 'a boy slave about 12 or 14 years of age beside a small quantity of powder, ball, paint, tobacco, etc.' Tsimshian slaves around Fort Simpson, Dunn noted in 1836, did the 'principal drudgery. These slaves, in barter, fetch a larger price to the northward than they do to the south; and are sold by the Nass tribe to the various inland tribes, for furs. These furs they again sell to the white traders for blankets, and other articles of use or luxury.'[56]

Douglas found, in July 1840, that slaves were the 'most highly prized' form of property among the Taku. Some people owned as many as twenty. Dunn recorded that among the Chilcat trading at Fort Taku, a slave was worth nine slaves. Slaves were traded to Taku from Kaigani and Stikine and exchanged for Chilcat furs, which were taken to Kaigani and sold to Americans or Russians. The easiest way for the company to obtain these furs would have been to enter the slave trade, but Douglas refused to do this. 'This detestable traffic,' he wrote, 'and the evils it gives rise to; are subjects of deep regret to us, but we know of no remedy within our power, or we would use it were it only for the sake of our own interest.' The Hudson's Bay Company had finally encountered 'a description of property that we cannot compete in.'[57] Douglas also found the 'abominable traffic in slaves' prevalent among all classes at Stikine. In many cases slaves were kept for the mere purpose of display, but they were 'also exceedingly useful as fishermen and hunters': 'The ladies too, slovenly as they are in their general habits, cannot condescend to exercise their tender hands, at any kind of work, and must also have their train of attendants to relieve them of domestic drudgery, which in their opinion is degrading and would involve the loss of cast.'[58]

Kaigani, in Russsian territory but frequented by American coasters, was the slave centre of the North West Coast. Dunn posed the following question to an English-speaking chief there: 'I asked him if he would like to go to America or England? He answered "No!" as he considered we were slaves – even our chiefs – who were always doing something from necessity; and as we were always at work for a living. "I have slaves," said he, "who hunt for me – paddle me in my canoes, – and my wives to attend upon me. Why should I wish to leave?"'[59]

British fur traders censured American captains for trading slaves between the Columbia River, Cape Flattery, and the North West Coast. In 1821 Peter Corney noted that

> I am sorry to say that the slave trade is carried on, on this coast, to a very great extent by the Americans. They buy slaves to the southward and take them to the northward, where they exchange them for the sea otter and other furs. If they cannot buy the slaves cheap, they make no scruple to carry them off by force. A Captain Ayres, of the ship *Mercury*, took twelve from the Columbia River in this manner, but while bearing down the coast, seven of them seized the whale-boat and ran from the ship; only one, however, arrived at the river.[60]

In 1829 Simpson wrote that American coasters bought slaves at Cape Flattery and the Straits of Juan de Fuca and took them to Haida territory, where they fetched between thirty and fifty beaver skins each. Simpson believed that slaves were 'the principal circulating medium on this Coast,' but there is no evidence that the HBC participated in the coastal slave trade.[61]

Slavery did, however, enter the HBC's forts as its lower Columbia and North West Coast operations grew more extensive. The presence of slaves in company forts resulted from domestic and work arrangements

with the local homeguard and other Indians. Company officials had difficulty eradicating slavery at its posts because slaves entered the fort sphere
through marriage. Fur traders' wives sometimes came with retinues of
slaves, and HBC employees also purchased slaves as servants, domestic
workers, and wives.

At first, slave labour was the only form of Native labour available to
the company. Tolmie, who arrived in 1833, recalled that the Indians of
the lower Columbia River and Puget Sound refused to work for the
company – 'any individual so-doing being reproached as placing himself
on the level of a slave.' Similarly, Scouler, in 1825, wrote that the
Chinook refused to cultivate potatoes because it was slaves' work:

> The Indians of the Columbia, who enjoy far greater opportunities for improve-
> ment than those of Skittegass, have as yet steadily refused to cultivate the
> ground, in spite of the example and encouragement of the settlers [fur traders],
> and have refused to grow the seeds that were offered them, while their pride
> urged, as an apology for their indolence, that it was the work of slaves to cul-
> tivate the ground.[62]

Slaves performed important functions in the Native economy of the
lower Columbia. 'Slaves do all the laborious work,' Alexander Ross wrote,
'and a Chinook matron is constantly attended to by two, three, or more
slaves, who are on all occasions obsequious to her will.' Slaves were food
producers, but they were also important in transport, as units of
exchange, and in hunting – which itself was a low-status occupation
among some coastal peoples. Chinook, Haida, and Tahltan ethnogra-
phies, for example, contain accounts of slaves hunting.[63]

Before the 1840s, slave labour was present and sometimes common in
HBC establishments. The slave of an Iroquois accompanied the Fraser
River expedition from Fort Vancouver in 1824, and they were prominent
in the Snake and Southern parties; on one trip Work took a slave with
him up the Snake. Simon Plomondon, later a member of the Oregon
Legislature, owned a slave at Nisqually in 1834.[64] At Cowlitz in 1842,
Father Bolduc noted that several other French Canadians had bought
slaves, and he condemned its universality in Native society:

> Who would have thought that slavery would be here in full vigor? However,
> nothing is truer, and what is more, they traffic in slaves as if they were low

animals. They do not regard them more than dogs (that is the name ordi-
narily given them). For a horse one can have a good slave, and, if he is not
worth much, one only gives a few blankets and a gun. Several Canadians buy
them to give them their freedom. The one who is now with me and who is
a good cook was bought for ten blankets. Although he is free, he has never
wished to leave M. Demers, who withdrew him from slavery.[65]

At Cowlitz, Demers wrote, 'Generally the women are treated as slaves;
they are assigned rough work, while the husband is occupied with
smoking or walking about.' In 1841 Simpson condemned the rampant
frequency and horrors of slavery among the Native people of Nisqually.
Slavery was also prevalent at Fort Langley.[66]

Company officials bought and kept slaves. 'Mr Manson purchased a
man slave from the Weetletook about a fortnight ago,' Tolmie noted in
his private Fort McLoughlin journal in 1834; 'The price paid was 10 R.B.
Blankets 3½ pt, ¼ Gal: Gunpowder, 50 balls, 20 leaves tobacco, 1 Pint
Pot 2nd hand, 3 Gals Mixed Rum, 1 Trading Gun – much worn. The
slave named Tom was employed with the people and occasionally in
hunting.'[67] Such transactions came to an end in 1833 with the Imperial
Emancipation Act, after which the company was answerable, at least
indirectly, to public opinion in Wilberforce's Britain. In 1835 McLoughlin fired Captain Thomas Pisk Kipling for keeping eleven slaves at Fort
George. Kipling had also paid five blankets for Chief Mossona's wife,
and McLoughlin concluded that he had been drinking.[68] In the company's eyes, it was acceptable to buy a slave in order to liberate him or
her as a servant or wife, but unacceptable to buy a slave to keep as a
slave.

Two visitors to Fort Vancouver in the late 1830s charged that slave
labour underlay many aspects of the fort's domestic economy and the
company's commercial operations on the Pacific. One was the Anglican
chaplain at Fort Vancouver, Herbert Beaver; the other was William
Slacum, an American government agent. 'I have seen more real slavery
in the short time I have been here, than in the eight years and a half
I was in the West Indies,' Beaver wrote from Fort Vancouver to a member of the HBC committee in November 1836. 'There are also Indians,
but I cannot say correctly the number, I think about forty, held in actual
bondage, having been purchased by persons in all classes of the Establishment.' Beaver determined the actual number of slaves at Fort Van-

couver to be thirty-two, eight belonging to officers and twenty-four to the 'Common Men.'[69] Beaver later told the Aborigines' Protection Society of London that HBC employees at Vancouver, and retired employees in the Willamette and Cowlitz rivers, held as many as ninety slaves altogether:

> The whole numbers of these wretched beings amounted to between 80 and 90. They were miserably clothed and fed ... I know of some of the men to be flogged by order of the officer, in charge of the establishment, and others to be cruelly ill-used by their owners. The women themselves, who were living with the lower class of the Company's servants, were much in the condition of slaves, being purchased by their Indian proprietors or relations, and not unfrequently re-sold amongst each other by their purchasers.[70]

When men from the fort married Native women, Beaver wrote, they brought slaves with them as 'female help.' 'As soon as a man takes one [a Native woman], he is obliged, even if she was previously a slave herself, to buy one or two to wait on her.' The domestic economy of Fort Vancouver was, therefore, based in part on slave labour. McLoughlin told Beaver that the slaves at the fort belonged to the Indian women, but Beaver called this a vain excuse, pointing out that the custom of the country permitted such women to retain their slaves even when they married company employees.[71]

The same issue was taken up by Slacum, who spent the winter of 1836-7 as a guest at Fort Vancouver. In his report to the American government, Slacum charged that slavery was prevalent in most aspects of the company's Columbia River operations, and that it originated in the extensive social relations existing between Native women and company employees:

> *Indian Slavery.* The price of a slave varies from eight to fifteen blankets. Women are valued higher than men. If a slave dies within six months of the time of purchase, the seller returns one-half the purchase money. As long as the Hudson Bay Company permit their servants to hold slaves, the institution of slavery will be perpetuated, as the price, eight to fifteen blankets, is too tempting for an Indian to resist. Many instances have occurred where a man has sold his own child. The chief factor at Vancouver says the slaves are the property of the women with whom their workmen live, and do not belong to the *men* in their employ, although I have known cases to the contrary. We

shall see how this reasoning applies. These women, who are said to be the owners of the slaves, are frequently bought themselves by the men with whom they live, when they are mere children; of course, they have no means to purchase, until their husbands *or their men* make the purchase from the proceeds of their labor; and *then* these women are considered the ostensible owners, which neither lessens the traffic, nor ameliorates the condition of the slave, while the Hudson Bay Company find it in their interest to encourage their servants to intermarry or live with the native women, as it attaches the men to the soil, and their offspring (half breeds) become in turn useful hunters and workmen at the different depots of the company. The slaves are generally employed to cut wood, hunt, and fish, for the families of the men employed by the Hudson Bay Company, and are ready for any extra work. Each man of the trapping parties has from two to three slaves, who assist to hunt, and take care of the horse and camp; they thereby save the company the expense of employing at least double the number of men that would otherwise be required on these excursions.[72]

James Douglas answered Herbert Beaver's charges during McLoughlin's 1838-9 leave of absence. The Governor and Committee were unaware that slavery was rampant on the Columbia River and at their Pacific coast depot, and Beaver's revelations promised to be a public-relations disaster in Britain. In a letter of October 1838 to the G&C, Douglas reported that cultural issues interfered with his attempts to suppress the traffic in slaves:

I regret, however, that the feeling among the Natives of this river, precludes every prospect of the immediate extinction of slavery, unless we resort to the very objectionable plan of forcible emancipation ... I do not feel justified in exposing our interests to the shock and excitement and desperate animosity which more active measures might preclude. Against our own people, I took a more active part, and denounced slavery as a state contrary to law; tendering to all unfortunate persons held as slaves, by British subjects, the fullest protection in the enjoyment of their natural rights.

Douglas went on to admit that there were indeed slaves at Fort Vancouver:

I fear that all my efforts have virtually failed in rooting out the practical evil, even within the precincts of this settlement. Of the persons ranking as slaves, some are children of tender age, others have grown up in ignorance of every useful art, whether of civilized or savage life, by which they might have to earn an independent livelihood, and all classes are so destitute and friendless, that they have, without exception, chosen the part of continuing with their present protectors. To have urged a forcible separation, in such circumstances, I must have provided them gratuitously, with food and clothing, as their spiritless labour is no value to the Company, and I feel reluctant to turn them loose into the forest, without any means of support.[73]

The trouble was not over. During the 1844-6 negotiations over the fate of Oregon, Slacum's report was publicized by an American senator, Caleb Cushing, who accused the HBC of keeping slaves at its western headquarters. McLoughlin admitted that the company had inherited slaves from Fort George when Fort Vancouver was opened in 1825; it was a problem that originated in the NWC era. He stated that John Cameron had liberated Fort George's slaves in the early 1820s, and that subsequently, 'I did not make the Servants Wives send their slaves away but availed myself of every opportunity to make them work, & pay them as other Indians. The consequence is, that our ploughing & harrowing is principally done by Indians and several of these Indians have claimed their liberty.' Slavery did not disappear; indeed, Fort Victoria, the new depot, was situated among Native cultures where slavery and slave raiding were prevalent. Perhaps fearing the repetition of charges like Beaver's and Slacum's, James Douglas, as colonial governor, vowed to abolish slavery on Vancouver Island.[74]

Fort Vancouver's traditions of labour and slavery were also carried over into the Willamette settlement by French Canadian and American settlers. Many settlers married liberated slaves or ones they had bought. Among the Chinook, de Mofras wrote, 'The price of a male slave is approximately the same as the price of four or five white woolen blankets either plain or gaudely striped, or two pounds of powder. Women, however, are somewhat more valuable. The majority of white colonists are married to Indian slaves whom they have purchased.' F.X. Matthieu of the Willamette recalled that most settlers were married to Clatsop or Chinook women or to their Metis daughters. An 1879 memoir by an American settler, Mr. Rees, supports these views: 'Nearly all the early settlers of French Prairie were the owners of a few of these slaves of both sexes; many of them were faithful laborers and the only valley Indians for many years following the early settlement who would condescend to do manual labour.' Historian Elsie Dennis concludes that the ownership and use of slaves by American settlers in the Willamette was very great: they did 'all the menial tasks of the household; made canoes; caught fish; planted and tended in the fields.'[75]

HBC employees of different ranks and backgrounds married or lived with Native and Metis women of all classes and cultures, from slaves to nobles. Altogether, several thousand Native women had some form of contact with British fur traders west of the Rockies before 1843, and not all of them were reciprocal or permanent relationships. In 1826, for example, Francis Ermatinger noted that he and John Work were in the habit of 'obtaining wives' wherever they went, but that Work excelled him because he made £100 a year compared to Ermatinger's £60. 'We ... can obtain a wife at every port, for a moderate charge, we come to. In this last sort of traffic, our friend Work, being fortunate enough to live upon a more juicey substance than myself, outdoes us all.'[76] Similarly, in 1825 Alexander Ross met a French Canadian returning home after forty-two years' service as a canoeman with the NWC and HBC. 'I have had twelve wives in the Country,' he boasted to Ross. Michel Laframboise, head of the Southern Party in the 1830s, boasted of having 'a wife in every tribe' between the Columbia River and California, and Modeste Demers reported that Native and Metis women were bought and sold at the Rendezvous.[77]

On the other hand, many alliances became permanent or semi-permanent. In 1829 Archibald McDonald of Langley noted that without some sort of domestic arrangement, 'there was no reconciling the men to the place.' On the Columbia, Roman Catholic missionaries married some fifty Kanaka labourers to their Native spouses, mainly Chinook and Cowlitz women. In October 1841 at Fort Stikine, Simpson recorded, with characteristic acuity and misogyny, that 'Fourteen or fifteen of the men of the establishment asked permission to take native wives; and leave to accept the worthless bargains was granted to all such as had the means of supporting a family. These matrimonial connections are a heavy tax on a post, in consequence of the increased demand for provisions, but form, at the same time, a useful link between the traders and the savages.'[78]

While Native traders, labourers, slaves, and women made their way for their own reasons into the company's palisades, they brought little with them apart from perishable commodities – and very little Native material culture, even stone items, seems to have existed at company posts. Regarding the excavation of Fort Vancouver, Louis Caywood wrote that 'Not a thing of Indian manufacture was found in connection with the excavation.' By contrast, over 100,000 objects of European origin, mainly beads, were retrieved.[79]

The company did not enter into land treaties with Indian people during the period of the joint occupancy of Oregon Territory. McLoughlin assured them that the company needed only a few sites for its posts, farms, and fisheries. He may or may not have told them that one day either Great Britain or the United States would assert absolute title to every square inch of their territory. McLoughlin's policy was recorded by Peter Burnett, a lawyer who came overland in 1843 and knew McLoughlin well:

> The doctor impressed the Indians with the fact that the company was simply a mercantile corporation, whose purpose was only trade with the natives; that its intention was only to appropriate to its exclusive use a few sites for its trading posts and small parcels of adjacent lands, sufficient to produce supplies for its people, thus leaving all the remainder of the country for the use and in the exclusive possession of the Indians; and that this possession of limited amounts of land by the company would be mutually beneficial.[80]

Such a policy was in effect in 1824, when the HBC obtained a 'formal cession' of the soil at Fort Colvile. Simpson recalled that the Colvile chief gave the company 'the land and the woods, because the whites would make better use of them than himself; but he had reserved the Chaudière Falls as necessary to his own people, remarking that the strangers, being able to get food out of stones and sand, could manage to live very well without fish.'[81]

Stones and soil also figured in a story related by Burnett:

> The shore of the Columbia River in front of Fort Vancouver was covered with cobble-stones, which were used by the company as ballast for its returning ships. The principal chief of the Indians concluded that the company ought to pay something for these stones; and one day, in the presence of a large crowd of his people (assembled, perhaps, for that purpose), he demanded payment of the doctor. Of course, the doctor was taken by surprise, but at

once comprehended the situation. He knew, if he consented to pay in this case, there would be no end of exactions in the future. How best to avoid the payment without giving offence was the question. He knew that the Indians possessed a keen sense of the ridiculous; and, after reflecting a moment, he picked up a cobble-stone and solemnly offered it to the chief, saying 'Eat this.' The Indians present at once saw how ridiculous it was to demand payment for that which was of no practical value to them, and set up a loud shout of derisive laughter. The chief was so ashamed of his silly demand that he walked off in silence, and never after that demanded payment for things of no value to him.[82]

FIGURE 26 *Indian Graves, Victoria* was sketched by American naval officer William McMurtrie in about 1853. [M. and M. Karolick Collection, Boston Museum of Fine Arts, C18868]

By 1843, then, everything in the Native world had a price: fur, provisions, labour, slaves, women, and land. All could be valued by HBC officials; most could be bought for blankets, Made Beaver, *haiqua*, or trade goods; and, excepting the human trade, most could be rendered into tangible exports for sale in global markets. Within a decade, anything could be bought for blankets, including treaty land on Vancouver Island, cobblestones and all. The company's exchange and labour policies continued unchanged into the colonial period in British Columbia.[83]

Conclusion

You can see it all here. It's all going out. The timber,
the grain, the coal, the sulphur ... We are a dispossessed people,
and we are rendered into poverty.

— LILLOOET CHIEF SAUL TERRY
ON THE VANCOUVER WATERFRONT, SEPTEMBER 1987[1]

In the late eighteenth century, British fur traders were obsessed with an idea: a British commerce extending across the North American continent to the west coast, and from there to Pacific markets. Alexander Mackenzie and his North West Company partners devised a scheme for the commercial development and territorial control of the Pacific region. They hoped to establish a combined fur trade and salmon fishery on the west coast, but in the end they exported only fur from beyond the Rocky Mountains. The NWC marketed fur directly in China, but their costly and unprofitable exports contributed to their merger with the Hudson's Bay Company in 1821.

After 1821, the well-capitalized HBC, led by George Simpson, succeeded in giving substance to this old idea of a British Pacific commerce. The fur traders from Hudson Bay erupted into a region with a mild and forgiving climate, an abundant resource base, and an impressive commercial potential. The new HBC was more successful than the NWC in locating profitable exports and markets on the Pacific coast. Under the energetic Simpson, the English company established a new administrative district west of the Rocky Mountains known as the Columbia Department. Fort Vancouver became headquarters for the company's extensive interior and coastal fur trades, from the Rockies to the Pacific, and from the Russian territories to the Gulf of California. But Simpson, like Mackenzie before him, looked irresistibly beyond the fur trade to the larger resources of the region. At Fort Vancouver, Simpson and his two most capable managers, John McLoughlin and James Douglas, initiated the HBC's new exports of wheat and flour, salmon, and timber to new Pacific markets in the Sandwich Islands, Sitka, and San

Francisco. They formed a regional economy on the Pacific coast, an economy largely independent of those to the east of the Rockies.

The European presence in the Columbia Department in 1843 was much more extensive than it had been in 1821. Simpson, master of the British fur trade strategies, visited the coast on three occasions, each time imposing policies that local HBC management put in place. On his first visit, he formulated a plan for economic survival. He ordered the extension of the fur trade throughout the department, a stop to waste and extravagance, and self-sufficiency in provisions. This entailed the development of secure salmon and agricultural trades. Simpson laid off extra employees, merged New Caledonia with the Columbia District, challenged American traders on the North West Coast and on the Columbia River, and foresaw the need to develop export trades with Pacific markets. By the time of his second visit, self-sufficiency in foodstuffs had been attained and the company was ready to embark on the export of surplus produce. Simpson reflected on these changes in 1837. 'Previous to 1821,' he wrote, 'the business of the Columbia department was very greatly limited; but it has since been very greatly extended and at much expense, and I am sorry to say, at a considerable sacrifice of life ... it now [includes] 22 trading establishments, besides several migratory, hunting and trading expeditions, and armed vessels on the north-west coast.'[2]

By the time of his third visit, the company had forced American traders to abandon the North West Coast and much of the southern interior. By defeating American competition, the company earned an effective commercial monopoly of the region. In 1844, Dunn summarized the HBC's achievement:

> In short, it may be said, that they have taken possession of every district within the whole region; which, throughout its wild and rugged parts, is dotted with their forts and establishments; and they exercise unrestrained trade and intercourse with all the native tribes; whereas the Americans, with the exception of a few missionary and agricultural establishments, have scarcely any possession or hold upon the country.[3]

American fur traders, both on the coast and in the interior, could offer no sustained competition against this powerful company with its effective commercial strategies, trained and efficient personnel, workable

'Indian policy,' financial backing, and emerging trans-Pacific commerce. In the 1830s, the company's workforce included former employees of Astor's Pacific Fur Company, Wyeth's Columbia River Fishing and Trading Company, Bryant & Sturgis of Boston, as well as many old Northwesters. At the same time, the HBC showed the Americans what could be done on the Pacific coast.

American traders and writers, like Washington Irving in the 1830s and 1840s, were well aware that British competition in the interior and Pacific coast fur trades had evicted them from the region. Yet they had no hesitation in portraying the HBC as a backward-looking fur trading concern standing in the way of their own progressive and patriotic commercial schemes. As Irving wrote:

> The resources of the country, too, while in the hands of a company restricted in its trade, can be but partially called forth: but in the hands of Americans, enjoying a direct trade with the East Indies, would be brought into quickening activity; and might soon realize the dream of Mr. Astor, in giving rise to a flourishing commercial empire.[4]

The Oregon Treaty of 1846 shocked company officials in the Columbia Department precisely because their commercial victory over the Americans had been so clear and one-sided. Their policies had kept American interest in the region at a largely theoretical stage for almost thirty years. The new boundary, however, bisected the department and cut the HBC's districts and transport routes in half. In December 1846, when Douglas heard the conditions of the treaty, he wrote to the HBC Governor and Committee: 'By this monstrous treaty all the Company's Establishments on the Columbia River, and to the Southward of that line, the Cowelits and Nisqually Districts, which were discovered and settled by British subjects, and are actually up to this point in a great measure, unknown to any other people, have been ceded without reservation to the United States.'[5]

Between 1813 and 1843, the Columbia Department was, for all practical purposes, a British commercial colony. Despite political joint status, British fur traders arrested every attempt by American fur traders to gain a foothold in the interior and on the Pacific coast, and the department remained, commercially, within the British imperial orbit. 'As long as the fur trade was the medium of rivalry,' historical geographer David Wishart concludes, 'British control of Oregon was never seriously threatened.'[6] But commercial victory by a British company did not translate into a British diplomatic victory. The 1846 treaty was an act of political compromise and appeasement bearing no relation to the North West and Hudson's Bay companies' commercial success over American traders west of the Rockies. The HBC's commercial achievement did not translate into a viable political argument on the British side. The Americans, by contrast, through the visits of Captain Gray, Lewis and Clark, the Pacific Fur Company, and boosters like Irving and the Oregon Trail immigrants, had a legitimate political claim to the Oregon territory even if their commercial achievement at the time of the treaty negotiations was almost negligible.

The HBC won every commercial battle it entered, but lost the political war of 1846. Two years later, however, the British government authorized the company's colonization of Vancouver Island, a bold and effective political gesture.[7] The company's success on Vancouver Island would help blunt the political expulsion from the Columbia.

By 1843, the company had expanded to its greatest territorial extent, largely as a result of fur trade extension west of the Rockies. The Columbia Department had reached its spatial maximum. The HBC controlled the trade of most of the cordillera: its activities extended from the Sacramento to the Stikine and Taku. The Northwesters had known only three main spheres of activity west of the Rockies: New Caledonia, the southern interior, and the lower Columbia. These regions were redefined by 1843: new districts were added, and all were integrated into the company's departmental business. The *Beaver* ventured into the reaches of coastal inlets (though the vessel usually traded on the inside passage), and the North West Coast, unknown to the NWC, was well under British commercial control. The company intercepted the extensive Native riverine east-west fur trade by establishing a chain of posts and a shipping department aligned on a north-south axis, ultimately directed to the London fur market.

The HBC invaded the resource-rich territory of the Native people of the whole region. Native people, who worked primarily as providers of pelts in 1821, were recruited by the company as traders and workers on the Pacific before 1843. They still provided furs, but increasingly they traded other things, and what they traded as provisions they later traded for export: salmon, herring, oolichan, sturgeon, whale and fish oil, cranberries, timber, shingles, masts, and spars. Their seasonal rounds could cope with such activities, but increasingly, they worked not within their traditional economy, but as traders and labourers within the company's provision and export economies. Native slaves also laboured for the company.

The company and its Native customers extended a trade language, Chinook: the language spread with the HBC's trade, and remained behind as an artifact of the HBC's presence. The company's monopoly, earned by defeating foreign competition, allowed it to impose uniform trade standards and a uniform 'Indian policy' over a vast area, which in turn allowed it to colonize Native economies and redirect Native produce. These were crucial years of transition between a largely Native world and a world intersected with the schedules of schooners, steamers, and general commerce.

The NWC's trade west of the Rockies had been essentially a seventeenth- and eighteenth-century riverine fur trade. By 1843, the region possessed the rudimentary materials of a nineteenth-century commercial economy: viable transport routes, growing export trades, accessible local markets, and a large and cheap labour supply. Although the company extended its fur trade everywhere west of the Rockies, the overall value of the trade reached its natural limit and was declining in some places. The company could not obtain more fur than the land or sea possessed. High-quality land mammal pelts were scarce on much of the mild and mountainous coast, and so, by the 1820s, were sea otter. Only the North West Coast posts – forts Simpson, McLoughlin, Stikine, and Taku – were established exclusively for the trade in furs. The others were formed as farms or depots. The fur trade of the newest depot, Fort Victoria, was very unpromising. Exports of country produce from the lower Columbia and Fraser rivers had increased steadily since the 1820s; together with retail sales of British goods at Oahu, Yerba Buena, and Fort Vancouver, they contributed at least £4,000 toward departmental profit. Douglas and Simpson examined coal, salmon, and timber resources on Vancouver Island with their export potential in mind.

Bulky commodities like lumber required Pacific markets if they were to emerge as profitable exports. The tropical trade route sought by

Dalrymple, Mackenzie, and the Northwesters was found in a quiet way in 1833 with the opening of the Oahu agency. After 1839, quantities of agricultural provisions, principally flour, were exported to Sitka; in 1841, the company opened a short-lived post at Yerba Buena for the hide, tallow, and retail trades. New exports and markets required new, largely waterborne transport. In the 1820s, the company created a marine department of six or seven ships that, by 1843, transported provisions and exports between the depot, the posts, and deep-sea markets. The ships had quite specialized functions: the steamship *Beaver* delivered foodstuffs to the Russians and traded fur along the coast for shipment to London on the annual vessel; another two vessels traded salmon and lumber to Oahu in exchange for salt, sugar, molasses, and other trade goods; others made the traditional voyage to London and back.

Faced with the possibility of an unfavourable boundary settlement, the company built a new depot on Vancouver Island in 1843 and prepared to develop a range of resources there and on the adjacent coast. The construction of Fort Victoria signalled the end of the southern, Columbia-based regional economy and the start of a northern economy, inaugurating a significant realignment of the company's Pacific activities. The year 1843 ended one commercial era and started another.

The HBC now operated two overlapping economies on the west coast. The first was the company's traditional economy, in which an annual ship collected Columbia Department furs for the London market. This economy was dominated by the valuable fur returns of the interior and the North West Coast. It had a parallel on Hudson Bay, where an English supply ship made an annual voyage for fur, just as it had since the late seventeenth century. Navigable only a month or two of the year, Hudson Bay had a rudimentary and seasonal coasting trade, no profitable local exports other than fur, a sparse Native population, and no local markets. But the difference between Hudson Bay and the Pacific coast lay in the coast's second economy, made up of regional and Pacific trades. Here the HBC exhibited impressive flexibility and creativity. After 180 years of exporting fur from the regions east of the Rockies, the company broadened its resource base to embrace new commodities and market conditions. The coastal shipping department functioned outside the London-Fort Vancouver fur axis; instead, this second economy exploited coastal resources and the wealth of Pacific markets. The main outlines were being drawn for a viable, maritime, regional economy on what is now the south coast of British Columbia – a regional economy with an unbroken conceptual genealogy going back to the Pacific ambitions of Dalrymple, Mackenzie, and the Northwesters. By contrast, the vast eastern districts were landlocked, isolated, and intemperate – and offered no comparable commercial opportunity until the railway era of the late nineteenth century.

The old and the new co-existed in the company's Pacific business. While the Columbia Department possessed some of the last and richest fur resources in interior North America, the HBC simultaneously developed a diverse economy on its coastal section. The fur trade of a district like New Caledonia was as traditional as the company could offer, while the business on the Pacific – a plateau and a mountain range away – left the fur trade behind in many places. Generalizations about a 'fur trade' era in British Columbia are inappropriate in the face of such stark regional differences.

The company's extended commercial and financial ventures on the Pacific contradict Arthur Ray's assertions that the HBC embarked on a diversification program only after 1870.[8] These ventures took place well in advance of those in the company's other departments. Rupert's Land was not the source of all new developments in HBC commercial practice. Indeed, clerks stationed on the Pacific subsequently returned to Rupert's Land with their new commercial knowledge intact. The demands of mercantile commerce, before industry as such, produced change in the nineteenth-century fur trade. Sales of fur on the London market, of course, remained of crucial financial importance, but in no way do they diminish the importance of the new Pacific exports and markets.[9]

The company's transformation required a large, immigrant labouring corps of engineers, blacksmiths, tinsmiths, bailiffs, millers, millwrights, carpenters, masons, sawyers, coopers, sailmakers, wheelwrights, and shipwrights. Others continued to fill the traditional positions – accountants, clerks, packers, builders, traders, interpreters, hunters, boatmen, voyageurs, labourers – but each year brought greater occupational diversity. Gradually, the diverse workforce of a nineteenth-century commercial economy was superimposed on an eighteenth-century fur trade. The potential for colonization with such a workforce was obvious. Indeed, formal colonization was probably inevitable, though owing to the border settlement, it would not be in the Willamette Valley despite the great number of retired employees there. In 1844, a Canadian missionary estimated that 'The Canadian population, country women and children, is about 1,000 souls, distributed about as follows: 600 at Wallamette, 100 at Vancouver, 100 at Cowlitz; the rest are scattered at the various posts of the Company.'[10] The non-Native population actively employed at the company's posts had tripled, from about 200 in 1821 to 600 in 1843. Most were French Canadians, Kanakas, and Scots, and all but a few lived with, or had married, Native or Metis women.

Demographically, the department was at a watershed in 1843. The company moved to the north just as the western-most segment of the Oregon Trail, formerly the HBC Snake Brigade Trail, became a reality for the expansionist Americans. McLoughlin recalled that 137 Americans had come in 1842, 875 in 1843, 1,475 in 1844, and 3,000 in 1845.[11] In 1844, the HBC even opened an agency in newly formed Oregon City. ('It is published everywhere in the United States that Oregon is an earthly paradise. That is what is bringing to us such a large number of Americans,' Father Bolduc wrote in 1845.[12]) Many received a guided tour to the promised land: immigrants' journals tell of assistance and provisions rendered by HBC guides and personnel, from Fort Hall to Fort Boise to Fort Nez Perces to Fort Vancouver – the mecca at the end of the trail.

The political status of the region in 1843 was no different than it had been in 1821. Over the next fifteen years, two British colonies – Vancouver Island (1849) and British Columbia (1858) – and two American territories – Oregon Territory (1848) and Washington Territory (1853) – would be carved out of what had been the Columbia Department. In 1843, the American presence on the Columbia River was taking semi-permanent form in the Oregon Provisional Government, and Simpson was apprehensive about the upcoming Oregon Treaty. But even the most unfavourable boundary settlement could not affect the operations of Fort Victoria, selected for its unhindered Pacific orientation, its access to local resources and coastal shipping, and its proximity to coastal provision centres. This was the Pacific entrepôt envisaged by Dalrymple and Mackenzie, and selected by Simpson as the centre of a diverse trade.

The next decade and a half (1843-58) witnessed serious attempts by the HBC to develop the resources of Vancouver Island. Victoria's commercial prominence would only be eclipsed forty years later by the completion of the Canadian Pacific Railway and the subsequent rise of the city of Vancouver, which, like its predecessor on the Columbia, would look as much to the interior as to the Pacific. The company's coastal economy could survive quite satisfactorily on its own, if necessary; it looked not eastward to the St. Lawrence or to Hudson Bay, but outward to London, Honolulu, and California, and indirectly to China and the Orient. Coastal resources were more accessible for development and export than interior resources. Fur traders on the Pacific thought there was enough salmon to feed all the people of Rupert's Land, enough potatoes to supply the Royal Navy, and enough spars for all Her Majesty's ships. By contrast, the inaccessibility of interior resources was brought home forcibly in 1844, when Archibald McDonald discovered silver and lead on Flat Bow (Kootenay) Lake. 'It is not probable that mining operations could be carried on to advantage at Flat Bow Lake,' wrote McLoughlin, 'the distance being about 600 miles from the sea coast, and the water navigation, so difficult, and dangerous, that the metal would have to be transported with packhorses, more than half the distance by land.' As late as 1876, the mine's wealth was similarly praised, but it was still considered too remote and inaccessible. Famous later as the Bluebell mine at Riondel, the deposit was not developed commercially for another four decades.[13]

Simpson's search for new exports on the Pacific was part of a larger continental resource development policy inaugurated in the late 1820s and early 1830s.[14] In 1828, he had hoped Red River would soon present 'a field for other pursuits and branches of Trade' in addition to the provision and fur trades; he later warned that 'without an export of some description it is impossible [that] a growing Settlement can prosper.'[15]

Led by Simpson, officials at Red River established three joint-stock companies at Red River between 1820 and 1833: the Buffalo Wool Company, capitalized at £2000; the Red River Tallow Company, capitalized at £1,000; and the Assiniboia Wool Company, capitalized at £6,000. To market their produce in London, Simpson built a 'Winter Road' between York Factory and Red River via Norway House and Lake Winnipeg, a distance of 300 miles as the crow flies. In 1830, he established an experimental farm to raise European crops and livestock, rear sheep, and prepare tallow, wool, hemp, and flax for the English market. All these attempts failed; they were plagued by wolves, grasshoppers, floods, managerial problems, and bitterly cold winters. Simpson expressed his frustration in 1830: 'Such a mass of confusion as never fell under my observation now presents itself.' Simpson's attempts to locate marketable exports at Red River failed mainly because of transport conditions: successful export commodities had to be plentiful, easily transportable, of high value, and of low weight to overcome isolation from Hudson Bay. Only animal pelts met all the criteria.[16]

These failures provide an instructive counterpoint to contemporary successes on the west coast, where conditions promoting a general commerce prevailed. As the Pacific coast became known, stark contrasts were drawn between it and Rupert's Land. Simpson mused on the potential of the Willamette Valley for cattle and stock raising in 1841: 'What advantage over the snows on the east side of the Rocky Mountains?'[17] In 1858, Edward Ermatinger reflected that Red River's disadvantages resulted from its being 'shut up in the middle of the continent without markets,' while Rupert's Land as a whole was 'cut off from access to the rest of the world, on three sides by desert & frozen seas & on the fourth by a hostile nation.' Why, Ermatinger asked, was Red River languishing while American settlements on the Columbia River prospered?

> The cause is that Red River, by nature, is in a great measure shut up in the middle of the continent without markets; while the Columbia, a magnificent stream, little inferior to the mighty St. Lawrence, running through the whole of the Oregon territory, affords facilities for commerce with every part of the world.
>
> The two places have no similarity the one to the other: in climate, soil, productions, & every physical character they are entirely different. A comparison between Norway and Italy would be about the parallel case: and the writer who stated that rich wine should be produced in the North of Europe because it is in Spain & Italy would not make a more silly assertion than the writer [who] ... states that because agricultural produce is abundantly raised in the Columbia, it might be raised equally well at Red River.[18]

On the Pacific coast, the HBC escaped the northern reality of cold northern winters and failed export trades. Only there would the company develop the general commerce anticipated in its charter in 1670. Popular stereotypes of the fur trade – images of voyageurs, frozen rivers, birchbark canoes – originated in a landlocked, northern place where animal pelts were the only profitable export.[19] Such images pertain to most of Canada, but not to the west coast, where hopes of an extended Pacific commerce had captured the imagination of fur trade visionaries for fifty years.

In their three decades of industrious solitude on the Pacific, the British fur traders established commercial patterns and certain official policies that would persist in the late nineteenth century. The essentials of British Columbia's coastal transport system were established during this time to extend the fur trade and service new export trades. The brief gold rushes of the 1850s and 1860s would not greatly alter the choices of labour, transport, commodity, and market devised by the HBC in the early years. Economic diversity would characterize the province just as it had the Columbia Department;[20] the regional economy is still based, equally, on logging, mining, fishing, and farming. After 1849, this economy would continue to operate under colonial and provincial management, and it would take British Columbians 150 years to deplete the abundant and varied resources of the coastline north of the forty-ninth parallel.

There was also continuity in Indian policy and personnel between the company, colony, and province. Indeed, fur traders Anderson, McKay, McKinlay, Blenkinsop, and Moffatt had notable second careers as Indian agents under the province and dominion.[21] Usages derived from the fur trade such as 'the interior' persist in British Columbia, though not in Washington or Oregon, a result of the HBC's evacuation of United States territory after 1846 and increased American settlement. After the Oregon Treaty the Americans, while distrustful of the HBC's continued presence, inherited with equanimity the resources, markets, and forms of labour devised by the company. The Americans would impose new political and social regimes upon this economic base, while the HBC moved its corporate culture – its skill, strategies, personnel, and vocabulary – to the north.

After the 1840s, company officials gradually abandoned the continental fur trade routes that had brought them to the coast in the first place, inaugurating forty years of isolation from the economy of the rest of

British North America. This isolation was heightened, and justified, by the success of the new regional economy. Between 1821 and 1843, the company's main external connections from the coast were, in order of importance, London, Hawaii, California, Hudson Bay, and Canada. Despite the presence on the Pacific of many French (and a few English) Canadian fur traders, contact with Rupert's Land and Canada became increasingly rare in the 1840s and 1850s. The island-based, colonial years between 1843 and 1871 encouraged this isolation. Only with Confederation and the completion of the Canadian Pacific Railway in 1886 would the vigorous transcontinental commerce of Simpson and the NWC visionaries be revived.[22]

During the fur trade period, the regional economy divided roughly into north coast, south coast, southern interior, and northern interior; indeed, as Anderson pointed out in 1872, the department's 'various divisions were distinguished by different names, most of which are still retained for local designation.' Native names – Okanagan, Kootenay, Kamloops, Nanaimo – were later applied to fur trade posts and eventually cities or whole regions. Even the name British Columbia, chosen by Queen Victoria in 1858 after a study of every available map of the territory, reflects a political and commercial inheritance from the vast and ultimately truncated Columbia Department.[23]

Abbreviations

BCHN   *British Columbia Historical News*
BCHQ   *British Columbia Historical Quarterly*
BCARS   British Columbia Archives and Record Service
CHSQ   *California Historical Society Quarterly*
DCB   *Dictionary of Canadian Biography*
HBCA   Hudson's Bay Company Archives
HBRS   Hudson's Bay Record Society
JRGS   *Journal of the Royal Geographical Society*
NAC   National Archives of Canada
OHQ   *Oregon Historical Quarterly*
PHR   *Pacific Historical Review*
PNQ   *Pacific Northwest Quarterly*
UBC   University of British Columbia
TRSC   *Transactions of the Royal Society of Canada*
WHQ   *Washington Historical Society*

Notes

Introduction

1 John Dunn, *History of the Oregon territory and British North-American fur trade; with an Account of the Habits and Customs of the Principal Native Tribes on the Northern Continent* (London: Edwards and Hughes 1844), 217.

2 Dunn, *History of Oregon territory*, 333. ·

3 Governor and Committee (hereafter G&C) to Haldane and Cameron, 4 September 1822, in R. Harvey Fleming, ed., *Minutes of Council, Northern Department of Rupert's Land, 1821-31*, with an introduction by H.A. Innis (Toronto: Champlain Society for the Hudson's Bay Record Society 1940) (hereafter HBRS 3) 335; Simpson to Andrew Colvile, 9 August 1824, HBRS 3, 243-4; Douglas to McLoughlin, 1 October 1840, Hudson's Bay Company Archives (hereafter HBCA), B.223/b/28, fos. 77-9; Alexander Forbes, *California: A History of Upper and Lower California from their first Discovery to the Present Time* ... (London: Smith, Elder and Co. 1839); Dunn, *History of Oregon territory*, 203.

4 The authority on the commercial strategies of the fur trade remains Harold A. Innis, *The Fur Trade in Canada: An Introduction to Canadian Economic History* (New Haven: Yale University Press 1930; revised edition, Toronto: University of Toronto Press 1956).

5 See, for example, Washington Irving, *The Rocky Mountains: Or, Scenes, Incidents, and Adventures in the Far West* ... Vol. 1 (Philadelphia: Carey, Lea, Blanchard 1837), 188-9.

6 For 'resource development' on the Pacific, see E.E. Rich, *Hudson's Bay Company 1670-1870* (hereafter *HBC*), Vol. 3 (Toronto: McClelland and Stewart 1960), 749, and Keith Ralston, 'Miners and Managers: The Organization of Coal Production on Vancouver Island by the Hudson's Bay Company, 1848-1862,' in E. Blanche Norcross, ed., *The Company on the Coast* (Nanaimo: Nanaimo Historical Society 1983), 42-55.

7 Innis, Introduction to HBRS, 3; E.E. Rich, ed., *The Letters of John McLoughlin from Fort Vancouver to the Governor and Committee, First Series, 1825-1838*, with an introduction by W. Kaye Lamb (London: HBRS 1941) (HBRS 4); E.E. Rich, ed., *The Letters of John McLoughlin from Fort Vancouver to the Governor and Committee, Second Series, 1839-1844*, with an introduction by W. Kaye Lamb (London: HBRS 1943) (HBRS 6); E.E. Rich, ed., *The Letters of John McLoughlin from Fort Vancouver to the Governor and Committee, Third Series, 1844-1846*, with an introduction by W. Kaye Lamb (London: HBRS 1944) (HBRS 7).

8 Frederick Merk, ed., *Fur Trade and Empire, George Simpson's Journal, Remarks Connected With the Fur Trade in the Course of a Voyage From York Factory to Fort George and Back to York, 1824-25* (Cambridge, MA: Harvard University Press 1931); E.E. Rich, ed., *Part of a Dispatch from George Simpson, Esq., Governor of Rupert's Land, to the Governor and Committee of the Hudson's Bay Company, London, March 1 1829, Continued and Completed March 24, and June 5, 1829* (London: Champlain Society for HBRS 1947) (HBRS 10); Glyndwr Williams, ed., *London Correspondence Inward from Sir George Simpson, 1841-42* (London: HBRS 1973) (HBRS 29).

9 Arthur J. Ray, *Indians in the Fur Trade: Their Role as Trappers, Hunters, and Middlemen in the Lands Southwest of Hudson Bay 1660-1870* (Toronto: University of Toronto Press 1974); Arthur J. Ray and Donald B. Freeman, *'Give Us Good Measure': An Economic Analysis of Relations between the Indians and the Hudson's Bay Company before 1773* (Toronto: University of Toronto Press 1978); Arthur J. Ray, *The Canadian Fur Trade in the Industrial Age* (Toronto: University of Toronto Press 1990).

10   James R. Gibson, *Imperial Russia in Frontier America: The Changing Geography of Supply of Russian America, 1784-1867* (New York: Oxford University Press 1976); *Farming the Frontier: The Agricultural Opening of the Oregon Country, 1786-1846* (Vancouver: UBC Press 1985); 'A Diverse Economy: The Columbia Department of the Hudson's Bay Company, 1821-1846,' *Columbia* (Summer 1991): 28-31; *Otter Skins, Boston Ships, and China Goods: The Maritime Fur Trade of the Northwest Coast, 1785-1841* (Montreal and Kingston: McGill-Queen's University Press 1992).

11   Barry M. Gough, *The Royal Navy and the Northwest Coast of North America, 1810-1914: A Study of British Maritime Ascendency* (Vancouver: UBC Press 1971); Barry M. Gough, *The Northwest Coast: British Navigation, Trade, and Discoveries to 1812* (Vancouver: UBC Press 1992); John S. Galbraith, *The Hudson's Bay Company as an Imperial Factor* (Toronto: University of Toronto Press 1957); Robin A. Fisher, *Contact and Conflict: Indian-European Relations in British Columbia, 1774-1890* (Vancouver: UBC Press 1977).

12   David J. Wishart, *The Fur Trade of the American West, 1807-1840. A Geographical Synthesis* (Lincoln and London: University of Nebraska Press 1979); John E. Sunder, *The Fur Trade on the Upper Missouri* (Norman, OK: University of Oklahoma Press 1993); James P. Ronda, *Astoria and Empire* (Lincoln, NE: University of Nebraska Press 1990); John Denis Haeger, *John Jacob Astor: Business and Finance in the Early Republic* (Indiana: Wayne State University Press 1991); Frederick Merk, *The Oregon Question: Essays in Anglo-American Diplomacy and Politics* (Cambridge, MA: Harvard University Press 1967); David M. Pletcher, *The Diplomacy of Annexation: Texas, Oregon, and the Mexican War* (Columbia, MS: University of Missouri Press 1973). See also Keith A. Murray, 'The Role of the Hudson's Bay Company in Pacific Northwest History,' in G. Thomas Edwards and Carlos A. Schwantes, eds., *Experience in a Promised Land* (Seattle: University of Washington Press 1986), 28-39.

CHAPTER 1: The North West Passage by Land

1   A.C. Anderson, 'A Compendium of the Province of British Columbia. Its Early History, General Features, Climate, Resources, Etc,' in *The British Columbia Directory for the Years 1882-83* (Victoria: R.T. Williams 1882), 2-26, 7.

2   This chapter owes much to Barry Gough's important book, *The Northwest Coast*.

3   Gough, *The Northwest Coast*, 13.

4   Rich, *HBC*, Vol. 1, 446, 448, 565.

5   On the British search for a North West Passage, see Lawrence J. Burpee, *The Search for the Western Sea* (Toronto: Musson 1908); Rich, *HBC*, Vol. 1, 446, 448, 462; Glyndwr Williams, *The British Search for the Northwest Passage* (London: Green and Company 1960); Gough, *The Northwest Coast*.

6   For the colonial American overland explorations, see Gough, *The Northwest Coast*, 154-5, 172; T.C. Elliott, 'The Origin of the Name Oregon,' *OHQ* 22, 2 (June 1921): 91-115; T.C. Elliott, 'Jonathan Carver's Source for the Name Oregon,' *OHQ* 23, 1 (March 1922): 53-69; James Ronda, 'Dreams and Discoveries: Exploring the American West, 1760-1815,' *William and Mary Quarterly* 46 (1989): 145-62.

7   Gough, *The Northwest Coast*, 31-62.

8   Gibson, *Otter Skins*, 23; Gough, *The Northwest Coast*, 70-1, 95, 127.

9   Gough, *The Northwest Coast*, 70, 87-103; Gibson, *Otter Skins*, 24; John Meares, *Voyages Made in the Years 1788 and 1789, from China to the North West Coast of America* (London 1790).

10   Gough, *The Northwest Coast*, 146-70.

11   Rich, *HBC*, Vol. 2, 131-2. On Pond's motives, see Rich, *HBC*, Vol. 2, 120, 131, 159; Campbell, *The North West Company*, 47, 59; Gough, *The Northwest Coast*, 172-80; Ronda, *Astoria and Empire*, 4-24.

12   Alexander Henry, 'A Proper Rout, by Land, to Cross the Great Continent of America from Quebec ...' [letter to Joseph Banks, 18 October 1781], quoted in Burpee, *The Search for the Western Sea*, 578-87, 584. See also Marjorie Wilkins Campbell, *The North West Company* (Toronto: Macmillan 1957), 47; and Ronda, *Astoria and Empire*, 25-9.

13   Alexander Dalrymple, *Plan for Promoting the Fur-Trade and Securing It to This Country by Uniting the Operations of the East India and Hudson's Bay Companies* (London 1789).

14 Rich, *HBC*, Vol. 2, 164; see also Gough, *The North West Coast*, 110. On the prohibitory East India Company monopoly, see Gough, *The Northwest Coast*, 172, and Gibson, *Otter Skins*, 25, 91-2. Parliament revoked the East India Company's monopoly of the British Indian trade in 1813 and terminated its monopoly altogether in 1833. Gibson, *Otter Skins*, 94, 247; Gough, *The Northwest Coast*, 195, 234 n. 76.

15 'Memorandum by Alexander Dalrymple on the Route for Discoveries,' 2 February 1790, in Burpee, *The Search for the Western Sea*, 589-90.

16 'Captain Holland's Plan to Explore from Quebec' [J.F. de B. Holland, c. July 1790], in Burpee, *The Search for the Western Sea*, 592-5; Gough, *The Northwest Coast*, 110.

17 Rich, *HBC*, Vol. 2, 164; Gough, *The Northwest Coast*, 110, 148-9.

18 Rich, *HBC*, Vol. 2, 202-3, 206-7, 210-11; Campbell, *The North West Company*, 70, 66-90; Gibson, *Otter Skins*, 26-7; Gough, *The Northwest Coast*, 180-1, 183-4. See also Grace Parker Morris, ed., 'Some Letters from 1792-1800 on the China Trade,' *OHQ* 42, 1 (March 1941): 48-87; A.S. Morton, ed., *The Journal of Duncan M'Gillivray of the North West Company at Fort George on the Saskatchewan, 1794-5* (Toronto: Macmillan 1929).

19 Howard T. Fry, *Alexander Dalrymple (1730-1808) and the Expansion of British Overseas Trade* (Toronto: University of Toronto Press 1970); Campbell, *The North West Company*, 63-7; Rich, *HBC*, Vol. 2, 157; Gough, *The Northwest Coast*, 110. See also Harold A. Innis, 'Peter Pond and the Influence of Captain James Cook on Exploration in the Interior of North America,' *TRHC*, Sec. 2 (1928): 131-41.

20 W. Kaye Lamb, ed., *The Journals and Letters of Sir Alexander Mackenzie* (Toronto: Macmillan 1970), 415-18; Rich, *HBC*, Vol. 2, 216, 221; Gough, *The Northwest Coast*, 183. Mackenzie had sent a similar statement to John Graves Simcoe in 1794. Campbell, *The North West Company*, 87-8.

21 Lamb, ed., *Mackenzie*, 417. Mackenzie's views were taken up by Alexander von Humboldt in his *Political Essay on the Kingdom of New Spain* ... Vol. 1 (London: Longman, Hurst, Rees, Orme, & Brown 1811), 20.

22 Lamb, ed., *Mackenzie*, 503-7. On these plans, see Arthur S. Morton, *A History of the Canadian West to 1870-71* ... (London: Thomas Nelson & Sons 1939), 520-2; Campbell, *The North West Company*, 129-31, 176-7; Gough, *The Northwest Coast*, 184-5.

23 Gough, *The Royal Navy*, 41-2; Barry M. Gough, ed., *To the Pacific and Arctic with Beechey: The Journal of Lieutenant George Peard of H.M.S. 'Blossom' 1825-1828* (Cambridge: Cambridge University Press 1973), 9.

24 Lamb, ed., *Mackenzie*, 14; Gough, *The Northwest Coast*, 183-5.

25 Mackenzie to British Board of Trade, 1809, quoted in Campbell, *The North West Company*, 177. See also Oscar O. Winther, 'Commercial Routes from 1792 to 1843 by Sea and Overland,' *OHQ* 42, 3 (September 1941): 230-46.

26 Gough, *The Northwest Coast*, 188; C.O. Ermatinger, ed., 'Edward Ermatinger's York Factory Express Journal, Being a Record of Journeys Made Between Fort Vancouver and Hudson Bay in the Years 1827-1828,' *TRSC*, Third Series (Ottawa: Royal Society 1912): 67-132, n. 83. See also A.C. Anderson, *The Dominion of the West. A Brief Description of the Province of British Columbia, Its Climate and Resources* (Victoria: Richard Wolfenden 1872), xxxvii-xxxviii. On Mackenzie's and Fraser's work in New Caledonia, see David V. Burley, J. Scott Hamilton, and Knut R. Fladmark, *Prophecy of the Swan: The Upper Peace River Fur Trade of 1794-1823* (Vancouver: UBC Press 1996), 27-33.

27 Irene M. Spry, 'Routes through the Rockies,' *The Beaver* 294 (Autumn 1963): 26-39.

28 Jefferson is quoted in D.W. Meinig, *The Great Columbia Plain: A Historical Geography, 1805-1910* (Seattle: University of Washington Press 1968), 32; see also Ronda, *Astoria and Empire*, 29-30. For the cartographic contribution of Lewis and Clark, see Carl I. Wheat, *Mapping the Transmississippi West*, Vol. 1 (San Francisco: Institute of Historical Geography 1958), 49-60.

29 Campbell, *The North West Company*, 85. The NWC had benefited indirectly from the terms of the Nootka Convention with Spain, which had given the British the rights to 'trade and dominion' on the North West Coast. Gough, *The Northwest Coast*, 191.

30 Mackenzie to British Board of Trade, 1809, quoted in Campbell, *The North West Company*,

177. For the NWC's 'Columbia Enterprise,' see Gough, *The Royal Navy*, 9-12, and A.S. Morton, 'The North West Company's Columbia Enterprise and David Thompson,' *CHR* 17 (1936): 266-88.

31 John Henry or Nathaniel Atcheson, supposed author(s), *On the Origins and Progress of the North-West Company of Canada, with a history of the fur trade, as connected with that concern* (London: Cox, Son, and Baylis 1811), 29-30, 36-7; see also Ronda, *Astoria and Empire*, 244-7.

32 Thompson, 1811, quoted in Richard Glover, *David Thompson's Narrative 1784-1812* (Toronto: Champlain Society 1962). See also Barbara Belyea, 'The "Columbian Enterprise" and A.S. Morton,' *BC Studies* 86 (1990): 3-27; Barbara Belyea, ed., *Columbia Journals of David Thompson* (Montreal and Kingston: McGill-Queen's University Press 1994).

33 Lamb, ed., *Mackenzie*, 10, 35. On the formation of the Pacific Fur Company, see Ronda, *Astoria and Empire*, 37-64.

34 Campbell, *The North West Company*, 57, 166-7. On the renegade Northwesters, see Washington Irving, *Astoria; or, Enterprise Beyond The Rocky Mountains*, Vol. 1 (London: Richard Bentley 1836), 53-4; Kenneth Wiggins Porter, *John Jacob Astor Business Man*, Vol. 1 (Cambridge, MA: Harvard University Press 1931), 30-1; and Ronda, *Astoria and Empire*, 36, 88-93.

35 Ross Cox, *Adventures on the Columbia River, Including The Narrative of a Residence of Six Years' on the West Side of the Rocky Mountains ...* (London: Henry Colburn and Richard Bentley 1831); Alexander Ross, *Adventures of the First Settlers on the Oregon or Columbia River: Being a Narrative of the Expedition Fitted out by John Jacob Astor, to Establish the Pacific Fur Company ...* (London: Smith, Elder and Co. 1849); Alexander Ross, *The Fur Hunters of the Far West; A Narrative of Adventures in the Oregon and Rocky Mountains* (London: Smith, Elder and Co. 1855); W. Kaye Lamb, ed., *Gabriel Franchère, Journal of a Voyage on the North West Coast of North America During the Years 1811, 1812, 1813 and 1814* (Toronto: Champlain Society 1969).

36 Fifteen of fifty-one members of Lewis and Clark's party had French names: Charles G. Clarke, *The Men of the Lewis and Clark Expedition* (Glendale, CA: Arthur H. Clarke 1970), 37-72. Irving, *Astoria*, Vol. 1, 214. On Crooks see William S. Lewis and Paul C. Phillips, eds., *The Journal of John Work a Chief-Trader of the Hudson's Bay Co. during His Expedition from Vancouver to the Flatheads and Blackfeet of the Pacific Northwest* (Cleveland: Arthur H. Clark 1923), 52.

37 Cox, *Adventures*, Vol. 1, 70, 208; Kenneth W. Porter, 'Roll of Overland Astorians,' *OHQ* 34, 2 (June 1933): 86. In its basic structure, personnel, and hierarchy, Astoria differed little from a NWC post. See Ronda, *Astoria and Empire*, 209-11.

38 Rich, *HBC*, Vol. 2, 248-50; Ross, *Adventures*, 5. See Morton, *A History*, 489, on the lack of originality in Astor's plan.

39 Dunn, *History of Oregon territory*, 219-20.

40 Ross, *The Fur Hunters*, Vol. 1, 1; Ross, *Adventures*, 85, 102.

41 Ross, *Adventures*, 153, 261, 283; Ross, *The Fur Hunters*, Vol. 1, 2. See also Ronda, Astoria and Empire, 95-7, 235-7, 286.

42 Ross, *Adventures*, 154, 241. On Astor's 1809 agreement with the Russian American Company, see Wishart, *The Fur Trade of the American West*, 117, and Ronda, *Astoria and Empire*, 65-86.

43 Hunt is quoted in Ross, *Adventures*, 241; see also 242, 245. Ronda, however, reports that Hunt was critical of the Scottish partners' decision to sell out to the NWC, *Astoria and Empire*, 285.

44 Ross, *Adventures*, 245, 252-4; Cox, *Adventures*, Vol. 1, 207-8; Ross, *The Fur Hunters*, Vol. 1, 2; Porter, *John Jacob Astor*, Vol. 1, 224-32; Ronda, *Astoria and Empire*, 264-5, 277-96.

45 Ross, *Adventures*, 219, 220, 252, 259. See T.C. Elliott, 'Sale of Astoria, 1813,' *OHQ* 33, 1 (March 1932): 43-50. On the formal return of Fort George to the United States in 1818, under the terms of the Treaty of Ghent, see Gough, *The Royal Navy*, 26-8 and Ronda, *Astoria and Empire*, 314-15.

46 Ross, *The Fur Hunters*, Vol. 1, 72; Cox, *Adventures*, Vol. 1, 64-5; Ross, *Adventures*, 100, 234-7; Philip Ashton Rollins, ed., *The Discovery of the Oregon Trail. Robert Stuart's Narrative of His Overland Trip Eastward from Astoria in 1812-13 ...* (New York: Charles Scribner's Sons

1935). Stuart is quoted in Meinig, *The Great Columbia Plain*, 43. On the Astorians' achievement, see Meinig, 39-43, 48-53.

47 Inglis, Ellice, & Co. to Henry Gouldburn, 2 August 1815, quoted in Katharine B. Judson, 'British Side of the Restoration of Fort Astoria - II,' *OHQ* 20, 4 (December 1919): 306; NWC partners, 18 July 1812, quoted in Gough, *The Northwest Coast*, 189; Simpson, quoted in Merk, *Fur Trade and Empire*, 278. See also Ross, *The Fur Hunters*, Vol. 1, 22; Corney, *Voyages in the Northern Pacific. Narrative of Several Trading Voyages from 1813 to 1818, Between the Northwest Coast of America, the Hawaiian Islands and China* ... (Honolulu: Thos. G. Thrum 1891; first published London 1821), 20-4, 31, 32; M. O'Neil, 'The Maritime Activities of the North West Company, 1813-1821,' *WHQ* 21 (1930): 243-67.

48 H. Lloyd Keith, 'The North West Company's "Adventure to the Columbia": A Reassessment of Financial Failure,' unpublished ms., 1989; Gough, *The Northwest Coast*, 189; Ross, *The Fur Hunters*, Vol. 1, 41.

49 Ross, *The Fur Hunters*, Vol. 1, 15, 72, 118, 198; see also Corney, *Voyages in the Northern Pacific*, 28.

50 Ross, *The Fur Hunters*, Vol. 1, 77, 156-8.

51 Ibid., 74, 291-2, 295. A few Iroquois had come overland with Astor's brigades. See Ronda, *Astoria and Empire*, 213.

52 Ross, *The Fur Hunters*, Vol. 1, 73-4.

53 Ibid., 158; W.T. Atkin, 'Snake Country Fur Trade, 1816-24,' *OHQ* 35, 4 (December 1934): 295-312; Ross, *The Fur Hunters*, Vol. 1, 158.

54 Ross, *The Fur Hunters*, Vol. 1, 100, 113, 190-1, 196-7.

55 Ibid., 73-4, 76.

56 Ibid., 117-18. Perkins and Company were the major American merchants in Canton. See Gibson, *Otter Skins*, 57-8, and Gough, *The Northwest Coast*, 63, 190. William McGillivray, 1816, is quoted in Hilary Russell, 'The Chinese Voyages of Angus Bethune,' *The Beaver* 307, 4 (Spring 1977): 31. On the Perkins contract, see also F.W. Howay, ed., 'William Sturgis: The Northwest Coast Trade,' *BCHQ* 8, 1 (January 1944): 25.

57 Rich, *HBC*, Vol. 3, 568; Keith, 'Adventure to the Columbia'; Galbraith, *Hudson's Bay Company*, 81-2; Gibson, *Otter Skins*, 26; Simpson to G&C [circa 1825], HBRS 10, 123-47.

58 Lewes to Simpson, 2 April 1822, quoted in Gibson, *Otter Skins*, 64; 331 n. 12; see also 26-7.

59 Rich, *HBC*, Vol. 3, 563-5, 568. Keith's figures (Table 1) show an aggregate loss of about £45,000. Keith, 'Adventure to the Columbia.' Gough attributes the company's impoverishment and eventual merger with the HBC to the East India Company monopoly. Gough, *The Northwest Coast*, 195.

60 See J. Neilson Barry, 'Agriculture in the Oregon Country 1795-1844,' *OHQ* 30, 2 (June 1929): 166.

61 Duncan McGillivray, 1808, is quoted in D.W. Moodie, 'The Trading Post Settlement of the Canadian North West,' *Journal of Historical Geography* 13 (1987): 360-74, 369; William McGillivray to John Strachan, 26 July 1821, is quoted in Campbell, *The North West Company*, 275.

62 Jamie Morton, *Fort St. James 1806-1914: A Century of Fur Trade on Stuart Lake*, Microfiche Report Series No. 367, (Ottawa: Canadian Parks Service 1988), 20, 34, 51.

63 Mary Cullen, 'Outfitting New Caledonia 1821-58,' in Carol M. Judd and Arthur J. Ray, eds., *Old Trails and New Directions: Papers of the Third North American Fur Trade Conference* (Toronto: University of Toronto Press 1980), 231-51; Bob Harris, Hartley Hatfield, and Peter Tassie, *The Okanagan Brigade Trail in the Southern Okanagan 1811 to 1849, Oroville, Washington to Westside, British Columbia* (Westside, BC: Wayside Press 1989), 3; Jean Webber, 'Fur Trading Posts in the Okanagan and Similkameen,' *Okanagan Historical Society* 57 (1993): 8-9.

64 HBRS 3, lxiv n. 4. Fort Alexandria was in New Caledonia District: Galbraith, *Hudson's Bay Company*, 119. The Pacific Fur Company's short-lived Shewaps post, founded in 1812, rivalled the NWC's post at Kamloops.

65 John Lee Lewes to Simpson, 2 April 1822, cited in Galbraith, *Hudson's Bay Company*, 81.

66 Wheat, *Mapping the Transmississippi West*, Vol. 2, 111.

67 Gough, *The Northwest Coast*, 188.

68 Corney, *Voyages in the Northern Pacific*, 80-1. See also Cox, *Adventures*, Vol. 1, 109-11.

69 For Columbia River place-names, see Marguerite Eyer Wilbur, ed., *Duflot de Mofras' Travels on the Pacific Coast*, Vol. 2 (Santa Anna, CA: Fine Arts Press 1937), 111; for Snake River place-names, see Wheat, *Mapping the Transmississippi West*, Vol. 2, 113.

70 Joseph William McKay, 'The Fur Trading System,' in R.E. Gosnell, ed., *The Year Book of British Columbia and Manual of Provincial Legislation* ... (Victoria 1897), 25.

71 Keith, 'Adventure to the Columbia.' See also Gordon Charles Davidson, *The North West Company* (New York: Russell & Russell 1967; first published 1918).

72 R. Cole Harris, ed., *Historical Atlas of Canada*, Vol. 1, (Toronto: University of Toronto Press 1987), plate 66; Gibson, *Otter Skins*, 29-35, 315.

73 Perkins and Company (Canton) to NWC [circa 1815-18], quoted in Keith, 'Adventure to the Columbia.'

74 James R. Gibson, 'Russian America in 1821,' *OHQ* 77, 2 (June 1976): 174-88; Gibson, *Otter Skins*, 18; Gough, *The Northwest Coast*, 69, 144-5, 164-5.

75 Morton, *A History*, 506; HBRS 3, xii; Galbraith, *Hudson's Bay Company*, 79; Gough, *The Royal Navy*, 28, 31. On the tenuous Spanish claim, see Gibson, *Farming the Frontier*, 257 n. 95.

76 John Floyd, 'Occupation of the Columbia River,' *OHQ* 8, 1 (March 1907): 62. For the 1818 negotiations, see Daniel Clayton, 'Whole Kingdoms for the Sake of a Harbour,' *Columbia* 9, 1 (Spring 1995): 38-44. For the early-nineteenth-century American vision of an overland 'Passage to India,' see Wishart, *The Fur Trade of the American West*, 115, and Ronda, *Astoria and Empire*, 327-37.

77 Corney, *Voyages in the Northern Pacific*, 29, 33, 72, 76, 81. On the NWC in California, see Cox, *Adventures*, Vol. 2, 50, and Alice Bay Maloney, 'Hudson's Bay Company in California,' *OHQ* 37, 1 (March 1936): 9-10.

78 James Keith to Colonel Perkins, 13 April 1821, Keith Papers, University of Aberdeen. I owe this reference to Dr. Lloyd Keith. On provisioning at Fort Astoria, see Ronda, *Astoria and Empire*, 204-7.

79 Innis, HBRS 3, xxx. On the merger, see Galbraith, *Hudson's Bay Company*, 7-8; Campbell, *The North West Company*, 267-77; William R. Sampson, *John McLoughlin's Business Correspondence, 1847-48* (Seattle: University of Washington Press 1973), xxiv-xxviii. For the principle of the agreement, see G&C to Williams, 26 February 1821, HBRS 3, 293. For the 26 March 1821 deed poll, see Morton, *A History*, 624-5, and [Hudson's Bay Company], *Copy of the Deed Poll Under the Seal of the Governor and Company of Adventurers of England Trading into Hudson's Bay, Bearing Date the Twenty-Sixth day of March 1821* (London: H.K. Causton 1821). For the exclusive licence dated 26 March 1821, see HBRS 2, 302-27.

80 At the height of the competitive era, the company had paid its shareholders dividends of 4 per cent: E.H. Oliver, ed., *The Canadian North-West; Its Early Development and Legislative Records: Minutes of the Council of the Red River Colony and the Northern Department of Rupert's Land* (Ottawa: Government Printing Bureau 1914-15), 135; Anderson, *Dominion of the West*, n. 92.

81 G&C to Simpson, 27 February 1822, HBRS 3, 301; Morton, *A History*, 695; Innis, *The Fur Trade in Canada*, 285-6; Ross, *The Fur Hunters*, Vol. 2, 230.

82 McKay, 'The Fur Trading System,' 21-2.

83 Arthur S. Morton, *Sir George Simpson, Overseas Governor of the Hudson's Bay Company* (Toronto: J.M. Dent & Sons 1944), 10; Rich, *HBC*, Vol. 2, 372; Vol. 3, 481; on Williams see Madge Wolfenden, ed., 'John Tod: "Career of a Scotch Boy,"'*BCHQ* 18, 3 and 4 (July-October 1954): 154. In 1826 Simpson replaced Williams as governor of the Southern Department, and in 1839 he received the official title of Governor-in-Chief of Rupert's Land. HBRS 3, xi.

84 W.S. Wallace, ed., *John McLean's Notes of a Twenty-five Years' Service in the Hudson's Bay Territory* (Toronto: Champlain Society 1932), 354, 386; Wolfenden, 'John Tod,' 146. Galbraith, *Hudson's Bay Company*, 18-19, provides a few instances when the G&C exercised their 'theoretical' control.

85 For the royal licence of 5 December 1821 and 'An Act for Regulating the Fur Trade,' see [Hudson's Bay Company], *Charters, Statutes, Orders in Council, etc, Relating to the Hudson's*

Bay Company (London: Hudson's Bay Company 1960), 93-102, 217. The grant 'prohibited every Subject of his Majesty, except ourselves, or persons authorised by Us, to trade with the Indians on the North West Coast of America to the Westward of the Stoney Mountains.' HBRS 3, 328-30.

86 Chester Martin, 'The Royal Charter,' *The Beaver* (June 1945): 26-35.

87 Douglas Leechman, 'Comodityes besides Furres,' *The Beaver* 304, 4 (Spring 1974): 46-52; E.E. Rich and A.M. Johnson, eds., *Hudson's Bay Letters Outward, 1679-1694* (London: HBRS 1948). Six of the adventurers of 1670 were fellows of the Royal Society of London, which tested the London market for buffalo hides and swan skins. R.P. Stearns, 'The Royal Society and the Company,' *The Beaver*, 276 (June 1945): 8-13.

88 Rich, *HBC*, Vol. 1, 597. On the different skills and advantages of the Montreal and Hudson Bay fur trades, see Richard Glover, 'The Difficulties of the HBC's Penetration of the West,' *CHR* 29, 3 (September 1948): 240-54.

89 See W. Stewart Wallace, *Documents Relating to the North West Company* (Toronto: Champlain Society 1934), 84-9.

90 McKay, 'The Fur Trading System,' 21.

91 Garry is quoted in Innis, *The Fur Trade in Canada*, 323. 'The spirit of enterprise which had leavened the Hudson's Bay Company after the coalition appears to have died out with the North-West Co partners, whose last representative on this coast, Sir James Douglas, had certainly contributed to the industries mentioned.' McKay, 'The Fur Trading System,' 23.

92 Ross, *The Fur Hunters*, Vol. 2, 6.

93 Wyeth is quoted in Lois Halliday McDonald, ed., *Fur Trade Letters of Francis Ermatinger: Written to his Brother Edward During his Service with the Hudson's Bay Company, 1818-1853* (Glendale, CA: Arthur H. Clark 1980), 169.

94 Grace Lee Nute, 'A Botanist at Fort Colvile,' *The Beaver*, 277 (September 1946): 28-31.

95 'Inventory of Goods Fort Vancouver Depot Spring 1844,' HBCA B.223/d/127, fo. 145.

CHAPTER 2: Managing a New Region

1 Simpson to G&C, 10 March 1825, HBCA A.12/1, fos. 109-48.

2 Between 1821 and 1825, New Caledonia District returns had averaged £9,607 a year, while those of the Columbia District averaged £22,702. York Factory, Accounts Current, 1821-26, HBCA B.239/d/286.

3 Gibson, *Otter Skins*, Table 1, 299-310. On the expiry of the Perkins contract, see T.C. Elliott, ed., 'Letter of Donald Mackenzie to Wilson Price Hunt,' *OHQ* 43, 3 (September 1942): 195.

4 Morton, *Fort St. James*, 19-20, 34, 36, 51.

5 G&C to Simpson, 27 February 1822, HBRS 3, 302-3; see also Galbraith, *Hudson's Bay Company*, 123; Morton, *Fort St. James*, 60-1; Gough, *The Royal Navy*, 32; Barry M. Gough, ed., *To the Pacific and Arctic*, 13.

6 Simpson to G&C, 16 July 1822, HBRS 3, 341; Simpson to G&C, 31 July 1822, HBRS 3, 343-4; Simpson to Cameron, 18 July 1822, HBRS 4, 414.

7 G&C to Haldane and Cameron, 4 September 1822, HBRS 3, 335.

8 'For many years past there has been a regular trade of fine beaver and fine otter skins from this market [London] to Russia, which it is well-known found their way to China through Kiachta. This shows that there must be a regular and constant demand for fine furs at high prices in some of the provinces of China.' William Smith to Messrs Perkins & Co, Canton, 9 April 1823, HBCA A.6/20, fos. 107-107d. See also Merk, *Fur Trade and Empire*, 192.

9 Keith, 'Adventure to the Columbia.'

10 In London, Simpson may also have consulted Corney. Corney, *Voyages in the Northern Pacific*, Introduction, 1.

11 'We are of opinion that a Vessel chartered every second year will answer the purpose for transporting outfit and returns ...' Simpson to G&C, 1 August 1823, HBCA A.12/1, fo. 11. The company may have wanted to avoid the commission fees charged by Perkins and the costly dependency on American merchants.

12 Corney, *Voyages in the Northern Pacific*, 3, 7, and following.

13 Innis, *The Fur Trade in Canada*, passim; Innis, introduction to HBRS 3.
14 Innis, introduction to HBRS 3. The company's 'frontier policies' were 'highly systematized after 1821.' Galbraith, *Hudson's Bay Company*, 10.
15 Simpson to Hargrave, 20 December 1843, Hargrave Papers, NAC.

CHAPTER 3: George Simpson and a New Pacific Commerce

1 Simpson to G&C, 10 March 1825, HBCA A.12/1, fos. 109-42.
2 On Simpson's Columbia policies, see Merk, *Fur Trade and Empire*, 47-73 and passim; Innis's introduction to HBRS 3, xxxi-lxxi; Rich, *HBC*, Vol. 3, 447-8, 557, 578-9; Meinig, *The Great Columbia Plain*, 68-76; Margaret A. Ormsby, *British Columbia: A History* (Toronto: Macmillan of Canada 1958), 51-7; McDonald, *Fur Trade Letters of Francis Ermatinger*, 52-60; Mary Cullen, *History of Fort Langley, 1827-96* (Ottawa: National Historic Parks and Sites 1979), 9-16; Gibson, *Farming the Frontier*, 7-27; Jean Barman, *The West Beyond the West: A History of British Columbia* (Toronto: University of Toronto Press 1991), 40-1.
3 Simpson to G&C, 8 September 1823, HBCA A.12/1, fos. 47-64. See also Arthur J. Ray, 'Some Conservation Schemes of the Hudson's Bay Company, 1821-50: An Examination of the Problems of Resource Management in the Fur Trade,' *Journal of Historical Geography* 1 (1975): 49-68.
4 HBRS 3, 319-25, 338, 388, 396, 424, 453; Simpson to G&C, 10 March 1825, HBCA A.12/1, fos. 109-48; Innis, *The Fur Trade in Canada*, 318. Critics thought Simpson pushed his 'strict system of economy' 'to the extreme of parsimony.' Wallace, *John McLean's Notes*, 239, 354, 360, 383.
5 Simpson to G&C, 8 September 1821, HBRS 3, 399; Ross, *The Fur Hunters*, Vol. 1, 15; McDonald to G&C, 6 April 1822, cited in Jean Murray Cole, *Exile in the Wilderness: The Biography of Chief Factor Archibald McDonald* (Don Mills: Burns & MacEachern 1979), 101; Simpson to G&C, 23 June 1823, HBRS 3, xxxi; Simpson to G&C, 10 August 1824, HBCA A.12/1, fos. 65, 69.
6 Simpson to G&C, 10 August 1824, HBCA A.12/1, fo. 69; Simpson to Andrew Colvile, 9 August 1824, HBRS 3, 243-4. See also Simpson to J.G. McTavish, 12 November 1822, HBRS 3, 424 and Simpson to G&C, 10 August 1824, HBCA A.12/1, fos. 97-8.
7 Otto Klotz, *Certain Correspondence of the Foreign Office and of the Hudson's Bay Company Copied from Original Documents, London 1898* (Ottawa: Government Printing Bureau 1899), 5.
8 Simpson, quoted in Rich, *HBC*, Vol. 3, 447. 'A small lake, appropriately enough known as the Committee's punch-bowl, sends its tribute, from one end to the Columbia, and from the other to the Mackenzie.' Thomas Simpson, *Narrative of the Discoveries on the North Coast of America; Afforded by the Officers of the Hudson's Bay Company During the Years 1836-39*, Vol. 1 (London: Richard Bentley 1843), 120.
9 Simpson to McLeod, 1 November 1824, McLeod Collection, NAC; Simpson to G&C, 10 March 1825, HBCA A.12/1, fo. 119; McLoughlin to G&C, 6 October 1825, HBRS 4, 16. Simpson (1824) is quoted in Merk, *Fur Trade and Empire*, 33-4.
10 Simpson to G&C, 27 October 1824, HBRS 3, xxxiii.
11 Simpson to G&C, 10 March 1825, HBCA A.12/1, fo. 119. The following discussion and quotations are based on this letter, a draft of which formed the basis of Merk's *Fur Trade and Empire*.
12 McLoughlin to Simpson, 20 March 1846, quoted in Frederick Merk, 'Snake Country Expedition, 1824-25. An Episode of Fur Trade and Empire,' *OHQ* 35, 2 (June 1934): 121-2; Simpson to G&C, 27 October 1824, HBRS 3, xxxiii.
13 W. Wilks, ed., *Journal kept by David Douglas, during his Travels in North America, 1823-1827* ... (London: W. Wesley & Son 1914), 103; Morag Maclachlan, 'The Founding of Fort Langley,' in E. Blanche Norcross, ed., *The Company on the Coast* (Nanaimo: Nanaimo Historical Society 1983) 16.
14 On the exotic assortment of trade goods at Fort George, see Keith, 'Adventure to the Columbia,' 31, n. 34 and HBRS 3, 53; on debts see McLoughlin to G&C, 14 November 1827, HBRS 4, 54.

15 Wilks, *Journal Kept by David Douglas*, 56, 103, 107; Simpson is cited in Pelly to Canning, 9 December 1825, in Klotz, *Certain Correspondence*, 12; Mackenzie is cited in Wilks, *Journal Kept by David Douglas*, 103; Dunn, *History of Oregon territory*, 141.
16 Simpson to G&C, 10 August 1824, HBCA A.12/1, fo. 69; Ross, *Adventures*, 101.
17 Wilks, *Journal Kept by David Douglas*, 127.
18 Ross, *The Fur Traders*, Vol. 1, 190-1, 196; Simpson to G&C, 10 March 1825, HBCA A.12/1; Simpson to G&C, 1824, quoted in Ormsby, *British Columbia*, 55. See also F.W. Howay, 'The Discovery of the Fraser River: The Second Phase,' *BCHQ* 4, 4 (October 1940): 247; Morag Maclachlan, 'The Founding of Fort Langley,' in E. Blanche Norcross, ed., *The Company on the Coast* (Nanaimo: Nanaimo Historical Society 1983), 11-13; T.C. Elliott, ed., 'Journal of John Work, November and December 1824,' *WHQ*, 3, 3 (July 1912): 198-228; Cullen, *Fort Langley*, 13-15; Morag Maclachlan, 'The Case for Francis Noel Annance,' *The Beaver* 73, 2 (April-May 1993): 35-9.
19 Simpson to G&C, 10 March 1825, HBCA A.12/1; Elliott, 'Journal of John Work, November and December 1824,' 223.
20 Simpson to G&C, 10 March 1825, HBCA A.12/1.
21 Ibid.
22 Ibid.
23 Ibid.
24 Ibid.
25 Ibid.
26 Ibid.
27 Ibid.
28 On McLoughlin's assignment to the Columbia, see Sampson, *McLoughlin's Business Correspondence*, xxviii-xxxi. Simpson thought McLoughlin was 'wanting in System & regularity.' Alice M. Johnson, 'System and Regularity,' *The Beaver* 291 (Summer 1960): 36-9. For Mackenzie's gun, see Wilks, *Journal Kept by David Douglas*, 243.
29 Simpson, *Narrative*, Vol. 1, 150-1. Simpson to G&C, 14 April 1825, quoted in Nute, 'A Botanist at Fort Colvile.'
30 McDonald, *Fur Trade Letters of Francis Ermatinger*, 119, 148-9; Simpson, *Narrative*, Vol. 1, 148; Anderson, *Dominion of the West*, n. 55; Duane Thomson, 'The Response of the Okanagan Indians to European Settlement,' *BC Studies* 101 (Spring 1994), 98-9; W.N. Sage, 'Peter Skene Ogden's Notes on Western Caledonia,' *BCHQ* 1, 1 (January 1937): 52, 55.
31 Simpson anticipated 'great benefits to arise from embarking with spirit, enterprize and perseverence on this fine field which the west side of the Continent presents to our view.' Simpson to G&C, August 1825, HBCA A.12/1, fo. 195.
32 Simpson to G&C, 1 September 1825, HBCA D.4/88, fos. 77-8; Simpson, 'The China Trade,' HBRS 10, 123-47; G&C to Simpson, 23 February 1826, HBRS 10, 137.
33 G&C to Simpson, 16 January 1828, HBRS 10, 145.
34 Simpson to G&C, 10 July 1828, HBCA D.4/92, fo. 25.
35 Glover, 'Hudson Bay to the Orient,' 51; HBRS 3, lxxiii; Galbraith, *Hudson's Bay Company*, 123-4; Gibson, *Otter Skins*, 28.
36 Simpson to G&C, 20 August 1826, HBCA A.12/1, fos. 238-89; 248.
37 Simpson to G&C, 5 September 1827, HBCA D.4/91, fo. 4.
38 Ross, *The Fur Hunters*, Vol. 1, 42; F.W. Howay, 'The Introduction of Intoxicating Liquors Amongst the Indians of the Northwest Coast,' *BCHQ* 6, 3 (July 1942): 157-70.
39 Simpson to G&C, 10 July 1828, HBRS 3, lxx.
40 G&C to Chief Factors in Charge of Columbia District, 22 July 1824, HBRS 4, 2. On the company's measures to engross the coastal trade and the arrival of the *William and Ann*, see Jonathan R. Dean, '"Those Rascally Spackaloids": The Rise of Gispaxlots Hegemony at Fort Simpson, 1832-40,' *BC Studies* 101 (Spring 1994): 41-78, 45-6.
41 John Scouler, 'Dr John Scouler's Journal of a Voyage to N.W. America,' *OHQ* 6, 2 (June 1905): 183; Maclachlan, 'The Founding of Fort Langley,' 13.
42 Scouler, 'Dr John Scouler's Journal,' 192, 194-5. 'This chief well remembers Mr Mears and

Captain Vancouver, and even speaks with gratitude of them. Maquina, a well-known character, is a stout healthy old man'; [John Scouler and David Douglas], 'Notices Respecting
Mr Scouler's and Mr Douglas's Recent Voyage to the North West Coast of America,' *Edinburgh Journal of Science* 5 (April-October 1826), 380.

43   Scouler and Douglas, 'Notices Respecting Mr Scouler's and Mr Douglas's Recent Voyage,'
      380.
44   Simpson to G&C, 20 August 1826, HBCA A.12/1, fos. 241-3.
45   McLoughlin to G&C, 6 October 1825, HBRS 4, 2-3, 18-19.
46   Simpson to G&C, 29 October 1826, HBCA A.12/12, fos. 83-5. On Simpson's hiring, see also
      Gibson, *Otter Skins* 65-7.
47   Innis, *The Fur Trade in Canada*, 298; John T. Walbran, *British Columbia Coast Names 1592-
      1906, to Which are Added a few Names in Adjacent United States Territory* (Ottawa: Govern-
      ment Printing Bureau 1909; reprinted by J.J. Douglas, Vancouver, 1971), 76; A. Simpson to
      McLoughlin, 20 March 1827, HBRS 4, 29 n. 1; Cullen, *Fort Langley*, 16-21; Maclachlan, 'The
      Founding of Fort Langley,' 13-14; Maureen Korman, 'The First Fort Langley,' *Canada West*
      7, 3 (September 1991): 84-91, 88. Desertion of freeman had prevented the establishment of
      the post in 1826: HBRS 3, lxix.
48   Simpson to G&C, 20 August 1826, HBCA A.12/1, fos. 241-2; Simpson to G&C, 10 July
      1828, HBCA D.4/92, fo. 67; McLoughlin to G&C, 10 July 1828, HBRS 4, 61. On the need
      to meet spring hunts, see also Gough, *The Northwest Coast*, 91.
49   It had 'the double object of securing a share of the Coasting Trade which had previously
      been monopolized by the Americans, and of possessing a Settlement on the Coast which
      would answer the purpose of a Depot, in the event of our being under the necessity of with-
      drawing from Fort Vancouver.' Simpson to G&C, 1 March 1829, in HBRS 10, 41.
50   Simpson to McLoughlin, 10 April 1825, HBRS 3, lxv-lxvi; Simpson to G&C, 25 July 1827,
      HBCA D.4/90; Simpson to G&C, 20 August 1826, HBCA A.12/1, fos. 238-89, 241-2.
51   Ormsby, *British Columbia*, 62; W. Kaye Lamb, ed., *The Letters and Journals of Simon Fraser
      1806-1808*, (Toronto: Macmillan 1960), 96, 109.
52   Simpson to G&C, 1 March 1829, HBRS 10, 38-9.
53   Ibid., 41.
54   McDonald to Governor and Council, Northern Department, 25 February 1830, HBCA
      D.4/123, fos. 66d-72 and Cullen, *Fort Langley*, 83-8; Cole Harris, 'The Fraser Canyon
      Encountered,' *BC Studies* 94 (Summer 1992): 5-28.
55   Simpson to G&C, 1 March 1829, in HBRS 10, 81-2.
56   Simpson to William Smith, 17 November 1828, HBRS 4, 95 n. 1.
57   Simpson to G&C, 1 March 1829, in HBRS 10, 78, 80.
58   Rich, *HBC*, Vol. 3, 610-11; Gibson, *Otter Skins*, 77.
59   G&C to Simpson, 27 February 1822, HBRS 3, 302-3; Stuart to McIntosh, 5 January 1823,
      quoted in Morton, *Fort St. James*, 66.
60   HBRS 3, 115; Morton, *Fort St. James*, 85-6, 95-6; Ormsby, *British Columbia*, 60; Simpson to
      G&C, 20 August 1826, HBCA A.12/1, fo. 245; Cullen, 'Outfitting New Caledonia,' 234; Min-
      utes of Northern Council, July 1828, HBRS 3, 214.
61   McKay, 'The Fur Trading System,' 25; Anderson, *The Dominion of the West*, 57.
62   Dunn, *History of Oregon territory*, 61-2.
63   Ermatinger, 'Edward Ermatinger's York Factory Express Journal'; Spry, 'Routes Through the
      Rockies'; Wilbur, *Duflot de Mofras' Travels*, Vol. 2, 89-92; Wilks, *Journal Kept by David Dou-
      glas*, 151.
64   Ross, *The Fur Hunters*, Vol. 1, 304; Edward Belcher, *Narrative of a Voyage Round the World,
      Performed in Her Majesty's Ship Sulphur, During the Years 1836-1842 ...* Vol. 1 (London: Henry
      Colburn 1843), 301.
65   Ogden is quoted in Galbraith, *Hudson's Bay Company*, 90-1; see also Morton, *A History*, 738-
      42; Simpson to G&C, 1822, HBRS 3, xlii. A frontier was 'the line where the area of monopoly
      touched the area of competition.' Galbraith, *Hudson's Bay Company*, 10. For the HBC's 1820s
      Snake policies, see also Wishart, *The Fur Trade of the American West*, 32, 127-31, 137.

66   Simpson to G&C, 1822, HBRS 3, lxiv, lv; Simpson to G&C, circa 10 March 1825, HBRS 3, xxxiii.
67   See Peter Skene Ogden, *Traits of American-Indian Life and Character* (London: Smith, Elder and Company 1853) [written 1838], 22; E.E. Rich, ed., *Peter Skene Ogden's Snake Country Journals 1824-25 and 1825-26* (London: HBRS 1950) (HBRS 13); Glyndwr Williams, ed., *Peter Skene Ogden's Snake Country Journals, 1827-28 and 1828-29* (London: HBRS 1971) (HBRS 23); and HBRS 28. Simpson is quoted in HBRS 3, xxxiii. In 1826 the G&C cautioned that Ogden 'on no account' should have trapped in American territory. G&C to McLoughlin, 20 September 1826, quoted in Merk, 'Snake Country Expedition,' 119. For John Work's 1825-32 career with the Snake Party, see Henry Drummond Dee, 'An Irishman in the Fur Trade: The Life and Journals of John Work,' *BCHQ* 7, 3 (October 1943): 240-53.
68   McLoughlin to Chief Factors and Chief Traders, Northern Factory, HBC, 10 August 1825, HBCA B.223/b/1, fo. 21; Simpson to McLoughlin, 9 July 1827, HBRS 3, lxviii.
69   Galbraith, *Hudson's Bay Company*, 177.
70   HBRS 3, lxviii-lxix; see also Galbraith, *Hudson's Bay Company*, 85-8, 96-9; Wishart, *The Fur Trade of the American West*, 41-79, 115-75.
71   Lewis and Phillips, *The Journal of John Work*, 37.
72   Ogden, *Traits*, 5. Smith was the first 'white man' to approach the Sacramento from east of the Rockies. Herman Leader, ed., 'A Voyage from the Columbia to California in 1840,' *CHSQ* 8, 2 (June 1929): 115 n. 85.
73   Simpson to Smith, 26 December 1828, quoted in Maurice S. Sullivan, ed., *The Travels of Jedediah Smith* (Santa Anna, CA: Fine Arts Press 1934), 137; A.R. McLeod, 'Particular Occurrences during a Voyage of about three Months, Southward of the Columbia' [6 September-10 December 1828], in Sullivan, *The Travels of Jedediah Smith*, 112-35, 152. On Smith's debacle and later plans, see also Simpson, *Narrative*, Vol. 1, 248-9; Ogden, *Traits*, 11-19; Lewis and Phillips, *The Journal of John Work*, 38. On the Umpqua incident, see also Nathan Douthit, 'The Hudson's Bay Company and the Indians of Southern Oregon,' *OHQ* 93, 1 (Spring 1992): 25-64, and John Phillip Reid, 'Restraints of Vengeance: Retaliation-in-Kind and the Use of Law in the Old Oregon Country,' *OHQ* 95, 1 (Spring 1994): 70-3.
74   'The posts on the Columbia were so meagre in their returns that the Snake expeditions were the chief source of profits.' Rich, *HBC*, Vol. 3, 620; Simpson to G&C, 1 March 1829, HBRS 10.
75   Alice Bay Maloney, ed., *Fur Brigade to the Bonaventura: John Work's California Expedition 1832-1833 For The HBC* (San Francisco: California Historical Society 1945), v; Wilks, *Journal Kept by David Douglas*, 66, 212, 213-39.
76   'Chief Trader McLeod with a small party has traced the coast to the southward of the Columbia about 120 miles and in that distance crossed three Rivers of considerable size in all of which he found vestiges of Beaver.' Simpson to G&C, 21 June 1827, HBCA D.4/90, fo. 6; Wilks, *Journal Kept by David Douglas*, 234.
77   This is based on McLeod's biography in HBRS 3, 448-9; Doyce B. Nunis, *The Hudson's Bay Company's First Fur Brigade to the Sacramento Valley: Alexander McLeod's 1829 Hunt* (Sacramento 1968); Maloney, *Fur Brigade to the Bonaventura*, v; Richard Dillon, *Siskiyou Trail: The Hudson's Bay Fur Company Route to California* (New York: McGraw Hill 1975).
78   Lewis A. McArthur, 'Oregon Geographic Names,' *OHQ* 28, 1 (March 1927): 104.
79   Simpson to G&C, 10 July 1828, HBCA D.4/92, fos. 68, 72-3;
80   Ibid.; Simpson to G&C, 1 March 1829, HBRS 10, 68-9.
81   Simpson to G&C, 14 June 1826, HBCA A.12/1, fos. 224-5; Simpson to G&C, 21 June 1827, HBCA D.4/90, fo. 6.
82   Simpson to Addington, 5 January 1826, HBRS 10, 169. Annual figures were as follows: 1821 (£25,715); 1822 (£31,726); 1823 (£32,720); 1824 (£40,952); and 1825 (£30,431). York Factory, Accounts Current 1821-1826, HBCA B.239/d/286. In the original, these are divided between Western Caledonia and Columbia.
83   Simpson to G&C, 10 July 1828, HBCA D.4/92, fos. 61, 81.
84   G&C to McLoughlin, 28 October 1829, HBRS 4, 37 n. 1; Simpson to G&C, 1 March 1829, HBRS 10, 72, 85-99, 109-10. See also Ormsby, *British Columbia*, 67, for these new plans.

CHAPTER 4: Nature Here Demands Attention

1   Duncan Finlayson, 'Trip Across to the Columbia 1831,' HBCA E.12/2, fos. 20-2.
2   'The number of goods produced in a north temperate climate in an area dominated by Pre-Cambrian formations, to be obtained with little difficulty in sufficient quantity and disposed of satisfactorily in the home market under prevailing transport conditions, was limited.' Innis, *The Fur Trade in Canada*, 384.
3   Dunn, *History of Oregon territory*, 202: 'The vast region extending between the Rocky Mountains and the Pacific Ocean is divided into two zones, distinctive as to climate, aspect, products.' Modeste Demers, 'General Notes on the Territory of the Columbia,' 13 February 1844, in Carl Landerholm, tr., *Notices & Voyages of the Famed Quebec Mission to the Pacific Northwest* ... (Portland, OR: Champoeg Press 1956), 176.
4   Harris, ed., *Historical Atlas of Canada*, Vol. 1, plates 4, 7, 8, 9, 17; A.L. Kroeber, *Cultural and Natural Areas of Native North America*, Vol. 1 (Berkeley: University of California Press 1939), 28-31, Map 8, Table 18; Knut Fladmark, *British Columbia Prehistory* (Ottawa: Archaeological Survey of Canada; National Museum of Man 1986), 6; Corneliis Groot and Leo Margolis., eds., *Pacific Salmon Life Histories* (Vancouver: UBC Press 1991).
5   In London, Scouler had talked to Archibald Menzies, Vancouver's botanist. John Scouler, 'Account of a Voyage to Madeira, Brazil, Juan Fernandez, and the Gallipagos Islands, Performed in 1824 and 1825 ...' *Edinburgh Journal of Science* 5 (April-October 1826): 195-214, 196; Wilks, *Journal Kept by David Douglas*, 51.
6   John Scouler, 'On the Temperature of the North West Coast of America,' *Edinburgh Journal of Science* 6 (November 1826-April 1827): 251-3.
7   Scouler, 'Observations on the Indigenous Tribes,' 217-18. Scouler even attributed linguistic differences to the character of the country. See John Scouler, 'On the Indian Tribes Inhabiting the North-West Coast of America,' *Journal of the Ethnographical Society of London* 1 (1848): 228-52, 239-40. Latham recorded forty-one vocabularies for Oregon Territory: R.G. Latham, 'The Language of the Oregon Territory,' *Journal of the Ethnological Society of London* 1 (1848): 154-66, 159.
8   Scouler, 'Observations on the Indigenous Tribes,' 216-18.
9   George Dixon, William Sturgis, and Silas Holbrook are quoted in Gibson, *Otter Skins*, 146-7. See also Gough, *The Northwest Coast*, 168.
10 S. Adams, 10 August 1822, quoted in Jonathan S. Green, *Journal of a Tour on the North West Coast of America in the Year 1829* (New York: Charles Frederick Heartman 1915), 22. The Coast Mountains were known originally as the North West Coast Range because they paralleled the line of the North West Coast. See Anderson, *Notes on North-Western America*, 2, 13, and Anderson, *Dominion of the West*, 5.
11 William Fraser Tolmie, 'Abstract of Meteorological Register Kept at Fort McLoughlin, Milbank Sound, B.C. ... during the Years 1833-34-35,' in Anderson, *Dominion of the West*, Appendix K, vii.
12 Simpson, *Narrative*, Vol. 1, 208.
13 Charles Bishop of the *Ruby*, quoted in Gibson, *Otter Skins*, 205; Meredith Gairdner, 'Meteorological Observations Made at Fort Vancouver from 7 June, 1833, to 31 May, 1834,' *Edinburgh New Philosophical Review* 20 (1836), 67-8. For an 1811 table of the weather at the mouth of the Columbia, see Ross, *Adventures*, 350-2.
14 Scouler, 'Account of a Voyage to Madeira, Brazil, Juan Fernandez, and the Gallipagos Islands,' 228-36, 230.
15 See Knut R. Fladmark, 'A Paleoecological Model for Northwest Coast Prehistory,' Archaeological Survey of Canada Mercury Series 43 (Ottawa: National Museum of Man 1975); K.R. Fladmark, 'Routes: Alternative Migration Corridors for Early Man in North America,' *American Antiquity* 44, 1 (1979): 55-69, 63-4.
16 John Scouler, quoted in John Richardson, *Fauna Boreali-Americana*, Vol. 3 (London: 1836), 159.
17 Wayne Suttles, *Coast Salish Essays* (Vancouver: Talonbooks 1987), 15-63.
18 Simpson, *Narrative*, Vol. 1, 193, 251; Anderson, 'Notes on the Indian Tribes,' 80. See also Fisher, *Contact and Conflict*, 81-3 and Elizabeth Vibert, 'Real Men Hunt Buffalo: Masculinity,

Race and Class in British Fur Traders' Narratives,' paper presented to the BC Studies Conference, 1994.

19   See Gibson, *Otter Skins*, 154, and Paul Kane, *Wanderings of an Artist Among the Indians of North America from Canada to Vancouver's Island and Oregon through the Hudson's Bay Company's Territory and Back Again* (London: Longman, Brown, Green, Longmans, and Roberts 1859), 126; W. Kaye Lamb, ed., *Gabriel Franchère*, 100.

20   Simpson to G&C, 10 March 1825, HBCA D.4/88, fos. 139-40. See also John McLoughlin, 'Fort Vancouver Report [1826-27],' HBRS 10, 233-7.

21   Kane, *Wanderings*, 147; Anderson, 'A Compendium of the Province of British Columbia,' 15; Richard A. Pierce, ed., *Russian America: Statistical and Ethnographical Information by Rear Admiral Ferdinand Petorich Wrangell ... Translated from the German Edition of 1839 ...* (Kingston: Limestone Press 1980), 13.

22   Mackenzie is quoted in Morton, *A History*, 416.

23   Lamb, ed., *The Letters and Journals of Simon Fraser*, 97-101, 99.

24   Alexander Caulfield Anderson, *Hand-book and Map to the Gold Regions of Frazer's and Thompson's Rivers ...* (San Francisco: J.J. Le Count 1858), 5-6, 20.

25   Anderson, 'A Compendium of the Province of British Columbia,' 6.

26   Anderson, 'Notes on the Indian Tribes,' 74.

27   Meredith Gairdner, 'Notes on the Geography of the Columbia River,' *Journal of the Royal Geographical Society* 2 (1841): 250-7; Simpson, *Narrative*, Vol. 1, 155; for descriptions of the dry country at the Dalles, see Richard Glover, ed., *David Thompson's Narrative 1784-1812* (Toronto: Champlain Society 1962), 355; Bernard DeVoto, ed., *The Journals of Lewis and Clark* (Boston: Houghton Mifflin 1953), 108-11; Anderson, *Handbook and Map*, 18; Simpson, *Narrative*, Vol. 1, 153; Meinig, *The Great Columbia Plain*, 3-20.

28   Finlayson, 'Trip Across to the Columbia 1831.'

29   'Table of the Weather at Fort Nez Percés, Forks of the Columbia River, for the Year 1822,' Ross, *The Fur Hunters*, Vol. 1, 324-32.

30   Wilks, *Journal Kept by David Douglas*, 340, 57, 129; P.J. De Smet, *Letters and Sketches: With a Narrative of a Years Residence Among the Indian Tribes of the Rocky Mountains* (Philadelphia: M. Fithian 1843), 218; Ermatinger, 'Edward Ermatinger's York Factory Express Journal,' 71 n. 3; Lamb, ed., *Gabriel Franchère*, 148; Simpson, *Narrative*, Vol. 1, 155, 164, 167-8; 'Frenchmen from Canada or Louisiana designate as cascades or chutes any point where the course of the river is interrupted by rocks, or where a portage ... must be made.' Wilbur, *Duflot de Mofras' Travels*, 54. On the Cascades, see also John K. Townsend, *Narrative of a Journey Across the Rocky Mountains to the Columbia River ...* (Philadelphia: Henry Perkins 1839), 164.

31   Glover, *David Thompson's Narrative*, 356-7, 363; Lamb, ed., *Gabriel Franchère*, 84, 97 n. 4, 100.

32   New Caledonia was 'that immense tract of land lying between the Coast Range and the Rocky Mountains, from 51° 30' to 57° of latitude north.' A.G. Morice, *The History of the Northern Interior of British Columbia* (Smithers, BC: Interior Stationery 1978) (first published 1904). Tod wrote that New Caledonia was situated between 53° and 57°, and between the Rockies and the Coast Mountains. Wolfenden, 'John Tod,' 156; Joseph McGillivray (1827) defined New Caledonia as extending from 51°30' north latitude to about 56° and west to 124°10', and Ross Cox (1831) wrote that it extended from 52° to 55° north. Cox, *Adventures on the Columbia River*, Vol. 2, 50, 360. Anderson wrote that Carrier hunting territory was 'the tract lying, approximately, between 52° and 57° north latitude and 120° and 127° west latitude.' A.C. Anderson, 'Notes on the Indian Tribes of British North America, and the Northwest Coast,' *The Historical Magazine* 7, 3 (March 1863) [written 1855]: 73-81, 75.

33   See Thomas W. Tanner, 'Fort Saint James,' in *Miscellaneous Papers: The Fur Trade*, manuscript report no. 131, (Ottawa: Parks Canada 1966), 149-64; Morton, *Fort St. James*, 40-3, 68-9, 102-4, 166-74; Modeste Demers (Fort Alexandria) to Mgr. the Bishop of Quebec, 20 December 1842, Landerholm, *Notices & Voyages*, 159; Fort Alexandria's population is from A.C. Anderson, cited in James Robert Anderson, 'Notes and Comments on Early Days and Events in British Columbia, Washington and Oregon,' BCARS, 108.

34   W. Kaye Lamb., ed., *Sixteen Years in the Indian Country: The Journal of Daniel Williams Harmon 1800-1816* (Toronto: Macmillan 1957); Alexander C. Anderson, 'Some Remarks upon
the Freezing of Streams in North America, in Connexion with the Supposed Congelation
of their Sources in High Latitude,' *Journal of the Royal Geographical Society* 15 (1845): 367-71,
371; W.N. Sage, 'New Caledonia: Siberia of the Fur Trade,' *The Beaver* 287 (Summer 1956):
24-9; Wallace, *John McLean's Notes*, 151; Anderson to editor, *Colonization Circular*, 3 January
1862, quoted in Anderson, *Dominion of the West*, Appendix G-2, xxxix; Modeste Demers
(Fort Alexandria), 20 December 1842, Landerholm, *Notices & Voyages*, 159. For NWC provisioning strategies in New Caledonia, see Jamie Morton, 'Conspicuous Production: Hudson's Bay Company Farms and Fisheries in British Columbia,' paper presented to the Great
River of the West Conference, Walla Walla, 1992, 3-5.

35   See David J. Spalding, 'The Early History of Moose (*Alces Alces*): Distribution and Relative Abundance in British Columbia,' Royal British Columbia Museum, *Contributions to
Natural Science* 11 (March 1990): 1-12.

36   David Douglas's 'fit for dogs' remark is from Douglas to William Hooker, 9 April 1833,
quoted in John Davies, ed., *Douglas of the Forests: The North American Journals of David Douglas* (Seattle: University of Washington Press 1980), 162; McLean is quoted in Leechman,
'Garden Seeds,' 30; on wages and general privation, see Morton, *Fort St. James*, 44; HBRS
3, 187, 213; Gibson, *Farming the Frontier*, 194.

37   Rich, *HBC*, Vol. 3, 616.

38   Wallace, *John McLean's Notes*, 174; Simpson is quoted in Rich, *HBC*, Vol. 3, 617.

39   The 1827 figure cited in Rich, 'The Fur Traders,' 46. On New Caledonia's farms and fisheries, see also Sage, ed., 'Peter Skene Ogden's Notes,' 51-2, 55.

40   Wolfenden, 'John Tod,' 227. See also Jeffrey W. Locke, 'No Salmon, No Furs: The Provisioning of Fort Kamloops, 1841-1849,' *British Columbia Historical News* 26, 2 (Spring 1993):
14-18.

41   Simpson to McLeod, 1 November 1824, McLeod papers, NAC; 'The country about Thompson's River is poor in Beaver and small furs; and the Natives are exceedingly indolent: for
the means of subsistence they depend chiefly on Salmon, which their River generally affords
in abundance.' Simpson to G&C, 1 March 1829, HBRS 10, 31; Rich, *HBC* 3, 618.

42   Joseph McGillivray to Ross Cox, February 1814, quoted in Cox, *Adventures on the Columbia
River*, Vol. 1, 263; Simpson, *Narrative*, Vol. 1, 155-6; Simpson to G&C, 25 November 1841,
HBRS 29, 54; Gibson, *Farming the Frontier*, 229; Archibald McDonald, [Report on the trade,
1827], in Miscellaneous Papers Relating to Fort Kamloops, BCARS; McDonald, 1829, quoted
in Ormsby, *British Columbia: A History*, 71. On the switch from beaver to marten skins, see
Henry F. Johnson, 'Fur Trading Days at Kamloops,' *BCHQ* 1, 3 (July 1937): 171-85, and Roger
Maier, 'Marten, Muskrats and Beaver: Fort Kamloops and the Hudson's Bay Company, 1822-
1856,' unpublished essay, University of Victoria, 1992. On the scarcity of furs, see Thomson,
'The Response of Okanagan Indians,' 99-100.

43   McLoughlin to G&C, 1 September 1826, HBRS 4, 31; Donald Mackenzie quoted in Ross,
Adventures, 218-19; Anderson, 'Notes on the Indian Tribes,' 77.

44   Trader Robert Campbell, quoted in Irving, *The Rocky Mountains*, Vol. 1, 213.

45   John Richardson, 'On the Frozen Soil of North America,' *Edinburgh New Philosophical Jour-
nal* 30 (1841): 110-26; Peter Warren Dease, 'On the Cultivation of the Cerealia in the High
Latitudes of North America,' *Edinburgh New Philosophical Journal* 30 (1841): 123-4; the
Englishmen quote is from Rich, *HBC*, Vol. 1, 541; for climate graphs, see Ray, *Indians in the
Fur Trade*, 42, 160.

46   D.W. Moodie, 'Gardening on Hudson Bay: The First Century,' *The Beaver* 309, 1 (Summer
1978): 54-9; Rich, *HBC*, Vol. 1, 177, 312, 378; Lewis H. Thomas, 'A History of Agriculture in
the Prairies to 1914,' *Prairie Forum* 1, 1 (April 1976): 31-45; Douglas Leechman, 'I Sowed Garden Seeds,' *The Beaver* (Winter 1970): 24-36, 26; Jody F. Decker, 'Scurvy at York. A Mysterious Affliction Lingered at the Bay,' *The Beaver* 69, 1 (February-March 1989): 42-8; E.E. Rich,
'The Fur Traders: Their Diet and Drugs,' *The Beaver* 307, 1 (Summer 1976): 42-53.

47   Morton, *A History*, 137; Rich, *HBC*, Vol. 1, 439, 494-5, 541-2, 603. Lyn Harrington, 'Triumph

of the Trumpeter,' *The Beaver* 286 (Winter 1955): 14-19; Rich, 'The Fur Traders,' 44. Geese were even domesticated at some bayside posts: Frits Pannekoek, 'Corruption at Moose,' *The Beaver* 309, 4 (Spring 1979): 5-11, and D.W. Moodie and Barry Kaye, 'Taming and Domesticating Native Animals of Rupert's Land,' *The Beaver* 307, 3 (Winter 1976): 10-19.

48   [George Simpson], 'Observations on Speeches in the House of Lords and House of Commons respecting the Hudson's Bay Company, Vancouver Island, &c. &c. by Sir George Simpson,' 28 March 1849, HBCA.

49   For a contemporary introduction to the Red River settlement, see Simpson, *Narrative*, 10-17; for the company's agricultural difficulties there, see Gibson, *Farming the Frontier*, 9-14.

50   Quoted in J.H. Pritchett, *The Red River Valley 1811-1849: A Regional Study* (Toronto: Ryerson Press 1942), 54.

51   Leechman, 'Garden Seeds,' 34; Riegert, *From Arsenic to DDT*, 23-8; G&C to Simpson, 7 June 1833, quoted in Lorne Hammond, 'Marketing Wildlife: The Hudson's Bay Company and the Pacific Northwest, 1821-49,' *Forest & Conservation History* 37 (January 1993): 17; Alexander Ross, *The Red River Settlement: Its Rise, Progress, and Present State* (London: Smith, Elder and Co. 1856), 49-50.

52   Simpson (n.d.) is quoted in Ralph Hedlin, 'Reluctant Beginnings of Western Commerce,' *The Beaver* (Summer 1959): 9; on 1820s self-sufficiency, see Innis in HBRS 3, xxxviii-xxxix; *Wisconsin Herald*, 15 September 1847, quoted in *The Beaver* 1, 4 (January 1921): 3. For a description of a Saskatchewan winter by Franchère, see Edward Ermatinger, *The Hudson's Bay Territories; A Series of Letters on this Important Question* (Toronto: Maclear, Thomas & Co. 1858), 7.

53   Cox, *Adventures*, Vol. 2, 211; Wilks, *Journal Kept by David Douglas*, 263, 265; Ermatinger, *The Hudson Bay Territories*, 9.

54   Ross, *The Fur Hunters*, Vol. 1, 70; McGillivray and Thompson are cited in Morton, *A History*, 10-11, 365; 'Norway House District Comparative View of Population & Surface 1843,' Donald Ross Papers, BCARS.

55   Thompson (circa 1818) is quoted in Wheat, *Mapping the Transmississippi West*, Vol. 2, 106; Ogden (1825) is quoted in HBRS 13, 205; Finlayson, 'Trip Across to the Columbia 1831.'

56   George Nelson is quoted in Sylvia Van Kirk, 'This Rascally & Ungrateful Country: George Nelson's Response to Rupert's Land,' in Richard C. Davis, ed., *Rupert's Land: a Cultural Tapestry* (Waterloo, ON: Waterloo University Press for the Calgary Institute for Humanities 1988), 113-30, 118; George Gladman to Edward Ermatinger, 5 August 1842, Ermatinger Papers, NAC.

CHAPTER 5: From Fort Vancouver to the Vermilion Sea

1   Francis Ermatinger to Robert Miles, 14 March 1826, in McDonald, *Fur Trade Letters of Francis Ermatinger*, 63.

2   Belcher is quoted in Gough, *The Royal Navy*, 47. See also McLoughlin to Simpson, 20 March 1846, quoted in Merk, 'Snake Country Expedition,' 107.

3   Dunn, *History of Oregon territory*, 133.

4   T.C. Elliott, ed., 'Extracts from the Emmons Journal,' *OHQ* 26, 3 (September 1925): 226

5   Townsend, *Narrative of a Journey*, 170.

6   Wallace, *John McLean's Notes*, 4.

7   [John McLoughlin], 'John McLoughlin – Statement to Parties in London [circa 1846],' *OHQ* 1, 2 (June 1900): 193-206; Irving, *The Rocky Mountains*, Vol. 2, 242-3.

8   A. Simpson to C. O'Gorman, 7 January 1831, HBCA D.4/125, fos. 103-4; [McLoughlin], 'John McLoughlin – Statement,' 193-206; D.W. Thompson to Josiah Marshall, 26 March 1829, quoted in Samuel Eliot Morison, 'New England and the Opening of the Columbia River Salmon Trade, 1830,' *OHQ* 28, 2 (June 1927); F.W. Howay, 'Brig Owhyhee in the Columbia, 1827,' *OHQ* 34, 4 (December 1933): 325-7; F.W. Howay, 'The Brig Owhyhee in the Columbia, 1829-30,' *OHQ* 35, 1 (March 1934): 10-21; Frances Fuller Victor, 'Flotsam and Jetsam of the Pacific. The Owhyhee, the Sultana, and the Mary Dacre,' *OHQ* 2, 1 (March 1901): 36-54, 38.

9   Townsend, *Narrative of a Journey*. On Wyeth's fur trading operations, see Wishart, *The Fur Trade of the American West*, 156-60.

10   Irving, *The Rocky Mountains*, Vol. 2, 241.
11   Townsend, *Narrative of a Journey*, 168, 177, 219; Irving, *Astoria*, Vol. 1, 160; John Ball, 'Across
     the Continent Seventy Years Ago,' *OHQ* 3, 1 (March 1902): 82-106.
12   Elliott, ed., 'Extracts from the Emmons Journal,' 272-3; George Barber Roberts, 'Letters to
     Mrs. F.F. Victor,' *OHQ* 63, 2-3 (June-September 1962): 231.
13   Wilks, *Journal Kept by David Douglas*, 140-1; between 1813 and 1821, Fort George's annual
     returns had held steady at between 2,500 and 3,000 pelts, most of which were traded from
     other places. Keith, 'Adventure to the Columbia.'
14   Corney, *Voyages in the Northern Pacific*, 68-9; Rollins, ed., *The Discovery of the Oregon Trail*,
     4-5; McLoughlin to G&C, 6 October 1825, HBRS 4, 15; McLoughlin to G&C, 1 Septem-
     ber 1826, ibid., 31; McLoughlin, 'Fort Vancouver Report [1826-27],' HBRS 10, 233-7; Simp-
     son to G&C, 25 July 1827, HBCA D.4/90; John Warren Dease, 'The Columbia Journal of
     John Warren Dease,' 10 October 1829, NAC. A company official later asserted that the Native
     people of the coast had been unable to trap animals before the coming of the company. C.H.
     French, 'Mr French Lectures,' *The Beaver* 2, 9 (June 1922): 38.
15   Ross, *The Fur Hunters*, Vol. 1, 71; Douglas to Kittson, 14 May 1838, HBCA B.223/ b/22, fos.
     12-13; Douglas to Birnie, 6 April 1838, HBCA B.223/b/22, fo. 5d.
16   On freemen, see Ross, *The Fur Hunters*, Vol. 1, 291-2, and Irving, *Astoria*, Vol. 1, 194-5. 'Our
     store at Fort George is only for Indians or at least all who deal there are supplied at Indian
     price ... the place where we have dealings with freemen is Vancouver where we pay them
     11/- for a made beaver.' McLoughlin to Birnie, 29 December 1840, HBCA B.223/b/27, fo.
     118. For the 'garden of the Columbia,' see Ross, *Adventures*, 100, 234.
17   [Alex-see], 'The Story of Alex-see of Suquash, B.C. Mohican-Iroquois Indian ... As
     recorded by Thos. P. Wicks, who heard it from the lips of Alex-see at the pioneer home of
     Ned Fregonne, an early settler on the Northern British Columbia Coast,' in Thomas P.
     Wicks, 'Pioneer Reminiscences of Thos. P. Wicks British Columbia Coast 1882. An auto-
     biography of Pioneer Life Amongst the Indians of Northern Vancouver Island,' compiled
     [by] Margaret Giles, City Archives, City Hall, Vancouver, 1939, 11-12.
18   Simpson to G&C, 25 November 1841, HBRS 29, 78; Alexander Lattie cited in Samuel C.
     Damon Journal, May 1849, Oregon Historical Society ms. no. 803. I owe this reference to
     Jamie Morton.
19   For a list of all Americans in Oregon since 1814, see [McLoughlin], 'John McLoughlin –
     Statement,' 193-206. On the continuing Snake policies, see Innis in HBRS 3, lxxiv, xxvii, lxvii.
     On Smith's explorations, see also Wheat, *Mapping the Transmississippi West*, Vol. 2, 119-39;
     Jedediah Smith, David E. Jackson, and W.L. Sublette to John H. Eaton, 29 October 1830,'
     OHQ 4, 4 (December 1903): 395-8; H.C. Dale, ed., *The Ashley-Smith Explorations and the Dis-
     covery of a Central Route to the Pacific, 1822-1829, with the Original Journals* (Cleveland: 1918).
20   D. Lee and J.H. Frost, *Ten Years in Oregon* (New York: J. Collard 1844), 78; John K. Townsend,
     Letter to *Newark Advertiser*, 26 January 1843, *OHQ* 4, 4 (December 1903): 400.
21   Edward Belcher, *Narrative of a Voyage Round the World, Performed in Her Majesty's Ship Sul-
     phur, During the Years 1836-1842* ... Vol. 1 (London: Henry Colburn 1843), 301; Thomas J.
     Farnham, *Travels in the Great Western Prairies* ... Vol. 2 (London: Richard Bentley 1843),
     257; Dunn, *History of Oregon territory*, 155.
22   Wallace, *John McLean's Notes*, 4. Policy was 'to lay waste the country, so as to offer no induce-
     ment to petty traders' (351); Belcher, *Narrative*, 301; Tolmie, 'History of Puget Sound and the
     Northwest Coast,' ts., Tolmie Papers, BCARS, 1878; Merk, 'Snake Country Expedition,' 107.
23   McLoughlin to Simpson, 1827, quoted in Merk, 'Snake Country Expedition,' 104; Ogden,
     Traits, 4. It was said to be 700 miles from the Green River to the mouth of the Colorado.
     'It is said ... that a party of trappers adventured so far down [the Colorado's?] deep dark
     chasm as to endanger their lives, and it was with the greatest difficulty that they extricated
     themselves from their almost hopeless dilemma.' Lee and Frost, *Ten Years in Oregon*, 119.
24   Irving, *The Rocky Mountains*, Vol. 1, 104; Vol. 2, 151; Townsend, *Narrative of a Journey*, 155. See
     also Farnham, *Travels in the Great Western Prairies*, Vol. 2, 151; for a description of the Flat-
     heads, Blackfeet, Snakes, Nez Perces, Piutes, see Dunn, *History of Oregon territory*, 311-31.

25 'A more dismal situation than that of this post can hardly be imagined. The fort is surrounded by a sandy desert, which produced nothing but wormwood.' Simpson, *Narrative*, Vol. 1, 161-2.

26 Wyeth to Messrs Tucker & Williams and Henry Hall, 8 November 1833, F.G. Young, ed., *The Correspondence and Journals of Captain Nathaniel J. Wyeth, 1831-6; A Record of Two Expeditions for the Occupation of the Oregon Country* ... (Eugene, Oregon: University of Oregon Press 1899), 78; Galbraith, *Hudson's Bay Company*, 101-7; Wishart, *The Fur Trade of the American West*, 159. Boisee, according to George Roberts, was a French word signifying thinly wooded. Roberts, 'Letters to Mrs. F.F. Victor,' 192.

27 On the hiring of Walker, see McDonald, *Fur Trade Letters of Francis Ermatinger*, 216 n. 36. See also McLoughlin to Douglas, March 1838, HBCA B.223/b/18, fos. 25-27d; Dunn, *History of Oregon territory*, 333. Inexperience and desertions also contributed to the failure of Wyeth's Fort Hall. See Richard G. Beidleman, 'Nathaniel Wyeth's Fort Hall,' *OHQ* 58, 3 (September 1957): 241-4.

28 On Flathead parties, see McDonald, *Fur Trade Letters of Francis Ermatinger*, 164, n. 35; for declining Snake returns, see Galbraith, *Hudson's Bay Company*, 95-6.

29 McDonald, *Fur Trade Letters of Francis Ermatinger*, 190, 219; Carl P. Russell, 'Wilderness Rendezvous Period of the American Fur Trade,' *OHQ* 42, 1 (March 1941): 1-47.

30 Irving, *The Rocky Mountains*, Vol. 1, 22.

31 William A. Slacum, 'Slacum's Report on Oregon 1836-7,' *OHQ* 13, 2 (June 1912): 190; F.G. Young, ed., 'Journal and Report by Dr. Marcus Whitman of His Tour of Exploration with Rev. Samuel Parker in 1835 Beyond the Rocky Mountains,' *OHQ* 28, 3 (Summer 1927), 247.

32 E.E. Rich and McLoughlin to Edward Ermatinger, 1834, HBRS 4, xcvii are quoted in McDonald, *Fur Trade Letters of Francis Ermatinger*, 151. n. 27, 155; Dunn, *History of Oregon territory*, 174.

33 Slacum, 'Slacum's Report,' 188; W.G.D. Stewart, *Altowan; or, Incidents of Life and Adventure in the Rocky Mountains* ... Vol. 2 (New York: Harper Brothers 1846), 87.

34 *Oregonian and Indians' Advocate*, December 1838, quoted in Carl P. Russell, 'Wilderness Rendezvous Period of the American Fur Trade,' *OHQ* 42, 1 (March 1941): 41; Ashel and Eliza Munger, 'Diary while Crossing the Plains, 1839,' *OHQ* 8, 4 (December 1907): 395-6. See also Wishart, *The Fur Trade of the American West*, 190-3.

35 Russell, quoted in McDonald, *Fur Trade Letters of Francis Ermatinger*, 183.

36 Simpson to G&C, November 1841, from HBRS 29, 58, quoted in McDonald, *Fur Trade Letters of Francis Ermatinger*, 239, 234; Russell, 'Wilderness Rendezvous,' 1-2.

37 Henry H. Spalding, 'A Letter by Henry H. Spalding from the Rocky Mountains,' *OHQ* 51, 2 (June 1950): 131.

38 James Henry Gilbert, *Trade and Currency in Early Oregon. A Study in the Commercial and Monetary History of the Pacific Northwest* (New York: Columbia University Press 1907), 25. For the 1841 date of collapse, see Demers, 'General Notes on the Territory of the Columbia,' 13 February 1844, Landerholm, *Notices & Voyages*, 186; for competition between the American companies, see Irving, *The Rocky Mountains*, Vol. 2, 159-78. In 1839, Farnham met Richardson in the Rockies, 'a remnant of the American Fur Company's trapping parties.' Farnham, *Travels in the Great Western Prairies*, Vol. 2, 72. See also Wishart, *The Fur Trade of the American West*, 165-6.

39 'Now, that beaver are scarce, there are only about fifty.' [McLoughlin], 'John McLoughlin – Statement,' 193-206.

40 Irving, *The Rocky Mountains*, Vol. 2, 242-3; Townsend, *Narrative of a Journey*, 182.

41 Wyeth is quoted in Robert C. Johnson, *John McLoughlin: 'Father of Oregon,'* (Portland, Oregon: Binfords & Mort 1958), 102-3.

42 Irving, *The Rocky Mountains*, Vol. 1, 226; Vol. 3, 171-2.

43 William Clark, '1830 Report on the Fur Trade by General William Clark,' *OHQ* 48, 1 (March 1947): 26.

44 Stewart, *Altowan*, Vol. 1, 61-2; Vol. 2, 102-3.

45 Townsend, *Narrative of a Journey*, 104.

46   De Smet, *Letters and Sketches*, 116-17. De Smet's observation about the HBC's prohibition of liquor in its Indian trade is not strictly accurate. In fact, the company sanctioned the sale of liquor in competitive regions. See clause 39 of HBC, 'Standing Rules and Regulations,' reprinted in Douglas MacKay, *The Honourable Company: A History of the Hudson's Bay Company* (London: Cassell and Company 1937), 406.

47   Clark, '1830 Report on the Fur Trade,' 26; Fred Wilbur Powell, 'Hall Jackson Kelley. Chapter 7,' *OHQ* 18, 1 (March 1917): 121; Townsend, *Narrative of a Journey*, 224-9; Dunn, *History of Oregon territory*, 175, 333; Dorothy Blakey Smith, ed., *James Douglas in California 1841 Being The Journal of a Voyage from the Columbia to California* (Vancouver: Librarian's Press 1965) 11; Simpson, *Narrative*, Vol. 1, 350. For revisionist views of the HBC's Indian policy, see Reid, 'Restraints of Vengeance,' and Cole Harris, 'Towards a Geography of Power in the Cordilleran Fur Trade,' *Canadian Geographer* 39, 2 (Summer 1995): 131-40.

48   See Lamb's introduction to HBRS 7, xviii-xxix; Maloney, *Fur Brigade to the Bonaventura*; Alice Bay Maloney, 'California Rendezvous,' *The Beaver* 275 (December 1944): 32-7; John S. Galbraith, 'A Note on the British Fur Trade in California, 1821-1846,' *Pacific Historical Quarterly* 24 (1955): 253-60.

49   Tolmie, 'History of Puget Sound and the Northwest Coast'; 'Memo. left with Lord Melbourne and the Right Honble. Charles P. Thompson,' 20 December 1837, Klotz, *Certain Correspondence*, 28. 'In 1821, getting hold in the West, the HBCo sent trapping and trading parties north, east, and south. During the first half of the thirties ... John Work led the party going to California.' Tolmie to James Swan, 27 March 1884, Swan Papers, UBC.

50   Maloney, *Fur Brigade to the Bonaventura*, v; Maloney, 'Hudson's Bay Company in California,' 11; Alexander Roderick McLeod, *The Hudson's Bay Company's First Fur Brigade to the Sacramento Valley: Alexander McLeod's 1829 Hunt* (Fair Oaks, CA: Sacramento Book Collectors Club 1968); Dee, 'An Irishman in the Fur Trade,' 253-6.

51   Maloney, *Fur Brigade to the Bonaventura*, iii.

52   See Dale, *The Ashley-Smith Explorations* and Thomas Coulter, *Notes on Upper California: A Journey from Monterey to the Colorado River in 1832* (Los Angeles: G. Dawson 1951).

53   Townsend, *Narrative of a Journey*, 173; Simpson to G&C, 10 August 1832, HBCA A.12/1, fo. 436; Demers, 'General Notes on the Territory of the Columbia,' 13 February 1844, Landerholm, *Notices & Voyages*, 179.

54   Dunn, *History of Oregon territory*, 197.

55   Wilbur, *Duflot de Mofras' Travels*, Vol. 2, 49-50; Charles Wilkes, 'Report on the Territory of Oregon 1842,' *OHQ* 12, 3 (September 1911): 277; Dunn, *History of Oregon territory*, 198.

56   Dunn, *History of Oregon territory*, 198.

57   Wilbur, *Duflot de Mofras' Travels*, Vol. 2, 18.

58   Anson S. Blake, 'The Hudson's Bay Company in San Francisco,' *CHSQ* 28, 3 (September 1949): Part 2, 255 n. 58. See also McLoughlin to Douglas, March 1838, HBCA B.223/b/18, fos. 25-27d. The company's Trinidad Bay plan may have originated in 1832-3, when Work explored the coast between San Francisco Bay and Eel River.

59   Erwin G. Gudde, *Californian Place Names. A Geographical Dictionary* (Berkeley: University of California Press 1949), 121, 198; Alice Bay Maloney, 'Peter Skene Ogden's Trapping Expedition to the Gulf of California 1829-30,' *California Historical Society Quarterly* 19, 4 (December 1940): 309. In 1841-2, Francis Ermatinger took the following route: Fort Vancouver to the source of Willamette, to the Calamet [Klamath], to the Pit Mountains [Pit River], to the Sacramento Valley, to a tributary of the Sacramento called 'Rivière la Cache,' to Sonoma, and to Yerba Buena. Simpson, *Narrative*, Vol. 1, 350-2.

60   Smith, *James Douglas in California*, 18. Finlayson to William Smith, 11 January 1834, HBCA B.223/b/9, fos. 50-1. Later, Douglas wrote that hunting in the San Joaquin Valley was in accordance to 'the letter of the Treaty' or 'convention.' Smith, *James Douglas in California*, xviii.

61   'This latter party noticed us in the Sacramento in 1837, but mistaking us for the Californians, were afraid to make themselves known.' Belcher, *Narrative*, Vol. 1, 301.

62   Forbes, *California*, 176-7. In 1830, Thomas McKay caught 'within months near Carquine'

more than 4,000 beaver worth two piasters a pound in California and £1 in London. Wilbur, *Duflot de Mofras' Travels*, Vol. 1, 246.

63 For San Joaquin orthography, see Leader, 'A Voyage from the Columbia,' 115 n. 85 and Smith, *James Douglas in California*, 9.

64 Wilbur, *Duflot de Mofras' Travels* Vol. 1, 245-6.

65 [Michel Laframboise], 'Notes on the Indian Tribes of the Upper and Lower Columbia. List of the nations on the lower part of the Columbia, and along the sea-coast southwards, from Michel la Framboise,' in Gairdner, 'Notes on the Geography of the Columbia River,' 255-6; Wilbur, *Duflot de Mofras' Travels*, Vol. 2, 18.

66 Bancroft, *History of California*, Vol. 3, 699, cited in Leader, 'A Voyage from the Columbia,' 105 n. 35. The *gente de razon* were 'the intelligensia, or the intelligent white class.' Wilbur, *Duflot de Mofras' Travels*, Vol. 1, 164.

67 Wilbur, *Duflot de Mofras' Travels*, Vol. 1, 174; Vol. 2, 17.

68 Ibid., Vol. 2, 20.

69 Work (Fort Vancouver) to Edward Ermatinger, 5 August 1832, quoted in Lewis and Phillips, eds., *The Journal of John Work*, 181; Blanchet quoted in Landerholm, *Notices & Voyages*, 29; on the character of the Southern Party, see also Demers in Landerholm, *Notices & Voyages*, 186-7.

70 Mikell de lores Wormell Warner, tr., and Harriet Duncan Munnick, ed., *Catholic Church Records of the Pacific Northwest* ... (St. Paul, OR: French Prairie Press 1972), A-46.

71 General Vallejo [circa 1838], HBRS 7, xxvii; Belcher, *Narrative*, Vol. 1, 129; McLoughlin to Douglas, March 1838, HBCA B.223/b/18, fos. 25-27d.

72 Sutter is quoted in Maloney, 'Hudson's Bay Company in California,' 16. Sutter had come overland and down the Snake, noting the company's methods. 'Capt. S. keeps a number of individuals a hunting Beaver and otter & has prohibited the H.B. Company from trapping on his property, he is also by subtile – but fair means securing the friendship of the Indian tribes about him.' [William Dunlop Brackenridge], 'Journal of William Dunlop Brackenridge, October 1-28 1841,' *California Historical Society Quarterly* 24, 4 (December 1945): 332.

73 Smith, *James Douglas in California*, 10; Thomas J. Farnham, *Travels in the Californias and Scenes in the Pacific Ocean* (New York: Saxton and Miles 1844), 383.

74 McLoughlin to Douglas, March 1838, HBCA B.223/b/18, fos. 25-27d; Douglas to G&C, 14 October 1839, HBRS 6, 225; McLoughlin (date not given by Blake), HBRS 6, 258, quoted in Blake, 'The Hudson's Bay Company in San Francisco,' (Part 2), 255 n. 57.

75 Simpson to G&C, 25 November 1841, HBRS 29, 77; McLoughlin to Douglas, 27 November 1840, HBCA B.223/b/27, fo. 108.

76 Smith, *James Douglas in California*, 9, 11; Douglas to Juan B. Alvarado, Governor General of Upper and Lower California, 11 January 1841, HBCA. Alvarado stipulated that half the men in the HBC party were to be 'Natives of the country.' Alvarado to Douglas, 13 January 1841, ibid., fos. 25-9.

77 Douglas to McLoughlin, 23 March 1841, from HBRS 6, 252, 256, quoted in Blake, 'The Hudson's Bay Company in San Francisco,' part 1, 98 and part 2, 255 n. 62. The company apparently obtained a grant of eleven square miles on the Sacramento River above the San Joaquin 'as a favor to one of its agents called Desportes MacKay,' but the land was not occupied. Wilbur, *Duflot de Mofras' Travels*, Vol. 1, 243. Alvarado made McKay a 'fine offer' to move to California 'to overawe the indians.' Roberts, 'Letters to Mrs. F.F. Victor,' 208, 235.

78 HBRS 4, 286 (1837); HBCA B. 223/b/31, fos. 149a-149b (1842 and 1843).

79 Simpson to McLoughlin, 1 and March 1842, from HBRS 29 and HBRS 6, 287, quoted in Blake, 'The Hudson's Bay Company in San Francisco,' Part 2, 254 n. 48 and 255.

80 Rae to Simpson, 27 August 1843, quoted in Simpson to G&C, 24 August 1844, HBCA A.12/2, fos. 337-9; fo. 338; McDonald, *Fur Trade Letters of Francis Ermatinger*, 251; Simpson to G&C, 20 June 1845, HBCA A.12/2 fo. 552.

81 The figure is from Galbraith, 'A Note.'

82 Irving, *The Rocky Mountains*, Vol. 1, 188-9; Vol. 2, 244.

83 Wyeth (1839) quoted in Beidleman, 'Nathaniel Wyeth's Fort Hall,' 250; Simpson to G&C, 20 June 1841, HBRS 29, 33.

CHAPTER 6: The North West Coast

1   Simpson to G&C, 26 August 1830, HBCA D.4/97, fo. 39.

2   Ermatinger, 'Notes,' 113. See also Dunn, *History of Oregon territory*, 227, and Cullen, *Fort Langley*, 23.

3   I have resurrected the original spelling and definition of 'North West Coast.' Like the North West Company and the North West Passage, it had two words; it was often abbreviated to N.W. or N-W Coast. I have retained the original spelling to avoid confusion with at least three other places: the 'Northwest,' the ethnographic 'Northwest Coast,' and the 'Pacific Northwest.' Montreal fur traders referred to the region north and west of the Great Lakes as the Northwest; anthropologists refer to the Northwest Coast ethnographic region as the coastline, including some interior territory, between California and Alaska; the American Pacific Northwest includes the states of Washington and Oregon.

4   Dunn identified the North West Coast as beginning at Cape Flattery, and Simpson defined it as the 'coast and islands extending northwards from Point Mudge.' Dunn, *History of Oregon territory*, 227, and Simpson to G&C, 25 November 1841, HBRS 29, 66-7. As late as 1843, Adam Thom defined the 'North-west Archipelago,' the 'Great Archipelago,' as stretching on the outer coast from Cape Flattery to Cape Spencer, and on the inner coast from the bottom of Puget Sound to Lynn Channel. Adam Thom, *The Claims to the Oregon Territory Considered* (London: Smith, Elder and Co. 1844), 2, 24.

5   Corney, *Voyages in the Northern Pacific*, 2. On the scarcity of both sea otter and 'land fur' on the Charlottes, see Green, *Journal of a Tour* 85 (25 May 1829), and Dunn, *History of Oregon territory*, 293. On the maritime fur traders' switch to continental pelts, see Gibson, *Otter Skins*, 61-2, 66, 133-6, 204, 240-2.

6   1835 returns were valued at £11,000; expenses were £3,000, leaving a profit of £8,000. 'This is the great beaver nursury, which continues to replace the numbers destroyed in the more exposed situations.' Wallace, *John McLean's Notes*, 185, 151, 174. See also Innis's remarks in HBRS 3, lxiv. McLean is quoted in Innis, *The Fur Trade in Canada*, 336.

7   For Fraser, see Gough, *The Northwest Coast*, 188; for Mackenzie, see T.A. Rickard, 'The Use of Iron and Copper by the Indians of British Columbia,' *BCHQ* 3, 1 (January 1939): 41-4; C.O. Ermatinger, 'The Columbia Department During the Hudson's Bay Regime,' ms., n.d. [circa 1850], Ermatinger Papers, NAC; Ogden, *Traits*, 92-3. See also Susan Marsden and Robert Galois, 'The Tsimshian, the Hudson's Bay Company and the Geopolitics of the Northwest Coast Fur Trade, 1787-1840,' *Canadian Geographer* 39, 2 (Summer 1995): 169-83.

8   Perkins and Company to NWC, n.d. [circa 1815-18], Keith, 'Adventure to the Columbia,' 13.

9   Finlayson to Hargrave, 10 March 1832, Glazebrook, *Hargrave Correspondence*, 88; Finlayson to McLoughlin, 10 September 1832, HBRS 4; Simpson to G&C, 25 November 1841, HBRS 29, 66-7. See also Ross, *The Fur Traders*, Vol. 1, 42.

10 Simpson to G&C, 26 August 1830, HBCA D.4/97, fos. 41-2.

11 HBRS 4, 358; Wallace *John McLean's Notes*, 4; Gibson, *Otter Skins*, 65-83; Dee, 'An Irishman in the Fur Trade,' 257-63. 'Coasting trade' was a term once applied to the coastal trade of the British Isles, Hudson Bay, and the eastern seaboard of the United States. More formally, it was known as the marine, country, naval, or shipping department or establishment.

12 Gough, *The Northwest Coast*, 69-126; W. Kaye Lamb, 'The Advent of the "Beaver,"' *The Beaver*, 2, 3 (July 1938): 163-84.

13 The Anglo-Russian convention set the southern boundary of Russian America at 55°40', its eastern limits along Portland canal to 56° north thence to the height of the mountains to the 141st parallel, and then to the Arctic. See Gough, *The Royal Navy*, 33, and Willard E. Ireland, 'The Evolution of the Boundaries of British Columbia,' *BCHQ* 3, 4 (October 1939): 263-82.

14 A. Simpson to C. O'Gorman, 7 January 1831, HBCA D.4/125, fos. 103-4.

15 Ibid.; Finlayson, 'Trip Across to the Columbia 1831.'

16 Rich, *HBC*, Vol. 3, 626; Simpson to Russian American Company, 20 March 1829, quoted in Donald C. Davidson, 'Relations of the Hudson's Bay Company with the Russian American Company on the Northwest Coast, 1829-1867,' *BCHQ* 5, 1 (January 1941): 35-6; Simp-

son to G&C, 18 July 1831, HBCA A.12/1, fos. 378-9. For transactions in 'Nass Grease' or 'Nass Oil,' see York Factory Country Produce Account Book, 1828-36, HBCA 239/d/491, fo. 81.

17 See Ogden to McLeod, 10 March 1831, quoted in Maloney, 'Peter Skene Ogden's Trapping Expedition,' 309-10, and Francis to Edward Ermatinger, 16 February 1831, McDonald, *Fur Trade Letters of Francis Ermatinger*, 141.

18 Douglas to McLeod, 12 March 1832, McLeod Papers, NAC; on the founding of Fort Simpson, see Walbran, *British Columbia Coast Names*, 395; Marius Barbeau, 'Old Port Simpson,' *The Beaver* 271 (September 1940): 20-23; Helen Meilleur, *A Pour of Rain. Stories from a West Coast Fort* (Victoria: Sono Nis Press 1980), 16.

19 McLoughlin to G&C, 20 October 1831, HBRS 4, 231-2; Simpson to G&C, 10 August 1832, HBCA A.12/1, fo. 431; on the *Lama*, see Walbran, *British Columbia Coast Names*, 395; on the Boston traders' knowledge, see Green, *Journal of a Tour* 61 (April 1829).

20 On Manson's 1832 voyages, see HBRS 1, 458, and Galois and Ray's plate in *Historical Atlas of Canada*, Vol. 2. On the relocation of Fort Simpson, see HBCA search file, and Walbran, *British Columbia Coast Names*, 396. Simultaneously, the people in New Caledonia explored toward the coast: Simon McGillivray, 'Journal of Voyage [from Stuart Lake] to Simpson's River by Land Summer 1833,' HBCA D.4/125, fos. 63-82.

21 Simpson to G&C, 25 November 1841, HBRS 29, 61-2; see also Simpson, *Narrative*, Vol. 1, 206. On contact with the Carrier, see Anderson, 'Notes on the Indian Tribes,' 74.

22 Finlayson to McLoughlin, 29 September 1836, HBCA B.223/b/12, fos. 16-17, and HBRS 4. See also Dunn, *History of Oregon territory*, 281-3; on the Chimseean 'circle of life,' see Douglas, 'Diary of a Trip to the Northwest Coast,' BCARS, 118.

23 Dunn, *History of Oregon territory*, 281-2.

24 Douglas to Work, 29 November 1838, HBCA B.223/b/22, fos. 39d-40; Work to Donald Ross, 27 November 1840, Donald Ross Papers, BCARS; Simpson to G&C, 25 November 1841, HBRS 29, 62.

25 Finlayson to McLoughlin, 29 September 1836, HBCA B.223/b/12, fos. 16-17, and HBRS 4; Simpson to G&C, 25 November 1841, HBRS 29, 62. On provisions, see Meilleur, *A Pour of Rain*; Gibson, *Otter Skins*, 210, 243-6, and Galois and Ray, 'Meat and Fish Traded at Fort Simpson, 1837,' plate of *Historical Atlas Of Canada*, Vol. 2.

26 Duncan Finlayson to John McLeod, 12 March 1832, McLeod Papers, NAC.

27 Simpson, *Narrative*, 202; Walbran, *British Columbia Coast Names*, 152, 45-7, 298.

28 Dunn, *History of Oregon territory*, 246. Dunn was trader there from June 1833 until the end of 1834.

29 Simpson to G&C, 21 July 1834, HBCA D.4/100, fo. 17.

30 Simpson, *Narrative*, Vol. 1, 202; William Fraser Tolmie, *The Journals of William Fraser Tolmie, Physician and Fur Trader* (Vancouver: Mitchell Press 1963). For a reconstruction of trade at the post in 1835, see Donald Mitchell, 'Sebassa's Men,' in Donald N. Abbott, ed., *The World is as Sharp as a Knife* (Victoria: British Columbia Provincial Museum 1981), 18-23.

31 Finlayson to McLoughlin, 29 September 1836, HBCA B.223/b/12, fos. 17-17d; also in HBRS 4. See also Dunn, *History of Oregon territory*, 251.

32 Charles Ross to Simpson, 1 October 1842, Charles Ross Correspondence, BCARS.

33 Scouler, 'Observations on the Indigenous Tribes,' 224.

34 McLoughlin to Finlayson and Work, 8 August 1836, HBCA B.223/b/15, fo. 59; Douglas to Manson, 21 June 1838, HBCA B.223/b/22, fo. 17.

35 Finlayson to McLoughlin, 29 September 1836, HBCA B.223/b/12, fos. 17-17d (also in HBRS 4); Simpson, *Narrative*, Vol. 1, 202; Simpson to G&C, 25 November 1841, HBRS 29, 61; Charles Ross to James Hargrave, 8 November 1842, Glazebrook, *Hargrave Correspondence*, 415. On Manson's garden, see Henry Drummond Dee, 'The Journal of John Work, 1835,' part 5, *BCHQ* 9, 2 (April 1945): 130.

36 McLoughlin to G&C, 5 August 1829, HBRS 4, 78-9, and see 118-19, 231 for this plan; McLoughlin to John McLeod, 1 February 1830, McLeod Papers, NAC.

37 George Blenkinsop to George Davidson, 25 May 1896, BCARS.

38 McNeill had found his 'independent mode of trading a failure.' Dunn, *History of Oregon territory*, 229. On his connection with Bryant & Sturgis, see Roberts, 'Letters to Mrs. F.F. Victor,' 192, 218 and Derek Pethick, *S.S. Beaver: The Ship That Saved the West* (Vancouver: Mitchell Press 1970), 28.

39 McLoughlin to G&C, 16 June and 17 July 1832, HBRS 4, 99, 117. On McNeill's hiring, see also Gibson, *Otter Skins*, 69.

40 Finlayson to Hargrave, 21 February 1833, Glazebrook, *Hargrave Correspondence*, 104-6.

41 Finlayson to McLoughlin, 10 September 1832, HBRS 4; McLoughlin to G&C, 28 October 1832, HBRS 4, 101.

42 G&C to Simpson, 1 March 1833, HBRS 4, 116 n. 5; McLoughlin to G&C, 28 May 1834, HBRS 4, 118-19. McLoughlin authorized second mate James Scarborough to 'step forward, and Declare himself Master' if the steamer 'falls in with an English Cruiser.' McLoughlin to Work, 14 November 1837, HBCA B.223/b/18, fo. 8.

43 Finlayson to McLoughlin, 29 September 1836, HBCA B.223/b/12, fos 17d-23d; also HBRS 4.

44 Simpson to G&C, 10 August 1832, HBCA A.12/1, fos. 431-6. The steamer was also to be used in 'surveying the harbours and inlets in the Straits of De Fuca and on the adjacent Coasts, and in towing our vessels in and out of the Columbia.' G&C to McLoughlin, 27 September 1843, HBRS 6, 310. See also Lamb, 'The Advent of the "Beaver,"' and Gibson, *Otter Skins*, 68.

45 G&C to Simpson, 5 March 1834, HBCA D.5/4, fo. 72. Seven permanent vessels or annual vessels from London were engaged in the Pacific trade in 1836. Alan Cameron, 'Ships of Three Centuries,' *The Beaver* 301 (Summer 1970): 13-14.

46 'Skokum': see McDonald to John McLeod, 25 January 1837, McLeod Papers, NAC; Simpson, *Narrative*, Vol. 1, 236. See also Walbran, *British Columbia Coast Names*, 40; Lamb, 'The Advent of the "Beaver"'; Pethick, *S.S. Beaver*.

47 Dunn, *History of Oregon territory*, 265; McLoughlin to Kittson, 9 June 1836, HBCA B.223/b/15, fo. 40; McLoughlin to Yale, 9 June 1836, HBCA B.223/b/15, fo. 41.

48 William Fraser Tolmie, 'Utilization of the Indians,' *The Resources of British Columbia* 1, 12 (February 1884): 7 (I owe this reference to John Lutz); Finlayson to McLoughlin, 29 September 1836, HBCA B.223/b/12, fos 17d-23d.

49 Dunn, *History of Oregon territory*, 265-6. Most furs sold at Fort McLoughlin were interior furs traded at Dean Channel and Bentinck Arm. Finlayson thought that the voyages of the *Beaver* 'will shut up that drain, and leave little to glean by vessels sailing along the coast.' Finlayson to McLoughlin, 29 September 1836, HBCA B.223/b/12, fos 17d-23d; also HBRS 4.

50 McLoughlin to Work, 13 March 1836, HBCA B.223/b/18, fos. 22d-23. On the Sebassa, see Dunn, *History of Oregon territory*, 274, and Mitchell, 'Sebassa's Men.'

51 Finlayson to McLoughlin, 29 September 1836, HBCA B.223/b/12, fos 17d-23d; also in HBRS 4.

52 Stations were places of commercial activity. A fishing station was a place where the company traded for salmon; a trading station (or simply 'station') was a place on the North West Coast where company vessels traded with Native people.

53 Simpson, *Narrative*, Vol. 1, 188, 236.

54 McLoughlin to Work, 8 December 1836, HBCA B.223/b/15, fo. 117; McLoughlin to Work, 16 June 1837, HBCA B.223/b/17, fo. 20.

55 Lorne Hammond, '"Any Ordinary Degree of System": The Columbia Department of the Hudson's Bay Company and the Harvesting of Wildlife, 1825-1849,' Master's thesis, University of Victoria, 1985, 64, and see also Fort Vancouver, Fur Trade Returns, Columbia District and New Caledonia, 1825-1857, BCARS; Tolmie to Swan, 30 December 1878, Swan Papers, UBC.

56 Simpson, *Narrative*, Vol. 1, 185, 240-1.

57 Scouler, 'Dr John Scouler's Journal,' 194-5; see also Green, *Journal of a Tour*, 100 and Dunn, *History of Oregon territory*, 244.

58 'Nearly all the furs of that part of the Island find their way to the Coquilts, and other places in Queen Charlotte Sound, where the navigation is confined, and [where] the Steam power

of the 'Beaver' works to advantage and confers a decided advantage over sailing vessels.' Douglas to Work, 21 June 1838, HBCA B.223/b/22, fos. 16-16d; see also Douglas to Work, 29 May 1839, HBCA B.223/b/24, fo. 18.

59 Douglas to Work, 21 June 1838, HBCA B.223/b/22, fos. 16-16d.

60 Douglas to Work, 29 November 1838, HBCA B.223/b/22, fo. 40d; Douglas to McLoughlin, 13 July 1840, quoted in Willard E. Ireland, 'James Douglas and the Russian American Company, 1840,' *BCHQ* 5, 1 (January 1941): 53-66; Douglas to McLoughlin, 1 October 1840, HBCA B.223/b/28, fos. 77-9; Simpson to G&C, 20 June 1841, HBCA D.4/109, fo. 26.

61 On the 1825 convention and the 1833 Stikine incident, see Belcher, *Narrative*, Vol. 1, 299; Ermatinger, 'Notes,' 117; Rich, *HBC*, Vol. 3, 610-11; Galbraith, *Hudson's Bay Company*, 134, 145-7; Gibson, *Otter Skins*, 77.

62 See Finlayson to Smith, 11 January 1834, HBCA B.223/b/9, fos. 51-2, and Ogden and Douglas to Simpson, 15 March 1847, HBCA B.223/b/36, fo. 4. On McLeod's 1834 trip from Fort Halkett on the Liard to the Stikine, see Morton, *A History*, 706.

63 Work to McLeod, 1 March 1834, McLeod Papers, NAC. The post would have allowed the company to 'extend the Trade to the British Territory North of 54.' McLoughlin to G&C, 14 March 1835, HBRS 4, 134-5; McLoughlin to Simpson, 1837, HBCA B.223/b/15, fos. 147-8. See also Davidson, 'Relations of the Hudson's Bay Company with the Russian American Company,' 39-43; W. Kaye Lamb, ed., 'McLoughlin's Statement of the Expenses in the "Dryad" Incident of 1834,' *BCHQ* 10, 4 (October 1946): 291-8.

64 On the Americans' earlier provisioning of Sitka and the background to the 'provision contract', see Gibson, *Otter Skins*, 79-80, 260-4; see also James R. Gibson, 'The "Russian Contract": The Agreement of 1838 [*sic*] Between the Hudson's Bay and Russian-American Companies,' in Richard A. Pierce, ed., *Russia in North America: Proceedings of the 2nd International Conference on Russian America* (Kingston: Limestone Press 1990), 157-80.

65 Oliver, *The Canadian North-West*, Vol. 2, 785; Simpson to G&C, 20 June 1841, HBCA D.4/109, fo. 21.

66 Douglas to McLoughlin, 1 October 1840, HBCA B.223/b/28, fos. 77-9. See also Douglas, 'Diary of a trip to the Northwest Coast,' 23-55.

67 Douglas (1840) reported by Simpson, *Narrative*, Vol. 1, 216; Douglas to McLoughlin, 1 October 1840, HBCA B.223/b/28, fos. 82-3. 'The Fort was built in the Spring of 1840 – It was abandoned in the Spring of 1843 – The Inlet on which it was built was named by Mr Douglas "Locality Inlet" situated about 30 miles south of the entrance of Takou River.' Roderick Finlayson to McKay, 27 December 1888, McKay Papers, BCARS. See also Wallace M. Olson, *A History of Fort Durham, Hudson's Bay Company Trading Post Located in Taku Harbour, 1840-1843, within the Boundaries of Juneau* (Juneau, AK: Heritage Research 1994).

68 Simpson, *Narrative*, Vol. 1, 214. Deer were so cheap that 'we absolutely make a profit on our consumption of provisions, the skin of the animals selling for much more than is paid for the whole carcase.' Simpson to G&C, 25 November 1841, HBRS 29, 64. On provision trades, see also Gibson, *Otter Skins*, 210, 243-6.

69 Douglas to McLoughlin, 1 October 1840, HBCA B.223/b/28, fos. 83-8. See also Douglas, 'Diary of a Trip to the Northwest Coast,' 47.

70 Simpson, *Narrative*, Vol. 1, 209-10. On the founding of Fort Stikine, see also Gibson, *Otter Skins*, 16, 79.

71 Douglas to McLoughlin, 1 October 1840, HBCA B.223/b/28, fos. 94-7.

72 Douglas to McLoughlin, 1 October 1840, HBCA B.223/b/28, fos. 94-7. Anderson noted that the Taku or Chilcat were 'in communication for the purposes of barter with the Chipewyans frequenting the posts of McKenzie's River.' Anderson, 'Notes on the Indian Tribes,' 75. For Basil Bottineau and Chief Shakes' 1845 ascent of the Stikine River, see Ogden and Douglas to Simpson, 15 March 1847, HBCA B.223/b/36, fo. 4.

73 Gibson, *Otter Skins*, 6-7, 13, 20, 179, 181, 259-60, 277. For the Russian and American sea otter hunts in California, see Adele Ogden, *The California Sea Otter Trade, 1784-1848* (Berkeley: University if California Press 1941), chapters 5-7.

74 Simpson to G&C, 5 September 1827, HBCA D.4/91, fo. 4; Simpson to G&C, 1 March 1829,

HBRS 10, 78; HBCA A.63/5, fo. 115; Scouler, 'Dr John Scouler's Journal,' 194-5; Dunn, *History of Oregon territory*, 244; A. Simpson to C. O'Gorman, 7 January 1831, HBCA D.4/125, fos. 103-4. The figure of 15,000 is from Howay, ed., 'William Sturgis,' 20.

75 Corney, *Voyages in the Northern Pacific*, 68-9; see also Gough, *The Northwest Coast*, 58.

76 Dunn, *History of Oregon territory*, 231-2.

77 McLoughlin to G&C, 6 October 1825, HBRS 4, 22. On the northern and southern species, see James R. Gibson, 'The Russian Fur Trade,' in Judd and Ray, *Old Trails and New Directions*, 217-30.

78 On Russian involvement, see Corney, *Voyages in the Northern Pacific*, 82-3; A. Simpson to C. O'Gorman, 7 January 1831, HBCA D.4/125, fos. 103-4; Wilbur, *Duflot de Mofras' Travels*, Vol. 2, 1-10; Finlayson to Smith, 11 January 1834, HBCA B.223/b/9, fos. 51-2.

79 Finlayson to Smith, 11 January 1834, HBCA B.223/b/9, fos. 51-2.

80 McLoughlin to Work, 8 December 1836, HBCA B.223/b/15, fo. 117; McLoughlin to Bancroft, 16 and 17 January 1837, HBCA B.223/b/15, fo. 126; McLoughlin to Simpson, 20 March 1837, HBCA B.223/b/15, fo. 146; McLoughlin to Robert Cowie, 5 June 1837, HBCA B.223/b/17, fo. 12d; Douglas to Pelly, 24 October 1838, HBCA B.223/b/22, fos. 33d-34.

81 McLoughlin to Pelly, 17 June 1836, HBCA B.223/b/12, fo. 44d; same to Bancroft, 5 June 1837, HBCA B.223/b/17, fos. 13-13d; same to Work, [n.d.], HBCA B.223/b/18, fo. 20d; Douglas to Bancroft, 24 October 1838, HBCA B.223/b/22, fos. 35-35d; same to Bancroft, 6 December 1838, HBCA B.223/b/22, fo. 43; same to Pelly, 24 October 1838, HBCA B.223/b/22, fos. 33d-34.

82 Pelly to Smith, 30 April 1839, HBCA A.11/61, fo. 52; J. Moltено to E. Grimes, January 1839, *The Hawaiian Spectator* 2,2 (April 1839): 236-38. On this incident, see also Meilleur, *A Pour of Rain*, 147-8.

83 Pelly and Allan to McLoughlin, 22 March 1843, HBCA B.223/b/30, fo. 22; McLoughlin to Pelly and Allan, 3 August 1843, HBCA B.223/b/30, fo. 30. On the decline, see Forbes, *California*, 176-7, 284, General Vallejo in HBRS 7, xxvii, and Ogden, *The California Sea Otter Trade*, chapter 7.

84 Simpson to G&C, 8 July 1839, HBCA D.4/106, fo.47; Simpson, *Narrative*, Vol. 1, 224.

85 New York *Gazette*, quoted in Galbraith, *Hudson's Bay Company*, 101.

86 Wyeth to Leon. Jarvis, 6 February 1832, Young, *The Wyeth Correspondence*, 32.

87 Wyeth to Mess. Tucker & Williams and Henry Hall Esq., 4 July and 8 November 1833, Wyeth to Mess. Joseph Baker & Son, 4 July 1833, in Young, *Wyeth Correspondence*, 60, 63, 78; Farnham, *Travels in the Great Western Prairies*, Vol. 2, 115; see also Howay, ed., 'William Sturgis,' 24.

88 James Gilchrist Swan, *The North-West Coast; or, Three Years' Residence in Washington Territory* (London: Sampson Low, Son, & Co. 1857), 96.

89 Gibson's figures for the 1830s are different from those below, owing to his inclusion of vessels freighting goods to Sitka. See Gibson, *Otter Skins*, 308-10, 76.

90 Finlayson to McLoughlin, 10 September 1832, HBRS 4; Simpson to G&C, 10 August 1832, HBCA A.12/1, fos. 431-6; Finlayson to McLeod, 12 March 1832, McLeod Papers, NAC.

91 McLoughlin to McLeod, 1 March 1832, McLeod Papers, NAC; Finlayson to Hargrave, 10 March 1832, Glazebrook, *Hargrave Correspondence*, 88.

92 Work reported on Ogden's 1832 activities to Ross, who repeated them to Robert Miles. Ross to Miles, 11 April 1833, Donald Ross Papers, BCARS.

93 'There were no Americans on the Coast this Season.' McLoughlin to Governor, Chief Factors and Traders, HBC, 9 September 1833, HBCA B.223/b/9, fo. 28.

94 McLoughlin to Manson, 20 December 1834, HBCA B.223/b/10, fo. 83; see also Simpson to G&C, 21 July 1834, HBCA D.4/100, fos. 10-11.

95 Finlayson to Smith, 11 January 1834, HBCA B.223/b/9, fos. 50-1. On pre-1830 exports of goods such as molasses, rice, tobacco, cloth, and beads to the coast (from Boston), see Gibson, *Otter Skins*, 185-6, 215-28.

96 Finlayson to Hargrave, 29 February, 1836, Glazebrook, *Hargrave Correspondence*, 230; Finlayson to McLoughlin, 29 September 1836, HBCA B.223/b/12, fos. 17d-23d; Dunn, *History of Oregon territory*, 285; Douglas to G&C, 18 October 1838, HBRS 4, 245-6; see also Dou-

glas to Chief Factors and Chief Traders, New Caledonia and Thompson's River Districts, 9 November 1838, HBCA B.223/b/22, fo. 36d.

97   See 'Movements of Hudson's Bay Company Vessels, 1837,' in Galois and Ray, 'The Fur Trade in the Cordillera, 1821-185' and 'Statement of Voyages, Performed by the Shipping, Attached to the Columbia Department, since 1842,' Fort Vancouver, 25 November 1844, HBCA B.223/b/31, fos. 192-3d.

98   Douglas to Simpson, 18 March 1838, HBRS 4, 274; Douglas to G&C, 18 October 1838, HBRS 4, 245.

99   Douglas to Chief Factors, Chief Traders, Northern Department, 6 September 1839, HBCA B.223/b/24, fo. 36d; Douglas to Hargrave, 26 February 1840, Glazebrook, *Hargrave Correspondence*, 311.

100   Simpson to G&C, 1 March 1842, HBRS 29, 110; Douglas to Simpson, 23 October 1843, HBCA D.5/9, fos. 114-21, quoted in 'Whales and Whaling' search file, HBCA; McLoughlin to Simpson, 7 April 1844, HBCA B.223/b/31, fo. 156 and also HBRS 6, 176-7; HBRS 7, 51; Douglas to Ross, 12 March 1844, Ross Papers, BCARS; Galbraith, *Hudson's Bay Company*, 451 n. 5; Gibson, *Otter Skins*, 82-3.

101   McLoughlin in HBRS 6, 24, cited in Gibson, *Farming the Frontier*, 78.

102   See Fort Vancouver, Fur Trade Returns, Columbia District and New Caledonia, 1825-1857, BCARS.

103   Douglas to Hargrave, 26 February 1840, Glazebrook, *Hargrave Correspondence*, 311.

104   Gibson, *Otter Skins*, xi, xii, 17, 267, 295.

105   Ibid, 61, 62, 66, 133-6, 204, 240-2, table 7, 315.

106   Simpson to G&C, 25 November 1841, in HBRS 29, 66-7. 'The N.W. Coast is now deserted,' wrote an American merchant in Oahu in December 1830; 'though there is good business to be done there if well managed. Land furs are more plentiful than ever.' John C. Jones to Josiah Marshall, 14 December 1830, quoted in Morison, 'New England and the Opening of the Columbia River Salmon Trade,' 129.

107   McLoughlin to Simpson, 20 March 1845, HBCA B.223/b/32, fo. 93; Douglas and Ogden to Simpson, 19 March 1846, HBCA B.223/b/34, fo. 28; Douglas and Ogden to Simpson, 15 March 1847, HBCA B.223/b/36, fo. 20; Ogden and Douglas to Simpson, 16 March 1848, HBCA B.223/b/37, fo. 16; Simpson to G&C, 24 June 1848, HBCA A.12/4, fo. 143.

108   The New York *Tribune*, 14 December 1842, quoted in *OHQ* 1,3 (September 1900): 334.

109   Gibson, *Farming the Frontier*, 224. Gibson's related assertion that the decline in the coastal and continental fur trades made the company's capture of the coast trade 'rather a hollow victory for Simpson' is equally questionable (Gibson, *Otter Skins*, 82); the decline in the continental fur trade did not begin to lower dividends until 1838 (MacKay, *The Honourable Company*, 328), and the coastal fur trade remained profitable for many years afterwards.

110   For a discussion of some of these policies and advantages, see Gibson, *Otter Skins*, 73-83, 123, 158.

111   McLoughlin to Simpson, 20 March 1843, quoted in Gibson, *Otter Skins*, 82; Herman Leader, ed., 'McLoughlin's Answer to Warre Report,' *OHQ* 33, 3 (September 1932): 225-6. American historians have echoed McLoughlin: Gilbert regarded American competition as 'fitful, and, for the most part, futile,' while Galbraith noted that 'after 1830 American sea captains had ceased to be a menace.' Gilbert, *Trade and Currency*, 23; Galbraith, *Hudson's Bay Company*, 177.

112   Dunn, *History of Oregon territory*, 220, 221, 227, 229.

CHAPTER 7: New Markets for New Exports

1   Thomas J. Farnham to J.R. Poinsett, 4 January 1840, in T. Jefferson Farnham, Correspondence Outward, BCARS.

2   Simpson to G&C, 1824, quoted in Ormsby, *British Columbia*, 60.

3   Pelly to Canning, 9 December 1825, Klotz, *Certain Correspondence*, 12; Corney, *Voyages in the Northern Pacific*, 72. See also Leechman, 'Garden Seeds,' 31-4, and James R. Gibson, 'Food for the Fur Traders: The First Farmers in the Pacific Northwest,' *Journal of the West* 7, 1

(1968): 18-30. For political motives behind the creation of this agricultural base, see G&C to Simpson, 16 January 1828, HBRS 3, lxvi.

4   Rich, *HBC*, Vol. 3, 657; see W. Kaye Lamb, 'John McLoughlin,' *DCB*, Vol. 8; McLoughlin to G&C, 20 November 1845, HBRS 7, 113.

5   Simpson to G&C, 1 March 1829 and G&C to McLoughlin, 28 October 1829, HBRS 10, 68-9, 97 n. 1, 235.

6   Gibson, *Farming the Frontier*, 38; McLoughlin to McLeod, 1 March 1833, McLeod Papers, NAC; Ball, 'Across the Continent,' 100; Francis to Edward Ermatinger, 14 March 1829, McDonald, *Fur Trade Letters of Francis Ermatinger*, 119; Roberts, 'Letters to Mrs. F.F. Victor,' 183.

7   H.H. Bancroft cited in Walbran, *British Columbia Coast Names*, 397; T.C. Elliott, ed., 'The Coming of the White Women, 1836,' part 2, *OHQ* 37, 3 (September 1936): 179.

8   Wyeth to Jarvis, 6 February 1832, Young, *The Wyeth Correspondence*, 32; Simpson to G&C, 21 July 1834, HBCA D.4/100, fo. 11.

9   Simpson to G&C, 10 June 1835, HBCA D.4/102, fo. 7.

10 On the company's activities in Hawaii, see Alexander Simpson, *The Sandwich Islands* (London: Smith, Elder & Co. 1843); Thomas G. Thrum, 'History of the Hudson's Bay Company's Agency in Honolulu,' *Hawaiian Historical Society* (1912): 43-59; G.V. Bennett, 'Early Relations of the Sandwich Islands to the Old Oregon Territory,' *Washington Historical Quarterly* 4 (April 1913): 116-26; Robert Watson, 'HBC in the Hawaiian Islands,' *The Beaver* (June 1930): 6-8; William P. St. Clair, Jr., 'Beaver in Hawaii,' *The Beaver* 272 (September 1941): 40-2; Alfred L. Lomax, 'Dr McLoughlin's Tropical Trade Route,' *The Beaver* 294 (Spring 1964): 10-15; Alexander Spoehr, 'Fur traders in Hawai'i: The Hudson's Bay Company in Honolulu, 1829-1861,' *The Hawaiian Journal of History* 20 (1986): 27-66.

11 Sheila P. Robinson, 'Men and Resources on the Northern Northwest Coast,' PhD diss., University of London, 1983, 186. On the islands' central role in the maritime fur trade, see also Gough, *The Northwest Coast*, 40, 54, 71, and Gibson, *Otter Skins*, 44-7. American traders developed a 'New Northwest Trade' at the Sandwich Islands before about 1830: Gibson, *Otter Skins*, 251-8, 281-4.

12 Corney, *Voyages in the Northern Pacific*, 36.

13 Simpson, *Narrative*, Vol. 2, 132, 137; for population estimates, see also Simpson to G&C, 1 March 1842, HBRS 29, 130 n. 2, and Gibson, *Otter Skins*, 287.

14 Corney, *Voyages in the Northern Pacific*, 36.

15 'List of Vessels at Oahu, from July 5, to Nov. 22 1835,' and 'Arrivals at Oahu, Sandwich Islands, Jan 1 Aug 1 1836,' HBCA A.11/61, fos. 3, 16. A passage of forty days from Fort Victoria to Honolulu was considered a 'very long voyage.' Pelly and Allan to G&C, 1 February 1846, HBCA A.11/62, fos. 88d-90. A passage of eight months from London to Fort Vancouver was considered 'protracted.' The three week figure is from Gibson, *Otter Skins*, 208.

16 McLoughlin to Aemilius Simpson, 13 November 1827, HBCA B.223/b/3, fo. 23; George Simpson to G&C, 1 March 1829, HBRS 10, 110.

17 Gough, *To the Pacific and Arctic*, 119 n. 1.

18 Simpson to G&C, 1 March 1829, HBRS 10, 75, 84, 86-7.

19 McLoughlin to G&C, 5 August 1829, HBRS 4, 77.

20 McLoughlin to McLeod, 1 February 1830, McLeod Papers, NAC; Finlayson to McLoughlin, 2 August 1832, HBCA B.223/b/8, fo. 41d.

21 Finlayson to Hargrave, 21 February 1833, Glazebrook, *Hargrave Correspondence*, 104-6.

22 Simpson to George Pelly, 26 November 1833, HBRS 4, 353; McLoughlin to G&C, 18 November 1834, HBRS 4, 124; Charlton to McLoughlin, 21 March 1835, HBCA B.223/b/11, fo. 112. On this first visit and the hiring of Charlton see also Spoehr, 'Fur Traders in Hawai'i,' 29-30.

23 HBCA A.11/62, fo. 91; Simpson to George Pelly, 26 November 1833, HBRS 4, 353. On the suspension of the EIC privilege, see Gough, *The Northwest Coast*, 234 n. 76, and Gibson, *Otter Skins*, 28.

24 Lomax, 'Tropical Trade Route,' 30; Simpson to G&C, 1 March 1842, HBRS 29, 126; William St. Clair, 'Beaver in Hawaii,' *The Beaver* 272 (September 1941): 41; Spoehr, 'Fur Traders,' 34.

For a detailed description of the islands, see Wilbur, *Duflot de Mofras' Travels*, Vol. 2, 36-44. Tolmie is quoted in Athelstan George Harvey, 'Meredith Gairdner: Doctor of Medicine,' *BCHQ* 9, 3 (April 1945): 89-112.

25 See Gough, *The Royal Navy*, 34-41.

26 G&C to McLoughlin, 4 December 1833, HBCA search file 'Timber.'

27 Simpson to G&C, 10 June 1835, HBCA D.4/102, fo. 16; G&C to McLoughlin, 8 December 1835, HBCA B.223/c/1, fos. 45d-46, and see also G&C to McLoughlin, 25 January 1837, HBCA B.223/c/1, fos. 58d-59.

28 McLoughlin to Edward Ermatinger, 1 February 1836, Ermatinger Papers, NAC; McLoughlin to Pelly, 15 November 1836, HBCA B.223/b/12, fo. 36 [lumber shed]; Pelly to Smith, 2 October 1836, HBCA A.11/61, fos. 14-15 [retail proposal]; McLoughlin to Pelly, 10 January 1838, HBCA B.223/b/18, fos. 11, 12d [Sangster]. On the retailing venture, see also Spoehr, 'Fur Traders,' 53.

29 They were known in the 1820s and 1830s as 'Owyhees' after the island of 'Owyhee' or 'Woahoo' (Oahu), but these terms disappeared and 'Sandwich Islanders' and 'Kanakas' appeared in the next two decades. 'Hawaii' and 'Hawaiians' seem to be 1850s names. For Kanakas on the coast, see Janice K. Duncan, 'Kanaka World Travellers and Fur Company Employees, 1785-1860,' *Hawaiian Journal of History* 7 (1973): 93-111; Spoehr, 'Fur Traders,' 32-4; Tom Koppel, *Kanaka, the Untold Story of Hawaiian Pioneers in British Columbia and the Pacific Northwest* (Vancouver: Whitecap Books 1995).

30 Simpson to G&C, 25 July 1827, quoted in HBRS 3, lxx.

31 Gibson, *Otter Skins*, 151-2, 212-13, 291; Ronda, *Astoria and Empire*, 111; Corney, *Voyages in the Northern Pacific*, 69, 73; Robert Carlton Clark, 'Hawaiians in Early Oregon,' *OHQ* 35, 1 (March 1934): 22-31; Pelly to Smith, 21 March 1840, HBCA A.11/61, fo. 53. See also George Verne Blue, 'A Hudson's Bay Company Contract for Hawaiian Labor,' *OHQ* 25 (1924): 72-5.

32 Jean Baptiste Bolduc (Honolulu) to 'Mr T.', 5 August 1842, quoted in Landerholm, *Notices & Voyages*, 133; *The Friend* (Honolulu), 1 September 1844, 79.

33 See Jean Barman, 'New Land, New Lives: Hawaiian Settlement in British Columbia,' *Hawaiian Journal of History* 29 (1995):1-32

34 Pelly and Mactavish to G&C, 10 January 1849, HBCA A.11/62, fo. 346. For 'Productions and Manufactures' and 'Trade' of the islands, see Simpson, *Narrative*, Vol. 2, 121-42.

35 McLoughlin to G&C, 6 October 1825, HBRS 4, 20-1; McLoughlin to G&C, 14 November 1827, HBRS 4, 54; Simpson to G&C, 10 July 1828, HBCA D.4/92, fo. 68; McLoughlin to A. Simpson, 24 June 1828, HBCA B.223/b/3, fo. 4 and McLoughlin to G&C, 11 August 1827, HBRS, 4, 51. For the Willamette salt springs, see Tolmie, *Journals*, 175.

36 Simpson, *Narrative*, Vol. 2, 127-8; see also Corney, *Voyages in the Northern Pacific*, 70; Spoehr, 'Fur Traders,' 57; Gibson, *Otter Skins*, 282.

37 Finlayson to Captain Grave, 2 August 1832, HBCA B.223/b/8, fo. 38; McLoughlin to Pelly, 18 November 1834, HBCA B.223/b/10; Pelly to McLoughlin, 21 March 1835, HBCA B.223/b/11, fo. 115; McLoughlin to Commander of the HBC'c Ship from England, 4 June 1835, HBCA B.223/b/11, fo. 18; McLoughlin to Yale, 4 June 1835, HBCA B.223/b/11, fo. 19; McLoughlin to Pelly, 10 January 1838, HBCA B.223/b/18, fos. 11, 12d. Shipments of salt from Fort Vancouver to Langley between 1838 and 1841 ranged from 600 to 840 bushels: HBCA C.7/177, fos. 64d, 68, 79, 84-5; Simpson to G&C, 6 July 1842, HBRS 29, 159.

38 Simpson, *Narrative*, Vol. 2, 122, 125-6. Ladd & Co was the 'principal manufacturer' of sugar: Pelly and Allan to G&C, 28 October 1843, HBCA A.11/62, fo. 6.

39 Fort McLoughlin offered molasses and rice in 1834: Tolmie, *Journals*, 312; see also Walbran, *British Columbia Coast Names*, 65.

40 McLoughlin to Charlton, 18 November 1830, HBCA B.223/b/6, fos. 21-2; Finlayson to W.G. Reid, 25 July 1832, HBCA B.223/b/8, fo.37; Reid to Finlayson, 26 and 27 July 1832, HBCA B.223/b/8, fos. 37-37d; Pierce and Thomas D. Hinckley to Finlayson, 4 January 1834, HBCA B.223/b/49; Finlayson to Smith, 11 January 1834, HBCA B.223/b/9, fos. 50-1; McLoughlin to Pelly, 10 January 1838, HBCA B.223/b/18, fos. 11, 12d.

41 'Invoice of Goods shipped on board the Brig Dryad ... June 9th 183' [HBCA]; Pelly to

Smith, 30 April 1839, HBCA A.11/61, fo. 51; McLoughlin to Pelly, 5 June 1837, HBCA B.223/b/17, fo. 14. French, previously of Canton, also supplied the Russian American Company at Sitka: Lamb, 'The Advent of the "Beaver,"' 175-6; Gibson, *Otter Skins*, 96; Galbraith, *Hudson's Bay Company*, 450 n. 50. For earlier tea exports from Canton, see Gibson, *Otter Skins*, 92-4.

42 Pelly to McLoughlin, 20 January 1836, HBCA B.223/b/11, fo. 123; McLoughlin to Pelly and Allan, 3 August 1843, HBCA B.223/b/30, fo. 28; McLoughlin to Pelly and Allan, 1 July 1844, HBCA B.223/b/31, fo. 114; McLoughlin to Charlton, 27 October 1831, HBCA B.223/b/7, fo. 9.

43 Kane, *Wanderings*, 153; 'Passengers to England [on *Eagle*]. Otakea che, Qu kee che, You akeeche, Japanese,' 15 November 1834, HBCA C.7/177, fo. 35. On this incident, see also Belcher, *Narrative* Vol. 1, 303-6; Anderson, 'Notes on the Indian Tribes,' 80-1; Anderson, *The Dominion of the West*, 101-2. In 1813, *Forester*, bound from London to the Columbia, found a 700-ton junk at the 49th parallel; three people were alive. The vessel had been 18 months at sea. Forbes, *California*, 299-300.

44 Finlayson to McLoughlin, 2 August 1832, HBCA B.223/b/8, fo. 42d; McLoughlin to Pelly, 3 October 1835, HBCA B.223/b/11, fo. 70; Pelly to McLoughlin, 20 January 1836, HBCA B.223/b/11, fo. 130; McLoughlin to Pelly, 6 June 1837, HBCA B.223/b/17, fo. 16d; McLoughlin to Pelly, 10 January 1838, HBCA B.223/b/18, fo. 13d. On Sandwich Islands coral exports, see also Joseph Schafer, ed., 'Documents Relative to Warre and Vavasour's Military Reconnaissance in Oregon, 1845-6,' *OHQ* 10, 1 (March 1909): 86

45 'There is a large amount of capital invested in the Northern Pacific Fisheries, there being upwards of 200 vessels, from almost every commercial country in Europe and America, at present, engaged in it.' Douglas to Ross, 12 March 1844, Ross Papers, BCARS. *Moby Dick or The White Whale* (1851), based on Herman Melville's voyages on an American Pacific whaler between 1840 and 1842, is set at this time, but Melville does not mention the merchants from Hudson Bay.

46 Simpson, *Narrative*, Vol. 2, 139, 141; Spoehr, 'Fur Traders,' 31.

47 Pelly to Smith, 30 April 1839, HBCA A.11/61, fo. 52; Pelly to Smith, 22 December 1838, HBCA A.11/61, fo. 48; see also [List of Goods shipped from Honolulu to London, 22 December 1838], HBCA B.191/z/1, fo. 66; Pelly to Smith, 30 April 1839, HBCA A.11/61, fo. 51-2; Pelly to Smith, 21 March 1840, HBCA A.11/61, fo. 53.

48 'Requisition for the Sandwich Islands. Outfit 1847. Shipment 1846,' HBCA A.11/62, fos. 101-6d; Pelly to McLoughlin, 21 March 1835, HBCA B.223/b/11, fo. 118.

49 Between 1840 and 1843, four batches of whalebone were exported for a total value of £123: Fort Vancouver Account Book, 1836-1860, HBCA B.223/d/212; the 1842 figure is from HBCA A.53/1. Barclay to Pelly and Allan, 18 September 1844, HBCA B.191/c/1, fo. 1; Pelly and Allan to G&C, 30 November 1845, HBCA A.12/62, fo. 79.

50 Simpson, *Narrative*, Vol. 2, 128; Pelly to Smith, 22 December 1838, HBCA A.11/61, fo. 48; [List of Goods shipped from Honolulu to London, 22 December 1838], HBCA B.191/z/1, fo. 66; Pelly to Smith, 30 April 1839, HBCA A.11/61, fo. 51. On the 1838 shipment, see also Spoehr, 'Fur Traders,' 123.

51 Douglas to G&C, 18 October 1838, HBRS 4, 267 and Douglas to Pelly, 24 October 1838, HBCA B.223/b/22, fo. 34. Oliver, *The Canadian North-West*, Vol. 2, 786; Simpson to G&C, 8 July 1839, HBCA D.4/106, fo.14. See also Spoehr, 'Fur Traders,' 30, 32, 35, 61 n 28.

52 Reginald Saw, 'Sir John H. Pelly, Bart., Governor, Hudson's Bay Company, 1822-1852,' *BCHQ* 13,1 (January 1949): 23-32; St. Clair, 'Beaver in Hawaii,' 41; Spoehr, 'Fur Traders' 37; Lomax, 'Tropical Trade Route,' 14. On earlier 'bills of exchange' (essentially cheques drawn on English banks), see Gibson, *Otter Skins*, 249.

53 Simpson to G&C, HBRS 6, 280; Simpson to G&C, 8 July 1839, HBCA D.4/106, fo. 14; Spoehr, 'Fur Traders,' 53; Simpson to G&C, 25 November 1841, HBRS 29, 88; Simpson, *The Sandwich Islands*, 50-1.

54 Simpson to G&C, 1 March 1842, HBRS 29, 128, 130, 131; Simpson, *Narrative*, Vol. 2, 127.

55 McLoughlin to Pelly, 5 June 1837, HBCA B.223/b/17, fo. 14; 'The Honourable Hudson's Bay Company in Account Current with George Pelly,' HBCA B.223/b/12, fos. 36-9, 48d-49;

McLoughlin to Simpson, 5 January 1836, HBCA B.223/b/15, fo. 67; McLoughlin to Pelly, 17 November 1836, HBCA B.223/b/12, fo. 52; Pelly and Allan to G&C, 10 August 1843, HBCA A.11/62, fo. 5.

56　'Account of Sales at the Sandwich Islands during four Months of Outfit 1844,' HBCA A.11/62, fo. 6; 'Statement of Sales on the Sandwich Islands as Part of Outfit 1844,' HBCA A.11/62, fo. 17; Pelly to William Smith, 30 April 1839, HBCA A.11/61, fo. 52. I have deleted half dollars from these figures.

57　Dugald Mactavish to Hargrave, 2 April 1842, Hargrave Papers, NAC.

58　Henry A. Price to Lewis F. Linn, 1 May 1842, quoted in *OHQ* 1,3 (September 1900): 329-30; Lomax, 'Tropical Trade Route,' 11; The *Polynesian* is quoted in St. Clair, 'Beaver in Hawaii,' 42; Spoehr, 'Fur Traders,' 31.

59　Farnham, *Travels in the Great Western Prairies*, Vol. 2, 258; Wilbur, *Duflot de Mofras' Travels*, Vol. 2, 88. For a voyage to Oahu in 1841, see Farnham, *Travels in the Californias*, 1-36.

60　From 1825-46, California was governed from Mexico; 1835-45 was the 'Decade of Revolution' in California, with nine governors in fifteen years. The 'Mexican War' between the US and Mexico lasted from 1846-8. Smith, *James Douglas in California*, xv-xvii; F.W. Beechey, *Narrative of a Voyage to the Pacific Beering's Strait ... in the Years 1825, 26, 27, 28* (London: Henry Colburn and Richard Bentley 1831), Vol. 1, 371. See also Gough, *The Royal Navy*, 41-5.

61　Smith, *James Douglas in California*, 29, 35-6; Gibson, *Otter Skins*, 19, 259-60; Forbes, *California*, 271-80, 284; Wilbur, *Duflot de Mofras' Travels*, Vol. 1, 255-9; Herman Leader, 'HBC in California,' *The Beaver* 279 (March 1949): 3-7; Irving, *The Rocky Mountains*, Vol. 2, 138; Simpson, *Narrative*, Vol. 1, 286-7.

62　Forbes, *California*, 264-6; Wilbur, *Duflot de Mofras' Travels*, Vol. 1, 255; Smith, *James Douglas in California*, 29.

63　Beechey, *Narrative*, Vol. 2, 395; Forbes, *California*, 264-5.

64　Richard Henry Dana, *Two Years Before the Mast. A Personal Narrative of Life at Sea* (Harmondsworth, Middlesex: Penguin 1981; first published 1840). On Bryant & Sturgis and the California hide and tallow trade, see Smith, *James Douglas in California*, 21-3 and Gibson, *Otter Skins*, 260; for American impressions of indolence, see Sullivan, *The Travels of Jedediah Smith*, 52 and [Peter H. Burnett], 'Letters of Peter H. Burnett,' *OHQ* 3, 4 (December 1902): 425.

65　Smith, *James Douglas in California*, 33; Simpson, *Narrative*, Vol. 1, 287, 288, 294, 295.

66　Belcher, *Narrative*, Vol. 1, 133; Forbes, *California*, vii, 286; Smith, *James Douglas in California*, 39; Francis to Edward Ermatinger, 4 March 1843, McDonald, *Fur Trade Letters of Francis Ermatinger*, 253; Mactavish to his mother, 14 November 1846, Hargrave papers, NAC.

67　McLoughlin to G&C, 1 September 1826, HBRS 4, 30; A. Simpson to C. O'Gorman, 7 January 1831, HBCA D.4/125, fos. 103-4. A. Simpson is cited in George Simpson to G&C, 18 July 1831, HBCA A.12/1, fos. 378-9; see also McLoughin to McDonald, 4 June 1831, HBCA B.223/b/7, fo. 2; Simpson, *Narrative*, Vol. 1, 364.

68　McLoughlin to G&C, 20 October 1831, HBRS 4, 231; Finlayson to Smith, 11 January 1834, HBCA B.223/b/9, fos. 50-1.

69　See Smith, *James Douglas in California*, 38; Russell M. Posner, 'A British Consular Agent in California: The Reports of James A. Forbes, 1843-1846,' *Southern California Quarterly* 53, 2 (June 1971): 101-12; Bancroft, *History of California*, Vol. 3, 743, cited in Leader, 'A Voyage from the Columbia to California; Wilbur, *Duflot de Mofras' Travels*, Vol. 1, 222.

70　Simpson to G&C, 21 July 1834, HBCA D.4/100, fos. 21-2.

71　McLoughlin gave Langtry letters of introduction, written five years earlier, by the G&C, to British merchants John Yates of Lima and Walford & Green of Valparaiso. McLoughlin to Captain Langtry, May 1834, HBCA B.223/b/10, fos. 19-21.

72　McLoughlin to G&C, 28 May 1834, HBRS 4, 120-5; McLoughlin to G&C, 18 November 1834, ibid., 125.

73　McLoughlin to McNeill, 30 July 1834, HBCA B.223/b/10, fo. 27; McLoughlin to G&C, 18 November 1834, HBRS 4, 125, 129; for the *Dryad* cargo, see HBCA A.11/61, fo. 4; G&C to McLoughlin, 8 December 1835, HBCA B.223/c/1, fo. 46.

74   Pelly to Smith, 14 March 1837, HBCA A.11/61, fo. 24; McLoughlin to Rae, 17 August 1837, HBCA B.223/b/17; McLoughlin to Pelly, 19 August 1837, HBCA B.223/b/17, fo. 29d; McLoughlin to Simpson, Chief Factors and Traders, 30 August 1837, HBCA B.223/b/17, fo. 31d; bill of lading enclosed in Pelly to Smith, 22 December 1838, HBCA A.11/61, fo. 48; bill of lading, HBCA B.191/z/1, fo. 66; Fort Vancouver Account Book, 1836-1860, HBCA B.223/d/212.

75   Forbes, *California*, 282.

76   The company, Tolmie recalled, 'had established an agency at Yerba Buena for the purchase of hides and tallow and the sale of European commodities.' Tolmie, 'History of Puget Sound and the North West Coast,' 8.

77   Oliver, *The Canadian North-West*, Vol. 2, 786; Alexander Simpson to McLoughlin, 1 October 1840, HBRS 6, 243-4; Smith, *James Douglas in California*, 27; Blake, 'The Hudson's Bay Company in San Francisco,' 110.

78   Alex Simpson to McLoughlin, 1 October 1840, HBRS 6, 244; Smith, *James Douglas in California*, xxii; Blake, 'The Hudson's Bay Company in San Francisco,' 98-9, 106 n. 6; Lansford Hastings, *The Emigrants' Guide to Oregon and California* (Princeton: Princeton University Press 1932; first published 1845), 109; Wilbur, *Duflot de Mofras' Travels*, Vol. 1, 227; Forbes, *California*, 166; Farnham, *Travels in the Californias*, 354-5.

79   Smith, *James Douglas in California*, xviii-xxiii, 1, 12, 27; Simpson to G&C, 25 November 1841, HBRS 29, 77; McLoughlin to Douglas, 27 November 1840, HBCA B.223/b/27, fo. 108. See also Donald Sage, 'Swirl of Nations – The HBC on the Pacific Coast in the Mid Nineteenth Century,' *The Beaver* (Spring 1963): 36.

80   Blake, 'The Hudson's Bay Company in San Francisco,' 103; Simpson, *Narrative*, Vol. 1, 304; Douglas to Juan B. Alvarado, Governor General of Upper and Lower California, 11 January 1841, and Alvarado to Douglas, 13 January 1841, quoted in Walter N. Sage, *Sir James Douglas and British Columbia* (Toronto: University of Toronto Press 1930), 106-8; Smith, *James Douglas in California*, 11, 27.

81   Douglas to McLoughlin, 23 March 1841, HBRS 6, 252-3.

82   Blake, 'The Hudson's Bay Company in San Francisco,' (Part 1), 99, 101, 108 n. 21; Sage, 'Swirl of Nations'; H.H. Bancroft, *History of California*, Vol. 4, 667-8, 710; Simpson to G&C, 1 March 1842, HBRS 29, 114; Simpson to Rae, 12 January 1842, HBRS 7, 76 n. 1; Smith, *James Douglas in California*, 16; Wilbur, *Duflot de Mofras' Travels*, Vol. 1, 227.

83   Mactavish to Hargrave, 2 April 1842, Glazebrook, *Hargrave Correspondence*, 383-4; Rae to William Smith, 1 November 1842, in Blake, 'The Hudson's Bay Company in San Francisco,' 255 n. 62; see also G&C to McLoughlin, 27 September 1843, HBRS 6, 314.

84   Wilbur, *Duflot de Mofras' Travels*, Vol. 1, 261, 256, 121.

85   Henry A. Price to Lewis F. Linn, 1 May 1842, *OHQ* 1, 3 (September 1900): 329-30.

86   Hastings, *The Emigrants' Guide*, 109.

87   Simpson, *Narrative*, Vol. 1, 327.

88   Ibid., 284; G&C to McLoughlin, 21 December 1842, HBRS 6, 298; McLoughlin to Rae, 29 May 1843, HBCA B.341/c/1, fo. 2.

89   Blake, 'The Hudson's Bay Company in San Francisco,' 253; Thomas Lowe to John F. Kennedy, 5 June 1852, in Thomas Lowe, Letters Outward 1852-1859, BCARS.

90   Davidson, 'Relations of the Hudson's Bay Company with the Russian American Company,' 39-43; John S. Galbraith, 'The Early History of the Puget's Sound Agricultural Company, 1838-43,' *OHQ* 55, 3 (September 1954): 234-5; 'New Archangel – Feeding the Population,' in Pierce, *Russian America*, 6

91   Finlayson to McLoughlin, 29 September 1836, HBCA B.223/b/12, fos. 17d-23d; also HBRS 4. One of the Honolulu merchants who supplied the Russians was William French. See Lamb, 'The Advent of the "Beaver,"' 175-6. The Russians had complained of the American liquor trade as early as 1808: Howay, 'The Introduction of Intoxicating Liquors,' 165.

92   Douglas to G&C, 18 October 1838, HBRS 4, 263; Alice M. Johnson, 'Simpson in Russia,' *The Beaver* 291 (Autumn 1960): 4-12, 11.

93   See HBCA F.29/2, fos. 162-70 for the original agreement of 6 February 1839. See also Innis,

The Fur Trade in Canada, 120, 142, 333; Reginald Saw, 'Treaty with the Russians,' *The Beaver* 289 (December 1948): 30-3; Ormsby, *British Columbia*, 76; Johnson, 'Simpson in Russia,'p. 58; HBRS 7, xi-xvii; Stephen M. Johnson, 'Wrangel and Simpson,' in Judd and Ray, *Old Trails and New Directions*, 207-16; Gibson, 'The Russian Contract.' A *fanega* was 'a dry measure whose capacity varied widely throughout Spain and her colonies. The Californian fanega was roughly 1.6 bushels.' Smith, *James Douglas in California*, 36.

94 Douglas, 'Diary of a Trip to the Northwest Coast,' 21; Davidson, 'Relations of the Hudson's Bay Company with the Russian American Company,' 49. See also [J.W. McKay], 'Fort Simpson in the Forties,' in W.W. Walkem, *Stories of Early British Columbia* (Vancouver: News-Advertiser 1914), 78.

CHAPTER 8: Columbia Country Produce

1 Francis (Thompson's River) to Edward Ermatinger, 4 March 1830, McDonald, *Fur Trade Letters of Francis Ermatinger*, 133.
2 Thomas Simpson, *Narrative*, 17-18.
3 McLoughlin, 'Fort Vancouver Report,' 1826-7, HBRS 10, 236.
4 Dugald Mactavish to William Mactavish, 19 October 1839, Glazebrook, *Hargrave Correspondence*, 307; Belcher, *Narrative*, Vol. 1, 294.
5 Louis R. Caywood, 'Excavating Fort Vancouver,' *The Beaver* 278 (March 1948): 4-7; Wilbur, *Duflot de Mofras' Travels*, Vol. 2, 98; 'Inventory of Goods Fort Vancouver Depot Spring 1844,' HBCA B.223/d/127, fo. 158; George Verne Blue, ed., 'Green's Missionary Report on Oregon, 1829,' *OHQ* 30, 3 (September 1929): 264. Roberts asserted that the HBC made 'whisky' from barley at its three stills at Fort Vancouver. Roberts, 'Letters to Mrs. F.F. Victor,' 197. McLoughlin to G&C, 31 October 1837, HBRS 4, 208.
6 Hastings, *The Emigrants' Guide*, 51.
7 Ogden, *Traits*, 213-18. For a description of the HBC's imports to Fort Vancouver, see Slacum, 'Slacum's Report,' 186-7; Wilbur, *Duflot de Mofras' Travels*, Vol. 2, 99; McKay, 'The Fur Trading System,' 24.
8 Farnham, *Travels in the Great Western Prairies*, Vol. 2, 266.
9 Douglas to G&C, 18 October 1838, HBRS 4, 260; Simpson, *Narrative* Vol. 1, 246; Landerholm, *Notices & Voyages*, 15 [January 1840]; Simpson to Hargrave, 1 July 1843, Hargrave Papers, NAC. On working hours and daily life, see also McKay, 'The Fur Trading System,' 22-3.
10 McLoughlin to Pambrun, September 1835, HBCA B.223/b/11, fo. 31.
11 Simpson, *Narrative*, Vol. 1, 245.Hastings, *The Emigrants' Guide*, 63. 'The larger ships usually leave London toward the end of April and December; reaching the Columbia River approximately four and one-half months later. Here they unload part of their cargo and take on wheat, timber, and planks, which they transport to the Hawaiian Islands, returning before bad weather sets in to Fort Langley on Puget Sound [*sic*], or to Fort Vancouver where they take on the remainder of their cargo for Europe.' Wilbur, *Duflot de Mofras' Travels*, Vol. 2, 88.
12 Belcher, *Narrative*, Vol. 1, 295.
13 McLoughlin to Simpson, 20 March 1837, HBCA B.223/b/15, fo. 78; the G&C appointed Douglas to 'the principal management of the Establishment of Fort Vancouver and the other Posts &c on the Coast, and of the Trapping Expeditions likewise of the Shipping.' McLoughlin to Douglas, March 1838, HBCA B.223/b/18, fo. 25-7d.
14 Simpson, *Narrative*, Vol. 1, 246; Archibald McKinlay, 'Narrative of a Chief Factor in the Hudson's Bay Company,' ms., 1878, BCARS. McKinlay was in the Columbia Department from as early as 1837.
15 [John Scouler and David Douglas], 'Notices respecting Mr Scouler's and Mr Douglas's recent Voyage to the North West Coast of America,' *Edinburgh Journal of Science* 5 (April-October 1826): 378-80, 379.
16 For people coming hundreds of miles, see Wilbur, *Duflot de Mofras' Travels*, Vol. 2, 59; for the use of salmon by the maritime fur traders, Pacific, and North West companies, see Gibson, *Otter Skins*, 205; Corney, *Voyages in the Northern Pacific*; Lamb, ed., *Gabriel Franchère*, 89-90, 100.

17   Dunn, *History of Oregon territory*, 120-1, 128, 264. Between the end of 1834 and the summer of 1836, Dunn was stationed at Fort Vancouver, and at Fort George as 'superintendent.'

18   Wilks, *Journal Kept by David Douglas*, 57; Corney, *Voyages in the Northern Pacific*, 61; Simpson to G&C, 10 March 1825, HBCA A.12/1, fo. 148 and [Burnett], 'Letters,' 421.

19   Simpson, *Narrative*, Vol. 1, 169. See also Townsend, *Narrative*, 252-3.

20   Wilks, *Journal Kept by David Douglas*, 127-8.

21   For the Cascade fishery, see Burnett, 'Letters of Peter H. Burnett,' 421; Simpson, *Narrative*, Vol. 1, 171; Douglas to G&C, 18 October 1838, HBRS 4, 267; 'Columbia District Country Produce Inventories Outfit 1837,' HBCA B.223/d/106, fo. 8; Henry Bridgman Brewster, 'The Log of the Lausanne,' part 3, *OHQ* 29, 4 (December 1928): 361; Elliott, ed., 'The Coming of the White Women,' 177. On the Fort Vancouver fishery, see Roberts, 'Letters to Mrs. F.F. Victor,' 205; Tolmie, 'Utilization of the Indians,' 7. On the Cowlitz fishery, see Douglas to G&C, 18 October 1838, HBRS 4, 264; and on the Willamette fishery, see Tolmie, 8 May 1833, *Journals*, 175.

22   Keith to Perkins, 13 April 1821, Keith Papers; Galbraith, *Hudson's Bay Company*, 183; Dunn, *History of Oregon territory*, 113-14; on Fort George as Fort Vancouver's 'outpost,' see Douglas to Chief Factors, Chief Traders, Northern Department, 6 September 1839, HBCA B.223/b/24, fo. 37d; Francis to Edward Ermatinger, 11 March 1833, McDonald, *Fur Trade Letters of Francis Ermatinger*, 163; Belcher, *Narrative*, Vol. 1, 289; on Birnie's duties as a pilot, see Townsend, *Narrative*, 182 and Wilbur, *Duflot de Mofras' Travels*, Vol. 2, 61.

23   Wilbur, *Duflot de Mofras' Travels*, Vol. 2, 62; De Smet, *Letters and Sketches*, 217; Dunn, *History of Oregon territory*, 166.

24   McLoughlin to John Dease, 23 July 1825, HBCA B.223/b/1, fo. 17.

25   Dunn, *History of Oregon territory*, 163-4.

26   Douglas to Birnie, 1 August 1838, HBCA B.223/b/22, fo. 23; HBCA C.7/177, fos. 40, 51; McLoughlin to Kipling, 14 March 1835, HBCA B.223/b/11, fo. 4; McLoughlin to Birnie, 6 July 1832, HBCA B.223/b/8, fos. 8d-9.

27   McLoughlin to Kipling, 30 June 1835, HBCA B.223/b/11, fo. 30; McLoughlin to Kipling, 10 August 1835, HBCA B.223/b/11, fo. 34; McLoughlin to Dunn, 29 August 1835, HBCA B.223/b/11, fo. 29; Douglas to Brotchie, 4 June 1838, HBCA B.223/b/22, fo. 14; Douglas to Birnie, 16 August 1838, HBCA B.223/b/22, fo. 25; Douglas to Humphreys, 8 September 1838, HBCA B.223/b/22, fo. 25; Douglas to Birnie, 29 May 1839, HBCA B.223/b/24, fo.20.

28   Douglas to Birnie, 23 June 1839, HBCA B.223/b/24, fo. 24d; Douglas to Birnie, 2 August 1839, HBCA B.223/b/24, fo. 29d; Douglas to Birnie, 29 August 1839, HBCA B.223/b/24, fo. 33.

29   McLoughlin to Birnie, 3 July 1840, HBCA B.223/b/27, fo. 41; McLoughlin to Birnie, 13 July 1840, HBCA B.223/b/27, fo. 45. In August, McLoughlin sent a man named Michel to Fort George 'in case you require any one to go to Chinook Bay': McLoughlin to Birnie, 3 August 1840, HBCA B.223/b/27, fo. 51; G&C to McLoughlin, 21 December 1842, HBRS 6, 302. For the salmon house at Fort George, see Thomas Vaughan, ed., 'Alexander Lattie's Fort George Journal, 1846,' *OHQ* 64, 3 (September 1963): 223 n. 5.

30   McLoughlin to Blanchette et al., 19 August 1840, HBCA B.223/b/27, fos. 57, 60-8; Nellie B. Pipes, ed., 'Journal of John H. Frost, 1840-43,' part 1, *OHQ* 35, 2 (March 1934): 60-1.

31   Ross, *Adventures*, 94; McLoughlin to G&C, 1 September 1826, HBRS 4, 37.

32   McLoughlin to McMillan, 19 October 1827, HBCA B.223/b/3, fo. 20; McLoughlin to McDonald, 31 March 1828, HBCA B.223/b/4, fo. 2; Simpson to G&C, 1 March 1829, HBRS 10, 75; McLoughlin to Manson, 18 August 1829, HBCA B.223/b/5, fo. 16; McLoughlin to G&C, 11 October 1830, HBRS 4, 88; McLoughlin to G&C, 24 November 1830, HBRS 4, 95.

33   McLoughlin to Charlton, 27 October 1831, HBCA B.223/b/7, fo. 9; HBCA 239/d/491, fo. 56 (1831 barrels were about twice the size of those of 1830); Finlayson to Reid, 25 July 1832, HBCA B.223/b/8, fos.36d-37; Reid to Finlayson, 26 July 1832, HBCA B.223/b/8, fo. 37; McLoughlin to Finlayson, 2 August 1833, HBCA B.223/b/9, fo. 18; Pierce and Hinckley to Finlayson, 4 January 1834, HBCA B.223/b/9, fo. 49.

34   G&C to McLoughlin, 4 December 1833, HBCA search file 'Timber'; G&C to McLoughlin, 8 December 1835, HBCA B.223/c/1, fos. 45d-46.

35 St. Clair, 'Beaver in Hawaii,' 40; James McCook, 'Sir George Simpson in the Hawaiian Islands,' *The Beaver* 307, 3 (Winter 1976): 47; Spoehr, 'Fur Traders,' 50; Simpson, *Narrative*, Vol. 1, 227; Pierce, ed., *Russian America*, 6, 13.

36 Finlayson to McLoughlin, 29 September 1836, HBCA B.223/b/12, fo. 24; St. Clair, 'Beaver in Hawaii,' 40; Douglas to G&C, 18 October 1838, HBRS 4, 267; 'Columbia District Country Produce Inventories Outfit 1837,' HBCA B.223/d/106, fo. 8.

37 Douglas to G&C, 18 October 1838, HBRS 4, 267; Pelly to Smith, 21 March 1840, HBCA A.11/61, fo. 53; McLoughlin to Alexander Simpson, 13 June 1840, HBCA B.223/b/27, fo. 35; McLoughlin to Spalding, 19 June 1840, HBCA B.223/b/27, fo. 36; McLoughlin to Pelly, 15 June 1840, HBCA B.223/b/27, fo. 33; McLoughlin to Pelly, 22 September 1840, HBCA B.223/b/27, fo. 76; HBCA C.7/177, fo. 82d.

38 McLoughlin to G&C, 1 September 1826, HBRS 4, 37; Wyeth to Mess. Joseph Baker & Son, 4 July 1833, Young, *Wyeth Correspondence*, 60; Morison, 'New England and the Opening of the Columbia River Salmon Trade,' 113-16, 130.

39 Wyeth to Mr Henry Hall and Mess. Ticker & Williams, 8 November 1833, Young, *Wyeth Correspondence*, 76.

40 McLoughlin to G&C, 10 January 1838, HBCA A.11/61, fo. 40; Townsend, *Narrative of a Journey*, 185, 219; McLoughlin to Ermatinger, 1 February 1835, Ermatinger Papers, NAC; McLoughlin to G&C, 30 September 1835, HBRS 4, 141; HBRS 4, 165-82; W.G. Rae to Hargrave, March 1836, Glazebrook, *Hargrave Correspondence*, 235; McLoughlin to Simpson, 20 March 1837, HBCA B.223/b/15, fos. 153-4.

41 Dunn, *History of Oregon territory*, 139.

42 McLoughlin to Birnie, 3 July 1840, HBCA B.223/b/27, fo. 41; McLoughlin to Birnie, 3 August 1840, HBCA B.223/b/27, fo. 51; McLoughlin to Governor, Chief Factors and Traders of HBC, 4 September 1840, HBCA B.223/b/27, fo. 38; [McLoughlin], 'John McLoughlin – Statement,' 193-206; Simpson to G&C, 21 July 1843, HBCA A,12/2, fo. 171; Avery Sylvester, 'Voyages of the Pallas and Chenamus, 1843-45,' part 2, *OHQ* 34, 4 (December 1933): 359-71.

43 Simpson to G&C, 25 November 1841, HBRS 29, 79; Simpson to G&C, 21 June 1843, HBCA A.12/2, fo. 171; Pelly and Allan to G&C, 7 August 1844, HBCA A.11/62, fo. 20; [McLoughlin], 'John McLoughlin – Statement,' 193-206; Wilbur, *Duflot de Mofras' Travels*, Vol. 2, 105.

44 Simpson to McLoughlin, 18 May 1842, HBRS 6, 289; G&C to McLoughlin, 27 September 1843, HBRS 6, 305; Pelly and Allan to G&C, 24 February 1844, HBCA A.11/62, fo. 15. London fishmongers, according to George Roberts, 'wanted something for the eye as well as the palate.' They wanted salmon with the head and backbone intact, '& the commonality would look with distrust upon salmon at a low price.' Roberts, 'Letters to Mrs. F.F. Victor,' 197.

45 Pelly and Allan to McLoughlin, 12 January 1843, HBCA B.223/b/30, fos. 18-19.

46 Pelly and Allan to G&C, 24 February 1844, HBCA A.11/62, fo. 15; Pelly and Allan to G&C, 24 September 1844, HBCA A.11/62, fos. 24-24d; Pelly and Allan to G&C, 5 March 1845, HBCA A.11/62, fos. 36-37d. McLoughlin had asked them to invest the proceeds of the Boston sale in tea, rice, or tobacco: McLoughlin to Pelly and Allan, 1 July 1844, HBCA B.223/b/31, fos. 113d-114. For later exports to Hawaii, see Richard Mackie, 'Colonial Land, Indian Labour, and Company Capital: The Economy of Vancouver Island, 1849-1858,' Master's thesis, University of Victoria, 1984, 26-41.

47 The G&C sent wheatmeal to Fort George in 1822 because they could not obtain Indian corn in London. G&C to Haldane and Cameron, 4 September 1822, HBRS 3, 335.

48 Neil M. Howison, 'Report of Lieutenant Neil M. Howison on Oregon 1846,' *OHQ* 14, 1 (March 1913): 51.

49 Douglas to Simpson, 18 March 1838, HBRS 4, 284.

50 Finlayson to McLoughlin, 2 August 1832, HBCA B.223/b/8, fo. 41d; McLoughlin to Ogden, 5 October 1832, HBRS 4, 314; HBCA C.7/177, fo. 36d; Pelly to McLoughlin, 21 March 1835, HBCA B.223/b/11, fo. 119; HBCA B.191/z/fo. 37; HBCA A.11/61, fo. 8; McLoughlin to Pelly, 17 June 1836, HBCA B.223/b/12, fo. 44; Finlayson to McLoughlin, 29 September 1836, HBRS 4; Pelly to Governor and Committee, 24 April 1838, HBCA A.11/61, fo. 38; Pelly to Smith, 22 December 1838, HBCA D.11/61, fo. 48; Pelly to Smith, 30 April 1839, HBCA A.11/61, fo.

51. In 1834, the grist and threshing mills were horse-powered: Townsend, *Narrative*, 171. A horse and an ox seem to have taken turns operating this primitive mill. 'It goes by horse power,' wrote Narcissa Whitman, 'but better so than no bread, or to grind by hand.' Elliott, ed., 'The Coming of the White Women,' 182. See also Townsend, *Narrative*, 171, and Powell, 'Hall Jackson Kelly,' 290.

51 Douglas to G&C, 18 October 1838, HBRS 4, 260, 265; Rich, *HBC*, Vol. 3, 693; Caywood, 'Excavating Fort Vancouver,' 4-7; Leonard Wiley, 'Mill Creek Site of Grist Mill of Hudson's Bay Company,' *OHQ* 43, 3 (September 1942): 282-5; Simpson, *Narrative*, Vol. 1, 171; Farnham to Poinsett, 4 January 1840, in Farnham, Correspondence Outward, BCARS; Farnham, *Travels in the Great Western Prairies*, Vol. 2, 266.

52 Douglas to G&C, 18 October 1838, HBRS 4, 241; Modeste Demers, 'General Notes on the Territory of the Columbia,' 13 February 1844, quoted in Landerholm, *Notices & Voyages*, 179; Simpson to G&C, 20 June 1844, HBCA A.11/2, fo. 380; Gibson, *Farming the Frontier*, 189; Mackie, 'The Colonization of Vancouver Island,' 37. On the growth of the French settlement at Willamette and its importance as a source of wheat, see Dunn, *History of Oregon territory*, 173-201; on the absence of coin and use of furs and wheat as currency, see H.S. Lyman, [ed.], 'Reminiscences of F.X. Matthieu,' *OHQ* 1, 1 (March 1900): 73-104, 102.

53 Finlayson to McLoughlin, 2 August 1832, HBCA B.223/b/8, fo. 41d; Pelly to McLoughlin, 21 March 1835, HBCA B.223/b/11, fo. 119; HBCA C.7/177, fo. 44; Pelly to Smith, 5 December 1835, HBCA A.11/61, fo. 1; HBRS 4, 152 n. 1; Finlayson to McLoughlin, 29 September 1836, HBRS 4; Pelly to Smith, 9 December 1838, HBCA D.11/61, fo. 48; Pelly to Smith, 30 April 1839, HBCA A.11/61, fo. 51; Simpson, *Narrative*, Vol. 1, 174; McDonald, *Fur Trade Letters of Francis Ermatinger*, 226. For the dairy, see also Elliott, ed., 'Extracts from the Emmons Journal,' 272-3, and Elliott, ed., 'The Coming of the White Women,' 182.

54 Lamb, ed., *Gabriel Franchère*, 89, 96; James Keith to Colonel Perkins, 13 April 1821, Keith Papers; Gibson, *Farming the Frontier*, 38; Finlayson to McLoughlin, 2 August 1832, HBCA B.223/b/8, fo. 41d; HBCA C.7/177, fo. 67; Belcher, *Narrative*, 302.

55 Wilks, *Journal Kept by David Douglas*, 103; Douglas quoted in William Morwood, *Traveller in a Vanished Landscape. The Life and Times of David Douglas* (London: Gentry Books 1973), 56; Finlayson, 'Trip Across to the Columbia 183'; Tolmie is quoted in Cole, *Exile in the Wilderness*, 168. On Gairdner, see Harvey, 'Meredith Gairdner.'

56 Barry M. Gough, 'Forests and Sea Power: A Vancouver Island Economy, 1778-1875,' *Journal of Forest History* 32 (1988): 117-24; Bryant & Sturgis to Harris, 30 May 1822, quoted in Gibson, *Otter Skins*, 243; Howay, 'The Brig Owhyhee in the Columbia, 1827,' 325-7. Lumber, the product of sawmills, included boards, planks, deals, rafters, spars, masts, shingles, and logs, but company employees, following the English usage, at first called most of these 'timber' until they adopted the Sandwich Islands usage. Deals, in England, were softwood boards or planks, usually of fir or pine. Graeme Wynn, *Timber Colony: A Historical Geography of Early Nineteenth Century New Brunswick* (Toronto: University of Toronto Press 1981), 3 n.

57 G&C to McLoughlin, 20 September 1826, 'Letterbook 621,' in HBCA search file 'Timber'; Aemilius Simpson to McLoughlin, 22 September 1828, quoted in Gibson, *Otter Skins*, 242; Green, *Journal of a Tour*, 61.

58 McLoughlin to McDonald, 31 March 1828, HBCA B.223/b/4, fo. 2; McLoughlin to Aemilius Simpson, 13 November 1827, HBCA B.223/b/3, fo. 23; Donald H. Clark, 'Sawmill on the Columbia,' *The Beaver* (June 1950): 42-4; Thomas K. Fleming, 'First Lumber Exports from the Pacific Coast,' *BCHN* 28, 2 (Spring 1995): 25-7, 40. Slacum, 'Slacum's Report,' 21.

59 McLoughlin to G&C, 14 July 1828, HBRS 4, 60, 62; Francis to Edward Ermatinger, 14 March 1829, McDonald, *Fur Trade Letters of Francis Ermatinger*, 121; Townsend, *Narrative of a Journey*, 171; Howay, 'The Brig Owhyhee in the Columbia, 1829-30,' 15; Simpson to G&C, 1 March 1829, HBRS 10, 84; St. Clair, 'Beaver in Hawaii,' 42; Spoehr, 'Fur Traders,' 48-9; 'List of men at Fort Vancouver 21st March 1833,' HBCA B.223/b/9, fo. 5; Simpson to G&C, 1 March 1829, HBRS 10, 84.

60 Douglas, 'Journal of a Journey from Fort Vancouver to York Factory and back 1835,' ms., BCARS; Clark, 'Sawmill on the Columbia,' 43; McLoughlin to G&C, 31 October 1837,

HBRS 4, 204; McLoughlin to Douglas, March 1838, HBCA B.223/b/18, fo. 25d. See also Elliott, ed., 'The Coming of the White Women,' 179, and Slacum, 'Slacum's Report,' 185.

61   McLoughlin to G&C, 14 July 1828, HBRS 4, 60, 62; Simpson to G&C, 1 March 1829, HBRS 10, 75, 84.

62   McLoughlin to G&C, 28 May 1834, HBRS 4, 120-5; Simpson to G&C, 26 August 1830, HBCA D.4/97, fo. 39.

63   Simpson to G&C, 1 March 1829, HBRS 10, 87.

64   G&C to McLoughlin, 28 October 1829, HBRS 4, 120 n. 1; see also Northern Council Minutes, July 1830, HBRS 3, 263.

65   J.E. Harriott to McLeod, 25 February 1831, McLeod Papers, NAC; McLoughlin to G&C, 11 October 1830, HBRS 4, 88; McLoughlin to G&C, 24 November 1830, HBRS 4, 95; McLoughlin to McDonald, 4 June 1831, HBCA B.223/b/7, fos. 1-2; Wilbur, *Duflot de Mofras' Travels*, Vol. 1, 259.

66   Manley Hopkins, *Hawaii: the Past, Present, and Future of its Island-Kingdom* ... (London: Longman, Green, Longman, and Roberts 1862), 34. Sandalwood 'has been nearly exhausted.' Simpson, *Narrative*, Vol. 2, 128; Spoehr, 'Fur Traders,' 48.

67   Belcher, *Narrative*, Vol. 1, 97. On this mill, see also Gibson, *Otter Skins*, 242.

68   Simpson to G&C, 1 March 1829, HBRS 10, 110; McLoughlin to G&C, 5 August 1829, HBRS 4, 76-7; McLoughlin to McLeod, 1 February 1830, McLeod Papers, NAC; McLoughlin to G&C, 11 October 1830, HBRS 4, 93; Charlton to McLoughlin, 27 January 1831, HBCA D.4/125, fos. 17d-19; McLoughlin to Charlton, 18 November 1830, HBCA B.223/b/6, fos. 21-2. On this first shipment to Oahu, see also Blue, ed., 'Green's Missionary Report,' 264-5.

69   Charlton to McLoughlin, 27 January 1831, HBCA D.4/125, fos. 17d-19.

70   McLoughlin to Simpson, 16 March 1831, HBRS 4, 226; Simpson to G&C, 18 July 1831, HBCA A.12/1, fo. 381; McLoughlin to Charlton, June 1832, HBCA B.223/b/8, fo. 5. Ibid.

71   Finlayson to McLoughlin, 2 August 1832, HBCA B.223/b/8, fo. 40d.

72   York Factory, Country Produce Account Books, 1828-36, HBCA 239/d/491, fos. 44, 56, 67, 68, 80; HBCA C.7/177, fos. 27d, 38d, 44d; Finlayson to Smith, 11 January 1834, HBCA B.223/b/9, fo. 52; Finlayson to Messrs Pierce and Hinckley, 17 January 1834, HBCA B.223/b/9, fo. 53; HBCA C.7/177, fo. 36d; McLoughlin to Pelly, 18 November 1834, HBCA B.223/b/11, fo. 72; HBCA B.191/z/1, fo. 37; McLoughlin to Kipling, 14 September 1835, HBCA B.223/b/11, fo. 46; HBRS 4, 152 n 1; HBCA A.11/61, fos. 2, 8, 18; McLoughlin to Work, 17 December 1834, HBCA B.223/b/10, fo. 81.

73   McLoughlin to Pelly, 14 March 1835, HBCA B.223/b/11, fos. 1-3.

74   Pelly to McLoughlin, 21 March 1835, HBCA B.223/b/11, fos. 116-20; Fred Wilbur Powell, 'Hall Jackson Kelley. Appendix,' *OHQ* 18, 4 (December 1917): 292.

75   Pelly to McLoughlin, 20 January 1836, HBCA B.223/b/11, fo. 125.

76   McLoughlin to G&C, 18 November 1834, HBRS 4, 124.

77   McLoughlin to Pelly, 12 October 1835, HBCA B.223/b/11, fo. 74; G&C to McLoughlin, 8 December 1835, HBCA B.223/c/1, fos. 45d-46.

78   Tim Ball, 'Timber: Adventurers at the Bay Struggled to Stay Warm,' *The Beaver* 67, 2 (March 1987): 45-56; David R. Dyck, 'The Company Diversifies. Loggers at Moose Factory,' *The Beaver* 77, 1 (February-March 1991): 29-34. See also Elaine Allan Mitchell, *Fort Timiskaming and the Fur Trade* (Toronto: University of Toronto Press 1977), 63; G&C to Williams and Simpson, 29 May 1822; Simpson to G&C, 25 August 1822, HBRS 3, 322, 374.

79   G&C to J.G. McTavish (Moose Factory), 4 March 1835; 'G&C to Jo. Brown, 21 October 1835, L.B. 661; 'G&C to J. Abernethy & Co, 3 February 1836 and G&C to Douglas, 15 November 1837, all paraphrased in HBCA search file, 'Timber.'

80   McLoughlin to Ermatinger, 1 February 1836, Ermatinger Papers, NAC; McLoughlin to Simpson, 4 April 1836, HBCA B.223/b/12, fo. 28; Pelly to Smith, 2 October 1836, HBCA A.11/61, fo. 14; McLoughlin to Simpson, 5 January 1836, HBCA B.223/b/15, fo. 67. On French's lumber trade at Sitka see Finlayson to McLoughlin, 29 September 1836, HBCA B.223/b/12, fo. 24; McLoughlin to Pelly, 10 January 1838, HBCA B.223/b/18, fo. 11. 'I do not wish to exact unreasonable prices, but I may expect reasonable profits, as all branches of business to be

inducted and continued successfully must become profitable in a less or more degree to the parties interested therein': McLoughlin to Pelly, 17 June 1836, HBCA B.223/b/12, fos. 42-42d;

81   Pelly to Smith, 1 January 1837, HBCA A.11/61, fo. 20; HBCA C.7/177, fos. 20, 54d; Fort Vancouver, [Country Produce], HBCA B.223/d/94; 'Columbia District Country Produce Inventories Outfit 1837,' HBCA B.223/d/106, fo. 8; *Sandwich Islands Gazette*, 5 August 1837, quoted in St. Clair, 'Beaver in Hawaii,' 40.

82   McLoughlin to Pelly, 17 June 1836, HBCA B.223/b/12, fos. 42-42d; McLoughlin to G&C, 9 April 1836, HBRS 4, 148; McLoughlin to R.F. Budge, 8 April 1836, HBCA B.223/b/15, fos. 8-9; McLoughlin to Simpson, 4 April 1836, HBCA B.223/b/12, fo. 28, 30.

83   McLoughlin to Eales, 8 April 1836, HBCA B.223/b/15, fos. 9-11; McLoughlin to Simpson, Chief Factors, Chief Traders, 30 August 1837, HBCA B.223/b/17, fo. 32; Pelly to Smith, 2 October 1836, HBCA A.11/61, fos. 14-15; G&C to Simpson, 15 February 1837, HBCA D.5/4, fo. 238d.

84   Pelly to Douglas, 30 April 1830, cited in Douglas to G&C, 18 October 1838, HBRS 4, 267; Pelly to G&C, 24 April 1838, HBCA A.11/61, fo. 38.

85   Pelly to Smith, 26 July 1838, HBCA A.11/61, fo. 43.

86   Pelly to Smith, 22 December 1838, HBCA A.11/61, fo. 48; Pelly to Smith, 30 April 1839, HBCA A.11/61, fos. 51-2; McLoughlin to Pelly, 11 November 1839, HBCA B.223/b/24, fo. 53d.

87   Douglas to G&C, 18 October 1838, HBRS 4, 259-60; 'Inventory of Goods Fort Vancouver Depot Spring 1844,' HBCA B.223/d/127, fo. 158; Douglas to Simpson, 18 March 1838, HBRS 4, 285.

88   Wilbur, *Duflot de Mofras' Travels*, Vol. 2, 99; Farnham, *Travels in the Great Western Prairies*, Vol. 2, 266; Charles Wilkes, *Narrative of the United States Exploring Expedition During the Years 1838, 1839, 1840, 1841 and 1842*, 5 Vols. (London: Wiley and Putnam 1845); Dunn, *History of Oregon territory*, 153; Farnham to Poinsett, 4 January 1840, in Farnham, Correspondence Outward. See also Elliott, ed., 'Extracts from the Emmons Journal,' 268, and Roberts, 'Letters to Mrs. F.F. Victor,' 206.

89   Douglas to G&C, 18 October 1838, HBRS 4, 259-60; Douglas to Simpson, 18 March 1838, HBRS 4, 285; Douglas to Pelly, 24 June 1839, HBCA B.223/b/24, fos. 21d, 22d-23; Pelly to Smith, 21 March 1840, HBCA A.11/61, fos. 53-6; Farnham to Poinsett, 4 January 1840, in Farnham, Correspondence Outward.

90   Pelly to Smith, 21 March 1840, HBCA A.11/61, fos. 53-4; McLoughlin to Pelly, 19 May 1840, HBCA B.223/b/27, fo. 19; McLoughlin to Pelly, 15 June 1840, HBCA B.223/b/27, fo. 33; HBCA C.7/177, fos. 77d, 82d; McLoughlin to Pelly and Alexander Simpson, 21 November 1840, HBCA B.223/b/27, fo. 105.

91   Simpson to G&C, 25 November 1841, HBRS 29, 87; Simpson to McLoughlin, 18 May 1842, HBRS 6, 290; G&C to McLoughlin, 27 September 1843, HBRS 6, 305.

92   Pelly and Allan to McLoughlin, 22 March 1843, HBCA B.223/b/30, fo. 21d; Clark, 'Sawmill on the Columbia,' 44.

93   Pelly and Allan to G&C, 28 October 1843, HBCA A.11/62, fo. 6.

94   See Mackie, 'Colonial Land, Indian Labour, and Company Capital.'

95   Simpson to G&C, 25 November 1841, HBRS 29, 78-9; Clark, 'Sawmill on the Columbia,' 43; Dugald Mactavish to Hargrave, 2 April 1842, Hargrave Papers, NAC.

96   Wilkes and Holmes are cited in Gibson, *Farming the Frontier*, 199, 200. Indian Trade profits declined from £3,295 in 1836, to £1,985 in 1837, to £1,187 in 1842, and to £2,274 in 1843; sale shop profits increased from £1,665 in 1836, to £1,613 in 1837, to £3,838 in 1842, and to £3,140 in 1843; the depot went from a £1,291 profit in 1836, to a loss in 1837 of £1,217, to a loss of £1,213 in 1842, to a loss in 1843 of £1,006. Fort Vancouver, Accounts Current, Outfit 1833, HBCA B.223/d/56; HBRS 4, 286; HBCA B.223/b/31, fos. 149a-149b; McLoughlin to Simpson, 20 March 1845, HBCA B.223/b/32, fo. 93.

CHAPTER 9: Beyond the Mere Traffic in Peltries

1   McDonald to McLeod, 15 January 1832, McLeod Papers, NAC.

2   McMillan to John McLeod, 21 January 1828, McLeod Papers, NAC; Simpson to G&C, 10 July 1828, HBCA D.4/92, fos. 66-7.

3   Simpson, *Narrative*, Vol. 1, 183, 244.

4   Simpson to G&C, 1 March 1829, HBRS 10, 42.

5   McDonald to Governor and Council, Northern Department, 25 February 1830, HBCA
     D.4/123, fos. 66d-72. The fort commanded, in trade, a 'vast extent of sea line.' Malcolm
     McLeod, *Peace River. A Canoe Voyage from Hudson's Bay to Pacific, by the late Sir George Simp-
     son; (Governor, Hon. Hudson's Bay Company) in 1828 Journal of the Late Chief Factor, Archibald
     McDonald (Hon. Hudson's Bay Company), who accompanied him* (Ottawa: J. Davie & Son,
     1872), 108. Named by Vancouver in 1792, the Gulf was renamed the Strait of Georgia by
     Captain Richards in 1865. Walbran, *British Columbia Coast Names*, 204-5.

6   McDonald, '1831,' quoted in Gibson, *Farming the Frontier*, 50; McDonald to Governor and
     Council of Northern Department, 25 February 1830, HBCA D.4/123, fo. 67; same to same,
     10 February 1831, HBCA D.4/125, fo. 114.

7   A. Simpson to C. O'Gorman, 7 January 1831, HBCA D.4/125, fos. 103-4; on the vessels, see
     Robert M. Galois, 'The Native Population of the Fort Langley Region, 1780-1857: A Demo-
     graphic Overview,' report submitted to Parks Canada, 1994, 7.

8   McDonald to McLeod, 15 January 1832, and Douglas to McLeod, 12 March 1832, McLeod
     Papers, NAC.

9   Simpson, *Narrative*, Vol. 1, 184; Hayman, *Robert Brown*, 47, 64.

10   Simpson to G&C, 25 November 1841, HBRS 29, 73-4; Yale to Simpson, 17 December 1845,
     quoted in Robie L. Reid, 'Early Days at Old Fort Langley,' *BCHQ* 1, 2 (April 1937): 79.

11   John Keast Lord, *The Naturalist in Vancouver Island and British Columbia* (London: Richard
     Bentley 1866), Vol. 1, 257. See McLeod, *Peace River*, 107-8; 'Extract from a Memorandum
     by the late James M. Yale, Esquire, formerly of the HBC, relating to the Fraser River
     Salmon,' Anderson, *The Dominion of the West*, Appendix, i; Dee, 'Journal of John Work,' 136;
     Roy I. Jackson, 'Sockeye from the Fraser,' *The Beaver* 283 (March 1953): 18-25.

12   Fur Trade Returns, Columbia District and New Caledonia, 1825-1857, BCARS.

13   On the fort's fishery, see F.L. Howay, 'Fort Langley, Historic HBC Post in British Columbia,'
     The Beaver 2, 2 (November 1921): 2-6, 4; Ormsby, *British Columbia*, 73; Reid, 'Early Days at
     Old Fort Langley,' 79-81; Robie Reid, ed., 'Fort Langley Correspondence: 1831-1858,' *BCHQ*
     3 (July 1937): 187-95; Robie Reid, 'Economic Beginnings in British Columbia,' *Transactions of
     the Royal Society of Canada* 30 (May 1936); Cullen, *Fort Langley*; Mackie, 'Colonial Land,' 24-
     46; Jamie Morton, *Fort Langley: An Overview of the Operations of a Diversified Fur Trade Post
     1848 to 1858 and the Physical Context in 1858* (Ottawa: Canadian Parks Service Microfiche Report
     Series No. 340, 1987); M.P. Shepard and A.W. Argue, *The Commercial Harvest of Salmon in
     British Columbia, 1820-1877* (Vancouver: Department of Fisheries and Oceans, 1989).

14   Aurelia Manson, 'Recollections of School Days,' BCARS; McMillan is cited in Simpson to
     G&C, 10 March 1825, HBCA A.12/1; Homer G. Barnett, *The Coast Salish of British Columbia*
     (Westport, CT: Greenwood Press 1975), 22; Fort Langley Journal, 1829-30, HBCA B.113/a/3,
     30 July 1829.

15   For the company's saltery at the mouth of the Chilliwack, see Cullen, *Fort Langley*, 50, and
     Richard Mayne, *Four Years in British Columbia and Vancouver Island ...* (London: John Mur-
     ray, 1862), 93; for Point Roberts, see Richard Rathbun, *A Review of the Fisheries in Con-
     tiguous Waters of the State of Washington and British Columbia* (Washington, DC: Govern-
     ment Printing Bureau 1899); for *bateaux*, see Anderson, *Handbook and Map*, 5, and Jamie
     Morton, 'Fort Langley Cooper's Shop Furnishing Plan,' unpublished manuscript, Calgary,
     Canadian Parks Service, Curatorial Services, 1988, 14-21.

16   McLoughlin to G&C, 1 September 1826, HBRS 4, 37; James McMillan, Fort Langley Jour-
     nal 1827-8, HBCA B.112/a/1 [27 July-2 August 1827]. 'The savages at one time used a wooden
     hook with a bone barb, but now they get supplied with steel fish-hooks by the Hudson's
     Bay Company.' Lord, *The Naturalist*, 259, 261. '125 Large Cod Hooks' were traded in 1829:
     McDonald to Governor and Council, Northern Department, 25 February 1830, HBCA
     D.4/123, fos. 66d-72.

17   Fort Langley Journal 1827-8 (26 September and 3 October 1827), HBCA B.113/a/1; McMil-
     lan to McLeod, 21 January 1828, McLeod Papers, NAC.

18   McLoughlin to McMillan, 31 March 1828, HBCA B.223/b/4, fo. 2; Fort Langley Journal
      1827-8 (27 September 1828), HBCA B.112/a/1; McMillan, 11 October 1828, quoted in McLeod,
      Peace River, 39.
19   Simpson to G&C, 1 March 1829, HBRS 10, 42; Fort Langley Journal 1829-30 (25 May 1829),
      HBCA B.112/a/3; McLoughlin to McDonald, 17 June 1829, HBCA B.223/b/5, fos. 4-5.
20   McDonald to McLoughlin, 23 October 1829, HBCA B.113/a/3; Fort Langley Journal 1829-
      30, 17-21 August 1829, HBCA B.112/a/3. See also 'Statement of Salmon Trade Fort Langley
      from 10th to 20th Augt 1829,' in McDonald to Governor and Council, Northern Depart-
      ment, 25 February 1830, HBCA D.4/123, fos. 66d-72; Fort Langley Journal 1827-8 (26 Septem-
      ber and 3 October 1827), HBCA B.113/a/1. These axes may have been analogous to nephrite
      celts used in wood-working. See Quentin Mackie, *The Taxonomy of Ground Stone Wood-
      working Tools* [British Archaeological Reports, International Series 613] (Oxford: Tempus
      Reparatum 1995), 4.
21   McDonald to Governor & Council, Northern Department, 25 February 1830, HBCA
      D.4/123, fos. 66-72; McDonald to Governor & Council, Northern Department, 10 Febru-
      ary 1831, HBCA D.4/125, fos. 62-3.
22   McDonald to Governor & Council, Northern Department, 25 February 1830, HBCA
      D.4/123, fos. 66-72; Cullen, *Fort Langley*, 86; Cole, *Exile in the Wilderness*, 148, 250; McLough-
      lin to McDonald, 7 July 1830, HBCA B.223/b/6, fos. 5-6; McDonald to McLoughlin, 14
      November 1829, HBCA B.113/a/3.
23   McDonald to Edward Ermatinger, 20 February 1831, quoted in Ormsby, *British Columbia*, 504
      n. 36; [McLoughlin], 'Mema. for Mr Finlayson,' [n.d., June 1832], HBCA B.223/b/8, fo. 5;
      McDonald to Governor & Council, Northern Department, 10 February 1831, HBCA D.4/125,
      fos. 62-3; J.E. Harriott to McLeod, 25 February 1831, and McDonald to McLeod, 20 Febru-
      ary 1831, McLeod Papers, NAC; McLoughlin to Simpson, 16 March 1831, HBRS 4, 226.
24   McDonald to Governor & Council, Northern Department, 10 February 1831, HBCA D.4/125,
      fos. 62-3; McDonald to McLeod, 20 February 1831, McLeod Papers, NAC.
25   McLoughlin to McDonald, 4 June 1831, HBCA B.223/b/7, fos. 1-2; McDonald to McLeod,
      15 January 1832, McLeod Papers, NAC; HBCA C.7/177, fo. 20 and McLoughlin to A. Simp-
      son, 13 August 1831, HBCA B.223/b/7, fo. 4d.
26   Finlayson to McLoughlin, 2 August 1832, HBCA B.223/b/8, fos. 41-41d. On the Lima mar-
      ket see Finlayson to W.G. Reid, 25 July 1832, HBCA B.223/b/8, fos. 36d-37; on Reid's voy-
      age to Valparaiso & Calloa, see Reid to Finlayson, 26 July 1832, HBCA B.223/b/8, fo. 37
      and Finlayson to Reid, 27 July 1832, HBCA B.223/b/8, fo. 37d.
27   Finlayson to McDonald, 2 August 1832, HBCA B.223/b/8, fo.39; see also Finlayson to Cap-
      tain Grave, 2 August 1832, HBCA B.223/b/8, fo. 38.
28   Charlton to McLoughlin, 21 March 1835, HBCA B.223/b/11, fo. 111. 'The minor streams [on
      the whole coast] swarm during the season with a small variety, known locally to the north-
      ward as the Squag-gan; inferior in richness to the larger fish, and therefore not so well
      adapted for salting, but nevertheless of excellent quality.' Anderson, *The Dominion of the
      West*, 31-2. Gibson confusingly identifies squaggan both as sockeye and as a 'bastard kind of
      salmon.' Gibson, *Otter Skins*, 210-11.
29   McLoughlin to McDonald, 5 July 1832, HBCA B.223/b/8; Tolmie, 10 September 1833, *Jour-
      nals*, 234-5; York Factory, Country Produce, Account Book, 1828-36, HBCA 239/d/491, fo.
      56; McLoughlin to Yale, 5 February 1834, HBCA B.223/b/10, fo. 91. On Fort Vancouver as
      a market see McLoughlin to Yale, 16 May 1834, HBCA B.223/b/10, fo. 14 and Cullen, *Fort
      Langley*, 96.
30   McLoughlin to G&C, 18 November 1834, HBRS 4, 130; McLoughlin to Yale, 14 September
      1834, HBCA B.223/b/10, fo. 45; McLoughlin to Yale, 4 June 1835, HBCA B.223/b/11, fo. 18.
31   Fort Langley Journal, 1829-30, HBCA B.113/a/3.
32   Jamie Morton, 'Over a Barrel. Coopering at Fort Langley,' *Canadian Collector* 20, 6 (Novem-
      ber 1985): 32-33.
33   Eight-gallon kegs were also made for cranberries and butter. Morton, 'Over a Barrel,' 32-3;
      Morton, 'Fort Langley Cooper's Shop,' 11, 13.

34 Morton, 'Fort Langley Cooper's Shop,' 8 n. 26, 9 n. 28, 36, quoting Fort Langley Journal, 5
    April 1830; McLoughlin to Kittson, 6 November 1835, HBCA B.223/b/11, fo. 77; McLoughlin
    to Yale, 6 November 1835, HBCA B.223/b/11, fo. 77; McLoughlin, 'Memorandum for Mr Yale,'
    HBCA B.223/b/24, fos. 59-60; McLoughlin to Yale, 22 February 1840, HBCA B.223/b/24, fos.
    66d-67.
35 The main source is HBCA C.7/177, fos. 44, 51, 54d, 60d, 70d. On the 1835 shipment, see
    also 'Account Sales at Woahoo pr. George Pelly of the Cargoes of the Ganymede & Dryad
    Consigned to him October 1835,' HBRS 4, 152 n. 1; 'The Honorable Hudson's Bay Com-
    pany in Account Current with George Pelly,' 21 July 1836, HBCA B.223/b/12, fos. 48d-49;
    'In Acct with George Pelly' 'By Salmon pr. Dryad,' June 30 [1836], HBCA A.11/61, fo. 18.
    For the 1836-7 shipments, see also Douglas to Simpson, 18 March 1838, HBRS 4, 281;
    Douglas to G&C, 18 October 1838, HBRS 4, 267; 'Columbia District Country Produce
    Inventories Outfit 1837,' HBCA B.223/d/106, fo. 8. Douglas to Yale, 21 November 1838,
    HBCA B.223/b/22, fo. 38.
36 McLoughlin to Yale, 6 March 1836, HBCA B.223/b/18, fo. 22; Douglas to Pelly, 4 December
    1838, HBCA B.223/b/22, fo. 41d; Douglas to Yale, 10 May 1839, HBCA B.223/b/24, fo. 14.
37 'Acct of Property Burnt with Fort Langley' enclosed in Yale to Simpson, 15 April 1840,
    HBCA B.223/b/28, fos. 53-5; Douglas, 'Diary of a Trip to the Northwest Coast,' 1; Yale to
    Simpson, 10 February 1841, James Murray Yale, Correspondence Outward, BCARS;
    McLoughlin to Pelly, 22 September 1840, HBCA B.223/b/27, fo. 76; McLoughlin to Dou-
    glas, 8 May 1840, HBCA B.223/b/27, fos. 13-14; McLoughlin to Yale, 30 May 1840, HBCA
    B.223/b/27, fo. 32; McLoughlin to Yale, 17 October 1840, HBCA B.223/b/27. fo. 92.
38 Simpson to G&C, 25 November 1841, HBRS 29, 73-4.
39 Reid, 'Early Days at Old Fort Langley,' 73, 81-2; Anderson, 'A Compendium of the Province
    of British Columbia,' 7; McLoughlin to G&C, 28 May 1834, HBRS 4, 118-19; McLoughlin
    to Yale, 2 October 1834, HBCA B.223/b/10, fo. 51; Douglas to Yale, 21 November 1838, HBCA
    B.223/b/22, fo. 38; Gibson, Farming the Frontier, 48-52; Simpson to G&C, 25 November 1841,
    HBRS 29, 74; Morton, 'Conspicuous Production,' 10-11, 19-23.
40 McLoughlin to McDonald, 17 June 1829, HBCA B.223/b/5, fo. 4; McDonald to McLough-
    lin, 14 September 1829, in Cole, Exile, 155, 251. See also McDonald to McLoughlin, 14
    November 1829, HBCA B.113/a/3.
41 McDonald to Governor & Council, Northern Department, 25 February 1830, HBCA
    D.4/123, fo. 71.
42 McLoughlin to McDonald, 7 July 1830, HBCA B.223/b/6, fo. 6; McDonald to Governor
    and Council, Northern Department, HBCA D.4/125, fo. 62d; Charlton to McLoughlin, 27
    January 1831, HBCA D.4/125, fos. 17d-1; HBCA C.7/177, fo. 33. In March 1835, Pelly asked
    McLoughlin for '100,000 Shingles about 18 Inches long and well made they would meet a
    Sale at $8 a thousand,' and he offered to send 'a specimen of those in demand here the Rus-
    sians seem very desirous of engrossing the whole Lumber supplies to this place.' Pelly to
    McLoughlin, 21 March 1835, HBCA B.223/b/11, fos. 118, 119.
43 Victor, 'Flotsam and Jetsam of the Pacific,' 38; John Dominis to Josiah Marshall, 14 June 1829,
    quoted in Morison, 'New England and the Opening of the Columbia River Salmon Trade,'
    123; Howay, 'The Brig Owhyhee in the Columbia, 1829-30,' 27; Green, Journal of a Tour, 100.
44 McLoughlin to G&C, 5 August 1829, HBRS 4, 78-9; McDonald to Governor and Coun-
    cil, Northern Department, 25 February 1830, HBCA D.4/123, fos. 66d-72. On the Clallum
    Expedition, see 'Old Memo Book and Journal of Edward Ermatinger,' Ermatinger Papers,
    NAC; Maclachlan, 'The Founding of Fort Langley,' 24-5; Francis Ermatinger, 'Earliest Expe-
    dition Against Puget Sound Indians,' Washington Historical Quarterly 1, 2 (January 1907).
45 Dominis to Marshall, 14 June 1829, quoted in Morison, 'New England and the Opening of the
    Columbia River Salmon Trade,' 123-4; McLoughlin to Heron, 20 July 1833, HBCA B.223/b/9,
    fo. 16; Dunn, History of Oregon territory, 231-2; Simpson to G&C, 1 March 1829, HBRS 10, 80.
46 McDonald to McLeod, 15 January 1832, McLeod Papers, NAC; York Factory, Country Pro-
    duce, Account Book, 1828-36, HBCA 239/d/491, fo. 67; Fort Vancouver, Accounts Current,
    1839-40, HBCA B.223/d/127, fo. 4.

47		Scouler, 'Account of a Voyage to Madeira, Brazil, Juan Fernandez, and the Gallapagos Islands,' 51-73, 70; James Douglas, 'Notes on the Tradition and Population of the Indians of the North West Coast,' c.1840, BCARS. On *haiqua*, see Robert M. Galois and Richard Mackie, 'A Curious Currency. Part 1: Haiqua Shells on the Northwest Coast in the 19th Century,' *The Midden* 22, 4 (October 1990): 1-3; Richard Mackie and Robert M. Galois, 'A Curious Currency. Part 2: The Hudson's Bay Company's Trade in Haiqua Shells,' *The Midden* 22, 5 (December 1990): 6-9; Gibson, *Otter Skins*, 9, 229-30.

48		Simpson, *Narrative*, Vol. 1, 196.

49		Roberts, 'Letters to Mrs. F.F. Victor,' 193.

50		Douglas to Kittson, 1 August 1838, HBCA B.223/b/22, fos. 22-22d; Douglas to Brotchie, 16 August 1838, HBCA B.223/b/22, fo. 24; Douglas to Scarborough, 13 May 1839, HBCA B.223/b/24, fo. 15. For 'Neah or Scarborough Bay,' see W. Colquhoun Grant, 'Description of Vancouver Island, By its First Colonist,' *Journal of the Royal Geographical Society*, Vol. 27 (1857), 268-320.

51		Simpson to G&C, 25 November 1841, HBRS 29, 78; McLoughlin to Heron, 18 June 1833, HBCA B.223/b/9, fo. 12.

52		McLoughlin to Heron, 20 July 1833, HBCA B.223/b/9, fo. 16.

53		Heron to Hargrave, 1 March 1834, Glazebrook, *Hargrave Correspondence*, 137; Douglas to G&C, 18 October 1838, HBRS 4, 261; Blanchet to Mgr. the Bishop of Quebec, 23 February 1841, Landerholm, *Notices & Voyages*, 62; Douglas to Kittson, 20 November 1838, HBCA B.223/b/22, fo. 37d; Douglas to Kittson, 1 August 1838, B.223/b/22, fos. 22-22d; Simpson to G&C, 25 November 1841, HBRS 29, 74.

54		McLoughlin to Governor, Chief Factors and Chief Traders, Northern Department, 29 August 1835, HBCA B.223/b/11, fo. 41; see also McLoughlin to G&C, 28 May 1834, HBRS 4, 119; McLoughlin to Kittson, 5 February 1835, HBCA B.223/b/10, fo. 93. Kittson had just traded a lot of *haiqua*.

55		Tolmie's diary, 12 May 1833, in Tolmie, *Journals*, 178-9. See also Galbraith, *Hudson's Bay Company*, 192-217; Gibson, *Otter Skins*, 79-80, 260-4.

56		Francis to Edward Ermatinger, 13 April 1829, McDonald, *Fur Trade Letters of Francis Ermatinger*, 123-4; Simpson to G&C, 10 August 1832, HBCA A.12/1, fo. 422.

57		'The Oragon Beef & Tallow Company,' in Simpson to G&C, 27 August 1834, HBCA D.4/100, fos. 30-1. See also Rich, *HBC*, Vol. 3, 661-2 and Gibson, *Farming the Frontier*, 79, and L.A. Wrinch, 'The Formation of the Puget's Sound Agricultural Company,' *WHQ* 24 (1933): 3-8

58		Simpson to G&C, 27 August 1834, HBCA D.4/100, fo. 2.

59		G&C to McLoughlin, 10 December 1834, HBRS 4, 137 n. 3.

60		'The present Factors & Traders will incur the expense of making a business, while the profits will go to others.' McLoughlin to G&C, 30 September 1835, HBRS 4, 137; see also Rich, *HBC*, Vol. 3, 661-2.

61		G&C, n.d., quoted in Gibson, *Farming the Frontier*, 86; Galbraith in HBRS 29, xxxvii, n. 2.

62		This is a case of Galbraith in 1973 misconstruing what he wrote in 1957, which was: 'The company's legal advisors expressed the opinion that the governor and committee could not, in conformity with the terms of the charter, invest any of the Company's capital in an association formed for agricultural purposes. Such action, they warned, might invalidate the charter. The dilemma was solved by the expedient of creating a satellite enterprise ...' Galbraith, *Hudson's Bay Company*, 198-9.

63		Rich, *HBC*, Vol. 3, 661-2, 685-7; Dunn, *History of Oregon territory*, 234; Galbraith in HBRS 29, xxxvii; Galbraith, 'The Early History of the Puget's Sound Agricultural Company,' 238.

64		Council Minute, quoted in Barker, *The Financial Papers of Dr. John McLoughlin*, 72-3.

65		Simpson, *Narrative*, Vol. 1, 178 [September 1841]; Tolmie, *Journals*, 195-6; Dunn, *History of Oregon territory*, 214; Kane, *Wanderings*, 142-3; Douglas, 'Diary of a Trip to the Northwest Coast,' 4-10.

66		Francis to Edward Ermatinger, 1 June 1837, McDonald, *Fur Trade Letters of Francis Ermatinger*, 200; Douglas to Chief Factors and Chief Traders, New Caledonia and Thompson's River Districts, 9 November 1838, HBCA B.223/b/22, fo. 36d; Douglas to G&C, 18

October 1838, HBRS 4, 249-51; Kittson, n.d., is quoted in Gibson, *Farming the Frontier*, 17. Hall Kelley claimed the HBC swapped Columbia lumber for California cattle. Powell, 'Hall Jackson Kelley. Appendix,' 292.

67 Simpson to Douglas, 8 January 1852, HBCA A.12/6, fo. 7. 'The Nisqually station answers the double purpose of a fur trading post and a pastoral establishment for the Puget Sound Company.' Simpson to G&C, 25 November 1841, HBRS 29, 98.

68 Simpson, *Narrative*, Vol. 1, 244 [October 1841]; McLoughlin to Douglas, March 1838, HBCA B.223/b/18, fo. 25d; Dunn, *History of Oregon territory*, 214.

69 Simpson to G&C, 20 June 1841, HBRS 29, 31-2; Simpson to G&C, 25 November 1841, ibid., 74; Puget's Sound Agricultural Company, Minute Book, 1839-1858, HBCA F.8/1; Kane, *Wanderings*, 142-3; 'Importation from the Columbia River, 1848,' HBCA A.63/5, fo. 159. See also Roberts, 'Letters to Mrs. F.F. Victor,' 205.

70 Gladman to Edward Ermatinger, 5 August 1842, Ermatinger Papers, NAC; Tod to Hargrave, 15 March 1843, Glazebrook, *Hargrave Correspondence*, 422-3; Puget's Sound Agricultural Company Minute Book, 1839-1858, HBCA F.8/1. On the initial profits and fate of the company, see Tolmie, 'History of Puget Sound and the North West Coast,' 23, and Mackie, 'Colonial Land,' 133-41.

71 McLoughlin to Smith, 7 September 1833, HBRS 4, 115; for Jolifie River and Cowlitz coal, see Tolmie, *Journals*, 186-90, 175; G&C to McLoughlin, 1 February 1834, HBRS 4, 132 n. 2; Simpson, *Narrative*, Vol. 1, 176; Schafer, ed., 'Documents Relative to Warre and Vavasour,' 55. In 1840 McLoughlin sent '1 Barrel Cowlitz Coal' to London: HBCA C.7/177, fo. 81d. 'Molybdenum. Discovery of a new metal,' *Daily Colonist*, 24 October 1882, 3.

72 Walbran, *British Columbia Coast names*, 477. See 'Memo re Coal on Vancouver Island,' Tolmie Papers, BCARS, and J.H. Kemble, 'Coals for the Northwest Coast, 1848-1850,' *BCHQ* 1 (1937): 121-31.

73 'There is in your vicinity a bed of Coal, from the specimen sent here by Dr Tolmie I suppose it would answer for the Steam Boat – Please get all the information you can about it.' McLoughlin to Manson, 15 November 1835, HBCA B.223/b/1, fo. 79. 'We set out for Newitie visited by the Quaquills – where the coals are situated.' Finlayson to McLoughlin, 29 September 1836, HBRS 4, 334-5. See also Lamb, 'The Advent of the "Beaver,"' 178.

74 Dunn, *History of Oregon territory*, 240.

75 Finlayson to McLoughlin, 16 February 1837, cited in McLoughlin to Simpson, 20 March 1837, HBCA B.223/b/15, fo. 147; 'Fort Simpson Outfit 1838 Country produce Remaining on hand Spring 1839,' HBCA B.223/d/127, fo. 3.

76 Douglas, 'Diary of a Trip to the Northwest Coast,' 16, 57-9; Douglas to McLoughlin, 1 October 1840, HBCA B.223/b/28, fos. 77-79; Simpson, *Narrative*, Vol. 1, 234-5.

77 McLoughlin 'To the Officer in charge of the HBCoy Establishment Mill Bank Sound or Fort Simpson.' About 13,000 shingles were produced at Fort Simpson in 1837 for post use, but these were not exported. Gibson, *Otter Skins*, 243.

78 Simpson, *Narrative*, Vol. 2, 183.

79 Simpson to McLoughlin, 18 May 1842, HBRS 6, 290; Simpson, *Narrative*, Vol. 1, 206; Douglas to McLoughlin, 1 October 1840, HBCA B.223/b/28, fo. 94; HBRS 29, 63 n. 4.

CHAPTER 10: Crisis in the Fur Trade

1 John Lee Lewes to Donald Ross, 20 December 1848, Donald Ross Papers, BCARS.

2 Innis, *The Fur Trade in Canada*, 384.

3 For falling beaver returns, see Gibson, *Farming the Frontier*, 201; for falling dividends, see MacKay, *The Honourable Company*, 378.

4 Innis, *The Fur Trade in Canada*, 4; Rich, *HBC*, Vol. 1, 109; for Mackenzie, see Gough, *The Northwest Coast*, 187; for beaver decline during the competitive era 1763-1821, see Ray, *Indians in the Fur Trade*, 117-23, and for the causes and effects in the beaver decline in the American fur trade, see Wishart, *The Fur Trade of the American West*, 31, 161.

5 Tolmie, *Journals*, 178-9 (12 May 1833). McLoughlin refers to the King's Posts on the north shore of the St. Lawrence.

6   Rich, *HBC*, Vol. 3, 495-7. See also Innis, *The Fur Trade in Canada*, 332; Francis and Morantz,
     Partners in Fur, 130-1; Gibson, *Farming the Frontier*, 200, 202; Gibson, *Otter Skins*, 82-3; Ham-
     mond, 'Marketing Wildlife,' 18-23; Robert M. Galois and Arthur J. Ray, 'The Fur Trade in
     the Cordillera, 1821-1857,' *Historical Atlas of Canada*, Vol. 2, Plate 16. Rich argued that profits
     were maintained while fur returns fell because, 'as trade fell off the indents were cut, and
     supplies to the Indians diminished, so that economy kept profits steady even in times of
     falling trade.' This, however, applies to fur trade districts alone. Rich, *HBC*, Vol. 3, 495-6.
7   Ian McTaggart Cowan and Charles J. Guiguet, *The Mammals of British Columbia* (Victo-
     ria: British Columbia Provincial Museum 1956); Douglas Cole and Bradley Lockner, eds.,
     To the Charlottes: George Dawson's 1878 Survey of the Queen Charlotte Islands (Vancouver: UBC
     Press 1993), 3, 107.
8   Wilkes, *Journal Kept by David Douglas*, 140-1 [19 August 1825]; Bishop George Hills diary,
     11 October 1860, Vancouver Theological College; Simpson, *Narrative*, Vol. 1, 184.
9   Innis, *The Fur Trade in Canada*, 332; Hammond, 'Marketing Wildlife,' 18-23; Moodie and
     Kaye, 'Taming and Domesticating Native Animals,' 17.
10   Simpson, *Narrative*, Vol. 1, 222; Ray, 'Some Conservation Schemes.' See also Francis and
     Morantz, *Partners in Fur*, 128-32; Innis, *The Fur Trade in Canada*, 325-7; Morton, *A History*,
     697-8; Ann Carlos, 'The Birth and Death of Predatory Competition in the North Ameri-
     can Fur Trade: 1810-1821,' *Explorations in Economic History* 19 (1982): 156-83.
11   Hammond, 'Marketing Wildlife,' 20; Simpson to G&C, 30 June 1829, quoted in Mitchell,
     Fort Timiskaming, 159; Wallace, *John McLean's Notes*, 353.
12   See Ian McTaggart Cowan, 'The Fur Trade and the Fur Cycle: 1825-1857,' *British Columbia
     Historical Quarterly* 2 (1938): 19-30; Charles Elton, *Voles, Mice and Lemmings: Problems in
     Population Dynamics* (Oxford: Oxford University Press 1942); Anne Morton, 'Charles Elton
     and the Hudson's Bay Company,' *The Beaver* 315, 4 (Spring 1985): 22-9; Hammond, 'Mar-
     keting Wildlife,' 18-19.
13   See Hugh Grant, 'Revenge of the Paris Hat,' *The Beaver* 68, 6 (December 1988-January
     1989): 37-44; G&C to Simpson, 11 March 1845, quoted in Hammond, 'Marketing Wildlife,'
     21. See also Gibson, *Otter Skins*, 83; Morton, *Sir George Simpson*, 189-90; Ross, *The Red River
     Settlement*, 220-1; Ray, 'Some Conservation Schemes,' 67.
14   Tod and Work are cited in Gibson, *Farming the Frontier*, 199; article 75 of Hudson's Bay
     Company, 'Standing Rules & Regulations,' (amendments), Donald Ross Papers, BCARS;
     Ross to Eden Colvile, 5 March 1851, ibid. 'Recollect it is not returns that bring profit so
     much as the price the furs sell for ...' McLoughlin to John McLeod, 1 February 1830,
     McLeod Papers, NAC.
15   Tolmie, *Journals*, 334 [2 January 1839]. On species mix, see Morton, *A History of the Canadian
     West*, 697-8; Harris, ed., *Historical Atlas*, Vol. 1, plate 61; Hammond, 'Marketing Wildlife,' 22.
16   Yale to Simpson, 10 January 1844, quoted in Galois, 'The Native Population of the Fort
     Langley Region,' 41.
17   G&C to McLoughlin, 27 September 1843, HBRS 6, 306. On poor fur sales, see also Gib-
     son, *Otter Skins*, 82.
18   Douglas to Hargrave (private), 10 February 1845, Hargrave Papers, NAC.
19   Simpson to G&C, 1 June 1843, quoted in Arthur L. Throckmorton, *Oregon Argonauts Mer-
     chant Adventurers on the Western Frontier* (Portland: Oregon Historical Society 1961), 40.
20   McDonald to James Douglas, 11 January 1841, quoted in Cole, *Exile in the Wilderness*, 211.
21   Tod [Thompson's River] to Hargrave, 15 March 1843, Glazebrook, *Hargrave Correspondence*,
     422-3; Finlayson to Ross (private), 16 December 1846, Donald Ross Papers, BCARS; John
     Lee Lewes is quoted in Anderson, 'Notes and Comments,' 118; Ross to Simpson (private),
     21 August 1848, Donald Ross Papers, BCARS.
22   Rich, *HBC*, Vol. 3, 495-7. For a complete list of dividends, see MacKay, *The Honourable Com-
     pany*, 374-9; see also Galbraith, *Hudson's Bay Company*, 432-3. On fur auction, demand, and final
     destinations, see Hammond, 'Marketing Wildlife.'
23   Alexander Simpson, *Life of Thomas Simpson*, quoted in Innis, *The Fur Trade in Canada*, 319
     n. 107; Wallace, *John McLean's Notes*, 346; Wilbur, *Duflot de Mofras' Travels*, Vol. 2, 106.

24   Robert Miles to John McLeod, 5 August 1832, McLeod Papers, NAC; Miles to Ermatinger, 25 July 1833, Edward Ermatinger Papers, NAC. Final profit was calculated only after all fur had been auctioned and overhead costs deducted. A post's 'apparent gain' was an estimate of total profit, based on past expenses and preliminary returns, and calculated before the fur had been sent to London.

25   See McLoughlin to G&C, 28 May 1834, HBRS 4, 119 and Rowand to Hargrave, 8 July 1840, Hargrave Papers, NAC.

26   London expenses amounted to £40,000 in 1832, £42,000 in 1833, £36,000 in 1838, and £45,000 in 1841. Shipping expenses (to York Factory and Fort Vancouver) were the largest of these, amounting to about £18,000 a year. George Gladman, 'Expenditure at Fenchurch Street on Account of the Fur Trade,' Donald Ross Papers, BCARS. 'I may say confidently that the Company's importations never exceeded £30,000 per annum ... When I say £30,000 this means total of English invoice including insurance & the usual charges.' Roberts, 'Letters to Mrs. F.F. Victor,' 231.

27   Wilbur, *Duflot de Mofras' Travels*, Vol. 2, 106; Simpson to G&C, 18 July 1831, HBCA A.12/1, fo. 383; Simpson to G&C, 10 June 1835, HBCA D.4/102, fo. 3; Simpson to Ross, 6 November 1841, Ross Papers, BCARS.

28   Douglas to Captain Shepherd, 28 May 1849, in Schofield, ed., *Report of the Provincial Archives Department* (1914), 75-6.

29   On the Snake Country's drastic fur declines of the late 1840s, see Louis S. Grant, 'Fort Hall under the Hudson's Bay Company, 1837-1856,' *OHQ* 40, 1 (March 1940): 37 n. 9.

30   E.g., Clouston to W.G. Smith, 5 December 1856, HBCA A.11/63, fos. 235-6; Tolmie to Swan, 30 December 1878, Swan Papers, UBC. Wilkes, in 1842, noted the differing results of the HBC's policies north and south of about the forty-eighth parallel. In the south, he wrote, fur-bearing animals had decreased 'owing to being hunted without regard to season. This is not, however, the case to the north, where the Company have been left to exercise their own rule and prevent the indiscriminate slaughter of old and young out of the proper season.' Wilkes, 'Report on the Territory of Oregon,' 287.

31   Rich, *HBC*, Vol. 3, 485, 819; Mackie, 'Colonial Land,' 216; Gibson, *Farming the Frontier*, 240 n. 1.

32   Wilbur, *Duflot de Mofras' Travels*, Vol. 2, 105, 107; Wilkes and Holmes are cited and quoted in Gibson, *Farming the Frontier*, 199-200; McDonald to Douglas, 11 January 1841, quoted in Cole, *Exile in the Wilderness*, 183. In 1855, Alexander Ross wrote that a century earlier the country had been rich in furs, but now 'the wild animals are completely swept away, and the Company, in a manner, as much occupied everywhere in farming operations as in the pursuits of hunting.' Ross, *The Red River Settlement*, 220-1.

33   Francis to Edward Ermatinger, 4 April 1844, McDonald, *Fur Trade Letters of Francis Ermatinger*, 260-2.

CHAPTER 11: Simpson's Reorganization

1   John Lee Lewes to James Hargrave, 1 April 1843, Glazebrook, *Hargrave Correspondence*, 429.

2   See Malcolm Clark Jr., *Eden Seekers: The Settlement of Oregon 1818-1862* (Boston 1981); William A. Bowen, *The Willamette Valley: Migration and Settlement on the Oregon Frontier* (Seattle: University of Washington 1978).

3   Aberdeen to Peel, 25 September 1844, quoted in Robert C. Clark, ed., 'Aberdeen and Peel on Oregon, 1844,' *OHQ* 34, 3 (September 1933): 237; Captain Gordon to Admiralty, 19 October 1845, quoted in Leslie M. Scott, 'Report of Lieutenant Peel on Oregon in 1845-46,' *OHQ* 29, 1 (March 1928): 69. See also Gough, *The Royal Navy*, 73.

4   For the guided tour, see, for example, Lee and Frost, *Ten Years in Oregon*, 121-210; T.C. Elliott, 'Richard ("Captain Johnny") Grant,' *OHQ* 36, 1 (March 1935): 8-13.

5   For a summary, see Lamb's introduction to HBRS 6, xvii-xviii.

6   In 1837, 218 French Canadians were stationed in the Columbia Department, while the Northern employed 157, the Montreal employed 132, and the Southern Department only 51. 'Memorandum by Edward Roberts, 19 March 1837,' cited in Galbraith, *Hudson's Bay Company*, 21, 434 n. 25.

7   Galbraith, *Hudson's Bay Company*, 82, 187, 189; G&C to Simpson, 16 January 1828, HBRS 3, lxvi; Ireland, 'The Evolution of the Boundaries of British Columbia,' 267; Clayton, 'Whole Kingdoms for the Sake of a Harbour,' 38-44. On the Treaty of Ghent and return of Fort George, see Ronda, *Astoria and Empire*, 305-15.
8   Simpson to G&C, 1 March 1829, HBRS 10, 41.
9   See Galbraith, *Hudson's Bay Company*, 177-91 and Gibson, *Farming the Frontier*, 187-205 for the political background to the Oregon Treaty.
10 See Meinig, *The Great Columbia Plain*, 76-114.
11 On Senator Benton's lobbying, see Ronda, *Astoria and Empire*, 327-35. Floyd, 'Occupation of the Columbia River'; Thomas S. Jessup, 'Occupation of the Columbia River,' [6 April 1824] *OHQ* 8, 3 (September 1907): 290-4; Jesse S. Douglas, ed., 'Matthews' Adventures on the Columbia. A Pacific Fur Company Document,' [December 1824] *OHQ* 40, 2 (June 1939): 105-48; Clark, '1830 Report on the Fur Trade'; Galbraith, 'The Early History of the Puget's Sound Agricultural Company,' 240, 251; Cornelius J. Brosnan, 'The Oregon Memorial of 1838,' *OHQ* 34,1 (March 1933): 68-77; Gough, *The Royal Navy*, 46-7; Norman Graebner, 'Maritime Factors in the Oregon Compromise,' *Pacific Historical Quarterly* 20 (November 1951): 331-46.
12 Simpson was also 'uneasy' about de Mofras's visit on behalf of the French government. Wilbur, *Duflot de Mofras' Travels*, Vol. 2, 102.
13 Farnham, *Travels in the Great Western Prairies*, Vol. 2, 260-1; Hall J. Kelley, *A Geographical Sketch of that Part of North America Called Oregon* ... (Boston: J. Howe 1830), 74-80.
14 See Frederick V. Holman, 'A Brief Account of the Oregon Provisional Government and What Caused Its Formation,' *OHQ* 13, 2 (June 1912): 89-139; Gibson, *Farming the Frontier*, 187-205.
15 On the river bar, see Alexander Spoehr, 'A Nineteenth Century Chapter in Hawaii's Maritime History: Hudson's Bay Company Merchant Shipping, 1829-1859,' *Hawaiian Journal of History* 22 (1988); on diseases, see James R. Gibson, 'Smallpox on the Northwest Coast, 1835-1838,' *BC Studies* 56 (Winter 1982-3): 61-2; on river drownings, see Gibson, *Farming the Frontier*, 195. The figure of 68 drowned is from Diane Eaton and Sheila Urbanek, *Paul Kane's Great Nor-West* (Vancouver: UBC Press 1995), 77.
16 Simpson to G&C, 10 August 1832, HBCA A.12/1, fo. 436.
17 Reid, 'Early Days at Old Fort Langley,' 73-5; Reid, ed., 'Fort Langley Correspondence,' 188-9; Tolmie, *Journals*, 229 [26 August 1833]; Heron to Hargrave, 1 March 1834, Glazebrook, *Hargrave Correspondence*, 137; for the effect on Fort Langley, see McLoughlin to Yale, 6 March 1836, HBCA B.223/b/18, fo. 22 and Ormsby, *British Columbia*, 73; on McLoughlin's opposition to a northern depot, see Galbraith, *Hudson's Bay Company*, 195, and Galbraith, 'The Early History of the Puget's Sound Agricultural Company,' 238-9.
18 G&C to Simpson, 5 March 1834, quoted in Lamb, 'The Founding of Fort Victoria,' *BCHQ* 7 (April 1943): 73.
19 McLoughlin to Work, 8 December 1836, HBCA B.223/b/15, fo. 117; Rich, *HBC*, Vol. 3, 718.
20 Douglas to Simpson, 18 March 1838, and McLoughlin to G&C, 15 November 1836, quoted in Lamb, 'The Founding of Fort Victoria,' 74-5.
21 Rich, *HBC*, Vol. 3, 678. See also Galbraith, *Hudson's Bay Company*, 196, and Steve A. Anderson, *Steilacoom Farm: The British Colonization of Puget Sound, 1841-1849* (Fort Steilacoom, WA: Historic Fort Steilacoom Association 1993).
22 'George Simpson to John Pelly 1837,' quoted in Gibson, *Farming the Frontier*, 75.
23 Simpson to J.H. Pelly, 1 February 1837, HBCA A.8/2, fo. 83, in HBCA search file 'Columbia District.'
24 G&C to Simpson, 15 February 1837, HBCA D.5/4, fo. 238d; Simpson to McLoughlin, Ogden, and Douglas, 16 June 1845, quoted in Lamb, 'The Founding of Fort Victoria,' 82. For Vancouver Island's special political status, see Gough, *The Royal Navy*, 52, 73.
25 Douglas to Ross, 12 March 1844, Donald Ross Papers, BCARS. See also Lamb in HBRS 7, 167 n. 1; Lamb, 'The Founding of Fort Victoria,' 77-8, 80-2.
26 On these proposals, see Gibson, *Farming the Frontier*, 190-4; Gibson, *Otter Skins*, 82.
27 Simpson to G&C, 25 November 1841, HBCA D.4/111, fo. 42; Simpson to G&C, 1 March 1842, HBRS 29, 117-19.

28 Simpson to Donald Ross, 6 November 1841, Ross Papers, BCARS.
29 Simpson to McLoughlin, 7 March 1842, HBRS 6, 287; Simpson to McLoughlin, 1 March 1842, quoted in Blake, 'The Hudson's Bay Company in San Francisco,' 255.
30 Simpson to McLoughlin, 3 March 1842, HBRS 6, 277; Simpson to G&C, 1 March 1842, HBRS 29, 114, 147.
31 Simpson to G&C, 25 November 1841, HBRS 29, 63-4.
32 Simpson to G&C, 25 November 1841, HBRS 29, 67-8.
33 Simpson to McLoughlin, 18 May 1842, HBRS 6, 288-94; G&C to McLoughlin, 21 December 1842, HBRS 6, 301.
34 Simpson to G&C, 25 November 1841, HBRS 29, 66-7; Simpson to G&C, 25 November 1841, HBRS 29, 61; G&C to McLoughlin, 21 December 1842, HBRS 6, 296. Simpson later referred to the 'total uselessness & want of means' in keeping forts McLoughlin and Taku open: Simpson to McLoughlin, 18 May 1842, HBRS 6, 290.
35 Simpson to Andrew Colvile (private), 15 November 1841, HBRS 6, xvii; Tod to Hargrave, March 1842, Glazebrook, *Hargrave Correspondence*, 371.
36 Simpson, *Narrative*, Vol. 2, 133-4 [March 1842]. The G&C were also enthusiastic about sales of Columbia produce at Oahu: G&C to McLoughlin, 21 December 1842, HBRS 6, 298-301. Simpson's decision to continue and expand the Oahu agency coincided with the British government's increased interest in the Sandwich Islands. See F.V. Longstaff and W. Kaye Lamb, 'The Royal Navy on the Northwest Coast, 1813-1850,' part 1, *BCHQ* 9, 1 (January 1945): 9, and Gough, *The Royal Navy*, 34-41.
37 Simpson to Ross, 6 November 1841, Ross Papers, BCARS; see also Simpson to G&C, 25 November 1841, HBRS 29, 87. For the tin concept, see Simpson to G&C, 10 March 1842, HBRS 29, 141.
38 Simpson to Ross, 6 November 1841, Donald Ross Papers, BCARS; James Douglas, 'Voyage Records, H.B.C. Ships, 1837-1844,' BCARS; Gough, *The Royal Navy*, 71, 80.
39 Simpson to G&C, 1 March 1842, HBRS 29, 107.
40 Ibid., 107-8. See also Lamb, 'The Founding of Fort Victoria,' 83, and Frederick Merk, 'The Oregon Pioneers and the Boundary,' *American Historical Review* 29, 4 (July 1924): 681-99.
41 'You have however the advantage of having Mr. Douglas for a correspondent, he writes a plain legible hand and will give you more news and information in one line than I can give in a sheet.' Ogden to Ross, 10 March 1848, Donald Ross Papers, BCARS.
42 Simpson to G&C, 1 March 1842, HBRS 29, 109; G&C to McLoughlin, 21 December 1842, HBRS 6, 296, 331.
43 Simpson to G&C, 1 March 1842, HBRS 29, 109-10; 'Substance of a Conversation with Captain Hoyer,' 1 March 1842, HBRS 29, 141-2. On the British Pacific whaling fleet, see Gough, *The Northwest Coast*, 196.
44 Simpson to McLoughlin, 18 May 1842, HBRS 6, 289; Simpson to G&C, 6 July 1842, HBRS 29, 166; for whale oil, see Fur Trade Returns, Columbia District and New Caledonia 1825-1857, BCARS; HBCA A.53/1; Fort Vancouver Account Book, 1836-1860, HBCA B.223/d/212. See also Bill Merilees, 'The Humpback Whales of Georgia Strait,' *Waters* 8 (1985): 11.
45 G&C to McLoughlin, 21 December 1842, HBRS 6, 297; Simpson to G&C, 21 June 1843, HBCA A.12/2, fo. 171; HBCA Search file, 'Oregon – Abernethy's Mill'; Simpson to G&C, 20 June 1844, HBCA A.12/2, fo. 374; Simpson to G&C, 20 June 1845, HBCA A.12/2, fo. 565; W. Kaye Lamb, 'Early Lumbering on Vancouver Island. Part 1: 1844-1855,' *BCHQ* 2 (January 1938): 31-53.
46 This is the theme of HBRS 7. In 1852, McLoughlin stated that for twenty years he had looked forward to living under the American flag. See [John McLoughlin], 'Letter of John McLoughlin to Oregon Statesman, June 8, 1852,' *OHQ* 8, 3 (September 1907): 295.
47 Simpson (Honolulu) to Ross, 12 March 1842, Donald Ross Papers, BCARS.
48 Ross to Simpson (draft), 15 August 1842, Donald Ross Papers, BCARS; Lewes to Hargrave, 1 April 1843, Glazebrook, *Hargrave Correspondence*, 429.
49 On the Spanish departure from Nootka, see Gough, *The Northwest Coast*, 165-6; Joseph William McKay, 'The Indians of British Columbia, a Brief Review of their Probable Ori-

gin, History, and Customs,' *British Columbia Mining Record* (Victoria and Vancouver 1899), 71-83, 79.

50   James Douglas, 'Diary of a Trip to Victoria,' 1-21 March 1843, BCARS, 13.

51   Bolduc (Cowlitz) to M.C., 15 February 1844, Landerholm, *Notices & Voyages*, 195; A.G. Morice, *History of the Catholic Church in Western Canada from Lake Superior to the Pacific (1659-1895)* (2 Vols.) (Toronto: Musson 1910), 292-3; Charles Ross to Hargrave, 10 January 1844, Hargrave Papers, NAC. In 1843, the Northern Council of Rupert's Land resolved that the new post was to be named Fort Victoria and to 'be erected on a scale sufficiently extensive to answer the purpose of the Depot'; Oliver, *The Canadian North-West*, Vol. 2, 862.

52   Agnes McKay, 'Recollections,' McKay Papers, BCARS; Thomas Lowe is cited in Walbran, *British Columbia Coast Names*, 512.

53   Kane, *Wanderings*, 144-66, 147 (Kane visited from April to June 1847); Mayne, *Four Years*, 22-3, 407; Simpson to G&C, 20 June 1844, HBCA A.12/2, fo. 374.

54   Douglas to Hargrave, 5 February 1843, Hargrave Papers, NAC; Simpson to Charles Ross, 20 June 1844, quoted in W. Kaye Lamb, 'Five Letters of Charles Ross, 1842-44,' *BCHQ* 7, 2 (April 1943): 117; Adam Dundas to the Secretary of State for the Colonies, 30 May 1848, in Papers Relating to the Colonization of Vancouver Island, 49.

55   Simpson to G&C, 1 March 1842, HBRS 29, 111-12; Simpson to G&C, 20 June 1844, HBCA A.12/2, fo. 374; Ross to Simpson, 10 January 1844, quoted in Lamb, 'Five Letters of Charles Ross,' 115; Ross to Hargrave, 10 January 1844, Hargrave Papers, NAC; Bowsfield, ed., *Fort Victoria Letters*, xxvii and xvii.

56   Kane, *Wanderings*, 145.

57   Simpson to G&C, 21 June 1843, HBCA A.12/2, fo. 171; Ormsby, *British Columbia*, 85.

58   Berthold Seemann, *Narrative of the Voyage of H.M.S. Herald, During the Years 1845-51* (London 1853), 102-3.

59   Lamb, 'The Founding of Fort Victoria,' 90; Fort Vancouver, Account Book, 1836-1860, HBCA B.223/d/212, fo. 217.

60   Peter Skene Ogden, Memorandum, 2 July 1852, HBCA A.12/6, fos. 120-121d. On Victoria's commercial advantages, see also Gough, *The Royal Navy*, 82.

61   Mackie, 'The Colonization of Vancouver Island,' 37-40. Charles Wilkes thought the United States should claim the whole of Oregon Territory. With a boundary at the forty-ninth parallel, he wrote, 'we should also give up what may be considered a storehouse of wealth in its forests, furs, and fisheries, containing an inexhaustible supply of the first and last of the best quality.' Wilkes, 'Report on the Territory of Oregon,' 294.

CHAPTER 12: The Native Foundation of Trade and Labour

1   Douglas to McLean, 26 December 1857, Fort Victoria, Correspondence Outward, 1856-1858, BCARS.

2   Harris, 'Towards a Geography of White Power.'

3   Corney, *Voyages in the Northern Pacific*; on west coast commodities, see Gibson, *Otter Skins*, 4, 5, 7-11, 231-8. Trade in the potent drug tobacco is worthy of serious study. 'In the wilds of America, ask the hardy voyager, ask the rude trapper, ask the dusky savage, from the bleak shore of Labrador to the remote coast of the Pacific, to name his greatest luxury – Tobacco, tobacco, tobacco: this and only this, is the great desideratum. With it in plenty all is well; without it, gloom and dullness instantly prevail.' Ogden, *Traits*, 97.

4   Galois and Mackie, 'A Curious Currency. Part 1'; Mackie and Galois, 'A Curious Currency. Part 2'; Gibson, *Otter Skins*, 229-30.

5   McKay, 'The Fur Trading System,' 24.

6   Ross, *Adventures*, 95.

7   Rich, *HBC*, Vol. 2, 109. On the introduction of blankets, see Morton, *A History*, 425, and Alice M. Johnson, 'Mons. Maugenest Suggests,' *The Beaver* 291 (Summer 1960): 36-9.

8   D.W. Thompson to Josiah Marshall, 7 November 1829, in Morison, 'New England and the Opening of the Columbia River Salmon Trade,' 125. In 1826, an American trader called blan-

kets the 'staple article' and duffles 'the most essential articles of trade.' Gibson, *Otter Skins*, 219; see also Fisher, *Contact and Conflict*, 6.

9   On HBC blankets as 'a unit of value by which the more valuable items, such as canoes, guns, fine skin garments, slaves, and native blankets, could be measured,' see Wayne Suttles, 'Post-Contact Culture Change among the Lummi Indians,' *BCHQ* 18, 1 & 2 (January-April 1954): 44.

10 Cole and Lockner, *To the Charlottes*, 129.

11 Simpson, *Narrative*, Vol. 1, 236; Kane, *Wanderings*, 153, 165-6.

12 Seemann, *Narrative*, quoted in Grant Keddie, 'Prehistoric Dogs of B.C.: Wolves in Sheeps' Clothing,' *The Midden* 25, 1 (February 1993): 3-4, 5. See also Suttles, 'Post-Contact Culture Change,' 44.

13 Sources: 1824-5 salmon: Merk, *Fur Trade and Empire*, 121; 1825 Fraser River: Maclachlan, 'The Founding of Fort Langley,' 21; 1834 Snake River: Townsend, *Narrative*, 138; 1834 slave: Lee and Frost, *Ten Years in Oregon*, 103; 1834 Fort Vancouver provisions: Townsend to *Newark Advertiser*, 401; 1835 *haiqua*: Galois and Mackie; 1836: H.H. Spalding to William Spalding et al., 2 October 1836, *OHQ* 13, 4 (December 1912), 375, and Elliott, 'The Coming of the White Women,' 175; 1837 N.W. Coast: Gibson, *Otter Skins*, 22; 1837 slave: Dunn, *History of Oregon territory*, 120; HBRS 4, 237-8; 1840 Fort George, 52, 56; 1840 NW Coast: Douglas, 'Diary of a Trip to the Northwest Coast,' 13, 15, 16, 118; 1843 pickets: above, ch. 9; 1846 canoe repair: Vaughan, 'Alexander Lattie's Fort George Journal,' 221; 1847: Kane at Victoria: *Wanderings*, 165-6.

14 Anderson, 'Notes on the Indian Tribes,' 77. Rich, *HBC*, Vol. 1, 494-5; on west coast homeguards, see Fisher, *Contact and Conflict*, 29-30. 'Constant reference to the Homeguard Indians in various journals was an indication of the dependence of the Company on the native population.' Innis, *The Fur Trade in Canada*, 134. Innis saw this dependence as a response to the expense and impracticality of importing food, and of the difficulty of growing food in a northern climate.

15 Simpson, *Narrative*, Vol. 1, 215. 'Strategically located groups quickly moved to occupy an economic space between spatially disparate fur producers and relatively immobile Euro-Canadian fur merchants.' R.M. Galois, 'The Worlds of Arthur Wellington Clah, 1855-1891: An outline,' unpublished paper presented to the BC Studies Conference, 1992, 6. For what Rich called the 'drift' of interior fur to Fort Simpson, see E.E. Rich, 'Trade Habits and Economic Motivation among the Indians of North America,' *The Canadian Journal of Economics and Political Science* 26 (1960): 41.

16 Near the Snake River in 1834, a traveller obtained a beaver skin worth $10 in Boston for 'a variety of little matters' worth twelve and a half cents. Townsend, *Narrative*, 138.

17 'Among the natives of the North-west coast, the features of the country, intersected by mountain ranges, or broken up into islands, rendered the tribes more sedentary; while at the same time, it permitted, and even from the diversity of its products required, some degree of commercial intercourse.' Scouler, 'On the Indian Tribes,' 239-40.

18 E.g., 'Standard of Trade Columbia River 1824-25,' Merk, *Fur Trade and Empire*, 174. 'Dependence of the Company on the Indian was closely related to the problem of reducing overhead.' Innis, *The Fur Trade in Canada*, 133.

19 Wayne Suttles, 'The Early Diffusion of the Potato among the Coast Salish,' *Coast Salish Essays*, 137-51; on their global significance, see R.N. Salamon, *The History and Social Influence of the Potato* (Cambridge: 1949).

20 Douglas to G&C, 14 October 1839, quoted in Reid, ed., 'Fort Langley Correspondence,' 190.

21 Leslie M. Scott, 'Indian Women as Food Providers and Tribal Counselors,' *OHQ* 52, 3 (September 1941): 208-19; Thomas Nuttall, 'Catalogue of Plants Collected Chiefly in the Valleys of the Rocky Mountains, near the Sources of the Columbia River,' *Journal of the Academy of Natural Sciences of Philadelphia* 7 (1834): 5-60. On Nuttall, see Ronda, *Astoria and Empire*, 317.

22 Simpson, *Narrative*, Vol. 1, 143-4.

23 See Gibson, *Otter Skins*, 243-6; Green, *Journal of a Tour*, 51; Dunn, *History of Oregon territory*, 294. See also Cole and Lockner, *To the Charlottes*, 54, 69, 107.

24   Scouler, 'Observations on the Indigenous Tribes,' 219. Scouler's observation that the Haida
     switched to commercial potato production with the decline of sea otter is pursued by Fisher,
     Contact and Conflict, 44; Sheila P. Robinson, 'Men and Resources on the Northern North-
     west Coast,' 251, 278-9; Gibson, *Otter Skins*, 243-6; Steven R. Acheson, 'In the Wake of the
     Iron People: A Case for Changing Settlement Strategies among the Kunghit Haida,' *Jour-
     nal of the Royal Anthropological Institute* 1, 2 (June 1995): 294.
25   Scouler, 'Account of a Voyage to Madeira, Brazil, Juan Fernandez, and the Gallipagos
     Islands,' 69-70; see also Scouler, 'Dr John Scouler's Journal,' 191.
26   Anderson, 'Notes on the Indian Tribes,' 75; John Work, 'Journal May 1835,' quoted in Mackay,
     'Pacific Coast Fur Trade,' 40; Simpson, *Narrative*, Vol. 1, 232; McLoughlin to G&C, 20
     November 1844, HBRS 7, 48.
27   The NWC's tradition was originally a French one. Trigger argues that fur traders in New
     France paved the way for colonization through good trading, employment, and cultural rela-
     tions with Native people. See Bruce Trigger, *Natives and Newcomers: Canada's 'Heroic Age'
     Reconsidered* (Montreal and Kingston: McGill-Queen's University Press 1985), 48-9, 298, 341.
28   Ray, 'The Hudson's Bay Company and Native People,' 343-4; Innis, *The Fur Trade in Canada*,
     308-12. See also Glen Makahonuk, 'Wage-Labour in the Northwest Fur Trade Economy 1760-
     1849,' *Saskatchewan History* 41, 1 (Winter 1985); for Indian labour at Red River colony, see Ray,
     Indians in the Fur Trade, 218-19, and Ute McEachran, 'The Reorganization of the Fur Trade
     after the "Merger" of the Hudson's Bay and North West Company, 1821-1826,' in P. Simpson-
     Housley, ed., *York University Department of Geography Paper Series* (York University 1988).
29   Sylvia Van Kirk, *Many Tender Ties: Women in Fur Trade Society 1670-1870* (Winnipeg: Wat-
     son and Dwyer 1980), 53, 73; McEachran, 'The Reorganization of the Fur Trade'; Paul This-
     tle, *Indian-European Relations in the Lower Saskatchewan Region to 1840* (Winnipeg: Uni-
     versity of Manitoba Press 1986), 91; Moodie and Kaye, 'Taming and Domesticating'; Moodie,
     'Gardening on Hudson Bay'; D. Wayne Moodie and Barry Kaye, 'Indian Agriculture in the
     Fur Trade Northwest,' *Prairie Forum* 11, 2 (Fall 1986): 176, 178; Tim Holzkamm, 'Ojibway
     Horticulture in the Upper Mississippi and Boundary Waters,' in Cowan, ed., *Papers of the
     Algonquian Conference*.
30   See Kathryn Bernick, 'A Post-Androcentric View of Fraser Delta Prehistory,' paper pre-
     sented to the Canadian Archaeological Association, Whitehorse, Yukon, May 1990; Scott,
     'Indian Women as Food Providers,' 211, 217; Lorraine Littlefield, 'Women Traders in the
     Maritime Fur Trade,' in Bruce Alden Cox, ed., *Native People, Native Lands* (Ottawa: Carle-
     ton University Press 1987), 173-85, and in the same volume, Jo-Anne Fiske, 'Fishing Is
     Women's Business: Changing Economic Roles of Carrier Men and Women,' 186-98;
     Jo-Anne Fiske, 'Colonization and the Decline of Women's Status: The Tsimshian Case,'
     Feminist Studies 17, 3 (1991): 509-35; Carol Cooper, 'Native Women of the Northern Pacific
     Coast: An Historical Perspective, 1830-1900,' *Journal of Canadian Studies* 27, 4 (Winter 1992-
     3): 44-75; Frieda Klippenstein, *The Role of the Carrier in the Fur Trade: A Report from His-
     torical and Anthropological Sources* (Canadian Parks Service, March 1992).
31   Carl Sauer, *The Early Spanish Main*; Corney, *Voyages in the Northern Pacific*, 44; Simpson,
     Narrative, Vol. 1, 316-17; Wilbur, *Duflot de Mofras' Travels*, Vol. 1, 134-5, 164, 245; Vol. 2, 4-
     5. See also James R. Gibson, 'European Dependence upon American Natives: The Case of
     Russian America,' *Ethnohistory* 25, 4 (Fall 1978): 359-85; Gibson, 'The Russian Fur Trade,'
     223-4; Victoria Wyatt, 'Alaskan Indian Wage Earners in the Nineteenth Century,' *PNQ* 78
     (January-April 1987): 43-9.
32   Tolmie, 'Utilization of the Indians,' 7.
33   Alexander Lattie, 'Particular Notes Extracted from Letters handy to refer to any Time,' c.
     May 1846, in Vaughan, 'Alexander Lattie's Fort George Journal,' 245; McKay, 'The Fur Trad-
     ing System,' 25. See also Lester A. Ross, *Fort Vancouver 1829-1860: A Historical Archaeologi-
     cal Investigation of the Goods Imported and Manufactured by the Hudson's Bay Company* (Van-
     couver, WA: National Park Service 1976), 148.
34   Corney, *Voyages in the Northern Pacific*, 56; Wilks, *Journal Kept by David Douglas*, 144;
     Townsend, *Narrative*, 238; Vaughan, 'Alexander Lattie's Fort George Journal,' 215.

35 Wilks, *Journal Kept by David Douglas*, 106; Wilbur, *Duflot de Mofras' Travels*, Vol. 1, 246; Tolmie, 'Utilization of the Indians,' 7; Townsend, *Narrative*, 160-1, 180; Schafer, ed., 'Documents Relative to Warre and Vavasour,' 43-4.

36 Roberts, 'Letters to Mrs. F.F. Victor,' 183; Tolmie, 'Utilization of the Indians,' 7; Vaughan, 'Alexander Lattie's Fort George Journal,' 215.

37 Lyman, 'Reminiscences of F.X. Matthieu,' 101; Douglas to G&C, 18 October 1838, HBRS 4, 265; Simpson, *Narrative*, Vol. 1, 249. When Americans arrived in large numbers on the lower Columbia after 1842, they found a large, cheap pool of Native labour available for farming, fishing, guiding, land clearing, cutting lumber, transport, loading ships, and carrying letters. See e.g. Nellie B. Pipes, ed., 'Journal of John H. Frost, 1840-43,' part 2, *OHQ* 35, 2 (June 1934): 139-67; Henry E. Reed, ed., 'Lovejoy's Pioneer Narrative, 1842-48,' *OHQ* 31, 3 (September 1930): 237-60.

38 William J. Samarin, 'Chinook Jargon and Pidgin Historiography,' *Canadian Journal of Anthropology* 5, 1 (Fall 1986): 23; J.V. Powell, 'Chinook Jargon and the Lexicographers,' *International Journal of American Linguistics* 56, 1 (January 1990): 137.

39 Robie L. Reid, 'The Chinook Jargon and British Columbia,' *BCHQ* 6, 1 (January 1942): 4; F.W. Howay, 'The Origins of the Chinook Jargon,' *BCHQ* 6, 4 (October 1942): 246; Roberts, 'Letters to Mrs. F.F. Victor,' 214; Wilbur, *Duflot de Mofras' Travels*, Vol. 2, 183. Anderson defined Chinook as the 'Language used by the different Indian Tribes, French and Half-Breeds.' Anderson, *Handbook and Map*, 25.

40 I am grateful to Anne Morton for showing me the Chinook vocabulary in the *Columbia's* Logbook, HBCA C.1/244. fo. 34; Anderson, *Handbook and Map*, 30.

41 Originally, there were two trading languages. As Tolmie explained: 'Before the HB Steamer "Beaver" in 1836 and later made it unprofitable for traders in sailing vessels to visit the Coast, a jargon consisting chiefly of broken Kygani and Tshatsinni Haida and English was the *lingua franca*, or medium of communication, between traders and indians as far south to my knowledge as Milbank Sound.' The language originated at Kaigani. Elsewhere, Tolmie referred to the Kaigani jargon as 'the "lingua franca" of the Northwest Coast fifty years ago and later, altho now in disuse generally, supplanted by a much changed Chinook Jargon.' In 1862, Richard Mayne similarly noted that the southern tribes universally understood Chinook, but the northern tribes did not. Tolmie to Swan, 30 December 1878 and 6 July 1879, Swan Papers, UBC; Green, *Journal of a Tour*, 40-1, and Anderson, 'Notes on the Indian Tribes,' 74; Mayne, *Four Years*, 244-5.

42 Tolmie, *Journals*, 213; G&C to [?] (n.d.) [1839], quoted in Gibson, *Farming the Frontier*, 117, and see also 88 and 179-86; Simpson, *Narrative*, Vol. 1, 179; 'Distribution List of Men at Cowlitz Farm 6 November 1843,' HBCA F.26/1, fo. 68; Puget's Sound Agricultural Company, 'Minute Book,' [1839-58], HBCA F.8/1. See also Thomas Vaughan, ed., 'The Cowlitz Farm Journal, 1847-51,' *OHQ* 63, 2 & 3 (June-September 1962), 112-74.

43 Tolmie to Joseph Howe, 6 October 1871, Tolmie Papers, BCARS.

44 Jamie Morton, '"Worthy of Commemoration in the Usual Form": Native Culture in the Interpretation of Fort Langley National Historic Site since 1924,' paper presented to the Chacmool Conference, 1992, 1-2; Maclachlan, 'The Founding of Fort Langley,' 27-8.

45 McLoughlin to Yale, 17 May 1834, HBCA B.223/b/10, fo. 17.

46 Denys Nelson, *Fort Langley 1827-1927: A Century of Settlement in the Valley of the Lower Fraser* (Vancouver: Art, Historical and Scientific Association of Vancouver 1927), 28; Anderson, *Handbook and Map*, 5. See Manson, 'Recollections,' for women in the salmon trade.

47 Ormsby, *British Columbia*, 92. I owe the Victoria journal reference to Cairn Crockford.

48 Mayne, *Four Years*, 146.

49 Charles Ermatinger, 'The Columbia,' 20; McDonald to John McLeod, 20 February 1831, McLeod Papers, NAC; Tolmie, *Journals*, 234; see Dee, ed., 'The Journal of John Work,' 138.

50 Kane, *Wanderings*, 171-2. In the 1840s, Joe McKay, then a postmaster, was in charge of the Nisqually-Victoria express system. See Alfred Stanley Deaville, *The Colonial Postage Systems and Postage Stamps of Vancouver Island and British Columbia, 1849-1871* (Victoria: Charles F. Banfield 1928), 17, 21.

51 Dunn, *History of Oregon territory*, 241, 271; Simpson, *Narrative*, Vol. 1, 192, 235. See also Galois, *Kwakwaka'wakw Settlements*, 200.

52 Personal communication, Bob Galois; Simpson, *Narrative*, Vol. 1, 231; Pelly to Smith, 30 April 1839, HBCA A.11/61, fo. 52; Simpson to McLoughlin, 18 May 1842, HBRS 6, 291-2.

53 Belcher, *Narrative*, Vol. 1, 301.

54 William Christie Macleod, 'Debtor and Chattel Slavery in Aboriginal North America,' *American Anthropologist* 27, 3 (July 1925): 375; Leland Donald, 'The Slave Trade on the North-west Coast of North America,' *Research in Economic Anthropology* 6 (1984): 121-58; Robert H. Ruby and John A. Brown, *Indian Slavery in the Pacific Northwest* (Spokane: Arthur H. Clark 1993).

55 Ogden, *Traits*, 67.

56 Dunn, *History of Oregon territory*, 273, 288; Tolmie, *Journals*, 313.

57 Douglas, 'Diary of a Trip to the Northwest Coast,' 36-7; Dunn, *History of Oregon territory*, 273, 288. For Taku slavery, see also Douglas to McLoughlin, 1 October 1840, HBCA B.223/b/28, fo. 91, and Simpson, *Narrative*, Vol. 1, 216.

58 Douglas, 'Diary of a Trip to the Northwest Coast,' 55.

59 Dunn, *History of Oregon territory*, 283, 287.

60 Corney, *Voyages in the Northern Pacific*, 67-8. On Ayres and his slaves, see also Scouler, 'Dr John Scouler's Journal,' 205.

61 Simpson to G&C, 1 March 1829, HBRS 10, 80. See Gibson, *Otter Skins*, 233-7, 277-8.

62 Tolmie, 'Utilization of the Indians,' 7; Scouler, 'Account of a Voyage to Madeira, Brazil, Juan Fernandez, and the Gallipagos Islands,' 51-73, 69-70. See also Scouler, 'Dr John Scouler's Journal,' 191, and his 'Observations on the Indigenous Tribes,' 219.

63 Ross, *Adventures*, 94; William Christie Macleod, 'Economic Aspects of Indigenous American Slavery,' *American Anthropologist* 30, 4 (October-December 1928): 640.

64 McDonald, *Fur Trade Letters of Francis Ermatinger*; Ermatinger, 'Edward Ermatinger's York Factory Express Journal,' 72; Elsie Frances Dennis, 'Indian Slavery in Pacific Northwest,' part 2, *OHQ* 31, 2 (June 1930), 192-3.

65 Bolduc, September 1842, Landerholm, *Notices & Voyages*, 149.

66 Demers, 'General Notes on the Territory of the Columbia,' 13 February 1844, Landerholm, *Notices & Voyages*, 186-7; for Fort Nisqually, see Simpson, *Narrative*, Vol. 1, 242-3; for Fort Langley, see Douglas to Yale, 21 November 1838, HBCA B.223/b/22, fo. 38, and Douglas to Yale, 10 May 1839, HBCA B.223/b/24, fo. 14d.

67 Tolmie, *Journals*, 310 (28 May 1834).

68 In 1835, the company, in response to the Slavery Emancipation Act, produced 'Regulations for Promoting Moral and Religious Improvement' in its Native dealings: see MacKay, *The Honourable Company*, 408-9. On the Kipling incident, see McLoughlin to Dunn, 11 September 1835, HBCA B.223/b/11, fo. 45. For slavery at Fort George, see Douglas to Birnie, 6 August 1838, HBCA B.223/b/22, fo. 23d.

69 Beaver to Benjamin Harrison, 15 November 1836 and 18 January 1837, in Thomas E. Jessett, ed., *Reports and Letters of Herbert Beaver 1836-1838* (Portland, OR: Champoeg Press 1959), 20, 31.

70 Herbert Beaver to Aborigines' Protection Society, circa 1842, in Aborigines' Protection Society, *Further Information Respecting the Aborigines* ... (Tract Relative to Aborigines, No. 8) (London: Edward Marsh 1842), 18.

71 Beaver to Harrison, 19 March and 2 October 1838, in Jessett, *Reports and Letters of Herbert Beaver*, 81, 132.

72 Slacum, 'Slacum's Report,' 191-2.

73 Douglas to G&C, 18 October 1838, HBRS 4, 237-8. See also Barry M. Gough, *Gunboat Frontier: British Maritime Authority and Northwest Coast Indians, 1846-90* (Vancouver: UBC Press 1984), 86.

74 McLoughlin, 'Remarks upon Mr Cushings Report ...' (circa 1845), HBRS 7, 275. 'Remember. The moral renovation of the place. Abolition of slavery within our limits. Lay down a principle and act upon it with confidence. To build a Church of Christ in this place.' James

Douglas, [memo, circa 1852], in Douglas Scrapbook, BCARS. On colonial attempts to abolish slavery, see Gough, *Gunboat Frontier*, 85-94. Dunn claimed that the Chinook custom of killing slaves at the death of high-ranking people had been stopped through the 'interposition' of the HBC, and another old employee, Ned Frigon, claimed that the Haida quit their slave raids into the Gulf of Georgia through the HBC's 'instrumentality.' Dunn, *History of Oregon territory*, 120; Frigon is cited in Thomas P. Wicks, 'Pioneer Reminiscences of Thos. P. Wicks British Columbia Coast 1882. An autobiography of Pioneer Life Amongst the Indians of Northern Vancouver Island,' compiled by Margaret Giles, City Archives, City Hall, Vancouver 1939, 22.

75 Wilbur, *Duflot de Mofras' Travels*, Vol. 2, 185; Lyman, 'Reminiscences of F.X. Matthieu,' 88-9; Rees is quoted in Dennis, 'Indian Slavery in Pacific Northwest,' part 2, 194; Dennis, 'Indian Slavery in Pacific Northwest,' part 3, *OHQ* 31, 3 (September 1930): 287-8.

76 Ermatinger alludes here to *Jack in his Element*, a song by English popular composer Charles Dibdin (1745-1814), which included the lines: 'In every mess I find a friend' and 'In every port a wife.' See *The Oxford Dictionary of Quotations* (London: Oxford University Press 1953), 173.

77 Ermatinger (Thompson's River) to Robert Miles, 14 March 1826, McDonald, *Fur Trade Letters of Francis Ermatinger*, 64; on Laframboise, see Warner and Munnick, *Catholic Church Records*, A-46; Ross, *The Fur Hunters*, Vol. 2, 236; Demers, 'General Notes on the Territory of the Columbia,' 13 February 1844, Landerholm, *Notices & Voyages*, 186. Duncan McDougall of the NWC paid ten blankets, ten guns, ten knives, and ten hatchets for a chief's daughter: Kane, *Wanderings*, 121. See also Van Kirk, *Many Tender Ties*, 73, 131-6, 166-7.

78 McDonald, 'Fort Langley Journal,' 3 March 1829, quoted in Mclachlan, 'The Founding of Fort Langley,' 17; Warner and Munnick, *Catholic Church Records*, index; Simpson, *Narrative*, Vol. 1, 231. See also John A. Hussey, 'The Women of Fort Vancouver,' *OHQ* 92, 3 (1991): 265-308, and Juliet Pollard, 'Growing Up Without the Means of Grace: Cultures and Children in the Pacific Northwest,' PhD diss., UBC, circa 1991.

79 Caywood, 'Excavating Fort Vancouver,' 4-7; Lester Ross, 'Hudson's Bay Company Glass Trade Beads: Manufacturing Types Imported to Fort Vancouver (1829-1860),' *The Bead Journal* 1, 2 (Fall 1974): 15-22.

80 Burnett, 'Recollections,' 97-8.

81 Simpson, *Narrative*, Vol. 1, 151.

82 Burnett, 'Recollections,' 97-8.

83 Wilson Duff, 'The Fort Victoria Treaties,' *BC Studies* 3 (Fall 1969): 3-57. For colonial Native labour, see Rolf Knight, *Indians at Work: An Informal History of Native Indian Labour in British Columbia* (Vancouver: New Star Books 1978); Rennie Warburton and Stephen Scott, 'The Fur Trade and Early Capitalist Development in British Columbia,' *Canadian Journal of Native Studies* 5, 1 (1985): 27-46; Rennie Warburton and David Coburn, eds., *Workers, Capital, and the State in British Columbia* (Vancouver, UBC Press 1988), 275-8; John Lutz, 'After the Fur Trade: The Aboriginal Labouring Class of British Columbia, 1849-1890,' *Journal of the Canadian Historical Association* 3 (1992), 69-94.

Conclusion

1 Quoted in Terry Glavin, 'Natives Fear Deck Stacked Against Them,' *Vancouver Sun*, 14 September 1987, D8.

2 Simpson to J.H. Pelly, 1 February 1837, quoted in HBCA search file 'Trade.'

3 Dunn, *History of Oregon territory*, 165.

4 Irving, *The Rocky Mountains*, Vol. 2, 245.

5 Douglas to G&C, HBRS 32, 2. 'Without their [the company's] exertions not a foot of land, on the west coast of America, would this day, own the sway of the British crown, and had a bolder spirit ruled the Aberdeen Cabinet in 1846, the Americans would never have set foot on the north bank of the Columbia, and we would not now be humble suppliants at the President's footstool, for the protection of rights, so hardly earned, by the best blood and treasure of the Company.' Douglas to Simpson, 12 October 1855, Fort Victoria, Correspondence Outward, 1850-1858, BCARS. 'We had at Vancouver no idea that the North side

of the Columbia would be abandoned. The treaty was very lame as far as the Company was concerned.' Roberts, 'Letters to Mrs. F.F. Victor,' 201.

6   Wishart, *The Fur Trade of the American West*, 14.

7   Mackie, 'The Colonization of Vancouver Island,' 5-8. On the 1846 negotiations, see Gibson, *Farming the Frontier*, 187-205.

8   Arthur J. Ray, *The Canadian Fur Trade in the Industrial Age* (Toronto: University of Toronto Press 1990), xvii and passim.

9   That profits might have been maintained by broadening the range of exports was a possibility not considered by Rich. In 1863, he wrote, 'The old Company had remained predominantly a fur-trading company. It was, indeed, as a fur-trading company that it earned its dividends and as a fur-trading company that it valued its assets.' Rich, *HBC*, Vol. 3, 816.

10 Landerholm, *Notices & Voyages*, 207.

11 McLoughlin, 'John McLoughlin – Statement,' 193-206.

12 Bolduc (Willamette) to M.T., 12 March 1845, Landerholm, *Notices & Voyages*, 239.

13 McLoughlin to Barclay, 23 November 1844, HBRS 7, 61-2. A sample was sent to London for examination by Heathfield & Burgess, Experimental Chemists, who confirmed a high proportion of silver. Cole, *Exile in the Wilderness*, 218, 255. 'A rich deposit of galena, yielding a moderate percentage of silver, exists on the Flat-bow Lake (Koutenais), but the position is too remote and inaccessible for its profitable working.' Anderson, *Notes on North-Western America*, 14. See also Jeremy Mouat, *Roaring Days: Rossland's Mines and the History of British Columbia* (Vancouver: UBC Press 1995), 5-6.

14 'The planned and purposeful production of a marketable staple [at Red River] was necessary, and Simpson, having once decided that a [staple] was necessary if the colony was to survive, made endless (and often costly) attempts to foster such products.' Rich, *HBC*, Vol. 3, 508.

15 Simpson to G&C, 10 July 1828, quoted in Alvin C. Gluek, 'Industrial Experiments in the Wilderness: A Sidelight in the Business History of the Hudson's Bay Company,' *Business History Review*, 32, 4 (Winter 1958): 425, and Gluek, *Minnesota and the Manifest Destiny of the Canadian Northwest* (Toronto: University of Toronto Press 1965), 23.

16 Simpson to G&C, 10 August 1832, HBCA A.12/1 fo. 422; G&C to Simpson, 5 March 1834, HBCA D.5/4, fos. 70d-71; 'Agreement with John Pritchard and others trading together under the firm of The Buffalo Wool Company, 17 May 1820,' HBCA; 'Sketch of the Route between York Factory and Red River Settlement &c Fall 1827,' HBCA B.235/a/10-11; Ross, *The Red River Settlement*, 136-8, 150; Simpson, *Narrative* Vol. 1, 57; Glazebrook, *The Hargrave Correspondence*, 46-51, 159; HBRS 3, 19, 210-11, 242, 258-9, 261-2, 280, 364, 392, 459; Robert Campbell, 'Sheep for Red River,' *The Beaver* 275 (March 1945): 40-4; Richard I. Ruggles, *A Country So Interesting. The Hudson's Bay Company and Two Centuries of Mapping, 1670-1870* (Montreal and Kingston: McGill-Queen's University Press 1991), plate 39; Morton, *A History*, 641-3, 662-3; Rich, *HBC*, Vol. 1, 461-2; Vol. 2, 310; Vol. 3, 488, 509-13; Alvin C. Gluek, 'The Fading Glory,' *The Beaver* 288 (Winter 1957): 50-5; Hedlin, 'Reluctant Beginnings'; Leechman, 'Garden Seeds'; Simpson (1830) is quoted in John A. Alwyn, 'Colony and Company Sharing the York Mainline,' *The Beaver* 310,1 (Summer 1979): 4-11.

17 Simpson, *Narrative*, Vol. 1, 250-1.

18 Ermatinger, 'Notes,' 96, 111, 120-1.

19 Simpson's successful diversification policies on the Pacific had smaller-scale counterparts on the Atlantic and St. Lawrence coasts. The HBC developed non-fur exports at Tadoussac, Mille-Vaches, Portneuf, Bersimes, Godbout, Sept Îsles, Mingan, Esquimaux Bay (Hamilton Inlet), and Ungava Bay. See Richard Mackie, 'Not the Fur Trade in Canada: George Simpson and Resource Development, 1820-1860,' paper presented to the Canadian Historical Association, Kingston, 1991.

20 British Columbia's 'economic development has been based on the successive emergence of new staples with the continued importance of the old.' 'Of all the Canadian regional economies which have evolved from non-agricultural staple-export origins only British Columbia has continued to be an economy directed by the export performance of the natural-resource sector.' Marr and Patterson, *Canada: An Economic History*, 445.

21 Richard Mackie, 'Joseph William McKay,' in Frances G. Halpenny, ed., *DCB*, Vol. 12
    (Toronto: University of Toronto Press 1990), 641-3 and 'George Blenkinsop,' in Ramsay
    Cook, *DCB*, Vol. 13 (Toronto: University of Toronto Press 1994), 87-9. 'The system pursued
    in this province, with regard to the Indian management, is roughly a modification of that
    traditionally followed by the North-West Company of a former day and the Hudson's Bay
    Company, with whom these were finally conjoined, in their dealings with the numerous
    tribes, from the Gulf of Saint Lawrence and the Frozen Ocean to the shores of the Pacific.'
    Anderson, 'A Compendium of the Province of British Columbia,' 13.

22 A point made by Innis and by Campbell, *The North West Company*, 279-80.

23 Anderson, *The Dominion of the West*, 1. 'If the name of New Caledonia is objected to as
    being already borne by another colony or island claimed by the French, it may be better to
    give the new colony west of the Rocky mountains another name. New Hanover, New Corn-
    wall and New Georgia appear from the maps to be names of subdivisions of that country,
    but do not appear on all maps. The only name which is given to the whole territory in
    every map the Queen has consulted is "Columbia," but as there exists also a Columbia in
    South America, and the citizens of the United States call their country also Columbia, at
    least in poetry, "British Columbia" might be, in the Queen's opinion, the best name.' Queen
    Victoria to Edward Bulwer Lytton, 24 July 1858, Walbran, *British Columbia Coast Names*, 63.

Bibliography

PRIMARY SOURCES

Unpublished

Anderson, James Robert. 'Notes and Comments on Early Days and Events in British Columbia, Washington, and Oregon.' Ts. BCARS

Dease, John Warren. 'The Columbia Journal of John Warren Dease, 1829.' NAC

Douglas, David. Journal 1823-1827

Douglas, James. 'Diary of a Trip to the Northwest Coast, April 22-October 2, 1840.' BCARS

———. 'Diary of a Trip to Victoria.' 1-21 March 1843. Ts. BCARS

———. 'Notes on the Tradition and Population of the Indians of the North West Coast.' BCARS

———. 'Notes Respecting Red River,' in his 'Journal of a Journey from Fort Vancouver to York Factory and Back 1835.' BCARS

———. [circa 1852], Scrapbook. n.d. BCARS

———. 'Voyage Records, H.B.C. Ships, 1837-1844.' BCARS

Ermatinger, C.O. 'The Columbia Department During the Hudson's Bay Regime.' Ms., n.d. [circa 1850]. Ermatinger Papers. NAC

Ermatinger, Edward. 'Notes on the Liverpool Financial Reform Association's tract entitled "The Hudson's Bay Company versus Magna Charta and the British People."' 15 September 1857. Ts., Ermatinger Papers. NAC

———. 'Old Memo Book and Journal of Edward Ermatinger.' Ermatinger Papers. NAC

———. Papers. NAC

Farnham, Thomas Jefferson. Correspondence Outward. BCARS

Finlayson, Duncan. 'Trip Across to the Columbia 1831.' Duncan Finlayson Papers. HBCA

Fort Kamloops [sic]. Miscellaneous Papers Relating to. BCARS

Fort Langley. Journal 1827-28. HBCA

———. Journal 1829-30. HBCA

Fort Vancouver. Account Book. 1836-1860. HBCA

———. Fur Trade Returns, Columbia District and New Caledonia, 1825-1857. BCARS

Fort Victoria. Correspondence Outward, 1856-1858. BCARS

———. Correspondence Outward, 1850-1858. BCARS

———. Journal, 1846-1850. HBCA

Hargrave, James. Papers. NAC

Hudson's Bay Company Archives

Keith, James. Papers. University of Aberdeen

Lowe, Thomas. Letters Outward 1852-1859. BCARS

Manson, Aurelia. 'Recollections of School Days.' Ms., BCARS

McKay, Agnes. 'Recollections.' McKay Papers. BCARS

McKay, Joseph William. Papers. BCARS

Mackenzie, Alexander. 'Journal of a Trip in the William and Ann, 1825.' HBCA B.223/a/1

McKinlay, Archibald. 'Narrative of a Chief Factor in the Hudson's Bay Company.' Ms., 1878. BCARS

McLeod, John. Papers. BCARS

———. Papers. NAC
Puget's Sound Agricultural Company. 'Minute Book.' [1839-1858]. HBCA
Ross, Charles. Correspondence [?] BCARS (A/B/40/R 735)
Ross, Donald. Papers. BCARS
Simpson, Aemilius. 'Log of the Cadboro.' HBCA C.1/218
Simpson, George. 'Observations on Speeches in the House of Lords and House of Commons
    respecting the Hudson's Bay Company, Vancouver Island, &c. &c. by Sir George Simpson.'
    28 March 1849. HBCA
Swan, James. Papers. UBC
Tod, John. 'The History of New Caledonia and the Northwest Coast.' 1874. Ts., BCARS
Tolmie, William Fraser. 'History of Puget Sound and the Northwest Coast.' 1878. Ts., Tolmie Papers.
    BCARS
———. Papers. BCARS
Wicks, Thomas 'Pioneer Reminiscences of Thos. Wicks British Columbia Coast 1882. An autobi-
    ography of Pioneer Life Amongst the Indians of Northern Vancouver Island.' Compiled by
    Margaret Giles, City Archives, City Hall, Vancouver, 1939
Yale, James Murray. Correspondence Outward. BCARS

Published

Aborigines' Protection Society. *Further Information Respecting the Aborigines* ... (Tract Relative to
    Aborigines, No. 8) London: Edward Marsh 1842
Anderson, Alexander Caulfield. 'A Compendium of the Province of British Columbia. Its Early His-
    tory, General Features, Climate, Resources, Etc.' In *The British Columbia Directory for the Years
    1882-83.* Victoria: R.T. Williams 1882, 2-26
———. *The Dominion of the West. A Brief Description of the Province of British Columbia, Its Climate
    and Resources.* Victoria: Richard Wolfenden 1872
———. *Hand-book and Map to the Gold Regions of Frazer's and Thompson's Rivers* ... San Francisco:
    J.J. Le Count 1858
———. 'Notes on the Indian Tribes of British North America, and the Northwest Coast.' *The His-
    torical Magazine* 8, 3 (March 1863) [written 1855]: 73-81
———. *Notes on North-Western America.* Montreal: Mitchell & Wilson 1876
———. 'Some Remarks upon the Freezing of Streams in North America, in Connexion with the
    Supposed Congelation of their Sources in High Latitude.' *Journal of the Royal Geographical
    Society* 15 (1845): 367-71
Ball, John. 'Across the Continent Seventy Years Ago.' *OHQ* 3, 1 (March 1902): 82-106
Bancroft, H.H. *History of California.* Santa Barbara: W. Hebberd 1963
Barker, Burt Brown, ed. *The Financial Papers of Dr. John McLoughlin.* Portland, OR: Oregon His-
    torical Society 1949
———, ed. *Letters of Dr. John McLoughlin, Written at Fort Vancouver 1829-1832.* Portland, OR: Bin-
    fords & Mort 1948
Beechey, F.W. *Narrative of a Voyage to the Pacific Beering's Strait ... in the Years 1825, 26, 27, 28.* 2 Vols.
    London: Henry Colburn and Richard Bentley 1831
Belcher, Edward. *Narrative of a Voyage Round the World, Performed in Her Majesty's Ship Sulphur,
    During the Years 1836-1842* ... 2 Vols. London: Henry Colburn 1843
Bell, Michael, ed. *Braves and Buffalo: Plains Indian Life in 1837.* Toronto: University of Toronto Press
    1973
Belyea, Barbara, ed. *Columbia Journals of David Thompson.* Montreal and Kingston: McGill-Queen's
    University Press 1994
Blue, George Verne, ed. 'Green's Missionary Report on Oregon, 1829.' *OHQ* 30, 3 (September 1929):
    259-71
———. 'A Hudson's Bay Company Contract for Hawaiian Labor.' *OHQ* 25 (1924): 72-5
Bowsfield, Hartwell, ed. *Fort Victoria Letters, 1846-1851.* Winnipeg: HBRS 1979 [HBRS 32]
[Brackenridge, William Dunlop]. 'Journal of William Dunlop Brackenridge, October 1-28 1841.'
    CHSQ 24, 4 (December 1945): 326-36

Brewster, Henry Bridgman. 'The Log of the Lausanne.' Part 3. *OHQ* 29, 4 (December 1928): 347-62

British and American Joint Commission for the Final Settlement of the Claims of the Hudson's Bay and Puget Sound Companies, *The Governor and Company of Adventurers of England Trading into Hudson Bay ... Submit the Following Memorial and Statement of their Claims Upon the United States.* N.p., [1865]

Brosnan, Cornelius J. 'The Oregon Memorial of 1838.' *OHQ* 34, 1 (March 1933): 68-77

[Burnett, Peter H]. 'Letters of Peter H. Burnett.' *OHQ* 3, 4 (December 1902): 398-426

Burnett, Peter H. 'Recollections and Opinions of an Old Pioneer.' *OHQ* 5, 1 (March 1904): 64-99

Campbell, Robert. 'Sheep for Red River.' *The Beaver* 275 (March 1945): 40-4

Clark, Robert C., ed. 'Aberdeen and Peel on Oregon, 1844.' *OHQ* 34, 3 (September 1933): 236-40

Clark, William. '1830 Report on the Fur Trade by General William Clark.' *OHQ* 48, 1 (March 1947): 25-33

Cole, Douglas, and Bradley Lockner, eds. *To the Charlottes: George Dawson's 1878 Survey of the Queen Charlotte Islands.* Vancouver: UBC Press 1993

Corney, Peter. *Voyages in the Northern Pacific. Narrative of Several Trading Voyages from 1813 to 1818, Between the Northwest Coast of America, the Hawaiian Islands and China ...* Honolulu: Thos. G. Thrum 1891; first published London 1821

Coulter, Thomas. *Notes on Upper California: A Journey from Monterey to the Colorado River in 1832.* Los Angeles: G. Dawson 1951

Cox, Ross. *Adventures on the Columbia River, Including The Narrative of a Residence of Six Years' on the West Side of the Rocky Mountains ...* 2 Vols. London: Henry Colburn and Richard Bentley 1831

Dale, H.C., ed. *The Ashley-Smith Explorations and the Discovery of a Central Route to the Pacific, 1822-1829, with the Original Journals.* Cleveland 1918

Dalrymple, Alexander. *Plan for Promoting the Fur-Trade and Securing it to This Country by Uniting the Operations of the East India and Hudson's Bay Companies.* London 1789

Dana, Richard Henry. *Two Years Before the Mast. A Personal Narrative of Life at Sea.* Harmondsworth, Middlesex: Penguin 1981

Davies, John. *Douglas of the Forests: The North American Journals of David Douglas.* Seattle: University of Washington Press 1980

Davies, K.G., ed. *Peter Skene Ogden's Snake County Journal, 1826-27.* London: HBRS 1961 [HBRS 3]

Dease, Peter Warren. 'On the Cultivation of the Cerealia in the High Latitudes of North America.' *Edinburgh New Philosophical Journal* 30 (1841): 123-4

Dee, Henry Drummond. 'The Journal of John Work, 1835.' Part 5. *BCHQ* 9, 2 (April 1945): 129-46

De Smet, P.J. *Letters and Sketches: With a Narrative of a Years Residence Among the Indian Tribes of the Rocky Mountains.* Philadelphia: M. Fithian 1843

————. *Oregon Missions and Travels over the Rocky Mountains in 1845-46.* New York: Edward Dunigan 1847

DeVoto, Bernard, ed. *The Journals of Lewis and Clark.* Boston: Houghton Mifflin 1953

Douglas, Jesse S., ed. 'Matthews' Adventures on the Columbia. A Pacific Fur Company Document.' [December 1824] *OHQ* 40, 2 (June 1939): 105-48

Duff, Wilson. 'The Fort Victoria Treaties.' *BC Studies* 3 (Fall 1969): 3-57

Dunn, John. *History of the Oregon territory and British North-American fur trade; with an Account of the Habits and Customs of the Principal Native Tribes on the Northern Continent.* London: Edwards and Hughes 1844

Elliott, T.C. 'Extracts from the Emmons Journal.' *OHQ* 26, 3 (September 1925): 263-73

————. 'Letter of Donald Mackenzie to Wilson Price Hunt.' *OHQ* 43, 3 (September 1942): 194-7

————. 'Sale of Astoria, 1813.' *OHQ* 33, 1 (March 1932): 43-50

————, ed. 'The Coming of the White Women, 1863' Part 2. *OHQ* 37, 3 (September 1936): 171-91

————, ed. 'Journal of John Work, November and December 1824.' *Washington Historical Quarterly* 3, 3 (July 1912): 198-228

Ermatinger, C.O., ed. 'Edward Ermatinger's York Factory Express Journal, Being a Record of Journeys Made Between Fort Vancouver and Hudson Bay in the Years 1827-1828.' *TRHS* Third Series (Ottawa: Royal Society 1912): 67-132

Ermatinger, Edward. *The Hudson's Bay Territories; A Series of Letters on this Important Question.* Toronto: Maclear, Thomas & Co. 1858

Ermatinger, Francis. 'Earliest Expedition Against Puget Sound Indians.' *WHQ* 1, 2 (January 1907)

Farnham, Thomas J. *Travels in the Californias and Scenes in the Pacific Ocean.* New York: Saxton and Miles 1844

———. *Travels in the Great Western Prairies* ... 2 Vols. London: Richard Bentley 1843

Fleming, R. Harvey, ed. *Minutes of Council, Northern Department of Rupert's Land, 1821-31.* Toronto: the Champlain Society for the HBRS 1940 [HBRS 3]

Floyd, John. 'Occupation of the Columbia River.' [25 January 1821] *OHQ* 8, 1 (March 1907): 51-75

Forbes, Alexander. *California: A History of Upper and Lower California from their first Discovery to the Present Time* ... London: Smith, Elder and Co. 1839

Gairdner, Meredith. 'Meteorological Observations Made at Fort Vancouver from 7 June, 1833, to 31 May, 1834.' *Edinburgh New Philosophical Review* 20 (1836): 67-8

———. 'Notes on the Geography of the Columbia River.' *Journal of the Royal Geographical Society* 2 (1841): 250-7

Gibson, James R. 'Russian America in 1821.' [Report by K.T. Khlebnikov] *OHQ* 77, 2 (June 1976): 174-88

Glazebrook, G. de T., ed. *The Hargrave Correspondence 1821-1843.* Toronto: Champlain Society 1938

Glover, Richard, ed. *David Thompson's Narrative 1784-1812.* Toronto: Champlain Society 1962

Gough, Barry M., ed. *To the Pacific and Arctic with Beechey. The Journal of Lieutenant George Peard of H.M.S. 'Blossom' 1825-1828.* Cambridge: Cambridge University Press 1973

Grant, W. Colquhoun. 'Description of Vancouver Island, By its First Colonist.' *Journal of the Royal Geographical Society* 27 (1857): 268-320

Great Britain, Parliament, House of Commons. *Report from the Committee Appointed to Inquire into the State and Conditions of the Countries Adjoining to Hudson's Bay and the Trade Carried on There.* London 1749

Green, Jonathan S. *Journal of a Tour on the North West Coast of America in the Year 1829.* New York: Charles Frederick Heartman 1915

Guide to the Province of British Columbia for 1877-8. Victoria: T.N. Hibben 1877

Hastings, Lansford. *The Emigrants' Guide to Oregon and California.* Princeton: Princeton University Press 1932; first published 1845

Hargrave, Joseph James. *Red River.* Montreal: J. Lovell 1871

Hayman, John, ed. *Robert Brown and the Vancouver Island Exploring Expedition.* Vancouver: UBC Press 1989

[Henry, John, or Nathaniel Atcheson, supposed author(s)]. *On the Origins and Progress of the North-West Company of Canada, with a history of the fur trade, as connected with that concern.* London: Cox, Son, and Baylis 1811

Hopkins, Manley. *Hawaii: the Past, Present, and Future of its Island-Kingdom* ... London: Longman, Green, Longman, and Roberts 1862

Howay, F.W., ed. 'William Sturgis: The Northwest Coast Fur Trade.' *BCHQ* 8, 1 (January 1944): 11-26

Howison, Neil M. 'Report of Lieutenant Neil M. Howison on Oregon 1846.' *OHQ* 14, 1 (March 1913): 1-60

Hudson's Bay Company. *Charters, Statutes, Orders in Council, etc, Relating to the Hudson's Bay Company.* London: Hudson's Bay Company 1960

———. *Colonization of Vancouver's Island* London: E. Couchman 1849

———. *Copy of the Deed Poll Under the Seal of the Governor and Company of Adventurers of England Trading into Hudson Bay, Bearing Date Twenty-Sixth Day of March 1821* ... London: H.K. Causton 1821

———. *Standing Rules and Regulations.* [1831]

Humboldt, Alexander von. *Political Essay on the Kingdom of New Spain* ... 5 Vols. London: Longman, Hurst, Rees, Orme, & Brown 1811

Irving, Washington. *Astoria; or, Enterprise Beyond The Rocky Mountains.* 3 Vols. London: Richard Bentley 1836

_____. *The Rocky Mountains: Or, Scenes, Incidents, and Adventures in the Far West* ... 3 Vols. (Philadelphia: Carey, Lea, Blanchard 1837

Jessett, Thomas E., ed. *Reports and Letters of Herbert Beaver 1836-1838.* Portland, OR: Champoeg Press 1959

Jessup, Thomas S. 'Occupation of the Columbia River.' [6 April 1824] *OHQ* 8, 3 (September 1907): 290-4

Kane, Paul. *Wanderings of an Artist Among the Indians of North America from Canada to Vancouver's Island and Oregon through the Hudson's Bay Company's Territory and Back Again.* London: Longman, Brown, Green, Longman, and Roberts 1859

Kelley, Hall J. *A Geographical Sketch of that Part of North America called Oregon* ... Boston: J. Howe 1830

Klotz, Otto. *Certain Correspondence of the Foreign Office and of the Hudson's Bay Company Copied from Original Documents, London 1898.* Ottawa: Government Printing Bureau 1899

Lamb, W. Kaye. 'Five Letters of Charles Ross, 1842-44.' *BCHQ* 7, 2 (April 1943): 103-18

_____, ed. *Gabriel Franchère, Journal of a Voyage on the North West Coast of North America During the Years 1811, 1812, 1813 and 1814.* Toronto: Champlain Society 1969

_____, ed. *The Journals and Letters of Sir Alexander Mackenzie.* Toronto: Macmillan 1970

_____, ed. *The Letters and Journals of Simon Fraser 1806-1808.* Toronto: Macmillan 1960

_____, ed. 'McLoughlin's Statement of the Expenses in the "Dryad" Incident of 1834.' *BCHQ* 10, 4 (October 1946): 291-8

_____, ed. *Sixteen Years in the Indian Country: The Journal of Daniel Williams Harmon 1800-1816.* Toronto: Macmillan 1957

Landerholm, Carl, tr. *Notices & Voyages of the Famed Quebec Mission to the Pacific Northwest* ... Portland, OR: Champoeg Press 1956

Latham, R.G. *The Ethnology of the British Colonies and Dependencies.* London: John Van Voorst 1851

_____. 'The Language of the Oregon Territory.' *Journal of the Ethnological Society of London* 1 (1848): 154-66

Leader, Herman, ed. 'McLoughlin's Answer to Warre Report.' *OHQ* 33, 3 (September 1932): 214-29

_____, ed. 'A Voyage from the Columbia to California in 1840.' *CHSQ* 8, 2 (June 1929): 97-115

Lee, D., and J.H. Frost. *Ten Years in Oregon.* New York: J. Collard 1844

Lewis, William S., and Paul C. Phillips, eds. *The Journal of John Work a Chief-Trader of the Hudson's Bay Co. during His Expedition from Vancouver to the Flatheads and Blackfeet of the Pacific Northwest.* Cleveland: Arthur H. Clark 1923

Lord, John Keast. 'American Furs: How Trapped and Traded.' *Eclectic Magazine* (April 1866): 445-52

_____. *The Naturalist in Vancouver Island and British Columbia.* 2 Vols. London: Richard Bentley 1866

Lyman, H.S., ed. 'Reminiscences of F.X. Matthieu.' *OHQ* 1, 1 (March 1900): 73-104

McDonald, Lois Halliday. *Fur Trade Letters of Francis Ermatinger: Written to his Brother Edward During his Service with the Hudson's Bay Company, 1818-1853.* Glendale, CA: Arthur H. Clark 1980

McKay, Joseph William. 'The Fur Trading System.' In *The Year Book of British Columbia and Manual of Provincial Legislation* ... Ed. R.E. Gosnell, 21-5. Victoria 1897

_____. 'The Indians of B8ritish Columbia, a Brief Review of their Probable Origin, History, and Customs.' *British Columbia Mining Record* (Victoria and Vancouver 1899): 71-83

McLeod, Alexander Roderick, *The Hudson's Bay Company's First Fur Brigade to the Sacramento Valley: Alexander McLeod's 1829 Hunt* (Fair Oaks, CA: Sacramento Book Collectors Club 1968

McLeod, Malcolm, ed. *Peace River. A Canoe Voyage from Hudson's Bay to Pacific, by the late Sir George Simpson; (Governor, Hon. Hudson's Bay Company) in 1828 Journal of the Late Chief Factor, Archibald McDonald (Hon. Hudson's Bay Company), who Accompanied Him.* Ottawa: J. Davie & Son 1872

McLoughlin, John. 'Letter of John McLoughlin to Oregon Statesman, June 8, 1852.' *OHQ* 8, 3 (September 1907): 294-9

[McLoughlin, John]. 'John McLoughlin. Statement to Parties in London [circa 1846].' *OHQ* 1, 2 (June 1900): 193-206

Major-Frégeau, Madeleine. *Overland to Oregon in 1845. Impressions of a Journey across North America by H.J. Warre.* Ottawa: Public Archives of Canada 1976

Maloney, Alice Bay, ed. *Fur Brigade to the Bonaventura John Work's California Expedition 1832-1833 for the HBC.* San Francisco: California Historical Society 1945

Martin, Chester. 'The Royal Charter.' *The Beaver* (June 1945): 26-35

Marx, Karl. *Capital. A Critique of Political Economy Vol. 1.* Chicago: Charles H. Kerr 1906

Mayne, Richard. *Four Years in British Columbia and Vancouver Island* ... London: John Murray 1862

Meares, John. *Voyages made in the Years 1788 and 1789, from China to the North West Coast of America.* London 1790

Merk, Frederick, ed. *Fur Trade and Empire, George Simpson's Journal, Remarks Connected With the Fur Trade in the Course of a Voyage From York Factory to Fort George and Back to York, 1824-25.* Cambridge, MA: Harvard University Press 1931

Minto, John. 'Reminiscences of Experiences on the Oregon Trail in 1844.' *OHQ* 2, 3 (September 1901): 209-54

Mitchell, Elaine Allan, ed. 'Clouston Goes to Pembina.' *The Beaver* 292 (Autumn 1961): 47-54

Monroe, Robert D. 'Two Early Views of Vancouver Island.' *The Beaver* 291 (Summer 1960): 12-14

Morris, Grace Parker, ed. 'Some Letters from 1792-1800 on the China Trade.' *OHQ* 42, 1 (March 1941): 48-87

Morton, A.S., ed. *The Journal of Duncan M'Gillivray of the North West Company at Fort George on the Saskatchewan, 1794-5.* Toronto: Macmillan 1929

Munger, Asahel, and Eliza Munger. 'Diary while Crossing the Plains, 1839.' *OHQ* 8, 4 (December 1907): 387-405

Munnick, Harriet Duncan, ed. *Catholic Church Records of the Pacific Northwest* ... Trans. Mikell de lores Wormell Warner. St. Paul, OR: French Prairie Press 1972

Nuttall, T. 'Catalogue of Plants Collected Chiefly in the Valleys of the Rocky Mountains, near the Sources of the Columbia River.' *Journal of the Academy of Natural Sciences of Philadelphia* 7 (1834): 5-60

Ogden, Peter Skene. *Traits of American-Indian Life and Character.* London: Smith, Elder and Company 1853 [written 1838]

Oliver, E.H., ed. *The Canadian North-West; Its Early Development and Legislative Records: Minutes of the Council of the Red River Colony and the Northern Department of Rupert's Land.* 2 Vols. Ottawa: Government Printing Bureau 1914-15

Pemberton, Joseph Despard. *Facts and Figures Relating to Vancouver Island and British Columbia, Showing What to Expect and How to get There.* London: Longman, Green, Longman, and Roberts 1860

Pierce, Richard A., ed. *Russian America: Statistical and Ethnographical Information by Rear Admiral Ferdinand Petorich Wrangell* ... *Translated from the German Edition of 1839* ... Kingston: The Limestone Press 1980

Pipes, Nellie B., ed. 'Journal of John H. Frost, 1840-43.' Part 2. *OHQ* 35, 2 (June 1934): 139-67

Posner, Russell M. 'A British Consular Agent in California: The Reports of James A. Forbes, 1843-1846.' *Southern California Quarterly* 53, 2 (June 1971): 101-12

Rathbun, Richard. *A Review of the Fisheries in Contiguous Waters of the State of Washington and British Columbia.* Washington, DC: Government Printing Bureau 1899

Reed, Henry E., ed. 'Lovejoy's Pioneer Narrative, 1842-48.' *OHQ* 31, 3 (September 1930): 237-60

Reid, Robie, ed. 'Fort Langley Correspondence: 1831-1858.' *BCHQ* 3 (July 1937): 187-95

Rich, E.E., ed. *Colin Robertson's Correspondence Book, Sept. 1817 to Sept. 1822.* London: Champlain Society for HBRS 1939 [HBRS 2]

———, ed. *George Simpson's Journal of Occurrences in the Athabaska Department and Report 1820-21.* Toronto: Champlain Society for the HBRS 1938 [HBRS 1]

———, ed. *The Letters of John McLoughlin from Fort Vancouver to the Governor and Committee, First Series, 1825-1838.* London: HBRS 1941 [HBRS 4]

———, ed. *The Letters of John McLoughlin from Fort Vancouver to the Governor and Committee, Second Series, 1839-1844* London: HBRS 1943 [HBRS 6]

———, ed. *The Letters of John McLoughlin from Fort Vancouver to the Governor and Committee, Third Series, 1844-1846.* London: HBRS 1944 [HBRS 7]

———, ed. *London Correspondence Inward from Eden Colvile, 1849-1852.* London: HBRS 1956 [HBRS 19]

_____, ed. *Part of a Dispatch from George Simpson, Esq., Governor of Rupert's Land, to the Governor and Committee of the Hudson's Bay Company, London, March 1 1829, Continued and Completed March 24, and June 5, 1829.* London: Champlain Society for the HBRS 1947 [HBRS 10]

_____, ed. *Peter Skene Ogden's Snake Country Journals 1824-25 and 1825-26.* London: HBRS 1950 [HBRS 13]

Rich, E.E., and A.M. Johnson, eds. *Hudson's Bay Letters Outward, 1679-1694.* London: HBRS 1948

Richardson, John. *Arctic Searching Expedition* ... London 1851

_____. *Fauna Boreali-Americana; or the Zoology of the Northern Parts of British America* ... Vol. 3. London 1836

_____. 'On the Frozen Soil of North America.' *Edinburgh New Philosophical Journal* 30 (1841): 110-26

Roberts, George Barber. 'Letters to Mrs. F.F. Victor.' [1878-83] *OHQ* 63, 2 & 3 (June-September 1962): 175-263

Rollins, Philip Ashton, ed. *The Discovery of the Oregon Trail. Robert Stuart's Narrative of his Overland Trip Eastward from Astoria in 1812-13* ... New York: Charles Scribner's Sons 1935

Ross, Alexander. *Adventures of the First Settlers on the Oregon or Columbia River: Being a Narrative of the Expedition Fitted out by John Jacob Astor, to Establish the Pacific Fur Company* ... London: Smith, Elder and Co. 1849

_____. *The Fur Hunters of the Far West; A Narrative of Adventures in the Oregon and Rocky Mountains.* 2 Vols. London: Smith, Elder and Co. 1855

_____. *The Red River Settlement: Its Rise, Progress, and Present State.* London: Smith, Elder and Co. 1856

Ruggles, Richard I. *A Country So Interesting: The Hudson's Bay Company and Two Centuries of Mapping, 1670-1870.* Montreal and Kingston: McGill-Queen's University Press 1991

Sage, W.N. 'Peter Skene Ogden's Notes on Western Caledonia.' *BCHQ* 1, 1 (January 1937): 45-56

Sampson, William R. *John McLoughlin's Business Correspondence, 1847-48.* Seattle and London: University of Washington Press 1973

Schafer, Joseph, ed. 'Documents Relative to Warre and Vavasour's Military Reconnaissance in Oregon, 1845-6.' *OHQ* 10, 1 (March 1909): 1-99

Schofield, E.O.S., ed. 'Papers Relating to the Colonization of Vancouver Island.' In Report of the Provincial Archives Department of the Province of British Columbia for the Year Ended December 31st 1913. Victoria: William H. Cullin 1914, 49-79

Scott, Leslie M. 'Report of Lieutenant Peel on Oregon in 1845-46.' *OHQ* 29, 1 (March 1928): 51-76

Scouler, John. 'Account of a Voyage to Madeira, Brazil, Juan Fernandez, and the Gallipagos Islands, Performed in 1824 and 1825 ...' *Edinburgh Journal of Science.* 5 (April-October 1826): 195-214

_____. 'Account of a Voyage to Madeira, Brazil, Juan Fernandez, and the Gallipagos Islands, Performed in 1824 and 1825, with a view of examining their Natural History.' *Edinburgh Journal of Science* 6, 1 (January 1827): 51-73

_____. 'Account of a Voyage to Madeira, Brazil, Juan Fernandez, and the Gallipagos Islands, Performed in 1824 and 1825, with a view of examining their Natural History.' *Edinburgh Journal of Science* 7, 2 (April 1827): 228-36

_____. 'Dr John Scouler's Journal of a Voyage to N.W. America.' *Quarterly of the Oregon Historical Society* 6, 2 (June 1905): 159-205

_____. 'Observations on the Indigenous Tribes of the N.W. Coast of America.' *Journal of the Royal Geographical Society* 11 (1841): 215-50

_____. 'On the Indian Tribes Inhabiting the North-West Coast of America.' *Journal of the Ethnographical Society of London* 1 (1848): 228-52

_____. 'On the Temperature of the North West Coast of America.' *Edinburgh Journal of Science* 6 (November 1826-April 1827): 251-53

[Scouler, John, and David Douglas]. 'Notices Respecting Mr Scouler's and Mr Douglas's Recent Voyage to the North West Coast of America.' *Edinburgh Journal of Science* 5 (April-October 1826): 378-80

Seemann, Berthold. *Narrative of the Voyage of H.M.S. Herald, During the Years 1845-51.* London 1853

Simpson, Alexander. *The Life and Travels of Thomas Simpson, the Arctic Discoverer.* London 1845

———. *The Sandwich Islands*. London: Smith, Elder & Co. 1843

Simpson, Sir George. *An Overland Journey Round the World, During the Years 1841 and 1842*. 2 Vols. London: H. Colburn 1847

Simpson, Thomas. *Narrative of the Discoveries on the North Coast of America; Afforded by the Officers of the Hudson's Bay Company During the Years 1836-39*. London: Richard Bentley 1843

Slacum, William A. 'Slacum's Report on Oregon 1836-7.' *OHQ* 13, 2 (June 1912): 175-224

Smith, Adam. *An Inquiry into the Nature and Causes of the Wealth of Nations*. Eds. R.H. Campbell, A.S. Skinner, and W.B. Todd. Oxford: Clarendon Press 1976

Smith, Dorothy Blakey, ed. *James Douglas in California 1841 Being The Journal of a Voyage from the Columbia to California*. Vancouver: Librarian's Press 1965

Smith, Jedediah S., David E. Jackson, and W.L. Sublette to John H. Eaton, 29 October 1830. *OHQ* 4, 4 (December 1903): 395-8

Spalding, Henry H. 'A Letter by Henry H. Spalding from the Rocky Mountains.' *OHQ* 51, 2 (June 1950): 127-33

———. 'H.H. Spalding to William Spalding et al., 2 October 1836.' *OHQ* 13, 4 (December 1912): 371-7

Stewart, Sir W.G.D. *Altowan; or, Incidents of Life and Adventure in the Rocky Mountains* ... Vol. 1. New York: Harper Brothers 1846

Sullivan, Maurice S., ed. *The Travels of Jedediah Smith*. Santa Anna, CA: Fine Arts Press 1934

Swan, James Gilchrist. *The North-West Coast; or, Three Years' Residence in Washington Territory*. London: Sampson Low, Son, & Co. 1857

Thom, Adam. *The Claims to the Oregon Territory Considered*. London: Smith, Elder and Co. 1844

Tolmie, William Fraser. *The Journals of William Fraser Tolmie, Physician and Fur Trader*. Vancouver: Mitchell Press 1963

———. 'Utilization of the Indians.' *The Resources of British Columbia* 1, 12 (1 February 1884): 7

Townsend, John K. Letter to *Newark Advertiser*, 26 January 1843. *OHQ* 4, 4 (December 1903): 399-402

———. *Narrative of a Journey Across the Rocky Mountains to The Columbia River* ... Philadelphia: Henry Perkins 1839

Vaughan, Thomas, ed. 'Alexander Lattie's Fort George Journal, 1846.' *OHQ* 64, 3 (September 1963): 197-245

———. 'The Cowlitz Farm Journal, 1847-51.' *OHQ* 63, 2 & 3 (June-September 1962): 112-74

Walbran, John T. *British Columbia Coast Names 1592-1906, to Which are Added a few Names in Adjacent United States Territory*. Ottawa: Government Printing Bureau 1909; reprinted by J.J. Douglas, Vancouver 1971

Walkem, W.W. *Stories of Early British Columbia*. Vancouver: News-Advertiser 1914

Wallace, W.S., ed. *John McLean's Notes of a Twenty-five Years' Service in the Hudson's Bay Territory*. Toronto: Champlain Society 1932

Wilbur, Marguerite Eyer, ed. *Duflot de Mofras' Travels on the Pacific Coast*. 2 Vols. Santa Anna, CA: Fine Arts Press 1937

Wilkes, Charles. *Narrative of the United States Exploring Expedition During the Years 1838, 1839, 1840, 1841 and 1842*. 5 Vols. London: Wiley and Putnam 1845

———. 'Report on the Territory of Oregon 1842.' *OHQ* 12, 3 (September 1911): 269-99

Wilks, W., ed. *Journal kept by David Douglas, during his Travels in North America, 1823-1827* ... (London: W. Wesley & Son 1914)

Williams, Glyndwr, ed. *London Correspondence Inward from Sir George Simpson, 1841-42*. London: HBRS 1973 [HBRS 29]

———. *Peter Skene Ogden's Snake Country Journals, 1827-28 and 1828-29*. London: HBRS 1971 [HBRS 28]

Wolfenden, Madge, ed. 'John Tod: "Career of a Scotch Boy."' *BCHQ* 18, 3 & 4 (July-October 1954): 133-238

Young, F.G., ed. *The Correspondence and Journals of Captain Nathaniel J. Wyeth, 1831-6; A Record of Two Expeditions for the Occupation of the Oregon Country* ... Eugene, OR: University of Oregon Press 1899

————, ed. 'Journal and Report by Dr. Marcus Whitman of His Tour of Exploration with Rev. Samuel Parker in 1835 Beyond the Rocky Mountains.' *OHQ* 28, 3 (Summer 1927): 239-57

NEWSPAPERS

Victoria Daily Colonist. 22 December 1907
Vancouver Sun. 14 September 1987: D8
Hawaiian Spectator. 2, 2 (April 1839): 236-8
The Friend (Honolulu). 1 September 1844: 79
Weekly Register London). 5 September 1849
Wisconsin Herald. 15 September 1847

SECONDARY SOURCES

Acheson, Steven R. 'In the Wake of the Iron People: A Case for Changing Settlement Strategies among the Kunghit Haida.' *Journal of the Royal Anthropological Institute* 1, 2 (June 1995): 273-99
Alwyn, John A. 'Colony and Company Sharing the York Mainline.' *The Beaver* 310, 1 (Summer 1979): 4-11
Anderson, Steve A. *Steilacoom Farm: The British Colonization of Puget Sound, 1841-1849.* Fort Steilacoom, WA: Historic Fort Steilacoom Association 1993
Atkin, W.T. 'Snake Country Fur Trade, 1816-24.' *OHQ* 35,4 (December 1934): 295-312
Ball, John. 'Across the Continent Seventy Years Ago.' *OHQ* 3, 1 (March 1902): 82-106
Ball, Tim. 'Timber: Adventurers at the Bay Struggled to Stay Warm.' *The Beaver* 67, 2 (March 1987): 45-56
Barbeau, Marius. 'Old Port Simpson.' *The Beaver* 271 (September 1940): 20-3
Barman, Jean. 'New Land, New Lives: Hawaiian Settlement in British Columbia.' *Hawaiian Journal of History* 29 (1995): 1-32
————. *The West Beyond the West: A History of British Columbia.* Toronto: University of Toronto Press 1991
Barnett, Homer G. *The Coast Salish of British Columbia.* Westport, CT: Greenwood Press 1975
Barry, J. Neilson. 'Agriculture in the Oregon Country 1795-1844.' *OHQ* 30, 2 (June 1929): 161-8
Beidleman, Richard G. 'Nathaniel Wyeth's Fort Hall.' *OHQ* 58, 3 (September 1957): 196-250
Belyea, Barbara. 'The "Columbian Enterprise" and A.S. Morton.' *BC Studies* 86 (1990): 3-27
Bennett, G.V. 'Early Relations of the Sandwich Islands to the old Oregon Territory.' *WHQ* 4 (April 1913) 116-26
Blake, Anson S. 'The Hudson's Bay Company in San Francisco.' Part 1. *CHSQ* 28, 2 (June 1949): 97-112
————. 'The Hudson's Bay Company in San Francisco.' Part 2. *CHSQ* 28, 3 (September 1949): 243-58
Bowen, William A. *The Willamette Valley: Migration and Settlement on the Oregon Frontier.* Seattle: University of Washington 1978
Burley, David V., J. Scott Hamilton, and Knut R. Fladmark. *Prophecy of the Swan: The Upper Peace River Fur Trade of 1794-1823.* Vancouver: UBC Press 1996
Cameron, Alan. 'Ships of Three Centuries.' *The Beaver* 301 (Summer 1970) 4-21
Campbell, Marjorie Wilkins. *The North West Company.* Toronto: Macmillan 1957
Carlos, Ann. 'The Birth and Death of Predatory Competition in the North American Fur Trade: 1810-1821.' *Explorations in Economic History* 19 (1982): 156-83
Caywood, Louis R. 'Excavating Fort Vancouver.' *The Beaver* 278 (March 1948): 4-7
Clark, Donald H. 'Sawmill on the Columbia.' *The Beaver* (June 1950): 42-4
Clark, Malcolm Jr. *Eden Seekers: The Settlement of Oregon 1818-1862.* Boston 1981
Clark, Robert Carlton. 'Hawaiians in Early Oregon.' *OHQ* 35, 1 (March 1934): 22-31
Clarke, Charles G. *The Men of the Lewis and Clark Expedition.* Glendale, CA: Arthur H. Clarke 1970
Clayton, Daniel. 'Geographies of the Lower Skeena.' *BC Studies* 94 (Summer 1992): 29-58
————. 'Whole Kingdoms for the Sake of a Harbour.' *Columbia* 9, 1 (Spring 1995): 38-44
Cole, Jean Murray. *Exile in the Wilderness: The Biography of Chief Factor Archibald McDonald.* Don Mills, ON: Burns & MacEachern 1979

Cooke, Alan. 'The Montagnais.' *The Beaver* 316, 1 (Spring 1985): 13-19

Cooper, Carol. 'Native Women of the Northern Pacific Coast: An Historical Perspective, 1830-1900.' *Journal of Canadian Studies* 27, 4 (Winter 1992-3): 44-75

Cowan, Ian McTaggart. 'The Fur Trade and the Fur Cycle: 1825-1857.' *BCHQ* 2 (1938): 19-30

Cowan, Ian McTaggart, and Charles J. Guiguet. *The Mammals of British Columbia*. Victoria: British Columbia Provincial Museum 1956

Cox, Bruce Alden, ed. *Native People, Native Lands*. Ottawa: Carleton University Press 1987

Crean, J.F. 'Hats and the Fur Trade.' *Canadian Journal of Economics and Political Science* 28 (1962): 373-86

Cullen, Mary. *History of Fort Langley, 1827-96*. Ottawa: National Historic Parks and Sites 1979

———. 'Outfitting New Caledonia, 1821-58.' In *Old Trails and New Directions*. Eds. Judd and Ray, 231-51. Toronto: University of Toronto Press 1980

Davidson, Donald C. 'Relations of the Hudson's Bay Company with the Russian American Company on the Northwest Coast, 1829-1867.' *BCHQ* 5, 1 (January 1941): 33-52

Davidson, Gordon Charles. *The North West Company*. New York: Russell & Russell 1967; first published 1918

Dean, Jonathan R. '"Those Rascally Spackaloids." The Rise of Gispaxlots Hegemony at Fort Simpson, 1832-40.' *BC Studies* 101 (Spring 1994): 41-78

Deaville, Alfred Stanley. *The Colonial Postage Systems and Postage Stamps of Vancouver Island and British Columbia, 1849-1871*. Victoria: Charles F. Banfield 1928

Decker, Jody F. 'Scurvy at York. A Mysterious Affliction Lingered at the Bay.' *The Beaver* 69, 1 (February-March 1989): 42-8

Dee, Henry Drummond. 'An Irishman in the Fur Trade: The Life and Journals of John Work.' *BCHQ* 7, 4 (October 1943): 229-70

Dennis, Elsie Frances. 'Indian Slavery in Pacific Northwest.' Part 2. *OHQ* 31, 2 (June 1930): 181-95; part 3, *OHQ* 31, 3 (September 1930): 285-96

Dillon, Richard. *Siskiyou Trail: The Hudson's Bay Fur Company Route to California*. New York: McGraw-Hill 1975

Douthit, Nathan. 'The Hudson's Bay Company and the Indians of Southern Oregon.' *OHQ* 93, 1 (Spring 1992): 25-64

Driver, Harold E. *Indians of North America*. Chicago: University of Chicago Press 1961

Duncan, Janice K. 'Kanaka World Travellers and Fur Company Employees, 1785-1860.' *Hawaiian Journal of History* 7 (1973), 93-111

Donald, Leland. 'The Slave Trade on the Northwest Coast of North America.' *Research in Economic Anthropology* 6 (1984): 121-58

Dyck, David R. 'The Company Diversifies. Loggers at Moose Factory.' *The Beaver* 77, 1 (February-March 1991): 29-34

Eaton, Diane, and Sheila Urbanek. *Paul Kane's Great Nor-West*. Vancouver: UBC Press 1995

Elliott, T.C. 'Jonathan Carver's Source for the Name Oregon.' *OHQ* 23, 1 (March 1922): 53-69

———. 'The Origin of the Name Oregon.' *OHQ* 22, 2 (June 1921): 91-115

———. 'Richard ("Captain Johnny") Grant.' *OHQ* 36, 1 (March 1935): 1-13

Elton, Charles. *Voles, Mice and Lemmings: Problems in Population Dynamics*. Oxford: Oxford University Press 1942

Fisher, Robin. *Contact and Conflict: Indian-European Relations in British Columbia, 1774-1890*. Vancouver: UBC Press 1977

Fiske, Jo-Anne. 'Colonization and the Decline of Women's Status: The Tsimshian Case.' *Feminist Studies* 17, 3 (1991): 509-35

———. 'Fishing is Women's Business: Changing Economic Roles of Carrier Men and Women.' In *Native People, Native Lands*. Ed. Bruce Cox, 186-98. Ottawa: Carleton University Press 1987

Fladmark, Knut R. *British Columbia Prehistory*. Ottawa: Archaeological Survey of Canada; National Museum of Man 1986

———. 'A Paleoecological Model for Northwest Coast Prehistory.' Archaeological Survey of Canada Mercury Series 43. Ottawa: National Museum of Man 1975

———. 'Routes: Alternative Migration Corridors for Early Man in North America.' *American Antiquity* 44, 1 (1979): 55-69

Fleming, Thomas K. 'First Lumber Exports from the Pacific Coast.' *BCHN* 28, 2 (Spring 1995): 25-7, 40

Francis, Daniel. 'Whaling on the Eastmain.' *The Beaver* 308, 1 (Summer 1977): 14-19

Francis, Daniel, and Toby Morantz. *Partners in Fur: A History of the Fur Trade in Eastern James Bay, 1600-1870*. Montreal and Kingston: McGill-Queen's University Press 1983

[French, C.H.]. 'Mr French Lectures.' *The Beaver* 2, 9 (June 1922): 38

Frenette, Jacques. 'Mingan au 19e Siècle: Cycles Annuels des Montagnais et Politiques Commerciales de la Compagnie de la Baie d'Hudson.' Canadian Museum of Civilization Mercury Series; Canadian Ethnology Service Papers No. 106. Ottawa: National Museums of Canada 1986

Fry, Howard T. *Alexander Dalrymple (1730-1808) and the Expansion of British Overseas Trade*. Toronto: University of Toronto Press 1970

Galbraith, John S. 'The Early History of the Puget's Sound Agricultural Company, 1838-43.' *OHQ* 55, 3 (September 1954): 234-59

———. *The Hudson's Bay Company as an Imperial Factor*. Toronto: University of Toronto Press 1957

———. 'A Note on the British Fur Trade in California, 1821-1846.' *Pacific Historical Quarterly* 24 (1955): 253-60

Galois, Robert. *Kwakwaka'wakw Settlements, 1775-1920: A Geographical Analysis and Gazetteer*. Vancouver: UBC Press 1994

Galois, Robert, and Richard Mackie. 'A Curious Currency. Part 1: Haiqua Shells on the Northwest Coast in the 19th Century.' *The Midden* 22, 4 (October 1990): 1-3

Galois, Robert, and Arthur J. Ray. 'The Fur Trade in the Cordillera, 1821-1857.' In *Historical Atlas of Canada*. Vol. 2, plate 16. Toronto: University of Toronto Press 1987

Gibson, James R. 'A Diverse Economy: The Columbia Department of the Hudson's Bay Company, 1821-1846.' *Columbia* (Summer 1991): 28-31

———. 'European Dependence upon American Natives: The Case of Russian America.' *Ethnohistory* 25, 4 (Fall 1978): 359-85

———. *Farming the Frontier: the Agricultural Opening of the Oregon Country, 1786-1846*. Vancouver: UBC Press 1985

———. 'Food for the Fur Traders: The First Farmers in the Pacific Northwest, 1805-1846.' *Journal of the West* 7, 1 (1968): 18-30

———. *Imperial Russia in Frontier America: The Changing Geography of Supply of Russian America, 1784-1867*. New York: Oxford University Press 1976

———. *Otter Skins, Boston Ships, and China Goods: The Maritime Fur Trade of the Northwest Coast, 1785-1841*. Montreal and Kingston: McGill-Queen's University Press 1992

———. 'The Russian Fur Trade.' In *Old Trails and New Directions*. Eds. Judd and Ray, 217-30. Toronto: University of Toronto Press 1980

———. 'Smallpox on the Northwest Coast, 1835-1838.' *BC Studies* 56 (Winter 1982-83): 61-81

Gilbert, James Henry. *Trade and Currency in Early Oregon. A Study in the Commercial and Monetary History of the Pacific Northwest*. New York: Columbia University Press 1907

Glover, Richard. 'The Difficulties of the HBC's Penetration of the West.' *CHR* 29, 3 (September 1948): 240-54

———. 'Hudson Bay to the Orient.' *The Beaver* 281 (December 1950): 47-51

Gluek, Alvin C. 'The Fading Glory.' *The Beaver* 288 (Winter 1957): 50-5

———. 'Industrial Experiments in the Wilderness: a Sidelight in the Business History of the Hudson's Bay Company.' *Business History Review*, 32, 4 (Winter 1958): 423-33

———. *Minnesota and the Manifest Destiny of the Canadian Northwest*. Toronto: University of Toronto Press 1965

Goodier, J.L. 'The Nineteenth-Century Fisheries of the Hudson's Bay Trading Posts on Lake Superior: a Biogeographical Study.' *Canadian Geographer* 28 (1984): 341-57

Gordon, C.H.M. 'Whale Hunting in James Bay.' *The Beaver* 3, 9 (June 1923): 340-1

Gough, Barry M. 'Forests and Sea Power: A Vancouver Island Economy, 1778-1875.' *Journal of Forest History* 32 (1988): 117-24

———. *Gunboat Frontier: British Maritime Authority and Northwest Coast Indians, 1846-90.* Vancouver: UBC Press 1984

———. *The Northwest Coast: British Navigation, Trade, and Discoveries to 1812.* Vancouver: UBC Press 1992

———. 'The North West Company's "Adventure to China."' *OHQ* 76, 4 (December 1975): 309-31

———. *The Royal Navy and the Northwest Coast of North America, 1810-1914: A Study of British Maritime Ascendency.* Vancouver: UBC Press 1971

Gower, R.H.G. Leveson. 'Later Voyages for Discovery of the Northwest Passage.' *The Beaver* 268, 2 (September 1937): 23-4

———. 'Voyages for Discovery of the Northwest Passage.' *The Beaver* 267, 1 (June 1936): 45-9

Graebner, Norman. 'Maritime Factors in the Oregon Compromise.' *Pacific Historical Quarterly* 20 (November 1951): 331-46

Grant, Hugh. 'Revenge of the Paris Hat.' *The Beaver* 68, 6 (December 1988-January 1989): 37-44

Grant, Louis S. 'Fort Hall under the Hudson's Bay Company, 1837-1856.' *OHQ* 40, 1 (March 1940): 34-9

Groot, Corneliis, and Leo Margolis, eds. *Pacific Salmon Life Histories.* Vancouver: UBC Press 1991

Gudde, Erwin G. *Californian Place Names. A Geographical Dictionary.* Berkeley: University of California Press 1949

Haeger, John Denis. *John Jacob Astor: Business and Finance in the Early Republic.* Detroit: Wayne State University Press 1991

Hammond, Lorne. 'Marketing Wildlife. The Hudson's Bay Company and the Pacific Northwest, 1821-49.' *Forest & Conservation History* 37 (January 1993): 14-25

Harrington, Lyn. 'Triumph of the Trumpeter.' *The Beaver,* 286 (Winter 1955): 14-19

Harper, J. Russell. *Paul Kane's Frontier.* Toronto: University of Toronto Press 1971

Harris, Bob, Hartley Hatfield, and Peter Tassie. *The Okanagan Brigade Trail in the Southern Okanagan 1811 to 1949, Oroville, Washington to Westside, British Columbia.* Westside, BC: Wayside Press 1989

Harris, R. Cole. 'The Fraser Canyon Encountered.' *BC Studies* 94 (Summer 1992): 5-28

———. 'Towards a Geography of Power in the Cordilleran Fur Trade.' *The Canadian Geographer* 39, 2 (Summer 1995): 131-40

———, ed. *Historical Atlas of Canada.* Vol. 1. Toronto: University of Toronto Press 1987

Harris, H.H. 'First Discovery of Coal in Western Canada.' *The Beaver* 6, 2 (March 1926): 70

Harvey, Athelstan George. *Douglas of the Fir. A Biography of David Douglas, Botanist.* Cambridge, MA: Harvard University Press 1947

———. 'Meredith Gairdner: Doctor of Medicine.' *BCHQ* 9, 3 (April 1945): 89-112

Hedlin, Ralph. 'Reluctant Beginnings of Western Commerce.' *The Beaver* (Summer 1959): 4-9

Holman, Frederick V. 'A Brief Account of the Oregon Provisional Government and What Caused Its Formation.' *OHQ* 13, 2 (June 1912): 89-139

Holzkamm, Tim. 'Ojibway Horticulture in the Upper Mississippi and Boundary Waters.' In *Papers of the Algonquian Conference.* Ed. W. Cowan.

Holzkamm, Tim E., Victor Lytwyn, and Leo G. Waisberg. 'Rainy River Sturgeon: An Ojibway Resource in the Fur Trade Economy.' *Canadian Geographer* 32, 3 (1988): 194-205

Howay, F.W. 'Fort Langley, Historic HBC Post in British Columbia.' *The Beaver* 2, 2 (November 1921): 2-6

———. 'Brig Owhyhee in the Columbia, 1827.' *OHQ* 34, 4 (December 1933): 324-9

———. 'The Brig Owhyhee in the Columbia, 1829-30.' *OHQ* 35, 1 (March 1934): 10-21

———. 'The Discovery of the Fraser River: The Second Phase.' *BCHQ* 4, 4 (October 1940): 245-52

———. 'The Introduction of Intoxicating Liquors Amongst the Indians of the Northwest Coast.' *BCHQ* 6, 3 (July 1942): 157-70

———. 'The Origins of the Chinook Jargon.' *BCHQ* 6,1 (October 1942): 225-50

Hussey, John A. *The History of Fort Vancouver and its Physical Structure.* Portland: Washington State Historical Society 1957

———. 'The Women of Fort Vancouver.' *OHQ* 92, 3 (1991): 265-308

Inglis, Richard I., and James C. Haggarty. 'Cook to Jewitt: Three Decades of Change in Nootka

Sound.' In *Le Castor Fait Tout: Selected Papers of the Fifth North American Fur Trade Conference.* Eds. Bruce Trigger, Toby Morantz, and Louise Dechene, 193-222. Montreal: St. Louis Historical Society 1987

Innis, Harold A. *The Fur Trade in Canada. An Introduction to Canadian Economic History.* New Haven: Yale University Press 1930; Revised edition Toronto: University of Toronto Press 1956
————. 'Peter Pond and the Influence of Captain James Cook on Exploration in the Interior of North America.' *TRHC* Sec. 2 (1928): 131-41

Ireland, Willard E. 'The Evolution of the Boundaries of British Columbia.' *BCHQ* 3, 4 (October 1939): 263-82
————. 'James Douglas and the Russian American Company, 1840.' *BCHQ* 5, 1 (January 1941): 53-66

Jackson, Roy I. 'Sockeye from the Fraser.' *The Beaver* 283 (March 1953): 18-25

Johnson, Alice M. 'Mons. Maugenest Suggests ...' *The Beaver* 287 (Summer 1956): 49-53
————. 'Simpson in Russia.' *The Beaver* 291 (Autumn 1960): 4-12
————. 'System and Regularity.' *The Beaver* 291 (Summer 1960): 36-9

Johnson, Henry F. 'Fur Trading Days at Kamloops.' *BCHQ* 1, 3 (July 1937): 171-85

Johnson, Robert C. *John McLoughlin: 'Father of Oregon.'* Portland, OR: Binfords & Mort 1958

Johnson, Stephen M. 'Wrangel and Simpson.' In *Old Trails and New Directions.* Eds. Judd and Ray, 207-16. Toronto: University of Toronto Press 1980

Judd, Carol M., and Arthur J. Ray. *Old Trails and New Directions: Papers of the Third North American Fur Trade Conference.* Toronto: University of Toronto Press 1980

Judson, Katharine B. 'British Side of the Restoration of Fort Astoria – II.' *OHQ* 20, 4 (December 1919): 305-30

Keddie, Grant. 'Prehistoric Dogs of B.C. Wolves in Sheeps' Clothing.' *The Midden* 25, 1 (February 1993): 3-5

Kemble, J.H. 'Coals for the Northwest Coast, 1848-1850.' *BCHQ* 1 (1937): 121-31

Klippenstein, Frieda. *The Role of the Carrier in the Fur Trade: A Report from Historical and Anthropological Sources.* Canadian Parks Service, March 1992

Knight, Rolf. *Indians at Work: An Informal History of Native Indian Labour in British Columbia.* Vancouver: New Star Books 1978

Koppel, Tom. *Kanaka, the Untold Story of Hawaiian Pioneers in British Columbia and the Pacific Northwest.* Vancouver: Whitecap Books 1995

Korman, Maureen. 'The First Fort Langley.' *Canada West* 7, 3 (September 1991): 84-91

Kroeber, A.L. *Cultural and Natural Areas of Native North America.* Vol. 1. Berkeley: University of California Press 1939

Lamb, W. Kaye. 'The Advent of the Beaver.' *The Beaver* 2, 3 (July 1938): 163-84
————. 'Early Lumbering on Vancouver Island. Part 1. 1844-1855.' *BCHQ* 2 (January 1938): 31-53
————. 'The Founding of Fort Victoria.' *BCHQ* 7, 2 (April 1943): 71-92
————. 'John McLoughlin.' In *Dictionary of Canadian Biography.* Vol. 8. Ed. Francess G. Halpenny, 575-81. Toronto: University of Toronto Press 1985

Lawson, Murray G. 'The Beaver Hat and the North American Fur Trade.' In *People and Pelts: Selected Papers of the Second North American Fur Trade Conference.* Ed. Malvina Bolus. Winnipeg: Peguis Publishers 1972

Leader, Herman. 'HBC in California.' *The Beaver* 279 (March 1949): 3-7

Leechman, Douglas. 'Comodityes Besides Furres.' *The Beaver* 304, 4 (Spring 1974): 46-52
————. 'I Sowed Garden Seeds.' *The Beaver* (Winter 1970): 24-36

Locke, Jeffrey W. 'No Salmon, No Furs: The Provisioning of Fort Kamloops, 1841-1849.' *BCHN* 26, 2 (Spring 1993): 14-18

Lomax, Alfred L. 'Dr McLoughlin's Tropical Trade Route.' *The Beaver* 294 (Spring 1964): 10-15

Longstaff, F.V., and W. Kaye Lamb. 'The Royal Navy on the Northwest Coast, 1813-1850.' Part 1. *BCHQ* 9, 1 (January 1945): 1-24

Lutz, John. 'After the Fur Trade: The Aboriginal Labouring Class of British Columbia, 1849-1890.' *Journal of the Canadian Historical Association* 3 (1992): 69-94

McArthur, Lewis A. 'Oregon Geographic Names.' *OHQ* 28, 1 (March 1927): 65-110

McCook, James. 'Sir George Simpson in the Hawaiian Islands.' *The Beaver* 307, 3 (Winter 1976): 46-53

McCullough, Allan B. *The Commercial Fishery of the Canadian Great Lakes.* Ottawa: National Historic Parks and Sites Branch 1989

McEachran, Ute [Schworer]. 'The Reorganization of the Fur Trade after the "Merger" of the Hudson's Bay and North West Company, 1821-1826.' In *York University Department of Geography Paper Series.* Ed. Simpson-Housley. Toronto: York University 1988

McIlwraith, T.F. *The Bella Coola Indians.* 2 Vols. Toronto: University of Toronto Press 1948

Mackay, Corday. 'Pacific Coast Fur Trade.' *The Beaver* (Summer 1955): 38-42

MacKay, Douglas. *The Honourable Company: A History of the Hudson's Bay Company.* London: Cassell and Company 1937

Mackie, Quentin. *The Taxonomy of Ground Stone Woodworking Tools.* British Archaeological Reports, International Series 613. Oxford: Tempus Reparatum 1995

Mackie, Richard. 'The Colonization of Vancouver Island, 1849-1858.' *BC Studies* 96 (Winter 1992-3): 1-40

——. and Robert M. Galois. 'A Curious Currency. Part 2: The Hudson's Bay Company's Trade in Haiqua Shells.' *The Midden* 22, 5 (December 1990): 6-9

Maclachlan, Morag. 'The Founding of Fort Langley.' In *The Company on the Coast.* Ed. E. Blanche Norcross, 9-28. Nanaimo: Nanaimo Historical Society 1983

Macleod, William Christie. 'Debtor and Chattel Slavery in Aboriginal North America.' *American Anthropologist* 27, 3 (July 1925): 370-81

——. 'Economic Aspects of Indigenous American Slavery.' *American Anthropologist* 30, 4 (October-December 1928): 632-50

Makahonuk, Glen. 'Wage-Labour in the Northwest Fur Trade Economy 1760-1849.' *Saskatchewan History* 41, 1 (Winter 1985

Maloney, Alice Bay. 'California Rendezvous.' *The Beaver* 275 (December 1944): 32-7

——. 'Hudson's Bay Company in California.' *OHQ* 37,1 (March 1936): 9-23

——. 'Peter Skene Ogden's Trapping Expedition to the Gulf of California 1829-30' *CHSQ* 19, 4 (December 1940): 308-16

Marr, William L., and Donald G. Paterson. *Canada: An Economic History.* Toronto: Macmillan 1980

Marsden, Susan, and Robert Galois. 'The Tsimshian, the Hudson's Bay Company, and the Geopolitics of the Northwest Coast Fur Trade, 1787-1840.' *Canadian Geographer* 39, 2 (Summer 1995): 169-83

Meilleur, Helen. *A Pour of Rain. Stories from a West Coast Fort.* Victoria: Sono Nis Press 1980

Meinig, D.W. *The Great Columbia Plain: A Historical Geography, 1805-1910.* Seattle: University of Washington Press 1968

Merilees, Bill. 'The Humpback Whales of Georgia Strait.' *Waters* 8 (1985): 7-24

Merk, Frederick. 'The Oregon Pioneers and the Boundary.' *American Historical Review* 29, 4 (July 1924): 681-99

——. *The Oregon Question: Essays in Anglo-American Diplomacy and Politics.* Cambridge, MA: Harvard University Press 1967

——. 'Snake Country Expedition, 1824-25. An Episode of Fur Trade and Empire.' *OHQ* 35, 2 (June 1934): 93-122

Mitchell, Donald. 'Sebassa's Men.' In *The World is as Sharp as a Knife.* Ed. Donald N. Abbott, 79-86. Victoria: British Columbia Provincial Museum 1981

Mitchell, Elaine Allan. 'Fort Timiskaming.' *The Beaver* 300 (Winter 1969): 18-23

——. *Fort Timiskaming and the Fur Trade.* Toronto: University of Toronto Press 1977

Moodie, D.W. 'Gardening on Hudson Bay: The First Century.' *The Beaver* 309, 1 (Summer 1978): 54-9

——. 'The Trading Post Settlement of the Canadian North West.' *Journal of Historical Geography* 13 (1987): 360-74

Moodie, D.W. and Barry Kaye. 'Indian Agriculture in the Fur Trade Northwest.' *Prairie Forum* 11, 2 (Fall 1986): 171-84

——. 'Taming and Domesticating Native Animals of Rupert's Land.' *The Beaver* 307, 3 (Winter 1976): 10-19

Morice, A.G. *History of the Catholic Church in Western Canada from Lake Superior to the Pacific* (1659-1895). 2 Vols. Toronto: Musson 1910

_____. *The History of the Northern Interior of British Columbia.* Smithers, BC: Interior Stationery 1978; first published 1904

Morison, Samuel Eliot. 'New England and the Opening of the Columbia River Salmon Trade, 1830.' *OHQ* 28, 2 (June 1927): 11-32

Morton, Anne. 'Charles Elton and the Hudson's Bay Company.' *The Beaver* 315, 4 (Spring 1985): 22-9

Morton, Arthur S. *A History of the Canadian West to 1870-71* ... London: Thomas Nelson & Sons 1939

_____. 'The North West Company's Columbia Enterprise and David Thompson.' *CHR* 17 (1936): 266-88

_____. *Sir George Simpson, Overseas Governor of the Hudson's Bay Company.* Toronto: J.M. Dent & Sons 1944

Morton, Jamie. 'Designed for Use. Hudson's Bay Company Country-made Furniture on the Pacific Slope.' *Canadian Collector* 20-6 (November 1985): 44-6

_____. *Fort Langley: An Overview of the Operations of a Diversified Fur Trade Post 1848 to 1858 and the Physical Context in 1858.* Microfiche Report Series No. 340. Ottawa: Environment Canada Parks 1988

_____. *Fort St. James 1806-1914: A Century of Fur Trade on Stuart Lake.* Microfiche Report Series No. 367. Ottawa: Canadian Parks Service 1988

_____. 'Over a Barrel: Coopering at Fort Langley.' *Canadian Collector* 20, 6 (November 1985): 32-3

_____. 'Post of Plenty.' *Horizon Canada* 7, 73 (August 1986): 1736-41

Morton, W.L. 'Donald A. Smith and Governor George Simpson.' *The Beaver* 392 (Autumn 1978): 4-9

Morwood, William. *Traveller in a Vanished Landscape. The Life and Times of David Douglas.* London: Gentry Books 1973

Mouat, Jeremy. *Roaring Days: Rossland's Mines and the History of British Columbia.* Vancouver: UBC Press 1995

Murray, Keith A. 'The Role of the Hudson's Bay Company in Pacific Northwest History.' In *Experience in a Promised Land.* Eds. G. Thomas Edwards and Carlos A. Schwantes, 28-39. Seattle: University of Washington Press 1986

Nelson, Denys. *Fort Langley 1827-1927: A Century of Settlement in the Valley of the Lower Fraser.* Vancouver: Art, Historical and Scientific Association of Vancouver 1927

Nunis, Doyce B. *The Hudson's Bay Company's First Fur Brigade to the Sacramento Valley: Alexander McLeod's 1829 Hunt.* Sacramento 1958

Nute, Grace Lee. 'A Botanist at Fort Colvile.' *The Beaver* 277 (September 1946): 28-31

Ogden, Adele. *The California Sea Otter Trade, 1784-1848.* Berkeley: University of California Press 1941

Olson, Wallace M. *A History of Fort Durham Hudson's Bay Company Trading Post Located in Taku Harbor, 1840-1843 Within the Boundaries of Juneau.* Juneau, AK: Heritage Research 1994

O'Neil, M., 'The Maritime Activities of the North West Company, 1813-1821.' *WHQ* 21 (1930): 243-67

Ormsby, Margaret A. *British Columbia: A History.* Toronto: Macmillan of Canada 1958

Pannekoek, Frits. 'Corruption at Moose.' *The Beaver* 309, 4 (Spring 1979): 5-11

Patterson, R.M. 'The Strangest Man I Ever Saw.' *The Beaver* 286 (Spring 1956): 26-9

Peters, Helen Bergen. *Painting During the Colonial Period in British Columbia 1845-1871.* Victoria: Sono Nis Press 1979

Pethick, Derek. *S.S. Beaver: The Ship That Saved the West.* Vancouver 1970

Pletcher, David M. *The Diplomacy of Annexation. Texas, Oregon, and the Mexican War.* Columbia, MS: University of Missouri Press 1973

Porter, Kenneth Wiggins. *John Jacob Astor: Business Man.* 2 Vols. Cambridge, MA: Harvard University Press 1931

_____. 'Roll of Overland Astorians, 1810-12.' *OHQ* 34, 2 (June 1933): 103-12

Powell, Fred Wilbur. 'Hall Jackson Kelley. Appendix.' *OHQ* 18, 4 (December 1917): 271-95

_____. 'Hall Jackson Kelley. Chapter 7.' *OHQ* 18, 1 (March 1917): 117-29

Powell, J.V. 'Chinook Jargon and the Lexicographers.' *International Journal of American Linguistics* 56, 1 (January 1990): 134-51

Power, Geoffrey. 'History of the Hudson's Bay Company Salmon Fisheries in the Ungava Bay Region.' *The Polar Record* 18, 113 (May 1976): 151-61

Pritchett, J.H. *The Red River Valley 1811-1849: A Regional Study.* Toronto: Ryerson Press 1942

Ralston, Keith. 'Miners and Managers: The Organization of Coal Production on Vancouver Island by the Hudson's Bay Company, 1848-1862.' In *The Company on the Coast.* Ed. E. Blanche Norcross, 42-55. Nanaimo: Nanaimo Historical Society 1983

Ray, Arthur J. *The Canadian Fur Trade in the Industrial Age.* Toronto: University of Toronto Press 1990

———. 'The Hudson's Bay Company and Native People.' In *History of Indian-White Relations.* Ed. Wilcomb E. Washburn, 335-52. Washington, DC: Smithsonian Institution 1988

———. *Indians in the Fur Trade: Their Role as Trappers, Hunters, and Middlemen in the Lands Southwest of Hudson Bay 1660-1870.* Toronto: University of Toronto Press 1974

———. 'Some Conservation Schemes of the Hudson's Bay Company, 1821-50: An Examination of the Problems of Resource Management in the Fur Trade.' *Journal of Historical Geography* 1 (1975): 49-68

Ray, Arthur J., and Donald B. Freeman. *'Give Us Good Measure': An Economic Analysis of Relations between the Indians and The Hudson's Bay Company before 1773.* Toronto: University of Toronto Press 1978

Reeves, Randall R., and Edward Mitchell. 'Hunting Whales in the St. Lawrence.' *The Beaver* 67, 4 (August-September 1987): 35-40

———. 'White Whale Hunting in Cumberland Sound.' *The Beaver* 312, 3 (Winter 1981): 42-9

Reid, John Phillip. 'Restraints of Vengeance: Retaliation-in-Kind and the Use of Law in the Old Oregon Country.' *OHQ* 95, 1 (Spring 1994): 48-92

Reid, Robie L. 'The Chinook Jargon and British Columbia.' *BCHQ* 6, 1 (January 1942): 1-12

———. 'Early Days at Old Fort Langley.' *BCHQ* 1, 2 (April 1937): 71-87

———. 'Economic Beginnings in British Columbia.' *Transactions of the Royal Society of Canada* 30 (May 1936): 89-108

Rich, E.E. 'The Colony of Rupert's Land.' *The Beaver* 309, 1 (Summer 1978): 4-12

———. 'The Fur Traders: Their Diet and Drugs.' *The Beaver* 307, 1 (Summer 1976): 42-53

———. *Hudson's Bay Company 1670-1870.* 3 Vols. Toronto: McClelland and Stewart 1960

———. 'Trade Habits and Economic Motivation among the Indians of North America.' *Canadian Journal of Economics and Political Science* 26 (1960): 35-53

Rickard, T.A. 'The Use of Iron and Copper by the Indians of British Columbia.' *BCHQ* 3, 1 (January 1939): 25-50

Riegert, Paul W. *From Arsenic to DDT: A History of Entomology in Western Canada.* Toronto: University of Toronto Press 1980

Ronda, James P. *Astoria and Empire.* Lincoln, NE: University of Nebraska Press 1990

———. 'Calculating Ouragon.' *OHQ* 94, 2-3 (Summer-Fall 1993): 121-40

———. 'Dreams and Discoveries: Exploring the American West, 1760-1815.' *William and Mary Quarterly* 46 (1989): 145-62

Ross, Lester A. *Fort Vancouver 1829-1860: A Historical Archaeological Investigation of the Goods Imported and Manufactured by the Hudson's Bay Company.* Vancouver, WA: National Park Service 1976

———. 'Hudson's Bay Company Glass Trade Beads: Manufacturing Types Imported to Fort Vancouver (1829-1860).' *The Bead Journal* 1, 2 (Fall 1974): 15-22

Rotstein, Abraham, and David K. Foot. *The Two Economies of the Hudson's Bay Company.* Toronto: Department of Economics and Institute for Policy Analysis, University of Toronto 1987

Ruby, Robert H. and John A. Brown. *Indian Slavery in the Pacific Northwest.* Spokane: Arthur H. Clark 1993

Russell, Carl P. 'Wilderness Rendezvous Period of the American Fur Trade.' *OHQ* 42, 1 (March 1941): 1-47

Russell, Hilary. 'The Chinese Voyages of Angus Bethune.' *The Beaver* 307, 4 (Spring 1977): 22-31

Sage, Donald. 'Swirl of Nations – The HBC on the Pacific Coast in the Mid Nineteenth Century.' *The Beaver* 293 (Spring 1963): 32-40

Sage, Walter. 'Geographic and Cultural Aspects of the Five Canadas.' Canadian Historical Association, *Report* (1937): 28-34

———. 'New Caledonia: Siberia of the Fur Trade.' *The Beaver* 287 (Summer 1956): 24-9

———. *Sir James Douglas and British Columbia.* Toronto: University of Toronto Press 1930

Salamon, R.N. *The History and Social Influence of the Potato.* Cambridge 1949

Samarin, William J. 'Chinook Jargon and Pidgin Historiography.' *Canadian Journal of Anthropology* 5, 1 (Fall 1986): 23-34

Sauer, Carl. *The Early Spanish Main.* Berkeley: University of California Press 1966

Saw, Reginald. 'Sir John H. Pelly, Bart., Governor, Hudson's Bay Company, 1822-1852.' *British Columbia Historical Quarterly* 13, 1 (January 1949): 23-32

———. 'Treaty with the Russians.' *The Beaver* 289 (December 1948): 30-3

Scott, Leslie M. 'Indian Women as Food Providers and Tribal Counselors.' *OHQ* 52, 3 (September 1941): 208-19

Shepard, M.P., and A.W. Argue. *The Commercial Harvest of Salmon in British Columbia, 1820-1877.* Vancouver: Department of Fisheries and Oceans 1989

Spalding, David J. 'The Early History of Moose (*Alces Alces*): Distribution and Relative Abundance in British Columbia.' Royal British Columbia Museum. *Contributions to Natural Science* 11 (March 1990): 1-12

Spoehr, Alexander. '"Fur Traders in Hawaii": The Hudson's Bay Company in Honolulu, 1829-1861.' *Hawaiian Journal of History* 20 (1986): 27-66

———. 'A Nineteenth Century Chapter in Hawaii's Maritime History: Hudson's Bay Company Merchant Shipping, 1829-1859.' *Hawaiian Journal of History* 22 (1988)

Spry, Irene M. 'Routes Through the Rockies.' *The Beaver* 294 (Autumn 1963): 26-39

St. Clair, William 'Beaver in Hawaii.' *The Beaver* 272 (September 1941): 40-2

Stearns, R. 'The Royal Society and the Company.' *The Beaver* 276 (June 1945): 8-13

Sunder, John E. *The Fur Trade on the Upper Missouri.* Norman, OK: University of Oklahoma Press 1993

Suttles, Wayne. *Coast Salish Essays.* Vancouver: Talonbooks 1987

———. 'Post-Contact Culture Change among the Lummi Indians.' *BCHQ* 18, 1 and 2 (January-April 1954): 29-102

Tanner, Adrian. 'The End of Fur Trade History.' *Queen's Quarterly* 90, 1 (Spring 1983): 176-91

Tanner, Thomas W. 'Fort Saint James.' In *Miscellaneous Papers: The Fur Trade*, ms. report no. 131. Ottawa: Parks Canada 1966

Thistle, Paul. *Indian-European Relations in the Lower Saskatchewan Region to 1840.* Winnipeg: University of Manitoba Press 1986

Thomas, Lewis H. 'A History of Agriculture in the Prairies to 1914.' *Prairie Forum* 1, 1 (April 1976): 31-45

Thomson, Duane. 'The Response of the Okanagan Indians to European Settlement.' *BC Studies* 101 (Spring 1994): 96-117

Tippett, Maria, and Douglas Cole. *From Desolation to Splendour: Changing Perceptions of the British Columbia Landscape.* Toronto: Clarke, Irwin & Company 1977

Throckmorton, Arthur L. *Oregon Argonauts Merchant Adventurers on the Western Frontier.* Portland: Oregon Historical Society 1961

Thrum, Thomas G. 'History of the Hudson's Bay Company's Agency in Honolulu.' *Hawaiian Historical Society* (1912): 43-59

Trigger, Bruce. *Natives and Newcomers: Canada's 'Heroic Age' Reconsidered.* Montreal and Kingston: McGill-Queen's University Press 1985

Van Kirk, Sylvia. *Many Tender Ties: Women in Fur Trade Society 1670-1870.* Winnipeg: Watson and Dwyer 1980

———. 'This Rascally & Ungrateful Country: George Nelson's Response to Rupert's Land.' In *Rupert's Land: a Cultural Tapestry.* Ed. Richard C. Davis, 113-30. Waterloo, ON: W.L.U.P. for the Calgary Institute for Humanities 1988

Victor, Frances Fuller. 'Flotsam and Jetsam of the Pacific. The Owyhee, the Sultana, and the Mary Dacre.' *OHQ* 2, 1 (March 1901): 36-54

Warburton, Rennie, and David Coburn, eds., *Workers, Capital, and the State in British Columbia.*
Vancouver: UBC Press 1988
———, and Stephen Scott. 'The Fur Trade and Early Capitalist Development in British Columbia.'
Canadian Journal of Native Studies 5, 1 (1985): 27-46
Watkins, M.H. 'A Staple Theory of Economic Growth.' *Canadian Journal of Economics and Political Science* 29 (1963) 141-58
Watson, Robert. 'HBC in the Hawaiian Islands.' *The Beaver* (June 1930): 6-8
Webber, Jean. 'Fur Trading Posts in the Okanagan and Similkameen.' *Okanagan Historical Society* 57 (1993): 6-33
Wheat, Carl I. *Mapping the Transmississippi West.* 2 vols. San Francisco: Institute of Historical Geography 1958
Wike, Joyce A. 'Problems in Fur Trade Analysis: the Northwest Coast.' *American Anthropologist* 60 (1958): 1086-1101
Wiley, Leonard. 'Mill Creek site of Grist Mill of Hudson's Bay Company.' *OHQ* 43, 3 (September 1942): 282-5
Williams, Glyndwr. *The British Search for the Northwest Passage.* London: Green and Company 1960
Wilson, Clifford 'Tadoussac, the Company, and the King's Posts.' *The Beaver* 266, 1 (June 1935): 8-12, 63, 66
Winther, Oscar O. 'Commercial Routes from 1792 to 1843 by Sea and Overland.' *OHQ* 42, 3 (September 1941): 230-46
Wishart, David J. *The Fur Trade of the American West, 1807-1840. A Geographical Synthesis.* Lincoln/London: University of Nebraska Press 1979
Wrinch, L.A. 'The Formation of the Puget's Sound Agricultural Company.' *WHQ* 24 (1933): 3-8
Wyatt, Victoria. 'Alaskan Indian Wage Earners in the Nineteenth Century.' *PNQ* 78 (January-April, 1987): 43-9
Wynn, Graeme. *Timber Colony: A Historical Geography of Early Nineteenth Century New Brunswick.* Toronto: University of Toronto Press 1981

THESES AND UNPUBLISHED PAPERS

Bernick, Kathryn. 'A Post-Androcentric View of Fraser Delta Prehistory.' Paper presented to the Canadian Archaeological Association, Whitehorse, Yukon, May 1990
Galois, R.M. 'The Worlds of Arthur Wellington Clah, 1855-1891: An Outline.' Unpublished paper presented to the BC Studies Conference, Victoria, 1992
Hammond, Lorne. '"Any Ordinary Degree of System": The Columbia Department of the Hudson's Bay Company and the Harvesting of Wildlife, 1825-1849.' MA thesis, University of Victoria, 1985
Hastings, Clifford. 'Mercantilism and Laissez-faire Capitalism in the Ungava Peninsula, 1670-1940: An Economic Geography of the Fur Trade.' MA thesis, McGill University, 1985
Keith, H. Lloyd. 'The North West Company's "Adventure to the Columbia": A Reassessment of Financial Failure.' Unpublished ms., 1989
Mackie, Richard. 'Colonial Land, Indian Labour, and Company Capital: the Economy of Vancouver Island, 1849-1858.' MA thesis, University of Victoria, 1984
———. 'Not the Fur Trade in Canada: George Simpson and Resource Development, 1820-1860.' Paper presented to the Canadian Historical Association, Kingston, 1991
Maier, Roger. 'Marten, Muskrats and Beaver: Fort Kamloops and the Hudson's Bay Company, 1822-1856.' Unpublished essay, University of Victoria, 1992
Morton, Jamie. 'Conspicuous Production: Hudson's Bay Company Farms and Fisheries in British Columbia.' Paper presented to the Great River of the West Conference, 1992
———. 'Fort Langley Cooper's Shop Furnishing Plan.' Unpublished ms., Calgary, Canadian Parks Service, Curatorial Services, 1988
———. '"Worthy of Commemoration in the Usual Form": Native Culture in the Interpretation of Fort Langley National Historic Site since 1924.' Paper presented to the Chacmool Conference, University of Calgary, 1992

Peers, Laura L. '"A Woman's Work is Never Done": Harold Hickerson, the Male Bias, and Ojibwa Ethnohistory.' Unpublished paper presented to the Rupertsland Research Centre Conference, Churchill, 1988

Pollard, Juliet. 'Growing Up Without the Means of Grace: Cultures and Children in the Pacific Northwest.' PhD dissertation, UBC, circa 1991

Robinson, Sheila. 'Men and Resources on the Northern Northwest Coast.' PhD dissertation, University of London, 1983

Schworer, Ute. 'The Reorganization of the Fur Trade of the Hudson's Bay Company after the "Merger" with the North West Company 1821 to 1826.' MA thesis, York University, 1987

Vibert, Elizabeth. 'Real Men Hunt Buffalo: Masculinity, Race and Class in British Fur Traders' Narratives.' Paper presented to the B.C. Studies Conference, 1994

Set in Caslon by Brenda and Neil West, BN Typographics West

Printed and bound in Canada by Friesens

Text design: Bev Leech

Cartography: Eric Leinberger